BECOMING AMERICANS

BECOMING AMERICANS

Four Centuries of Immigrant Writing

Edited by
ILAN STAVANS

Foreword by
PETE HAMILL

A Special Publication of The Library of America

Some of the material in this volume is reprinted
with the permission of holders of copyright and publishing rights.
Acknowledgments are on page 707.

Distributed to the trade by Penguin Group (USA) Inc.
and in Canada by Penguin Books Canada, Ltd.

Book design by Fearn Cutler de Vicq

Library of Congress Control Number: 2009929080

ISBN: 978-1-59853-051-3

First Printing

Printed in the United States of America

BECOMING AMERICANS:
Four Centuries of Immigrant Writing

is published with support from

MARTIN E. SEGAL

MARK KRUEGER CHARITABLE TRUST

LEWIS-SEBRING FAMILY FOUNDATION

LUCIUS LITTAUER FOUNDATION

H. AXEL SCHUPF

CONTENTS

FOREWORD

I mmigrants made the United States of America into a great nation. Yes: that's a cliché. But it is also a fundamental social and historical truth.

Across four centuries, the steady arrival of millions of immigrants into North America created a human alloy, in which different metals combined to make something stronger than each individual component. At first, the majority came from Europe, although their individual stories could be quite different. There were exiles among them (with plans to return home), refugees waiting out the savageries of war, and above all, immigrants hoping to start new lives. Many were in flight from hunger or bigotry or tyranny. Others chose America because they refused to kneel before kings or czars. A small number were fleeing family scandals, or the police, or personal rejection. For many, the Atlantic journey to the port of New York offered an almost existential opportunity: to become whatever persons they wanted to be.

They received many gifts upon arrival: work and housing, and that healing indifference that doesn't care whether you are Catholic, Protestant, or Jew, as long as you play by the rules. This certainly applied to the great wave of Eastern European Jews, Italians, and Irish who arrived toward the end of the 19th century. The present for those new arrivals was often scary, and disappointing, but almost all of them carried stoic visions of the future in their meager luggage. They did some of the worst jobs in this country so that their American children would never have to do them. Their children would be taller than their parents. They would be better educated. And most important, they would be free. For all of their lives.

The immigrants and their children could see where America failed to realize this vision. All had to face the great stain of slavery and its aftermath. Those Americans with roots in Africa were not fully free regardless of what the Emancipation Proclamation told them. Legally sanctioned segregation, exploitation, and bigotry lasted another century before African Americans— aided by a smaller number of the descendants of other immigrants—began to tear down so many old walls.

To be sure, we must all beware of sentimentalizing the tale of the immigrants. As with all human beings, there were few saints among them, and many sinners. In the ethnic ghettos life was never easy. There were con men among them, and gangsters, who preyed on their own people. Alcohol wrecked too many of them. Families often tottered and collapsed. But in spite of everything, most endured. And each immigrant wave gave the United States great gifts in return: music, laughter, theater, vaudeville, big time sports, food, and language. Because of them, irony became essential to the American style, a way of expressing the difference between what was promised and what was delivered. Americans are people who learned to laugh at themselves, sometimes through tears.

Becoming American was never simple, however, especially when some of the Americans already here sought to obstruct the process. In the 1840s, the Know Nothing movement spread like a virus from a minority of the Anglo-Saxon majority. Immigrants were killed in the violent streets of New York. Hope itself too often lay wounded. Some ideological descendants of the Know Nothings are around today, blathering on cable television and the Internet. But in that same 19th century, there was a growing awareness among the Anglo-Saxon majority that every immigrant life actually contained a story. Too often, the immigrants couldn't tell their own stories because they were illiterate or too exhausted by long hours of work to put pen to paper. That is why so many immigrant stories were written by their American children, or by strangers with compassion in their hearts. But many new arrivals did struggle successfully to find the voice and time and energy to tell their valuable stories—over 80 of them are gathered in this volume. Today the United States is in the midst of the largest immigrant wave in a century. We are hearing now from Americans whose origins are in the Dominican Republic, China, Haiti, South Korea, the Ukraine, and Mexico. Even more, and almost certainly different, literary gifts are surely coming.

The passions of anti-immigrant rhetoric are certain to rise and fall and rise again, as the American alloy changes. But it would be good for the zealots to read this extraordinary volume and learn again that their own ancestors fought a similar war for ethnic or religious purity, and lost. Perhaps then they will remember: the huge statue of a woman in New York harbor, holding aloft the torch of liberty, that enduring sculpted symbol of the United States of America, is an immigrant from France.

Pete Hamill

INTRODUCTION

T he United States, as we are often reminded, is a nation of immigrants,
and immigrants have dramatically shaped its literature. Phillis Wheatley, Jacob Riis, Isaac Bashevis Singer, Vladimir Nabokov, Czeslaw Milosz, Junot Díaz—a few of the most noted from various backgrounds—have brought
transforming influences and flavors to the American canon. But the immigrant strain of American writing embraces far more than a few outstanding, isolated voices. As this volume demonstrates, it is a rich and complex
body of work with much to tell us about a story we may think we already
know. As central as immigration is to the American story, important strands
of the narrative have been hidden from view, buried beneath long-standing
metaphors such as the melting pot. By gathering first-person accounts, many
by less familiar writers, this anthology represents a reclamation project, an
excavation of a submerged tradition. The volume's scope brings into relief the
continuities and disruptions within that tradition. Together these writers tell
a more jagged and variegated tale than the one often heard in the national
conversation about immigration.

Spanning four centuries, *Becoming Americans* gathers writing by 85
immigrants from 45 countries of origin; the selections are arranged chrono-
logically by date of arrival, illustrating not only how the views of immigrants
have changed, but also how America itself has evolved. All the writing is by
immigrants except for the last entry, by Richard Rodriguez, whose parents
came from Mexico. This coda speaks for the second generation that must

negotiate the legacy bestowed on it: the divided self of the parents, the need to feel comfortable in both the land and the language.

The book is a record of the immigrant experience—mostly distilled as memoir, sometimes as fiction—that reveals the wealth of reasons for immigrating and the daunting obstacles to overcome, from the journey itself to the shock and spectacle of first arrival to the ongoing struggle to master the complexities of American life. It shows, at times, the inspiring capacity of ordinary men and women to adapt and prosper. Other selections, by contrast, give voice to disappointment and protest, as in Gottlieb Mittelberger's invective on the miseries of 18th-century Pennsylvania or Edwidge Danticat's harrowing account of her uncle's death while in the custody of immigration authorities.

A note on parameters: The editorial focus of this anthology is on immigrants from other countries, not on the nation's internal migration. Hence, the northbound journey of African Americans following emancipation as well as the forced relocation of American Indians during the 19th century have not been included. Hawaiians and the Inuit are not, by this definition, immigrants either. Puerto Ricans pose a different kind of challenge. With the signing of the Jones Act in 1917, Puerto Rico became a commonwealth (in Spanish an *estado libre asociado*), and the status of the island's men and women became that of immigrants on the mainland. Conversely, people of Mexican descent in the United States are not always immigrants. The boundaries drawn following the Mexican-American War (1846–48) account for the presence of a large number of Latinos in the Southwest.

In sum, this anthology becomes something greater than its parts: a new kind of American history, a history whose themes can often be gleaned, as in many of these selections, from the individual truths of imaginative literature, not only in the poems of detained Chinese immigrants on California's Angel Island but also in the contemporary fiction of Dinaw Mengestu and Aleksandar Hemon. Traditional narratives of American history often reflect an insider's perspective, focusing more on responses to the immigrants' arrival and assimilation—or perceived lack thereof—than on the immigrants' own experiences and varied perspectives on their new home. Here, in contrast, is a liminal portrait of America, one rendered from the outside looking in, or, more accurately, from the outside becoming in.

Each case, each circumstance is different; each era of American life has had its particular pressures and expectations. The writing collected in this volume is not only diverse but also, inevitably, complex. Each immigrant must deal in different ways, depending on era and circumstance, with unforeseeable and sometimes agonizing rites of transition and transformation. But a few nearly universal elements persist. At its core, all immigrant writing is built around an odyssey. The arc is that of a personal journey from a place called home in search of another place to call home, a journey unavoidably filled with obstacles. Fundamental questions arise: Who am I? Where do I belong? And, crucially: Who is this writing meant for? In what medium can it be most fully expressed? For most, the immigrant experience means living in at least two different languages, the mother tongue and English. Often the immigrant's odyssey involves giving up a language and adopting another one. The mediation of passing from one language to another may involve self-censorship: there are things an audience for one tongue might understand that an audience for another might not. It is this verbal dilemma that leads, in writers such as Eva Hoffman and Ariel Dorfman, to an abundance of word games, etymological reflections, linguistic somersaults.

Physical displacement and linguistic differences are only the most obvious challenges. Immigrants must negotiate subtle degrees of meaning in social mores and systems of value. The complexity is frequently compounded by the need to function, within their families, in some kind of harmony with the place and the values left behind, or else run the risk of seeming to betray their own origins. The simplest choices—of work, pastime, or courtship—can call into question basic identity. It is not simply a matter of adjusting to the realities of America but of forging, however locally and privately, a new reality in which the claims of the new world and the old find at least a tenuous balance.

One major fault line that divides the writers in this anthology runs straight through the family. At least in the autobiographical writings, the immigrants who give an account of their coming to America as adults tend to reflect on a successful fulfillment of their hopes and ambitions. If history is a tale proverbially told by its winners, then the immigrant memoir tends to be the story of an ultimately happy fate, as initial hardships yield to a comfortable and perhaps gently ambivalent adaptation to life in the United States. Immigrant children have different, and in a way more representative, stories to tell. Their parents may not have succeeded in adjusting to American life, and their difficulties take on a particular intensity within the family, where longed-for continuities with the Old Country are precariously—even quixotically—maintained against the onslaught of the American world outside the home. Unlike their parents, those who immigrate as children often possess a kind of double consciousness, allowing them especially sharp insights into the ongoing struggle between native and adopted cultures that strikes at the core of the immigrant's being.

Recent writers, too, possess a hybrid perspective, a consequence of a world in which revolutions in telecommunications and travel have made contact with their home countries an unexceptional, nearly banal phenomenon. The boundaries between homeland and adopted country are much more porous than they have ever been, and immigrant writing during the last quarter-century shows a shrewd awareness of the new conundrums of our globalized age. The reflections of writers such as Josip Novakovich, Marie Arana, Gary Shteyngart, and Eva Hoffman, to name a few, on their split identities are no less trenchant for being expressed with wit, irony, and a cosmopolitan sense of the absurd.

As many of these writers in this anthology reveal, the dilemma of assimilation is never completely resolved. Each partial resolution is an invention, the result of a fresh confrontation with an environment whose coordinates and ground rules are always subtly shifting. In the end, of course, immigrants and the America in which they must find their way are irrevocably altered by the encounter, and each change generates further changes within the society and within each immigrant family. In immigrant literature there is never simple acceptance but rather a constant questioning, a weighing of contradictory and compelling appeals, a never-ending examination of what really comprises a national identity.

That is why this anthology, built out of the individual experiences of immigrants over four hundred years, becomes in the end a rich portrait of America itself, captured in the shock and vibrancy of first collisions, seen with fresh eyes and from unanticipated and not infrequently unflattering angles. The process of assimilating—not necessarily to the demands of the America already in place but to the full force of one's meeting with it—is a work that is never done. That continuing process is in fact at the very heart of American life.

The tidy expression, redolent of the fait accompli, that "America is a nation of immigrants" only hints at a deeper truth: America is a nation *becoming*. The American experiment in self-government, the idea that a people could reconstitute themselves as a nation, has from the beginning been mirrored by, and reinforced by, the immigrant's belief that he or she could be reconstituted. There is something deeply transformational in the idea of America. This book is a testimony to its historic and continuing power.

One must not make too much of the notion of American exceptionalism—the idea that the United States is unique in its historical character and destiny—but it must be acknowledged that the way immigration has become part of American life and culture is not quite comparable to what has prevailed elsewhere, at least up to the present. It may be that now—in light of the massive migration from developing countries to the industrial and post-industrial worlds—we are entering an age in which something like the American experience will be repeated elsewhere. But too often, so far, the experience in other countries has been one of xenophobic mistrust and rancor. While the history of immigration in the United States is bumpy at best, the emotion most often invoked about it is gratitude: not only have newcomers been thankful for the opportunity to remake themselves, but the native-born population has in the end extended respect to the outsiders who have become their fellow citizens. In that regard, at least, the United States is a model.

As an epigraph for this anthology, I offer what is perhaps the country's most famous literary treatment of the theme of immigration, Emma Lazarus's "The New Colossus." For a century this sonnet, written in 1883 and now inscribed at the base of the Statue of Liberty, greeted ships filled with hopeful newcomers from the Old World. Lazarus's family were Sephardic Jews from Portugal who immigrated during the colonial period. The poem does not overtly discuss immigration policy—then as now a much contested question—but it affirms the idea of the United States as a safe haven for the downtrodden. This inscription on its base gives a special meaning to a statue that—as its full title, "Liberty Enlightening the World," indicates—was intended as a celebration of freedom. With her poem Lazarus affirmed the profound connection between the ideas of freedom and immigration.

The New Colossus

Not like the brazen giant of Greek fame,
With conquering limbs astride from land to land;
Here at our sea-washed, sunset gates shall stand
A mighty woman with a torch, whose flame
Is the imprisoned lightning, and her name
Mother of Exiles. From her beacon-hand
Glows world-wide welcome; her mild eyes command
The air-bridged harbor that twin cities frame.
"Keep, ancient lands, your storied pomp!" cries she
With silent lips. "Give me your tired, your poor,
Your huddled masses yearning to breathe free,
The wretched refuse of your teeming shore.
Send these, the homeless, tempest-tost to me,
I lift my lamp beside the golden door!"

Ilan Stavans

To Libby and Harvey Rosenberg,
who opened the door for me

RICHARD FRETHORNE

The story of immigration to America begins largely in silence. Before 1820 approximately 11 million people crossed the Atlantic from Europe and Africa to North and South America and the Caribbean. Of these, nearly three quarters—some eight million—came against their will, as slaves. In the English colonies about 750,000 men, women, and children arrived before 1700; of these, some 350,000 were African slaves, and as many as 200,000 were indentured servants who, like Richard Frethorne, were deemed by law and social convention the property of their masters for a period of time, usually four to seven years, in exchange for transport across the Atlantic and maintenance. From this great majority of immigrants to early America, very few voices come down to us today. Frethorne's 1623 letters from Jamestown, Virginia, to his parents in England—there were three in all, and they constitute all that is known about him—are a rare and invaluable communication, allowing us to hear the desperation behind the silence.

Letter to His Mother and Father

LOVING AND KIND FATHER AND MOTHER:
My most humble duty remembered to you, hoping in god of your good health, as I myself am at the making hereof. This is to let you understand that I your child am in a most heavy case by reason of the country, [which] is such that it causeth much sickness, [such] as the scurvy and the bloody flux and diverse other diseases, which maketh the body very poor and weak. And when we are sick there is nothing to comfort us; for since I came out of the ship I never ate anything but peas, and loblollie (that is, water gruel). As for deer or venison I never saw any since I came into this land. There is indeed some fowl, but we are not allowed to go and get it, but must work hard both early and late for a mess of water gruel and a mouthful of bread and beef. A

mouthful of bread for a penny loaf must serve for four men which is most pitiful. [You would be grieved] if you did know as much as I [do], when people cry out day and night—Oh! That they were in England without their limbs— and would not care to lose any limb to be in England again, yea, though they beg from door to door. For we live in fear of the enemy every hour, yet we have had a combat with them . . . and we took two alive and made slaves of them. But it was by policy, for we are in great danger; for our plantation is very weak by reason of the death and sickness of our company. For we came but twenty for the merchants, and they are half dead just; and we look every hour when two more should go. Yet there came some four other men yet to live with us, of which there is but one alive; and our Lieutenant is dead, and [also] his father and his brother. And there was some five or six of the last year's twenty, of which there is but three left, so that we are fain to get other men to plant with us; and yet we are but 32 to fight against 3000 if they should come. And the nighest help that we have is ten mile of us, and when the rogues overcame this place [the] last [time] they slew 80 persons. How then shall we do, for we lie even in their teeth? They may easily take us, but [for the fact] that God is merciful and can save with few as well as with many, as he showed to Gilead. And like Gilead's soldiers, if they lapped water, we drink water which is but weak.

And I have nothing to comfort me, nor is there nothing to be gotten here but sickness and death, except [in the event] that one had money to lay out in some things for profit. But I have nothing at all—no, not a shirt to my back but two rags (2), nor clothes but one poor suit, nor but one pair of shoes, but one pair of stockings, but one cap, [and] but two bands [collars]. My cloak is stolen by one of my fellows, and to his dying hour [he] would not tell me what he did with it; but some of my fellows saw him have butter and beef out of a ship, which my cloak, I doubt [not], paid for. So that I have not a penny, nor a penny worth, to help me too either spice or sugar or strong waters, without the which one cannot live here. For as strong beer in England doth fatten and strengthen them, so water here doth wash and weaken these here [and] only keeps [their] life and soul together. But I am not half [of] a quarter so strong as I was in England, and all is for want of victuals; for I do protest unto you that I have eaten more in [one] day at home than I have allowed me here for a week. You have given more than my day's allowance to a beggar at the door;

and if Mr. Jackson had not relieved me, I should be in a poor case. But he like a father and she like a loving mother doth still help me.

For when we go to Jamestown (that is 10 miles of us) there lie all the ships that come to land, and there they must deliver their goods. And when we went up to town [we would go], as it may be, on Monday at noon, and come there by night, [and] then load the next day by noon, and go home in the afternoon, and unload, and then away again in the night, and [we would] be up about midnight. Then if it rained or blowed never so hard, we must lie in the boat on the water and have nothing but a little bread. For when we go into the boat we [would] have a loaf allowed to two men, and it is all [we would get] if we stayed there two days, which is hard; and [we] must lie all that while in the boat. But that Goodman Jackson pitied me and made me a cabin to lie in always when I [would] come up, and he would give me some poor jacks [fish] [to take] home with me, which comforted me more than peas or water gruel. Oh, they be very godly folks, and love me very well, and will do anything for me. And he much marvelled that you would send me a servant to the Company; he saith I had been better knocked on the head. And indeed so I find it now, to my great grief and misery; and [I] saith that if you love me you will redeem me suddenly, for which I do entreat and beg. And if you cannot get the merchants to redeem me for some little money, then for God's sake get a gathering or entreat some good folks to lay out some little sum of money in meal and cheese and butter and beef. Any eating meat will yield great profit. Oil and vinegar is very good; but, father, there is great loss in leaking. But for God's sake send beef and cheese and butter, or the more of one sort and none of another. But if you send cheese, it must be very old cheese; and at the cheesemonger's you may buy very good cheese for twopence farthing or halfpenny, that will be liked very well. But if you send cheese, you must have a care how you pack it in barrels; and you must put cooper's chips between every cheese, or else the heat of the hold will rot them. And look whatsoever you send me—be it never so much—look, what[ever] I make of it, I will deal truly with you. I will send it over and beg the profit to redeem me; and if I die before it come, I have entreated Goodman Jackson to send you the worth of it, who hath promised he will. If you send, you must direct your letters to Goodman Jackson, at Jamestown, a gunsmith. (You must set down his freight, because there be more of his name there.)

Good father, do not forget me, but have mercy and pity my miserable case. I know if you did but see me, you would weep to see me; for I have but one suit. (But [though] it is a strange one, it is very well guarded.) Wherefore, for God's sake, pity me. I pray you to remember my love to all my friends and kindred. I hope all my brothers and sisters are in good health, and as for my part I have set down my resolution that certainly will be; that is, that the answer of this letter will be life or death to me. Therefore, good father, send as soon as you can; and if you send me any thing let this be the mark.

ROT   Richard Frethorne,
                                            Martin's Hundred

THOMAS TILLAM

Between 1629 and 1641 some 20,000 English men, women, and children came to New England. Demographically, this migration, known in filiopietistic New England as the Great Migration, was unlike any other to the New World in the 17th century. Families, not single men, predominated, most of middling status and sharing similar regional origins and dissenting, or Puritan, sensibilities. Thomas Tillam (died after 1668) arrived in 1638, and his poem gives lyric expression to the optimism, hope, and trust in providence—tinged, always, with an anxious regard for the snares of sin—that characterized the foundation of the Puritan commonwealths in America. For whatever reason—most likely an espousal of Baptist beliefs anathema to the orthodox leaders in Massachusetts—Tillam returned to England; between 1661 and 1667 he helped to establish a communal sect in Heidelberg, Germany.

Upon the First Sight of New England
June 29, 1638

Hail holy land wherein our holy Lord
hath planted his most true and holy word;
Hail happy people who have dispossessed
yourselves of friends, and means, to find some rest
for your poor wearied souls, oppressed of late
for Jesus' sake, with envy, spite, and hate;
To you that blessed promise truly's given
of sure reward, which you'll receive in Heaven.
Methinks I hear the lamb of God thus speak:
Come my dear little flock, who for my sake
have left your country, dearest friends, and goods
and hazarded your lives o'th raging floods.

Possess this country; free from all annoy
here I'll be with you, here you shall enjoy
my Sabbaths, sacraments, my ministry
and ordinances in their purity.
But yet beware of Satan's wily baits;
he lurks among you, cunningly he waits
to catch you from me. Live not then secure
but fight 'gainst sin, and let your lives be pure.
Prepare to hear your sentence thus expressed:
Come ye my servants of my Father Blessed.

JAMES REVEL

More than 30,000 people convicted of crimes in England were transported to America during the 17th and 18th centuries. Historians speculate as to whether James Revel (flourished c. 1659–1680) actually was one such felon describing his own experience in verse, or whether this poem is an imaginative work in a lively tradition of cautionary transportation tales much favored then in England (a tradition that achieved its most popular expression in Daniel Defoe's 1722 novel *Moll Flanders*). Historical details about the conditions endured by indentured servants in Virginia in the 1670s establish reason to assume a measure of authenticity. The ballad was widely published as a broadside in the 18th century and, remarkably, in 1823, with only minor changes, mostly of place names, it was republished in Scotland as "a sorrowful account of his fourteen years transportation to Botany Bay, in New South Wales."

The Poor Unhappy Transported Felon's Sorrowful Account of His Fourteen Years Transportation at Virginia in America

PART I.

My loving countrymen pray lend an ear,
To this relation that I bring you here,
My present sufferings at large I will unfold,
Altho' it's strange, 'tis true as e'er was told.
　Of honest parents I did come tho' poor,
Who besides me had children never more,
Near temple-bar was born their darling son,
In virtue's paths he for some time did run.
　My parents in me took a vast delight,

And sent me unto school to read and write,
And cast accompts likewise as it appears,
Until that I was aged thirteen years.

Then to a tin man I was apprentice bound,
My master and my mistress good I found,
They lik'd me well, my business I did mind,
From me my parents comfort hop'd to find.

My master near unto Moorfields did dwell,
Here into wicked company I fell,
To wickedness I quickly was inclin'd,
So soon is tainted any youthful mind.

I from my master then did run away,
And rov'd about the streets both night and day,
Did with a gang of thieves a robbing go,
Which fill'd my parents hearts with grief and woe.

At length my master got me home again,
And us'd me well in hopes I might reclaim,
My father tenderly to me did say,
My dearest child why did you run away.

If you had any cause at all for grief,
Why came you not to me to seek relief,
I well do know you did for nothing lack,
Food for the belly, and cloaths for the back.

My mother said, son, I did implore,
That you will from your master go no more,
Your business mind, your master don't forsake,
Lest you again to wicked courses take.

I promis'd fair, but yet could not refrain,
But to my old companions went again;
For vice when once, alas! it taints the mind,
Is not soon rooted out again we find.

With them a thieving I again did go,
But little did my tender parents know,
I followed courses which did seem most vile,

My absence griev'd them being their only child.
   A wicked life I liv'd I must confess,
In fear and dread, and great uneasiness,
Which does attend those actions most unjust,
For thieves can never one another trust.
   Strong liquor banished the thoughts of fear,
But justice stopped us in our full career,
One night was taken up one of our gang,
Who five impeach'd, and three of them were hang'd.
   I was one of the five was try'd and cast,
Yet transportation I did get at last,
A just reward for my vile actions base,
So justice overtook me at the last.
   My father vex'd, my mother she took on,
And said, alas! alas! my only son,
My father said, it cuts me to the heart,
To think on such a cause as this we part.
   To see him grieve pierced my very soul,
My wicked case I sadly did condole,
With grief and shame my eyes did overflow,
And had much rather choose to die than go.
   In vain I grieved and in vain my parents wept,
For I was quickly sent on board the ship,
With melting kisses, and a heavy heart,
I from my parents then did part.

PART II.

In a few days we left the river quite,
And in short time of land we lost the sight,
The captain and the sailors us'd us well,
But kept us under lest we should rebel.
   We were in number much about threescore
A wicked lousy crew as e'er went o'er,
Oaths and tobacco with us plenty were,

Most did smoak, but all did curse and swear
    Five of our number in the passage dy'd,
Who were cast into the ocean wide,
And, after sailing seven weeks and more,
We at Virginia all were put on shore.

    Then to refresh us we were all well clean'd,
That to our buyers we might the better seem;
The things were given that did to each belong,
And they that had clean linen put it on.

    Our faces shav'd, comb'd our wigs and hair,
That we in decent order might appear,
Against the Planters did come us to view,
How well they lik'd this fresh transported crew.

    The women from us separated stood,
As well as we by them to be thus view'd,
And in short time some men up to us came,
Some ask'd our trade, others ask'd our name.

    Some view'd our limbs turning us round,
Examining like horses if we were sound,
What trade my lad, said one to me,
A tin-man sir. That will not do for me.

    Some felt our hands, others our legs and feet,
And made us walk to see if we were compleat.
Some view'd our teeth, to see if they were good,
And fit to chew our hard and homely food.

    If any like our limbs, our looks and trades,
Our captain then a good advantage make,
For they a difference make it doth appear,
'Twixt those of seven and those of fourteen years.

    Another difference too there is allow'd,
Those who have money will have favour shew'd;
But if no cloaths nor money they have got,
Hard is their fate, and hard will be their lot.

    At length a grim old man unto me came,

He ask'd my trade, likewise my name,
I told him I a tin-man was by trade,
And not eighteen years of age I said.
   Likewise the cause I told which brought me here,
And for fourteen years transported were;
And when from me he this did understand,
He bought me of the captain out of hand.

PART III.

Down to the harbour I was took again,
On board a ship loaded with chains;
Which I was forc'd to wear both night and day,
For fear I from the sloop should run away.
   My master was a man but of ill fame,
Who first of all a transport thither came,
In Rapahannock county he did dwell,
In Rapahannock river known full well.
   When the ship was laden and home sent,
An hundred miles we up the river went,
The weather cold, and very hard my fare,
My lodgings on the deck both hard and bare.
   At last to my new master's house I came,
To the town of Wicowoco call'd by name,
Here my European cloaths were took from me,
Which never after I could ever see.
   A canvas shirt and trowzers me they gave,
A hop sack frock in which I was a slave,
No shoes or stockings had I for to wear,
Nor hat nor cap my head and feet were bare.
   Thus dress'd, into the field I next did go,
Among tobacco plants all day to hoe,
At day break in the morn our work begun,
And lasted till the setting of the sun.
   My fellow slaves were five transports more,

With eighteen negroes which is twenty four,
Besides four transport women in the house,
To wait upon his daughter and his spouse.
　　We and the negroes both alike did fare,
Of work and food we had an equal share,
And in a piece of ground called our own,
The food we eat first by ourselves is sown.
　　No other time to us they will allow,
But on a Sunday we the same must do,
Six days we slave for our master's good,
The seventh is to produce our homely food,
　　And when we a hard day's work have done,
Away unto the mill we must be gone,
'Till twelve or one o'clock a grinding corn,
And must be up by day light in the morn.
　　And if you get in debt with any one,
It must be paid before from thence you come,
In publick places they'll put up your name,
As every one their just demands may claim.
　　But if we offer for to run away,
For every hour we must serve a day,
For every day a week, they're so severe,
Every week a month, every month a year.
　　But if they murder, rob or steal while there,
They're straitway hang'd the laws are so severe,
For by the rigour of that very law,
They are kept under and do stand in awe.

PART IV.

At last it pleased God I sick did fall,
But I no favour could receive at all,
For I was forc'd to work while I could stand,
Or hold the hoe within my feeble hand.
　　Much hardship then I did endure,
No dog was ever nursed so before,

More pity then the negro slaves bestow'd,
Than my inhuman brutal master show'd.

Oft on my knees the Lord I did implore,
To let me see my native land once more,
For through his grace my life I would amend,
And be a comfort to my dearest friends.

Helpless and sick and left alone,
I by myself did use to make my moan,
And think upon my former wicked ways,
That had brought me to this wretched case.

The Lord who saw my grief and smart,
And my complaint, he knew my contrite heart,
His gracious mercy did to me afford,
My health again was unto me restor'd.

It pleas'd the Lord to grant to me such grace,
That tho' I was in such a barbarous place,
I serv'd the Lord with fervency and zeal,
By which I did much inward comfort feel.

Now twelve years had passed thus away,
And but two more by law I had to stay,
When death did my cruel master call,
But that was no relief to me at all.

The Widow would not the plantation hold,
So we and that were to be sold,
A Lawyer who at James town did dwell,
Came for to see and lik'd it very well.

He bought the negroes who for life are slaves,
But no transported felons would he have,
So we were put like sheep into the fold,
Unto the best bidder to be sold.

PART V.

A Gentleman who seemed very grave,
Said unto me, how long are you a slave,
Not two years quite, I unto him reply'd,

That is but very short indeed, he cry'd.

He ask'd my trade, name and whence I came,
And what vile fact had brought me to this shame,
I told him all, at which he shook his head,
I hope you have seen your folly now he said.

I told him yes, and truly did repent,
But what made me most of all relent,
That I should to my parents prove so wild,
Being their darling and their only child.

He said no more but from me short did turn,
While from my eyes the tears did trickling run,
To see him to my overseer to go,
But what he said to him, I do not know,

He straitway came unto me again,
And said, no longer you must here remain,
For I have bought you of this man said he,
Therefore prepare yourself to go with me.

I went with him, my heart opprest with woe,
Not knowing him or where I must go,
But was surprized very much to find,
He used me so tenderly and kind.

He said he would not use me as a slave,
But as a servant if I'd well behave,
And if I pleas'd him when my time expir'd,
He'd send me home again if I requir'd.

My kind new master did at James-town dwell,
By trade a cooper and liv'd very well,
I was his servant on him to attend,
Thus God unlook'd for raised me a friend.

PART VI.

Thus did I live in plenty, peace and ease,
Having none but my master to please,
And if at any time he did ride out,

I with him rode the country round about.

And in my heart I often griev'd to see,
So many transport felons there to be,
Some who in England have liv'd fine and brave,
Were like horses forc'd to trudge and slave.

At length my fourteen years expir'd quite,
Which fill'd my very soul with fond delight,
To think I should no longer there remain,
But to old England once return again.

My master for me did express much love,
And as good as his promise he did prove,
He got me ship'd and I came home again,
With joy and comfort tho' I went with pain.

My father and mother well I found,
Who to see me with joy did abound,
My mother over me did weep with joy,
My father cry'd, once more I see my boy.

Whom I thought dead, but does alive remain,
And is returned to me once again,
I hope God has so wrought upon thy mind,
No more to wickedness thoul't be inclin'd,

I told him all the dangers I went thro',
Likewise my sickness, and my hardships too,
Which fill'd their tender hearts with sad surprize,
While melting tears ran trickling from their eyes,

I begg'd of them from all grief to refrain,
Since God had brought me to their home again,
The Lord unto me so much grace would give,
To work for you both while I do live.

My countrymen take warning e'er too late,
Lest you shou'd share my unhappy fate,
Altho' but little crimes you here have done,
Think of seven or fourteen years to come.

Forc'd from your friends and country to go,

Among the Negroes to work at the hoe,
Indifferent countries void of all relief,
Sold for a slave because you prov'd a thief.
  Now young men all with speed your lives amend
Take my advice, as one that is your friend,
For tho' so slight you do make of it here,
Hard is your lot if you once get there.

AYUBA SULEIMAN DIALLO

In the late 17th and 18th centuries, the Atlantic slave trade capitalized on, and over time greatly exacerbated, an internal system of slave-trading in sub-Saharan Africa. In 1730 Ayuba Suleiman Diallo (1701–1773), a member of the Muslim merchant elite of the Senegambian region (in present-day Senegal), traveled to the West African coast to sell two people and purchase paper and other commodities; he was kidnapped, transported to Maryland, and sold into slavery. Attempting escape, he was captured and imprisoned at the Kent County Courthouse where he impressed a lawyer named Thomas Bluett. After a translator was found who spoke Ayuba's native Wolof, his freedom was purchased and he was sent to England where he became known as Job ben Solomon. After spending some months there, Ayuba returned to his home in Africa, one of very few slaves to make such a circuit. His narrative, compiled and published by Bluett, is one of the earliest first-person accounts of the Atlantic slave trade.

from

Some Memoirs of the Life of Job,

**The Son of Solomon, the High Priest of Boonda in Africa;
Who Was a Slave About Two Years in Maryland;
and Afterwards Being Brought to England, Was Set Free,
and Sent to His Native Land in the Year 1734**

SECT. 1.
**An Account of the Family of JOB; his Education; and the more
remarkable Circumstances of his Life, before he was taken Captive.**

JOB's Countrymen, like the Eastern People and some others, use to design themselves by the Names of their Ancestors, and in their Appellations mention their Progenitors several Degrees backward; tho' they also have

Sirnames for distinguishing their particular Families, much after the same
Manner as in *England*. JOB's Name, in his own Country, is HYUBA, BOON
SALUMENA, BOON HIBRAHEMA; *i.e.* JOB, the Son of *Solomon*, the Son of
Abraham. The Sirname of his Family is *Jallo*.

JOB, who is now about 31 or 32 Years of age, was born at a Town called
Boonda in the County of *Galumbo* (in our Maps *Catumbo*) in the Kingdom of
Futa in *Africa*; which lies on both Sides the River *Senegal*, and on the south
Side reaches as far as, the River *Gambia*. These two Rivers, JOB assured me,
run pretty near parallel to one another, and never meet, contrary to the Posi-
tion they have in most of our Maps. The Eastern Boundary of the Kingdom
of *Futa* or *Senega* is the great Lake, called in our Maps *Lacus Guarde*. The
Extent of it, towards the North, is not so certain. The chief City or Town of
it is *Tombut*; over against which, on the other side of the River, is *Boonda*, the
Place of JOB's Nativity.

About fifty Years ago *Hibrahim*, the Grandfather of JOB, founded the Town
of *Boonda*, in the Reign of *Bubaker*, then King of *Futa*, and was, by his Permission, sole Lord Proprietor and Governor of it, and at the same Time High
Priest, or *Alpha*; so that he had a Power to make what Laws and Regulations
he thought proper for the Increase and good Government of his new City.
Among other Institutions, one was, that no Person who flies thither for Protection shall be made a Slave. This Privilege is in force there to this Day, and
is extended to all in general, that can read and know God, as they express it;
and it has contributed much to the Peopling of the Place, which is now very
large and flourishing. Some time after the Settlement of this Town *Hibrahim*
died; and, as the Priesthood is hereditary there, *Salumen* his Son, the Father
of JOB, became High Priest. About the same time *Bubaker* the King dying,
his Brother *Gelazi*, who was next Heir, succeeded him. *Gelazi* had a Son,
named *Sambo*, whom he put under the Care of *Salumen*, JOB's Father, to
learn the *Koran* and *Arabick* Language. JOB was at this Time also with his
Father, was Companion to *Sambo*, and studied along with him. *Sambo*, upon
the Death of *Gelazi*, was made King of *Futa*, and reigns there at present.
When JOB was fifteen Years old, he assisted his Father as *Emaum*, or Sub-
priest. About this Age he married the Daughter of the Alpha of *Tombut*, who
was then only eleven Years old. By her he had a Son (when she was thirteen
Years old) called *Abdolah*; and after that two more Sons, called *Hibrahim* and

Sambo. About two Years before his Captivity he married a second Wife, Daughter of the Alpha of *Tomga*; by whom he has a Daughter named *Fatima*, after the Daughter of their Prophet *Mahommed*. Both these Wives, with their Children, were alive when he came from Home.

SECT. II.
Of the Manner of his being taken Captive;
and what followed upon it, till his Return.

In February, 1730. JOB's Father hearing of an *English* Ship at *Gambia* River, sent him, with two Servants to attend him, to sell two Negroes and to buy Paper, and some other Necessaries; but desired him not to venture over the River, because the Country of the *Mandingoes*, who are Enemies to the People of *Futa*, lies on the other side. JOB not agreeing with Captain *Pike* (who commanded the Ship, lying then at *Gambia*, in the Service of Captain *Henry Hunt*, Brother to Mr. *William Hunt*, Merchant, in *Little Tower-Street*, *London*) sent back the two Servants to acquaint his Father with it, and to let him know that he intended to go farther. Accordingly, having agreed with another Man, named *Loumein Yoas*, who understood the *Mandingoe* Language, to go with him as his Interpreter, he crossed the River *Gambia*, and disposed of his Negroes for some Cows. As he was returning Home, he stopp'd for some Refreshment at the House of an old Acquaintance; and the Weather being hot, he hung up his Arms in the House, while he refresh'd himself. Those Arms were very valuable; consisting of a Gold-hilted Sword, a Gold Knife, which they wear by their Side, and a rich Quiver of Arrows, which King *Sambo* had made him a Present of. It happened that a Company of the *Mandingoes*, who live upon Plunder, passing by at that Time, and observing him unarmed, rush'd in, to the Number of seven or eight at once, at a back Door, and pinioned JOB, before he could get to his Arms, together with his Interpreter, who is a Slave in *Maryland* still. They then shaved their Heads and Beards, which JOB and his Man resented as the highest indignity; tho' the *Mandingoes* meant no more by it, than to make them appear like Slaves taken in War. On the 27th of *February*, 1730. they carried them to Captain *Pike* at *Gambia*, who purchased them; and on the first of *March* they were put on Board. Soon after JOB found means to acquaint Captain *Pike* that he was the same Person that came to trade with him a few Days before, and after what Manner he had been taken. Upon this Captain *Pike* gave him leave to redeem himself and his Man; and JOB sent to an Acquaintance of his Father's, near *Gambia*, who promised to send to JOB's Father, to inform him of what had happened, that he might take some Course to have him set at Liberty. But it being a Fortnight's journey between that Friend's House and his Father's, and the Ship sailing in about a Week after, JOB was brought with the rest of the Slaves to *Annapolis* in *Maryland*, and delivered to Mr. *Vachell Denton*, Factor to Mr. *Hunt*, before mentioned. JOB heard since, by Vessels that came from *Gambia*, that his Father sent down several Slaves, a little after Captain *Pike* sailed, in order to procure his Redemption; and that *Sambo*, King of *Futa*, had made War upon the *Mandingoes*, and cut off great Numbers of them, upon account of the Injury they had done to his Schoolfellow.

Mr. *Vachell Denton* sold JOB to one Mr. *Tolsey* in *Kent* Island in *Maryland*, who put him to work in making Tobacco; but he was soon convinced that JOB had never been used to such Labour. He every Day shewed more and more Uneasiness under this Exercise, and at last grew sick, being no way able to bear it; so that his Master was obliged to find easier Work for him, and therefore put him to tend the Cattle. JOB would often leave the Cattle, and withdraw into the Woods to pray; but a white Boy frequently watched him, and whilst he was at his Devotion would mock him, and throw Dirt in his Face. This very much disturbed JOB, and added to his other Misfortunes; all which were increased by his Ignorance of the *English* Language, which prevented his complaining, or telling his Case to any Person about him. Grown in some measure desperate, by reason of his present Hardships, he resolved to travel at a Venture; thinking he might possibly be taken up by some Master, who would use him better, or otherwise meet with some lucky Accident, to divert or abate his Grief. Accordingly, he travelled thro' the Woods, till he came to the County of *Kent*, upon *Delaware Bay*, now esteemed Part of *Pensilvania*; altho' it is properly a Part of *Maryland*, and belongs to my Lord *Baltimore*. There is a Law in force, throughout the Colonies of *Virginia, Maryland, Pensilvania*, &c. as far as *Boston* in *New England*, viz. That any Negroe, or white Servant who is not known in the County, or has no Pass, may be secured by any Person, and kept in the common Gaol, till the Master of such Servant shall fetch him. Therefore JOB being able to give no Account of himself, was put in Prison there.

This happened about the Beginning of *June*, 1731. when I, who was attending the Courts there, and had heard of JOB, went with several Gentlemen to the Gaoler's House, being a Tavern, and desired to see him. He was brought into the Tavern to us, but could not speak one Word of *English*. Upon our Talking and making Signs to him, he wrote a Line or two before us, and when he read it, pronounced the Words *Allah* and *Mahommed*; by which, and his refusing a Glass of Wine we offered him, we perceived he was a *Mahometan*, but could not imagine of what Country he was, or how he got thither; for by his affable Carriage, and the easy Composure of his Countenance, we could perceive he was no common Slave.

When JOB had been some time confined, an old Negroe Man, who lived in that Neighbourhood, and could speak the *Jalloff* Language, which JOB also understood, went to him, and conversed with him. By this Negroe the Keeper was informed to whom JOB belonged, and what was the Cause of his leaving his Master. The Keeper thereupon wrote to his Master, who soon after fetch'd him home, and was much kinder to him than before; allowing him a Place to pray in, and some other Conveniencies, in order to make his Slavery as easy as possible. Yet Slavery and Confinement was by no means agreeable to JOB, who had never been used to it; he therefore wrote a Letter in *Arabick* to his Father, acquainting him with his Misfortunes, hoping he might yet find Means to redeem him. This Letter he sent to Mr. *Vachell Denton*, desiring it might be sent to *Africa* by Captain *Pike*; but he being gone to *England*, Mr. *Denton* sent the Letter inclosed to Mr. *Hunt*, in order to be sent to *Africa* by Captain *Pike* from *England*; but Captain *Pike* had sailed for *Africa* before the Letter came to Mr. *Hunt*, who therefore kept it in his own Hands, till he should have a proper Opportunity of sending it. It happened that this Letter was seen by *James Oglethorpe*, Esq; who, according to his usual Goodness and Generosity, took Compassion on JOB, and gave his Bond to Mr. *Hunt* for the Payment of a certain Sum, upon the Delivery of JOB here in *England*. Mr. *Hunt* upon this sent to Mr. *Denton*, who purchas'd him again of his Master for the same Money which Mr. *Denton* had formerly received for him; his Master being very willing to part with him, as finding him no ways fit for his Business.

He lived some time with Mr. *Denton* at *Annapolis*, before any Ship could stir out, upon account of the Ice that lay in all the Rivers of *Maryland* at that Time. In this Interval he became acquainted with the Reverend Mr. *Henderson*, a Gentleman of great Learning, Minister of *Annapolis*, and Commissary to the Bishop of *London*, who gave JOB the Character of a Person of great Piety and Learning; and indeed his good Nature and Affability gain'd him many Friends besides in that Place.

In *March*, 1733, he set sail in the *William*, Captain *George Uriel* Commander; in which Ship I was also a Passenger. The Character which the Captain and I had of him at *Annapolis*, induced us to teach him as much of the *English* Language as we could, he being then able to speak but few Words of it, and those hardly intelligible. This we set about as soon as we were out at Sea, and in about a Fortnight's Time taught him all his Letters, and to spell almost any single Syllable, when distinctly pronounced to him; but JOB and my self falling sick, we were hindered from making any greater Progress at that Time. However, by the Time that we arrived in *England*, which was the latter End of *April*, 1733. he had learned so much of our Language, that he was able to understand most of what we said in common Conversation; and we that were used to his Manner of Speaking, could make shift to understand him tolerably well. During the Voyage, he was very constant in his Devotions; which he never omitted, on any Pretence, notwithstanding we had exceeding bad Weather all the time we were at Sea. We often permitted him to kill our fresh Stock, that he might eat of it himself; for he eats no Flesh, unless he has killed the Animal with his own Hands, or knows that it has been killed by some *Mussulman*. He has no Scruple about Fish; but won't touch a bit of Pork, it being expresly forbidden by their Law. By his good Nature and Affability he gained the good Will of all the Sailors, who (not to mention other kind Offices) all the way up the Channel shewed him the Head Lands and remarkable Places; the Names of which JOB wrote down carefully, together with the Accounts that were given him about them. His Reason for so doing, he told me, was, that if he met with any *Englishman* in his Country, he might by these Marks be able to convince him that he had been in *England*.

GOTTLIEB MITTELBERGER

Between 1710 and 1775 some 100,000 Germans immigrated to the American colonies, many drawn by a steady stream of rose-colored promotional material circulating throughout the German states. By the time of the first federal census in 1790, German-Americans constituted fully a third of the population of Pennsylvania. The majority of these immigrants came as "redemptioners" who were afforded passage on credit but were sold into indentured servitude if they were unable to make payment shortly after their arrival. Gottlieb Mittelberger (1715–1779?) arrived in Philadelphia in October 1750 aboard the *Osgood*, along with 500 of his fellow countrymen. With fortunes better than most, he settled as an organist and schoolmaster in New Providence, outside Philadelphia. Disillusioned and determined to challenge the promoters of German colonization, he returned to Germany in 1754 to write an exposé of the harsh realities of the Atlantic passage and of settlement in a still largely undeveloped land. The translation of the passage that follows is by Oscar Handlin and John Clive.

from
Journey to Pennsylvania

In the month of May 1750 I left my birthplace Enzweihingen in the district of Vaihingen for Heilbronn, where an organ was waiting for me, ready to be shipped to Pennsylvania. With this organ I took the usual route down the Neckar and the Rhine to Rotterdam in Holland. From Rotterdam I sailed with a transport of approximately 400 souls—Württemberger, Durlacher, Palatines, and Swiss, etc.—across the North Sea to Cowes in England; and, after a nine-day stopover there, across the Atlantic, until at last on the tenth of October 1750 I landed in Philadelphia, the capital of Pennsylvania.

I made careful inquiries into the conditions of the county. And what I am going to describe in this book I partly found out for myself, and partly heard from reliable people who know what they were talking about. I should no doubt have been able to report and to recount more if, at the time, I had ever considered publishing anything about Pennsylvania. But I always thought myself far too feeble to do that sort of thing. It was only the misfortunes I encountered on my voyage to and fro (for in the country itself things went well with me, because l was able to earn a living right away, and could easily support myself well) and the nasty tricks the Newlanders wanted to play on me and my family, as I shall relate further on, that first gave me the idea not to keep what I knew to myself.

But what really drove me to write this little book was the sad and miserable condition of those traveling from Germany to the New World, and the irresponsible and merciless proceedings of the Dutch traders in human beings and their man-stealing emissaries—I mean the so-called Newlanders. For these at one and the same time steal German people under all sorts of fine pretexts, and deliver them into the hands of the great Dutch traffickers in human souls. From this business the latter make a huge profit, and the Newlanders a smaller one.

This, as I say, is the principal reason for my publishing this little book. In fact, I had to take a solemn oath to write it. For before I left Pennsylvania, when it became known that I wanted to return to Württemberg, numerous Württemberger, Durlacher, and Palatines (a great many of whom live there and spend their days moaning and groaning about ever having left their native country) begged me with tears and uplifted hands, and even in the name of God, to publicize their misery and sorrow in Germany. So that not only the common people but even princes and lords might be able to hear about what happened to them; and so that innocent souls would no longer leave their native country, persuaded to do so by the Newlanders, and dragged by them into a similar kind of slavery. And so I vowed to the great God, and promised those people to reveal the entire truth about it to people in Germany, according to the best of my knowledge and ability.

I hope, therefore, that my dear countrymen and indeed all of Germany will be no less concerned to get news and factual information about how far it is to Pennsylvania and how long it takes to get there; about what the journey costs, and what discomforts and dangers one has to undergo in the bargain; about what happens when the people arrive in America well or ill; about how they are sold and scattered around; and, finally, about what conditions in general are like. I conceal neither good nor bad aspects; and thus I hope that the world, liking an honest man, will look on me as impartial and truthful. Once people have read all this I have no doubt that those who might still have some desire to go over there will stay at home and will carefully avoid this long and difficult voyage and the misfortunes connected with it; since such a journey will mean for most who undertake it the loss of all they possess, of freedom and peace, and for some the loss of their very lives and, I can even go so far as to say, of the salvation of their souls.

To travel from Durlach or Württemberg as far as Holland and the open sea one must reckon on a trip of 200 hours. From there across the sea to England as far as Cowes, where all ships drop anchor before they finally begin the great ocean crossing, another 150 hours. From there over 100 hours until one completely loses sight of England. Then across the Atlantic, that is from land to land, as the sailors put it, 1,200 hours. Finally from the first sight of land in Pennsylvania to Philadelphia, over 40 hours. Altogether such a journey adds up to 1,700 hours or 1,700 French miles.

This journey lasts from the beginning of May until the end of October, that is, a whole six months, and involves such hardships that it is really impossible for any description to do justice to them. The reason for this is that the Rhine boats must pass by thirty-six different customs houses between Heilbronn and Holland. At each of these all the ships must be examined, and these examinations take place at the convenience of the customs officials. Meanwhile, the ships with the people in them are held up for a long time. This involves a great deal of expense for the passengers; and it also means that the trip down the Rhine alone takes from four to six weeks.

When the ships with their passengers arrive in Holland they are there held up once again for from five to six weeks. Because everything is very expensive in Holland the poor people must spend nearly all they own during this period. In addition various sad accidents are likely to occur here. I have, for instance, seen with my own eyes two of the children of a man trying to board ship near Rotterdam meet sudden death by drowning.

In Rotterdam, and to some extent also in Amsterdam, the people are packed into the big boats as closely as herring, so to speak. The bedstead of one person is hardly two feet across and six feet long, since many of the boats carry from four to six hundred passengers, not counting the immense amount of equipment, tools, provisions, barrels of fresh water, and other things that also occupy a great deal of space.

Because of contrary winds it sometimes takes the boats from two to four weeks to make the trip from Holland to Cowes. But, given favorable winds, that voyage can be completed in eight days or less. On arrival everything is examined once more and customs duties paid. It can happen that ships have to ride at anchor there from eight to fourteen days, or until they have taken on full cargoes. During this time everyone has to spend his last remaining money and to consume the provisions that he meant to save for the ocean voyage, so that most people must suffer tremendous hunger and want at sea where they really feel the greatest need. Many thus already begin their sufferings on the voyage between Holland and England.

When the ships have weighed anchor for the last time, usually off Cowes in Old England, then both the long sea voyage and misery begin in earnest. For from there the ships often take eight, nine, ten, or twelve weeks sailing to Philadelphia, if the wind is unfavorable. But even given the most favorable winds, the voyage takes seven weeks.

During the journey the ship is full of pitiful signs of distress—smells, fumes, horrors, vomiting, various kinds of sea sickness, fever, dysentery, headaches, heat, constipation, boils, scurvy, cancer, mouth-rot, and similar afflictions, all of them caused by the age and the highly-salted state of the food, especially of the meat, as well as by the very bad and filthy water, which brings about the miserable destruction and death of many. Add to all that shortage of food, hunger, thirst, frost, heat, dampness, fear, misery, vexation, and lamentation as well as other troubles. Thus, for example, there are so many lice, especially on the sick people, that they have to be scraped off the bodies. All this misery reaches its climax when in addition to everything else one must also suffer through two to three days and nights of storm, with everyone convinced that the ship with all aboard is bound to sink. In such misery all the people on board pray and cry pitifully together.

In the course of such a storm the sea begins to surge and rage so that the waves often seem to rise up like high mountains, sometimes sweeping over the ship; and one thinks that he is going to sink along with the ship. All the while the ship, tossed by storm and waves, moves constantly from one side to the other, so that nobody aboard can either walk, sit, or lie down and the tightly packed people on their cots, the sick as well as the healthy, are thrown every which way. One can easily imagine that these hardships necessarily affect many people so severely that they cannot survive them.

I myself was afflicted by severe illness at sea, and know very well how I felt. These people in their misery are many times very much in want of solace, and I often entertained and comforted them with singing, praying, and encouragement. Also, when possible, and when wind and waves permitted it, I held daily prayer meetings with them on deck, and, since we had no ordained clergyman on board, was forced to administer baptism to five children. I also held services, including a sermon, every Sunday, and when the dead were buried at sea, commended them and our souls to the mercy of God.

Among those who are in good health impatience sometimes grows so great and bitter that one person begins to curse the other, or himself and the day of his birth, and people sometimes come close to murdering one another. Misery and malice are readily associated, so that people begin to cheat and steal from one another. And then one always blames the other for having undertaken the voyage. Often the children cry out against their parents, husbands against wives and wives against husbands, brothers against their sisters, friends and acquaintances against one another.

But most of all they cry out against the thieves of human beings! Many groan and exclaim: "Oh! If only I were back at home, even lying in my pigsty!" Or they call out: "Ah, dear God, if I only once again had a piece of good bread or a good fresh drop of water." Many people whimper, sigh, and cry out pitifully for home. Most of them become homesick at the thought that many hundreds of people must necessarily perish, die, and be thrown into the ocean in such misery. And this in turn makes their families, or those who were responsible for their undertaking the journey, often-times fall almost into despair—so that it soon becomes practically impossible to rouse them from their depression. In a word, groaning, crying, and lamentation go on aboard day and night; so that even the hearts of the most hardened, hearing all this, begin to bleed.

One can scarcely conceive what happens at sea to women in childbirth and to their innocent offspring. Very few escape with their lives; and mother and child, as soon as they have died, are thrown into the water. On board our ship, on a day on which we had a great storm, a woman about to give birth and unable to deliver under the circumstances, was pushed through one of the portholes into the sea because her corpse was far back in the stern and could not be brought forward to the deck.

Children between the ages of one and seven seldom survive the sea voyage; and parents must often watch their off-spring suffer miserably, die, and be thrown into the ocean, from want, hunger, thirst, and the like. I myself, alas, saw such a pitiful fate overtake thirty-two children on board our vessel, all of whom were finally thrown into the sea. Their parents grieve all the more, since their children do not find repose in the earth, but are devoured by the predatory fish of the ocean. It is also worth noting that children who have not had either measles or smallpox usually get them on board the ship and for the most part perish as a result.

On one of these voyages a father often becomes infected by his wife and children, or a mother by her small children, or even both parents by their children, or sometimes whole families one by the other, so that many times numerous corpses lie on the cots next to those who are still alive, especially when contagious diseases rage on board.

Many other accidents also occur on these ships, especially falls in which people become totally crippled and can never be completely made whole again. Many also tumble into the sea.

It is not surprising that many passengers fall ill, because in addition to all the other troubles and miseries, warm food is served only three times a week, and at that is very bad, very small in quantity, and so dirty as to be hardly palatable at all. And the water distributed in these ships is often very black, thick with dirt, and full of worms. Even when very thirsty, one is almost unable to drink it without loathing. It is certainly true that at sea one would often spend a great deal of money just for one good piece of bread, or one good drink of water—not even to speak of a good glass of wine—if one could only obtain them. I have, alas, had to experience that myself. For toward the end of the voyage we had to eat the ship's biscuit, which had already been spoiled for a long time, even though in no single piece was there more than the size of a thaler that was not full of red worms and spiders' nests. True, great hunger and thirst teach one to eat and drink everything—but many must forfeit their lives in the process. It is impossible to drink sea water, since it is salty and bitter as gall. If this were not the case, one could undertake such an ocean voyage with far less expense and without so many hardships.

When at last after the long and difficult voyage the ships finally approach land, when one gets to see the headlands for the sight of which the people on board had longed so passionately, then everyone crawls from below to the deck, in order to look at the land from afar. And people cry for joy, pray, and sing praises and thanks to God. The glimpse of land revives the passengers, especially those who are half-dead of illness. Their spirits, however weak they had become, leap up, triumph, and rejoice within them. Such people are now willing to bear all ills patiently, if only they can disembark soon and step on land. But, alas, alas!

When the ships finally arrive in Philadelphia after the long voyage only those are let off who can pay their sea freight or can give good security. The others, who lack the money to pay, have to remain on board until they are purchased and until their purchasers can thus pry them loose from the ship. In this whole process the sick are the worst off, for the healthy are preferred and are more readily paid for. The miserable people who are ill must often still remain at sea and in sight of the city for another two or three weeks—which in many cases means death. Yet many of them, were they able to pay their debts and to leave the ships at once, might escape with their lives.

Before I begin to describe how this commerce in human beings takes place I must report what the voyage to Philadelphia or Pennsylvania costs. Any one older than ten years has to pay £10, or 60 florins, for the passage from Rotterdam to Philadelphia. Children between five and ten pay half fare, that is to say £5, or 30 florins. All children under the age of five get free passage. In return the passengers are transported across the ocean; and as long as they are at sea, they get their board, however bad it is (as I reported above).

All this covers only the sea voyage; the cost of land transportation from home to Rotterdam, including the Rhine passage, comes to at least 40 florins no matter how economically one tries to live on the way. This does not include the expenses of any extraordinary contingencies. I can assure readers of this much—that many travelers on the journey from their homes to Philadelphia spent 200 florins, even with all possible thrift.

This is how the commerce in human beings on board ship takes place. Every day Englishmen, Dutchmen, and High Germans come from Philadelphia and other places, some of them very far away, sometime twenty or thirty or forty hours' journey, and go on board the newly arrived vessel that has brought people from Europe and offers them for sale. From among the healthy they pick out those suitable for the purposes for which they require them. Then they negotiate with them as to the length of the period for which they will go into service in order to pay off their passage, the whole amount of which they generally still owe. When an agreement has been reached, adult persons by written contract bind themselves to serve for three, four, five, or six years, according to their health and age. The very young, between the ages of ten and fifteen, have to serve until they are twenty-one, however.

Many parents in order to pay their fares in this way and get off the ship must barter and sell their children as if they were cattle. Since the fathers and mothers often do not know where or to what masters their children are to be sent, it frequently happens that after leaving the vessel, parents and children do not see each other for years on end, or even for the rest of their lives.

People who arrive without the funds to pay their way and who have children under the age of five, cannot settle their debts by selling them. They must give away these children for nothing to be brought up by strangers; and in return these children must stay in service until they are twenty-one years old. Children between five and ten who owe half-fare, that is, thirty florins, must also go into service in return until they are twenty-one years old, and can neither set free their parents nor take their debts upon themselves. On the other hand, the sale of children older than ten can help to settle a part of their parents' passage charges.

A wife must be responsible for her sick husband and a husband for his sick wife, and pay his or her fare respectively, and must thus serve five to six years not only for herself or himself, but also for the spouse, as the case may be. If both should be ill on arrival, then such persons are brought directly from the ship into a hospital, but not until it is clear that no purchaser for them is to be found. As soon as they have recovered, they must serve to pay off their fare, unless they have the means immediately to discharge the debt.

It often happens that whole families—husband, wife, and children—being sold to different purchasers, become separated, especially when they cannot pay any part of the passage money. When either the husband or the wife has died at sea, having come more than halfway, then the surviving spouse must pay not only his or her fare, but must also pay for or serve out the fare of the deceased.

When both parents have died at sea, having come more than halfway, then their children, especially when they are still young and have nothing to pawn or cannot pay, must be responsible for their own fares as well as those of their parents, and must serve until they are twenty-one years old. Once free of service, they receive a suit of clothing as a parting gift, and if it has been so stipulated the men get a horse and the women a cow.

When a servant in this country has the opportunity to get married he has to pay £5 to £6, that is, 30 to 36 florins for every year that he would still have had to serve. But many who must purchase and pay for their brides in this manner come to regret their purchases later. They would just as soon surrender their damnably expensive wares again and lose their money into the bargain.

No one in this country can run away from a master who has treated him harshly and get far. For there are regulations and laws that ensure that runaways are certainly and quickly recaptured. Those who arrest or return a fugitive get a good reward. For every day that someone who runs away is absent from his master he must as a punishment do service an extra week, for every week an extra month, and for every month a half year. But if the master does not want to take back the recaptured runaway, he is entitled to sell him to someone else for the period of as many years as he would still have had to serve.

Occupations vary, but work is strenuous in this new land; and many who have just come into the country at an advanced age must labor hard for their bread until they die. I will not even speak of the young people. Most jobs involve cutting timber, felling oak trees, and levelling, or as one says there, clearing, great tracts of forest, roots and all. Such forest land, having been cleared in this way, is then laid out in fields and meadows. From the best wood that has been felled people construct railings or fences around the new fields. Inside these, all meadows, all lawns, gardens, and orchards, and all arable land are surrounded and enclosed by thickly cut wood planks set in zigzag fashion one above the other. And thus cattle, horses, and sheep are confined to pasture land.

Our Europeans who have been purchased must work hard all the time. For new fields are constantly being laid out; and thus they learn from experience that oak tree stumps are just as hard in America as they are in Germany. In these hot regions there is particularly fulfilled in them that with which the Lord God afflicted man in the first book of Moses, on account of his sin and disobedience, namely: "Thou shalt eat thy bread in the sweat of thy brow." Thus let him who wants to earn his piece of bread honestly and in a Christian manner and who can only do this by manual labor in his native country stay *there* rather than come to America.

For, in the first place, things are no better in Pennsylvania. However hard one may have had to work in his native land, conditions are bound to be equally tough or even tougher in the new country. Furthermore the emigrant has to undertake the arduous voyage, which means not only that he must suffer more misery for half a year than he would have to suffer doing the hardest labor, but also that he must spend approximately two hundred florins which no one will refund to him. If he has that much money, he loses it; if he does not have it, he must work off his debt as a slave or as a miserable servant. So let people stay in their own country and earn their keep honestly for themselves and their families. Furthermore, I want to say that those people who may let themselves be talked into something and seduced into the voyage by the thieves of human beings are the biggest fools if they really believe that in America or Pennsylvania roasted pigeons are going to fly into their mouths without their having to work for them.

How sad and miserable is the fate of so many thousand German families who lost all the money they ever owned in the course of the long and difficult voyage, many of whom perished wretchedly and had to be buried at sea and who, once they have arrived in the new country, saw their old and young separated and sold away into places far removed one from the other! The saddest aspect of all this is that in most instances parents must give away their young children getting nothing in return. For such children are destined never to see or recognize parents, brothers, and sisters again, and, after they have been sold to strangers, are not brought up in any sort of Christian faith.

In Pennsylvania there exist so many varieties of doctrines and sects that it is impossible to name them all. Many people do not reveal their own particular beliefs to anyone. Furthermore there are many hundreds of adults who not only are unbaptized, but who do not even want baptism. Many others pay no attention to the Sacraments and to the Holy Bible, or even to God and His Word. Some do not even believe in the existence of a true God or Devil, Heaven or Hell, Salvation or Damnation, the Resurrection of the Dead, the Last Judgment and Eternal Life, but think that everything visible is of merely natural origin. For in Pennsylvania not only is everyone allowed to believe what he wishes; he is also at liberty to express these beliefs publicly and freely.

Thus when young people not raised in the fundamentals of religion must go into service for many years with such freethinkers and unbelievers and are not permitted by these people to attend any church or school, especially when they live far away from them, then such innocent souls do not reach a true knowledge of the Divine and are brought up like heathen or Indians.

The ocean voyage is sometimes dangerous for those people who bring money and effects with them from home, because at sea much is often spoiled by inrushing water. And sometimes they are robbed on board by dishonest people. Thus such once-wealthy folk are to have really unhappy experiences. . . .

J. HECTOR ST. JOHN DE CRÈVECOEUR

When France lost the siege of Quebec in 1759, military surveyor Michel-Guillaume Saint-Jean de Crèvecoeur (1735–1813) headed south instead of returning to his native Normandy, settling at Pine Hill in Orange County, New York, and becoming a prosperous—and increasingly loyalist—gentleman farmer. He wrote a dozen essays about colonial life in which he defined the American character. Unlike many earlier accounts by newcomers presenting disappointing and at times miserable conditions, Crèvecoeur was one of the first to celebrate the country as a magnet for potential settlers. It is Crèvecoeur who gives us the melting pot metaphor. Forced to flee during the American Revolution, he returned to France where he published these essays to great acclaim: in French in 1781 and a year later in English as *Letters from an American Farmer*. He came back to the new United States as a consul in 1783, continued to write about the American scene, and remained in his sometime adoptive country for another ten years before returning to France.

from

Letters from an American Farmer

I wish I could be acquainted with the feelings and thoughts which must agitate the heart and present themselves to the mind of an enlightened Englishman, when he first lands on this continent. He must greatly rejoice that he lived at a time to see this fair country discovered and settled; he must necessarily feel a share of national pride, when he views the chain of settlements which embellishes these extended shores. When he says to himself, this is the work of my countrymen, who, when convulsed by factions, afflicted by a variety of miseries and wants, restless and impatient, took refuge here. They brought along with them their national genius, to which they principally owe what liberty they enjoy, and what substance they possess. Here he sees the industry of his native country displayed in a new manner, and traces in their works the embrios of all the arts, sciences, and ingenuity which flourish in Europe. Here he beholds fair cities, substantial villages, extensive fields, an immense country filled with decent houses, good roads, orchards, meadows, and bridges, where an hundred years ago all was wild, woody and uncultivated! What a train of pleasing ideas this fair spectacle must suggest; it is a prospect which must inspire a good citizen with the most heartfelt pleasure. The difficulty consists in the manner of viewing so extensive a scene. He is arrived on a new continent; a modern society offers itself to his contemplation, different from what he had hitherto seen. It is not composed, as in Europe, of great lords who possess every thing, and of a herd of people who have nothing. Here are no aristocratical families, no courts, no kings, no bishops, no ecclesiastical dominion, no invisible power giving to a few a very visible one; no great manufacturers employing thousands, no great refinements of luxury. The rich and the poor are not so far removed from each other as they are in Europe. Some few towns excepted, we are all tillers of the earth, from Nova Scotia to West Florida. We are a people of cultivators, scattered over an immense territory, communicating with each other by means of good roads and navigable rivers, united by the silken bands of mild government, all respecting the laws, without dreading their power, because they are equitable. We are all animated with the spirit of an industry which is unfettered and unrestrained, because each person works for himself. If he travels through our rural districts he views not the hostile castle, and the haughty mansion, contrasted with the clay-built hut and miserable cabbin, where cattle and men help to keep each other warm, and dwell in meanness, smoke, and indigence. A pleasing uniformity of decent competence appears throughout our habitations. The meanest of our log-houses is a dry and comfortable habitation. Lawyer or merchant are the fairest titles our towns afford; that of a farmer is the only appellation of the rural inhabitants of our country. It must take some time ere he can reconcile himself to our dictionary, which is but short in words of dignity, and names of honour. There, on a Sunday, he sees a congregation of respectable farmers and their wives, all clad in neat homespun, well mounted, or riding in their own humble waggons. There is not among them an esquire, saving the unlettered magistrate. There he sees a parson as simple as his flock, a farmer who does not riot on the labour of others. We have no princes, for whom we toil, starve, and bleed: we are the most perfect society now existing in the world. Here man is free as he ought to be; nor is this pleasing equality so transitory as many others are. Many ages will not see the shores of our great lakes replenished with inland nations, nor the unknown bounds of North America entirely peopled. Who can tell how far it extends? Who can tell the millions of men whom it will feed and contain? for no European foot has as yet travelled half the extent of this mighty continent!

The next wish of this traveller will be to know whence came all these people? they are a mixture of English, Scotch, Irish, French, Dutch, Germans, and Swedes. From this promiscuous breed, that race now called Americans have arisen. The eastern provinces must indeed be excepted, as being the unmixed descendents of Englishmen. I have heard many wish that they had been more intermixed also: for my part, I am no wisher, and think it much better as it has happened. They exhibit a most conspicuous figure in this great and variegated picture; they too enter for a great share in the pleasing perspective displayed in these thirteen provinces. I know it is fashionable to reflect on them, but I respect them for what they have done; for the accuracy and wisdom with which they have settled their territory; for the decency of their manners; for their early love of letters; their ancient college, the first in this hemisphere; for their industry; which to me who am but a farmer, is the criterion of everything. There never was a people, situated as they are, who with so ungrateful a soil have done more in so short a time. Do you think that the monarchical ingredients which are more prevalent in other governments, have purged them from all foul stains? Their histories assert the contrary.

In this great American asylum, the poor of Europe have by some means met together, and in consequence of various causes; to what purpose should they ask one another what countrymen they are? Alas, two thirds of them had no country. Can a wretch who wanders about, who works and starves, whose life is a continual scene of sore affliction or pinching penury; can that man call England or any other kingdom his country? A country that had no bread for him, whose fields procured him no harvest, who met with nothing but the frowns of the rich, the severity of the laws, with jails and punishments; who owned not a single foot of the extensive surface of this planet? No! urged by a variety of motives, here they came. Every thing has tended to regenerate them; new laws, a new mode of living, a new social system; here they are become men: in Europe they were as so many useless plants, wanting vegetative mould, and refreshing showers; they withered, and were mowed down by want, hunger, and war; but now by the power of transplantation, like all other plants they have taken root and flourished! Formerly they were not numbered in any civil lists of their country, except in those of the poor; here they rank as citizens. By what invisible power has this surprising metamorphosis been performed? By that of the laws and that of their industry. The laws, the indulgent laws, protect them as they arrive, stamping on them the symbol of adoption; they receive ample rewards for their labours; these accumulated rewards procure them lands; those lands confer on them the title of freemen, and to that title every benefit is affixed which men can possibly require. This is the great operation daily performed by our laws. From whence proceed these laws? From our government. Whence the government? It is derived from the original genius and strong desire of the people ratified and confirmed by the crown. This is the great chain which links us all, this is the picture which every province exhibits, Nova Scotia excepted. There the crown has done all; either there were no people who had genius, or it was not much attended to: the consequence is, that the province is very thinly inhabited indeed; the power of the crown in conjunction with the musketos has prevented men from settling there. Yet some parts of it flourished once, and it contained a mild harmless set of people. But for the fault of a few leaders, the whole were banished. The greatest political error the crown ever committed in America, was to cut off men from a country which wanted nothing but men!

What attachment can a poor European emigrant have for a country where he had nothing? The knowledge of the language, the love of a few kindred as poor as himself, were the only cords that tied him: his country is now that which gives him land, bread, protection, and consequence: *Ubi panis ibi patria*, is the motto of all emigrants. What then is the American, this new man? He is either an European, or the descendant of an European, hence that strange mixture of blood, which you will find in no other country. I could point out to you a family whose grandfather was an Englishman, whose wife was Dutch, whose son married a French woman, and whose present four sons have now four wives of different nations. *He* is an American, who leaving behind him all his ancient prejudices and manners, receives new ones from the new mode of life he has embraced, the new government he obeys, and the new rank he holds. He becomes an American by being received in the broad lap of our great *Alma Mater*. Here individuals of all nations are melted into a new race of men, whose labours and posterity will one day cause great changes in the world. Americans are the western pilgrims, who are carrying along with them that great mass of arts, sciences, vigour, and industry which began long since in the east; they will finish the great circle. The Americans were once scattered all over Europe; here they are incorporated into one of the finest systems of population which has ever appeared, and which will hereafter become distinct by the power of the different climates they inhabit. The American ought therefore to love this country much better than that wherein either he or his forefathers were born. Here the rewards of his industry follow with equal steps the progress of his labour; his labour is founded on the basis of nature, *self-interest*; can it want a stronger allurement? Wives and children, who before in vain demanded of him a morsel of bread, now, fat and frolicsome, gladly help their father to clear those fields whence exuberant crops are to arise to feed and to clothe them all; without any part being claimed, either by a despotic prince, a rich abbot, or a mighty lord. Here religion demands but little of him; a small voluntary salary to the minister, and gratitude to God; can he refuse these? The American is a new man, who acts upon new principles; he must therefore entertain new ideas, and form new opinions. From involuntary idleness, servile dependence, penury, and useless labour, he has passed to toils of a very different nature, rewarded by ample subsistence.—This is an American.

PHILLIS WHEATLEY

In 1761, when she was seven or eight years old, Phillis Wheatley (c. 1753–1784) was kidnapped from her home in the Senegambian region of West Africa and brought to Boston, Massachusetts, where she was purchased by John Wheatley, a wealthy tailor, as a servant for his wife, Susanna. Taught to read, Phillis soon demonstrated a prodigious mastery of scripture and began to write verse. She published her first poem, an elegy "On the Death of the Rev. Mr. George Whitefield," in 1770, and became a literary sensation, first in Boston, and later in London, where she traveled in 1773 to publish her first book, *Poems on Various Subjects*. "On being brought from Africa to America" is perhaps the best known poem by this young African slave who is today the best known American poet of the colonial period. Its apparent celebration of her own forced immigration to America might puzzle, but her challenge to her white audience, driven home with a play of words keyed to the sugar trade that destroyed the lives of so many Africans, remains profoundly powerful.

On being brought from Africa to America

'Twas mercy brought me from my *Pagan* land,
Taught my benighted soul to understand
That there's a God, that there's a *Saviour* too:
Once I redemption neither sought nor knew.
Some view our sable race with scornful eye,
"Their colour is a diabolic die."
Remember, *Christians*, *Negros*, black as *Cain*,
May be refin'd, and join th' angelic train.

JOHN JAMES AUDUBON

Born in Haiti, the son of a French merchant and a French chamber-maid (who died the year he was born), Jean Rabine—or some years later John James Audubon (1785–1851)—invented a variety of stories to explain his origins. At the age of three he was sent to Nantes, France, to live with his father's family. It was during his relatively carefree childhood there that he began to collect natural curiosities. The slave uprising in Haiti prevented him from returning to the island to oversee his father's sugar plantations. Instead at the age of 18, in part to avoid conscription into Napoleon's army, he came to the United States to manage property his father had purchased at Mill Grove, near Norristown, Pennsylvania. It was here that he fell in love with Lucy Bakewell, the daughter of his neighbor, and began his intense lifelong fascination with birds. The passage included here is taken from a short autobiographical account that Audubon had originally written for his sons; "Myself" was published by his daughter in *Scribner's* in March 1893.

from

Myself

I was within a few months of being seventeen years old, when my step-mother, who was an earnest Catholic, took into her head that I should be confirmed; my father agreed. I was surprised and indifferent, but yet as I loved her as if she had been my own mother,—and well did she merit my deepest affection,—I took to the catechism, studied it and other matters pertaining to the ceremony, and all was performed to her liking. Not long after this, my father, anxious as he was that I should be enrolled in Napoleon's army as a Frenchman, found it necessary to send me back to my own beloved country, the United States of America, and I came with intense and indescribable pleasure.

On landing at New York I caught the yellow fever by walking to the bank at Greenwich to get the money to which my father's letter of credit entitled me. The kind man who commanded the ship that brought me from France, whose name was a common one, John Smith, took particular charge of me, removed me to Morristown, N.J., and placed me under the care of two Quaker ladies who kept a boarding-house. To their skilful and untiring ministrations I may safely say I owe the prolongation of my life. Letters were forwarded by them to my father's agent, Miers Fisher of Philadelphia, of whom I have more to say hereafter. He came for me in his carriage and removed me to his villa, at a short distance from Philadelphia and on the road toward Trenton. There I would have found myself quite comfortable had not incidents taken place which are so connected with the change in my life as to call immediate attention to them.

Miers Fisher had been my father's trusted agent for about eighteen years, and the old gentlemen entertained great mutual friendship; indeed it would seem that Mr. Fisher was actually desirous that I should become a member of his family, and this was evinced within a few days by the manner in which the good Quaker presented me to a daughter of no mean appearance, but toward whom I happened to take an unconquerable dislike. Then he was opposed to music of all descriptions, as well as to dancing, could not bear me to carry a gun, or fishing-rod, and, indeed, condemned most of my amusements. All these things were difficulties toward accomplishing a plan which, for aught I know to the contrary, had been premeditated between him and my father, and rankled the heart of the kindly, if somewhat strict Quaker. They troubled me much also; at times I wished myself anywhere but under the roof of Mr. Fisher, and at last I reminded him that it was his duty to install me on the estate to which my father had sent me.

One morning, therefore, I was told that the carriage was ready to carry me there, and toward my future home he and I went. You are too well acquainted with the position of Mill Grove for me to allude to that now; suffice it to say that we reached the former abode of my father about sunset. I was presented to our tenant, William Thomas, who also was a Quaker, and took possession under certain restrictions, which amounted to my not receiving more than enough money per quarter than was considered sufficient for the expenditure of a young gentleman.

Miers Fisher left me the next morning, and after him went my blessings, for I thought his departure a true deliverance; yet this was only because our tastes and educations were so different, for he certainly was a good and learned man. Mill Grove was ever to me a blessed spot; in my daily walks I thought I perceived the traces left by my father as I looked on the even fences round the fields, or on the regular manner with which avenues of trees, as well as the orchards, had been planted by his hand. The mill was also a source of joy to me, and in the cave, which you too remember, where the Pewees were wont to build, I never failed to find quietude and delight.

Hunting, fishing, drawing, and music occupied my every moment; cares I knew not, and cared naught about them. I purchased excellent and beautiful horses, visited all such neighbors as I found congenial spirits, and was as happy as happy could be. A few months after my arrival at Mill Grove, I was informed one day that an English family had purchased the plantation next to mine, that the name of the owner was Bakewell, and moreover that he had several very handsome and interesting daughters, and beautiful pointer dogs. I listened, but cared not a jot about them at the time. The place was within sight of Mill Grove, and Fatland Ford, as it was called, was merely divided from my estate by a road leading to the Schuylkill River. Mr. William Bakewell, the father of the family, had called on me one day, but, finding I was rambling in the woods in search of birds, left a card and an invitation to go shooting with him. Now this gentleman was an Englishman, and I such a foolish boy that, entertaining the greatest prejudices against all of his nationality, I did not return his visit for many weeks, which was as absurd as it was ungentlemanly and impolite.

Mrs. Thomas, good soul, more than once spoke to me on the subject, as well as her worthy husband, but all to no import; English was English with me, my poor childish mind was settled on that, and as I wished to know none of the race the call remained unacknowledged.

Frosty weather, however, came, and anon was the ground covered with the deep snow. Grouse were abundant along the fir-covered ground near the creek, and as I was in pursuit of game one frosty morning I chanced to meet Mr. Bakewell in the woods. I was struck with the kind politeness of his manner, and found him an expert marksman. Entering into conversation, I

admired the beauty of his well-trained dogs, and, apologizing for my dis-
courtesy, finally promised to call upon him and his family.

Well do I recollect the morning, and may it please God that I may never
forget it, when for the first time I entered Mr. Bakewell's dwelling. It happened that he was absent from home, and I was shown into a parlor where
only one young lady was snugly seated at her work by the fire. She rose on
my entrance, offered me a seat, and assured me of the gratification her father
would feel on his return, which, she added, would be in a few moments, as she
would despatch a servant for him. Other ruddy cheeks and bright eyes made
their transient appearance, but, like spirits gay, soon vanished from my sight;
and there I sat, my gaze riveted, as it were, on the young girl before me, who,
half working, half talking, essayed to make the time pleasant to me. Oh! may
god bless her! It was she, my dear sons, who afterward became my beloved
wife, and your mother. Mr. Bakewell soon made his appearance, and received
me with the manner and hospitality of a true English gentleman. The other
members of the family were soon introduced to me, and "Lucy" was told to
have luncheon produced. She now arose from her seat a second time, and her
form, to which I had previously paid but partial attention, showed both grace
and beauty; and my heart followed every one of her steps. The repast over,
guns and dogs were made ready.

Lucy, I was pleased to believe, looked upon me with some favor, and I
turned more especially to her on leaving. I felt that certain *"je ne sais quoi"*
which intimated that, at least, she was not indifferent to me.

LORENZO DA PONTE

Immigration encourages, if indeed it does not require, a capacity for self-invention and re-invention. By any standard Lorenzo Da Ponte (1749–1838), whose picaresque *Memoirs* recount his colorful life in the cultural capitals of *ancien régime* Europe, came well prepared. Born Emanuel Conegliano to a Jewish family in Ceneda in the Republic of Venice (now Vittorio Veneto, Italy), at 14 he renamed himself after the bishop who baptized him when his widowed father converted himself and his three sons to Roman Catholicism in order to remarry. As portrayed in his *Memoirs* (inspired by those of his friend Giacomo Casanova), Da Ponte was a good-hearted, somewhat heedless soul who careened back and forth from poverty to prosperity while taking on a great many roles: priest, teacher, gambler, publisher, bookseller, bordello operator, political exile, poet at the court of Austrian Emperor Joseph, impresario of the London opera, librettist of Mozart's *The Marriage of Figaro, Così fan tutte,* and *Don Giovanni.* The far-flung nature of Da Ponte's career reminds us that the 17th and 18th centuries were a time of unprecedented mobility for the peoples of Europe. The journey across the Atlantic was often just the most dramatic stage in a larger pattern of movement that prepared immigrants for the challenges of the New World. Da Ponte's challenges in America would be many, but at his death he could claim the distinction of being Columbia University's first professor of Italian.

from
Memoirs

My passage from London to Philadelphia was long, disastrous and full of annoyances and strain. It lasted not less than eighty-six days, over the entire course of which I was without all those comforts, which my age, my state of mind, and a tremendous voyage at sea, might seem to have required, to make it endurable, if not a pleasure. I had heard tell that to get to America, it was sufficient for me to pay a certain sum to the captain of the vessel on which I embarked; and that he would then provide me with the necessaries. That may have been well enough for people who met honest captains, courteous and well bred and concerned to do everything possible to make the voyage pleasant for the passengers. I fell into the clutches of a rascal from Nantucket, whose accustomed business was whale-fishing and who treated his passengers like the vilest sailors, whom, in turn, he treated exactly like those monsters of the sea. He had with him only the coarsest provisions and of these he was a very sparing dispenser. My first mistake was to pay him forty-four guineas before setting foot on his ship, without contracts or papers, and without making adequate investigation; asking nothing else of him than to be taken to Philadelphia and fed. At the dinner hour, I began to foresee what my fate was to be. The meal was made ready on the deck aft. A rickety old table of worm-eaten pineboards, a tablecloth blacker than a charcoal-burner's shirt; three plates of nicked china, and three rusty iron knives and forks were the sweet preludes to the approaching feast. Messire the Nantucketer took a seat, invited me to sit down opposite him and in a few minutes the African cook arrived with a great wooden bowl in one hand and a pewter platter in the other, which he silently deposited on the table, and, lowering his head, departed.

"Odoardo," cried my aquatic host in a loud voice, "Odoardo! Come to dinner!"

At the second call, "Mr. Odoardo" appeared, emerging from the vessel's cabin where he had been sleeping for some hours. He nodded his head a little and, without speaking to me or looking at me, sat down to the captain's right. His strange appearance did not leave me time to look at what that bowl contained. "Odoardo" was the image of a sleeping Bacchus, save that he was dressed like a miller in working garb, his *quondam* white linen according perfectly with the charcoal-burner's shirt and with the tablecloth of our Typhoïs. The latter, meantime, had set in front of me a little pewter plate with several spoonfuls of a broth he had scooped from the sailoresque bowl; a broth which I had at first sight taken for the water from boiled chestnuts. Observing that I sat gazing at it without eating, he said:

"What, Mr. Italiano, aren't you going to have some chicken soup?"

I was very hungry, and I am especially fond of chicken. I turned my eyes upon that dear bird! Let any hungry soul imagine my state of mind, when, staring at the object before me, I thought I saw not so much a boiled fowl as a crow that had lost its feathers in an argument with a cat. I allowed my two companions to riot at will among such appetizing tid-bits. I swooped down upon a huge piece of English cheese, which, to my good luck, lay at my right, and made a meal of it. Mr. Abissai Haydn, as the captain was named, looked at me a little sourly, gaped, and said nothing; but, noticing that a bottle of wine was also within my reach and fearing that I might treat it as I had treated the cheese, *la bocca sollevò dal fiero pasto*, got up from the place where he was sitting, gathered that bottle between his fins, drew out the cork, gave a little glass of it to me, and another to our friend the flour-grinder, recorked the bottle, put it under lock and key, and strode away whistling.

That, more or less, was the manner in which this harpooner of whales treated me during all that double Lent of mine; save that, instead of broth of chestnut water, or crow-chicken, every day there appeared either a bit of dried meat or a slice of salt pork, the mere sight of which would have been enough to banish the hunger of Count Ugolino. To cap the climax of my woe, I had not brought a bed with me. I was obliged, therefore, to make a kind of litter of the shirts and clothes I had with me in order not to ease my aged limbs on the hard wood of a very narrow niche on which one would have rested badly even with mattresses and pillows.

Despite all these hardships I arrived safe and sound in Philadelphia on the morning of the fourth of June. I hurried to the house of Captain Collet, who had brought my family to America. There I learned that they had settled in New York. I left about two o'clock in the afternoon, and reached that city on the following morning toward sunrise. I knew the name of the street, but not the number of the house, where my people were living. I went a short distance down the street and knocked at a door to ask for information. By a strange and delightful coincidence, it happened to be the very house in which they were staying. There is no need of telling how I was received. They had already begun to fear a shipwreck in view of the extraordinary length of my passage, and especially on account of the dangers of the Atlantic Ocean quite usual at a season when navigation is prodigiously impeded by floating masses of ice. In fact, not many days before my arrival, the *Jove* had gone down, with the loss of many lives.

After some days of quiet amid the tender rejoicings of my family, I turned, without losing time, to business. Very little had I brought with me from London: a box of violin strings, a number of Italian classics of scant worth, several copies of a very fine Virgil, several of Davila's History, and from forty to fifty dollars in cash. Such the treasures which I had been able to rescue from the talons of usurers, constables, lawyers, enemies and treacherous friends in London, where for eleven years I had followed the occupation of bookseller, printer, manager's agent and opera poet! My wife, however, had brought with her from six to seven thousand dollars, not saved by me, however.

Fear of diminishing or consuming so tenuous a capital by sitting too long with folded hands, induced me to embrace the counsel of a man who, I supposed, was perfectly familiar with the line of business he was urging me to undertake.* I turned grocer accordingly; and let him who has a grain of sense imagine how I must have laughed at myself every time my poet's hand was called upon to weigh out two ounces of tea, or measure half a yard of "pigtail,"† now to a cobbler, now to a teamster, or pour out, in exchange for three cents, a morning dram, which was not, however, the *dramma* of the *Cosa rara* nor that of the *Nozze di Figarò*!‡ So goes the world! Yet in spite of that, if the occupation I had assumed was not very dignified, my purse was not the loser by it.

My troubles began early in September. Yellow fever broke out at that time and obliged me to depart from that city with my family. I withdrew to Elizabeth Town where I bought a little house and garden, and continued in trade. Unfortunately I took a licentious wastrel into business with me: and the consequence may be easily guessed. What with his exorbitant expenditure, and the calamity of having to deal with the foremost rascals in Jersey, in a short

*It was my wife's father who gave me the advice in question, thus becoming the innocent cause of my first misfortune in America. L. Da P.

†"Pigtail" was a kind of plug tobacco. L. Da P.

‡"Dram," Italian *una dramma*, a sip of liquor. The difference from *un dramma* (an opera) is in the gender, not in the price. Some people will see my joke! L. Da P.

time everything had gone up in smoke. I then dissolved the partnership. It was found that he was in my debt to the amount of a thousand dollars, for which he gave me three notes payable in one, two and three years. But on the maturity of the first, he fled to Jamaica.* I was about ready to abandon commerce when a little dinner of rather original device brought me to that decision very suddenly. It is an instructive little story, and quite novel. I will tell it briefly, without comment.

I owed a balance of one hundred and twenty dollars to an Irish grocer in New York. Chancing to be in that city, I called on him, and asked him to go over our accounts. There were some mistakes, and it would take some time to rectify them. Everything, however, was tranquilly attended to. After a time, his wife called him to dinner, and he insisted, almost using force, that I should dine with him. We talked little of business as we ate. I told him, merely, that I had left a variety of country produce in the hands of a merchant in New York and that I would instruct the merchant in question to sell them to him, paying him what I owed.

To that the Irishman made no reply, but called to his clerk to bring a bottle of wine and whispered a few words in the man's ear, beckoning to him, then, to withdraw. I drank a small glass of the wine with him, and we went back to our accounts. There was still a difference of thirty dollars in our calculations. I, in fact, did not owe him more than one hundred and twenty dollars. He was asking for a hundred and fifty. Night coming on, I told him that my presence was necessary in Elizabeth Town and that I had to be going, but would return to New York in a day or two and settle my bill with him. He made no reply to that either, but going, coming, talking of this and that, he seemed to be seeking pretexts to detain me. To succeed the better he went and got the bottle, drank "to my good health," insisted that I drink to his, and in some minutes the clerk was back, panting and dripping with sweat. The Irishman then told me that I could go or stay, just as I found convenient. He held out his hand. I shook it, and departed.

I had not gone forty paces when I felt a heavy hand clap down on my shoulder and a stentorian voice cry:

*I must give the scoundrel's name; H. Micheli. L. Da P.

"You are my prisoner!"

I turned and could see that the constable who was arresting me was the clerk of my generous host of the sour dinner!

I asked him who he was and what he wanted of me.

"I am a deputy sheriff," he replied, "I ask you for the one hundred and fifty dollars you owe Mr. John Mackinly, or else bail from two owners of real property for your appearance at the proper time. If you cannot do either the one thing or the other, you will be pleased to accompany me to prison!"

I said I would make no comment on this story. I shall do as I said, leaving the comment to my readers. I deposited several objects of value in the hands of Messrs. Bradhurst & Field, respectable grocers in New York. They went bail for me. A few days later I paid that man one hundred and twenty dollars which was all that I owed him. I did not see him or hear of him for more than four years. One day, however, I picked up a newspaper and read the following paragraph:

"John Mackinly was killed in Savannah yesterday morning, by a stroke of lightning!"

I will make no comment on that either!

On returning to Elizabeth Town, that dinner and that Irish bottle gave me such a terrible indigestion that I could not bear the mention of business. I sold as best I could such merchandise as was left me and set out to pay my debts. The income from the sale of my stock was not sufficient to pay all of them, so I sold my house and garden which I had hoped was to be the peaceful shelter of my declining years. I then disposed of several objects which had served to ornament the house or persons in the family, and, between the first of December to the first of January, I had the satisfaction of paying three thousand four hundred dollars to my creditors. Thus, in the sixtieth year of my life, I did not hesitate a single moment to despoil myself of everything, in order to pay not my own debts, but those of an imprudent man whom I, more imprudent than he, had declared my partner in business, though he had cheated me in London a long time before. Those were mistakes for which I neither ask nor deserve pity!

Without help, money, friends, what could I do, what plans should I make in order to support a family that depended entirely on my labors? I returned to New York and I began to examine whether I could somehow make a living along the lines of Italian or Latin letters. In a few days I learned that as far as the Italian language and literature were concerned, they were about as well known in this city as Turkish or Chinese. As for Latin I found that it was cultivated generally and that "gentlemen in America thought they knew enough not to need the instruction of an Italian Latinist." Those were the very words that an American gentleman used in speaking to me a few days after my return from Jersey to New York. Of them I shall speak more at length at the opportune moment. Will my reader just bear them in mind!

I was almost hopeless of success, when the good genius of Italian literature willed that, as I was passing in front of the shop of the late M. Riley, bookseller on Broadway, it occurred to me to enter. I approached his counter and asked him if he had any Italian books in his store.

"I have a few," he replied, "but no one ever asks for them."

While we stood chatting, an American gentleman approached and joined our conversation. I was soon aware from his remarks that he was admirably read in a variety of literature. Coming by chance to allude to the language and literature of my country, I took occasion to ask him why they should be so little studied in a country as enlightened as I believed America to be.

"Oh sir," he replied, "modern Italy is not, unfortunately, the Italy of ancient times. She is not that sovereign queen which gave to the ages and to the world emulators, nay rivals, of the supreme Greeks."

He was then pleased to inform me that "five or at the most six" were the writers of fame, of whom the country of those great men could boast over the past six centuries. I asked him, not without a sarcastic smile, to name those authors; and he: "Dante, Petrarch, Boccaccio, Ariosto, Tasso, . . ." And he stopped: "To tell the truth, I cannot recall the sixth."

He had been counting the names off on his fingers; he halted, accordingly, with his little finger held tightly between the forefinger and the thumb of his right hand, like a person thinking. I laid hold on those fingers and said, gaily:

"You will not let go of that finger for a whole month, if you allow me to hold your hand like this till I shall have finished naming one by one the great men of the last six centuries in Italy!"

"We do not know them," he said.

"So I observe!" I replied. "But do you suppose a teacher of Italian would find any favor and encouragement . . . ?"

The bookseller who had been listening to our conversation, broke in vivaciously:

"There's not the slightest doubt of that!"

"If that be the case," said I quickly, "I shall be the fortunate Italian to make known to gentlemen in America the merits of his language, and the number and deserts of his greatest men of letters!"

Within three days, twelve of the most cultivated youths and maidens in New York were taking Italian lessons of me. The fifteenth day of December in the year 1807, I began my first career as a teacher in New York, under the happiest auspices, in the house of the venerable Bishop Moore ever of sweet, dear and honored memory to me. It was there that I laid the cornerstone of my fortunate edifice. The first to adorn it luminously were those incomparable young men, his son and his nephew; then Mr. John M. Vicker and Mr. E. Pendleton, four gentlemen whose knowledge, good manners, and Christian and social virtues are most justly appreciated by the noble and populous city of New York. The example of persons so illustrious could not but produce the most excellent impression upon the remainder of the citizens. In less than a month I had twenty-four young people to teach. Since, at the moment of my present writing,* I could count more than five hundred, it does not seem to me à propos to mention the names of them all

benchè scritti nel cor tutti li porto,
a mia gloria, a mia gioia, a mio conforto.

The kindness with which my lessons were listened to, the regularity with which they were attended, and the extraordinary favor accorded both to me and to the language of my country, in a short time created such an enthusiasm among the more studious young people of the town that, for my second trimester, I could only with the greatest difficulty provide for the number of

---

*The moment when I first printed these Memoirs. Later on, between the years 1826 and 1830, the number of pupils who learned Italian from me doubled. L. Da P.

my pupils. It seemed, however, that Providence were giving me a strength, a steadfastness, a courage that my advanced years could not supply. It was not long before I had the supreme pleasure of hearing that very learned gentleman who had not been able to remember the sixth of our classics, solemnly sing his recantation, and see him transformed into one of the most fiery and zealous promoters and patrons of the Italian language and of Italian authors, who, at his example and advice, were read, studied, and admired by the liveliest and keenest talents of both sexes.

Perceiving, to my unbounded joy, such general enthusiasm in the young people of those days, I neglected no means nor allurement to add fuel to the fire, and foment it. There were not in New York at that time any booksellers who had Italian books on their shelves. I erred, in the first edition of these Memoirs, in saying I imported a chosen number of classical works from various countries in Europe. It is true that I mentioned such hopes and desires to a certain bookseller in Genoa; but I had no other reply than that he would forward me the books on receipt of their cost—the sum amounted to a little more than ninety dollars (such the first encouragement the egregious booksellers of Italy gave me). It was my dear brother, Paolo, by no means rich, and harassed by terrible worries, who sent me the first series of our classics. I distributed them among my pupils, incited them to read and ponder them, and in less than three years I had the pure delight of seeing the libraries and the desks of studious Americans ornamented with the flower of our literature which was making its first appearance in this country.

I then proposed and succeeded in establishing day and evening assemblies in which no other language than Italian was spoken, where the most beautiful passages of our orators and poets were read aloud or recited from memory and where we performed little comedies or operas composed by me for the most dignified and respected young ladies in the city. The effect of such exercises was truly marvelous. They added the delight of amusement to the flame of general enthusiasm for the study of this beautiful language, and served at the same time to facilitate the acquisition and the practice of it. We once gave on a little stage I set up in my own house, the *Mirra* of the great

Alfieri. Our audience was made up of one hundred and fifty persons who had all been introduced by me to the study of the Italian language within a space of three years. The delight occasioned by that divine production, and the general approbation of it is not to be described. I was obliged to repeat it the following evening to greater applause and before a greater number of spectators.

FANNY KEMBLE

Frances (Fanny) Kemble was born into a family of English actors in 1809. Her stage debut as Juliet at Covent Garden in 1829 was a sensation. For three years she played leading parts in London before traveling to New York City with her father, where the two began a barnstorming theatrical tour around the country ("nothing finer did ever stage exhibit," thought Walt Whitman in *Specimen Days*). In 1834 she married Pierce Butler, a Georgia slaveholder, and gave up the stage, and the following year she published her *Journal of Residence in America*, the first two of what would be eight volumes of published journals. The Butlers' marriage was never a success, due in large part to Fanny's outspoken views on abolition and women's rights; they were divorced in 1848. During the Civil War she published her *Journal of a Residence on a Georgian Plantation* (1863), hoping to sway public opinion in England against the Confederate cause. Kemble died in London in 1893.

from
Journals

New York City
September 3, 1832

T he houses are almost all painted glaring white or red; the other favourite colours appear to be pale straw colour and grey. They have all green venetian shutters, which give an idea of coolness, and almost every house has a tree or trees in its vicinity, which looks pretty and garden-like. We reached our inn,—the gentlemen were waiting for us, and led us to our drawing-room. I had been choking for the last three hours, and could endure no more, but sobbed like a wretch aloud.

There was a piano in the room, to which I flew with the appetite of one who has lived on the music of the speaking-trumpet for a month; that, and some iced lemonade and cake, presently restored my spirits. I went on playing and singing till I was exhausted, and then sat down and wrote journal. Mr. [William Hodgkinson, son of one of the Duke of Norfolk's tenants who befriended the Kembles on his emigration to Boston] went out and got me Sir Humphrey Davy's *Salmonia*, which I had been desiring, and he had been speaking of, on board ship.

At five o'clock we all met once more together to dinner. Our drawing-room being large and pleasant, the table was laid in it. 'Tis curious how an acquaintanceship of thirty days has contrived to bind together in one common feeling of kindness and good-fellowship persons who never met before, who may never meet again. Tomorrow we all separate to betake ourselves each to our several paths; and as if loath to part company, they all agreed to meet once more on the eve of doing so, probably for ever. How strongly this clinging principle is inherent in our natures! These men have no fine sympathies of artificial creation, and this exhibition of *adhesiveness* is in them a real, and heart-sprung feeling. It touched me—indeed it may well do so; for friends of thirty days are better than utter strangers, and when these my shipmates shall be scattered abroad, there will be no human being left near us whose face we know, or whose voice is familiar to us. Our dinner was a favourable specimen of eating as practised in this new world; everything good, only in too great a profusion, the wine drinkable, and the fruit beautiful to look at; in point of flavour it was infinitely inferior to English hot-house fruit, or even fine espalier fruit raised in a good aspect.

Everything was wrapped in ice, which is a most luxurious necessary in this hot climate; but the things were put on the table in a slovenly, outlandish fashion; fish, soup, and meat, at once, and puddings, and tarts, and cheese, at another once; no finger glasses, and a patched table-cloth,—in short, a want of that style and neatness which is found in every hotel in England. The waiters, too, reminded us of the half-savage highland lads that used to torment us under that denomination in Glasgow—only that they were wild Irish instead of wild Scotch. The day had cleared, and become intensely hot, towards evening softening and cooling under the serene influences of the loveliest moon imaginable. The streets were brilliantly lighted, the shops through the trees, and the people parading between them, reminded me very much of the Boulevards. We left the gentlemen, and went down stairs, where

I played and sang for three hours. On opening the door, I found a junta of men sitting on the hall floor, round it, and smoking. Came up for coffee; most of the gentlemen were rather elated,—we sang, and danced, and talked, and seemed exceedingly loath to say good-by. I sat listening to the dear Doctor's theory of the nature of the soul, which savoured infinitely more of the spirituality of the bottle than of immaterial existences, I heard him descant very tipsily upon the vital principle, until my fatigue getting fairly the better of my affection for him, I bade our remaining guests good night, and came to bed.

New York City

September 5, 1832

I have been in a sulky fit half the day, because people will keep walking in and out of our room without leave or license, which is coming a great deal too soon to Hope's idea of Heaven. I am delighted to see my friends, but I like to tell them so, and not that they should take it for granted . . .

Came home up Broadway, which is a long street of tolerable width, full of shops, in short the American Oxford road, where all people go to exhibit themselves, and examine others. The women that I have seen hitherto have all been very gaily dressed, with a pretension to French style, and a more than English exaggeration of it. They all appear to me to walk with a French shuffle, which, as their pavements are flat, I can only account for by their wearing shoes made in the French fashion, which are enough in themselves to make a waddler of the best walker that ever set foot to earth. Two or three were pretty girls, but the town being quite empty, these are probably bad specimens of the graces and charms that adorn Broadway in its season of shining . . . to the Theatre. Wallack [British actor and contemporary of John Kemble] was to act in *The Rent Day*. Mercy how strange I felt as I once more set foot in a theatre; the sound of the applause set my teeth on edge. The house is pretty though rather gloomy, well formed, about the size of the Haymarket, with plenty of gold carving, and red silk about it, looking rich and warm. The audience was considerable, but all men; scarce, I should think, twenty women in the dress circle, where, by the bye, as well as in the private boxes, I saw men sitting with their hats on . . . I cried most bitterly during the whole piece, for as in his very first scene Wallack asks his wife if she will go with him to America, and she replies, "What, leave the farm?" I set off from thence and ceased no more . . .

New York City

September 6, 1832

These democrats are as title-sick as a banker's wife in England. My father told me to-day, that Mr. [Philip Hone, former mayor and prominent businessman], talking about the state of the country, spoke of the lower orders finding their level; now this enchants me, because a republic is a natural anomaly; there is nothing republican in the construction of the material universe; there be highlands and lowlands, lordly mountains as barren as any aristocracy, and lowly valleys, as productive as any labouring classes. The feeling of rank, of inequality, is inherent in us, a part of the veneration of our natures; and like most of our properties seldom finds its right channels—in place of which it has created artificial ones suited to the frame of society into which the civilized world has formed itself. I believe in my heart that a republic is the noblest, highest, and purest form of government; but I believe that according to the present disposition of human creatures, 'tis a mere beau ideal, totally incapable of realization. What the world may be fit for six hundred years hence, I cannot exactly perceive—but in the mean time, 'tis my conviction that America will be a monarchy before I am a skeleton.

One of the curses of living at an inn in this unceremonious land: Dr. [Charles Mifflin, a prominent physician] walked in this evening, accompanied by a gentleman, whom he forthwith introduced to us. I behaved very *ill*, as I always do on these occasions; but 'tis an impertinence, and I shall take good care to certify such to be my opinion of these free and easy proceedings. The man had a silly manner, but he may be a genius for all that. He abused General Jackson, and said the cholera was owing to his presidency; for that Clay had predicted, that when he came into power, battle, pestilence, and famine would come upon the land: which Prophecy finds its accomplishment thus: they have had a war with the Indians, the cholera has raged, and the people, flying from the infected cities to the country, have eaten half the farmers out of house and home. This hotel reminds me most extremely of our "iligant" and untidy apartments in dear nasty Dublin, at the Shelbourne. The paper in our bedroom is half peeling from the walls, our beds are without curtains, then to be sure there are pier looking-glasses, and one or two pieces of showy French furniture in it. 'Tis customary, too, here, I find, for men to sleep three or four in a room; conceive an Englishman shown into a dormitory for half-a-dozen! I can't think how they endure it; but, however, I have a fever at all those things . . .

New York City

September 9, 1832

After dinner, sat looking at the blacks parading up and down; most of them in the height of the fashion, with every colour in the rainbow about them. Several of the black women I saw pass had very fine figures; (the women here appear to me to be remarkably small, my own being, I should think, the average height): but the contrast of a bright blue, or pink crape bonnet, with the black face, white teeth, and glaring blue whites of the eyes, is beyond description grotesque. The carriages here are all, to my taste, very ugly; hung very high from the ground, and of all manner of ungainly, old-fashioned shapes. Now this is where, I think, the Americans are to be quarreled with: they are beginning, at a time, when all other nations are arrived at the highest point of perfection, in all matters conducive to the comfort and elegance of life; they go into these countries; into France, into our own dear little snuggery, from whence they might bring models of whatever was most excellent, and give them to their own manufacturers, to imitate or improve upon. When I see these awkward, uncomfortable vehicles, swinging through the streets, and think of the beauty, the comfort, the strength, and lightness of our English built carriages and cabs, I am much surprised at the want of emulation and enterprise, which can be satisfied with inferiority, when equality, if not superiority, would be so easy . . .

New York City

September 13, 1932

The destruction of the original inhabitants of a country by its discoverers, always attended, as it is, with injustice and cruelty, appears to me one of the most mysterious dispensations of Providence.

The chasing, enslaving, and destroying creatures, whose existence, however inferior, is as justly theirs, as that of the most refined European is his;

who for the most part, too, receive their enemies with open-handed hospitality, until taught treachery by being betrayed, and cruelty by fear; the driving
the child of the soil off it, or, what is fifty times worse, chaining him to till it;
all the various forms of desolation which have ever followed the landing of
civilized men upon uncivilized shores; in short, the theory and practice of
discovery and conquest, as recorded in all history, is a very singular and
painful subject of contemplation.

'Tis true, that cultivation and civilization, the arts and sciences that render life useful, the knowledge that ennobles, the adornments that refine existence, above all, the religion that is its most sacred trust and dear reward, all
these, like pure sunshine and healthful airs following a hurricane, succeed
the devastation of the invader; but the sufferings of those who are swept
away are not the less, and though I believe that good alone is God's result, it
seems a fearful proof of the evil wherewith this earth is cursed, that good
cannot progress but over such a path. No one, beholding the prosperous and
promising state of this fine country, could wish it again untenanted of its
enterprising and industrious possessors; yet even while looking with admiration at all that they have achieved, with expectation amounting to certainty
to all that they will yet accomplish; 'tis difficult to refrain from bestowing
some thoughts of pity and of sadness upon those, whose homes have been
overturned, whose language has past away, and whose feet are daily driven
further from those territories of which they were once sole and sovereign
lords. How strange it is to think, that less than one hundred years ago, these
shores, resounding with the voice of populous cities—these waters, laden
with the commerce of the wide world, were silent wildernesses, where sprang
and fell the forest leaves, where ebbed and flowed the ocean tides from day to
day, and from year to year in uninterrupted stillness; where the great sun,
who looked on the vast empires of the east, its mouldering kingdoms, its
lordly palaces, its ancient temples, its swarming cities, came and looked
down upon the still dwelling of utter loneliness, where nature sat enthroned
in everlasting beauty, undisturbed by the far off din of worlds "beyond the
flood" . . .

New York City

September 15, 1832

The women here, like those of most warm climates, ripen very early, and decay proportionately soon. They are, generally speaking, pretty, with good complexions, and an air of freshness and brilliancy, but this I am told is very evanescent; and whereas, in England, a woman is in the full bloom of health and beauty from twenty to five-and-thirty; here, they scarcely reach the first period without being faded, and looking old. They marry very young, and this is another reason why age comes prematurely upon them. There was a fair young thing at dinner today who did not look above seventeen, and she was a wife. As for their figures, like those of French women, they are too well dressed for one to judge exactly what they are really like: they are, for the most part, short and slight, with remarkably pretty feet and ancles; but there's too much pelerine and petticoat, and "de quoi" of every sort to guess anything more.

New York City

September 20, 1832

. . . By the bye, Essex [an African American whom they met on shipboard] called this morning to fetch away the captain's claret jug; he asked my father for an order [of theater tickets], adding, with some hesitation, "It must be for the gallery, if you please, sir, for people of colour are not allowed to go to the pit, or any other part of the house." I believe I turned black myself, I was so indignant. Here's aristocracy with a vengeance! . . .

New York City

September 21, 1832

. . . My own opinion of poor Mr. Keppel [Romeo to her Juliet] is that no power on earth or in heaven can make him act decently; however, of course, I did not object to his trying again; he did not swamp me the first night, so I don't suppose he will the fifth. We dined at five; just before dinner received a most delicious bouquet, which gladdened my very heart with its sweet smell and lovely colours: some of the flowers were strangers to me. After dinner, Colonel [Sibell, otherwise unidentified] called, and began pulling out heaps of newspapers, and telling us a long story about Mr. Keppel, who it seems has been writing to the papers to convince them and the public that he is a good actor, at the same time throwing out sundry hints which seem aimed our way, of injustice, oppression, hard usage, and the rest on't . . . Came to bed in a tremendous dudgeon. The few critiques that I have seen upon our acting have been, upon the whole, laudatory. One was sent to me from a paper called the Mirror, which pleased me very much; not because the praise in it was excessive, and far beyond my deserts, but that it was written with great taste and feeling, and was evidently not the produce of a common press hack . . .

New York City
September 22, 1832

Went into a shop to order a pair of shoes. The shopkeepers in this place with whom I have hitherto had to deal, are either condescendingly familiar, or insolently indifferent in their manner. Your washerwoman sits down before you, while you are *standing* speaking to her; and a shop boy bringing things for inspection, not only sits down, but keeps his hat on in your drawing-room. The worthy man to whom I went for my shoes was so amazingly ungracious, that at first I thought I would go out of the shop; but recollecting that I should probably only go farther and fare worse, I gulped, sat down, and was measured. All this is bad: it has its origin in a vulgar misapprehension, which confounds ill breeding with independence, and leads people to fancy that they elevate themselves above their condition by discharging its duties and obligations discourteously . . .

New York City
September 24, 1832

At the end of the play, the clever New Yorkians actually called for Mr. Keppel! and this most worthless clapping of hands, most worthless bestowed upon such a worthless object, is what, by the nature of my craft, I am bound to care for; I spit at it from the bottom of my soul! Talking of applause, the man who acted Bedamar to-night thought fit to be two hours dragging me off the stage, in consequence of which I had to scream, "Jaffier, Jaffier," till I thought I should have broken a blood-vessel; on my remonstrating with him upon this, he said, "Well, you are rewarded, listen:" the people were clapping and shouting vehemently; this is the whole history of acting and actors. We came home tired, and thoroughly disgusted, and found no supper. The cooks, who do not live in the house, but come and do their work, and depart home whenever it suits their convenience, had not thought proper to stay to prepare any supper for us: so we had to wait for the readiest things that could be procured out of doors for us—this was pleasant—very! At last appeared a cold, boiled fowl, and some monstrous oysters, that looked for all the world like an antediluvian race of oysters, "for in those days there were giants." Six mouthfuls each; they were well-flavoured, but their size displeased my eye, and I swallowed but one, and came to bed . . .

JOHN McELGUN

John McElgun's 1873 novel *Annie Reilly; or, The Fortunes of an Irish Girl in New York* follows two young immigrants—James O'Rourke and the Annie of the title—from Munster in southern Ireland to Liverpool and then New York City, where their separate, harrowing stories finally and happily reconnect. Subtitled "A Tale Founded on Fact," the novel vividly documents the injustices and indignities that typified the experience of those who left Ireland in the steerage of "coffin ships" in the wake of the Great Famine. The failure of Ireland's staple potato crop in the 1840s, compounded by persistent social, economic, and political disasters, led to the death or exodus to the United States and elsewhere of some 3 million men and women by the mid-1850s. Arriving somewhat later—at Castle Garden, New York City's Emigrant Landing Depot from 1855 until the opening of Ellis Island in 1892—James and Annie would have been part of a smaller but still massive transatlantic wave. After the famine the departure of sons and daughters became almost an expected rite of passage in Ireland.

About John McElgun, the author of *Annie Reilly*, almost nothing definitive is known. He notes in his preface that his depiction of Liverpool's "man-catchers," who preyed on helpless passengers, "falls short of what I have actually witnessed myself." Perhaps a John McElgun (or McAlgun, or McGunn, or thereabouts, surnames being a frequent minor casualty of the Atlantic crossing) will be recoverable in immigration and other records currently being digitized in the United States and Ireland, and a history of this notable writer's career can begin to be pieced together.

from

Annie Reilly

A fter a comparatively safe and speedy passage, James O'Rourke reached New York. It was one of those mellow days in the early fall when everything looks so serene and calm that the anxious passengers were landed. How beautiful New York Harbor looked! The waters seemed asleep on the bosom of the bay, save where disturbed by the lively ferry-boats ploughing their way backwards and forwards, in every direction, and the little snorting tugs, puffing in and out here and there, busy as bees of a June morning. A number of large, majestic-looking ships, that had just come in from all ports of the world, lay out in the stream, looking weary after their long voyage.

It being early day, the passengers were not delayed at Castle Garden overnight, except such as chose to wait for friends who were expecting them. James had no friends, and he walked into the streets and up along Broadway, wondering at the size, and beauty, and cheerful look of the buildings along that noble thoroughfare. It was at the time of day when Broadway is at its liveliest, lined with wagons, carriages, carts, and drays, and the sidewalk so crowded with people hurrying along that it is impossible for any of them to make much speed. James walked on—he knew not where—looking on himself as the most lonely and friendless of the great throng. At length he came to what seemed to him a neglected waste of ground, which, having mortally offended the city in some way, was left behind, forgotten, haggard, and cheerless. Near the centre of this waste stood a large building in a half-finished state, looking so dreary that the ill fate of the neighborhood seemed to have visited it at last.

A number of men were standing around the doors or sitting on the steps of the building, and all looking so much like men that had nothing to do, that James thought it might not inconvenience any of them much to tell him where he might find work. So approaching a gentleman with a wide-leafed straw hat, a tight-fitting coat, much too short for him, and very long, wide pantaloons, who stood on the end of a row picking his teeth, James asked:

"Please, sir, can you tell me where I may find employment? I am a stranger here."

"Most undoubtedly, sir; follow me," said the gentleman, putting his toothpick in his vest pocket. "Come along, sir."

James, delighted beyond measure at this sudden good luck, hurried after his new friend, but found it no very easy task to keep up with him. He had such a happy method of diving past crowds which jostled against the other that he had once or twice to wait for him on the corner. At length the gentleman swept into a low, narrow door in one of the side streets, and when James rushed in after him, he found him seated behind a neat little desk, looking as composed as if he had been sitting there since morning.

"So you want employment, do you?" said he, surveying James from head to foot.

"Yes, sir," replied the latter.

"What kind do you prefer?" said he, opening a book which lay on the desk before him. "We have a variety."

"Well, sir," replied James with a smile, "I am not afraid of any kind of work, but would of course prefer whichever pays best."

"Let me see," said the other, closing his eyes and resting his chin on his hand, "let me see. You are strong enough to work in a dry-goods store?"

"You mean, sir—"

"I mean what you call a cloth-shop in the Old Country."

"Oh! yes; I beg your pardon, sir," said James, greatly elated. "Certainly I am, sir."

"You landed this morning, eh?" said the gentleman.

"This morning, sir?"

"Any friends in New York?"

"No, sir."

"All alone, eh?"

"Quite so, sir."

"Well, now, sir, I'll tell you what I'll do. You give me three dollars, and I'll send you right up to the establishment."

James felt greatly surprised at this, for he really thought the gentleman was an extensive employer himself. He had never heard of an "intelligence office," and was quite at a loss what to think. He couldn't be a swindler, having such a handsome place.

"No; he *must* be an employer, and probably wants this money as security for a day or two, till he sees how I get on," thought James.

And looking at the gentleman again, and seeing him busy writing, and apparently utterly oblivious of his presence, was confirmed in this latter idea.

"I'll pay the money, sir," said he, taking from his pocket a few shillings and one half-crown, which was his entire store.

The gentleman thought it most remarkable, but nevertheless it was true, that the coins when changed into dollars amounted to just the required number and ten cents over. So he swept it into a drawer, and, throwing a ten-cent stamp on the desk, drew a piece of paper to him, and, having written a few words on it with violet ink, handed it to James. The latter glanced at it and said:

"What way am I to go there, sir?"

"You see I am so busy, or I would take you up myself. But, anyway, all you have to do is to cross over five blocks to your right, then down a long street you'll see with a marble building on the up-town corner, then one block to your right, then take the cars—you know the street-cars—and ride eleven blocks more, and any one can point out Van Sleuthers & Duckey's dry-goods store to you. Go inside, and show them that address, and you're all right."

James thanked him, left the office, and went in search of Van Sleuthers & Duckey's.

That he did not find it, and that there was no such firm in the city, it is needless to say. He had been swindled out of the last penny by an "intelligence agent"; and after travelling up and down the streets, looking at every sign, stopping to make enquiries at every clothing establishment, he found himself at nightfall close by the East River, footsore, weary, and dejected. He sat down on a log on one of the docks, and, covering his eyes with his hands, began to think over his forlorn, desolate state.

In a large city, without a friend, without one face he had ever known, without a single penny in his pocket. Where to spend the night or get a morsel to eat he knew not; he had spent the ten cents riding up and down in search of Van Sleuthers & Duckey's. He sat a prey to these thoughts for some time, till, raising his head, he saw coming leisurely towards him, from the direction of the street, a man in his shirt-sleeves, smoking a large briar-wood pipe.

As he approached, James could see he was of his own race, and made up his mind to speak to him. This was no difficult matter, for the stranger came on, puffing like an engine, and, sitting down beside him remarked it was a fine night.

O'Rourke saw at once, from his large, rough hands, that he belonged to the working-class, and, observing his neat white shirt and black tie, and everything he wore so clean, thought of the miserable appearance of the English working-men.

"You're not long out from the ould counthry, I think," said he kindly.

"No, indeed," said James. "I came ashore this morning."

"Well, well," said the man, moving close to him, "I am glad to see any one so late from the ould dart. How is things there now; anything better?"

"Oh! much the same as usual," replied James. "Improvements come very slowly in Ireland."

"That's so, that's so, me friend," said the other, with a sigh. "But the people an't starving as they wor when I left there?"

"Not so bad as that now," said James.

"Do you live around here?" asked the stranger, after a pause.

"I have no home," said James, drawing back his head a little.

"No home," said the other, "and a greenhorn; why, that's rough. I suppose be that ye mane you haven't got any money neither."

"Not a penny," was the reply.

Then James told him how he had been cheated by the intelligence agent.

"You're not the first who has been fleeced by thim robbers," said the other in a rage. "They swindle dozens of poor innocent people every day, and you'll niver hear of one of thim bein' arristed. But," added he, checking himself, "it can't be helped now, and I'll niver see one of my countrymen that desarves it out in the streets at night while I have a room; so you must come wid me to-night. The ould woman 'ill find some place for you to sleep."

James thanked him again and again, and, after enjoying a smoke from his pipe, they walked up the dock and along the street a little way, till they came to a somewhat neat-looking brick house with a wooden stoop. The man entered, and both went up a flight of very clean but carpetless stairs to the third story, and, turning the knob of the door, entered a tidily furnished room of comfortable dimensions. Over the wooden mantel-piece hung a handsome engraving of Archbishop Hughes, side by side with another of St. Patrick, and on the opposite wall hung a picture of Killarney Lakes. Several other pictures, some of Irish clergy, some of American, were fastened round the walls, all very tastefully arranged.

There was no person in the room on their entrance, and the man, seeing James look closely at the archbishop's likeness, began to tell numerous stories of his kindness and benevolence. After some time, a woman came in, carrying a basket on her arm; and from the appearance of her face, and the trim, cleanly way in which she was clad, James knew at once whose taste had arranged the room.

"Well, well, Terence, and what a man you are," said she, laying down the basket, and looking at her husband with a smile, "to leave housekeeping."

"Oh! in troth, I was afraid she'd begin to screech whin ye'd be gone, Bridget, so I left her inside with Mrs. Kearney. She stays as quiet wid her as wid yourself," said her husband.

"Oh! just so; anything to get rid of the job. But keep quiet now; she's asleep in Mrs. Kearney's arms, and I'll bring her in and put her in the cradle."

The woman left the room, and soon returned, carrying in her arms a little babe of a few months old, and, shaking her hand at her husband to say nothing, lest he should rouse the infant, went through the passage-way into another room.

The man conversed with James for awhile, then, telling him he'd be back in a moment, followed his wife. Both soon returned, and James could see from the kind, sympathetic look the woman gave him that her husband had been telling his story.

"Excuse me," said the man, "but ye haven't tould me yer name."

James told him.

"In troth, and a good name it is. My own is Terence McManus, and this is Mrs. McManus, and that sleepy youngster ye seen a minute ago is Mary McManus. So we know each other all roun' now, and are quite at our aise."

The agreeable, honest, good-natured manner of the man did make James feel much easier in mind than he had felt for some time. Mrs. McManus prepared a good meal, of which all three partook. This over, they sat together, and talked over matters in the old and new country. One important point to James came out from this conversation, and that was he learned that his host, who worked along the docks, being what is commonly called a 'longshoreman, would find him employment at the same business the following day.

HANS MATTSON

Organized emigration from Sweden to America began around 1638 when a small settlement, New Sweden, was established in what is now Wilmington, Delaware. But it was not until the mid-19th century that Swedes began to arrive in the United States in significant numbers, prompted by economic hardship and rigid social stratification at home and the lure of freedom, jobs, and available farmland on the American prairies. Hans Mattson (1832–1893), born in Skåne, was on the leading edge of this great wave, arriving in 1851; he soon became a notable advocate of Swedish immigration, publishing letters about his new country in the Swedish press and officially appointed as Minnesota immigration agent from 1866 to 1870. Mattson then served as Minnesota's secretary of state (1870–72 and 1887–91) and edited newspapers such as *Minnesota Stats Tidning*. Here, in excerpts from his 1891 autobiography *Reminiscences: The Story of an Emigrant*—published first in Sweden as *Minnen af Öfverste H. Mattson* (1890)—Mattson looks back on the beginnings of his life in America. At the age of 18, with no English, little money, and a background that had ill-prepared him for hard labor, he is forced to turn repeatedly to strangers for help—an experience that informs a deeply liberal sense of duty to others, in the land of "no free lunch."

from
The Story of an Immigrant

At that time America was little known in our part of the country, only a few persons having emigrated from the whole district. But we knew that it was a new country, inhabited by a free and independent people, that it had a liberal government and great natural resources, and these inducements were sufficient for us. My parents readily consented to my emigration, and, having made the necessary preparations, my father took my friend Eustrom and myself down to the coast with his own horses, in the first part of May, 1851. It was a memorable evening, and I shall never forget the last farewell to my home, in driving out from the court into the village street, how I stood up in the wagon, turned towards the dear home and waved my hat with a hopeful hurrah to the "folks I left behind." A couple of days' journey brought us to a little seaport, where we took leave of my father and boarded a small schooner for the city of Gothenburg.

At that time there were no ocean steamers and no emigrant agents; but we soon found a sailing vessel bound for America on which we embarked as passengers, furnishing our own bedding, provisions and other necessaries, which our mothers had supplied in great abundance. About one hundred and fifty emigrants from different parts of Sweden were on board the brig Ambrosius. In the middle of May she weighed anchor and glided out of the harbor on her long voyage across the ocean to distant Boston.

We gazed back at the vanishing shores of the dear fatherland with feelings of affection, but did not regret the step we had taken, and our bosoms heaved with boundless hope. At the age of eighteen, the strong, healthy youth takes a bright and hopeful view of life, and so did we. Many and beautiful were the air-castles we built as we stood on deck, with our eyes turned towards the promised land of the Nineteenth century. To some of these castles our lives have given reality, others are still floating before us.

The good brig Ambrosius landed us in Boston on June 29, 1851, but during the voyage about one-half of the passengers were attacked by small-pox and had to be quarantined outside the harbor. My good friend and I were fortunate enough to escape this plague; but instead of this was I taken sick with the ague on our arrival at Boston.

Now, then, we were in America! The new, unknown country lay before us, and it seemed the more strange as we did not understand a word of the

English language. For at that time the schools of Sweden paid no attention to English, so that although I had studied four languages, English, the most important of all tongues, was entirely unknown to me.

The first few weeks of our stay in Boston passed quietly and quickly, but the ague grew worse and my purse was getting empty. My friend, however, had more money than I, and as long as he had a dollar left he divided it equally between us. I cannot resist the temptation to relate a seriocomical escapade of this period, one that to many will recall similar occurrences in their own experience as immigrants ignorant of the language of the country.

In Gothenburg we had become acquainted with a bright young man from Vexiö, Janne Tenggren by name, who had also served in the army. When we met him he had already bought a ticket on a sailing vessel bound for New York, so that we could not make the voyage together. But we agreed to hunt each other up after our arrival in America. We left Sweden about the same time with the understanding that if we arrived first we should meet him in New York, and if he arrived first he should go to Boston to meet us there.

About a week after our arrival in Boston, we heard that the vessel on which he had embarked had arrived, and I immediately left for New York to fulfill our promise. But, unfortunately, I found he had already gone west, so I bought a return ticket to Boston the same day. The journey was by steamboat to Fall River, thence by rail to Boston. We left New York in the evening. I remained on the deck, and went to sleep about ten o'clock on some wooden boxes. About eleven o'clock I awoke, saw the steamer laying to, and, supposing we were at Fall River, hurried off and followed the largest crowd, expecting thus to get to the railroad depot. Striking no depot, however, I returned to the harbor, only to find the steamer gone, and everybody but myself had vanished from the pier.

There I stood, in the middle of the night, without money, ignorant of the language, and not even knowing where I was! Tired and discouraged I finally threw myself down on a wooden box on the sidewalk, and went to sleep. About five o'clock in the morning a big policeman aroused me by poking at me with his club. This respectable incarnation of social order evidently took me for a tramp or a madman, and as he could not obtain any intelligible information from me in any language known to him, he took me to a small shoe store kept by a German.

Fortunately, my acquaintance with the German language was sufficient to enable me to explain myself, and I soon found that I had left the steamer several hours too early; that the name of this place was New London, that another steamer would come past at the same time the next night, so that all I had to do was to wait for that steamer and go to Boston on the same ticket.

I spent the day in seeing the city and chatting with my friend, the shoe maker, and in the evening returned to the wharf to watch for the Boston steamer.

This being my ague day, I had violent attacks of ague and fever, so that I was again forced to lie down to rest on the same wooden box, and again went to sleep. After a while I was aroused by the noise of the approaching steamer; rushed on board in company with some other passengers, and considered myself very fortunate when reflecting that I would surely be in Boston the next morning. I had made myself familiar with the surroundings during the day, and when the steamer started, I noticed that it directed its course towards New York, instead of Boston. I had no money to pay my fare to New York, could neither borrow nor beg, and so I crawled down in a little hole in the fore part of the steamer, where the tackles and ropes were kept, thus, fortunately, escaping the notice of the ticket collector.

The next evening I again embarked for Boston and finally arrived safely at my destination.

We stayed in Boston several weeks, and during that time my ague caused a heavy drain on our small treasury. We had no definite plan, did not know what to do, and as we had never been used to any kind of hard work, matters began to assume a serious aspect, especially in regard to myself. But then, as now, the hope of many a young man was the Great West which, at that time, was comparatively little known even in Boston. Toward the close of the month of July we, therefore, went to Buffalo, which was as far as our money would carry us. Here we put up at a cheap boarding house kept by a Nor-wegian by name of Larson, with whom we stopped while trying to get work. But having learned no trade and being unused to manual labor, we soon found that it was impossible to get a job in the city; so we left our baggage at the boarding house and started on foot for a country place named Hamburg, some ten miles distant, where we learned that two of our late companions across the ocean had found employment. On the road to Hamburg, about dusk, we reached a small house by the wayside, where we asked for food and shelter. I was so exhausted that my friend had to support me in order to reach the house. We found it occupied by a Swedish family, which had just sat down to a bountiful supper. Telling them our condition, we were roughly told to clear out; in Sweden, they said, they had had enough of gentlemen and would have nothing to do with them here.

We retraced our steps with sad hearts until a short distance beyond the house we found an isolated barn partly filled with hay. There was no one to object, so we took possession and made it our temporary home. I am glad to say that during a long life among all classes of people, from the rudest barbarians to the rulers of nations, that family of my own countrymen were the only people who made me nearly lose faith in the nobler attributes of man. I have an excuse, however, for this conduct in the fact that in the mother-country, which they had left a year before, they had probably been abused and exasperated on account of the foolish class distinction then existing there. They evidently belonged to that class of tenants who were treated almost like slaves. The following day we found our late companions a mile from our barn, both working for a farmer at $15.00 per month, which was then considered big wages. They were older men and accustomed to hard labor, so that their situation was comparatively easy. They received us kindly and procured work for Eustrom with the same farmer, while I, still suffering with the ague, could not then attempt to work, and therefore returned to my castle in the meadow, (the hay-barn). There I remained about a week living on berries which I found in the neighboring woods and a slice of bread and butter, which Eustrom brought me in the evening, when, with blistered hands and sore back, he called to comfort me and help build better air castles for the future.

A council was finally held among us four, and it was decided to send me back to Buffalo with a farmer who was going there the following morning. One of the men, Mr. Abraham Sandberg, on parting gave me a silver dollar, with the injunction to give it to someone who might need it worse than I, whenever I could do so. I have never met Abraham again; but I have regarded it as a sacred duty to comply with his request, and, in case these lines should come before his eyes I wish to let him know that my debt has been honestly paid.

On reaching the old hoarding house in Buffalo the landlord promised that he would send me to a hospital where I could receive proper treatment and care. I made up a little bundle of necessary underwear, and in an hour a driver appeared at the door; I was lifted into the cart and off we went through the muddy streets to the outskirts of the city, where I was duly delivered at a large building which I supposed to be the hospital. It was near evening, and I was brought into a large dining-room, with a hundred others or more, served with supper, corn mush and molasses water, after which I was shown to a bed in a large room among many others. I suffered with fever, and for the first time in my life with loneliness. Exhausted nature finally took out its due, and I slept soundly until awakened in the morning by a loud sound of a gong. As soon as dressed I walked out in the yard, or lawn, back of the building. On one side was a high plank fence, behind which I heard some strange sounds. I found a knot-hole, and, peeping through this, I observed another lawn, on which were many people. They were strange looking; I never saw any like them before. Some were swinging, some dancing, others shouting, singing and weeping and behaving in a most out-of-the-way manner. I wondered and wondered, and finally it dawned upon me that it must be a lunatic asylum. It was, in fact, as I since learned, the county poor farm, where one part was used for the lunatics and the other for paupers like myself. Has it come to this? I asked myself; is this the goal of all my ambition and hopes? Going back to the room, where I had slept, I stealthily took my little bundle, slipped out through a side door into a back yard, found a gate open and was soon in the street. I started on a run with all the power in me, as if pursued by all the furies of paupers and lunatics, never stopping until I was near the old boarding house, where I was taken in exhausted and in deep despair. I would have killed the landlord for deceiving me if I had been able to do so. One good thing resulted from the sad experience of that day: the mental shock on dis-covering where I was, cured me for the time being of the ague.

The next day my friend returned from Hamburg, where he could no longer get any employment on account of his blistered hands, and poor health in gen-eral. We now put our wise heads together and agreed that we had already had enough of the West for the time being. Having plenty of good clothes, bedding, revolvers and other knick-knacks, we sold to our landlord whatever we could spare, in order to raise money enough to pay our way back to Boston.

During our stay in Buffalo, our renowned countrywoman, Jenny Lind, happened to give a concert there. We were standing on the street where we could see the people crowd into the theatre, but that was all we could afford, and we never heard her sing. Our host advised us to go and ask her for help; but our pride forbade it.

At this time the Swedes were so little known, and Jenny Lind, on the other hand, so renowned in America, that the Swedes were frequently called "Jenny Lind men," this designation being often applied to myself.

Having purchased tickets for Albany, we returned East in the month of August. I still remember how we rode all night in a crowded second-class car, listening to the noisy merry-making of our fellow-passengers; but we understood very little of it, for up to this time we had lived exclusively among our own countrymen, and learned only a few English words—a mistake, by the way, which thousands of immigrants have made and are still making.

Arriving at Albany, we sat down by an old stone wall near the railroad depot, to talk over our affairs. Fate had been against us while we remained together, and we probably depended too much upon each other. Accordingly, we decided to part for some time and try our luck separately; and if one of us met with success he would, of course, soon be able to find a position for the other. We decided by drawing lots that Eustrom should go to Boston and I to New York. When we had bought our tickets there remained one dollar, which we divided, and we left for our respective places of destination the same evening.

Our landlord in Buffalo had given us the address of a sailors' boarding-house in New York, which was also kept by a Norwegian by the same name of Larson. So when I left the Hudson River steamer early the next morning, I paid my half-dollar to a drayman, who took me to said boarding house. I found Mr. Larson to be a kind, good-natured man, told him my difficulties right out, and asked him to let me stop at his house until I could find something to do. He agreed to this, and for a week or so I tried my best to get work. But, when asked what kind of work I could do, I was compelled to answer that I had learned no trade, but that I would gladly try to learn anything and do anything whatever, even sweep the streets, if necessary. As a result of my protracted sickness, I was so weak and exhausted that nobody thought I would be able even to earn my bread. As to easy or intellectual work, I had no earthly chance, as long as I did not know the English language. Finally Mr. Larson took me to a ship-owner's office. I still remember that a Norwegian captain was cruel enough to remark in my hearing, that he did not intend to take any half-dead corpses along with him to sea.

After two weeks of fruitless efforts to get work for me, my host finally declared that he could not very well keep me any longer, because his accommodations were crowded with paying customers; nevertheless, he allowed me to sleep in the attic free of charge, while I had to procure my food as best I could, which I also did for another two weeks. Being a convalescent, I had a ravenous appetite, and, indeed, I found how hard it is to obtain food without having anything to pay for it. Of the few articles of clothing which I brought with me from Buffalo, I had to sacrifice one after another for subsistence. When all other means were exhausted, I was compelled to go to the kitchen-doors and tell my desperate and unfortunate condition by signs, and more than one kind-hearted cook gave me a solid meal.

Tramps! In our day there is a great deal of talk about tramps, and it has become customary, to brand as a tramp, any poor wandering laborer who seeks work. There are undoubtedly many who justly deserve this title; but I think there are tramps who are not to blame for their deplorable condition, and who deserve encouragement and friendly assistance, for I have been one of them myself, without any fault or neglect on my part. It always provokes me to hear a young or inexperienced person use the expression "tramp" so thoughtlessly, and in such a sweeping manner. Long ago I made up my mind that no tramp should ever leave my door without such aid as my resources would allow. It is better to give to a thousand undeserving, than to let one unfortunate but deserving suffer.

I arrived in Boston about the middle of December, and, when I returned to the old boarding house, I spoke English so well that my acquaintances hardly believed it possible that I could be the same person. Mr. Eustrom was now working as wood polisher. He had made many friends and lived happily and contented on $4 a week. By strict economy these wages sufficed for board, lodging, and clothes.

It happened to be an unfavorable time of the year when I arrived, however, and many men who had been employed during the summer were now discharged at the approach of winter. Mr. Eustrom's employer had a good friend in New Hampshire, an old Swedish sailor, Anderson by name, who was farming up there. He promised to let me come and live with him and do whatever chores I could until something might turn up the next spring.

A few days afterwards I went by rail to Contocook where I was met by Mr. Anderson, who took me out to his hospitable home a couple of miles from the town. This Anderson was a remarkable man. Having no education to speak of, he was a better judge of human nature and practical affairs of life than any other man I ever met. He was pleased with me, and said he wished I would sit down in the evening and tell him about Sweden, and explain to him what I had learned at school. Poor Anderson! He had one fault, rum got the better of him, and it was cheap in New England at that time, only sixteen cents a gallon. He bought a barrel of it at a time, and did not taste water as long as the rum lasted.

The day after my arrival he asked me if I would like to go with him into the woods to help cut some logs. Of course I would, and we took our axes and started off. It was a very cold December day, and I had thin clothes and no mittens. Mr. Anderson went to cut down a tree, and I commenced to work at one which was already felled. This was the first time I swung an axe in earnest, and after a short while I felt that my hands were getting cold. But I made up my mind not to stop until the log was finished. By holding the axe handle very tight it stopped the circulation of the blood through my fingers, and when I finally stopped and dropped the axe I could not move my fingers, for eight of them were frozen stiff. Mr. Anderson now took off his cap, filled it with snow, put my hands into the snow, and thus we ran to the house as fast as our legs would carry us. The doctor tried his very best; but, nevertheless, in a few days the flesh and the nails began to peel off, and two doctors decided to amputate all the fingers on my right hand. Fortunately I did not give my consent, but told them that I would rather die of gangrene than live without hands, for my future depended exclusively on them.

My friend Eustrom, having heard of my misfortune, soon came to visit me, and brought with him an old Irish woman who was something of a doctor, and cured my hands by means of a very simple plaster which she prepared herself. But I was forced into complete inactivity for more than three months, during which time I was entirely helpless, and had to be washed, dressed, and fed like an infant. But, as to me, the old proverb has always proved true: "When things are at the worst they'll mend." There were men and women in my accidental home who willingly tended to me in my trouble. May God bless them for it! In the latter part of March, Mr. Anderson, who had always treated me with the greatest kindness, quite unexpectedly told me that I was now able to work again and could try to get a place with some other family in the neighborhood, because he could not keep me any longer.

Our nearest neighbor was a genuine Yankee, Daniel Dustin by name. He was very rich, well read, liberal minded, respectable and honest, but so *close* that he would scarcely let his own family have enough food to eat, and his wife was even more stingy. Mr. Dustin agreed to let me work for my board until spring, and then he would give me five dollars a month, which offer I cheerfully accepted. He immediately took me out into the woods to chop wood for the summer, and he was to haul it home. The new, tender muscles and nails on my fingers made wood chopping very painful to me, and I could feel every blow of the axe through my entire body. Never has any man worked so hard for me, when I afterwards hired help for good wages, as I worked for my board here; and, by the way, this board consisted chiefly of potatoes and corn meal cake. When the spring work commenced I got five dollars a month, and had to get up at five o'clock in the morning to do the chores, and then work in the field from seven in the morning until dark.

CARL SCHURZ

The eventfulness of the life of Carl Schurz (1829–1906) can be gauged by the fact that the following excerpt from his memoirs, recounting his first impressions of New York City as a newly arrived 23-year-old, comprises the first few pages of the *second* volume. The only suggestion here of old-world adventure is an oblique reference to serving as an aide-de-camp at the siege of Rastatt during the 1848 revolution in Germany. The bravery and enthusiasm he exhibited as a German democratic nationalist was to be of a piece with the harrowing vicissitudes of his new-world life. The following extract marks a relatively tranquil interlude in this extraordinary progression. From German democrat to American orator, to staunch Republican and friend of Lincoln, Civil War brigadier, journalist, senator, and secretary of the Interior—there was very little in the American political realm Schurz left untouched. The alacrity with which he embraced the highest ideals and promises of his adopted country is reflected in a speech he delivered to a group of German immigrants at the 1893 World's Fair in Chicago. "Our character," he said, "should take on the best of that which is American, and combine it with the best of that which is German. By doing this, we can best serve the American people and their civilization." We find him in the last few years of his life, as he wrote these memoirs, a fervent anti-imperialist, his principles uncompromised to the end, still living by his well-known dictum: "My country, right or wrong; if right, to be kept right; and if wrong, to be set right."

from
Reminiscences

O n the 17th of September, 1852, my young wife and I entered the harbor of New York on board the fine packet-ship "City of London" after a voyage of twenty-eight days. There were at that period steamers—although only a few of them—regularly running between England and the United States. But a friend of ours who had visited this country several times had told us that a good, large sailing-ship was safer than a steamer, and more comfortable to persons liable to sea-sickness. Thus persuaded, we chose the packet "City of London," a fine ship of about two thousand tons, magnificent to look at. And we did not repent of our choice. Our stateroom was large and commodious, the captain, although a thoroughly sea-bred man, polite and attentive, the table not bad, and the traveling company agreeable. There were several hundred emigrants in the steerage, but only about twenty passengers in the cabin, among them a Yale professor and several New York merchants. I was not able to converse in English; but as the Yale professor spoke some German, and two or three of the New York merchants some French, there was amusing and instructive entertainment enough.

Having determined to make the United States my permanent home, I was resolved to look at everything from the brightest side, and not to permit myself to be discouraged by any disappointment.

I knew that my buoyant Rhenish blood would help me much. But I was not so sure as to whether my young wife, whose temperament was not so sanguine as mine and who had grown up in easier conditions and in constant contact with sympathetic people, would be able as readily and cheerfully as I to accept the vicissitudes of life in a new country and a strange social atmosphere. But we were young—I twenty-three years old, and my wife eighteen —and much might be hoped from the adaptability of youth. Still, I was anxious that the first impression of the new country should be bright and inspiring to her. And that wish was at once gratified in the highest degree. The day on which we arrived in New York harbor could not have been more glorious. The bay and the islands surrounding it were radiant with sunlit splendor. When we beheld this spectacle, so surprisingly entrancing after a four-weeks' journey over the waste of waters, our hearts fairly leaped with joy. We felt as if we were entering, through this gorgeous portal, a world of peace and happiness.

As we skirted the shore of Staten Island, with its fine country houses and green lawns and massive clumps of shade trees, a delightful picture of comfort and contentment—Staten Island was then still a favorite summering place—I asked one of my fellow-passengers what kind of people lived in those charming dwellings. "Rich New Yorkers," said he. "And how much must a man have to be called a rich New Yorker?" I asked. "Well," he answered, "a man who has something like $150,000 or $200,000 or an assured income of $10,000 or $12,000 would be considered wealthy. Of course, there are men who have more than that—as much as a million or two, or even more." "Are there many such in New York?" "Oh, no, not many; perhaps a dozen. But the number of people who might be called 'well to do' is large." "And are there many poor people in New York?" "Yes, some; mostly newcomers, I think. But what is called poverty here would, in many cases, hardly be called poverty in London or Paris. There are scarcely any hopelessly poor here. It is generally thought here that nobody need be poor."

In the changing course of time I have often remembered this conversation.

It was not easy to find a place of rest for our first night in the New World. We had heard of the Astor House as the best hostelry in New York. But the Astor House was full to overflowing, and so our carriage had laboriously to work its way from hotel to hotel, through the confusion of omnibuses and drays and other vehicles, up the thundering Broadway. But in none of them did we find a vacant room until finally we reached Fourteenth Street, where the Union Square Hotel, which has subsequently been turned into a theater and then into a hotel again, called the Morton House, offered to us a hospitable abode—a very plainly furnished room, but sufficient for our needs.

The recollection of our first dinner at the Union Square Hotel is still vivid in my mind. It was a table d'hôte, if I remember rightly, at five o'clock in the afternoon. Dinner-time was announced by the fierce beating of a gong, an instrument which I heard for the first time on that occasion. The guests then filed into a large, bare dining-room with one long row of tables. Some fifteen or twenty negroes, clad in white jackets, white aprons, and white cotton gloves, stood ready to conduct the guests to their seats, which they did with broad smiles and curiously elaborate bows and foot scrapings. A portly colored head-waiter in a dress coat and white necktie, whose manners were strikingly grand and patronizing, directed their movements. When the guests were seated, the head-waiter struck a loud bell; then the negroes rapidly filed out and soon reappeared carrying large soup tureens covered with bright silver covers. They planted themselves along the table at certain intervals, standing for a second motionless. At another clang of their commander's bell they lifted their tureens high up and then deposited them upon the table with a bump that made the chandeliers tremble and came near terrifying the ladies. But this was not the end of the ceremony. The negroes held fast with their right hands to the handles of the silver covers until another stroke of the bell resounded. Then they jerked off the covers, swung them high over their heads, and thus marched off as if carrying away their booty in triumph. So the dinner went on, with several repetitions of such proceedings, the negroes getting all the while more and more enthusiastic and bizarre in their performances. I was told that like customs existed at other hotels, but I have never seen them elsewhere executed with the same perfection as at our first dinner in America. It may well be believed that they then astonished us greatly.

I remember well our first walk to see the town:—the very noisy bustle on the principal streets; the men, old and young, mostly looking serious and preoccupied, and moving on with energetic rapidity; the women also appearing sober-minded and busy, although many of them were clothed in loud colors, red, green, yellow, or blue of a very pronounced glare; the people, although they must have belonged to very different stations in life, looking surprisingly alike in feature and expression as well as habit; no military sentinels at public buildings; no soldiers on the streets; no liveried coachmen or servants; no uniformed officials except the police. We observed huge banners stretched across the street, upon which were inscribed the names of Pierce and King as the Democratic, and Scott and Graham as the Whig, candidates for the presidency and the vice-presidency—names which at that time had, to me, no meaning, except that they indicated the impending presidential election and the existence of competing political parties. As to the American politics of the day, I had received only some vague impressions through my conversations with various persons. My friend Kinkel, who had visited the United States in 1851 in the interest of the revolutionary movement in Europe, had been received by President Fillmore and had described him to me as a "freundlicher und wohlwollender Greis" (an amiable and benevolent old gentleman). Of the political parties he could tell me only that they both seemed to be dominated by the slave-holders, or at least to be afraid of the slavery question, and that most of the Germans in the United States were on the side of the Democrats, because they were attracted by the name of democracy and because they believed that the Democratic party could be more surely depended upon to protect the rights of the foreign-born citizens. The news articles about American politics which I had read in European papers had been, as they mostly have remained to the present day, well-nigh valueless to everyone not personally acquainted with American affairs, and my conversations with my fellow-passengers had given me little light on the then existing situation. It presented itself to me like a dense fog in which I saw shadowy figures indistinctly moving.

We spent two or three days in trying to see what "sights" there were in the city, and we found that there were none in the line of museums, or picture galleries, or remarkable public or private buildings. Barnum's museum of curiosities, on the corner of Broadway and Ann Street, opposite St. Paul's Church, was pointed out to us as a thing really worth seeing. In the shop-windows on Broadway we observed nothing extraordinary. The theaters we could not enjoy because I did not understand English. The busy crowds thronging the streets were always interesting, but strange: not a familiar face among them. A feeling of lonesomeness began to settle upon us.

Then my young wife fell ill. I called in an old American doctor who lived in the hotel. He seemed to be a man of ability; he certainly was very genial and kind. He knew some French, and thus we could converse. As the illness of my wife became known in the hotel, a spirit of helpfulness manifested itself among the guests, which surprised and touched me deeply—that American helpfulness which was then, and, I trust, is now, one of the finest and most distinguishing characteristics of this people. Gentlemen and ladies, one after another, called upon us to ask whether they could be of any service. Some of the ladies, in fact, now and then relieved me from my watch at my wife's bedside to give me an hour's breathing time in the open air. I then walked up and down or sat on a bench in the little park of Union Square, which was surrounded by a high iron railing. Union Square was, at that period, far "up town." There were above Fourteenth Street many blocks or clumps of houses with large gaps between them, but, as far as I can remember, no continuous, solidly built-up streets. Madison Square showed many vacant lots, there being a field partly planted with corn and enclosed by a picket fence where the Fifth Avenue Hotel now stands. Wandering circuses used to pitch their tents on that spot. But although far up town, Union Square had its share of noisy bustle.

There, then, in that little park, I had my breathing spells, usually in the dusk of evening. They were among the most melancholy hours of my life. There I was in the great Republic, the idol of my dreams, feeling myself utterly lonesome and forlorn. The future lay before me wrapped in an impenetrable cloud. What I had seen was not so different from Europe as I had vaguely expected, and yet it was strange and mysterious. Would my experiences here realize the ideal I had conceived, or would they destroy it? I had to struggle hard against these gloomy musings, and finally I roused myself to the thought that in order to get into sympathy with the busy life I saw around me, I must become active in it, become *of it*—and that, the sooner the better.

During my wife's illness, which lasted nearly a fortnight, I had exchanged letters with some of my German friends in Philadelphia, especially with my "chum" of former days, Adolph Strodtmann, who had established a small German bookshop there and published a little German weekly paper—*Die Locomotive,*—and with Dr. Heinrich Tiedemann, a brother of the unfortunate Colonel Tiedemann, the Governor of Rastatt, on whose staff I had served as aide-de-camp during the siege of that fortress. Dr. Tiedemann had settled down in Philadelphia as a physician and was in good practice. My wife and I longed for the face of a friend; and as there was nothing to hold us in New York, we resolved to visit Philadelphia, not with any purpose of permanent settlement, but thinking that it might be a good place for a beginning of systematic study. This it proved to be. We soon found among the recently immigrated Germans, and also among Americans, a sympathetic social intercourse, and with it that cheerfulness of mind which encourages interest in one's surroundings.

My first task was to learn English in the shortest possible time. I have, of late years, frequently had to answer inquiries addressed to me by educators and others concerning the methods by which I acquired such knowledge of the language and such facility in using it as I possess. That method was very simple. I did not use an English grammar. I do not think I ever had one in my library. I resolutely began to read—first my daily newspaper, which happened to be the *Philadelphia Ledger*. Regularly every day I worked through editorial articles, the news letters and despatches, and even as many of the advertisements as my time would allow. The *Philadelphia Ledger*, which has since become a very excellent, influential, and important organ of public opinion, was at that time a small and ill-printed sheet, rather colorless in politics, which entertained its readers largely with serious editorial dissertations on such innocent subjects as "The Joys of Spring," "The Beauties of Friendship," "The Blessings of a Virtuous Life," and the like—sometimes a little insipid, but usually very respectable in point of style. Then I proceeded to read English novels. The first one I took up was "The Vicar of Wakefield." Then followed Walter Scott, Dickens, and Thackeray; then Macaulay's historical essays, and, as I thought of preparing myself for the legal profession, Blackstone's "Commentaries," the clear, terse and vigorous style of which I have always continued to regard as a very great model. Shakespeare's plays, the enormous vocabulary of which presented more difficulties than all the rest, came last. But I did my reading with the utmost conscientiousness. I never permitted myself to skip a word the meaning of which I did not clearly understand, and I never failed to consult the dictionary in every doubtful case.

At the same time I practiced an exercise which I found exceedingly effective. I had become acquainted with the "Letters of Junius" through a German translation, and was greatly fascinated by the brilliancy of this style of political discussion. As soon as I thought myself sufficiently advanced in the knowledge of the language, I procured an English edition of Junius and translated a considerable number of the letters from the English text into German in writing; then I translated, also in writing, my German translation back into English, and finally compared this re-translation with the English original. This was very laborious work, but, so to speak, I felt in my bones how it helped me. Together with my reading, it gave me what I might call a sense of the logic and also of the music of the language.

When I began to write in English—letters or other more pretentious compositions—it happened to me not infrequently that in reading over what I had written I stopped at certain forms of expression I had used, doubting whether they were grammatically correct. I then sometimes tried to substitute other forms; but almost invariably I found, upon consulting competent authority, that the phrase as I had, following my instinct, originally put it down, was better than the substitute. In less than six months after I had begun this course of study I was sufficiently advanced to carry on a conversation in English about subjects not requiring a wide knowledge of technical terms, with tolerable ease, and to write a decent letter.

Since becoming known as a speaker and writer in English as well as in German, I have often been asked by persons interested in linguistic studies or in psychological problems, whether while speaking or writing I was thinking in English or in German, and whether I was constantly translating from one language into the other. The answer was that, when speaking or writing in English, I was thinking in English; and, when speaking or writing in German, I was thinking in German; and when my mind followed a train of thought which did not require immediate expression in words, I was unconscious of what language I was thinking in.

I have also often been asked in which language I preferred to think and write. I always answered that this depended on the subject, the purpose, and the occasion. On the whole, I preferred the English language for public speaking, partly on account of the simplicity of its syntactic construction, and partly because the pronunciation of the consonants is mechanically easier and less fatiguing to the speaker. I have preferred it also for the discussion of political subjects and of business affairs because of its full and precise terminology. But for the discussion of philosophical matters, for poetry, and for familiar, intimate conversation I have preferred the German. And beyond this, I have found that about certain subjects, or with certain persons who understood both English and German equally well, I would rather speak in English or in German, as the case might be, without clearly knowing the reason why. It was a matter of feeling which cannot be exactly defined.

"Here in America," I wrote to my friend, "you can see daily how little a people needs to be governed. There are governments, but no masters; there are governors, but they are only commissioners, agents. What there is here of great institutions of learning, of churches, of great commercial institutions, lines of communication, etc., almost always owes its existence, not to official authority, but to the spontaneous co-operation of private citizens. Here you witness the productiveness of freedom. You see a magnificent church—a voluntary association of private persons has founded it; an orphan asylum built of marble—a wealthy citizen has erected it; a university—some rich men have left a large bequest for educational purposes, which serves as a capital stock, and the university then lives, so to speak, almost on subscriptions; and so on without end. We learn here how superfluous is the action of governments concerning a multitude of things in which in Europe it is deemed absolutely indispensable, and how the freedom to do something awakens the desire to do it."

Although I am well aware of its crudities of expression, its inaccuracies of statement, and of the incompleteness of its presentation of American conditions, I quote this letter because it portrays fairly well the workings of the mind of a young man who has been suddenly transplanted from the Old World—its ways of thinking, its traditional views of life, its struggles, illusions, and ideals—into a new world where he witnesses the operation of elementary forces in open daylight, and the realities of free government in undisguised exhibition. I endeavored to get at the essence of truly democratic life, and I still believe that, notwithstanding some errors in the detail of my observations, my general conclusions as to the vital element of democratic institutions were correct.

JACOB RIIS

The early immigrant experience of Danish-born Jacob Riis (1849–
1914), recounted in his 1901 autobiography *The Making of an American*,
puts one in mind of Emerson's model young American: the "sturdy lad
. . . who in turn tries all the professions, who *teams it, farms it, peddles,*
keeps a school, preaches, edits a newspaper. . . ." Riis, who came to the
United States in 1870, in part because he was spurned by the woman he
loved, worked for the next several years with an almost superhuman
doggedness at various jobs: as a carpenter (the trade to which he had
been apprenticed in Copenhagen), farmer, peddler, miner. Always hungry, often homeless, he kept himself afloat by drawing on the crafts he
had learned in his homeland, his command of English, and a sense of
superiority over blacks, Asians, Italians, and other newly arrived immigrants from Southern and Eastern Europe. After several years of this
itinerant life, Riis found steady work as a police reporter for the *New
York Tribune* in 1877. He was horrified by the wretched conditions of
slum life and, animated with a proselyte's zeal, made it his life's work to
bring them to public attention. First lecturing in churches and theaters,
then writing newspaper articles, all culminated in the work for which he
is best known, *How the Other Half Lives* (1890), notable for its words as
well as for the accompanying photographs, interior shots of tenements
and dives which flash photography made possible. The book proved immensely popular and soon brought him to the attention of Theodore
Roosevelt, with whom he would collaborate on Progressive Era reform
projects for the next 20 years and who called Riis "the best American I
ever knew."

from

The Making of an American

T he steamer *Iowa*, from Glasgow, made port, after a long and stormy voyage, on Whitsunday, 1870. She had come up during the night, and cast
anchor off Castle Garden. It was a beautiful spring morning, and as I looked
over the rail at the miles of straight streets, the green heights of Brooklyn, and
the stir of ferryboats and pleasure craft on the river, my hopes rose high that
somewhere in this teeming hive there would be a place for me. What kind of
a place I had myself no clear notion of. I would let that work out as it could. Of
course I had my trade to fall back on, but I am afraid that is all the use I
thought of putting it to. The love of change belongs to youth, and I meant to
take a hand in things as they came along. I had a pair of strong hands, and
stubbornness enough to do for two; also a strong belief that in a free country,
free from the dominion of custom, of caste, as well as of men, things would
somehow come right in the end, and a man get shaken into the corner where
he belonged if he took a hand in the game. I think I was right in that. If it took
a lot of shaking to get me where I belonged, that was just what I needed. Even
my mother admits that now. To tell the truth, I was tired of hammer and saw.
They were indissolubly bound up with my dreams of Elizabeth that were now
gone to smash. Therefore I hated them. And straightway, remembering that
the day was her birthday, and accepting the fact as a good omen, I rebuilt my
air-castles and resolved to try on a new tack. So irrational is human nature at
twenty-one, when in love. And isn't it good that it is?

In all of which I have made no account of a factor which is at the bottom
of half our troubles with our immigrant population, so far as they are not of
our own making: the loss of reckoning that follows uprooting; the cutting
loose from all sense of responsibility, with the old standards gone, that makes
the politician's job so profitable in our large cities, and that of the patriot and
the housekeeper so wearisome. We all know the process. The immigrant has
no patent on it. It afflicts the native, too, when he goes to a town where he is
not known. In the slum it reaches its climax in the second generation, and
makes of the Irishman's and the Italian's boys the "toughs" who fight the
battles of Hell's Kitchen and Frog Hollow. It simply means that we are crea-

tures of environment, that a man everywhere is largely what his neighbors and his children think him to be, and that government makes for our moral good too, dreamers and anarchists to the contrary notwithstanding. But, simple as it is, it has been too long neglected for the safety of the man and of the State. I am not going to discuss here plans for mending this neglect, but I can think of three that would work; one of them does work, if not up to the top notch—the public school. In its ultimate development as the neighborhood centre of things, I would have that the first care of city government, always and everywhere, at whatever expense. An efficient parish districting is another. I think we are coming to that. The last is a rigid annual enrolment—the school census is good, but not good enough—for vaccination purposes, jury duty, for military purposes if you please. I do not mean for conscription, but for the ascertainment of the fighting strength of the State in case of need—for anything that would serve as an excuse. It is the enrolment itself that I think would have a good effect in making the man feel that he is counted on for something; that he belongs as it were, instead of standing idle and watching a procession go by, in which there is no place for him; which is only another way of saying that it is his right to harass it and levy tribute as he can. The enrolment for voting comes too late. By that time he may have joined the looters' army.

So as properly to take my own place in the procession, if not in the army referred to, as I conceived the custom of the country to be, I made it my first business to buy a navy revolver of the largest size, investing in the purchase exactly one-half of my capital. I strapped the weapon on the outside of my coat and strode up Broadway, conscious that I was following the fashion of the country. I knew it upon the authority of a man who had been there before me and had returned, a gold digger in the early days of California; but America was America to us. We knew no distinction of West and East. By rights there ought to have been buffaloes and red Indians charging up and down Broadway. I am sorry to say that it is easier even to-day to make lots of people over there believe that, than that New York is paved, and lighted with electric lights, and quite as civilized as Copenhagen. They will have it that it is in the wilds. I saw none of the signs of this, but I encountered a friendly policeman, who, sizing me and my pistol up, tapped it gently with his club and advised me to leave it home, or I might get robbed of it. This, at first blush, seemed to confirm my apprehensions; but he was a very nice policeman, and took time to explain, seeing that I was very green. And I took his advice and put the revolver away, secretly relieved to get rid of it. It was quite heavy to carry around.

I had letters to the Danish Consul and to the President of the American Banknote Company, Mr. Goodall. I think perhaps he was not then the president, but became so afterward. Mr. Goodall had once been wrecked on the Danish coast and rescued by the captain of the lifesaving crew, a friend of my family. But they were both in Europe, and in just four days I realized that there was no special public clamor for my services in New York, and decided to go West. A missionary in Castle Garden was getting up a gang of men for the Brady's Bend Iron Works on the Allegheny River, and I went along. We started a full score, with tickets paid, but only two of us reached the Bend. The rest calmly deserted in Pittsburg and went their own way. Now here was an instance of what I have just been saying. Not one of them, probably, would have thought of doing it on the other side. They would have carried out their contract as a matter of course. Here they broke it as a matter of course, the minute it didn't suit them to go on. Two of them had been on our steamer, and the thought of them makes me laugh even now. One was a Dane who carried an immense knapsack that was filled with sausages, cheese, and grub of all kinds when he came aboard. He never let go of it for a moment on the voyage. In storm and sunshine he was there, shouldering his knapsack. I think he slept with it. When I last saw him hobbling down a side street in Pittsburg, he carried it still, but one end of it hung limp and hungry, and the other was as lean as a bad year. The other voyager was a jovial Swede whose sole baggage consisted of an old musket, a blackthorn stick, and a barometer glass, tied up together. The glass, he explained, was worth keeping; it might some day make an elegant ruler. The fellow was a blacksmith, and I mistrust that he could not write.

Adler and I went on to Brady's Bend. Adler was a big, explosive German who had been a reserve officer, I think, in the Prussian army. Fate had linked us together when on the steamer the meat served in the steerage became so bad as to offend not only our palates, but our sense of smell. We got up a demonstration, marching to see the captain in a body, Adler and I carrying a tray of the objectionable meat between us. As the spokesman, I presented the case briefly and respectfully, and all would have gone well had not the hot blood of Adler risen at the wrong moment, when the captain was cautiously exploring the scent of the rejected food. With a sudden upward jerk he caused that official's nose to disappear momentarily in the dish, while he exploded in voluble German. The result was an instant rupture of diplomatic relations. Adler was put in the lock-up, but set free again immediately. He spent the rest of the voyage in his bunk shouting dire threats of disaster impending from the "Norddeutsche Consul," once he reached New York. But we were all too glad to get ashore to think of vengeance then.

Adler found work at the blast-furnace, while I was set to building huts for the miners on the east bank of the river where a clearing had been made and called East Brady. On the other side of the Allegheny the furnaces and rolling mills were hidden away in a narrow, winding valley that set back into the forest-clad hills, growing deeper and narrower with every mile. It was to me, who had been used to seeing the sun rise and set over a level plain where the winds of heaven blew as they listed, from the first like a prison. I climbed the hills only to find that there were bigger hills beyond—an endless sea of swelling billows of green without a clearing in it. I spent all Sunday roaming through it, miles and miles, to find an outlook from which I might see the end; but there was none. A horrible fit of homesickness came upon me. The days I managed to get through by working hard and making observations on the American language. In this I had a volunteer assistant in Julia, the pretty, barefooted daughter of a coal-miner, who hung around and took an interest in what was going on. But she disappeared after I had asked her to explain what setting one's cap for any one meant. I was curious because I had heard her mother say to a neighbor that Julia was doing that to me. But the evenings were very lonesome. The girl in our boarding-house washed dishes always to one tune, "The Letter that Never Came." It was not a cheerful tune and not a cheerful subject, for I had had no news from home since I left. I can hear her yet, shrieking and clattering her dishes, with the frogs yelling accompaniment in the creek that mumbled in the valley. I never could abide American frogs since. There is rest in the ko-ax, ko-ax! of its European brother, but the breathless yi! yi! of our American frogs makes me feel always as if I wanted to die—which I don't.

In making the clearing, I first saw an American wood-cutter swing an axe, and the sight filled me with admiration for the man and the axe both. It was a "double-bitter," and he a typical long-armed and long-limbed backwoodsman. I also had learned to use the axe, but anything like the way he swung it, first over one, then over the other shoulder, making it tell in long, clean cuts at every blow, I had never dreamt of. It was splendid. I wished myself back in Copenhagen just long enough to tell the numskulls there, who were distrustful of American tools, which were just beginning to come into the market, that they didn't know what they were talking about. Of course it was reasonable that the good tools should come from the country where they had good use for them.

There was a settlement of honest Welshmen in the back hills, and the rumor that a Dane had come into the valley reached it in due course. It brought down a company of four sturdy miners, who trudged five miles over bad land of a Sunday to see what I was like. The Danes who live in Welsh song and story must have been grievous giants, for they were greatly disgusted at sight of me, and spoke their minds about it without reserve, even with some severity, as if I were guilty of some sort of an imposition on the valley.

It could hardly have been this introduction that tempted me to try coalmining. I have forgotten how it came about—probably through some temporary slackness in the building trade; but I did try, and one day was enough for me. The company mined its own coal. Such as it was, it cropped out of the hills right and left in narrow veins, sometimes too shallow to work, seldom affording more space to the digger than barely enough to permit him to stand upright. You did not go down through a shaft, but straight in through the side of a hill to the bowels of the mountain, following a track on which a little donkey drew the coal to the mouth of the mine and sent it down the incline to run up and down a hill a mile or more by its own gravity before it reached the place of unloading. Through one of these we marched in, Adler and I, one summer morning with new pickaxes on our shoulders and nasty little oil lamps fixed in our hats to light us through the darkness where every second we stumbled over chunks of slate rock, or into pools of water that oozed through from above. An old miner whose way lay past the fork in the tunnel where our lead began showed us how to use our picks and the timbers to brace the slate that roofed over the vein, and left us to ourselves in a chamber perhaps ten feet wide and the height of a man.

We were to be paid by the ton, I forget how much, but it was very little, and we lost no time getting to work. We had to dig away the coal at the floor with our picks, lying on our knees to do it, and afterward drive wedges under the roof to loosen the mass. It was hard work, and, entirely inexperienced as we were, we made but little headway. As the day wore on, the darkness and silence grew very oppressive, and made us start nervously at the least thing. The sudden arrival of our donkey with its cart gave me a dreadful fright. The friendly beast greeted us with a joyous bray and rubbed its shaggy sides against us in the most companionable way. In the flickering light of my lamp I caught sight of its long ears waving over me—I don't believe I had seen three donkeys before in my life; there were none where I came from—and heard that demoniac shriek, and I verily believe I thought the evil one had come for me in person. I know that I nearly fainted.

That donkey was a discerning animal. I think it knew when it first set eyes on us that we were not going to overwork it; and we didn't. When, toward evening, we quit work, after narrowly escaping being killed by a large stone that fell from the roof in consequence of our neglect to brace it up properly, our united efforts had resulted in barely filling two of the little carts, and we had earned, if I recollect aright, something like sixty cents each. The fall of the roof robbed us of all desire to try mining again. It knocked the lamps from our hats, and, in darkness that could almost be felt, we groped our way back to the light along the track, getting more badly frightened as we went. The last stretch of way we ran, holding each other's hands as though we were not men and miners, but two frightened children in the dark.

As we emerged from the damp gap in the mountain side, the sunset was upon the hills. Peaceful sounds came up from the valley where the shadows lay deep. Gangs of men were going home from the day's toil to their evening rest. It seemed to me that I had been dead and had come back to life. The world was never so wondrous fair. My companion stood looking out over the landscape with hungry eyes. Neither of us spoke, but when the last gleam had died out in the window of the stone church we went straight to the company's store and gave up our picks. I have never set foot in a coal mine since, and have not the least desire to do so.

EDITH MAUDE EATON

Edith Maude Eaton (1865–1914) occupies a prominent place in Chinese-American letters. She was, as one recent editor puts it, "the first person of Chinese descent in the United States to write and publish work about Chinese-American life." But Eaton's connection to the main threads of Chinese immigrant experience was entirely atypical, and her identity was a complicated subject that occupied her throughout her life and career. The daughter of an English merchant father and a Chinese mother adopted and educated by English missionaries, she came to the United States from England as a young girl in the early 1870s and found herself an outsider both in Chinatown and in the Anglo-American neighborhoods where she was raised. She was asked by a local newspaper to report on the Chinese immigrant community and found herself—as she recounts in her 1890 essay "Leaves from the Mental Portfolio of an Eurasian"—"called upon to fight their battles." Later in California "broadminded" literary friends encouraged her to trade on her nationality and work up an exotic persona: "if I wish to succeed in literature in America I should dress in Chinese costume, carry a fan in my hand, wear a pair of scarlet beaded slippers. . . . Instead of making myself familiar with the Chinese Americans around me, I should discourse on my spirit acquaintance with Chinese ancestors. . . ." Under her pen name Sui Sin Far she wrote for a popular American audience perhaps not ready to hear the more realistic voices one finds in the poems of Chinese immigrants detained on Angel Island (see pp. 163–65). Eaton was, however, a constant and forceful advocate for the rights of the "race" she chose to adopt, in a nation increasingly xenophobic about the Chinese. *Mrs. Spring Fragrance*, the 1912 story collection from which the title story is included here, offers more than mere *chinoiserie*: her questions about love, tradition, and the meaning of "assimilation" in a new nation are still resonant almost a century later.

Mrs. Spring Fragrance

I

W hen Mrs. Spring Fragrance first arrived in Seattle, she was unacquainted with even one word of the American language. Five years later her husband, speaking of her, said: "There are no more American words for her learning." And everyone who knew Mrs. Spring Fragrance agreed with Mr. Spring Fragrance.

Mr. Spring Fragrance, whose business name was Sing Yook, was a young curio merchant. Though conservatively Chinese in many respects, he was at the same time what is called by the Westerners, "Americanized." Mrs. Spring Fragrance was even more "Americanized."

Next door to the Spring Fragrances lived the Chin Yuens. Mrs. Chin Yuen was much older than Mrs. Spring Fragance; but she had a daughter of eighteen with whom Mrs. Spring Fragrance was on terms of great friendship. The daughter was a pretty girl whose Chinese name was Mai Gwi Far (a rose) and whose American name was Laura. Nearly everybody called her Laura, even her parents and Chinese friends. Laura had a sweetheart, a youth named Kai Tzu. Kai Tzu, who was American-born, and as ruddy and stalwart as any young Westerner, was noted amongst baseball players as one of the finest pitchers on the Coast. He could also sing, "Drink to me only with thine eyes," to Laura's piano accompaniment.

Now the only person who knew that Kai Tzu loved Laura and that Laura loved Kai Tzu, was Mrs. Spring Fragrance. The reason for this was that, although the Chin Yuen parents lived in a house furnished in American style, and wore American clothes, yet they religiously observed many Chinese customs, and their ideals of life were the ideals of their Chinese forefathers. Therefore, they had betrothed their daughter, Laura, at the age of fifteen, to the eldest son of the Chinese Government school-teacher in San Francisco. The time for the consummation of the betrothal was approaching.

Laura was with Mrs. Spring Fragrance and Mrs. Spring Fragrance was trying to cheer her.

"I had such a pretty walk today," said she. "I crossed the banks above the beach and came back by the long road. In the green grass the daffodils were blowing, in the cottage gardens the currant bushes were flowering, and in the air was the perfume of the wallflower. I wished, Laura, that you were with me."

Laura burst into tears. "That is the walk," she sobbed, "Kai Tzu and I so love; but never, ah, never, can we take it together again."

"Now, Little Sister," comforted Mrs. Spring Fragrance, "you really must not grieve like that. Is there not a beautiful American poem written by a noble American named Tennyson, which says:

> 'Tis better to have loved and lost,
> Than never to have loved at all?"

Mrs. Spring Fragrance was unaware that Mr. Spring Fragrance, having returned from the city, tired with the day's business, had thrown himself down on the bamboo settee on the veranda, and that although his eyes were engaged in scanning the pages of the *Chinese World*, his ears could not help receiving the words which were borne to him through the open window.

> " 'Tis better to have loved and lost,
> Than never to have loved at all,"

repeated Mr. Spring Fragrance. Not wishing to hear more of the secret talk of women, he arose and sauntered around the veranda to the other side of the house. Two pigeons circled around his head. He felt in his pocket, for a li-chi which he usually carried for their pecking. His fingers touched a little box. It contained a jadestone pendant, which Mrs. Spring Fragrance had particularly admired the last time she was down town. It was the fifth anniversary of Mr. and Mrs. Spring Fragrance's wedding day.

Mr. Spring Fragrance pressed the little box down into the depths of his pocket.

A young man came out of the back door of the house at Mr. Spring Fragrance's left. The Chin Yuen house was at his right.

"Good evening," said the young man. "Good evening," returned Mr. Spring Fragrance. He stepped down from his porch and went and leaned over the railing which separated this yard from the yard in which stood the young man.

"Will you please tell me," said Mr. Spring Fragrance, "the meaning of two lines of an American verse which I have heard?"

"Certainly," returned the young man with a genial smile. He was a star student at the University of Washington, and had not the slightest doubt that he could explain the meaning of all things in the universe.

"Well," said Mr. Spring Fragrance, "it is this:

'Tis better to have loved and lost,
Than never to have loved at all."

"Ah!" responded the young man with an air of profound wisdom. "That, Mr. Spring Fragrance, means that it is a good thing to love anyway—even if we can't get what we love, or, as the poet tells us, lose what we love. Of course, one needs experience to feel the truth of this teaching."

The young man smiled pensively and reminiscently. More than a dozen young maidens "loved and lost" were passing before his mind's eye.

"The truth of the teaching!" echoed Mr. Spring Fragrance, a little testily. "There is no truth in it whatever. It is disobedient to reason. Is it not better to have what you do not love than to love what you do not have?"

"That depends," answered the young man, "upon temperament."

"I thank you. Good evening," said Mr. Spring Fragrance. He turned away to muse upon the unwisdom of the American way of looking at things.

Meanwhile, inside the house, Laura was refusing to be comforted.

"Ah, no! no!" cried she. "If I had not gone to school with Kai Tzu, nor talked nor walked with him, nor played the accompaniments to his songs, then I might consider with complacency, or at least without horror, my approaching marriage with the son of Man You. But as it is—oh, as it is—!"

The girl rocked herself to and fro in heartfelt grief.

Mrs. Spring Fragrance knelt down beside her, and clasping her arms around her neck, cried in sympathy:

"Little Sister, oh, Little Sister! Dry your tears—do not despair. A moon has yet to pass before the marriage can take place. Who knows what the stars may have to say to one another during its passing? A little bird has whispered to me—"

For a long time Mrs. Spring Fragrance talked. For a long time Laura listened. When the girl arose to go, there was a bright light in her eyes.

II

Mrs. Spring Fragrance, in San Francisco, on a visit to her cousin, the wife of the herb doctor of Clay Street, was having a good time. She was invited everywhere that the wife of an honorable Chinese merchant could go. There was much to see and hear, including more than a dozen babies who had been born in the families of her friends since she last visited the city of the Golden Gate. Mrs. Spring Fragrance loved babies. She had had two herself, but both had been transplanted into the spirit land before the completion of even one moon. There were also many dinners and theatre-parties given in her honor. It was at one of the theatre-parties that Mrs. Spring Fragrance met Ah Oi, a young girl who had the reputation of being the prettiest Chinese girl in San Francisco, and the naughtiest. In spite of gossip, however, Mrs. Spring Fragrance took a great fancy to Ah Oi and invited her to a tête-à-tête picnic on the following day. This invitation Ah Oi joyfully accepted. She was a sort of bird girl and never felt so happy as when out in the park or woods.

On the day after the picnic Mrs. Spring Fragrance wrote to Laura Chin Yuen thus:

> My Precious Laura,—May the bamboo ever wave. Next week I accompany Ah Oi to the beauteous town of San José. There will we be met by the son of the Illustrious Teacher, and in a little Mission, presided over by a benevolent American priest, the little Ah Oi and the son of the Illustrious Teacher will be joined together in love and harmony—two pieces of music made to complete one another.
>
> The Son of the Illustrious Teacher, having been through an American Hall of Learning, is well able to provide for his orphan bride and fears not the displeasure of his parents, now that he is assured that your grief at his loss will not be inconsolable. He wishes me to waft to you and to Kai Tzu—and the little Ah Oi joins with him—ten thousand rainbow wishes for your happiness.
>
> My respects to your honorable parents, and to yourself, the heart of your loving friend,
>
> Jade Spring Fragrance

To Mr. Spring Fragrance, Mrs. Spring Fragrance also indited a letter:

Great and Honored Man,—Greeting from your plum blossom,* who is desirous of hiding herself from the sun of your presence for a week of seven days more. My honorable cousin is preparing for the Fifth Moon Festival, and wishes me to compound for the occasion some American "fudge," for which delectable sweet, made by my clumsy hands, you have sometimes shown a slight prejudice. I am enjoying a most agreeable visit, and American friends, as also our own, strive benevolently for the accomplishment of my pleasure. Mrs. Samuel Smith, an American lady, known to my cousin, asked for my accompaniment to a magniloquent lecture the other evening. The subject was "America, the Protector of China!" It was most exhilarating, and the effect of so much expression of benevolence leads me to beg of you to forget to remember that the barber charges you one dollar for a shave while he humbly submits to the American man a bill of fifteen cents. And murmur no more because your honored elder brother, on a visit to this country, is detained under the roof-tree of this great Government instead of under your own humble roof. Console him with the reflection that he is protected under the wing of the Eagle, the Emblem of Liberty. What is the loss of ten hundred years or ten thousand times ten dollars compared with the happiness of knowing oneself so securely sheltered? All of this I have learned from Mrs. Samuel Smith, who is as brilliant and great of mind as one of your own superior sex.

For me it is sufficient to know that the Golden Gate Park is most enchanting, and the seals on the rock at the Cliff House extremely entertaining and amiable. There is much feasting and merry-making under the lanterns in honor of your Stupid Thorn.

I have purchased for your smoking a pipe with an amber mouth. It is said to be very sweet to the lips and to emit a cloud of smoke fit for the gods to inhale.

Awaiting, by the wonderful wire of the telegram message, your

---

*The plum blossom is the Chinese flower of virtue. It has been adopted by the Japanese, just in the same way as they have adopted the Chinese national flower, the chrysanthemum.

gracious permission to remain for the celebration of the Fifth Moon Festival and the making of American "fudge," I continue for ten thousand times ten thousand years,

Your ever loving and obedient woman,

J<small>ADE</small>

P.S. Forget not to care for the cat, the birds, and the flowers. Do not eat too quickly nor fan too vigorously now that the weather is warming.

Mrs. Spring Fragrance smiled as she folded this last epistle. Even if he were old-fashioned, there was never a husband so good and kind as hers. Only on one occasion since their marriage had he slighted her wishes. That was when, on the last anniversary of their wedding, she had signified a desire for a certain jadestone pendant, and he had failed to satisfy that desire.

But Mrs. Spring Fragrance, being of a happy nature, and disposed to look upon the bright side of things, did not allow her mind to dwell upon the jadestone pendant. Instead, she gazed complacently down upon her bejeweled fingers and folded in with her letter to Mr. Spring Fragrance a bright little sheaf of condensed love.

III

Mr. Spring Fragrance sat on his doorstep. He had been reading two letters, one from Mrs. Spring Fragrance, and the other from an elderly bachelor cousin in San Francisco. The one from the elderly bachelor cousin was a business letter, but contained the following postscript:

> Tsen Hing, the son of the Government schoolmaster, seems to be much in the company of your young wife. He is a good-looking youth, and pardon me, my dear cousin;—but if women are allowed to stray at will from under their husbands' mulberry roofs, what is to prevent them from becoming butterflies?

"Sing Foon is old and cynical," said Mr. Spring Fragrance to himself. "Why should I pay any attention to him? This is America, where a man may speak to a woman and a woman listen, without any thought of evil."

He destroyed his cousin's letter and re-read his wife's. Then he became very thoughtful. Was the making of American fudge sufficient reason for a wife to wish to remain a week longer in a city where her husband was not?

The young man who lived in the next house came out to water the lawn.

"Good evening," said he. "Any news from Mrs. Spring Fragrance?"

"She is having a very good time," returned Mr. Spring Fragrance.

"Glad to hear it. I think you told me she was to return the end of this week."

"I have changed my mind about her," said Mr. Spring Fragrance. "I am bidding her remain a week longer, as I wish to give a smoking party during her absence. I hope I may have the pleasure of your company."

"I shall be delighted," returned the young fellow. "But, Mr. Spring Fragrance, don't invite any other white fellows. If you do not I shall be able to get in a scoop. You know, I'm a sort of honorary reporter for the *Gleaner*."

"Very well," absently answered Mr. Spring Fragrance.

"Of course, your friend the Consul will be present. I shall call it 'A high-class Chinese stag party!' "

In spite of his melancholy mood, Mr. Spring Fragrance smiled.

"Everything is 'high-class' in America," he observed.

"Sure!" cheerfully assented the young man. "Haven't you ever heard that all Americans are princes and princesses, and just as soon as a foreigner puts his foot upon our shores, he also becomes of the nobility—I mean, the royal family."

"What about my brother in the Detention Pen?" dryly inquired Mr. Spring Fragrance.

"Now, you've got me," said the young man, rubbing his head. "Well, that is a shame—'a beastly shame,' as the Englishman says. But understand, old fellow, we that are real Americans are up against that—even more than you. It is against our principles."

"I offer the real Americans my consolations that they should be compelled to do that which is against their principles."

"Oh, well, it will all come right some day. We're not a bad sort, you know. Think of the indemnity money returned to the Dragon by Uncle Sam."

Mr. Spring Fragrance puffed his pipe in silence for some moments. More than politics was troubling his mind.

At last he spoke. "Love," said he, slowly and distinctly, "comes before the, wedding in this country; does it not?"

"Yes, certainly."

Young Carman knew Mr. Spring Fragrance well enough to receive with calmness his most astounding queries.

"Presuming," continued Mr. Spring Fragrance—"presuming that some friend of your father's, living—presuming—in England—has a daughter that he arranges with your father to be your wife. Presuming that you have never seen that daughter, but that you marry her, knowing her not. Presuming that she marries you, knowing you not.—After she marries you and knows you, will that woman love you?"

"Emphatically, no," answered the young man.

"That is the way it would be in America that the woman who marries the man like that—would not love him?"

"Yes, that is the way it would be in America. Love, in this country, must be free, or it is not love at all."

"In China, it is different!" mused Mr. Spring Fragrance.

"Oh, yes, I have no doubt that in China it is different."

"But the love is in the heart all the same," went on Mr. Spring Fragrance.

"Yes, all the same. Everybody falls in love sometime or another. Some"—pensively—"many times."

Mr. Spring Fragrance arose.

"I must go down town," said he.

As he walked down the street he recalled the remark of a business acquaintance who had met his wife and had had some conversation with her: "She is just like an American woman."

He had felt somewhat flattered when this remark had been made. He looked upon it as a compliment to his wife's cleverness; but it rankled in his mind as he entered the telegraph office. If his wife was becoming as an American woman, would it not be possible for her to love as an American woman—a man to whom she was not married? There also floated in is memory the verse which his wife had quoted to the daughter of Chin Yuen. When the telegraph clerk handed him a blank, he wrote this message:

"Remain as you wish, but remember that 'Tis better to have loved and lost, than never to have loved at all.'"

*

When Mrs. Spring Fragrance received this message, her laughter tinkled like falling water. How droll! How delightful! Here was her husband quoting American poetry in a telegram. Perhaps he had been reading her American poetry books since she had left him! She hoped so. They would lead him to understand her sympathy for her dear Laura and Kai Tzu. She need no longer keep from him their secret. How joyful! It had been such a hardship to refrain from confiding in him before. But discreetness had been most necessary, seeing that Mr. Spring Fragrance entertained as old-fashioned notions concerning marriage as did the Chin Yuen parents. Strange that that should be so, since he had fallen in love with her picture before *ever* he had seen her, just as she had fallen in love with his! And when the marriage veil was lifted and each beheld the other for the first time in the flesh, there had been no disillusion—no lessening of the respect and affection, which those who had brought about the marriage had inspired in each young heart.

Mrs. Spring Fragrance began to wish she could fall asleep and wake to find the week flown, and she in her own little home pouring tea for Mr. Spring Fragrance.

IV

Mr. Spring Fragrance was walking to business with Mr. Chin Yuen. As they walked they talked.

"Yes," said Mr. Chin Yuen, "the old order is passing away, and the new order is taking its place, even with us who are Chinese. I have finally consented to give my daughter in marriage to young Kai Tzu."

Mr. Spring Fragrance expressed surprise. He had understood that the marriage between his neighbor's daughter and the San Francisco schoolteacher's son was all arranged.

"So 'twas," answered Mr. Chin Yuen; "but it seems the young renegade, without consultation or advice, has placed his affections upon some untrustworthy female, and is so under her influence that he refuses to fulfil his parents' promise to me for him."

"So!" said Mr. Spring Fragrance. The shadow on his brow deepened.

"But," said Mr. Chin Yuen, with affable resignation, "it is all ordained by Heaven. Our daughter, as the wife of Kai Tzu, for whom she has long had a loving feeling, will not now be compelled to dwell with a mother-in-law and where her own mother is not. For that, we are thankful, as she is our only one and the conditions of life in this Western country are not as in China. Moreover, Kai Tzu, though not so much of a scholar as the teacher's son, has a keen eye for business and that, in America, is certainly much more desirable than scholarship. What do you think?"

"Eh! What!" exclaimed Mr. Spring Fragrance. The latter part of his companion's remarks had been lost upon him.

That day the shadow which had been following Mr. Spring Fragrance ever since he had heard his wife quote, "'Tis better to have loved," etc., became so heavy and deep that he quite lost himself within it.

At home in the evening he fed the cat, the bird, and the flowers. Then, seating himself in a carved black chair—a present from his wife on his last birthday—he took out his pipe and smoked. The cat jumped into his lap. He stroked it softly and tenderly. It had been much fondled by Mrs. Spring Fragrance, and Mr. Spring Fragrance was under the impression that it missed her. "Poor thing!" said he. "I suppose you want her back!" When he arose to go to bed he placed the animal carefully on the floor, and thus apostrophized it:

"O Wise and Silent One, your mistress returns to you, but her heart she leaves behind her, with the Tommies in San Francisco."

The Wise and Silent One made no reply. He was not a jealous cat.

Mr. Spring Fragrance slept not that night; the next morning he ate not. Three days and three nights without sleep and food went by.

There was a springlike freshness in the air on the day that Mrs. Spring Fragrance came home. The skies overhead were as blue as Puget Sound stretching its gleaming length toward the mighty Pacific, and all the beautiful green world seemed to be throbbing with springing life.

Mrs. Spring Fragrance was never so radiant.

"Oh," she cried light-heartedly, "is it not lovely to see the sun shining so clear, and everything so bright to welcome me?"

Mr. Spring Fragrance made no response. It was the morning after the fourth sleepless night.

Mrs. Spring Fragrance noticed his silence, also his grave face.

"Everything—everyone is glad to see me but you," she declared, half seriously, half jestingly

Mr. Spring Fragrance set down her valise. They had just entered the house.

"If my wife is glad to see me," he quietly replied, "I also am glad to see her!"

Summoning their servant boy, he bade him look after Mrs. Spring Fragrance's comfort.

"I must be at the store in half an hour," said he, looking at his watch. "There is some very important business requiring attention."

"What is the business?" inquired Mrs. Spring Fragrance, her lip quivering with disappointment.

"I cannot just explain to you," answered her husband.

Mrs. Spring Fragrance looked up into his face with honest and earnest eyes. There was something in his manner, in the tone of her husband's voice, which touched her.

"Yen," said she, "you do not look well. You are not well. What is it?"

Something arose in Mr. Spring Fragrance's throat which prevented him from replying.

"O darling one! O sweetest one!" cried a girl's joyous voice. Laura Chin Yuen ran into the room and threw her arms around Mrs. Spring Fragrance's neck.

"I spied you from the window," said Laura, "and I couldn't rest until I told you. We are to be married next week, Kai Tzu and I. And all through you, all through you—the sweetest jade jewel in the world!"

Mr. Spring Fragrance passed out of the room.

"So the son of the Government teacher and little Happy Love are already married," Laura went on, relieving Mrs. Spring Fragrance of her cloak, her hat, and her folding fan.

Mr. Spring Fragrance paused upon the doorstep.

"Sit down, Little Sister, and I will tell you all about it," said Mrs. Spring Fragrance, forgetting her husband for a moment.

When Laura Chin Yuen had danced away, Mr. Spring Fragrance came in and hung up his hat.

"You got back very soon," said Mrs. Spring Fragrance, covertly wiping away the tears which had begun to fall as soon as she thought herself alone.

"I did not go," answered Mr. Spring Fragrance. "I have been listening to you and Laura."

"But if the business is very important, do not you think you should attend to it?" anxiously queried Mrs. Spring Fragrance.

"It is not important to me now," returned Mr. Spring Fragrance. "I would prefer to hear again about Ah Oi and Man You and Laura and Kai Tzu."

"How lovely of you to say that!" exclaimed Mrs. Spring Fragrance, who was easily made happy. And she began to chat away to her husband in the friendliest and wifeliest fashion possible. When she had finished she asked him if he were not glad to hear that those who loved as did the young lovers whose scerets she had been keeping, were to be united; and he replied that indeed he was; that he would like every man to be as happy with a wife as he himself had ever been and ever would be.

"You did not always talk like that," said Mrs. Spring Fragrance slyly. "You must have been reading my American poetry books!"

"American poetry!" ejaculated Mr. Spring Fragrance almost fiercely, "American poetry is detestable, *abhorrable!*"

"Why! why!" exclaimed Mrs. Spring Fragrance, more and more surpised.

But the only explanation which Mr. Spring Fragrance vouchsafed was a jadestone pendant.

ABRAHAM CAHAN

Abraham Cahan (1860–1951) arrived in the United States at age 21 with a well-developed political consciousness. Forced to flee Velizh, a Lithuanian town now in Russia, where he had been teaching public school and where he was suspected of engaging in radical activities, he headed straight for New York City, and within several years he had learned enough English to start writing articles for local newspapers. With the help of William Dean Howells—who called him a "new star of realism"—his first novel, *Yekl, A Tale of the New York Ghetto*, was published in 1896. A year later he founded what was to prove his most enduring legacy, the *Jewish Daily Forward*. Under his leadership the newspaper softened its ideological edge, becoming less polemical and intellectual, and geared itself more toward Yiddish-speaking workers and their families. It was, in the words of Ronald Sanders, "the immigrants' friend and confidant . . . a patient and omniscient father, wise in the ways of America." Cahan's masterpiece, *The Rise of David Levinsky*, appeared in 1917, and is considered to be one of the most significant literary products of the great wave of Jewish immigration between 1880 and 1924. H. L. Mencken observed, "It is a fine feat to write a first-rate novel, but it is also a fine feat to steer a great newspaper from success to success in difficult times. He has done both." The following excerpt is taken from Cahan's five-volume autobiography, *Bleter fun mayn leben*, written in Yiddish between 1926 and 1931. The English translation, by Leon Stein, Abraham P. Conan, and Lynn Davison and entitled *The Education of Abraham Cahan*, was published in 1969.

from
The Education of Abraham Cahan

W e arrived in Philadelphia on the 6th of June, 1882.
The realization that I was in America filled me with elation. I had moved from the ordinary world into a special world—America. But I spied a cat on the pier and almost cried out, "Look, a cat, just like at home," and then I knew that America was in the same world as Russia, Austria, Germany. My anxiety eased.

We were received in a large building by representatives of the Hebrew Emigrant Aid Society. With them were also some government officials, none of whom wore yellow trousers or high hats; nor were any of them especially tall.

We were taken to a second-floor room, seated around large tables and given food. The place looked like a big stable and the entire scene smacked of charity and the barracks. My heart grew even heavier when they began to register us. I felt we were being treated like recruits at a Russian summons to military service.

Then, while we waited, I gathered a collection from among my fellow immigrants in order to give "Mister" a present. As he left us I said to him in English, "Good-bye!" And suddenly I was gripped by a love for the ship on which, for almost two weeks, we had been together on our crossing.

Later that evening we were taken to a railroad station. I remember little of our trip to New York, only that several stops were made on the way and that day was breaking as it ended.

I remember that in the semidarkness we were led into a large, high-ceilinged, beautiful hall. A long row of windows, flooded with light, stretched along the wall. It was like a magic palace, and when it suddenly began to move I was astounded.

This was a ferryboat. At the time I would not have known what to call it because this floating palace in no way resembled the miserable contraption of planks which is pulled by ropes across the Vilia in Vilna or the Dvina in Velizh.

The ferryboat docked in New York, at historic Castle Garden, for several decades the landing place of immigrants. Today, Castle Garden, at the Battery, houses an aquarium. Off in the distance one can still see the large steamers heading for Europe.

In those days, before restrictive immigration laws, newcomers were not long detained. They were registered by the authorities and let go. If they had nowhere to go they could remain at Castle Garden until they found a place. But they were always free to go when they wished.

The main office of the Hebrew Emigrant Aid Society was on State Street, directly opposite Castle Garden. When I arrived there I was interviewed by an American Jew who conversed with me in German, which neither of us spoke well. Unable to communicate effectively, we were uneasy with each other. I departed with a strong impression that he was a heartless bourgeois. And he probably suspected that I was a wild Russian. That is what they called us immigrants at that time, sometimes even to our faces.

This inability to understand each other affected the relationship between the Russian-Jewish immigrants and the American Yahudim or German Jews who had crossed over years earlier. Later I realized that there were Yahudim who fervently wished to help us stand on our own two feet in the new homeland.

The reports of the pogroms had stirred them deeply and accounted for their participation in the immigrant society. But agreement between us was practically impossible. It wasn't only the differences in our daily language and manner of speaking that got in the way. That wouldn't have been so bad. It was deeper differences in inherited concepts and customs that separated us. With the best intentions in the world and with gentle hearts they unknowingly insulted us.

Solomon Menaker took me back to Castle Garden. There I slept during my first night in America. The beds were bad and the air as acrid as if a thousand cats dwelt there. We spent almost the entire night talking but I remember very little of what we said.

I remember my first day in the Jewish part of the city. I walked along East Broadway in the late afternoon. Old, white-bearded men sat on some of the stoops and the skullcaps on their heads made me feel at home.

The Jewish quarter was very small. East Broadway then had stores where Jewish customer peddlers bought their stock which they then sold on the installment plan to their non-Jewish white and black customers while going from door to door. There were a number of such stores also on Canal Street and in this respect the neighborhood has not changed completely.

A few Jewish families had moved into houses along East Broadway at Clinton and Montgomery Streets. Only a few years earlier this had been a purely native American section of East Broadway, even an aristocratically American section. At the time of my arrival the elder William Vanderbilt was the nation's wealthiest millionaire. And at the time of his marriage his residence was on East Broadway. Up until shortly before my arrival even the mayor of New York, who seldom belongs to the aristocracy, lived close by.

The dollar nobility—the millionaires—were still a novelty in America. Before the Civil War, the population of the country consisted chiefly of farmers and small and middle-rank businessmen. There were few giant cities or giant factories. The change after the Civil War was a rapid one. It is hard to believe that all this happened only about sixty years ago.

Today, New York has a building that is fifty-three stories high. Buildings with twenty and thirty floors are commonplace in dozens of other cities. But when I arrived in the United States no building was taller than eight stories.

The number of Jewish families diminished as one moved away from East Broadway toward Henry Street to Madison, Monroe and finally to Cherry Street where there were no Jews at all. In the other direction, the Jewish quarter, with a mixture of Irish and Germans, extended north to Delancey Street.

There were not yet any Jewish cafes or restaurants at the time of my arrival. I remember a German-owned and a French-owned cafe on Grand Street. On that same street, between Allen and Orchard Streets was Ridley's, the large department store which drew customers from all parts of the city. Further along Grand Street was Lord and Taylor, the famous store that now operates on Fifth Avenue and 38th Street.

Jewish sweatshop garment workers had established on Hester Street a market for operators, basters, half-basters, finishers and pressers. To this market came contractors, seeking to hire help. The place was known as the "chazer market" or "pig market." Hester Street had earlier been inhabited by the Germans and the Irish.

At the time of my arrival the main Jewish neighborhood was bound by East Broadway, Grand Street, Suffolk Street and Allen Street. A smaller center was at Bayard and Mott Streets. The Irish had moved toward the East River section of the area.

The Germans had resettled above Houston Street. In the hot summer evenings the stoops along Second Avenue and its side streets were filled with German men, women and children, reading German newspapers, conversing in German. The area had a distinctly German atmosphere, with beer halls, delicatessen stores and even an occasional German bookstore.

The Bowery was inhabited by the most dangerous law-breakers. Criminals and outcasts made it their neighborhood, and the cheapest prostitutes strolled its sidewalks. Nearby Chrystie, Forsythe and Eldridge Streets were no better in the evenings. Irish, Germans and Americans lived there along with a few Jews and no Italians.

These were the days before electrically powered trolley cars, and only horse-drawn cars moved along the main streets. The one on East Broadway was a small blue car drawn by a single small horse. The driver was also the conductor.

He stood on his platform at the front end of the car, directly behind the horse. Near him was a glass receptacle into which those who boarded his car dropped a nickel which the conductor would then examine. If you needed change he would open the small door behind him through which he handed change to the new passenger. He had small envelopes with the exact change counted out in advance for a dollar, a quarter or a dime. The car would not move until all who had boarded it had paid their fares.

I had my first experience with the elevated railroad the day after my arrival, and it showed that I was still very much a greenhorn. I climbed the stairs and purchased my ticket with my nickel. I had the ticket but I didn't know what to do with it. As I moved toward the platform the ticket collector stopped me. Motioning with his finger, he tried to indicate to me that should I drop the ticket in the box in front of him.

Unfortunately, his gestures seemed strange to me, for the gesture of an American has an "accent" that makes it different from the same kind of gesture by a Jew in Vilna. For this reason I couldn't understand him. He grabbed my hand and began to shake it over his box with the intention of prying the ticket from my grip. I thought he was ridiculing me so I held fast to my ticket. Finally, I understood.

One of the first things I had to do was find my socialist friends from Vilna. I was impatient to learn from them about the arrests in Vilna. In Liverpool I had learned that they had joined the Kiev Am Olam group. In this country its headquarters was in Greenpoint, a remote part of Brooklyn. So I set forth with the address and travel details in my pocket.

First I crossed the East River on the ferryboat. Then I boarded a two-tiered horsecar and took a seat on the upper level. (The Brooklyn elevated line had not yet been completed.) From that perch, and with my Liverpool dictionary in my hand, I peered out at the street signs and selected from them words whose meaning I then searched for in my dictionary.

When I arrived at my destination my Vilna friends were astounded and overjoyed to see me. We conversed for hours and they told me about the raids and the arrests and their decision to emigrate. They had arrived in the United States on May 30.

I also learned that while they remained hopeful they were also disappointed by the reports that the attempt to establish a commune colony had not yet worked out well. In the group I found my old friends, Saul Badanes, Solomon Menaker, the older of the Caspe brothers, a number of Jewish workers and Alexander Harkavy, later known as the compiler of an English-Jewish dictionary and as an author of textbooks for immigrants.

The city had no subways. Automobiles, phonographs and motion pictures were still things to dream about. There were some telephones and there was one bridge binding the city—Brooklyn Bridge—but it was not yet open.

Paris and London seem to be unchanging. But New York is always changing, always being torn down and built up and changing. The city at this time was one-third the size it is now and its tallest buildings were no more than eight stories high. Yet, she was a giant to me, as now, her past diminished by growth, she is all the more a giant. Such crowds as were to be seen on Broadway in the vicinity of Brooklyn Bridge and Fulton Street were the largest I had ever encountered in my life.

The Jewish section of the city was itself a center of great variety. There were Russian and Polish Jews, German-American Jews called Yahudim, many of them from Posen, which was the Polish part of Germany. There were Jews from Germany itself. And there were American-born Jews. During my first years in the United States a few Yahudim were still living in the neighborhood of East Broadway. But most of the richer Posen and German Jews had already moved uptown.

About two years after my arrival, the Young Men's Hebrew Association, with headquarters uptown, opened a branch on East Broadway. American-born boys from German-Jewish families joined.

A Yahudi is an impossibility today in the Jewish section. But in those years they owned almost all the small stores and many of the larger ones on Grand Street. With the arrival of the first immigrants from Russia, they began to move further uptown. Actually it was not our coming that caused them to go. When one becomes rich one moves uptown. So it goes even today. Fiftieth Street was far uptown.

Before my arrival not many Jews emigrated from Russia to America. The exceptions were Jews from Kalisz and Suwalki, near the German border. They were the core of the Jewish population on the East Side. Almost all the peddlers and the customer peddlers, as well as the storekeepers on East Broadway and on Canal Street who sold them the clothes, the cloth, the furniture and the jewelry that they peddled, were from the province of Suwalki. Many of the thirty to forty thousand Jewish workers in the city, including a large group of Jews from western Poland, were employed in tailoring men's clothing. The women's cloak trade was small, having only recently been started in the United States. Formerly, better cloaks were imported from Germany. Most women wore shawls.

The first cloak shops were established by the Yahudim, who were not themselves tailors but who hired as their cutters, operators and pressers the Jews coming over from Poland and Lithuania.

There were very few intellectuals among the earlier immigrant Jews from Russia and Austria. The newcomers from Suwalki included some talmudic Jews. These aristocrats of the East Side could frequently be heard arguing a passage from the Talmud in the peddler stores on East Broadway.

For all practical purposes, the city had no high schools. Even had they then existed I am not certain that the Jewish newcomers would have sent their children to them. But they did send them to the public grade schools. The Jewish young men at City College were from the Yahudi families. They spoke English, almost no Yiddish and thought of going into business after completing school.

There was little of the thirst for higher education which one finds among Jewish youth today. Jewish cultural life was dominated by Old-World Jewishness and newly acquired, primitive Americanism.

The popular impression that the first Jewish immigrants were mainly criminals who had fled criminal actions in the old country is an enormous exaggeration. I encountered a few toughies; but most of the immigrants were honest, plain people and, with the exception of the minority of talmudic Jews, uneducated.

Under conditions in the new homeland, even the small-time, old-country lawbreakers took advantage of the opportunity to live decent lives. But others took the opposite path, forgetting the decent ways of their old homeland and becoming swindlers in the new. This happens to immigrants all over the world as, separated from friends and family, they face new and untried experiences.

At the time of my arrival, the country still echoed with the sensationalism of the murder committed by a very pious Jew named Pesach Rubinstein, a jewelry peddler from the province of Kovno. He was famous throughout the Jewish section for his piety. But he had become infatuated with his niece. Then, fearing that his relations with her would be revealed, he persuaded her one day to come with him to the deserted fields and meadows of far-off Brownsville, in Brooklyn. There, with a cigarmaker's knife, he killed her. His crime remained his secret.

But she came to him in a dream, shouting the place where her body lay. Terrorized by the realization that his sin would be magnified by the fact that she had not received Jewish burial and that she would therefore haunt him and finally choke out his life, Rubinstein confessed his guilt. The police traced the knife to him. He was tried, found guilty, and sentenced to death. In the Tombs prison he took his own life.

*

With the coming of the new immigrants one began to hear Russian spoken on the streets of the East Side. Once, a woman passing by as a friend and I were conversing in Russian on East Broadway, turned on us with disgust and spat out: "Tfu! The nerve, actually talking Russian! Wasn't it bad enough that you had to hear that dirty language in Russia?"

Even the uneducated immigrants could speak Russian, although they preferred Yiddish. But the intellectual minority spoke only Russian among themselves. This was a new thing in New York and it was because we were the first Russian-Jewish intellectuals in the United States.

We had brought something more than just this new way of conversing. In our hearts we also brought our love for enlightened Russian culture. We had transported from Russia the banner of idealism, scarred and blood-stained in the Russian revolutionary movement.

We could feel the resistance of the old-fashioned Suwalki Jews to the spirit of our new movement. They considered us to be atheists and lunatics; we intellectuals thought of them as ignorant, primitive people.

We were a small minority. Most of our own fellow immigrants shared the suspicions felt by the Suwalki Jews. The Jewish masses in the old country knew little about socialism. Socialist ideas were fenced in by a wall of guns and gallows, by censorship and the fear of the police. The formation of the Jewish Workers' Bund in Vilna was still fifteen years off. A mere handful of Jewish workers in Vilna had grasped the meaning of socialism—and almost all of this handful had come to America.

After my arrival it took me just three days to realize that the establishment of commune colonies was not really my dream. I was not fascinated by village life, by the prospect of laboring on the soil. On the contrary, I felt strongly drawn to the life of the city. My heart beat to its rhythms, and as the heart feels so thinks the head.

More than feeling was involved when one weighed the chances of a communist farm colony in the United States. I expressed my opinion on this so sharply that I found myself quarreling about it with some of my idealistic friends.

Several years earlier William Frey, a Russian revolutionary follower of Chernishevsky, became converted to idealistic communism as opposed to revolution by force. He gave up his career and came to America where he soon became an advocate of Auguste Comte's "religion of humanity." In line with that "religion," he preached against every revolutionary movement, even against the workers' struggle for higher wages and a shorter work week.

In the 1870s, the revolutionary Russian journal, *Vperiod*, published in Switzerland, contained a long letter from Frey about communist colonies in the United States. The letter had been sent from Kansas where Frey and his followers were operating a commune on a farm.

The editor of *Vperiod* had replied in the same issue and had argued that the instrument for overthrowing the capitalist system was a great mass movement, not ineffective, small communist colonies. The editor complimented the communards for their hard work and their devotion but said that their colony was like a plant being nurtured under glass by artificial means. The fate of humanity could not be made to depend on such artificial means. Revolution must proceed by natural means.

I read this exchange in *Vperiod* long after it had occurred, and it opened my eyes. I remembered the fable I had read in a Russian reader for children about the fool who tries to clinch the sale of a house by offering a brick as a sample.

Socialism could not be achieved through sample colonies. What did such a colony prove as it struggled to survive, surrounded by a vast capitalist country, dependent on capitalist transportation and capitalist banks and capitalist stores and competing with capitalist farmers? An entirely new structure was needed. What good was a sample brick?

In my arguments with followers of the commune idea I cited all the previous attempts in the United States to establish commune farms and noted that only the Quakers had succeeded.

I told my friends, sometimes in heated arguments, that they were wasting their time and their energy on an impossible dream. I counted myself out of the group for I had begun to feel around me the seething life of a great American city. Formerly I had only read about capitalism. Now it surrounded me on all sides.

New York had a German-language socialist daily newspaper called the *New Yorker Volkszeitung*. For us it was a real treasure. In Russia such a publication was a secret and dangerous enterprise, circulated underground and issued irregularly. But here it was issued regularly every day and openly circulated!

This newspaper was the reason some of us learned German even before we learned English. It played a major role in our intellectual development. Every day we could read in its pages challenging Marxist interpretations of the news.

In the old country we had been limited to the few booklets and pamphlets that had circulated secretly. But in the United States we received through the *New Yorker Volkszeitung* a daily Marxist commentary on life and politics. And every day the unreal nature of commune colonies became increasingly clear to me.

I also began to attend the German-language meetings addressed by the editors of the *New Yorker Volkszeitung*. I remember the first German workers meeting I attended in a hall on Second Avenue near Houston Street. In a fever of excitement, I followed as best I could the inspiring German talks by editors Sergius Schevitsch and Alexander Jonas. Schevitsch was a German baron from Latvia. He had been educated in Russia and could speak and write French, Italian and English as well as Russian and German. He was married to Elena von Racowita for whom Ferdinand Lassalle died in a duel.

I have no words sufficient to describe the deep excitement this first meeting stirred in me. How could I even think of deserting this seething, stimulating life in the midst of the struggles of the workers and take off, instead, for some far-off puny colony which had as much chance of overthrowing capitalism as a fly has of pushing over an elephant? The dream of an instant earthly paradise dissolved. The *New Yorker Volkszeitung* and the German-language socialist meetings took its place.

I felt America's freedom every minute. I breathed freer than I had ever breathed before. But all the time I was saying to myself, "All of this is a capitalist prison." And the confusion in my brain was compounded by the fact that in the first few months in America I worked like a slave at my first jobs.

From Russia, where distribution of socialist literature was a secret task evoking the terror of Siberian exile, I had brought the notion that to be dedicated to the cause required the underground performance of such prohibited tasks. Therefore I planned to print socialist propaganda leaflets, to post myself in the street in front of the shops and factories and to distribute them to the workers. This had the taste of underground conspiracy, although there was no risk in doing it here.

I longed to persuade myself that by distributing such socialist leaflets I would be leading the life of a Russian revolutionary in the United States. The word "leaflet" had a sacred sound. It was "forbidden fruit" even though it was not forbidden. In years to come, hundreds of others, for the same reason, experienced the same illusion. And because there was no secret socialist movement in the United States, they looked upon the native movement with contempt.

What kind of socialism could it be without conspiracy? What good was the fruit if it wasn't forbidden? The power of deeply rooted beliefs is greater than the power of logic and common sense. Socialism itself teaches that the special circumstances of each time and each place must be taken into account in formulating tactics. But the romantic stimulation of danger is powerful. If all is permissible and danger is absent, socialism becomes diluted and revolutionary heroism becomes impossible.

LUDWIG LEWISOHN

In the following excerpt from his 1922 autobiography *Up Stream: An American Chronicle*, an impressionable eight-year-old Ludwig Lewisohn (1883–1955) arrives in a small South Carolina town from his native Berlin. He also begins to recognize, in retrospect, a problem that would continue to occupy him until his death: a sense of "alienation from my own race" as well as from the small local Jewish community of which he was nominally a member. A few chapters further—now a convert to Methodism and a high-school valedictorian—the young Lewisohn imagines he has become "an American, a Southerner, and a Christian," and even notes in himself a "distinct and involuntary hostility to everything either Jewish or German." Later life taught Lewisohn to see the limits of the assimilation he once imagined himself to have achieved and to prize the ethnic heritage that his upbringing had largely denied him. Indeed, he returned to the broader subject of Jewish experience throughout his varied and prolific literary career, writing books and articles on Jewish subjects, including *Israel* (1925), *This People* (1933), *The Answer: The Jew and the World* (1939), and *The American Jew: Character and Destiny* (1950). He also edited the Zionist journal *New Palestine* from 1944 to 1948 and in 1948 was one of the first professors at newly founded Brandeis University, where he taught until his death.

from

Up Stream: An American Chronicle

THE AMERICAN SCENE

I

T he Suevia, scheduled to reach New York on the ninth day, did not arrive until the fifteenth. Not a fleck of sunshine all those days; a sky almost black, a piping wind, a turbulent sea dashing up in huge steel-gray waves with bottle-green under-curves and fierce, white, fang-like edges. A primae-val, chaotic, brutal sea. The great ship quivered and creaked and wheezed; the water slapped against the port-holes and ran down the round, dim panes; almost hourly the propeller was punched clear above sea-level and whirred with a naked, metallic grind. . . . My mother was hopelessly sea-sick the whole time; my father and I led a dim, nebulous existence, when possible on deck, when not, in the red-carpeted saloon. But the sea got hold of the inner-most core of my mind; it became part of my life, and in inland places I have often caught myself tense with desire after its tang and roar.

Our land-fall was still gray but quiet. Afar off lay a dim, hook-like shore. The voyage had liberated my father's mind from terror and madness. He was so strengthened and cheered that even my mother smiled. To come to land at all seemed, after our tremendous experience, almost like coming home. But the pier at Hoboken was rough and wild, a place of hoarse cries and brute haste and infernal confusion. A kindly German-American fellow-passenger helped us; saw to it that our luggage was not unduly searched and put us in a rumbling hack on our way to an hotel. It was Meyer's Hotel, a comfortable, unpretentious place. We were worn out and rested well during our first night on American soil under the strange mosquito-bars.

The place where my uncle lived and whither we were bound lay far away in the South Atlantic States. But my father and mother thought that we ought to rest for a day or two and see a city so great and famous as New York. A curious timidity kept us, however, from venturing far through the grime and rattle. We crossed the Brooklyn Bridge, I know, and saw the gilt dome of the World Building, then the tallest structure on this hemisphere, and the ele-vated railroad. But we did not go up town nor into the financial section, drifted somehow into a lake of mud shaken by trucks and drays on Canal Street and retreated to Hoboken.

Being ill-advised we took ship again and spent nearly fifty hours on a coast-wise voyage South. We could eat no food. Negro stewards served it and over it was the strange flavor of bananas and Concord grapes. There was no storm or gloom now. But the brilliantly radiant sea was rough and choppy and the steamer small. The weather grew milder and milder and when we steamed into Queenshaven harbor the day was like spring.

The bay is one of the most beautiful in the world. In its fold lies the old city with its gardens and verandahs and its few slender spires. Golden-green islands extend its curves. The coloring of sea and sky, in whatever mood, is of so infinite and delicate a variety as though the glow and splendor of all the jewels in the world had been melted there. And over city and bay lies a rich quietude that steals upon the heart through the liquid softness of that untroubled air. I heard my father and mother speak of the beauty of the scene; my own sense of it must have been vague. But I cannot disassociate that early vision from an hundred later ones. For that city and bay came to mean my boyhood and youth, high passion and aspiration, and later a grief that darkened my life. I close my eyes: I can see every stone of the old city, every wave of the bay. But my mind sees both garbed in a cruel and unearthly sweetness. My bodily eyes could endure to see neither of them any more. . . . Friends of my uncle who were commissioned to meet us missed the boat. My father summoned his scraps of English, hired a four-wheeler and took us to the Queenshaven Hotel. There these people found us, astonished that my parents had not yet acquired the habits of poverty but had gone boldly to the best hotel in the city. They took us to their house where the children astonished me by speaking English. It did not seem to me nearly so curious in grown persons. I stared at the tattered Negroes in the yard, almost too tired to be impressed by any strangeness. In the afternoon our friends took us to our train, shoved us into a day-coach and hurried off.

I recall vividly the long, shabby, crowded car and its peculiar reek of peanuts, stale whiskey and chewing-tobacco. Half of the passengers were burly negroes who gabbled and laughed weirdly. The white men wore broad-rimmed wool-hats, whittled and spat and talked in drawling tones. I very distinctly shared my parents' sense of the wildness, savagery and roughness of the scene, their horrified perception of its contrast to anything they had ever known or seen. Soon the dark fell and at the wayside stations queer, pan-like lamps flared up in reddish ribbands of fire. At one station a group of men entered carrying tall cudgels. They opened jack-knives and proceeded to peel and devour these cudgels. My mother grew almost hysterical; my father racked his mind and discovered some half-forgotten information on the subject of sugar-cane. . . . At ten o'clock we reached Saint Mark's and trudged out of the car. A man with heavy moustaches and clad in a red sweater lifted me from the platform. From my previous experience of life I judged him to be a porter or a cabby. To my disgust and amazement he called me by name and kissed me on the mouth. It was my uncle.

II

In 1890 the village of St. Mark's in South Carolina was raw; it had more than a touch of wildness and through its life there ran a strain of violence. It consisted of two principal streets, running diagonally to each other and of half a dozen lesser streets that trailed off into cotton-fields and pine-forests. There was a cotton-seed oil mill, a saw mill and twenty to thirty general merchandise stores. Three or four of these were housed in one-story buildings of red brick. For the rest the village was built of wood and many of the houses were unpainted, showing the browned and weather-beaten boards. There was a Methodist Church and a Baptist Church, each with a grave-yard behind it. North of the village straggled a Negro grave-yard, its graves decorated with colored pebbles, bits of iridescent glass and the broken shards of cheap vases. Here and there, behind houses or in chance lanes were small, black, one-roomed huts inhabited by Negro women. These women were in domestic service in the village and, as I learned later, plied, in addition and quite openly, an equally ancient but less honest trade. Despite eight or ten bar-rooms the streets were quiet except on Saturday. Then the village flared into life. Many hundreds of Negroes came in from the sparsely settled country; they rode in on horses or mules or oxen or drove rough carts and primitive wagons, and were themselves generally clad in garments of which the original homespun had disappeared in a mass of gaudy patches. They traded and drank and, child-like, spent their money on foolish things—perfumes and handsome whips and sweets. Toward dusk they reeled in a hot turmoil and filled the air with that characteristic odor of peanuts and stale whiskey and chewing tobacco.

I watched the village life with a deep sense of its strangeness but almost without astonishment. Soon I was merged into it and felt quite at home. No, not quite. During at least a year, at lengthening intervals of course, I felt a sharp nostalgia for the land of my birth and its life. Suddenly, at the edge of the forest, a sense of grief would overcome me. Somewhere beyond those dark trees, beyond leagues of country, beyond the ocean, lay our home. . . . And I would weep bitterly. And still, in my maturer years the edge of a forest or else a few solitary trees at a great distance bring back to me that old sense of wistfulness and yearning—no longer for definite scenes or associations, but for the mystery of delight I have not known, beauty I have not seen, peace I have sought in vain. . . .

The Southern country-side awakened in me, child that I was, a rich, an almost massive joy in nature. About a mile beyond the lonely little railroad station with its bales of cotton and acrid-smelling sacks of yellow guano lay the "red hills." These hills were not very high; I could climb them easily; they were covered with very tall, very straight pine-trees that seemed to me shaft-like and sky-piercing. Through a fold of the hills ran a rapid, very shallow little brook over a bed of clean, bright pebbles. In spring the dogwood showed its white blossoms there; in the mild Southern autumn a child could lie on the deep layers of brownish pine-needles and play with the aromatic cones and gaze up at the brilliant blue of the sky.

The summer stirred me deeply. I had been used to the cool, chaste, frugal summers of the North. Here the heat smote; the vegetation sprang into rank and hot luxuriance—noisome weeds with white ooze in their stems and bell-like pink flowers invaded the paths and streets. I felt a strange throbbing, followed by sickish languor and a dumb terror at the frequent, fierce thunderstorms. Both my intelligence and my instincts ripened with morbid rapidity and I attribute many abnormalities of temper and taste that are mine to that sudden transplantation into a semi-tropical world. . . .

I was a thorough child nevertheless and delighted in certain acquisitions which the new world brought me—a percussion cap pistol, a mouth organ, a Jew's harp. Nor did I give up my old life. My books had been saved and, one day, my father discovered that he had forgotten a small balance in the Deutsche Bank. For this money he ordered books from Germany, and I came into possession of a set of very red volumes: the marvelous chap-books of the Reformation age—Griseldis, Genoveva, Robert the Devil, Dr. Faustus— naive and knightly or magical and grim; and of two slimmer volumes called Beckers Erzahlungen aus der Alten Welt, which contained the Iliad and the Odyssey in simple, lucid German prose. In the reading of these, especially of the Odyssey, culminated the imaginative joys of my childhood. I do not know Greek; I cannot read Homer in the original. Yet I am sure that I know what Homer is. In a plain room behind the store in which apples and cloth and furniture and ploughshares and rice and tinned fish were sold to chattering Negroes, I sat with my book and clearly heard

"The surge and thunder of the Odyssey"

and saw Nausikaa and her maidens, white limbed and fair, on the shore of the wine-dark sea, and dwelt with Odysseus on the island of Callypso and returned home with him to Ithaca—not without tears—and listened to the twanging bow-string that sped the avenging arrows. The wood-cut that was the frontispiece of the little volume showed Hermes on his mission of command to Circe. Above floats the god with his staff and his winged cap and sandals. Below him stretches the immeasurable stream of ocean. In the background, small and far but very clear, lies an island with a tiny fane of Doric columns. I gazed at the picture for hours and knew the freshness, the grace and the clarity of that morning of the world.

III

My uncle and aunt received us into their queer little house which was huddled, as though for protection, against the shop. The walls of the house were of the rudest; the wind blew through knot-holes in the timber. My father and mother were bitterly disappointed. My uncle had sent the St. Mark's Herald to Berlin and my father, who did not understand the art and vocabulary of town-booming nor the society items of an American village newspaper, assumed that St. Mark's was a town of some importance and my uncle a prominent citizen. And here he had come to a squalid village, the guest of a man well-enough liked by his fellow citizens but wretchedly poor. My aunt, moreover, though a woman of some kindly qualities, was a Jewess of the Eastern tradition, narrow-minded, given over to the clattering ritual of pots and pans—"meaty" and "milky"—and very ignorant. On the very evening of our arrival, having at last withdrawn to the one spare bed-room, my father and mother looked blankly at each other. A chill wind blew in thin, keen streams through chinks in the bare, wooden wall, the geese squawked loudly in the muddy yard, my aunt was heard scolding her little girls in a mixture of Yiddish and English, a little, unshaded kerosene lamp made the grim room look all the gloomier. My mother sat down on the springless bed, a picture of desolation. The sudden plunge unnerved her. All through the voyage we had lived on our accustomed plane of civilized comfort. Only here did the descent begin.

She had one consolation that apparently justified the whole adventure. My father was a changed man. From now on and for many years he was full of energy and buoyancy, splendidly patient and brave, always ready to cheer her in her fits of loneliness and depression. He had shaken off the morbid inhibitions and immediately started out into the village to see what he could do.

The people of the village, storekeepers, a few retired farmers, three physicians, three or four lawyers, came of various stocks—English, Scotch-Irish, German, even French and Dutch. But they were all descended from early nineteenth century settlers and had become thorough Americans. Everybody belonged to either the Baptist or the Methodist church. The Methodists were, upon the whole, more refined, had better manners than the Baptists and were less illiterate. Among all the villagers there was a moderate amount of hard drinking and a good deal of sexual irregularity, especially with Mulatto women. I have since wondered that there was not more. The life was sterile and monotonous enough. They were all kindly, even the rougher ones, not very avaricious, no drivers of hard bargains, given to talking about shooting but doing very little of it. (During the two years of our residence two men were shot and in each case upon extreme provocation.) Also so far as their light went, they were liberal. This was well illustrated by the position of the Jews in the village. Of these there were about ten families, all recent immigrants, and so aliens in speech and race and faith. Most of them, moreover, were quite prosperous. Yet between them and these Southern villagers the relations were hearty and pleasant and consolidated by mutual kindness and tolerance. Only one Jew and that was my father, was looked upon with some suspicion by the severer among his Gentile neighbors. The reason was curious and significant; he did not perform the external rites of the Jewish faith and, upon entering a fraternal life insurance order, he smiled and hesitated when asked to affirm categorically his belief in a personal God.

He soon saw that there was nothing to be done in St. Mark's except add another to the existing shops. But since nearly every one seemed to have prospered and since the quiet and the easy, democratic atmosphere of the place appealed to him, he hesitated but little. Help and good advice were offered alike by Jew and Gentile and, at the end of a few months, we were installed in some pleasant rooms beside one of the few brick stores on Main Street. There was the usual heterogeneous stock of food and implements, furniture and dry-goods. My mother went to Queenshaven and bought adequate furniture for our little home.

Although she yearned very bitterly for her native land, her friends and kin, for music and for all the subtle supports of the civilization in which she was so deeply rooted, life opened fairly enough. Domestic service cost next to nothing, food was plentiful and cheap. Even friends were not wanting. Our landlord and his family, prominent members of the Methodist church, saw soon enough that my father and mother were of a different mental type and of different antecedents from the other Jews in St Mark's. There followed an exchange of visits. Mrs. C. gave my mother much good advice, explained to her many American ways and manners that seemed very strange, and tried to console her in regard to her most burning and immediate problem—that of my education. This friendship led to others. And so when summer came, we who had no vegetable garden—and would have been just as helpless had we had one—received daily attentions from our Gentile friends: baskets of tomatoes or okra or sweet-corn or bell-pepper. And one friend, a very aged physician who liked and admired my mother and had a dim but steady perception of her profound spiritual isolation, sent her weekly a great basketful of roses. My father, at the same time, found a congenial companion in a young lawyer. The two played chess together and from him my father borrowed Shakespeare and Byron, Dickens and Thackeray and Scott with whose works he was, like all educated Germans, thoroughly familiar and whom he now read with avidity in their own language. We saw a good deal of my uncle and his family and their friends. But culturally we really felt closer to the better sort of Americans in the community, and so there began in those early days that alienation from my own race which has been the source to me of some good but of more evil.

MARY ANTIN

"Although I have written a genuine personal memoir," says Mary Antin (1881–1949) in the introduction to *The Promised Land*, "I believe its
chief interest lies in the fact that it is illustrative of scores of unwritten
lives." Raised by a well-to-do family of Jewish shopkeepers in a *shtetl* in
modern-day Belarus, Antin enjoyed a relatively tranquil and enlightened
childhood until she was about nine, when the family business collapsed
and an influx of Jews fleeing pogroms elsewhere in Russia made it impossible for them to find work. Her father immigrated to Boston in 1891,
and his wife and children followed three years later. Antin's natural intelligence, ferocious curiosity, and religious skepticism ensured her a quick
and eager assimilation into her adopted country. Within a short time,
Antin (now "Mary," no longer "Mashke") had managed to learn to read
and write English with great facility and get an essay published in *Primary Education* magazine. She later graduated from Radcliffe College.
Her 1912 memoir, from which this excerpt is taken, was immensely popular: during her lifetime it went through 34 printings and sold almost
85,000 copies. Along with Abraham Cahan's fiction, *The Promised Land*
is considered by many to mark the beginning of Jewish literature in
America. Despite this early triumph, she only wrote one other book—
They Who Knock at Our Gates (1914), which argued for an unrestricted
immigration policy—and a handful of essays. In 1918 the separation
from her husband, the death of her father, and the general xenophobic
tenor of wartime American life brought on a nervous breakdown from
which she never fully recovered. In later years she tried to reconcile her
Jewish heritage with the ecumenical American God her heart belonged
to: "In all those places where race lines are drawn, I shall claim the Jewish
badge; but in my Father's house of many mansions I shall continue a free
spirit."

from

The Promised Land

The public school has done its best for us foreigners, and for the country, when it has made us into good Americans. I am glad it is mine to tell how the miracle was wrought in one case. You should be glad to hear of it, you born Americans; for it is the story of the growth of your country; of the flocking of your brothers and sisters from the far ends of the earth to the flag you love; of the recruiting of your armies of workers, thinkers, and leaders. And you will be glad to hear of it, my comrades in adoption; for it is a rehearsal of your own experience, the thrill and wonder of which your own hearts have felt.

How long would you say, wise reader, it takes to make an American? By the middle of my second year in school I had reached the sixth grade. When, after the Christmas holidays, we began to study the life of Washington, running through a summary of the Revolution, and the early days of the Republic, it seemed to me that all my reading and study had been idle until then. The reader, the arithmetic, the song book, that had so fascinated me until now, became suddenly sober exercise books, tools wherewith to hew a way to the source of inspiration. When the teacher read to us out of a big book with many bookmarks in it, I sat rigid with attention in my little chair, my hands tightly clasped on the edge of my desk; and I painfully held my breath, to prevent sighs of disappointment escaping, as I saw the teacher skip the parts between bookmarks. When the class read, and it came my turn, my voice shook and the book trembled in my hands. I could not pronounce the name of George Washington without a pause. Never had I prayed, never had I chanted the songs of David, never had I called upon the Most Holy, in such utter reverence and worship as I repeated the simple sentences of my child's story of the patriot. I gazed with adoration at the portraits of George and Martha Washington, till I could see them with my eyes shut. And whereas formerly my self-consciousness had bordered on conceit, and I thought myself an uncommon person, parading my schoolbooks through the streets, and swelling with pride when a teacher detained me in conversation, now I grew humble all at once, seeing how insignificant I was beside the Great.

As I read about the noble boy who would not tell a lie to save himself from punishment, I was for the first time truly repentant of my sins. Formerly I had fasted and prayed and made sacrifice on the Day of Atonement, but it was more than half play, in mimicry of my elders. I had no real horror of sin, and I knew so many ways of escaping punishment. I am sure my family, my neighbors, my teachers in Polotzk—all my world, in fact—strove together, by example and precept, to teach me goodness. Saintliness had a new incarnation in about every third person I knew. I did respect the saints, but I could not help seeing that most of them were a little bit stupid, and that mischief was much more fun than piety. Goodness, as I had known it, was respectable, but not necessarily admirable. The people I really admired, like my Uncle Solomon, and Cousin Rachel, were those who preached the least and laughed the most. My sister Frieda was perfectly good, but she did not think the less of me because I played tricks. What I loved in my friends was not inimitable. One could be downright good if one really wanted to. One could be learned if one had books and teachers. One could sing funny songs and tell anecdotes if one travelled about and picked up such things, like one's uncles and cousins. But a human being strictly good, perfectly wise, and unfailingly valiant, all at the same time, I had never heard or dreamed of. This wonderful George Washington was as inimitable as he was irreproachable. Even if I had never, never told a lie, I could not compare myself to George Washington; for I was not brave—I was afraid to go out when snowballs whizzed—and I could never be the First President of the United States.

So I was forced to revise my own estimate of myself. But the twin of my new-born humility, paradoxical as it may seem, was a sense of dignity I had never known before. For if I found that I was a person of small consequence, I discovered at the same time that I was more nobly related than I had ever supposed. I had relatives and friends who were notable people by the old standards,—I had never been ashamed of my family,—but this George Washington, who died long before I was born, was like a king in greatness, and he and I were Fellow Citizens. There was a great deal about Fellow Citizens in the patriotic literature we read at this time; and I knew from my father how he was a Citizen, through the process of naturalization, and how I also was a citizen by virtue of my relation to him. Undoubtedly I was a Fellow Citizen, and George Washington was another. It thrilled me to realize what sudden greatness had fallen on me; and at the same time it sobered me, as with a sense of responsibility. I strove to conduct myself as befitted a Fellow Citizen.

Before books came into my life, I was given to star-gazing and day-dreaming. When books were given me, I fell upon them as a glutton pounces on his meat after a period of enforced starvation. I lived with my nose in a book, and took no notice of the alternations of the sun and stars. But now, after the advent of George Washington and the American Revolution, I began to dream again. I strayed on the common after school instead of hurrying home to read. I hung on fence rails, my pet book forgotten under my arm, and gazed off to the yellow-streaked February sunset, and beyond, and beyond. I was no longer the central figure of my dreams; the dry weeds in the lane crackled beneath the tread of Heroes.

What more could America give a child? Ah, much more! As I read how the patriots planned the Revolution, and the women gave their sons to die in battle, and the heroes led to victory, and the rejoicing people set up the Republic, it dawned on me gradually what was meant by *my country*. The people all desiring noble things, and striving for them together, defying their oppressors, giving their lives for each other—all this it was that made *my country*. It was not a thing that I *understood*; I could not go home and tell Frieda about it, as I told her other things I learned at school. But I knew one could say "my country" and *feel* it, as one felt "God" or "myself." My teacher, my schoolmates, Miss Dillingham, George Washington himself could not mean more than I when they said "my country," after I had once felt it. For the Country was for all the Citizens, and *I was a Citizen*. And when we stood up to sing "America," I shouted the words with all my might. I was in very earnest proclaiming to the world my love for my new-found country.

> "I love thy rocks and rills,
> Thy woods and templed hills."

Boston Harbor, Crescent Beach, Chelsea Square—all was hallowed ground to me. As the day approached when the school was to hold exercises in honor of Washington's Birthday, the halls resounded at all hours with the strains of patriotic songs; and I, who was a model of the attentive pupil, more than once lost my place in the lesson as I strained to hear, through closed doors, some neighboring class rehearsing "The Star-Spangled Banner." If the doors happened to open, and the chorus broke out unveiled—

"O! say, does that Star-Spangled Banner yet wave
O'er the land of the free, and the home of the brave?"—

delicious tremors ran up and down my spine, and I was faint with suppressed enthusiasm.

Where had been my country until now? What flag had I loved? What heroes had I worshipped? The very names of these things had been unknown to me. Well I knew that Polotzk was not my country. It was *goluth*—exile. On many occasions in the year we prayed to God to lead us out of exile. The beautiful Passover service closed with the words, "Next year, may we be in Jerusalem." On childish lips, indeed, those words were no conscious aspiration; we repeated the Hebrew syllables after our elders, but without their hope and longing. Still not a child among us was too young to feel in his own flesh the lash of the oppressor. We knew what it was to be Jews in exile, from the spiteful treatment we suffered at the hands of the smallest urchin who crossed himself; and thence we knew that Israel had good reason to pray for deliverance. But the story of the Exodus was not history to me in the sense that the story of the American Revolution was. It was more like a glorious myth, a belief in which had the effect of cutting me off from the actual world, by linking me with a world of phantoms. Those moments of exaltation which the contemplation of the Biblical past afforded us, allowing us to call ourselves the children of princes, served but to tinge with a more poignant sense of disinheritance the long humdrum stretches of our life. In very truth we were a people without a country. Surrounded by mocking foes and detractors, it was difficult for me to realize the persons of my people's heroes or the events in which they moved. Except in moments of abstraction from the world around me, I scarcely understood that Jerusalem was an actual spot on the earth, where once the Kings of the Bible, real people, like my neighbors in Polotzk, ruled in puissant majesty. For the conditions of our civil life did not permit us to cultivate a spirit of nationalism. The freedom of worship that was grudgingly granted within the narrow limits of the Pale by no means included the right to set up openly any ideal of a Hebrew State, any hero other than the Czar. What we children picked up of our ancient political history was confused with the miraculous story of the Creation, with the supernatural legends and hazy associations of Bible lore. As to our future, we Jews in Polotzk had no national expectations; only a life-worn dreamer here and there hoped to die in Palestine. If Fetchke and I sang, with my father, first making sure of our audience, "Zion, Zion, Holy Zion, not forever is it lost," we did not really picture to ourselves Judæa restored.

So it came to pass that we did not know what *my country* could mean to a man. And as we had no country, so we had no flag to love. It was by no far-fetched symbolism that the banner of the House of Romanoff became the emblem of our latter-day bondage in our eyes. Even a child would know how to hate the flag that we were forced, on pain of severe penalties, to hoist above our housetops, in celebration of the advent of one of our oppressors. And as it was with country and flag, so it was with heroes of war. We hated the uniform of the soldier, to the last brass button. On the person of a Gentile, it was the symbol of tyranny; on the person of a Jew, it was the emblem of shame.

So a little Jewish girl in Polotzk was apt to grow up hungry-minded and empty-hearted; and if, still in her outreaching youth, she was set down in a land of outspoken patriotism, she was likely to love her new country with a great love, and to embrace its heroes in a great worship. Naturalization, with us Russian Jews, may mean more than the adoption of the immigrant by America. It may mean the adoption of America by the immigrant.

On the day of the Washington celebration I recited a poem that I had composed in my enthusiasm. But "composed" is not the word. The process of putting on paper the sentiments that seethed in my soul was really very dis-composing. I dug the words out of my heart, squeezed the rhymes out of my brain, forced the missing syllables out of their hiding-places in the dictionary. May I never again know such travail of the spirit as I endured during the fevered days when I was engaged on the poem. It was not as if I wanted to say that snow was white or grass was green. I could do that without a dictionary. It was a question now of the loftiest sentiments, of the most abstract truths, the names of which were very new in my vocabulary. It was necessary to use polysyllables, and plenty of them; and where to find rhymes for such words as "tyranny," "freedom," and "justice," when you had less than two years' acquaintance with English! The name I wished to celebrate was the most difficult of all. Nothing but "Washington" rhymed with "Washington." It was a most ambitious undertaking, but my heart could find no rest till it had proclaimed itself to the world; so I wrestled with my difficulties, and spared not ink, till inspiration perched on my penpoint, and my soul gave up its best.

When I had done, I was myself impressed with the length, gravity, and nobility of my poem. My father was overcome with emotion as he read it. His hands trembled as he held the paper to the light, and the mist gathered in his eyes. My teacher, Miss Dwight, was plainly astonished at my performance, and said many kind things, and asked many questions; all of which I took very solemnly, like one who had been in the clouds and returned to earth with a sign upon him. When Miss Dwight asked me to read my poem to the class on the day of celebration, I readily consented. It was not in me to refuse a chance to tell my schoolmates what I thought of George Washington.

I was not a heroic figure when I stood up in front of the class to pronounce the praises of the Father of his Country. Thin, pale, and hollow, with a shadow of short black curls on my brow, and the staring look of prominent eyes, I must have looked more frightened than imposing. My dress added no grace to my appearance. "Plaids" were in fashion, and my frock was of a red-and-green "plaid" that had a ghastly effect on my complexion. I hated it when I thought of it, but on the great day I did not know I had any dress on. Heels clapped together, and hands glued to my sides, I lifted up my voice in praise of George Washington. It was not much of a voice; like my hollow cheeks, it suggested consumption. My pronunciation was faulty, my declamation flat. But I had the courage of my convictions. I was face to face with twoscore Fellow Citizens, in clean blouses and extra frills. I must tell them what George Washington had done for their country—for *our* country—for me.

I can laugh now at the impossible metres, the grandiose phrases, the verbose repetitions of my poem. Years ago I must have laughed at it, when I threw my only copy into the wastebasket. The copy I am now turning over was loaned me by Miss Dwight, who faithfully preserved it all these years, for the sake, no doubt, of what I strove to express when I laboriously hitched together those dozen and more ungraceful stanzas. But to the forty Fellow Citizens sitting in rows in front of me it was no laughing matter. Even the bad boys sat in attitudes of attention, hypnotized by the solemnity of my demeanor. If they got any inkling of what the hail of big words was about, it must have been through occult suggestion. I fixed their eighty eyes with my single stare, and gave it to them, stanza after stanza, with such emphasis as the lameness of the lines permitted.

> He whose courage, will, amazing bravery,
>> Did free his land from a despot's rule,
> From man's greatest evil, almost slavery,
>> And all that's taught in tyranny's school,
> Who gave his land its liberty,
>> Who was he?

> 'T was he who e'er will be our pride,
>> Immortal Washington,
> Who always did in truth confide.
>> We hail our Washington!

The best of the verses were no better than these, but the children listened. They had to. Presently I gave them news, declaring that Washington

> Wrote the famous Constitution; sacred's the hand
> That this blessed guide to man had given, which says, "One
> And all of mankind are alike, excepting none."

This was received in respectful silence, possibly because the other Fellow Citizens were as hazy about historical facts as I at this point. "Hurrah for Washington!" they understood, and "Three cheers for the Red, White, and Blue!" was only to be expected on that occasion. But there ran a special note through my poem—a thought that only Israel Rubinstein or Beckie Aronovitch could have fully understood, besides myself. For I made myself the spokesman of the "luckless sons of Abraham," saying—

> Then we weary Hebrew children at last found rest
> In the land where reigned Freedom, and like a nest
> To homeless birds your land proved to us, and therefore
> Will we gratefully sing your praise evermore.

The boys and girls who had never been turned away from any door because of their father's religion sat as if fascinated in their places. But they woke up and applauded heartily when I was done, following the example of Miss Dwight, who wore the happy face which meant that one of her pupils had done well.

The recitation was repeated, by request, before several other classes, and the applause was equally prolonged at each repetition. After the exercises I was surrounded, praised, questioned, and made much of, by teachers as well as pupils. Plainly I had not poured my praise of George Washington into deaf ears. The teachers asked me if anybody had helped me with the poem. The girls invariably asked, "Mary Antin, how could you think of all those words?" None of them thought of the dictionary!

If I had been satisfied with my poem in the first place, the applause with which it was received by my teachers and schoolmates convinced me that I had produced a very fine thing indeed. So the person, whoever it was,—perhaps my father—who suggested that my tribute to Washington ought to be printed, did not find me difficult to persuade. When I had achieved an absolutely perfect copy of my verses, at the expense of a dozen sheets of blue-ruled note paper, I crossed the Mystic River to Boston and boldly invaded Newspaper Row.

It never occurred to me to send my manuscript by mail. In fact, it has never been my way to send a delegate where I could go myself. Consciously or unconsciously, I have always acted on the motto of a wise man who was one of the dearest friends that Boston kept for me until I came. "Personal presence moves the world," said the great Dr. Hale; and I went in person to beard the editor in his armchair.

From the ferry slip to the offices of the "Boston Transcript" the way was long, strange, and full of perils; but I kept resolutely on up Hanover Street, being familiar with that part of my route, till I came to a puzzling corner. There I stopped, utterly bewildered by the tangle of streets, the roar of traffic, the giddy swarm of pedestrians. With the precious manuscript tightly clasped, I balanced myself on the curbstone, afraid to plunge into the boiling vortex of the crossing. Every time I made a start, a clanging street car snatched up the way. I could not even pick out my street; the unobtrusive street signs were lost to my unpractised sight, in the glaring confusion of store signs and advertisements. If I accosted a pedestrian to ask the way, I had to speak several times before I was heard. Jews, hurrying by with bearded chins on their bosoms and eyes intent, shrugged their shoulders at the name "Transcript," and shrugged till they were out of sight. Italians sauntering behind their fruit carts answered my inquiry with a lift of the head that made their earrings gleam, and a wave of the hand that referred me to all four points of the compass at once. I was trying to catch the eye of the tall policeman who stood grandly in the middle of the crossing, a stout pillar around which the waves of traffic broke, when deliverance bellowed in my ear.

"Herald, Globe, Record, *Tra-avel-er!* Eh? Whatcher want, sis?" The tall newsboy had to stoop to me. "Transcript? Sure!" And in half a twinkling he had picked me out a paper from his bundle. When I explained to him, he good-naturedly tucked the paper in again, piloted me across, unravelled the end of Washington Street for me, and with much pointing out of landmarks, headed me for my destination, my nose seeking the spire of the Old South Church.

I found the "Transcript" building a waste of corridors tunnelled by a maze of staircases. On the glazed-glass doors were many signs with the names or nicknames of many persons: "City Editor"; "Beggars and Peddlers not Allowed." The nameless world not included in these categories was warned off, forbidden to be or do: "Private—No Admittance"; "Don't Knock." And the various inhospitable legends on the doors and walls were punctuated by frequent cuspidors on the floor. There was no sign anywhere of the welcome which I, as an author, expected to find in the home of a newspaper.

I was descending from the top story to the street for the seventh time, trying to decide what kind of editor a patriotic poem belonged to, when an untidy boy carrying broad paper streamers and whistling shrilly, in defiance of an express prohibition on the wall, bustled through the corridor and left a door ajar. I slipped in behind him, and found myself in a room full of editors.

I was a little surprised at the appearance of the editors. I had imagined my editor would look like Mr. Jones, the principal of my school, whose coat was always buttoned, and whose finger nails were beautiful. These people were in shirt sleeves, and they smoked, and they didn't politely turn in their revolving chairs when I came in, and ask, "What can I do for you?"

The room was noisy with typewriters, and nobody heard my "Please, can you tell me." At last one of the machines stopped, and the operator thought he heard something in the pause. He looked up through his own smoke. I guess he thought he saw something, for he stared. It troubled me a little to have him stare so. I realized suddenly that the hand in which I carried my manuscript was moist, and I was afraid it would make marks on the paper. I held out the manuscript to the editor, explaining that it was a poem about George Washington, and would he please print it in the "Transcript."

There was something queer about that particular editor. The way he stared and smiled made me feel about eleven inches high, and my voice kept growing smaller and smaller as I neared the end of my speech.

At last he spoke, laying down his pipe, and sitting back at his ease.

"So you have brought us a poem, my child?"

"It's about George Washington," I repeated impressively. "Don't you want to read it?"

"I should be delighted, my dear, but the fact is—"

He did not take my paper. He stood up and called across the room.

"Say, Jack! here is a young lady who has brought us a poem—about George Washington.—Wrote it yourself, my dear?—Wrote it all herself. What shall we do with her?"

Mr. Jack came over, and another man. My editor made me repeat my business, and they all looked interested, but nobody took my paper from me. They put their hands into their pockets, and my hand kept growing clammier all the time. The three seemed to be consulting, but I could not understand what they said, or why Mr. Jack laughed.

A fourth man, who had been writing busily at a desk near by, broke in on the consultation.

"That's enough, boys," he said, "that's enough. Take the young lady to Mr. Hurd."

Mr. Hurd, it was found, was away on a vacation, and of several other editors in several offices, to whom I was referred, none proved to be the proper editor to take charge of a poem about George Washington. At last an elderly editor suggested that as Mr. Hurd would be away for some time, I would do well to give up the "Transcript" and try the "Herald," across the way.

A little tired by my wanderings, and bewildered by the complexity of the editorial system, but still confident about my mission, I picked my way across Washington Street and found the "Herald" offices. Here I had instant good luck. The first editor I addressed took my paper and invited me to a seat. He read my poem much more quickly than I could myself, and said it was very nice, and asked me some questions, and made notes on a slip of paper which he pinned to my manuscript. He said he would have my piece printed very soon, and would send me a copy of the issue in which it appeared. As I was going, I could not help giving the editor my hand, although I had not experienced any handshaking in Newspaper Row. I felt that as author and editor we were on a very pleasant footing, and I gave him my hand in token of comradeship.

I had regained my full stature and something over, during this cordial interview, and when I stepped out into the street and saw the crowd intently studying the bulletin board I swelled out of all proportion. For I told myself that I, Mary Antin, was one of the inspired brotherhood who made newspapers so interesting. I did not know whether my poem would be put upon the bulletin board; but at any rate, it would be in the paper, with my name at the bottom, like my story about "Snow" in Miss Dillingham's school journal. And all these people in the streets, and more, thousands of people—all Boston!—would read my poem, and learn my name, and wonder who I was. I smiled to myself in delicious amusement when a man deliberately put me out of his path, as I dreamed my way through the jostling crowd; if he only *knew* whom he was treating so unceremoniously!

When the paper with my poem in it arrived, the whole house pounced upon it at once. I was surprised to find that my verses were not all over the front page. The poem was a little hard to find, if anything, being tucked away in the middle of the voluminous sheet. But when we found it, it looked wonderful, just like real poetry, not at all as if somebody we knew had written it. It occupied a gratifying amount of space, and was introduced by a flattering biographical sketch of the author—the *author!*—the material for which the friendly editor had artfully drawn from me during that happy interview. And my name, as I had prophesied, was at the bottom!

When the excitement in the house had subsided, my father took all the change out of the cash drawer and went to buy up the "Herald." He did not count the pennies. He just bought "Heralds," all he could lay his hands on, and distributed them gratis to all our friends, relatives, and acquaintances; to all who could read, and to some who could not. For weeks he carried a clipping from the "Herald" in his breast pocket, and few were the occasions when he did not manage to introduce it into the conversation. He treasured that clipping as for years he had treasured the letters I wrote him from Polotzk.

Although my father bought up most of the issue containing my poem, a few hundred copies were left to circulate among the general public, enough to spread the flame of my patriotic ardor and to enkindle a thousand sluggish hearts. Really, there was something more solemn than vanity in my satisfaction. Pleased as I was with my notoriety—and nobody but I knew how exceedingly pleased—I had a sober feeling about it all. I enjoyed being praised and admired and envied; but what gave a divine flavor to my happiness was the idea that I had publicly borne testimony to the goodness of my exalted hero, to the greatness of my adopted country. I did not discount the homage of Arlington Street, because I did not properly rate the intelligence of its population. I took the admiration of my schoolmates without a grain of salt; it was just so much honey to me. I could not know that what made me great in the eyes of my neighbors was that "there was a piece about me in the paper"; it mattered very little to them what the "piece" was about. I thought they really admired my sentiments. On the street, in the schoolyard, I was pointed out. The people said, "That's Mary Antin. She had her name in the paper." *I* thought they said, "This is she who loves her country and worships George Washington."

To repeat, I was well aware that I was something of a celebrity, and took all possible satisfaction in the fact; yet I gave my schoolmates no occasion to call me "stuck-up." My vanity did not express itself in strutting or wagging the head. I played tag and puss-in-the-corner in the schoolyard, and did everything that was comrade-like. But in the schoolroom I conducted myself gravely, as befitted one who was preparing for the noble career of a poet.

I am forgetting Lizzie McDee. I am trying to give the impression that I behaved with at least outward modesty during my schoolgirl triumphs, whereas Lizzie could testify that she knew Mary Antin as a vain, boastful, curly-headed little Jew. For I had a special style of deportment for Lizzie. If there was any girl in the school besides me who could keep near the top of the class all the year through, and give bright answers when the principal or the school committee popped sudden questions, and write rhymes that almost always rhymed, *I* was determined that that ambitious person should not soar unduly in her own estimation. So I took care to show Lizzie all my poetry, and when she showed me hers I did not admire it too warmly. Lizzie, as I have already said, was in a Sunday-school mood even on week days; her verses all had morals. My poems were about the crystal snow, and the ocean blue, and sweet spring, and fleecy clouds; when I tried to drag in a moral it kicked so that the music of my lines went out in a groan. So I had a sweet revenge when Lizzie, one day, volunteered to bolster up the eloquence of Mr. Jones, the principal, who was lecturing the class for bad behavior, by comparing the bad boy in the schoolroom to the rotten apple that spoils the barrelful. The groans, coughs, a-hem's, feet shufflings, and paper pellets that filled the room as Saint Elizabeth sat down, even in the principal's presence, were sweet balm to my smart of envy; I didn't care if I didn't know how to moralize.

When my teacher had visitors I was aware that I was the show pupil of the class. I was always made to recite, my compositions were passed around, and often I was called up on the platform—oh, climax of exaltation!—to be interviewed by the distinguished strangers; while the class took advantage of the teacher's distraction, to hold forbidden intercourse on matters not prescribed in the curriculum. When I returned to my seat, after such public audience with the great, I looked to see if Lizzie McDee was taking notice; and Lizzie, who was a generous soul, her Sunday-school airs notwithstanding, generally smiled, and I forgave her her rhymes.

Not but what I paid a price for my honors. With all my self-possession I had a certain capacity for shyness. Even when I arose to recite before the customary audience of my class I suffered from incipient stage fright, and my voice trembled over the first few words. When visitors were in the room I was even more troubled; and when I was made the special object of their attention my triumph was marred by acute distress. If I was called up to speak to the visitors, forty pairs of eyes pricked me in the back as I went. I stumbled in the aisle, and knocked down things that were not at all in my way; and my awkwardness increasing my embarrassment I would gladly have changed places with Lizzie or the bad boy in the back row; anything, only to be less conspicuous. When I found myself shaking hands with an august School-Committeeman, or a teacher from New York, the remnants of my self-possession vanished in awe; and it was in a very husky voice that I repeated, as I was asked, my name, lineage, and personal history. On the whole, I do not think that the School-Committeeman found a very forward creature in the solemn-faced little girl with the tight curls and the terrible red-and-green "plaid."

These awful audiences did not always end with the handshaking. Sometimes the great personages asked me to write to them, and exchanged addresses with me. Some of these correspondences continued through years, and were the source of much pleasure, on one side at least. And Arlington Street took notice when I received letters with important-looking or aristocratic-looking letterheads. Lizzie McDee also took notice. *I* saw to that.

O. E. RØLVAAG

Ole Edvart Rølvaag (1876–1931) was born to a fishing family on Dønna Island off the coast of Norway. His family was poor but literate, and he received a decent public school education. At 20 he immigrated to his uncle's farm in Elk Point, South Dakota. The quiet heartbreak that animates this passage from *The Third Life of Per Smevik*, a semi-autobiographical novel published in 1912, reflects the contrast between the wind-swept fjords and sparkling waters of Rølvaag's youth and the endless expanses of the Dakota prairies he now had to work. Rolvaag devoted his later life to the preservation of Norwegian culture in America, both as the head of the Norwegian department at St. Olaf College in Minnesota (where he taught from 1906 until his death) and as one of the founders of the Society for Norwegian Language and Culture. He also published numerous books, all in Norwegian. His last and most popular book was translated into English as *Giants in the Earth*. A portrait of the struggles faced by Norwegian immigrants, it was a Book-of-the-Month Club selection on its publication in 1927, and had sold 80,000 copies by the end of the year. The translation is by Ella Valborg Tweet and Solveig Zempel.

from
The Third Life of Per Smevik

South Dakota
DEAR BROTHER ANDREAS,   May 15, 1901

Hearty thanks for writing so soon. From the tone of your letter, I can hear how lonely and empty the house has become since Mother left. Well, you know that is to be expected. There is no use in complaining, for that won't bring her back, not that you complain so much; it rather seems that you say too little. It's not in the lines I read your unhappiness, but between them.

Yes, it is sad to think that she had neither one of her boys with her in her last hour; you were in Lofoten and I was here in America. I am certain that she missed us, and missed us very much. At the time of her death, I dreamt about her two nights in a row. The dream was the same both nights, except that it was much clearer the second night. It was so vivid then that I couldn't sleep any more. I got up, lit the lamp and sat down to study, but that didn't help. My thoughts turned constantly to Mother; I simply could not keep them away from her. So I got dressed and slipped quietly from my room out into the cold, moonlit winter night. There I took a long walk and let my thoughts wander undisturbed to Mother and home, and many other things far off in Norway.

What did I dream? I dreamt that I stood on the other side of Smevik bay, and on the hillside by our house I saw Mother, dressed in her Sunday best. It looked as if she was ready to go somewhere far away. She waved at me and called to me to come across the bay so she could say good-bye. The dream was so vivid that I recognized the clothes she was wearing; I heard her voice clearly. Only one thing seemed strange about the dream. Over the bay, the house, Mother, and the whole scene there lay a supernatural peace and still-ness. It was because of this that I could hear her words so clearly across the distance of the bay, yet she spoke in her normal tone of voice. Wasn't it strange that I should have had that dream two nights in a row, just at that time? Can you explain it? Did she, perchance, get permission to pass by here on the way to the heavenly home to bid her son farewell? If anyone should be granted such a wish, it would have to be Mother.

So you have begun to think seriously about coming to America? In that connection you ask many questions, some of which are rather difficult to answer. The old saying that, "One fool can ask more questions than ten wise men can answer," again shows itself to be true. Now you know that no offense was meant by this remark. You ask me to explain what you eventually would gain by coming to America. That is much easier said than done. Why don't you turn the question around and ask what you would lose? The latter I can probably answer more easily than the former. I am still too much of a newcomer to be able to discuss with any justice all the advantages this country has to offer the immigrant. It is possible that the answer I give now would not be the same twenty or forty years hence; nor do I know how my children, grandchildren and great-grandchildren will come to see the matter. What advantages will they have because I came to America? I ought to know all these things in order to give you a fair answer. Just now I had a brilliant idea. Last year at a Fourth of July celebration (Fourth of July is America's Seventeenth of May) I heard a speech on the theme: "What is gained and what is lost, upon exchanging the Fatherland for the new land." I have a copy of this speech. For the most part I am in complete agreement with it, and since the speech answers your questions much better than I can, I will send you some excerpts from it. You must read them with due consideration. Please let Father read them too.

"We who are assembled here today for this occasion are adopted children, that is, the majority of us are. We have sprung from a different root, and have come from another people. Hence, this festive day cannot have the same significance for us that it will have for our descendants. Even though we are foreign children, we wish to help celebrate this country's national holiday. It is our right and our duty. It is our right because the adopted child belongs to the family and has the same rights as the natural child. It is our duty to celebrate the Fourth of July because we ought to show our new mother honor on her birthday. But let us honor her in a worthy manner, brothers. Let our homage be such that she will understand more clearly that noble blood flows in the veins of the children she took to herself from the Northland—and let us prove to her that her family has been enriched by much good human material.

"We are adopted children. Let us today dwell a little on that truth, for it is a solemn truth and we do well to remind ourselves of it often. America is our country, but not our Fatherland. When the ship bearing us or our parents sailed westward into the unknown, when Norway's gray coast with its snow covered peaks sank into the sea, then our Fatherland sank with it. As such it exists for us no more. When we came here and received our citizenship papers and became Americans, we swore obedience and allegiance to the United States of America; but at the same time we forswore all our citizen's rights in that impoverished land we had left behind—in truth a serious oath! Thus were we adopted. Thus you and I exchanged our Fatherland for a new land.

"And now in this festive hour, I think that you and I ought to try to come to a clearer understanding of what was gained and what was lost in this exchange. It is time that we immigrants come to some conclusion about this, if we haven't already done so.

"Broadly speaking we can certainly say that much was lost, but also that much was received in return. Quoting the poet we may say:

> "Stort har jeg mistet, men stort jeg fik,
> Bedst var det kan hende, det gik som det gik,
> Og saa faar du ha tak da Gud."

> "Much have I lost, but much I received,
> Perhaps it was best that it happened this way,
> Thank you then, O God."

"Yes, truly there has been much won and much lost. There are large figures on both sides of the balance sheet. If I were to ask any of you at this very moment which was the greater—the loss or the gain—most of you would doubtless reply the gain, and that may very well be correct. You have beautiful, well kept farms here. You have built fine houses. Undeniably most of you have done well. There is wealth in the Norwegian settlements of the northwest today, no doubt about that. But these things have certainly not come of themselves; you have not gotten them for nothing; you have had to struggle hard and suffer much need before you got to where you now stand. Let us pause a moment and consider what these things have cost. You have experienced all the struggles and privations that the pioneer life had to offer. Thirty or forty years ago it wasn't so easy for a poor family to come here. In the old country you had a home, at least most of you did. Although that home was ever so poor and humble, it was possible with work and frugality to live there. This home you abandoned and came to a strange continent. But, the promised land was no paradise; there was no shortage of land, but it was wild and the wilderness had to be cleared. A hole was dug in the hillside. This dug-out became the home where you lived both summer and winter. Then the land was cleared and plowed but it went slowly—so terribly slowly—for there were no tools, no horses, only two bare hands to do all the work, and how unspeakably tired they often became. The family increased; there were new mouths crying for food, more bodies to clothe. You worked early and late to keep body and soul together, and to retain the land on which you had settled. This is but a small portion of what your present wealth has cost you.

"But why bring out all these dark memories? Let us also recall the brighter ones, for it was not all toil and suffering and poverty. From the long years of hardship, you have reaped rich blessings; God has in full measure rewarded your labors. Success came slowly, but it came; the small fields grew bit by bit; one piece of machinery was acquired, then another, then several. The oxen were traded for horses. The dugout was replaced by a shanty. Thus things have improved little by little until now—yes, what do we see now? The shanties have disappeared. Instead there are magnificent houses and farm buildings of all kinds. It can be said in all truthfulness that you have become wealthy. And this prosperity is the first thing I will mention as a gain in your exchange of your Fatherland for this new country. It cannot be denied that many of you could have become prosperous in Norway, too, if you had expended as much energy and labor with as much ambition and enterprise as you have done since you came here.

"Right here, in connection with this idea, I want to mention another benefit which you have received in this exchange: the practical grasp of things that you were forced to adopt when you came here. Also, you were forced to pay attention to time. Here you soon realized that the old saying, 'Time is money,' is more than just talk. No matter how dearly we love our friends and relatives over there, we have to admit that the great majority of them do not understand the value of really economical intensive work. The way they waste and fritter away time! Neither is that enterprising spirit—that shrewd, progressive, food-producing ambition—so well developed in them. Or have you forgotten how you never saw any other way of doing the work than the methods your father and grandfather and forefathers for generations had used? If you had done things the same way here, there would have been hard times and starvation in this country, too.

"Let us consider a few more of the advantages you received in the exchange. There is the great personal growth you experienced by coming to a new land, and mingling with foreign people. It is very fruitful to blend one's own ideas with those of strangers. By this process you received new thoughts which unconsciously became a part of yourselves. Your outlook was broadened and you developed more than you realized. This was a hard school as we shall later see, but it was a good school. And easy or difficult, it was an unavoidable necessity in order to survive over here.

"The fourth benefit we received when we exchanged our Fatherland for this new country was the great freedom which we enjoy here, both civil and religious. From a purely theoretical point of view, Norway is more democratic than America, and yet it can be truthfully said that no human beings under the sun enjoy the same freedoms as the American farmer. His independence is almost boundless. The only masters he knows are the sun and the rain, and the tax commissioner. Anyway the taxes are so reasonable in this country that no one need complain about them. It is quite different in many European countries where taxes are so high that it is difficult for rich and poor alike to stand up under the burden.

"But the greatest advantage that we received when we exchanged our Fatherland for this country is the rich variety of opportunities this land has to offer each individual. No matter how poor a young man may be, no matter how humble his ancestry, if he has the courage and the will power he can succeed. There are innumerable examples of Askeladden, the poor little ash boy, winning the princess and half the kingdom. Let us look at a few. The great railroad king, Jim Hill, began with just his bare hands and became a millionaire. John Lind, one of America's ablest politicians, emigrated to this country as a poor fourteen-year-old boy; at one time he ran a threshing machine in eastern Minnesota. And Knute Nelson, the boy from Voss who reached as high a position in government as it is possible for an immigrant to reach, was once a shepherd boy. When the Civil War broke out General Grant was earning his living by hauling cordwood. President Andrew Johnson was the son of a tailor, and he himself worked as a tailor's apprentice. And one of the greatest of all of history's great men, Abraham Lincoln, first saw the light of day in a simple log cabin in Kentucky. But why mention all these names? You will find them on nearly every page of this country's history. And if you look at this country's intellectual leaders, you will meet the same sight again. Thousands upon thousands of young men, with no other help except a pair of strong hands and an undaunted spirit, have struggled through school after school until they finally reached their longed-for goal. It is not only the Yankee boy who has accomplished this. No, it can be said without boasting, and it should be said with pride, that the lad from the foreign land—the adopted child, for whom the difficulties have been even greater—has accomplished it just as often, if not oftener, and just as well, if not better, than the native son. And these rich and varied opportunities for the individual are, in my opinion, the greatest of all the benefits we received when we exchanged our Fatherland for this country.

"However, there were not just advantages to this exchange. Wealth is a great earthly benefit; an extensive civil and religious liberty is certainly a blessing; rich opportunities for each individual is one of the Creator's gifts to mankind. But life is more than food, earthly happiness is more than civic freedom, and God's greatest gift to man is not first and foremost great opportunities. When I consider all that we forfeited in this exchange, all the other things that make life worth living and that fill the years with true happiness, then I wonder at times if what we gave in exchange was not worth more than what we received. Let us turn the page now and see what we find on the other side of the ledger.

"The first loss, I find, is that ennobling and uplifting influence which a mighty and magnificent nature has on the human mind. All eminent men who have studied this question agree that the natural environment exerts a great influence on us. It must be so! Why otherwise do you decorate your houses? Why otherwise do you mothers polish your kitchens every day? You cannot bear to see things disorderly and dirty. Why can't you bear this? Because it makes you depressed and discouraged. So it is with the nature that surrounds us, with this difference, perhaps, that the impressions of nature work on us more unconsciously for they remain the same day after day, year in and year out. Now you must not infer that I believe America has no natural beauty, for it certainly has. The West is, after all, famous in that respect. Even the prairies of the Middle West have their beauty. When we, for example, sit out on the porch on a warm midsummer evening and listen to the rustling of the half-ripened grain, when we hear how this rustling blends harmoniously with the monotonous tones of the crickets, the grasshoppers and the frogs—then the prairie is truly beautiful. There is no doubt about that. And yet this beauty is insignificant compared with that of your Fatherland. This is proven by the ever-increasing stream of tourists who visit Norway each year. There is almost unanimous agreement that nowhere else have they found such an impressive, such a sublime beauty as they find there. They could scarcely say anything else either, for all extremes of nature are found in Norway. There the brilliant summer reaches its hand to the eternal glaciers of the polar regions. And the northern summer nights! No, not night at all, but day—an enchanted fairy day. Time and time again artists have tried to capture on canvas that blending of light and color which the northern summer night spreads over land and sea, but to no avail. The traveler will find mountain peaks as wild as any in Switzerland. He will find mountain chains so majestic that they compare favorably with the Alps; fjords, of which the Scots have seen no equal; and beyond these, he can find valleys whose charm reminds him of Italy. Over the entire landscape lie the deep organ tones of the rivers and the waterfalls. Then there is the sea—so powerful, so melancholy, so awe-inspiring in its anger, and so bewitching in its calmness. There are folks from Western Norway in this gathering, I see. They know how true this is. I remember so well my first weeks in America, in the eastern part of Wisconsin. Near the farm where I worked were some high, wild hills. On my first Sunday there (I had had my first lesson in milking that evening) I scrambled up through the weeds and brush to the top of the highest hill. The sweat ran and the nettles burned my face, but I went on nevertheless. When I finally reached the top, I stood completely still and stared out and out; my eye wandered over the entire horizon as I searched and hunted in vain for the sea. I am not ashamed to say that as I walked home that night I was not far from tears. This one incident shows in a way what power the Norwegian nature has had upon me. And I, for my part, believe it to be an indisputable fact that the reason Norway has produced so many artists in various fields can be attributed largely to her magnificent nature. The prairie has not yet produced any really great artist.

"This loss that I have mentioned, great as it is, is a small thing compared with another: We lost our Fatherland—the bitterest, the heaviest, the most irreparable loss of all. To lose one's Fatherland—exactly what is meant by that? Ah, brothers, that is more than you and I can bear to speak about today. Anyway, I am sure you know what it means. Or have you forgotten that parting so many, many years ago? Don't you remember how unspeakably difficult it was? Oh yes, you remember it well. One doesn't easily forget his farewell to family and friends, and the last handclasp with his gray-haired father and mother. And when the cottage on the hill and the church spire disappeared from view, and your eyes became misty, then a strange heaviness fell upon your heart. This is not to be wondered at for then the most tender and sensitive heart strings snapped. These things are not easily forgotten. They usually remain in one's memory as long as one lives. The Norwegians are a very warm hearted people, it is said, and for this reason they feel such a loss very keenly.

"Giving up our Fatherland means more than getting a wound that can never be healed in this life. It also means that we have forfeited spiritual contact with our own people and our own nation. And that, brothers, is a very severe loss. It is difficult to live among a strange people, a people with a completely different outlook on life than our own. It is painful to always feel that you are a stranger among strangers. You've never felt that, you say? No that isn't to be expected out here in these large Norwegian settlements where everything is nearly the same as you were accustomed to in the old country. But how many thousands and thousands are there in our large cities who have experienced this, do you suppose? How many fine Norwegians have landed in an insane asylum for just this reason? All that coldness, strangeness, and homesickness—that sick, hurting, gnawing longing—drove them finally into madness, either that or into vice. For there were times when the longing for home and family had to be deadened, and so it was deadened in the dives of the big city. This has happened to many a fine Norwegian youth. But even though it hasn't always gone quite so badly—and thank God it doesn't—yet this feeling of forever being a stranger is an unpleasant companion. It follows one as faithfully as a shadow. Even in the midst of happiness, it may come forth and cast its darkness over everything. This feeling of being an alien causes a discordant note even in the most joyful laughter.

"These that we have mentioned here are cruel losses, irreparably cruel. But if we had lost no more than this, there would be little reason to complain, especially when we remember what we won. Let us take a closer look at the balance sheet.

"When we severed our ties with our Fatherland, we became not only strangers among strangers, but we were cut off from our own nation and became strangers to our own people. Our pulse no longer throbs in rhythm with the hearts of our own kindred. We have become strangers; strangers to those we left, and strangers to those we came to. The Fatherland to which we had centuries of inherited rights, we have given away, and we of the first generation can never get another. Let me repeat: We have become outsiders to the people we left, and we are also outsiders among the people to whom we came. Thus we have ceased to be a harmonious part of a greater whole; we have become something apart, something torn loose, without any organic connections either here in America or over in Norway. Our souls can no longer burn with genuine national enthusiasm. That uplifting and ennobling of the spirit which every true citizen experiences in a national crisis can never be felt by us. In short, we have become rootless. One of our most important nerves has been cut. We are alienated. This speech is perhaps unclear to some of you. Let me, therefore, ask a question or two: Have you ever felt that you are a real American? Do you feel that the American people are really your people? A small, a very small percentage of Norwegian-Americans seem to feel that way but I doubt that they really do, deep down in their hearts. This I know, most of us do not; we are simply unable to. As a result, we can never enter into the public life of this country to the degree that our education and intelligence give us the unquestionable right to. Well then, suppose we sold out and went back to Norway to live. Would we not feel at home then, we who are so Norwegian in all respects? No, herein lies the greatest tragedy of all. We would feel like strangers there too. For a few, it seems to work out, but for the great majority who try, it proves unsuccessful. They believed themselves to be Norwegians, but soon discovered they were not. Here they had acquired attitudes, unconsciously perhaps, that didn't fit into the conditions they found over there. First, they tried to become Americans, but found they couldn't; then they wanted to become Norwegians again, but found that to be equally impossible. Herein lies the tragedy of emigration. If you give up your Fatherland for good, it can never be regained; neither can you get another in its place, no matter what you do.

"Whenever I think these thoughts, tragic as they are, I am reminded of an anecdote from Osterdal that the Norwegian writer J. B. Bull tells. There was a gypsy who traveled about between the villages there. The man's name was Mikkel. He was handy and clever as most gypsies are, and since he could do just about anything people asked him, he was nicknamed Tinker Mikkel. Once he came to a pastor's farm where there were many children, as is fitting and proper. At this farm they had a music box, but it played only one tune—a waltz. Every now and then one of the children would go over and wind it up. The pastor's wife finally became sick and tired of this continual waltz, so she asked Mikkel one day as he strolled into the farm if he couldn't take the waltz tune out and put in a hymn instead. Yes, Tinker Mikkel would try, so he took the music box and disappeared for a week. 'Well, how did it go?' asked the wife, when Mikkel returned with the box. 'Did you get the hymn tune in?' Tinker Mikkel scratched his head as he replied, 'Well, I don't really know. I got the hymn in, but it was harder to get the waltz out.' When they wound up the box and let it play, out came the strangest music they had ever heard. It was a hymn melody in waltz time. Now and then came snatches of the hymn, then a bit of the waltz, then both hymn and waltz together. Thus it is with us foreign born here in this country: we are neither the one nor the other, we are both at the same time.

"And still we haven't accounted for everything in the ledger. No, there are some figures left so large we can scarcely comprehend them. And if we talked for days on this theme, we could not tell everything. The truth is this, brothers, that no one can ever fully explain what it means to lose his Fatherland. We can have a more or less clear feeling of it, but this feeling we cannot express in words. We lost the inexpressible! The saddest of all is that one never realizes these things before it is too late. If people in the Old Country could see things as you and I do, then it would not be long until that stream of emigrants would be nearly dried up . . ."

Then the speaker went on to show that the loss was greater than the gain not only for the first generation, but also for the second and the third, and that it was impossible for anyone to say definitely when this loss could be fully overcome.

But I won't copy that part of the speech. You aren't married and perhaps never will be either, so you're not particularly interested in the second and third generations. Besides I can't write any more; I have been copying this speech for two evenings now and I'm tired of it. You must read it thoughtfully. I believe what the speaker says is true. I've been thinking the same thoughts myself; perhaps this is why I liked the speech so well.

You can understand that I will not tell you to come to America. No, I won't even advise you to do it. I will just say that you need never worry about food and clothing. They just seem to come by themselves.

I had a letter from Uncle Hans some time ago; he advised me to get you and Father to come here this fall. He says that both of you can stay with him all winter, and you won't have to do a thing. He thinks it is best for you to hold an auction immediately, and come as soon as possible. Then you can avoid going to Lofoten this winter and Father won't have to be alone. This is not bad advice; if you really intend to come, the sooner the better. But let me know as soon as you have made any final decision.

In just two weeks I'm through here. It is sad to be so alone. All my classmates are now busy sending invitations to relatives and friends, and getting ready for commencement activities. I don't have anyone to invite except Uncle Hans, and he says he can't come. On the other hand, I have the honor of giving a speech at the graduation ceremony. Well, that honor doesn't mean much to me, since none of my own people can get pleasure from it.

Right after graduation I am going to North Dakota to teach parochial school. I don't know yet how long I will be there. You can send my letters to Uncle Hans, and he will forward them to me.

May God help and guide you to make the right decision about coming to America.

Your affectionate brother,
P. A. Smevik

ANZIA YEZIERSKA

Teenage Anzia Yezierska (c. 1885–1970) immigrated to America with her family from a Polish *shtetl* in what is now Belarus (then part of the Russian Empire) and settled in the burgeoning Jewish community on the Lower East Side of Manhattan in the late 1890s. She was immediately put to work in a sweatshop, but attended night school where she quickly learned English and eventually earned a scholarship to Columbia University, graduating in 1904 with a bachelor's degree in domestic science. Her first book, *Hungry Hearts*, a collection of stories documenting the plight of Jewish immigrant women, was made into a movie by Samuel Goldwyn soon after it was published in 1920. Yezierska then moved to Hollywood, and although she was making enough money for studio publicists to call her "the sweatshop Cinderella," she spent only a year on the West Coast before returning to New York City to continue writing novels and stories. *Children of Loneliness*, the story collection from which this excerpt from the title story is taken, was published in 1923. Here we have a poignant illustration of that "inversion of social relations" that Mary Antin talks about in *The Promised Land*: when the first generation "must step down from their throne of parental authority, and take the law from their children's mouths."

from
Children of Loneliness

"Oh, Mother, can't you use a fork?" exclaimed Rachel as Mrs. Ravinsky took the shell of the baked potato in her fingers and raised it to her watering mouth.

"Here, *Teacherin* mine, you want to learn me in my old age how to put the bite in my mouth?" The mother dropped the potato back into her plate, too wounded to eat. Wiping her hands on her blue-checked apron, she turned her glance to her husband, at the opposite side of the table.

"Yankev," she said bitterly, "stick your bone on a fork. Our *teacherin* said you dassn't touch no eatings with the hands."

"All my teachers died already in the old country," retorted the old man. "I ain't going to learn nothing new no more from my American daughter." He continued to suck the marrow out of the bone with that noisy relish that was so exasperating to Rachel.

"It's no use," stormed the girl, jumping up from the table in disgust; "I'll never be able to stand it here with you people."

"'You people?' What do you mean by 'you people?'" shouted the old man, lashed into fury by his daughter's words. "You think you got a different skin from us because you went to college?"

"It drives me wild to hear you crunching bones like savages. If you people won't change, I shall have to move and live by myself."

Yankev Ravinsky threw the half-gnawed bone upon the table with such vehemence that a plate broke into fragments.

"You witch you!" he cried in a hoarse voice tense with rage. "Move by yourself! We lived without you while you was away in college, and we can get on without you further. God ain't going to turn his nose on us because we ain't got table manners from America. A hell she made from this house since she got home."

"*Shah!* Yankev *leben*," pleaded the mother, "the neighbors are opening the windows to listen to our hollering. Let us have a little quiet for a while till the eating is over."

But the accumulated hurts and insults that the old man had borne in the one week since his daughter's return from college had reached the breaking-point. His face was convulsed, his eyes flashed, and his lips were flecked with froth as he burst out in a volley of scorn:

"You think you can put our necks in a chain and learn us new tricks? You think you can make us over for Americans? We got through till fifty years of our lives eating in our own old way—"

"Wo is me, Yankev *leben*!" entreated his wife. "Why can't we choke our-selves with our troubles? Why must the whole world know how we are tearing ourselves by the heads? In all Essex Street, in all New York, there ain't such fights like by us."

Her pleadings were in vain. There was no stopping Yankev Ravinsky once his wrath was roused. His daughter's insistence upon the use of a knife and fork spelled apostasy, Anti-Semitism, and the aping of the Gentiles.

Like a prophet of old condemning unrighteousness, he ran the gamut of denunciation, rising to heights of fury that were sublime and godlike, and sinking from sheer exhaustion to abusive bitterness.

"*Pfui* on all your American colleges! *Pfui* on the morals of America! No respect for old age. No fear for God. Stepping with your feet on all the laws of the holy Torah. A fire should burn out the whole new generation. They should sink into the earth, like Korah."

"Look at him cursing and burning! Just because I insist on their changing their terrible table manners. One would think I was killing them."

"Do you got to use a gun to kill?" cried the old man, little red threads darting out of the whites of his eyes.

"Who is doing the killing? Aren't you choking the life out of me? Aren't you dragging me by the hair to the darkness of past ages every minute of the day? I'd die of shame if one of my college friends should open the door while you people are eating."

"You—you—"

The old man was on the point of striking his daughter when his wife seized the hand he raised.

"*Mincha!* Yankev, you forgot *Mincha!*"

This reminder was a flash of inspiration on Mrs. Ravinsky's part, the only thing that could have ended the quarreling instantly. *Mincha* was the prayer just before sunset of the orthodox Jews. This religious rite was so automatic with the old man that at his wife's mention of *Mincha* everything was immediately shut out, and Yankev Ravinsky rushed off to a corner of the room to pray.

"*Ashrai Yoishwai Waisahuh!*"

"Happy are they who dwell in Thy house. Ever shall I praise Thee. *Selah!* Great is the Lord, and exceedingly to be praised; and His greatness is unsearchable. On the majesty and glory of Thy splendor, and on Thy marvelous deeds, will I meditate."

The shelter from the storms of life that the artist finds in his art, Yankev Ravinsky found in his prescribed communion with God. All the despair caused by his daughter's apostasy, the insults and disappointments he suffered, were in his sobbing voice. But as he entered into the spirit of his prayer, he felt the man of flesh drop away in the outflow of God around him. His voice mellowed, the rigid wrinkles of his face softened, the hard glitter of anger and condemnation in his eyes was transmuted into the light of love as he went on:

"The Lord is gracious and merciful; slow to anger and of great lovingkindness. To all that call upon Him in truth He will hear their cry and save them."

Oblivious to the passing and repassing of his wife as she warmed anew the unfinished dinner, he continued:

"Put not your trust in princes, in the son of man in whom there is no help." Here Reb Ravinsky paused long enough to make a silent confession for the sin of having placed his hope on his daughter instead of on God. His whole body bowed with the sense of guilt. Then in a moment his humility was transfigured into exaltation. Sorrow for sin dissolved in joy as he became more deeply aware of God's unfailing protection.

"Happy is he who hath the God of Jacob for his help, whose hope is in the Lord his God. He healeth the broken in heart, and bindeth up their wounds."

A healing balm filled his soul as he returned to the table, where the steaming hot food awaited him. Rachel sat near the window pretending to read a book. Her mother did not urge her to join them at the table, fearing another outbreak, and the meal continued in silence.

The girl's thoughts surged hotly as she glanced from her father to her mother. A chasm of four centuries could not have separated her more completely from them than her four years at Cornell.

"To think that I was born of these creatures! It's an insult to my soul. What kinship have I with these two lumps of ignorance and superstition? They're ugly and gross and stupid. I'm all sensitive nerves. They want to wallow in dirt."

She closed her eyes to shut out the sight of her parents as they silently ate together, unmindful of the dirt and confusion.

"How is it possible that I lived with them and like them only four years ago? What is it in me that so quickly gets accustomed to the best? Beauty and cleanliness are as natural to me as if I'd been born on Fifth Avenue instead of the dirt of Essex Street."

A vision of Frank Baker passed before her. Her last long talk with him out under the trees in college still lingered in her heart. She felt that she had only to be with him again to carry forward the beautiful friendship that had sprung up between them. He had promised to come shortly to New York. How could she possibly introduce such a born and bred American to her low, ignorant, dirty parents?

"I might as well tear the thought of Frank Baker out of my heart," she told herself. "If he just once sees the pigsty of a home I come from, if he just sees the table manners of my father and mother, he'll fly through the ceiling."

Timidly, Mrs. Ravinsky turned to her daughter.

"Ain't you going to give a taste the eating?"

No answer.

"I fried the *lotkes* special' for you—"

"I can't stand your fried, greasy stuff."

"Ain't even my cooking good no more either?" Her gnarled, hard-worked hands clutched at her breast. "God from the world, for what do I need yet any more my life? Nothing I do for my child is no use no more."

Her head sank; her whole body seemed to shrivel and grow old with the sense of her own futility.

"How I was hurrying to run by the butcher before everybody else, so as to pick out the grandest, fattest piece of *brust!*" she wailed, tears streaming down her face. "And I put my hand away from my heart and put a whole fresh egg into the *lotkes*, and I stuffed the stove full of coal like a millionaire so as to get the *lotkes* fried so nice and brown; and now you give a kick on everything I done—"

"Fool woman," shouted her husband, "stop laying yourself on the ground for your daughter to step on you! What more can you expect from a child raised up in America? What more can you expect but that she should spit in your face and make dirt from you?" His eyes, hot and dry under their lids, flashed from his wife to his daughter. "The old Jewish eating is poison to her; she must have *trefa* ham—only forbidden food."

Bitter laughter shook him.

"Woman, how you patted yourself with pride before all the neighbors, boasting of our great American daughter coming home from college! This is our daughter, our pride, our hope, our pillow for our old age that we were dreaming about! This is our American *teacherin*! A Jew-hater, an Anti-Semite we brought into the world, a betrayer of our race who hates her own father and mother like the Russian Czar once hated a Jew. She makes herself so refined, she can't stand it when we use the knife or fork the wrong way; but her heart is that of a brutal Cossack, and she spills her own father's and mother's blood like water."

Every word he uttered seared Rachel's soul like burning acid. She felt herself becoming a witch, a she-devil, under the spell of his accusations.

"You want me to love you yet?" She turned upon her father like an avenging fury. "If there's any evil hatred in my soul, you have roused it with your cursed preaching."

"*Oi-i-i!* Highest One! pity Yourself on us!" Mrs. Ravinsky wrung her hands. "Rachel, Yankev, let there be an end to this knife-stabbing! *Gottuniu!* my flesh is torn to pieces!"

Unheeding her mother's pleading, Rachel rushed to the closet where she kept her things.

"I was a crazy idiot to think that I could live with you people under one roof." She flung on her hat and coat and bolted for the door.

Mrs. Ravinsky seized Rachel's arm in passionate entreaty.

"My child, my heart, my life, what do you mean? Where are you going?"

"I mean to get out of this hell of a home this very minute," she said, tearing loose from her mother's clutching hands.

"Wo is me! My child! We'll be to shame and to laughter by the whole world. What will people say?"

"Let them say! My life is my own; I'll live as I please." She slammed the door in her mother's face.

"They want me to love them yet," ran the mad thoughts in Rachel's brain as she hurried through the streets, not knowing where she was going, not caring. "Vampires, bloodsuckers fastened on my flesh! Black shadow blighting every ray of light that ever came my way! Other parents scheme and plan and wear themselves out to give their child a chance, but they put dead stones in front of every chance I made for myself."

With the cruelty of youth to everything not youth, Rachel reasoned:

"They have no rights, no claims over me like other parents who do things for their children. It was my own brains, my own courage, my own iron will that forced my way out of the sweatshop to my present position in the public schools. I owe them nothing, nothing, nothing."

POEMS BY CHINESE IMMIGRANTS

The history of Chinese immigration to the United States is a volume in itself. Faced with brutal work, discrimination, and then restrictive entry laws, the lure of a better life in America must have been extraordinarily compelling. The passage of the Chinese Exclusion Act in 1882 meant that virtually all arrivals from China—and with the Immigration Act of 1917 from elsewhere in southern and eastern Asia—would not be welcome. When the U.S. Immigration Station on Angel Island in San Francisco Bay began operation in 1910 it served primarily as a detention center for Asians who would soon be returned to their home countries. The anonymous selection that follows come from *Island*, a 1991 anthology of writings by Chinese immigrants on Angel Island from 1910 to 1940. The book was edited and translated by Him Mark Lai, Genny Lim, and Judy Yung.

The gold and silver of America is very appealing.
Jabbing an awl into the thigh in search of glory,
I embarked on the journey.
Not only are my one-thousand pieces of gold already depleted, but
My countenance is blackened. It is surely for the sake of the family.

Four days before the Qiqiao Festival,
I boarded the steamship for America.
Time flew like a shooting arrow.
Already, a cool autumn has passed.
Counting on my fingers, several months have elapsed.
Still I am at the beginning of the road.
I have yet to be interrogated.
My heart is nervous with anticipation.

Everyone says travelling to North America is a pleasure.
I suffered misery on the ship and sadness in the wooden building.
After several interrogations, still I am not done.
I sigh because my compatriots are being forceably detained.

By One from Xiangshan

Originally, I had intended to come to America last year.
Lack of money delayed me until early autumn.
It was on the day that the Weaver Maiden met the Cowherd
That I took passage on the *President Lincoln.*
I ate wind and tasted waves for more than twenty days.
Fortunately, I arrived safely on the American continent.
I thought I could land in a few days.
How was I to know I would become a prisoner suffering in the wooden
    building?
The barbarians' abuse is really difficult to take.
When my family's circumstances stir my emotions, a double stream
    of tears flow.
I only wish I can land in San Francisco soon,
Thus sparing me this additional sorrow here.

Instead of remaining a citizen of China, I willingly became an ox.
I intended to come to America to earn a living.
The Western styled buildings are lofty; but I have not the luck to live in
them.
How was anyone to know that my dwelling place would be a prison?

Poem by One Named Xu From Xiangshan Encouraging the Traveler

Just talk about going to the land of the Flowery Flag and my countenance
fills with happiness.
Not without hard work were 1,000 pieces of gold dug up and gathered
together.
There were words of farewell to the parents, but the throat choked up first.
There were many feelings, many tears flowing face to face, when parting
with the wife.

Waves big as mountains often astonished this traveller.
With laws harsh as tigers, I had a taste of all the barbarities.
Do not forget this day when you land ashore.
Push yourself ahead and do not be lazy or idle.

MENOTTI PELLEGRINO

Little is known about Menotti Pellegrino, including his birth, arrival, and death dates. He was probably born in Sicily and came to New York City's Lower East Side in the early years of the 20th century. In 1903 he published a novel in Italian, *I misteri di New York* (translated here by Ann Goldstein as *The Mysteries of New York*). Pellegrino presents the city as a place of stunning extremes, a mixture of the brutal and the vital, hardly an instant safe haven for the tens of thousands of Italian immigrants who have to struggle through the tangles of poverty, crime, and corruption in order to survive in their new home.

from
The Mysteries of New York

NEW YORK! The sigh of every derelict of the old world; the refuge of hearts longed for by the delinquent; the cradle of fortune sought by the disinherited of all peoples.

NEW YORK! Chaos, where hope and disillusion swirl, gold and tin, virtue and vice, wealth and misery; and the greedy hand of every newcomer gropes as it attempts to seize the good part and often ends up grasping only the bad. The enigma, where through the whole gamut of base and shameful acts one sees the insolent boor rise, while the wellborn person who refuses to join in the prevailing corruption falls. The anomaly in which guilt is bowed down; crime, prostitution, promiscuity, and theft are crowned, and shame, honesty, and justice are derided or pitied. The altar of the Almighty Dollar, where everything is traded and measured, from heart to mind; where love and honor, every affection, every feeling, by which everything is inspired, on which every-thing hinges, at which everything genuflects, are only things with a price.

NEW YORK is the synthetic word, it is America for the majority of the innumerable worshippers of the powerful Almighty Dollar. In fact, among all those thousands of immigrants who from every part of Europe and elsewhere converge on the great metropolis, a considerable number always remain there, even to the detriment of their own capacities, which would find greater opportunities in spreading out into the other states of the American union.

NEW YORK will be the first land on which our eyes, tired of the sight of the sea, rest, said a traveler with an aristocratic air, leaning on the rail of the first-class bridge of an English steamship, to a fair woman with a shapely figure and majestic bearing, whose beautiful eyes, of a bright, enchanting black, along with the evidently unusual pallor of her cheeks, revealed traces of fear, which had caused those eyes to widen.

※　※

Bowery!

It's not only a street, it's a world in itself.

There exist all the layers of human society.

Surely if one were to seek in the world a city thoroughfare of equal classicism, of equal importance as the Bowery of New York, one would fail in the undertaking.

Broad enough for more than four separate trolley tracks, with shoulders wide enough to be streets themselves, in addition to spacious sidewalks on both sides, surmounted by the high tracks of the elevated trains that run noisily up and down, at intervals of perhaps a minute, it has no repose at night, nor the peace of repose.

In the long line of disparate buildings, in that whole long linked extension, you would not find the habitation of a family.

Hotels, furnished rooms, clubs, theaters, stores, warehouses, factories, schools, credit institutions, banks, and next door to one another countless bars always full of drinkers, shops for every kind of article, workshops for strange objects, antique stores, anatomical museums, displays of mummies, of freaks, of talking machines, instruments that play by themselves, and a crowd of the curious, always new, pressing in to admire, and a rabble of pickpockets, always active, taking from the more intent admirers whatever it can, in spite of the sign, in block letters, in the entryway of every attraction: Watch out for pickpockets.

At all hours of the day, in the deafening noise of the elevated trains, in the continuous rhythmic rolling of the trolleys, a flow of people goes up and down that sidewalk, among them the artisan hurrying to work, the prostitute who seems to follow her shadow and hopes only to be followed, the girl on her way to the factory nibbling an apple or chewing gum, the idler who is looking for a swindle, the street peddler, the newsboy, the junk dealer, the man hurrying by as if he feared to be sullied, the grande dame who avoids looking at the passersby, pulling a small dog with her little finger burdened by a large diamond.

And the drunk, who tacking this way and that cries, threatens, or sings; the cop who is in close conversation with a young woman, while others, pairing up after making an agreement, where is the more and the less, climb the steps of one of the many taverns; two ragged vagabonds having a fist-fight who act like athletes in a ring of spectators; the pimp who pretends to be attentively admiring something in a shopwindow, while in fact waiting to make his offering to the first who approaches; the secret policeman who collects his weekly bribe from the peddlers, while his partner, under some pretext or other, arrests any among them who refuse.

Greatness, splendor, wealth, depravity, filth, misery—all find confused yet typical expression on the Bowery.

At night the actors and the scene change, but they are no less characteristic than the figures, the things of the day.

If the number of passersby who are hurrying about their business is less, the noise of trolleys and trains is the same, and the number of women seeking adventure, stationed at every corner, in every doorway, near the pillars of the elevated tracks, is greater, until the dawn hours of the morning, when like bats they go home, as if fleeing the light. They offer themselves to whoever passes by, leading him to a dark area, dragging him to the entrance of a hotel, starting a conversation as they skillfully steal the watch of the fool who's been caught, then leaving him waiting in vain in a room where they've brought him, after cadging the agreed-on price before fulfilling the bargain.

The men who, lacking any sense of honor, strangers to every virtue, live on these women, eat off their flesh, covering themselves to the last abuse, often follow them, and when the inexperienced fellow falls into their hands and is led into a suitable bar, they fall like wolves on a sheep, like falcons on a sparrow, and strip him of everything and beat him, if he resists, and divide the spoils with the owner of the place.

The shouts, the obscene cries of the drunks, the vulgar scenes around the improvised stalls selling fried or boiled food that a crowd of strange customers devours on the sidewalk, the frequent arrival of the ambulance, announced by the ringing of its electric bell, to pick up someone who has been injured—these are all things typical of night on the Bowery.

LUDOVICO CAMINITA

Not much is known about Ludovico Caminita's early life, other than he was born in Italy and came to the United States in 1902. When the Red Scare gripped America in 1920, anarchists, communists, socialists, would-be revolutionaries, labor leaders, and other activists and dissidents were rounded up for imprisonment and even deportation—just for holding seemingly unpatriotic political views. Caminita, living at the time among radicalized Italian-American industrial workers in Paterson, New Jersey, was sent to Ellis Island for three years. There he wrote an account of his incarceration and his anarchist views, published in 1924 as *Nell'isola delle lagrime: Ellis Island* (translated here by Ann Goldstein as *On the Island of Tears: Ellis Island*). Despite significant disillusion, Caminita never lost his affection for the place that had welcomed him as an immigrant—where he "had enjoyed so much and suffered so much"— and in his later years adopted more moderate views.

from
On the Island of Tears: Ellis Island

S unday passed monotonously. We were tired from the long night, and our thoughts were with our families. We spoke from one cell to another, at long intervals and without much interest. Every so often a guard came along, called a name, and gave the prisoner cigars or cigarettes that his relatives had brought.

The wife of the weaver who had lodged and fed Joe Termini, and given him money, thought that he was a prisoner with us, and had had the idea of bringing him some cigarettes. Poor thing! All alone, and far from his comfortable mother, he surely felt, more than the others, the burden of unexpected imprisonment!

"The cigars are for my husband, the cigarettes for Joe Termini."

"Joe Termini? But he's a spy for the federal agents! Who knows where the bum is now!" exclaimed the guard.

You can imagine the amazement of the poor woman!

They brought us breakfast, lunch, and dinner from a nearby restaurant, paid for, of course, by the federal government. I, who with my frequent travels was used to American cooking, considered those meals tasty. The others, who had never left their native dinner tables, received that food like a penance. "Oatmeal" and coffee with milk to a Piedmontese, or a Neapolitan!

Monday came as a relief. We didn't know what they would do with us, but we hadn't slept for two days, and the thought that we would be able to lie down on some mattress or other, at home or in prison or on the island, consoled us a little.

During the wait the minutes seemed like hours. Every time a guard entered we all expected to be called. And it was a great disappointment when instead he called us to deliver a package.

I received underwear and cigarettes.

"Who brought them?" I asked the guard.

"Your wife."

"That's impossible; my wife can't leave the house; she's sick."

"I tell you, she did bring them. The chief recognized her. And she's outside there, in the crowd, waiting for you to come out. They are pitiful, poor women! Since six in the morning they've been out there, and it's six degrees below zero. Such is life!"

He went off shaking his head and repeating: "Yes, such is life!"

I stood there for some minutes gripping the iron bars, then I threw myself on the bedsprings and hid my face in my overcoat so that my cellmate wouldn't see the tears that I couldn't hold back. I wept for the woman who walked heroically at my side, a smile of comfort on her lips, always ready to support me in difficult moments, along the Via Crucis of my fate, lined with thorns. I wept for the wives of the others, frail, innocent creatures, true victims of that judicial error made for the sake of ignoble profit by the new priests of the class struggle, who wore soft hats and fluttering black ties.

Around two o'clock the chief of the local police made a tour of inspection and stopped in front of my cell. He was in plainclothes. He asked me how I was doing, if breakfast and lunch had been good, and urged me not to be discouraged.

"I'm sorry about this mistake. I knew it the night they brought you here, because the federal agents wanted to do everything secretly—they wouldn't trust us. I hope that it will all turn out to be a soap bubble in the end."

"Thank you. I know that our wives have been waiting a long time for us, out in the street, in the cold. Couldn't you let them have shelter?"

"I would do it happily, because the poor creatures really are a pitiful sight; but the federal agents won't allow it. They're already irritated because I allowed you to get cigarettes and clean underwear."

"If I am not mistaken, you are the chief here, not the federal agents."

"Yes, but I would be opposing those people just for a matter of a few minutes. Be patient. Now they'll take you away. I hope that it will all come to nothing, and that you will soon return to your families. Goodbye; rather, see you again. Cheer up!"

A few minutes later the federal agents came to get us. They were agitated. Why? They handcuffed us two by two and lined us up. I was with a young man from the Romagna who had been in the United States only a few months, and who had a pretty little wife and a sweet baby. He knew a few phrases of bad English, and had a confused idea of their meaning. He was an apprentice weaver by day and a typesetter by night. He was small of stature, lively, and talked a lot, too much, but since he had nothing in his mind but an inexhaustible reservoir of jokes, not all decent, he couldn't talk about anything else. He was always laughing. He was so empty-headed that his friends called him a sucker. And he laughed at it. Even that day, he had not lost his stupid good humor, for, knowing that he was innocent of any possible or imaginable crime, he was convinced that within a few hours he would be freed and would be able to recount to one and all his extraordinary adventure in America.

My left wrist was bound to his right by a handcuff, and we were made to leave by a rear door of the building, which opened into a courtyard. There the agents stopped us; they moved my companion in chains a step away, making our arms straighten, and leaving me to face the lens of a camera. An agent ordered me to take off my hat. I refused.

When this function was over, which all great personages must submit to today, we were put on a police bus, with two federal agents and four uniformed local policemen, and the bus departed, bell ringing.

At the sound of that bell, our wives, followed by the crowd, ran to greet us, but they were stopped by a line of police, who were armed with heavy clubs, because they were afraid of a rebellion. I and my companion scrutinized the crowd, but it was so dense and fluctuating that it was impossible to see our wives.

It was only a few blocks from where we were to the train station. All along the way the sidewalks were lined with people, who hailed us waving caps and handkerchiefs. A policeman said to a federal agent, "You see? We told you that public opinion is with them. You wanted to put on this show because you don't know the place."

My companion in misfortune, happy in his ignorance, began waving his left hand in response to the crowd, and cried, "Goodbye! Goodbye!"

One could imagine oneself a truly important person at that moment. One of the federal agents, less restrained than the others, shouted at him: "Shut up!" and he, drunk on his quarter of an hour of sudden popularity, shouted back at him: "Shut up you!"

The agent became furious and quickly landed a punch across his face. Not satisfied with that, he pulled out a blackjack and was about to strike the unfortunate gusher of jokes, not all decent, when a policeman grabbed him by the wrist saying: "You damn fool, you want to get us lynched?"

The agent remembered the crowd, put the blackjack back in his pocket, and giving the prisoner a look like an angry hyena said: "When we get to the island I'll kill you."

The poor man didn't understand, but when I translated the threat into Italian, the color drained from his face, he bent his head, and remained silent.

When we arrived at the train station, the agents wouldn't let us go in because the waiting room was extremely crowded. They backed us up against a wall, under the overhang of the roof, and planted themselves in front of us, so that no one could get near us. Behind us was a window that opened into the waiting room. I looked through the glass and saw that people were thronging to see us. One man had a folded newspaper in his hand, and I could read some bits of the large-type headline: "Arrest . . . Deport . . ." Without a doubt, that newspaper was referring to us. The man understood my wish and unfolded the first page. I read the giant red letters of the headline:

"The king of the anarchists arrested with twenty of his followers—he is to be expelled from the United States."

A subhead in black:

"For eighteen years he has escaped the police searches."

Another, in italic:

"Arms, hand grenades, and dynamite confiscated from his house."

The king of the anarchists, according to the paper, was me!

And prominently displayed was the picture of an ugly mug in a beret, with no collar, who surely had been dug up in the depths of the Bowery, and the paper was passing him off as me.

After about ten minutes the other detainees arrived on foot and were herded under the roof.

I knew that in America reporters took special courses in journalism at the university, where they studied the best means for arousing the morbid curiosity of readers. But I had never imagined that their impudence had no limits. The mob was looking for a human beast surrounded by its terrifying followers and was finding neither the one nor the others. It saw some well-dressed people, with a very civilized appearance, handcuffed.

What a disappointment!

Suddenly there was a scuffle. I saw Grandi's wife, a small woman; Pietro Baldisserotti's wife, tall and robust, with big muscles; and the woman who had brought cigars for her husband and cigarettes for Joe Termini struggling with the federal agents. The three women wanted to break through the police cordon to get to us; they seemed to have lost their senses. They must have suffered mightily to abandon themselves to that open, irresistible rebellion. More than eight hours on the sidewalk in six-degree-below-zero weather! And all they wanted was to be near their husbands for a few moments and say some words of comfort. The crowd expressed its sympathy for those poor women by hurling taunting remarks and cutting insults at the agents. These put up with it, but they did not dare to react with violence.

Finally one of them took out a blackjack.

For those who do not know it, this insidious weapon is a ball of lead tied to the end of a strip of flexible leather. The law strictly prohibits the use of this weapon, even for the police, but there are none who do not carry one openly.

The agent, obviously annoyed, threatened the wife of Baldisserotti, and now the women became furious. But they were three against a group of strong men, armed with every weapon, including the most powerful: the certainty of going unpunished.

The crowd began to shout; one soul, a little bolder than the others, raised his fists at the agents. Then a detective sergeant from Paterson, a certain Billy Hughes, known for his great courage, rushed over to me.

"Mr. Caminita, tell your friends to urge their wives to be patient. What's going to happen if the federal agents get out their automatics?"

"If you let them come through, everything will work out for the best."

"But the agents have explicit orders. I'm afraid there will be a bloodbath."

"You ask them, in our name, to submit for the sake of their husbands."

The sergeant hurried off to communicate our request, and did so in such a way that the women could see us. We made them a sign to calm down, showing them our handcuffed wrists to indicate that we could not give them any help. They understood. Mrs. Grandi called to us, in English, so that the agents could understand: "We wish to go into the station to buy tickets, what right have these brutes to keep us out."

An Italian American detective from Paterson, De Luccia, also helped to soothe them.

The police officers had a lot of trouble trying to pacify some men who were threatening to start a fight.

Finally some calm was restored.

My eyes sought my wife. I saw her. We smiled at each other. And we continued to smile; but suddenly she couldn't keep up the effort to control herself. She hid her face in a handkerchief.

Knowing that she was so ill, I felt that exposing herself to the intense cold was a suicide in disguise.

The Paterson police began to criticize the federal agents, calling them agents provocateurs.

"It's a needless cruelty," said one.

"It's a stupid put-on," the detective sergeant concluded.

Finally the train arrived. We exchanged looks and smiles with our families, and we departed.

During the trip—an hour—my companion, the cheerful young fellow whom his friends called by a name that I cannot transcribe, was cheerful no longer. He glanced sidelong at the agent who had threatened to kill him as soon as we arrived at the island the way a dog looks from under the table at his master who he expects is going to beat him. He didn't dare to speak. Finally he said to me in a low voice, and without turning his head:

"When we get to the island, that big ape is going to get me, right?"

"I don't think so."

"Oh, yes he's going to give me a thrashing. How he's keeping an eye on me! But I didn't mean to offend him. I don't know myself why I told him to shut up himself. Out of the damn habit of always saying 'Shut up yourself' when people tell me to be quiet."

For the entire journey he did nothing but annoy me with his whining.

When we arrived in New York, the agents lined us up and walked us down to South Ferry. People stopped to stare at us, thinking perhaps that we were, at the least, a gang of bandits captured in the wild West.

The pavement was covered with ice, and in order to keep from slipping we had to perform miracles of balance, each tugging on the other's wrist. The handcuffs stuck to our skin like icicles. My hands were frozen. My gloves were of no use. I was afraid that the tips of my ears would freeze, and every so often I rubbed them with my free hand. The agents cursed the cold and took it out on us.

That march of a mile and a quarter was endless. When we boarded the warm ferry boat, it seemed to us we were in paradise.

The boat set off, and during the crossing I watched, heartsick, as New York receded; New York, the great, immense, beautiful metropolis, where I had enjoyed so much and suffered so much; New York, that I loved the way one loves the city of one's birth!

As we approached Ellis Island, I saw through the window the huge, beautiful, proud statue of Liberty that stands near the Island of Tears, and there came to mind the words of Madame Roland, uttered on the gallows, as she looked at the statue of Liberty standing before her.

HENRY ROTH

The literary reputation of Henry Roth (1906–1995) rests almost entirely on *Call It Sleep*, the semi-autobiographical novel from which the excerpt below is taken. Its prologue describes the last leg of the 1907 journey from Tsymenytsia (at the northeastern extremity of the Austro-Hungarian Empire, now in Ukraine) to the United States by the author's stand-in, David Schearl, and his mother. The book narrates the life as well as the psychological and spiritual development of a child of Jewish immigrants growing up in New York City, and marks an important transition in Jewish-American immigrant writing from the gritty naturalism of Abraham Cahan and Anzia Yezierska to the more introspective works of Saul Bellow and Philip Roth. *Call It Sleep* was received favorably upon its publication in 1934 but soon fell into obscurity until 1964, when a paperback reprint received a glowing encomium by Irving Howe on the front page of the *New York Times Book Review*. The novel became a national bestseller. In the interim Roth had worked, with varying degrees of enthusiasm, as a teacher, precision metal grinder, waterfowl farmer, and psychiatric aide. Now, with the financial independence afforded by a grant from the National Institute of Arts and Letters, he and his wife, Muriel, were able to travel extensively and move from their Maine farm to Albuquerque, New Mexico. Here he finished his last work—*Mercy of a Rude Stream*—just before he died.

from

Call It Sleep

PROLOGUE

*(I pray thee ask no questions
this is that Golden Land)*

T he small white steamer, Peter Stuyvesant, that delivered the immigrants from the stench and throb of the steerage to the stench and the throb of New York tenements, rolled slightly on the water beside the stone quay in the lee of the weathered barracks and new brick buildings of Ellis Island. Her skipper was waiting for the last of the officials, laborers and guards to embark upon her before he cast off and started for Manhattan. Since this was Saturday afternoon and this the last trip she would make for the week-end, those left behind might have to stay over till Monday. Her whistle bellowed its hoarse warning. A few figures in overalls sauntered from the high doors of the immigration quarters and down the grey pavement that led to the dock.

It was May of the year 1907, the year that was destined to bring the greatest number of immigrants to the shores of the United States. All that day, as on all the days since spring began, her decks had been thronged by hundreds upon hundreds of foreigners, natives from almost every land in the world, the joweled close-cropped Teuton, the full-bearded Russian, the scraggly-whiskered Jew, and among them Slovack peasants with docile faces, smooth-cheeked and swarthy Armenians, pimply Greeks, Danes with wrinkled eyelids. All day her decks had been colorful, a matrix of the vivid costumes of other lands, the speckled green-and-yellow aprons, the flowered kerchief, embroidered homespun, the silver-braided sheepskin vest, the gaudy scarfs, yellow boots, fur caps, caftans, dull gabardines. All day the guttural, the high-pitched voices, the astonished cries, the gasps of wonder, reiterations of gladness had risen from her decks in a motley billow of sound. But now her decks were empty, quiet, spreading out under the sunlight almost as if the warm boards were relaxing from the strain and the pressure of the myriads of feet. All those steerage passengers of the ships that had docked that day who were permitted to enter had already entered—except two, a woman and a young child she carried in her arms. They had just come aboard escorted by a man.

About the appearance of these late comers there was very little that was unusual. The man had evidently spent some time in America and was now bringing his wife and child over from the other side. It might have been thought that he had spent most of his time in lower New York, for he paid only the scantest attention to the Statue of Liberty or to the city rising from the water or to the bridges spanning the East River—or perhaps he was merely too agitated to waste much time on these wonders. His clothes were the ordinary clothes the ordinary New Yorker wore in that period—sober and dull. A black derby accentuated the sharpness and sedentary pallor of his face; a jacket, loose on his tall spare frame, buttoned up in a V close to the throat; and above the V a tightly-knotted black tie was mounted in the groove of a high starched collar. As for his wife, one guessed that she was a European more by the timid wondering look in her eyes as she gazed from her husband to the harbor, than by her clothes. For her clothes were American— a black skirt, a white shirt-waist and a black jacket. Obviously her husband had either taken the precaution of sending them to her while she was still in Europe or had brought them with him to Ellis Island where she had slipped them on before she left.

Only the small child in her arms wore a distinctly foreign costume, an impression one got chiefly from the odd, outlandish, blue straw hat on his head with its polka dot ribbons of the same color dangling over each shoulder.

Except for this hat, had the three newcomers been in a crowd, no one probably, could have singled out the woman and child as newly arrived immigrants. They carried no sheets tied up in huge bundles, no bulky wicker baskets, no prized feather beds, no boxes of delicacies, sausages, virgin-olive oils, rare cheeses; the large black satchel beside them was their only luggage. But despite this, despite their even less than commonplace appearance, the two overalled men, sprawled out and smoking cigarettes in the stern, eyed them curiously. And the old peddler woman, sitting with basket of oranges on knee, continually squinted her weak eyes in their direction.

The truth was there was something quite untypical about their behavior. The old peddler woman on the bench and the overalled men in the stern had seen enough husbands meeting their wives and children after a long absence to know how such people ought to behave. The most volatile races, such as the Italians, often danced for joy, whirled each other around, pirouetted in an ecstasy; Swedes sometimes just looked at each other, breathing through open mouths like a panting dog; Jews wept, jabbered, almost put each other's eyes out with the recklessness of their darting gestures; Poles roared and gripped each other at arm's length as though they meant to tear a handful of flesh; and after one pecking kiss, the English might be seen gravitating toward, but never achieving an embrace. But these two stood silent, apart; the man staring with aloof, offended eyes grimly down at the water—or if he turned his face toward his wife at all, it was only to glare in harsh contempt at the blue straw hat worn by the child in her arms, and then his hostile eyes would sweep about the deck to see if anyone else were observing them. And his wife beside him regarding him uneasily, appealingly. And the child against her breast looking from one to the other with watchful, frightened eyes. Altogether it was a very curious meeting.

They had been standing in this strange and silent manner for several minutes, when the woman, as if driven by the strain into action, tried to smile, and touching her husband's arm said timidly, "And this is the Golden Land." She spoke in Yiddish.

The man grunted, but made no answer.

She took a breath as if taking courage, and tremulously, "I'm sorry, Albert, I was so stupid." She paused waiting for some flicker of unbending, some word, which never came. "But you look so lean, Albert, so haggard. And your mustache—you've shaved."

His brusque glance stabbed and withdrew. "Even so."

"You must have suffered in this land." She continued gentle despite his rebuke. "You never wrote me. You're thin. Ach! Then here in the new land is the same old poverty. You've gone without food. I can see it. You've changed."

"Well that don't matter," he snapped, ignoring her sympathy. "It's no excuse for your not recognizing me. Who else would call for you? Do you know anyone else in this land?"

"No," placatingly. "But I was so frightened, Albert. Listen to me. I was so bewildered, and that long waiting there in that vast room since morning. Oh, that horrible waiting! I saw them all go, one after the other. The shoemaker and his wife. The coppersmith and his children from Strij. All those on the Kaiserin Viktoria. But I—I remained. To-morrow will be Sunday. They told me no one could come to fetch me. What if they sent me back? I was frantic!"

"Are you blaming me?" His voice was dangerous.

"No! No! Of course not Albert! I was just explaining."

"Well then let me explain," he said curtly. "I did what I could. I took the day off from the shop. I called that cursed Hamburg-American Line four times. And each time they told me you weren't on board."

"They didn't have any more third-class passage, so I had to take the steerage—"

"Yes, now I know. That's all very well. That couldn't be helped. I came here anyway. The last boat. And what do you do? You refused to recognize me. You don't know me." He dropped his elbows down on the rail, averted his angry face. "That's the greeting I get."

"I'm sorry, Albert," she stroked his arm humbly. "I'm sorry."

"And as if those blue-coated mongrels in there weren't mocking me enough, you give them that brat's right age. Didn't I write you to say seventeen months because it would save the half fare! Didn't you hear me inside when I told them?"

"How could I, Albert?" she protested. "How could I? You were on the other side of that—that cage."

"Well why didn't you say seventeen months anyway? Look!" he pointed to several blue-coated officials who came hurrying out of a doorway out of the immigration quarters. "There they are." An ominous pride dragged at his voice. "If he's among them, that one who questioned me so much, I could speak to him if he came up here."

"Don't bother with him, Albert," she exclaimed uneasily. "Please, Albert! What have you against him? He couldn't help it. It's his work."

"Is it?" His eyes followed with unswerving deliberation the blue-coats as they neared the boat. "Well he didn't have to do it so well."

"And after all, I did lie to him, Albert," she said hurriedly trying to distract him.

"The truth is you didn't," he snapped, turning his anger against her. "You made your first lie plain by telling the truth afterward. And made a laughing-stock of me!"

"I didn't know what to do." She picked despairingly at the wire grill beneath the rail. "In Hamburg the doctor laughed at me when I said seventeen months. He's so big. He was big when he was born." She smiled, the worried look on her face vanishing momentarily as she stroked her son's cheek. "Won't you speak to your father, David, beloved?"

The child merely ducked his head behind his mother.

His father stared at him, shifted his gaze and glared down at the officials, and then, as though perplexity had crossed his mind he frowned absently. "How old did he say he was?"

"The doctor? Over two years—and as I say he laughed."

"Well what did he enter?"

"Seventeen months—I told you."

"Then why didn't you tell them seventeen—" He broke off, shrugged violently. "Baah! You need more strength in this land." He paused, eyed her intently and then frowned suddenly. "Did you bring his birth certificate?"

"Why—" She seemed confused. "It may be in the trunk—there on the ship. I don't know. Perhaps I left it behind." Her hand wandered uncertainly to her lips. "I don't know. Is it important? I never thought of it. But surely father could send it. We need only write."

"Hmm! Well, put him down." His head jerked brusquely toward the child. "You don't need to carry him all the way. He's big enough to stand on his own feet."

She hesitated, and then reluctantly set the child down on the deck. Scared, unsteady, the little one edged over to the side opposite his father, and hidden by his mother, clung to her skirt.

"Well, it's all over now." She attempted to be cheerful. "It's all behind us now, isn't it, Albert? Whatever mistakes I made don't really matter any more. Do they?"

"A fine taste of what lies before me!" He turned his back on her and leaned morosely against the rail. "A fine taste!"

They were silent. On the dock below, the brown hawsers had been slipped over the mooring posts, and the men on the lower deck now dragged them dripping from the water. Bells clanged. The ship throbbed. Startled by the hoarse bellow of her whistle, the gulls wheeling before her prow rose with slight creaking cry from the green water, and as she churned away from the stone quay skimmed across her path on indolent, scimitar wing. Behind the ship the white wake that stretched to Ellis Island grew longer, raveling wanly into melon-green. On one side curved the low drab Jersey coast-line, the spars and masts on the waterfront fringing the sky; on the other side was Brooklyn, flat, water-towered; the horns of the harbor. And before them, rising on her high pedestal from the scaling swarmy brilliance of sunlit water to the west, Liberty. The spinning disk of the late afternoon sun slanted behind her, and to those on board who gazed, her features were charred with shadow, her depths exhausted, her masses ironed to one single plane. Against the luminous sky the rays of her halo were spikes of darkness roweling the air; shadow flattened the torch she bore to a black cross against flawless light—the blackened hilt of a broken sword. Liberty. The child and his mother stared again at the massive figure in wonder.

The ship curved around in a long arc toward Manhattan, her bow sweeping past Brooklyn and the bridges whose cables and pillars superimposed by distance, spanned the East River in diaphanous and rigid waves. The western wind that raked the harbor into brilliant clods blew fresh and clear—a salt tang in the lull of its veerings. It whipped the polka-dot ribbons on the child's hat straight out behind him. They caught his father's eye.

"Where did you find that crown?"

Startled by his sudden question his wife looked down. "That? That was Maria's parting gift. The old nurse. She bought it herself and then sewed the ribbons on. You don't think it's pretty?"

"Pretty? Do you still ask?" His lean jaws hardly moved as he spoke. "Can't you see that those idiots lying back there are watching us already? They're mocking us! What will the others do on the train? He looks like a clown in it. He's the cause of all this trouble anyway!"

The harsh voice, the wrathful glare, the hand flung toward the child frightened him. Without knowing the cause, he knew that the stranger's anger was directed at himself. He burst into tears and pressed closer to his mother.

"Quiet!" the voice above him snapped.

Cowering, the child wept all the louder.

"Hush, darling!" His mother's protecting hands settled on his shoulders.

"Just when we're about to land!" her husband said furiously. "He begins this! This howling! And now we'll have it all the way home, I suppose! Quiet! You hear?"

"It's you who are frightening him, Albert!" she protested.

"Am I? Well, let him be quiet. And take that straw gear off his head."

"But Albert, it's cool here."

"Will you take that off when I—" A snarl choked whatever else he would have uttered. While his wife looked on aghast, his long fingers scooped the hat from the child's head. The next instant it was sailing over the ship's side to the green waters below. The overalled men in the stern grinned at each other. The old orange-peddler shook her head and clucked.

"Albert!" his wife caught her breath. "How could you?"

"I could!" he rapped out. "You should have left it behind!" His teeth clicked, and he glared about the deck.

She lifted the sobbing child to her breast, pressed him against her. With a vacant stunned expression, her gaze wandered from the grim smouldering face of her husband to the stern of the ship. In the silvery-green wake that curved trumpet-wise through the water, the blue hat still bobbed and rolled, ribbon stretched out on the waves. Tears sprang to her eyes. She brushed them away quickly, shook her head as if shaking off the memory, and looked toward the bow. Before her the grimy cupolas and towering square walls of the city loomed up. Above the jagged roof tops, the white smoke, whitened and suffused by the slanting sun, faded into the slots and wedges of the sky. She pressed her brow against her child's, hushed him with whispers. This was that vast incredible land, the land of freedom, of immense opportunity, that Golden Land. Again she tried to smile.

"Albert," she said timidly, "Albert."

"Hm?"

"Gehen vir voinen du? In Nev York?"

"Nein. Bronzeville. Ich hud dir schoin geschriben."

She nodded uncertainly, sighed . . .

Screws threshing, backing water, the Peter Stuyvesant neared her dock— drifting slowly and with canceled momentum as if reluctant.

MOYSHE-LEYB HALPERN

Born in Zlotshev in Galicia (in what is now Poland), Moyshe-Leyb Halpern (1886–1932) had a traditional Jewish upbringing and early education but later studied in secular Polish schools. At the age of 12 he was taken to Vienna to study commercial art but in 1907 returned home to become a writer. A year later he immigrated to the United States. His passion for poetry led him to connect with Yiddish writers in New York City, where he soon emerged as one of the better known literary modernists of the Di Yunge ("the young ones") movement. His poetry collections include *In nyu york* (*In New York*, 1919) and *Di goldene pave* (*The Golden Peacock*, 1924). He made his living as a freelance journalist and led an itinerant life, moving from Detroit to Cleveland, from Los Angeles to Boston. The poem here, taken from *In nyu york*, offers a grim picture of the immigrant experience, concluding somberly with "A gallows for me in the Golden Land." Translator Kathryn Hellerstein notes that in Yiddish the word "golden" means "endearing, warm, good" as well as "wealthy, valuable, or promising."

In the Golden Land

—Mama, why, oh, why do you hold
    That everything here is changed into gold,
    That gold is made from iron and blood,
    Night and day, from iron and blood?

—My son, you cannot hide from a mother—
    Mama finds out, mama feels, with a shudder:
    You don't have enough meat or bread—
    In the Golden Land you aren't properly fed.

—Mama, does it come into your head,
That people here throw away bread?
That on an overgenerous earth,
Things may lose their golden worth?

—I don't know, son, but my heart cries—
From here your face looks dark as the night
And your eyelids fall shut drowsily
Like the eyes of a man dying for sleep.

—Mama, surely you have heard
Of trains, that, racing under the earth,
Drag us from bed at the break of dawn
And late at night bring us home again.

—Son, I don't know. It hurts deep and high.
Just yesterday when we said good-bye
You were healthy, young, and strong—
I need to see now that nothing's wrong.

—Mama, why do you suck my blood?
You're hurting me, and it does no good.
Why are you crying? Do you see at all
What I envision—a high dark wall?

—Why shouldn't I cry over you, my son?
God and mother both forgotten!
Now your own life is a wall that stands
Blocking your way in the Golden Land.

—Mama, you're right. We are far and gone.
A golden chain . . . and an iron chain . . .
For you, in heaven, a golden throne,
A gallows for me in the Golden Land.

ERNESTO GALARZA

Ernesto Galarza (1905–1984), scholar, writer, poet, and activist, fled
Mexico with his family just as the Mexican revolution was breaking out
in 1910. By 1911 he had begun his schooling in Sacramento, California,
and by the time he was eight his command of English allowed him to act
as an interpreter for older *chicanos*. After graduating from Occidental
College on a full scholarship in 1927, he began master's work at Stanford
University followed by doctoral study at Columbia University. From 1936
to 1947 he served first as education specialist and then as chief of the
labor section for the Pan-American Union in Washington, D.C. For the
next 13 years he worked as field organizer for both the National Farm
Labor Union and the National Agricultural Workers Union; he was particularly concerned with the abuses of the *bracero* or day-laborer system,
whereby farm owners were able to depress wages and undermine farm
labor unions. After 1960 Galarza devoted his time to writing, but never
lost touch with the labor movement, working as a consultant for government agencies, charities, and political organizations. His autobiography,
Barrio Boy, was published in 1971.

from
Barrio Boy

I n a corner of the musty lobby of the Hotel Español, we waited until it was
our turn to talk with the manager. The place was filled with people stack-
ing and moving luggage, some talking in Spanish, others in English and
other strange tongues. The manager wore a long white apron and a blue beret
and spoke *gachupín* like the Spaniards of Mazatlán. He led us to a back room,
took our baggage claim check, showed us the dining room and returned later
with our tin trunk.

The hotel was a prison, even more confining than the alley in Tucson. We were frightened by the traffic of mule teams, wagons, and the honking auto-mobiles that passed by continuously. From our view in the lobby the street was a jumble. Up and down from the doorway of the hotel all we could see were shops and stores, warehouses and saloons, hotels and restaurants, few ladies and no children. Sacramento, I decided, was an ugly place, not like the vineyards and the eucalyptus trees with pastel colored trunks we had seen from the train.

For breakfast in the hotel kitchen we drank coffee with buttered hard rolls. Lunch was not served and since we were afraid to venture into the street, we did not eat. Supper was served in a room without windows, at a long table crowded with people who lived in the hotel and outsiders who came for meals. It was served by the manager, who was also the cook. Up and down both sides of the table he poured boiling soup out of a kettle into our plates, forked out pieces of meat, sawed thick chunks of bread from loaves as long as my arm, and poured wine. It was a noisy table, with loud talk and the clatter of dishes and the burly *gachupines* slurping soup. But it was a show to us, funny and very un-Mexican.

In the corner of the lobby nearest the street window we sat for hours on a wooden bench, watching the pedestrians closely. At last we saw the two we were waiting for. Gustavo and José passed by the window, looked in, and stepped inside. With a shout I charged them and wedged myself between their legs, where I held tight. The three exchanged greetings.

"How are you, sister?"

"Very well. How have things been with you?"

After a little weeping by Doña Henriqueta we stood and looked at one another. My uncles were dressed in blue bib overalls and work jackets of the same stuff with brass buttons, and caps. Gustavo was the shorter of the two, chunky and thick-shouldered. Jose was thin all over—neck, arms, fingers, and face.

They paid our hotel bill and we gathered our things. We stepped into the cold drizzly street, my uncles carrying the suitcases and tin trunk and holding me by the hands. With the two of them on either side and Doña Hen-riqueta behind me I trotted confidently through the scurrying crowd on the sidewalks, the rumbling drays and the honking automobiles. I was beginning to lose my fear of Sacramento.

It was a short walk from the hotel to the house where we turned in, the tallest I had ever seen. A wide wooden stairway went up from the sidewalk to a porch on the second story, and above that another floor, and still higher a gable as wide as the house decorated with carvings and fretwork. The porch balustrade was in the same gingerbread style of lattice work and the wooden imitation of a fringe between the round pillars. We walked up the stairway and the three of us waited while José went inside.

He came back with the landlady. She was certainly a gringo lady—two heads taller than Gustavo, twice as wide as José, square-jawed, rosy-faced, a thin nose with a small bulge on the end and like all Americans, with rather large feet. She had a way of blinking when she smiled at us.

Standing as straight as the posts of the porch and holding her shoulders square and straight across she seemed to me more like a general than a lady.

Mostly with blinks and hand motions and a great many ceremonial smiles, we were introduced to Mrs. Dodson, who led us into the house, down some narrow, dark stairs and to the back of the first floor where she left us in our new apartment.

It consisted of one large room, a kitchen and a closet that had been a bathroom from which all the fixtures had been removed except the bathtub. Directly behind the kitchen was a cramped back yard enclosed on three sides by a board fence like all the other American fences I had already seen—dirty gray planks, streaked and cracked. Rising from the yard there was a steep wooden stairway resting on cement blocks. It made a right angle at the second story and turned back toward the house, continuing to the third floor. The stairway had panels on each side and a landing on each floor. From the yard the fire escape looked like a ladder into the wild blue yonder. Since people rarely used it, and the panels made private cubicles of the landings, I discovered that I could use them as private crow's nests from which I could survey the *barrio*'s back yards for blocks around.

The apartment was furnished. In the living room there were three single beds, a clothes closet as high as the ceiling, an oil stove, a round dining table covered with checkered linoleum, a chest of drawers, and some chairs. In the kitchen there was a gas stove on a wooden platform, a table, a bench, and a dish closet next to the sink. A small icebox on the back porch dripped into a rubber tube to the ground through a hole in the floor. The bathtub in the big closet was covered with boards and a mattress on top of them. This was to be my room. It had no windows but an electric cord with a small bulb and a print curtain over the door connecting with the kitchen gave me quarters of my own.

We reached the front door through a long gloomy hall that opened on the street porch, from which we stepped to the sidewalk over a boardwalk. Along one side of the house there was an open corridor between the house and the fence, by which we got to the toilet and bathroom that all the tenants on the first floor used. We were enclosed from the street by a picket fence flanking the stairs, set off by a scraggly peach tree on each side. Because our rooms were dank and cheerless we sat on the porch or stood behind the picket fence, street watching, when the weather permitted. Mrs. Dodson's apartment was on the second floor back, with a door to a side porch from which she could look out over the yard and the street. This was the command post of 418 L Street, our refuge in a strange land.

Since Gustavo and José were off to work on the track early the next morning after our arrival, it was up to us to tidy the apartment and get the household into shape. As usual when we moved into a new place, we dusted and swept and scrubbed floors, doors, woodwork, windows, and every piece of furniture. Mrs. Dodson provided us with cans of a white powder that was sprinkled on everything that needed cleaning—cans with the picture of an old lady dressed in wooden shoes, a swinging skirt, and white bonnet.

The Americans, we discovered, put practically everything in cans on which they pasted fascinating labels, like *La Vieja Dotch Klen-ser*. Doña Henriqueta admired the bright colors and the delicious pictures of fruits and vegetables. We spelled and sounded out as well as we could the names of unfamiliar foods, like corn flakes and Karo syrup. On the kitchen shelf we arranged and rearranged the boxes and tins, with their displays of ingenious designs and colors, grateful that the Americans used pictures we knew to explain words that we didn't.

Once the routine of the family was well started, my mother and I began to take short walks to get our bearings. It was half a block in one direction to the lumber yard and the grocery store; half a block in the other to the saloon and the Japanese motion picture theater. In between were the tent and awning shop, a Chinese restaurant, a secondhand store, and several houses like our own. We noted by the numbers on the posts at the corners that we lived between 4th and 5th streets on L.

Once we could fix a course from these signs up and down and across town we explored farther. On Sixth near K there was the Lyric Theater with a sign that we easily translated into Lírico. It was next to a handsome red stone house with high turrets, like a castle. Navigating by these key points and following the rows of towering elms along L Street, one by one we found the post office on 7th and K; the cathedral, four blocks farther east; and the state capitol with its golden dome.

It wasn't long before we ventured on walks around Capitol Park which reminded me of the charm and the serenity of the Alameda in Tepic. In some fashion Mrs. Dodson had got over to us that the capitol was the house of the government. To us it became El Capitolio or, as more formally, the Palacio de Gobierno. Through the park we walked into the building itself, staring spellbound at the marble statue of Queen Isabel and Christopher Columbus. It was awesome, standing in the presence of that gigantic admiral, the one who had discovered America and Mexico and Jalcocotán, as Doña Henriqueta assured me.

After we had thoroughly learned our way around in the daytime we found signs that did not fail us at night. From the window of the projection room of the Lyric Theater a brilliant purple light shone after dark. A snake of electric lights kept whipping round and round a sign over the Albert Elkus store. K Street on both sides was a double row of bright show windows that led up to the Land Hotel and back to Breuner's, thence down one block to the lumber yard, the grocery store, and our house. We had no fear of getting lost.

These were the boundaries of the lower part of town, for that was what everyone called the section of the city between Fifth Street and the river and from the railway yards to the Y-street levee. Nobody ever mentioned an upper part of town; at least, no one could see the difference because the whole city was built on level land. We were not lower topographically, but in other ways that distinguished between Them, the uppers, and Us, the lowers. Lower Sacramento was the quarter that people who made money moved away from. Those of us who lived in it stayed there because our problem was to make a living and not to make money. A long while back, Mr. Howard, the business agent of the union told me, there had been stores and shops, fancy residences, and smart hotels in this neighborhood. The crippled old gentleman who lived in the next room down the hall from us, explained to me that our house, like the others in the neighborhood, had been the home of rich people who had stables in the back yards, with back entrances by way of the alleys. Mr. Hansen, the Dutch carpenter, had helped build such residences. When the owners moved uptown, the back yards had been fenced off and subdivided, and small rental cottages had been built in the alleys in place of the stables. Handsome private homes were turned into flophouses for men who stayed one night, hotels for working people, and rooming houses, like ours.

Among the saloons, pool halls, lunch counters, pawnshops, and poker parlors was skid row, where drunk men with black eyes and unshaven faces lay down in the alleys to sleep.

The lower quarter was not exclusively a Mexican *barrio* but a mix of many nationalities. Between L and N Streets two blocks from us, the Japanese had taken over. Their homes were in the alleys behind shops, which they advertised with signs covered with black scribbles. The women walked on the street in kimonos, wooden sandals, and white stockings, carrying neat black bundles on their backs and wearing their hair in puffs with long ivory needles stuck through them. When they met they bowed, walked a couple of steps, and turned and bowed again, repeating this several times. They carried babies on their backs, not in their arms, never laughed or went into the saloons. On Sundays the men sat in front of their shops, dressed in gowns, like priests.

Chinatown was on the other side of K Street, toward the Southern Pacific shops. Our houses were old, but those in which the Chinese kept stores, laundries, and restaurants were older still. In black jackets and skullcaps the older merchants smoked long pipes with a tiny brass cup on the end. In their dusty store windows there was always the same assortment of tea packages, rice bowls, saucers, and pots decorated with blue temples and dragons.

In the hotels and rooming houses scattered about the *barrio* the Filipino farm workers, riverboat stewards, and houseboys made their homes. Like the Mexicans they had their own poolhalls, which they called clubs. Hindus from the rice and fruit country north of the city stayed in the rooming houses when they were in town, keeping to themselves. The Portuguese and Italian families gathered in their own neighborhoods along Fourth and Fifth Streets southward toward the Y-street levee. The Poles, Yugo-Slavs, and Koreans, too few to take over any particular part of it, were scattered throughout the *barrio*. Black men drifted in and out of town, working the waterfront. It was a kaleidoscope of colors and languages and customs that surprised and absorbed me at every turn.

Although we, the foreigners, made up the majority of the population of that quarter of Sacramento, the Americans had by no means given it up to us. Not all of them had moved above Fifth Street as the *barrio* became more crowded. The bartenders, the rent collectors, the insurance salesmen, the mates on the river boats, the landladies, and most importantly, the police— these were all gringos. So were the craftsmen, like the barbers and printers, who did not move their shops uptown as the city grew. The teachers of our one public school were all Americans. On skid row we rarely saw a drunk wino who was not a gringo. The operators of the pawnshops and second-hand stores were white and mostly Jewish.

For the Mexicans the barrio was a colony of refugees. We came to know families from Chihuahua, Sonora, Jalisco, and Durango. Some had come to the United States even before the revolution, living in Texas before migrating to California. Like ourselves, our Mexican neighbors had come this far moving step by step, working and waiting, as if they were feeling their way up a ladder. They talked of relatives who had been left behind in Mexico, or in some far-off city like Los Angeles or San Diego. From whatever place they had come, and however short or long the time they had lived in the United States, together they formed the *colonia mexicana*. In the years between our arrival and the First World War, the *colonia* grew and spilled out from the lower part of town. Some families moved into the alley shacks east of the Southern Pacific tracks, close to the canneries and warehouses and across the river among the orchards and rice mills.

The *colonia* was like a sponge that was beginning to leak along the edges, squeezed between the levee, the railroad tracks, and the river front. But it wasn't squeezed dry, because it kept filling with newcomers who found families who took in boarders: basements, alleys, shanties, run-down rooming houses and flop joints where they could live.

Crowded as it was, the *colonia* found a place for these *chicanos*, the name by which we called an unskilled worker born in Mexico and just arrived in the United States. The *chicanos* were fond of identifying themselves by saying they had just arrived from *el macizo*, by which they meant the solid Mexican homeland, the good native earth. Although they spoke of *el macizo* like homesick persons, they didn't go back. They remained, as they said of themselves, *pura raza*. So it happened that José and Gustavo would bring home for a meal and for conversation workingmen who were *chicanos* fresh from *el macizo* and like ourselves, *pura raza*. Like us, they had come straight to the *barrio* where they could order a meal, buy a pair of overalls, and look for work in Spanish. They brought us vague news about the revolution, in which many of them had fought as *villistas*, *huertistas*, *maderistas*, or *zapatistas*. As an old *maderista*, I imagined our *chicano* guests as battle-tested revolutionaries, like myself.

As poor refugees, their first concern was to find a place to sleep, then to eat and find work. In the *barrio* they were most likely to find all three, for not knowing English, they needed something that was even more urgent than a room, a meal, or a job, and that was information in a language they could understand. This information had to be picked up in bits and pieces—from families like ours, from the conversation groups in the poolrooms and the saloons.

Beds and meals, if the newcomers had no money at all, were provided—in one way or another—on trust, until the new *chicano* found a job. On trust and not on credit, for trust was something between people who had plenty of nothing, and credit was between people who had something of plenty. It was not charity or social welfare but something my mother called *asistencia*, a helping given and received on trust, to be repaid because those who had given it were themselves in need of what they had given. *Chicanos* who had found work on farms or in railroad camps came back to pay us a few dollars for *asistencia* we had provided weeks or months before.

Because the *barrio* was a grapevine of job information, the transient *chicanos* were able to find work and repay their obligations. The password of the barrio was *trabajo* and the community was divided in two—the many who were looking for it and the few who had it to offer. Pickers, foremen, contractors, drivers, field hands, pick and shovel men on the railroad and in construction came back to the *barrio* when work was slack, to tell one another of the places they had been, the kind of *patrón* they had, the wages paid, the food, the living quarters, and other important details. Along Second Street, labor recruiters hung blackboards on their shop fronts, scrawling in chalk offers of work. The grapevine was a mesh of rumors and gossip, and men often walked long distances or paid bus fares or a contractor's fee only to find that the work was over or all the jobs were filled. Even the chalked signs could not always be relied on. Yet the search for *trabajo*, or the *chanza*, as we also called it, went on because it had to.

We in the *barrio* considered that there were two kinds of *trabajo*. There were the seasonal jobs, some of them a hundred miles or more from Sacramento. And there were the closer *chanzas* to which you could walk or ride on a bicycle. These were the best ones, in the railway shops, the canneries, the waterfront warehouses, the lumber yards, the produce markets, the brick kilns, and the rice mills. To be able to move from the seasonal jobs to the close-in work was a step up the ladder. Men who had made it passed the word along to their relatives or their friends when there was a *chanza* of this kind.

It was all done by word of mouth, this delicate wiring of the grapevine. The exchange points of the network were the places where men gathered in small groups, apparently to loaf and chat to no purpose. One of these points was our kitchen, where my uncles and their friends sat and talked of *el macizo* and of the revolution but above all of the *chanzas* they had heard of.

There was not only the everlasting talk about *trabajo*, but also the never-ending action of the *barrio* itself. If work was action the *barrio* was where the action was. Every morning a parade of men in oily work clothes and carrying lunch buckets went up Fourth Street toward the railroad shops, and every evening they walked back, grimy and silent. Horse drawn drays with low platforms rumbled up and down our street carrying the goods the city traded in, from kegs of beer to sacks of grain. Within a few blocks of our house there were smithies, hand laundries, a macaroni factory, and all manner of places where wagons and buggies were repaired, horses stabled, bicycles fixed, chickens dressed, clothes washed and ironed, furniture repaired, candy mixed, tents sewed, wine grapes pressed, bottles washed, lumber sawed, suits fitted and tailored, watches and clocks taken apart and put together again, vegetables sorted, railroad cars unloaded, boxcars iced, barges freighted, ice cream cones molded, soda pop bottled, fish scaled, salami stuffed, corn ground for masa, and bread ovened. To those who knew where these were located in the alleys, as I did, the whole *barrio* was an open workshop. The people who worked there came to know you, let you look in at the door, made jokes, and occasionally gave you an odd job.

This was the business district of the *barrio*. Around it and through it moved a constant traffic of drays, carts, bicycles, pushcarts, trucks, and high-wheeled automobiles with black canvas tops and honking horns. On the tailgates of drays and wagons, I nipped rides when I was going home with a gunnysack full of empty beer bottles or my gleanings around the packing sheds.

Once we had work, the next most important thing was to find a place to live we could afford. Ours was a neighborhood of leftover houses. The cheapest rents were in the back quarters of the rooming houses, the basements, and the run-down clapboard rentals in the alleys. Clammy and dank as they were, they were nevertheless one level up from the barns and tents where many of our *chicano* friends lived, or the shanties and lean-to's of the migrants who squatted in the "jungles" along the levees of the Sacramento and the American rivers.

Barrio people, when they first came to town, had no furniture of their own. They rented it with their quarters or bought a piece at a time from the secondhand stores, the *segundas*, where we traded. We cut out the ends of tin cans to make collars and plates for the pipes and floor moldings where the rats had gnawed holes. Stoops and porches that sagged we propped with bricks and fat stones. To plug the drafts around the windows in winter, we cut strips of corrugated cardboard and wedged them into the frames. With squares of cheesecloth neatly cut and sewed to screen doors holes were covered and rents in the wire mesh mended. Such repairs, which landlords never paid any attention to, were made *por mientras*, for the time being or temporarily. It would have been a word equally suitable for the house itself, or for the *barrio*. We lived in run-down places furnished with seconds in a hand-me-down neighborhood all of which were *por mientras*.

We found the Americans as strange in their customs as they probably found us. Immediately we discovered that there were no *mercados* and that when shopping you did not put the groceries in a *chiquihuite*. Instead everything was in cans or in cardboard boxes or each item was put in a brown paper bag. There were neighborhood grocery stores at the corners and some big ones uptown, but no *mercado*. The grocers did not give children a *pilón*, they did not stand at the door and coax you to come in and buy, as they did in Mazatlán. The fruits and vegetables were displayed on counters instead of being piled up on the floor. The stores smelled of fly spray and oiled floors, not of fresh pineapple and limes.

Neither was there a plaza, only parks which had no bandstands, no concerts every Thursday, no Judases exploding on Holy Week, and no promenades of boys going one way and girls the other. There were no parks in the *barrio*; and the ones uptown were cold and rainy in winter, and in summer there was no place to sit except on the grass. When there were celebrations nobody set off rockets in the parks, much less on the street in front of your house to announce to the neighborhood that a wedding or a baptism was taking place. Sacramento did not have a *mercado* and a plaza with the cathedral to one side and the Palacio de Gobierno on another to make it obvious that there and nowhere else was the center of the town.

It was just as puzzling that the Americans did not live in *vecindades*, like our block on Leandro Valle. Even in the alleys, where people knew one another better, the houses were fenced apart, without central courts to wash clothes, talk and play with the other children. Like the city, the Sacramento *barrio* did not have a place which was the middle of things for everyone.

In more personal ways we had to get used to the Americans. They did not listen if you did not speak loudly, as they always did. In the Mexican style, people would know that you were enjoying their jokes tremendously if you merely smiled and shook a little, as if you were trying to swallow your mirth. In the American style there was little difference between a laugh and a roar, and until you got used to them you could hardly tell whether the boisterous Americans were roaring mad or roaring happy.

It was Doña Henriqueta more than Gustavo or José who talked of these oddities and classified them as agreeable or deplorable. It was she also who pointed out the pleasant surprises of the American way. When a box of rolled oats with a picture of red carnations on the side was emptied, there was a plate or a bowl or a cup with blue designs. We ate the strange stuff regularly for breakfast and we soon had a set of the beautiful dishes. Rice and beans we bought in cotton bags of colored prints. The bags were unsewed, washed, ironed, and made into gaily designed towels, napkins, and handkerchiefs. The American stores also gave small green stamps which were pasted in a book to exchange for prizes. We didn't have to run to the corner with the garbage; a collector came for it.

With remarkable fairness and never-ending wonder we kept adding to our list the pleasant and the repulsive in the ways of the Americans. It was my second acculturation.

The older people of the *barrio*, except in those things which they had to do like the Americans because they had no choice, remained Mexican. Their language at home was Spanish. They were continuously taking up collections to pay somebody's funeral expenses or to help someone who had had a serious accident. Cards were sent to you to attend a burial where you would throw a handful of dirt on top of the coffin and listen to tearful speeches at the graveside. At every baptism a new *compadre* and a new *comadre* joined the family circle. New Year greeting cards were exchanged, showing angels and cherubs in bright colors sprinkled with grains of mica so that they glistened like gold dust. At the family parties the huge pot of steaming tamales was still the center of attention, the *atole* served on the side with chunks of brown sugar for sucking and crunching. If the party lasted long enough, someone produced a guitar, the men took over and the singing of *corridos* began.

In the *barrio* there were no individuals who had official titles or who were otherwise recognized by everybody as important people. The reason must have been that there was no place in the public business of the city of Sacramento for the Mexican immigrants. We only rented a corner of the city and as long as we paid the rent on time everything else was decided at City Hall or the County Court House, where Mexicans went only when they were in trouble. Nobody from the *barrio* ever ran for mayor or city councilman. For us the most important public officials were the policemen who walked their beats, stopped fights, and hauled drunks to jail in a paddy wagon we called *La Julia*.

The one institution we had that gave the *colonia* some kind of image was the *Comisión Honorífica*, a committee picked by the Mexican Consul in San Francisco to organize the celebration of the *Cinco de Mayo* and the Sixteenth of September, the anniversaries of the battle of Puebla and the beginning of our War of Independence. These were the two events which stirred everyone in the *barrio*, for what we were celebrating was not only the heroes of Mexico but also the feeling that we were still Mexicans ourselves. On these occasions there was a dance preceded by speeches and a concert. For both the *cinco* and the sixteenth queens were elected to preside over the ceremonies.

Between celebrations neither the politicians uptown nor the *Comisión Honorífica* attended to the daily needs of the *barrio*. This was done by volunteers—the ones who knew enough English to interpret in court, on a visit to the doctor, a call at the county hospital, and who could help make out a postal money order. By the time I had finished the third grade at the Lincoln School I was one of these volunteers. My services were not professional but they were free, except for the IOU's I accumulated from families who always thanked me with "God will pay you for it."

My clients were not *pochos*, Mexicans who had grown up in California, probably had even been born in the United States. They had learned to speak English of sorts and could still speak Spanish, also of sorts. They knew much more about the Americans than we did, and much less about us. The *chicanos* and the *pochos* had certain feelings about one another. Concerning the *pochos*, the *chicanos* suspected that they considered themselves too good for the *barrio* but were not, for some reason, good enough for the Americans. Toward the *chicanos*, the *pochos* acted superior, amused at our confusions but not especially interested in explaining them to us. In our family when I forgot my manners, my mother would ask me if I was turning *pochito*.

Turning *pocho* was a half-step toward turning American. And America was all around us, in and out of the *barrio*. Abruptly we had to forget the ways of shopping in a *mercado* and learn those of shopping in a corner grocery or in a department store. The Americans paid no attention to the Sixteenth of September, but they made a great commotion about the Fourth of July. In Mazatlán Don Salvador had told us, saluting and marching as he talked to our class, that the *Cinco de Mayo* was the most glorious date in human history. The Americans had not even heard about it.

In Tucson, when I had asked my mother again if the Americans were having a revolution, the answer was: "No, but they have good schools, and you are going to one of them." We were by now settled at 418 L Street and the time had come for me to exchange a revolution for an American education.

The two of us walked south on Fifth Street one morning to the corner of

Q Street and turned right. Half of the block was occupied by the Lincoln School. It was a three-story wooden building, with two wings that gave it the shape of a double-T connected by a central hall. It was a new building, painted yellow, with a shingled roof that was not like the red tile of the school in Mazatlán. I noticed other differences, none of them very reassuring.

We walked up the wide staircase hand in hand and through the door, which closed by itself. A mechanical contraption screwed to the top shut it behind us quietly.

Up to this point the adventure of enrolling me in the school had been carefully rehearsed. Mrs. Dodson had told us how to find it and we had circled it several times on our walks. Friends in the *barrio* explained that the director was called a principal, and that it was a lady and not a man. They assured us that there was always a person at the school who could speak Spanish.

Exactly as we had been told, there was a sign on the door in both Spanish and English: "Principal." We crossed the hall and entered the office of Miss Nettie Hopley.

Miss Hopley was at a roll-top desk to one side, sitting in a swivel chair that moved on wheels. There was a sofa against the opposite wall, flanked by two windows and a door that opened on a small balcony. Chairs were set around a table and framed pictures hung on the walls of a man with long white hair and another with a sad face and a black beard.

The principal half turned in the swivel chair to look at us over the pinch glasses crossed on the ridge of her nose. To do this she had to duck her head slightly as if she were about to step through a low doorway.

What Miss Hopley said to us we did not know but we saw in her eyes a warm welcome and when she took off her glasses and straightened up she smiled wholeheartedly, like Mrs. Dodson. We were, of course, saying nothing, only catching the friendliness of her voice and the sparkle in her eyes while she said words we did not understand. She signaled us to the table. Almost tiptoeing across the office, I maneuvered myself to keep my mother between me and the gringo lady. In a matter of seconds I had to decide whether she was a possible friend or a menace. We sat down.

Then Miss Hopley did a formidable thing. She stood up. Had she been standing when we entered she would have seemed tall. But rising from her chair she soared. And what she carried up and up with her was a buxom superstructure, firm shoulders, a straight sharp nose, full cheeks slightly molded by a curved line along the nostrils, thin lips that moved like steel springs, and a high forehead topped by hair gathered in a bun. Miss Hopley was not a giant in body but when she mobilized it to a standing position she seemed a match for giants. I decided I liked her.

She strode to a door in the far corner of the office, opened it and called a name. A boy of about ten years appeared in the doorway. He sat down at one end of the table. He was brown like us, a plump kid with shiny black hair combed straight back, neat, cool, and faintly obnoxious.

Miss Hopley joined us with a large book and some papers in her hand. She, too, sat down and the questions and answers began by way of our interpreter. My name was Ernesto. My mother's name was Henriqueta. My birth certificate was in San Blas. Here was my last report card from the Escuela Municipal Numero 3 para Varones of Mazatlán, and so forth. Miss Hopley put things down in the book and my mother signed a card.

As long as the questions continued, Doña Henriqueta could stay and I was secure. Now that they were over, Miss Hopley saw her to the door, dismissed our interpreter and without further ado took me by the hand and strode down the hall to Miss Ryan's first grade.

Miss Ryan took me to a seat at the front of the room, into which I shrank—the better to survey her. She was, to skinny, somewhat runty me, of a withering height when she patrolled the class. And when I least expected it, there she was, crouching by my desk, her blond radiant face level with mine, her voice patiently maneuvering me over the awful idiocies of the English language.

During the next few weeks Miss Ryan overcame my fears of tall, energetic teachers as she bent over my desk to help me with a word in the pre-primer. Step by step, she loosened me and my classmates from the safe anchorage of the desks for recitations at the blackboard and consultations at her desk. Frequently she burst into happy announcements to the whole class. "Ito can read a sentence," and small Japanese Ito, squint-eyed and shy, slowly read aloud while the class listened in wonder: "Come, Skipper, come. Come and run." The Korean, Portuguese, Italian, and Polish first graders had similar moments of glory, no less shining than mine the day I conquered "butterfly," which I had been persistently pronouncing in standard Spanish as boo-ter-flee. "Children," Miss Ryan called for attention. "Ernesto has learned how to pronounce *butterfly!*" And I proved it with a perfect imitation of Miss Ryan. From that celebrated success, I was soon able to match Ito's progress as a sentence reader with "Come, butterfly, come fly with me."

Like Ito and several other first graders who did not know English, I received private lessons from Miss Ryan in the closet, a narrow hall off the classroom with a door at each end. Next to one of these doors Miss Ryan placed a large chair for herself and a small one for me. Keeping an eye on the class through the open door she read with me about sheep in the meadow and a frightened chicken going to see the king, coaching me out of my phonetic ruts in words like *pasture, bow-wow-wow, hay,* and *pretty,* which to my Mexican ear and eye had so many unnecessary sounds and letters. She made me watch her lips and then close my eyes as she repeated words I found hard to read. When we came to know each other better, I tried interrupting to tell Miss Ryan how we said it in Spanish. It didn't work. She only said "oh" and went on with *pasture, bow-wow-wow,* and *pretty.* It was as if in that closet we were both discovering together the secrets of the English language and grieving together over the tragedies of Bo-Peep. The main reason I was graduated with honors from the first grade was that I had fallen in love with Miss Ryan. Her radiant, no-nonsense character made us either afraid not to love her or love her so we would not be afraid, I am not sure which. It was not only that we sensed she was with it, but also that she was with us.

Like the first grade, the rest of the Lincoln School was a sampling of the lower part of town where many races made their home. My pals in the second grade were Kazushi, whose parents spoke only Japanese; Matti, a skinny Italian boy; and Manuel, a fat Portuguese who would never get into a fight but wrestled you to the ground and just sat on you. Our assortment of nationalities included Koreans, Yugoslavs, Poles, Irish, and home-grown Americans.

Miss Hopley and her teachers never let us forget why we were at Lincoln: for those who were alien, to become good Americans; for those who were so born, to accept the rest of us. Off the school grounds we traded the same insults we heard from our elders. On the playground we were sure to be marched up to the principal's office for calling someone a wop, a chink, a dago, or a greaser. The school was not so much a melting pot as a griddle where Miss Hopley and her helpers warmed knowledge into us and roasted racial hatreds out of us.

At Lincoln, making us into Americans did not mean scrubbing away what made us originally foreign. The teachers called us as our parents did, or as close as they could pronounce our names in Spanish or Japanese. No one was ever scolded or punished for speaking in his native tongue on the playground. Matti told the class about his mother's down quilt, which she had made in Italy with the fine feathers of a thousand geese. Encarnación acted out how boys learned to fish in the Phillipines. I astounded the third grade with the story of my travels on a stagecoach, which nobody else in the class had seen except in the museum at Sutter's Fort. After a visit to the Crocker Art Gallery and its collection of heroic paintings of the golden age of California, someone showed a silk scroll with a Chinese painting. Miss Hopley herself had a way of expressing wonder over these matters before a class, her eyes wide open until they popped slightly. It was easy for me to feel that becoming a proud American, as she said we should, did not mean feeling ashamed of being a Mexican.

The Americanization of Mexican me was no smooth matter. I had to fight one lout who made fun of my travels on the *diligencia*, and my barbaric translation of the word into "diligence." He doubled up with laughter over the word until I straightened him out with a kick. In class I made points explaining that in Mexico roosters said "qui-qui-ri-qui" and not "cock-a-doodle-doo," but after school I had to put up with the taunts of a big Yugoslav who said Mexican roosters were crazy.

But it was Homer who gave me the most lasting lesson for a future American.

Homer was a chunky Irishman who dressed as if every day was Sunday. He slicked his hair between a crew cut and a pompadour. And Homer was smart, as he clearly showed when he and I ran for president of the third grade.

Everyone understood that this was to be a demonstration of how the American people vote for president. In an election, the teacher explained, the candidates could be generous and vote for each other. We cast our ballots in a shoe box and Homer won by two votes. I polled my supporters and came to the conclusion that I had voted for Homer and so had he. After class he didn't deny it, reminding me of what the teacher had said—we could vote for each other but didn't have to.

CLAUDE McKAY

The youngest of 11 children, Jamaica-born Claude McKay (1889–
1948) was trained as a cabinetmaker but instead joined the island's con-
stabulary. In 1912 he published two collections of dialect verse, *Songs of
Jamaica* and *Constab Ballads,* and he used the prize money they earned to
come to the United States to study at Tuskegee Institute and later at Kansas State University. The racism he encountered as a black immigrant
made him politically active and sympathetic to communism—but also at
times nostalgic for the seemingly idyllic island he had left. In 1914 McKay
moved to New York City and became an integral part of the Harlem Re-
naissance. His poetry collection *Harlem Shadows,* which is the source of
the two selections included here, appeared in 1922. Later that year McKay
left the U.S., traveled for two years in the Soviet Union (which he admired) and remained in Europe until 1934. His writing also includes the
impressive jazz-influenced novel *Home to Harlem* (1928).

The Tropics in New York

Bananas ripe and green, and ginger-root,
   Cocoa in pods and alligator pears,
And tangerines and mangoes and grape fruit,
   Fit for the highest prize at parish fairs,

Set in the window, bringing memories
   Of fruit-trees laden by low-singing rills,
And dewy dawns, and mystical blue skies
   In benediction over nun-like hills.

My eyes grew dim, and I could no more gaze;
   A wave of longing through my body swept,
And, hungry for the old, familiar ways,
   I turned aside and bowed my head and wept.

America

Although she feeds me bread of bitterness,
And sinks into my throat her tiger's tooth,
Stealing my breath of life, I will confess
I love this cultured hell that tests my youth!
Her vigor flows like tides into my blood,
Giving me strength erect against her hate.
Her bigness sweeps my being like a flood.
Yet as a rebel fronts a king in state,
I stand within her walls with not a shred
Of terror, malice, not a word of jeer.
Darkly I gaze into the days ahead,
And see her might and granite wonders there,
Beneath the touch of Time's unerring hand,
Like priceless treasures sinking in the sand.

LOUIS ADAMIC

Born Alojzij Adamic in Blato, Slovenia (then part of the Austro-Hungarian Empire), the oldest of nine children of Catholic peasants, Louis Adamic (1899–1951) arrived in the United States in 1913. After working in the mailroom of a Slovenian newspaper in New York, he was naturalized as a citizen in 1918, joined the U.S. Army, and published his first short story under a pseudonym. He settled in California and continued his literary efforts with the essay "The Truth about Los Angeles" (1927) and became part of a literary milieu that included Upton Sinclair, Mary Austin, Carey McWilliams, and Robinson Jeffers. His left-wing politics informed his first full-length book, *Dynamite: The Story of Class Violence in America* (1931). But it was the experience of immigration that provided him with his true subject, about which he would write prolifically and with a decidedly personal slant. *Laughing in the Jungle*, excerpted here, was the first of his memoirs to reflect on his own acculturation and the position of the immigrant in American life. A Guggenheim grant enabled him to return to Slovenia, now part of Yugoslavia, and write *The Native's Return* (1935), followed by two immigrant novels—*Grandsons* (1935) and *Cradle of Life* (1936)—and *My America* (1938), a lively hodgepodge of personal impressions animated by what Alfred Kazin called "an outsider's curiosity and a vibrant democratic paternalism." Because of his fusion of reportage and autobiography, Adamic is often regarded as a precursor of the New Journalism of the 1960s.

from
Laughing in the Jungle

As a boy of nine, and even younger, in my native village of Blato, in Carniola—then a Slovenian duchy of Austria and later a part of Yugoslavia —I experienced a thrill every time one of the men of the little community returned from America.

Five or six years before, as I heard people tell, the man had quietly left the village for the United States, a poor peasant clad in homespun, with a mustache under his nose and a bundle on his back; now, a clean-shaven *Amerikanec*, he sported a blue-serge suit, buttoned shoes very large in the toes and with india-rubber heels, a black derby, a shiny celluloid collar, and a loud necktie made even louder by a dazzling horseshoe pin, which, rumor had it, was made of gold, while his two suitcases of imitation leather, tied with straps, bulged with gifts from America for his relatives and friends in the village. In nine cases out of ten, he had left in economic desperation, on money borrowed from some relative in the United States; now there was talk in the village that he was worth anywhere from one to three thousand American dollars. And to my eyes he truly bore all the earmarks of affluence. Indeed, to say that he thrilled my boyish fancy is putting it mildly. With other boys in the village, I followed him around as he went visiting his relatives and friends and distributing presents, and hung onto his every word and gesture.

Then, on the first Sunday after his homecoming, if at all possible, I got within earshot of the nabob as he sat in the winehouse or under the linden in front of the winehouse in Blato, surrounded by village folk, ordering wine and *klobase*—Carniolan sausages—for all comers, paying for accordion-players, indulging in tall talk about America, its wealth and vastness, and his own experiences as a worker in the West Virginia or Kansas coal-mines or Pennsylvania rolling-mills, and comparing notes upon conditions in the United States with other local *Amerikanci* who had returned before him.

Under the benign influence of *cvichek*—Lower Carniolan wine—and often even when sober, the men who had been in America spoke expansively, boastfully, romantically of their ability and accomplishments as workers and of the wages they had earned in Wilkes-Barre or Carbondale, Pennsylvania, or Wheeling, West Virginia, or Pueblo, Colorado, or Butte, Montana, and generally of places and people and things and affairs in the New World. The men who returned to the village, either to stay or for a visit, were, for the most part, natural men of labor—men with sinewy arms and powerful backs— "Bohunks," or "Hunkies," so called in the United States—who derived a certain brawny joy and pride from hard toil. Besides, now that they had come home, they were no longer mere articles upon the industrial labor market, "working stiffs" or "wage slaves," as radical agitators in America referred to them, but adventurers, distant kinsmen of Marco Polo safely returned from a far country, heroes in their own eyes and the eyes of the village; and it was natural for them to expand and to exaggerate their own exploits and enlarge upon the opportunities to be found in America. Their boasting, perhaps, was never wholly without basis in fact. . . .

I remember that, listening to them, I played with the idea of going to America when I was but eight or nine.

My notion of the United States then, and for a few years after, was that it was a grand, amazing, somewhat fantastic place—the Golden Country—a sort of Paradise—the Land of Promise in more ways than one—huge beyond conception, thousands of miles across the ocean, untellably exciting, explosive, quite incomparable to the tiny, quiet, lovely Carniola; a place full of movement and turmoil, wherein things that were unimaginable and impossible in Blato happened daily as a matter of course.

In America one could make pots of money in a short time, acquire immense holdings, wear a white collar, and have polish on one's boots like a *gospod*—one of the gentry—and eat white bread, soup, and meat on weekdays as well as on Sundays, even if one were but an ordinary workman to begin with. In Blato no one ate white bread or soup and meat, except on Sundays and holidays, and very few then.

In America one did not have to remain an ordinary workman. There, it seemed, one man was as good as the next. There were dozens, perhaps scores, or even hundreds of immigrants in the United States, one-time peasants and workers from the Balkans—from Carniola, Styria, Carinthia, Croatia, Banat, Dalmatia, Bosnia, Montenegro, and Serbia—and from Poland, Slovakia, Bohemia, and elsewhere, who, in two or three years, had earned and saved enough money working in the Pennsylvania, Ohio, or Illinois coal-mines or steel-mills to go to regions called Minnesota, Wisconsin, and Nebraska, and there buy sections of land each of which was larger than the whole area owned by the peasants in Blato. . . . Oh, America was immense—*immense!*

I heard a returned *Amerikanec* tell of regions known as Texas and Oklahoma where single farms—*renche* (ranches), he called them—were larger than the entire province of Carniola! It took a man days to ride on horseback from one end of such a ranch to the other. There were people in Blato and in neighboring villages who, Thomas-like, did not believe this, but my boyish imagination was aflame with America, and I believed it. At that time I accepted as truth nearly everything I heard about America. I believed that a single cattleman in Texas owned more cattle than there were in the entire Balkans. And my credulity was not strained when I heard that there were gold-mines in California, and trees more than a thousand years old with trunks so enormous that it required a dozen men, clasping each other's hands, to encircle them with their arms.

In America everything was possible. There even the common people were "citizens," not "subjects," as they were in Austria and in most other European countries. A citizen, or even a non-citizen foreigner, could walk up to the President of the United States and pump his hand. Indeed, that seemed to be a custom in America. There was a man in Blato, a former steel-worker in Pittsburgh, who claimed that upon an occasion he had shaken hands and exchanged words with Theodore Roosevelt, to whom he familiarly referred as "Tedi"—which struck my mother very funny. To her it seemed as if some one had called the Pope of Rome or the Emperor of Austria by a nickname. But the man assured her, in my hearing, that in America everybody called the President merely "Tedi."

Mother laughed about this, off and on, for several days. And I laughed with her. She and I often laughed together.

※　※

The day I spent on Ellis Island was an eternity. Rumors were current among immigrants of several nationalities that some of us would be refused admittance into the United States and sent back to Europe. For several hours I was in a cold sweat on this account, although, so far as I knew, all my papers were in order, and sewed away in the lining of my jacket were twenty-five dollars in American currency—the minimum amount required by law to be in the possession of every immigrant before entering the country. Then, having rationalized away some of these fears, I gradually worked up a panicky feeling that I might develop measles or smallpox, or some other such disease. I had heard that several hundred sick immigrants were quarantined on the island.

The first night in America I spent, with hundreds of other recently arrived immigrants, in an immense hall with tiers of narrow iron-and-canvas bunks, four deep. I was assigned a top bunk. Unlike most of the steerage immigrants, I had no bedding with me, and the blanket which some one threw at me was too thin to be effective against the blasts of cold air that rushed in through the open windows; so that I shivered, sleepless, all night, listening to snores and dream-monologues in perhaps a dozen different languages.

The bunk immediately beneath mine was occupied by a Turk, who slept with his turban wound around his head. He was tall, thin, dark, bearded, hollow-faced, and hook-nosed. At peace with Allah, he snored all night, producing a thin wheezing sound, which occasionally, for a moment or two, took on a deeper note.

I thought how curious it was that I should be spending a night in such proximity to a Turk, for Turks were traditional enemies of Balkan peoples, including my own nation. For centuries Turks had forayed into Slovenian territory. Now here I was, trying to sleep directly above a Turk, with only a sheet of canvas between us.

Soon after daybreak I heard him suddenly bestir himself. A moment later he began to mutter something in Turkish, and clambered out of his bed in a hurry. He had some difficulty extricating himself, for there was not more than a foot between his and my bunk, and in his violent haste rammed a sharp knee in the small of my back. I almost yelled out in pain.

Safely on the floor, the Mohammedan began to search feverishly in a huge sack which contained his belongings, and presently pulled out a narrow, longish rug and carefully spread it on the floor between two tiers of bunks.

This done, he stretched himself several times, rising on his toes, cleared his throat, rubbed his beard, adjusted his turban, which was slightly askew; whereupon, oblivious of my wide-eyed interest, he suddenly crashed to his knees on the floor with a great thud. Next he lifted his long arms ceilingward and began to bow toward the east, touching the carpet with his brow, the while mumbling his sun-up prayer to Allah.

At first I did not know what to think of the Mussulman's doings. Then, slowly realizing what it was all about, the scene struck me as immensely funny. Sleepy and cold though I was, I had to pull the blanket over my head, lest the worshiper hear me laughing.

*

Late in the afternoon of the last day of 1913 I was examined for entry into the United States, with about a hundred other immigrants who had come on the *Niagara*.

The examiner sat bureaucratically—very much in the manner of officials in the Old Country—behind a great desk, which stood upon a high platform. On the wall above him was a picture of George Washington. Beneath it was an American flag.

The official spoke a bewildering mixture of many Slavic languages. He had a stern voice and a sour visage. I had difficulty understanding some of his questions.

At a small table, piled with papers, not far from the examiner's desk, was a clerk who called out our names, which, it seemed, were written on the long sheets of paper before him.

When my turn came, toward dusk, I was asked the usual questions. When and where was I born? My nationality? Religion? Was I a legitimate child? What were the names of my parents? Was I an imbecile? Was I a prostitute? (I assume that male and female immigrants were subjected to the same questionnaire.) Was I an ex-convict? A criminal? Why had I come to the United States?

I was questioned as to the state of my finances and I produced the required twenty-five dollars.

What did I expect to do in the United States? I replied that I hoped to get a job. What kind of job? I didn't know; any kind of job.

The inspector grunted vaguely. "And who is this person, Stefan—Stefan Radin—who is meeting you here?"

I answered that Stefan Radin was the brother of a friend of mine, now dead.

Then the inspector waved me out of his presence and the clerk motioned me to go back and sit on one of the benches near by.

I waited another hour. It got dark and the lights were turned on in the room.

Finally, after dozens of other immigrants had been questioned, Steve

Radin was called into the examining-room and asked, in English, to state his relationship to me.

He answered, of course, that he was not related to me at all.

Whereupon the inspector fairly pounced upon me, speaking the dreadful botch of Slavic languages. What did I mean by lying to him? He said a great many other things which I did not understand. I did comprehend, however, his threat to return me to the Old Country. It appeared that America had no room for liars: America was glad to welcome to its shores only decent, honest, truthful people.

My heart pounded.

Finally it occurred simultaneously to me and to Steve Radin that the man must be laboring under some misapprehension. And, truly, before another minute elapsed it turned out that the clerk had made a mistake by entering on my paper that I had declared Stefan Radin was my uncle. How the mistake had occurred I do not know; perhaps the clerk had confused my questionnaire form with some one else's.

Finally, perceiving the error, the examiner's face formed in a grimace and, waving his hand in a casual gesture, he ordered me released.

Steve Radin picked up my bag and, in the confusion, I barely remembered to say good-by to Peter Molek, who was going to Pennsylvania.

I was weak in the knees and just managed to walk out of the room, then downstairs and onto the ferryboat. I had been shouted at, denounced as a liar by an official of the United States on my second day in the country, before a roomful of people, including Steve Radin, whom, so far, I had merely glimpsed.

But the weakness in my knees soon passed. I laughed, perhaps a bit hysterically, as the little Ellis Island ferryboat bounded over the rough, white-capped waters of the bay toward the Battery.

Steve Radin gaped at me. Then he smiled.

I was in New York—in America.

Narodni Glas, like most Bohunk newspapers, was perennially in financial doldrums. Every few months it was in danger of going under.

When I had been assistant editor for about three months, and the circulation of the paper was showing an especially swift decline, I suggested to the publisher and Mr. Zemlar that they send me on a "trip around the United States." I proposed to visit the larger Slovenian *kolonije* in the industrial centers, see how our people lived, write of their problems as immigrants, their social and cultural life and their working conditions, and solicit subscriptions. Some of the other Bohunk newspapers had traveling correspondents and subscription solicitors. My chief motive in wanting to travel, of course, was not to put the paper on its feet, but to see the country.

The publisher at first hesitated, then decided to try me out for a month, in which period I was to cover Pennsylvania and Ohio. I first went to Forest City, in the anthracite country of Pennsylvania. Peter Molek lived there. He was glad to see me and we had a long talk.

"What did I tell you?" he said. "America *is* good for you." He was impressed with my English, which by now I spoke rather passably, and the fact that I wrote for a newspaper.

Molek's health was about the same as when he returned to the United States. He was no longer a colliery watchman. He had recently married a middle-aged Slovenian widow with five children. Her husband, a friend of Molek's, had been killed in a mine. Her insurance money had amounted to a couple of thousand dollars, and with this money Molek and she had just started a grocery and vegetable store which promised well.

Forest City was then a town of eight thousand inhabitants, Slovenians predominating with nearly five hundred families. Molek was more or less acquainted with all of them, and helped me to get among them, see how they lived, and secure their subscriptions.

Molek also knew many Slovenians in the neighboring coal towns—Carbondale, Pittston, Scranton, Wilkes-Barre—and gave me letters to them or merely suggested that I call and tell them I was a friend of his. They, in turn, sent me to other Slovenians living farther on, in western Pennsylvania and Ohio. Thus I had no difficulty finding my own people in the grimy industrial cities and towns of those states.

All the places were bleak, unharmonious, with immense coal-heaps, cin-

der-piles in front of houses, and stinking rubbish-dumps, tin cans and discarded machinery everywhere. But, of course, more than in the looks of
places I was interested in the manner of living among my countrymen, the
Slovenians and other Bohunks.

The great majority of immigrants who plunged into the turmoil of America,
from the most intelligent to the least, were naturally bewildered, or numbed
by the impact of the country upon their senses and their minds. Their first
concern upon arrival was to find people of their own nationality, in whose
midst they might orient themselves. One could seldom, if ever, get a job in
one's old line. In America there was no stability, which was almost the key-
note of life in the European countries before the World War. With machinery
being improved from day to day, the job that one found carried with it no security. One might lose it from week to week, almost from hour to hour, and
one could seldom base on its continuation any plans for the future. The more
pronounced the difference in language, ways, and conditions in America and
in the immigrant's own country, the more urgent it was for him to seek out his
countrymen.

In the case of the Slavic immigrants eighteen or twenty years ago, at
which time they came over in a steady stream, the first, although not the most
important, difficulty arose in making the people here—native-born Americans and aliens of other nationalities—understand who they were and
whence they hailed. The difficulty lay basically in the fact that many of them
were not clear on the point themselves. If a Slovenian was asked what his
nationality was, he very likely replied that he was a Kranjec or Krainer or
Carniolan, from Kranjsko (German, *Krain*; English, *Carniola*). Only a few
Czechs, Styrian Germans, and Italians from Trieste and Giorizia knew what
he meant. It was as if a citizen from some such obscure state as Nevada, arriving in Belgrade or Lublyana, announced that his nationality was Nevadan.
If he really knew what he was, he declared himself a Slovenian, but that, to
the average American, Irishman, or Scandinavian, meant no more than
Carniolan.

The poor Bohunk then proceeded to explain, perhaps with the aid of a
map, that the Slovenians were a small Slavic nation, first cousins, one might

say, to the Czechs, Poles, and Russians, inhabiting a little country within Austria which the Hapsburgs, with their Machiavellian *divide et impera* policy, had cut up into three tiny provinces, Carniola, Carinthia, and Styria. But before he was through explaining, presto! he was an "Austrian," which, in a sense, was correct. Where his people had larger colonies, as in Cleveland, Forest City, Wilkes-Barre, Carbondale, Pittsburgh, and Chicago, they were known also as Krainers or Granners (Carniolans).

By a similar process, the Croatians, too, became "Austrians," though, since Croatia used to be a part, not of Austria, but of Hungary, that was never true in any sense. Even the Serbs and Montenegrins, who appeared to speak the same language as the Croats, were labeled "Austrians," and the Yugoslav languages became the "Austrian" tongue. The Czechs, always conscious of their nationality, never hesitated to state what they were. In consequence, though they had been under Austrian rule longer than the Yugoslavs, they were never Austrians in America, but either Czechs or Bohemians.

The Poles, with their dramatic historical background, which included the participation of a number of their countrymen in the American Civil War, had no trouble making anyone understand who they were and where they came from. They were Poles or, at worst, Polacks. American-born Polish children, in some cases even of the second generation, usually showed pride in their origin, and if their family names were at all pronounceable, retained them. In this case they differed from all the other Bohunks save the Bohemians. (I write in the past tense because immigration is ended and immigrants are vanishing in the melting-pot.)

The Serbians, too, with a historical background as bloody, though perhaps not as splendid, as that of the Poles and the Czechs, were a proud people; but most of them never intended to stay here permanently, and so they made no emphatic objection to being called Austrians. On the other hand, the German Austrians who were Austrians before anyone else, insisted strenuously that they were Germans, no doubt because they hated being included with such lowly rabble as the Croatians, Slovenians, Slovaks, and Serbians in the American-made "Austrian" nationality.

From that viewpoint the Viennese Germans' objection to being known as Austrians was perhaps not unjustified, for Croatia, Bosnia, Herzegovina, Lika, Banat, Dalmatia, Montenegro, and southern Serbia sent to America, for the most part, simple peasants who lacked any definite nationalistic consciousness, and who, next to tilling the earth and fishing, were interested only in fighting, love- and verse-making, drinking, dancing, singing, strumming the *gusle* or *tamburice*, and, last but not least, keeping on the good side of Yahweh. They thought of themselves as fighters, lovers, poets, dancers, singers, and children of the Almighty before it occurred to them that they were also members of definite national and political groups. They were very proud of their endurance at hard physical labor, their reproductive powers (their women were used to very frequent child-bearing), their singing voices, and their ability to carry liquor like men.

The Slovenians, the smallest of Slavic nations, were, next to the Czechs, the most cultured and civilized of Bohunks. Many of those who came to America, even among the peasants of the lowest economic order, were well aware of their nationality and cultural superiority, and, like the German-speaking subjects of His Apostolic Majesty, resented being classed with the "Austrians." But in the United States census figures they were counted, along with the Croatians and the Yugoslav groups, as Austrians.

Ten or fifteen years ago, if one came to an American city and inquired for the Croatian or Slovenian colony, one found that no such thing was known. When one explained that one really sought the "Austrians," the stranger consulted would, with a gesture of disdain, direct one to take such-and-such street-car, ride to the end of the line, and then walk a few blocks; there, in "Hunkytown," lived the "Austrians," or Bohunks, in low, unpainted shacks or bleak-looking apartment-houses along unpaved streets that swarmed with unclean children in torn garments.

The Bohunks indeed were "dung." But their natural health, virility, and ability to laugh served, from time to time, to help them transcend their lowly status in the American scheme of things. On Saturday nights and Sunday afternoons the men got together, and, apart from the prim and proper "better element," sang, played their stringed instruments and accordions, drank, fought, shouted, laughed, and roared to their hearts' content.

CHARLES CHAPLIN

An icon of cinema, Charles Chaplin (1889–1977) first visited the
United States as an actor touring with Fred Karno's London-based vaudeville troupe. During the tour, as he relates in the following excerpt from
his youthful memoir *Charlie Chaplin's Own Story*, he caught the attention of movie mogul Mack Sennett, who hired him to work for Keystone
Films in Hollywood. Chaplin's admiration of the "continual wonder" of
the United States here gives no hint of the eventual difficulties he would
experience with his adopted country. Because of his leftist political sympathies and personal conduct, he was informed by the Attorney General
in 1952 during a vacation in England that he would have to endure an
inquiry regarding his "moral worth" before being permitted re-entry into
the United States. Chaplin opted to stay in Europe, settling in Switzerland and returning to America only once, in 1972, to accept an honorary
Academy Award.

from

Charlie Chaplin's Own Story

N ow, since I was twenty at the time, four years ago, when I stood on the
deck of the steamer and saw America rising into view on the horizon, it
may seem strange to some persons that I had no truer idea of this country
than to suppose just west of New York a wild country inhabited by American
Indians and traversed by great herds of buffalo. It is natural enough, however, when one reflects that I had spent nearly all my life in London, which is,
like all great cities, a most narrow-minded and provincial place, and that my
only schooling had been the little my mother was able to give me, combined
later with much eager reading of romances. Fenimore Cooper, your own
American writer, had pictured for me this country as it was a hundred years

ago, and what English boy would suppose a whole continent could be made over in a short hundred years?

So, while the steamer docked, I stood quivering with eagerness to be off into the wonders of that forest of skyscrapers which is New York, with all the sensations of a boy transported to Mars, or any other unknown world, where anything might happen. Indeed, one of the strangest things—to my way of thinking—which I encountered in the New World, was brought to my attention a moment after I landed. At the very foot of the gangplank Mr. Reeves, the manager of the American company, who was with me, was halted by a very fat little man, richly dressed, who rushed up and grasped him enthusiastically by both hands.

"Velgome! Velgome to our gountry!" he cried. "How are you, Reeves? How goes it?"

Mr. Reeves replied in a friendly manner, and the little man turned to me inquiringly. "Who's the kid?" he asked.

"This is Mr. Chaplin, our leading comedian," Mr. Reeves said, while I bristled at the word "kid." The fat man, I found, was Marcus Loew, a New York theatrical producer. He shook hands with me warmly and asked immediately, "Vell, and vot do you think of our gountry, young man?"

"I have never been in Berlin," I said stiffly. "I have never cared to go there," I added rudely, resenting his second reference to my youth.

"I mean America. How do you like America? This is our gountry now. We're all Americans together over here!" Marcus Loew said with real enthusiasm in his voice, and I drew myself up in haughty surprise. "My word, this *is* a strange country," I said to myself. Foreigners, and all that, calling themselves citizens! This is going rather far, even for a republic, even for America, where anything might happen.

That was the thing which most impressed me for weeks. Germans, it seemed, and English and Irish and French and Italians and Poles, all mixed up together, all one nation—it seemed incredible to me, like something against all the laws of nature. I went about in a continual wonder at it. Not even the high buildings, higher even than I had imagined, nor the enormous, flaming electric signs on Broadway, nor the high, hysterical, shrill sound of the street traffic, so different from the heavy roar of London, was so strange to me as this mixing of races. Indeed, it was months before I could become accustomed to it, and months more before I saw how good it is, and felt glad to be part of such a nation myself.

We were playing a sketch called *A Night in a London Music-Hall*, which probably many people still remember. I was cast for the part of a drunken man, who furnished most of the comedy, and the sketch proved to be a great success, so that I played that one part continuously for over two years, traveling from coast to coast with it twice.

The number of American cities seemed endless to me, like the little boxes the Chinese make, one inside the other, so that it seems no matter how many you take out, there are still more inside. I had imagined this country a broad wild continent, dotted sparsely with great cities—New York, Chicago, San Francisco—with wide distances between. The distances were there, as I expected, but there seemed no end to the cities. New York, Buffalo, Pittsburgh, Cincinnati, Columbus, Indianapolis, Chicago, St. Louis, Kansas City, Omaha, Denver—and San Francisco not even in sight yet! No Indians, either.

Toward the end of the summer we reached San Francisco the first time, very late, because the train had lost time over the mountains, so that there was barely time for us to reach the Orpheum and make up in time for the first performance. My stage hat was missing, there was a wild search for it, while we held the curtain and the house grew a little impatient, but we could not find it anywhere. At last I seized a high silk hat from the outraged head of a man who had come behind the scenes to see Reeves and rushed on to the stage. The hat was too loose. Every time I tried to speak a line it fell off, and the audience went into ecstasies. It was one of the best hits of the season, that hat.

It slid back down my neck, and the audience laughed; it fell over my nose, and they howled; I picked it up on the end of my cane, looked at it stupidly and tried to put the cane on my head, and they roared. I do not know the feelings of its owner, who for a time stood glaring at me from the wings, for when at last, after the third curtain call, I came off holding the much dilapidated hat in my hands, he had gone. Bareheaded, I suppose, and probably still very angry.

After the show I came out on the street into a cold gray fog, which blurred the lights and muffled the sound of my steps on the damp pavement, and, drawing great breaths of it into my lungs, I was happy. "For the lova Mike!" I said to Reeves, being very proud of my American slang. "This is a little bit of all right, what? Just like home, don't you know! What do you know about that!" And I felt that, next to London, I liked San Francisco, and was sorry we were to stay only two weeks.

We returned to New York, playing return dates on the "big time" circuits, and I almost regretted the close of the season and the return to London. The night we closed at Keith's I found a message waiting for me at the theater.

"We want you in the pictures. Come and see me and talk it over. Mack Sennett."

"Who's Mack Sennett?" I asked Reeves, and he told me he was with the Keystone motion-picture company. "Oh, the cinematographs!" I said, for I knew them in London, and regarded them as even lower than the music-halls. I tore up the note and threw it away.

"I suppose we're going home next week?" I asked Reeves, and he said he thought not; the "little big time" circuits wanted us and he was waiting for a cable from Karno.

Early next day I called at his apartments, eager to learn what he had heard, for I wanted very much to stay in America another year, and saw no way to do it if Karno recalled the company. I did not think again of the note from Sennett, for I did not regard seriously an offer to go into the cinematographs. I was delighted to hear that we were going to stay, and left New York in great spirits, with the prospect of another year with *A Night in a London Music-Hall* in America.

Twelve months later, back in New York again, I received another message from Mr. Sennett, to which I paid no more attention than to the first one. We were sailing for London the following month. One day, while I was walking down Broadway with a chance acquaintance, we passed the Keystone offices and my companion asked me to come in with him. He had some business with a man there. I went in, and was waiting in the outer office when Mr. Sennett came through and recognized me.

"Good morning, Mr. Chaplin, glad to see you! Come right in," he said cordially, and, ashamed to tell him I had not come in reply to his message, that indeed I had not meant to answer it at all, I followed him into his private office. I talked vaguely, waiting for an opportunity to get away without appearing rude. At last I saw it.

"Let's not beat about the bush any longer," Mr. Sennett said. "What salary will you take to come with the Keystone?" This was my chance to end the interview, and I grasped it eagerly.

"Two hundred dollars a week," I said, naming the most extravagant price which came into my head.

"All right," he replied promptly. "When can you start?"

FELIPE ALFAU

One of the great literary rediscoveries of the past quarter century has been the work of the Barcelona-born writer Felipe Alfau (1902–1999), who came to the United States in 1916. Set largely in Madrid, Alfau's first novel, *Locos: A Comedy of Gestures*, was written in 1928 but not published until 1936, and even then was available only by special order from the publisher. Predictably, the novel fell into near-total obscurity despite good reviews. Mary McCarthy recalled: "I was enamored of that book and never forgot it. . . . I used to ask about him whenever I met a Spaniard; not one knew his name." A serendipitous discovery in a used bookstore by an editor led to the 1988 reissue of *Locos* and, because of its enthusiastic reception, the publication in 1990 of Alfau's other novel, *Chromos*, written in 1948. Centered on a group of Spanish Americans, including Alfau himself, in Manhattan in the 1930s, *Chromos* was hailed for its wit, lyricism, and inventiveness, and was nominated for the National Book Award. In considering what it means to be an "American-iard," Alfau brings to his immigration story a distinctively playful modernism reminiscent of Calvino, Svevo, and Nabokov.

from
Chromos

The moment one learns English, complications set in. Try as one may, one cannot elude this conclusion, one must inevitably come back to it. This applies to all persons, including those born to the language and, at times, even more so to Latins, including Spaniards. It manifests itself in an awareness of implications and intricacies to which one had never given a thought; it afflicts one with that officiousness of philosophy which, having no business of its own, gets in everybody's way and, in the case of Latins, they lose that racial characteristic of taking things for granted and leaving them to their own devices without inquiring into causes, motives or ends, to meddle indiscreetly into reasons which are none of one's affair and to become not only self-conscious, but conscious of other things which never gave a damn for one's existence.

In the words of my friend Don Pedro, of whom more later, this could never happen to a Spaniard who speaks only Spanish. We are more direct but, according to him, when we enter the English-speaking world, we find the most elementary things questioned, growing in complexity without bounds; we experience, see or hear about problems which either did not exist for us or were disposed of in what he calls that brachistological fashion of which we are masters: nervous breakdowns, social equality, marital maladjustment and beholding Oedipus in an unfavorable light, friendships with those women intellectualoids whom Don Pedro has baptized perfect examples of feminine putritude, psychoneuroses, anal hallucinations, etc., leading one gently but forcibly from a happy world of reflexes of which one was never aware, to a world of analytical reasoning of which one is continuously aware, which closes in like a vise of missionary tenacity and culminates in such a collapse of the simple as questioning the meaning of meaning.

According to Don Pedro, a Spaniard speaking English is indeed a most incongruous phenomenon and the acquisition of this other language, far from increasing his understanding of life, if this were possible, only renders it hopelessly muddled and obscure. He finds himself encumbered with too much equipment for what had been, after all, a process as plain as living and while perhaps becoming glib and searching if oblique and indirect, in discussing culturesque fads and interrelated topics of doubtful value even in the English market, he gradually loses his capacity to see and think straight until he emerges with all other English-speaking persons in complete incapacity to understand the obvious. It is disconcerting.

Dr. de los Rios does not agree with Don Pedro and suggests that complications generally set in whenever one learns anything, but I want to believe that this argument is churlish, eclectic and inconvenient to the purpose of my reasoning.

Rather I am inclined to side with Don Pedro who, being among other things an authority on tauromachia and therefore often expressing himself in such terms, announces that de los Rios belongs to that very castizo class

of Spaniards who always neutralize the charge of extremism with a philosophical veronica and whose lemma should be: to tame the enraged bull of
radicalism with the cool cape of tolerance.

But perhaps here one should abandon such considerations to say something about these two individuals.

Dr. José de los Rios was an old friend. I had known him since Spain where
he had gained good fame as a general physician. Then he had begun to spe-
cialize in things of the nerves and the mind; he published several technical
books that were very successful outside Spain; he lectured in various countries and was at present one of the leading neurologists in the world. It was
as such that he had come to this country where we had resumed a friendship
which to me, considering his eminent position in the world of science, was a
source of great pride and an honor as undeserved as unquestioned. Through
him I had met Don Pedro here, but the two of them seemed to have known
each other for centuries.

Don Pedro Guzman O'Moore Algoracid was his very full name, at once
sonorous, lofty and unconvincing. The Guzman part very Castilian, the other
requires no explanation for the English reader and the last starkly Moorish.
Of somber countenance and attire, with Mephistophelian suggestions of a
clowning Dracula flashing out of the night in a Spanish cloak he favored,
weather permitting, he boasted of pure unadulterated Irish and Moorish
blood and ancestry which, according to his genealogical chemistry, made him
the most castizo Spaniard.

Due to an accident in his youth interpreted as the agent which had
changed the course of his life, he enjoyed a marked limp, thus justifying his
other prop and inseparable companion: a formidable walking stick with all
the disquieting protuberances of a shillelagh. I understood in a general way
that in Spain he had been a very promising musician and possibly that the
accident had had something to do with his abandoning all serious thoughts
of music, but what I knew was that at present he was the best-known Spanish bandleader in these parts, often referred to as the Emperor of Latin
American music and the Svengali of Swing. In the rendering of tangos, conducted like all his music, through justifiable affectation, with his shillelagh,
he was peerless and he played them all with such an exaggerated rhythm
that, in his own words, they all sounded like someone sawing a heavy log.

With a liberal education proudly shared between the University of Dublin and Salamanca's Colegio de Nobles Irlandeses, his multiple personality was at present divided into two main hemispheres: one, that of an eccentric and temperamental bandleader intended for his well-paying public; the other, that of a character of recondite and esoteric accomplishments, reserved for his Spanish friends. A familiar figure in those sections of New York referred to for expediency's sake as Broadway and Harlem and the widely scattered Spanish quarters in the city, such as Cherry and Columbia streets, radio announcers, commentators and feature writers, with blissful disregard for Castilian dignity, had shortened his name to Pete Guz, which had stuck and as such he was known to the American public and there was nothing anyone could do about it, though Dr. de los Rios had cleverly amalgamated his name and personality into the nickname of the Moor and this is what most of his Spanish friends always called him, with the exception of some who, because of his biting comments, referred to him as Don Pedro el Cruel. He was changeable and he was complicated and, in his manner of speaking, it would have been interesting to trace the wanderings of this complex variable over the subconscious plane and evaluate the integral of his real conclusions. To me, he was an absurd combination of a slightly daffy Irish-Moorish Don Quixote with sinister overtones of Beelzebub and the only Irishman I ever heard speak English with an Andalusian brogue.

He laid what to me appeared ridiculous claims to his past, but for that matter he always spoke of everything in the most fantastic manner. He told of remarkable exploits of his ancestors in Ireland and often told of a grandfather who had returned to Spain from Africa with a monumentally archaic and rusty key to reopen the house of his ancestors in Granada only to find that the lock had since been changed, whence he climbed in through an open window, and he also referred to the year 1492 as that fateful dark day when Spain had committed its two greatest strategical errors: the expulsion of the Moors and the discovery of the Americas. In the beginning I had taken all this phantasmagoria with reservations mixed with that suspiciousness which most Spaniards feel for one another when they meet outside of Spain which makes us think that any Spaniard claiming to be so must be an imposter, particularly if he claims to come from Madrid, to the point that we never believe that anyone comes from there, as if it were an empty city or a place which no one can ever leave. It seems that to be from Spain is quite a claim, but to come from Madrid is unbelievable. I have been doubted so much that now I say that I am a Latin American and save myself a good deal of trouble. This is something that we frequently do when abroad, so that one has the strange situation of two Spaniards posing before each other as Latin Americans and both being surprised at their accent and suspecting that after all the parents of both were gallegos. I think this is very foolish and take this opportunity to advise all my countrymen who read this to carry their passports with them at all times and thus squelch any doubts as to their nationality and if they come from Madrid, to run to the nearest consulate and there have the fact stated in bold type.

However, Dr. de los Rios's attitude gradually conquered my misgivings. He who had always impressed me with his affable skepticism listened to the Moor's tales without batting an eye and with a manner that tended to lend credence to them and I began to think that perhaps the Moor was a true living legend and not something on the other side of the footlights.

They were very different, these two men, and they represented two fundamental types of Spaniards. It has been said many times that Cervantes portrayed the two main types of Spaniards with Don Quixote and Sancho Panza, but speaking in the manner of de los Rios, one ventures to believe that this is somewhat specious because one can find two such main types in any other country and they really divide humanity into two classes, which fact possibly constitutes their greatness, but in the case of these two contemporary men, the division was part of the national history and structure. It was ethnological and racial within the same country, one showing the Visigoth and the other the Moorish influences.

Yet these two different men shared one national characteristic: neither one showed even remotely his real age. Although I do not think they would much mind, I will not divulge it but will content myself with our classical and noncommittal saying: they were younger than God. They belonged to a class common in our country which is ageless and eons of time can only succeed in mummifying. Dr. de los Rios had not changed physically since I first met him, except for a few white hairs lost in his blond mane, mustache and goatee. Spiritually is another thing. While I remember him many years ago in Spain alive with an adventuresome scientific outlook and eager for risky and modern experimentalism often fired into whimsicalities by a tremendous imagination and moral courage that easily overcame medical conventionalities and politics, he had settled—not materially, mind you, but morally—into a cold realism which under a mist of indifference was vaster and relentless as destiny in its heuristic approach to all problems. As for the Moor, I believe he had been born with the same thick iron gray hair which he wore cut very short and brushed forward like the schoolboys of my childhood, or like that of an anachronic bootblack who had just offered to polish our shoes and got a tip from de los Rios for not doing it.

We were in Bryant Park and Dr. de los Rios spoke of his inability to allow anyone to polish his shoes and Don Pedro instantly seized on the subject to elaborate and generalize. Typical of the two men was that the virtuous implication which in Dr. de los Rios had become the modest description of an individual case of personal failing, grew with the Moor to transcendental proportions of social and national attitudes surging into patriotic boastfulness embodied in himself, even if done with careful indirectness. No matter what he spoke about, and that was many things, he sounded as if he were talking of himself. It seemed as though his personality and viewpoint approached a subject, elbowed their way into its midst and then exploded in vociferous and violent altercation, dispersing everything to remain there alone, with nothing to say, the enemy ignominiously routed in a battle which it had never fought.

From this it was but a step to his favorite subject of assault: an obsession with the position of the Spaniard in the world, with more assurance in Spain and with more complications in foreign lands—all right, in this country. His bad foot resting lightly on the bench where de los Rios and I sat, his shillelagh hovered above us like the sword of Damocles and he spoke down on us in a way all his own. It was intimate and kidding and disconcerting and it bounced along on hypnotic expressions and necromantic gestures, presenting the obvious as an incantation, his sentences disconnected and frequently unfinished, bifurcating, darting from one thing to another, like a school of herringbones which have not stopped swimming and the whole interrupted almost rhythmically by a stroke of laughter with a rising inflection ending in a protracted cough. He held and shook before us like a marionette his straw man: the "Americaniard."

This, a word of his own composition, he had begun originally to employ when referring to Spaniards in the Americas and at one time might have included Latin Americans, but he had gradually varied the meaning until at present it applied to Spaniards in New York and then by association even to other foreigners, especially of Latin origin, in the same circumstances. It implied a certain attitude and behavior of the emigrant, incapable of standing up under the pressure of a majority, and referred more to physical and spiritual deportment than to a condition. Knowing the Moor as I imagined I did, I don't think that it was flattering.

"He is a queer bird, the Americaniard; yes sir, very queer—while adaptability was a natural virtue, he overdoes it to the point of being chameleonic, but the expert eye can detect—and what an ape— His health never suffered when he was at home, but the moment he learns a little English, he begins to consult the directory for physicians and psychoanalysts. You ought to know . . . ," he addressed the placid Dr. de los Rios, ". . . yes, he is quick to seize upon all types of unheard-of ailments to use them as so many alibis for his traditional laziness which he imagines, naively enough, to be reprehensible in his new surroundings, wants to be a regular guy, and in the end finds himself prostrate in the recumbent company of the conquering majority. He is a beaten individual with delusions of mediocrity whose defeat has gone to his head and he has no match when playing the ingratiating role of repentant foreigner— He is unique, this Americaniard. He learns to be good-naturedly patronizing toward animals, minorities and foreigners in general, provided they are not his countrymen; speaks of cooperation, and dispensing advice freely to anyone who wants it or not fills him with overflowing well-being and kindly superiority. His childhood having been nursed with wine, he nevertheless learns to backslap and shake hands at the slightest alcoholic provocation. He becomes a freethinker and a liberal, but eats fish on Fridays served with the excuse that it is fresher, and he quotes the Bible. I tell you— the pharisee. Trying to run away from himself, he is always running into mirrors and endeavoring to make the best of his imagined prison. Doesn't know what it's all about—"

He concentrated on me: "You should write a book about the Americaniards, somebody should, but you have not written for a long time—anyway you could not write anymore about your people in Spain—have been too long away, forgotten too much—don't know what it's all about and you could not write about Americans—don't know enough—impossible ever to understand another people. I could not understand them when I first came and every day I understand them less. We meet, we talk, but neither knows what it's all about—total confusion. My English was abominable when I arrived and every day I speak it worse—impossible; can't understand a damn thing."

I have it on good authority that his English was perfect, but he had nursed an invincible accent and an unassailable syntax. He continued: "To write about the Americans would be presumptuously impolite and besides the competition would be formidable both in quality and quantity. . . ." He waved at the public library, the proximity of which probably had something to do with the turn of the conversation, or rather monologue: "Why, between all the publishers, they put out so much that they could pump that whole structure full every year from top to bottom—yes, that should be out of the question. . . ."

I was about to interpolate something but he slapped the intention in mid-air. "Now, about the Americaniards, that is different. You should be an author-ity on the subject by now."

Dr. de los Rios raised a restraining hand: "Leave this fellow alone, you infidel Moor. He wants no trouble and has been making an honest living for a long time as it is. Don't tempt him."

"Of course, to the rescue, Dr. Jesucristo"; this was his established rejoin-der for the nickname of the Moor. "To save a soul from a minor intellectual crime," he addressed me, "snatch yourself away from the sanctimonious hands. Don't let him rob you of eternal condemnation and besides what in-deed more shrewdly appropriate, more shamelessly opportunistic in these good old days of the Latinamericanization of the United States? In this age of good-neighbor policy, which began in the days of the tango and then forti-fied with daiquiris, rum and Coca-Cola and tequila, cavorted through the rumba, the conga, to wind up with the crying jag of the ay, ay, ay?" He sang it and took a few dancing steps despite his bad leg, oblivious of the perplex-ity of passersby and his stick pointed to the former Sixth Avenue. Then he became sober and his criticism of the Americas more pointed.

Feeling well-stocked with demagogic ammunition of irresistible clichés, I thought of mentioning the tactlessness of such comments coming from one who had been so successful, at least financially, in both continents through the frequent tours with his band and was almost ready to use even the one about if you don't like it here why don't you go back . . . , which even Dr. de los Rios had pronounced unanswerable, but well I knew what his disarming answer would be: "We Spaniards reserve the patriarchal privilege to criticize, advise and even scold, by the divine right of the discoverer, the conqueror, and having staked first claim in lofty defiance of the patented rights of the Vikings with their winged helmets and immodest, though ruggedly exposed knees, which we, fully clothed, dressed formally, Christianly and uncomfortably, decline to take seriously." Furthermore, I knew that he would blast me with his remarks on the Indian and his past and present distribution over the Americas; quoting the well-known saying that one example is worth one hundred arguments, he would deluge me with one hundred devastating examples and I, not well versed on the subject, could never find an adequate rebuttal. He had gained such confidence that the last time I fell into the argumentative trap he simply squirted through his teeth the three words "the American Indian" and I gave up.

Unhindered by my unspoken objections he went on with his paradoxical theory of a country accused of imperialism and being invaded by a pacific penetration to the tune of popular torrid music, twice imported Afro-Antillean tempos and tropical concoctions, a fanciful parallel on a soporific smoke screen of narcotics blown ahead over the Orient to gently overcome resistance and render it droolingly happy in its surrender—the devil's own lullaby. All strange, transoceanic parallels indeed to be used as tracks on which to launch his theory of the Latinamericanization of the United States.

But is this the new conquest of the Americas, by the Americas and for the Americas? This mutual transcontinental, translinguistic, transracial osmosis? If so, it is a far cry from the conquistadores to these frightened hybrids, from those who knocked down the door of a new world, to those who knock at the door of a richer world, and the majority of which are lost in a subterraneal labyrinth, like slaves in a mine, to trade their machete for a dishrag, or if more fortunate, though less radical, to transform and adjust their guitar and castanets asymptotically to the afrodisiacuban rattle of the maracas. It is a far, heartrending cry from those Spaniards to these Americaniards.

And yet the Latinamericanization of the United States may be but a special case of its internationalization, as Dr. José de los Rios points out when he remarks that it is an even longer cry from Alexander, Phidias or Archimedes, to a modern Greek running a small shop in some obscure corner of New York, or from the proverbial Asiatic splendor to one of these Chinese laundries. No modern liner has the dignity of the *Pinta*, the *Niña* or the *Santa Maria*, but neither does the bullet have the dignity of the arrow, nor the airplane the dignity of the eagle. And even so, I insist that the objection is temporizing and disregards the main issue by generalizing a secondary, common characteristic. Unquestionably there is sadness in the final surrender and dissolution of any nationality that has come to less, which are most. Witness the mummies and other relics resting in museums of lands other than those where they lived. But what makes the case of the Spaniard especially sad and poignant is the obvious historical associations. I feel that this case must be considered very specially and that it has undeniable priority because after all they were the discoverers of this new world. This is what makes the irony so blatant and leads one to think even more soberly and with more melancholy, that one could have begun all this by parodying a famous speech by a famous North American, something like this:

"Twenty-score and many years ago, my forefathers came to the Americas . . . ," but the rest would be very different and I invite the reader to collaborate, to frame in his mind and consider carefully what might follow; the motives and the ends; one springing from idealism, risking—and perhaps succumbing to—disillusionment: ". . . whether that nation or any nation so conceived and so dedicated, can long endure"—the other running from fate or destiny and doomed to bitter realization.

We were walking east and at the corner of the public library turned and began to walk down the avenue. The Moor changed the subject abruptly by the simple expedient of taking up the new one and suggesting with enthusiasm that we go atop the Empire State Building. He praised the building, the view from its top, spoke like a barker, mentioning that it owed its existence to a great politician whom he admired greatly and considered so castizo that he should have been born in Madrid. He said it would give me perspective to write what he had suggested: "You will see the Americaniards scurrying about below—and many others, yes sir, many others." He said it very confidentially as one imparting the secret of the ages.

Dr. de los Rios stopped short: "Let's not and stop importuning this fellow. First you frighten him with your ghosts of complications that beset us in an English-speaking environment and now . . . ," he turned to me: "Don't sell your soul to this devil. There is still time. Don't follow him." He saw me weaken, waver, ready to succumb under the hypnotic spell of the Moor who stood there shamelessly making passes, exorcisms and incantations, right in front of the library, and then Dr. de los Rios was magnanimous: "All right; go and sin no more. But I will not sanction this with my presence. In fact, since we left that bench I have been debating whether to go in there and look up one or two things, which I have been intending to do for some time." He turned suddenly and went up the steps of the library with extraordinary lightness and agility.

No sooner was he gone than the dark sleeve of the Moor closed over my shoulders like the cloak of Satan, propelling me along to my doom, and he renewed his assault. I was endeavoring to think up objections and I knew there were plenty, but I was confused. Vaguely I thought that the task he proposed was well beyond my ability, that to choose representative characters from the imposing array of what he called the Americaniards and to put them on paper was as much above my head and meager stock of diligence as the building toward which we were walking, but I'd swear that the sly Moor was reading my mind. The master promoter of intellectual pranks was in full command.

"Don't worry about that. You do not have to use new ones. Use any old ones you may have about. In fact, you must have smuggled some already without the immigration authorities being the wiser—on paper. Know what I mean?" He held me at arm's length without interrupting our syncopated walk. "And I know where we can find them and you too know the place." I was dizzy and was sure that I was walking in my sleep and dreaming. The monotonous beating of the bare end of his shillelagh against the pavement must have been instrumental in the hypnosis. "We will go back there, but after dark. First we go up and look and wait, and then when night falls, we go down back there. The prophecies say that your little smug intellectual crime must be thus perpetrated, without attenuating circumstances, thus it will be lower, more revolting, more dastardly and—more fascinating." So help me, he actually hissed the last words loudly, with bestial mockery.

Never a match for him, I was lost. Staggering drunkenly under my opprobrium, I blubbered hopelessly, inaudibly: "Haven't got a typewriter," but I knew that all resistance was useless and this last gesture as pitiful as trying to save oneself from a conflagration by spitting on it.

"I'll get you one, if I have to get your own out of hock—" and on he swept me.

Entering the elevator had a quality of sepulchral irrevocability, of being walled alive, of the catafalque, and I knew that I was at his mercy, in his mental grip and certain that he was thinking through me, but that he must have found me a very crude tool. The momentary increase in weight in this minimum of space equated the sensation of motion to zero, or compensated it by creating the feeling of moving in opposite directions simultaneously. All the time that we were going up, we were falling with constant acceleration and this made one think of the misleading and pitiful attempts at propagandizing relativity. Then the slight pressure in the ears brought anticipation reflecting in the future, childhood reminiscences of Verne, Wells and Flammarion and when finally one emerged, it was like coming out of a long anesthetic, with a gasp and a vertigo at the explosion of the view which reached dangerously near the confines of pleasure.

Don Pedro ambled about and took his position here and there, frowning his contemplation almost truculently and when he stopped, hunched, holding his stick in both hands, he looked like a bird of prey, perched, poised, ready to dive, but then he only waved his arm downward like a readying dark wing and pointed in silence. Thus we stood and looked, never uttering a word, and then night began to arch and close over us like a dome from the East.

Manhattan looked like a quarry. The conglomeration of buildings seemed to point, to call and appeal and crowd about this leader for guidance, their sharp outlines reaching vainly, and with nightfall the quarry was a mine shining with gold that increased in profusion and brightness and gradually overflowed and ran in rivers to the hazy horizons. Under the crescent moon glowing like the lamp of Aladdin, one could not help thinking of it as the gold mine which has lured and swallowed so many, and the buildings continued to call and appeal temptingly and dangerously, until nothing but the lights could be seen. Down on the prism of the sidewalks, they were diffused reflection of livid dancing polarization, the streets spectral bands. This was the light fantastic on the sidewalks of New York and as each star appeared above, it found its reflection below, until the city had become a multiplying mirror of the sky.

And at last, to wake up from the dream or sink further into it, his fateful words: "Time to go."

If the building had become a medieval castle and he had descended clinging to the outside walls . . . but we went down by way of the elevator with the sinking sensation that often startles and makes one jump in bed when falling asleep.

Everything was foreordained and all inevitable. The old but well-kept Hispano-Suiza that slid to a stop before us, quietly, dark and foreboding like a hearse. The uncanny timing, everything suggested Satanism and witchcraft, the dragnet of Lucifer.

No doubt his Cuban boy was at the wheel as usual and this was one reassuring contact with friendly reality. He was a simpático fellow in perennial good humor and with a well-developed incapacity to take anything seriously. Probably well-trained in his native and tough school of voodoo and the evil eye, he was hardened by his association with the Moor and could keep his equanimity under the most trying circumstances. But I could only guess that he was there because the dividing curtain was drawn and we might as well have been driven by a ghost. I ventured to suggest meekly that the place might have been torn down, but the Moor answered in cryptic jest that we were returning to the past by the fourth perpendicular and I would find everything as I had left it. Nothing more was said and the drive across town and then down the West Side was swift and deliberate with all the ephemeral finality of a blackout.

One block from our destination we got out and before I had time to look into the driver's compartment, the car drove away. We walked along the dark street and I tried to lag behind, to find one last desperate excuse, but the Moor took hold of my arm and marched me until we were in front of the old basement. Then came the blinding flash of hope:

"But the key. I am sure I don't have it."

"Seek and thou shall find; haa—"

Inserting one's hand in one's pocket and finding it empty is conceded to create the deepest consternation, but this was worse; the key was there and I was crushed.

"But suppose that someone has moved in since."

"Don't worry. It is empty all right." And I knew that he was right, that he was master and this was destiny, that there was no escape: "Go and get it over with. It won't take long."

"Aren't you coming in?"

"No. I'll wait for you out here and act as a lookout." The shameless conspiracy of it, the insulting confabulatory implication: "But give me a cigarette. I am all out of them." The crowning insult.

I gave him the cigarette and lighted it for him endeavoring to postpone things—the nadir of abjection—but then the conviction that I was dreaming decided me to sleep the thing through to certain awakening and calmly I inserted a key which I had never expected to use again. As I did this, the last hopeful and irrelevant memory of the Moor's ancestor returning to Granada ran through my mind, but the door opened easily and swung inward without a squeak.

The street outside had been dark enough, but the room was pitch-black. I still held the matches in my hand and lit one. There was no furniture, and as I advanced toward the far wall, I felt my shadow creeping and growing behind me and bending with the ceiling as if to pounce.

Ever since I had entered the former neighborhood and as we approached this house, the tense anticipation had been growing at a rate suggesting the law of the inverse square which I had often heard Don Pedro mention, and on entering the room, it exploded with the full force of memories that were overpowering as the present multiplied by their distance.

I looked around carefully, keeping my vigilant shadow unmolested behind and above me, like a cobra. The stains and cracks on the walls became those of bare stone, creating confusing and bizarre designs like those of a sarcophagus. Some old calendar chromos still clung to them: one showing a man with calañes and short jacket serenading a young lady with high comb and very black, mournful eyes at a window with bars and profusely surrounded by flowers; another was a chapel with a recumbent bullfighter dying on a couch with a beshawled woman, her head buried in his bloody chest and all around the austere, stoic, classical countenances of the loyal members of his cuadrilla and a tearful old lady staring her reproach at the altar and the eternal old priest withholding discreetly his understanding and faith and soothing blessing, but attentive to the duties of his office in performing the last rites; chromos that had once been brilliantly bursting with color and drama, but were now faded and desecrated by fly stains; chromos in disrepute.

The bookcase with its books was still at the far wall, the only piece of furniture left in that room once abandoned in the great divide of life. I reached for one of the books, felt the thick dust on it and pulled. A cockroach crawled over my hand and I let go of the book. It fell on the floor where it lay open and I fancied I saw more bugs run out of it in all directions. They ran up the walls, over and under the chromos which in the uncertain light of the match seemed to oscillate painfully, to grow dolefully animated and gather the deceptive depth of a reverie, reaching for the cracks, the shadows in the walls as if to pull them like a shroud over their shame, to resume their disturbed sleep, and as the walls seemed to recede, the shadows running through them like waves, merged with the pictures to form a confused tapestry depicting people and scenes that came to life, but more like things remembered or imagined, because the walls were no longer there.

BERNARDO VEGA

The *Memoirs of Bernardo Vega*, published posthumously in 1977, provides an invaluable account of the early phase of Puerto Rican migration to New York City, where Vega (1885–1965) arrived in 1916. He was a *tabaquero* (cigar-factory worker), labor organizer, political activist, writer, and founder of the Spanish-language newspaper *Gráfico*. By his own account, Vega wrote his *Memoirs* while "still filled with indignation and anger over the ridiculous hardships to which we were subjected. . . . It pained me to see so many good, cultivated people subjected to shameful treatment and forced to accept injustice in order to stay alive."

from
Memoirs of Bernardo Vega

FROM MY HOMETOWN CAYEY TO SAN JUAN, AND HOW I ARRIVED IN NEW YORK WITHOUT A WATCH

Early in the morning of August 2, 1916, I took leave of Cayey. I got on the bus at the Plaza and sat down, squeezed in between passengers and suitcases. Of my traveling companions I remember nothing. I don't think I opened my mouth the whole way. I just stared at the landscape, sunk in deep sorrow. I was leaving a girlfriend in town . . .

But my readers are very much mistaken if they expect a sentimental love story from me. I don't write to pour my heart out—confessions of love bore me to death, especially my own. So, to make a long story short, the girl's parents, brothers, relatives, and well-wishers declared war on me. That's not exactly why I decided to leave, but that small-town drama of Montagues and Capulets did have an influence. Anyway, I left Cayey that hot summer, heavy of heart, but ready to face a new life.

From an early age I had worked as a cigar-roller in a tobacco factory. I had just turned thirty, and although it was not the first time I had left my hometown, never before had I put the shores of Puerto Rico behind me. I had been to the capital a few times. But now it meant going farther, to a strange and distant world. I hadn't the slightest idea what fate awaited me.

In those days I was taller than most Puerto Ricans. I was white, a peasant from the highlands (a *jíbaro*), and there was that waxen pallor to my face so typical of country folk. I had a round face with high cheekbones, a wide, flat nose, and small blue eyes. As for my lips, well, I'd say they were rather sensual, and I had strong, straight teeth. I had a full head of light chestnut hair, and, in contrast to the roundness of my face, I had square jaws. All in all, I suppose I was rather ugly, though there were women around who thought otherwise.

I did not inspire much sympathy at first sight, I'm sure of that. I have never made friends easily. No doubt my physical appearance has a lot to do with it. I hadn't been living in New York for long before I realized how difficult it was for people to guess where I came from. Time and again I was taken for a Polish Jew, or a Tartar, or even a Japanese . . . God forgive my dear parents for my human countenance, which was after all the only thing they had bequeathed me!

I arrived in San Juan at around ten o'clock in the morning. I ordered the driver to take me to El Comercio, a cheap hotel I knew of on Calle Tetuán. I left my suitcase and went out for a walk in the city.

The sun warmed the pavements of the narrow streets. I longed for the morning chill of my native Toa valley. I decided to go for a ride in a trolley car and say goodbye to an old schoolteacher of mine. To her I owed my first stop. Her name was Elisa Rubio and I have fond memories of her to this day. In her little house in Santurce she told me glowing things about the United States and praised my decision to emigrate. I would have a chance to study there. To this day, after all these years, her exaggerated praise echoes in my mind: "You have talent and ambition. You will get ahead, I am sure. And you'll become famous." Heaven forgive my well-meaning teacher.

On my return to the old section of San Juan, I spent the afternoon taking leave of my comrades. There was Manuel F. Rojas, who had been elected secretary general of the Partido Socialista at the constituent assembly recently held in Cayey, my hometown, which I had attended as a delegate. With him were Santiago Iglesias, Prudencio Rivera Martínez, and Rafael Alonso

Torres . . . They all were unhappy about my decision to leave because of the loss it would be for our newly organized workers' movement. But they did not try hard to dissuade me. As socialists, we dig our trenches everywhere in the world.

I returned to the little hotel tired and sweaty. Before going up to my room I bought the daily newspapers—*La Correspondencia*, *El Tiempo*, *La Democracia*. In shirtsleeves, I threw myself onto my bed and plunged into the latest events of the day.

In those days our newspapers were not as big as they are today—none were over twelve pages. The news, especially about foreign affairs, did not take up much space. But our native writers waxed eloquent in endless polemics—original commentaries, sharp criticism, and plenty of our local humor. They reflected the life of the whole society—or rather, of its ruling class—with uneven success, but in any case they were more truthful than they are today, for sure.

Night fell, and I washed up, dressed, and went back out in the street. I had a long conversation with Benigno Fernández García, the son of a prestigious Cayey family. We talked about the European war, in which the United States was soon to be involved. Then I returned to my hotel, went to bed, and tried to sleep, but it was impossible. My mind was full of memories and my heart ached. Until then I had been acting like a robot, or a man under the influence of drugs. Now, alone in the darkness of my room, I recalled my mother's tears, the sad faces of my little brothers . . . I just couldn't get to sleep.

Once again I went back into the streets. It had rained. A pleasant breeze blew through the city. The bright moon lit up the streets. The damp pavements glistened. And I took to walking, up one street and down another, in an intimate chat with the cobblestones of that city which means so much to Puerto Ricans.

Dawn caught me by surprise, seated on one of the benches in the Plaza de Armas now and then looking up at the big clock. The cheerful rattle of the first trolley car brought me back to sad reality. Within a few minutes the bold tropical sun had taken possession of San Juan, and the streets were crowded with people. Gentlemen in jackets and hats left home to go to work. But the largest crowds were made up of people flocking in from the countryside, dealers in agricultural produce. Cornflakes had not yet replaced corn on the cob, though things were already headed in that direction.

The hours passed quickly. At around two in the afternoon I boarded the boat, the famous *Coamo* which made so many trips from San Juan to New York and back. I took a quick look at my cabin, and went right back up on deck. I did not want to lose a single breath of those final minutes in my country, perhaps the last ones I would ever have.

Soon the boat pushed off from the dock, turned, and began to move slowly toward El Morro castle at the mouth of the harbor. A nun who worked at the women's home was waving *adiós* from high up on the ramparts; I assumed she meant it for me. As soon as we were on the open sea and the boat started to pitch, the passengers went off to their cabins, most of them already half seasick. Not I. I stayed up on deck, lingering there until the island was lost from sight in the first shadows of nightfall.

The days passed peacefully. Sunrise of the first day and the passengers were already acting as though they belonged to one family. It was not long before we came to know each other's life stories. The topic of conversation, of course, was what lay ahead: life in New York. First savings would be for sending for close relatives. Years later the time would come to return home with pots of money. Everyone's mind was on that farm they'd be buying or the business they'd set up in town . . . All of us were building our own little castles in the sky.

When the fourth day dawned even those who had spent the whole trip cooped up in their cabins showed up on deck. We saw the lights of New York even before the morning mist rose. As the boat entered the harbor the sky was clear and clean. The excitement grew the closer we got to the docks. We recognized the Statue of Liberty in the distance. Countless smaller boats were sailing about in the harbor. In front of us rose the imposing sight of skyscrapers—the same skyline we had admired so often on postcards. Many of the passengers had only heard talk of New York, and stood with their mouths open, spellbound . . . Finally the *Coamo* docked at Hamilton Pier on Staten Island.

First to disembark were the passengers traveling first class—businessmen, well-to-do families, students. In second class, where I was, there were the emigrants, most of us *tabaqueros*, or cigar workers. We all boarded the ferry that crossed from Staten Island to lower Manhattan. We sighed as we set foot on solid ground. There, gaping before us, were the jaws of the iron dragon: the immense New York metropolis.

All of us new arrivals were well dressed. I mean, we had on our Sunday best. I myself was wearing a navy blue woolen suit (or *flus*, as they would say back home), a borsalino hat made of Italian straw, black shoes with pointy toes, a white vest, and a red tie. I would have been sporting a shiny wristwatch too, if a traveling companion hadn't warned me that in New York it was considered effeminate to wear things like that. So as soon as the city was in sight, and the boat was entering the harbor, I tossed my watch into the sea . . . And to think that it wasn't long before those wristwatches came into fashion and ended up being the rage!

And so I arrived in New York, without a watch.

THE TRIALS AND TRIBULATIONS OF AN
EMIGRANT IN THE IRON TOWER OF BABEL
ON THE EVE OF WORLD WAR I

The Battery, which as I found out later is what they call the tip of lower Manhattan where our ferry from Staten Island docked, was also a port of call for all the elevated trains. The Second, Third, Sixth, and Ninth Avenue lines all met there. I entered the huge station with Ambrosio Fernández, who had come down to meet me at the dock. The noise of the trains was deafening, and I felt as if I was drowning in the crowd. Funny, but now that I was on land I started to feel seasick. People were rushing about every which way, not seeming to know exactly where they were headed. Now and then one of them would cast a mocking glance at the funny-looking travelers with their suitcases and other baggage. Finally there I was in a subway car, crushed by the mobs of passengers, kept afloat only by the confidence I felt in the presence of my friend.

The train snaked along at breakneck speed. I pretended to take note of everything, my eyes like the golden deuce in a deck of Spanish cards. The further along we moved, and as the dingy buildings filed past my view, all the visions I had of the gorgeous splendor of New York vanished. The skyscrapers seemed like tall gravestones. I wondered why, if the United States was so rich, as surely it was, did its biggest city look so grotesque? At that moment I sensed for the first time that people in New York could not possibly be as happy as we used to think they were back home in Cayey.

Ambrosio rescued me from my brooding. We were at the 23rd Street station. We got off and walked down to 22nd Street. We were on the West Side. At number 228 I took up my first lodgings. It was a boarding house run by Mrs. Arnao, the place where Ambrosio was living.

On my first day in New York I didn't go out at all. There was a lot to talk about, and Ambrosio and I had lengthy conversations. I told him the latest from Puerto Rico, about our families and friends. He talked about the city, what life was like, what the chances were of finding a job . . . To put it mildly, an utterly dismal picture.

Ambrosio himself was out of work, which led me to ask myself, "Now, if Ambrosio is out of a job, and he's been here a while and isn't just a cigar-worker but a silversmith and watchmaker to boot, then how am I ever going to find anything?" My mind began to cloud over with doubts; frightening shadows fell over my immediate future. I dreaded the thought of finding myself out in the streets of such a big, inhospitable city. I paid the landlady a few weeks' rent in advance. Then, while continuing my conversation with Ambrosio, I took the further precautionary measure of sewing the money for my return to Puerto Rico into the lining of my jacket. I knew I only had a few months to find work before winter descended on us. If I didn't, I figured I'd send New York to the devil and haul anchor.

Word was that Mrs. Arnao was married to a Puerto Rican dentist, though I never saw hide nor hair of the alleged tooth-puller around the house. She was an industrious woman and her rooming house was furnished in elegant taste. She had a flair for cooking and could prepare a delectable dinner, down to the peapods. At the time I arrived her only other boarder was Ambrosio, which led me to suspect that she wasn't doing too well financially.

But in those days you didn't need much to get by in New York. Potatoes were selling for a fraction of a cent a pound; eggs were fifteen cents a dozen; a pound of salt pork was going for twelve cents, and a prime steak for twenty cents. A nickel would buy a lot of vegetables. You could pick up a good suit for $10.00. With a nickel fare you could get anywhere in the city, and change from one line to another without having to pay more.

The next day I went out with Ambrosio to get to know New York. We headed for Fifth Avenue, where we got on a double-decker bus. It was the first time I had ever been on one of those strange contraptions! The tour was terrific. The bus went uptown, crossed over on 110th Street and made its way up Riverside Drive. At 135th Street we took Broadway up to 168th Street, and then St. Nicholas Avenue to 191st. From our comfortable seats on the upper deck we could soak in all the sights—the shiny store windows, then the mansions, and later on the gray panorama of the Hudson River.

In later years I took the same trip many times. But I was never as impressed as I was then, even though on other occasions I was often in better company. Not to say that Ambrosio wasn't good company, don't get me wrong!

At the end of our tour, where we got off the bus, was a little park. We strolled through it, reading the inscriptions commemorating the War of Independence. We couldn't help noticing the young couples kissing right there in public. At first it upset me to witness such an embarrassing scene. But I quickly realized that our presence didn't matter to them, and Ambrosio confirmed my impression. What a difference between our customs back home and the behavior of Puerto Rican men and women in New York!

We returned by the same route, but got off the bus at 110th Street. We walked up Manhattan Avenue to 116th, which is where the León brothers—Antonio, Pepín, and Abelardo—were living. They owned a small cigar factory. They were part of a family from Cayey that had emigrated to New York back in 1904. The members of that family were some of the first Puerto Ricans to settle in the Latin *barrio* of Harlem. In those days the Nadals, Matienzos, Pietris, Escalonas, and Umpierres lived there too; I also knew of a certain Julio Ortíz. In all, I'd say there were some one hundred and fifty Puerto Ricans living in that part of the city around the turn of the century.

Before our countrymen, there were other Hispanics here. There was a sizable Cuban colony in the last quarter of the nineteenth century, members of the Quesada, Arango, and Mantilla families, as well as Emilia Casanova de Villaverde. They must have been people of some means, since they lived in apartments belonging to Sephardic Jews on 110th Street facing Central Park.

As I was saying, when I took up residence in New York in 1916 the apartment buildings and stores in what came to be known as El Barrio, "our" barrio, or the Barrio Latino, all belonged to Jews. Seventh, St. Nicholas, and Manhattan avenues, and the streets in between, were all inhabited by Jewish people of means, if not great wealth. 110th Street was the professional center of the district. The classy, expensive stores were on Lenox Avenue, while the more modest ones were located east of Fifth Avenue. The ghetto of poor Jews extended along Park Avenue between 110th and 117th and on the streets east of Madison. It was in this lower class Jewish neighborhood that some Puerto Rican and Cuban families, up to about fifty of them, were living at that time. Here, too, was where a good many Puerto Rican cigarworkers, bachelors for the most part, occupied the many furnished rooms in the blocks between Madison and Park.

On Park Avenue was an open-air market where you could buy things at low prices. Early in the morning the vendors would set up their stands on the sidewalk under the elevated train, and in the afternoon they would pack up their goods for the night. The marketplace was dirty and stank to high heaven, and remained that way until the years of Mayor Fiorello La Guardia, who put the market in the condition it is in today.

Many of the Jews who lived there in those days were recent immigrants, which made the whole area seem like a Tower of Babel. There were Sephardic Jews who spoke ancient Spanish or Portuguese; there were those from the Near East and from the Mediterranean, who spoke Italian, French, Provençal, Roumanian, Turkish, Arabic, or Greek. Many of them, in fact, could get along in five or even six languages. On makeshift shelves and display cases, hanging from walls and wire hangers, all kinds of goods were on display. You could buy everything from the simplest darning needle to a complete trousseau. For a quarter you could get a used pair of shoes and for two or three cents a bag of fruit or vegetables.

At the end of our visit to this neighborhood, Ambrosio and I stopped off for dinner at a restaurant called La Luz. We were attracted by the Spanish name, though the owner was actually a Sephardic Jew. The food was not prepared in the style that was familiar to us, but we did notice that the sauces were of Spanish origin. The customers who frequented the place spoke Castilian Spanish. Their heated discussions centered on the war raging in Europe. From what I could gather, most of them thought that the United

States would soon be involved in the conflict, and that the Germans would be defeated in the end.

I was impressed by the restaurant because it was so hard to believe that it was located in the United States. There was something exotic about the atmosphere. The furniture and decor gave it the appearance of a café in Spain or Portugal. Even the people who gathered there, their gestures and speech mannerisms, identified them as from Galicia, Andalusia, Aragon, or some other Iberian region. I began to recognize that New York City was really a modern Babylon, the meeting point for peoples from all over the world.

At this time Harlem was a socialist stronghold. The Socialist Party had set up a large number of clubs in the neighborhood. Young working people would get together not only for political purposes but for cultural and sports activities and all kinds of parties. There were two major community centers organized by the party: the Harlem Terrace on 104th Street (a branch of the Rand School), and the Harlem Educational Center on 106th between Madison and Park. Other cultural societies and a large number of workers' cooperatives also worked out of these centers. Meetings and large indoor activities were held at the Park Palace, an auditorium with a large seating capacity. Outdoor public events were held at the corner of 110th Street and Fifth Avenue. All kinds of political, economic, social, and philosophical issues were discussed there; every night speakers aired their views, with the active participation of the public.

Housing in that growing neighborhood was for the most part owned by people who lived there. In many buildings the owners lived in one apartment and rented out the rest. There was still little or no exploitation of tenants by absentee landlords who had nothing to do with the community. The apartments were spacious and quite comfortable. They were well maintained precisely because the owners themselves lived in the buildings. Clearly, the Jewish people who lived in Harlem back then considered it their neighborhood and felt a sentimental attachment to it. Several generations had grown up there; they had their own schools, synagogues, and theaters . . . But all of this changed rapidly during the war and in the years to follow.

It was late, almost closing time, when we reached the León brothers' little cigar factory. Antonio, the eldest, harbored vivid memories of his little hometown of Cayey, which he had left so many years ago. His younger brothers,

Pepín and Abelardo, had emigrated later but felt the same kind of nostalgia. There we were, pining for our distant homeland, when Ambrosio finally brought up the problem at hand: my pressing need for work. "Work, here?" the elder brother exclaimed. "This dump hardly provides for us!" Thus, my dream of rolling cigars in the León brothers' little factory was shattered. My tribulations in the iron Tower of Babel had begun.

PROLETARIANS EXTEND A HAND, BUT HUNGER PINCHES AND THERE IS NO REMEDY BUT TO WORK IN A WEAPONS FACTORY

The following day Ambrosio and I began the challenging task of looking for work. We set out for the neighborhood where the bulk of the cigarworkers then lived: the blocks along Third Avenue, between 64th and 106th streets. Spread out over this large area were a lot of Puerto Ricans. There were also a lot in Chelsea, and up on the West Side of Manhattan, which is where the ones with money lived.

After Manhattan, the borough with the largest concentration of Puerto Ricans was Brooklyn, in the Boro Hall area, especially on Sand, Adams, and Pearl streets, and over near the Navy Yard. Puerto Rican neighborhoods in the Bronx and the outlying parts of Manhattan were still unknown.

Between 15th and 20th streets on the East Side there were the boarding houses that served as residences primarily for Puerto Rican *tabaqueros*. I especially remember the houses owned by Isidro Capdevila and Juan Crusellas. They were where Francisco Ramos, Félix Rodríguez Infanzón, Juan Cruz, Lorenzo Verdeguez, Pedro Juan Alfaro, and Alfonso Baerga were staying.

In 1916 the Puerto Rican colony in New York amounted to about six thousand people, mostly *tabaqueros* and their families. The broader Spanish-speaking population was estimated at 16,000.

There were no notable color differences between the various pockets of Puerto Ricans. Especially in the section between 99th and 106th, there were quite a few black *paisanos*. Some of them, like Arturo Alfonso Schomburg, Agustín Vázquez, and Isidro Manzano, later moved up to the black North American neighborhood. As a rule, people lived in harmony in the Puerto Rican neighborhoods, and racial differences were of no concern.

That day we visited a good many cigar factories. The men on the job were friendly. Many of them even said they would help us out if we needed it. That's how cigarworkers were, the same in Puerto Rico as in Cuba, the same in Tampa as in New York. They had a strong sense of *compañerismo*— we were all brothers. But they couldn't make a place for us at the worktable of any factory.

I spent the days that followed going around the city and visiting places of interest. A "card-carrying" socialist, I made my way down to the editors of the *New York Call*, the Socialist Party paper which back then had a circulation in the hundreds of thousands. I showed a letter of introduction given to me by Santiago Iglesias before I left San Juan, and they welcomed me like a brother. Some of the editorial staff spoke our language and showed great interest in the situation in Puerto Rico. We talked about the conditions of the workers, strikes, and the personality of Iglesias . . . They insisted that I come back that afternoon to talk to Morris Hillquit, the leader of the party.

My conversation with Comrade Hillquit centered around the question of the political sovereignty of Puerto Rico. In his opinion, our country should be constituted as a republic, while maintaining friendly relations with the United States. He told me that was what he advised Santiago Iglesias. "I do not understand," he added, "how that political position could not appear in the program of the Partido Socialista of Puerto Rico."

I left very impressed by my meetings with the North American comrades. A few days later I introduced myself to the Socialist Section of Chelsea. The secretary was an Irishman by the name of Carmichael. He attended to me in a friendly fashion and signed me up as a member, after which he introduced me to a comrade by the name of Henry Gotay. A sailor by trade, Henry was a descendant of Felipe Gotay, that celebrated Puerto Rican who commanded one of the regiments of Narciso López' army in its final and unsuccessful invasion on Cuba. Henry in turn introduced me to Ventura Mijón and Emiliano Ramos, two Puerto Rican *tabaquero* militants. They belonged to an anarchist group led by Pedro Esteves and associated with the newspaper *Cultura Proletaria*, the organ of the Spanish anarchists in New York.

In Henry's judgment, Mijón, Ramos, and Esteves were simply degrading their own intelligence and wasting their time preaching such a utopian cause. Henry was a man of deep socialist convictions. I had lunch that day with him and Carmichael at a Greek place on 27th Street and Eighth Avenue. It was an interesting experience—it was the first time I ever drank whisky. As I was not used to alcoholic beverages, I got very drunk and my two new friends had to carry me home. That was the first time I was dead drunk in New York!

Liquor in those years was dirt cheap. A hearty shot of the best brand went for a dime. All the bars had what was called "free lunch," with an endless assortment of tidbits free for the taking: cheese, ham, smoked fish, eggs, potatoes, onions, olives . . . I must admit I was a frequent client of those taverns in my needier days. I would nurse my ten-cent shot and stuff my face with free goodies. What a shame when a few years later prohibition put an end to those paradises of the poor!

My drunk cost me several days in bed. All I had to do was take a drink of water and the whisky would roll around in my stomach and I'd be drunk all over again. But once I was back on my feet I headed straight for the Socialist Club. I was there often, and Carmichael, Henry, and I became close friends. They helped me straighten out some personal problems and went to great lengths to find me a job. But times were very bad. There simply was no work, and with every passing day I saw my situation grow bleaker and bleaker . . . "As a last resort," my friend said, "when your money runs out and you can't pay your rent, bring your belongings here and sleep in the club. And as for food, don't worry about that either. There'll be some here for you. The party has an emergency fund for cases like this." Those words gave me such a lift!

In the following days I visited Local 90 of the Cigarmakers' Union, which was a local led by the "progressives" in the union. Jacob Ryan held the post of secretary. I showed him my "travel card," establishing me as a member of the Puerto Rico chapter of the International Cigarmakers' Union/A.F.L. I wasn't given much of a welcome; my meeting with the secretary was cold and formal.

I immediately started attending union meetings at the hall up on 84th Street off Second Avenue. There I met many countrymen who had been living in New York since the end of the century. The militancy of those Puerto Rican cigarmakers had been a decisive factor in the election of progressive candidates to leading positions in the local.

Despite all my efforts, after more than a month in New York I was still unemployed. If I didn't find something soon I knew I'd be in serious straits.

How much longer could I stretch the little money I had? The bills I had sewn into the lining of my jacket were of course sacred, so I decided to resort to an employment agency and "buy" a job. Yes, sure, I had already been warned of all the traps set to catch the innocent. I knew how mercilessly they would swindle foreigners by "selling" them imaginary jobs. But I had to turn somewhere, and even the slightest hope was better than none. So I showed up, along with my friend Ambrosio, who was also still out of work, at one of those infamous agencies. We paid our $15.00 and set our hopes on the employment due us.

Day in, day out, we would go to the agency and be sent off to some remote "workplace." More often than not it turned out that the street number, and even the street, was completely unknown to anyone. Other times we would track down the address, only to find an abandoned building. We would of course go back to the agency and explain what had happened, but they would only treat us like idiots who couldn't even find our way around town. Finally it began to dawn on us that we were being made fools of.

One day I woke up with that *jíbaro* spirit boiling in my blood. When we got there, the agency was full of innocent new victims. I went straight up to the man in charge and raised holy hell. I yelled at him—partly in English but mostly in Spanish—and demanded my money back immediately. A few Spaniards heard the noise and joined me in a loud chorus, demanding the return of their money too. Two employees of the agency grabbed me by the arms and tried to throw me down the stairs. But the Spaniards jumped to my defense. Finally the boss of the place, afraid of a serious scandal and police involvement, gave all of us our money back.

At the next meeting of the Socialist Club I recounted my experience at the employment agency, and it was decided to make a complaint to the authorities. I later found out that they did in fact conduct an investigation, and that the agency had its license suspended. The fact is, though, that the injustices of those infamous agencies continued, and that Puerto Ricans became their most favored prey.

In those years, and for a long time to come, the Socialist Party, the Cigarmakers' Union, and the Seamen's Union were the only groups that were concerned about defending foreign workers. The other labor unions either showed no interest, or were too weak to do anything, as in the case of the Dressmakers' Union, which later became the powerful International Ladies' Garment Workers' Union. It should also be mentioned that the Fur and Leather Workers' Union showed its solidarity with the struggles of foreign workers.

Socialist influence was strong among the Jews. Many of their organizations worked with the Socialist Party and the labor unions. Most outstanding of all were the Jewish Workmen's Circle and the liberal-minded newspaper *Forward*.

I began to move in these circles and go to a lot of their activities. Truth is, though, that as far as finding work is concerned none of it did me any good. On top of that, the landlady at our rooming house, Mrs. Arnao, began to ask us every single day whether or not we had found work. Even though we would pay her religiously every week, she started to have an unpleasant look on her face.

At the same time, the warm hospitality we had enjoyed at the boarding house was cooling down. There was not such a variety of food as in our first days there. The rooms weren't cared for as carefully as they had been at the beginning. The hatchet finally fell on a Friday, after dinner. Suddenly Mrs. Arnao informed us that she was thinking of going away on a trip and that we would have to move out.

Figuring that misery makes poor company, Ambrosio and I decided to part ways. We headed off in different directions. Before long word had it that my friend had found work in a gunpowder factory. As for me, I took up lodgings at the house of a certain Rodríguez, a cigarmaker from Bayamón who had a boarding house on East 86th Street. It was actually the first floor of a modern building. The apartment was spacious and comfortable. The roomers in the house were mostly Hungarians and Czechs. The style of life in the neighborhood was strictly European, filled with traces of old Vienna, Berlin, and Prague.

Mr. Rodríguez' wife was an excellent Puerto Rican woman. To her misfortune, however, her husband drank whisky the way a camel drinks water. When he was sober he was mild-mannered and good natured, but when he took to drinking, which was usually the case, he liked to pick fights.

Several Puerto Ricans were also staying in the house, very good people to be sure. Many others of the same caliber came by to visit. Among them I got to know Paco Candelas, J. Amy Sanjurjo, J. Correa, Pablo Ortíz, and Pepe

Lleras. It was a pleasant neighborhood: the atmosphere was neat and clean, the people friendly and open-minded. Everyone would express themselves in their own tongue. Most people spoke English, but poorly, and always with a foreign accent.

There were excellent restaurants in the neighborhood. You had your choice—Hungarian, German, Czech, Italian, Montenegran . . . Quite a few of them would imitate the style of cafés in Vienna and Bohemia. The area was full of good-looking women, especially Hungarian. A lot were blonde, though you'd also see dark-haired ones with that distinctive gypsy beauty! I must admit that it was those women, who looked so much like the ones from my home country, that most appealed to the romantic side of me. But what could a man do who was out of work and down to his last pennies?

But I enjoyed the neighborhood anyway. On 86th Street there were five theaters where they not only showed films but put on live shows. I loved the diversity of people. Nearby was the German colony, where the socialists were active in all community affairs. There were many meeting places there, most notably the Labor Temple. Down a little ways was the Czech area, with its center of activity being the Bohemian National Hall (*Narodni Budova*), between First and Second avenues. The followers of Beneš and Masaryk used to meet there before Czechoslovakia became an independent state.

Around the time that I went to live in that part of town a good many Puerto Ricans were beginning to move in too. Many Hispanics, especially Cubans from the time of José Martí, lived on those streets. Right in the heart of that area, in fact, at 235 East 75th Street, is where our illustrious country-man Sotero Figueroa lived for many years.

It certainly was a good thing that I liked the neighborhood, because the truth is that my situation was desperate. Winter was near and I didn't even have adequate clothing. As fall set in I spent my days feeling the lining of my jacket and that precious return fare to Puerto Rico. But I wasn't about to give up until the eleventh hour . . .

One morning my fellow townsman Pepe Lleras invited me to go with him to Kingsland over in New Jersey. My good friend Lleras, who was also unemployed, convinced me that the only place we would be able to find work was in the munitions industry. So off we went to one of those immense plants. When asked in the personnel office if we had any experience, we said yes. I was so set on landing something that I almost went so far as to say I had grown up playing with gunpowder!

That was my first job in the United States. The war in Europe was at its height. The Germans had just suffered a setback at Verdun. In the United States, war material was being produced in enormous quantities. The work in the munitions plant was very hard. Only those hardened by rigorous labor could stand it. It really was too much for the soft hands of *tabaqueros* like ourselves. They would work us for eight hours without a break. Even to do your private business you had to get permission from the lead man of the work crew, and he would only relieve you for a few short minutes. Never before had I experienced, or even witnessed, such brutal working conditions.

Pepe and I would be out of the house at five in the morning. It took us almost two hours to get there. The work day started at seven and we would spend the whole day surrounded by all kinds of grenades and explosives. Most of the workers were Italians of peasant stock, tough as the marble of their country. There were also a lot of Norwegian, Swedish, and Polish workers, most of them as strong as oxen . . . Pepe Lleras and I, though better built than the average Puerto Rican, were beaten to a pulp after two weeks.

On the way home we would collapse onto the seat of the train like two drunks, and when we got home we hardly even felt like eating. Our hands were all beaten and bloody and felt like they were burning. After massaging each other's backs, we would throw ourselves into bed like tired beasts of burden. At the crack of dawn, feeling as though we had hardly slept more than a few minutes, we'd be up and off to another day's labor.

One day—we hadn't been there long—we met up with a stroke of hard luck. We used to get there a few minutes before work began to change into our work clothes. It so happened that one afternoon at the end of the day we couldn't find our street clothes. We complained to the man in charge, but he only responded sneeringly, "What do you think this is, a bank or something? If your clothes are stolen, that's your tough luck."

It sure was our tough luck. The clothes that were stolen were the only good clothes we had, and for me the loss was greater still—for along with my suit jacket went my passage money back to Puerto Rico. It was as though my return ship had gone up in flames.

LOUIS CHU

Louis Chu (1915–1970) and his family left China's Guangtong Province in 1924 and settled in Newark, New Jersey. Chu earned a master's degree in sociology from New York University and served with the Army Signal Corps in China during World War II. After the war he returned to China and married; the couple then moved to New York City, where Chu opened a record store, hosted a daily radio program in the 1950s, and worked as an administrator for a Chinese-American community center. He also took writing courses at the New School for Social Research and began submitting his work to magazines and publishers. Despite five rejections his novel *Eat a Bowl of Tea* was eventually published in 1961 but was virtually unnoticed. It has since been acknowledged as an essential Chinese-American novel, eschewing exotic stereotypes and dealing incisively with fraught familial relationships and the psychosexual difficulties of Chinese men. It appears that almost all of Chu's other fiction has not survived.

from
Eat a Bowl of Tea

To Mei Oi the novelty of New York soon wore off. Chinatown turned out to be less glamorous than she had pictured it. Buildings are buildings everywhere. New York lacked the intimacy of a rural village. She could not go over to Lane Four to borrow a porcelain dish for her cooking. In the village there is always something going on. Market days. Weddings. Hair-cut banquets. Planting. Harvesting. The Moon Festival. There is a oneness, a togetherness. A sense of belonging. A proud identity. In a village everybody knows everybody else.

New York for Mei Oi was a strange land. She knew no one outside of her immediate family. There was no one to visit. Ben Loy's aunt lived in Chicago, and Wing Sim's wife lived in Connecticut. She was alone at home while her husband worked. Added to this loneliness, she was sorrowing over the abrupt termination of her brief honeymoon. What had begun in the ecstasy of love was lost. Love had tumbled off the high pedestal of married bliss. As a pathetic substitute for ardor, Ben Loy usually took his wife to see a movie uptown on his days off. Sometimes, but seldom, he would take her to one of the local Chinese theaters when the film was exceptionally good. Other times they would go shopping or sight-seeing around New York. They saw the Statue of Liberty, the Empire State Building, the Museum of Natural History, Times Square. All these they did not have in rural Sunwei.

Ben Loy wanted to please his wife. If she hinted that a dress in a window looked nice, he got it for her. During the six months since her arrival in New York, he had bought her an expensive watch at one of the credit jewelers uptown. Wah Gay, acting the part of the proud father-in-law, had given her a diamond ring and a pair of gold bracelets. Ben Loy had given her a hair dryer, too. On his days off he even cooked for her.

But the gestures of affection from her husband could not make Mei Oi a happy woman. She was restless. One day after dinner she said to her husband, "Many women from China are now working in sewing shops in Chinatown. May I go out and get a job too?"

"I don't want you to work," replied Ben Loy firmly, taken aback by the suddenness of the question.

"Other housewives can work, why . . ."

"When a group of women get together," said Ben Loy, "they do nothing but gossip. And when they do, there's bound to be trouble." The request made him feel insecure. If his wife worked, he reasoned, she would come in contact with all sorts of people, both good and bad. He had heard of a woman who ran away with the boss of a sewing shop not long ago.

"I'll just keep quiet," said Mei Oi, disappointed. "I won't talk to them."

"That's what you say," retorted Ben Loy.

"It's a lot easier to pass the time away when one is working," said Mei Oi, dabbing at her eyes with a handkerchief. She ran from the kitchen to the bedroom, leaving the dishes undone in the sink.

"*Moi Moi*, please don't cry." Ben Loy hurried to her side.

"I'm not like others," she burst out crying. "Others are kept busy with their little ones."

Ben Loy put his arms around her and kissed her, stroking her soft black hair until she was quieter.

"Promise me one thing," she sobbed. "Promise me you'll go to see a doctor."

"I'll go next week," he replied sullenly, more conscious than ever before of his inadequacy. "Don't worry, I'll go."

"Go and ask your father if I could go to work too," she managed between sobs.

"Okay, I'll go next week," said Ben Loy.

The next week, when Ben Loy dropped in to see his father, he found him alone in the clubhouse. "Got a letter for you," he said.

"*Ah Sow* is well these days?" the father asked, accepting the letter.

"Hao, hao," replied Ben Loy.

He motioned for Ben Loy to sit down. "*Ah Sow* has come home for about six months now . . . more than six months," he began slowly. "Do you have any news for me?"

"What news should I have?" retorted Ben Loy irritably. "What news do you want?"

"I'm referring to your wife," said Wah Gay, rather gravely now. "Maybe *she* has some news for me." He waited for Ben Loy to answer. But the son only stared at the blank wall, then at the doorway, as if he wished someone would come in to interrupt the conversation.

"Your mother in her last letter to me asked me the same thing," continued the father. "Asked if I have any news for her concerning you two. Both your mother and I are getting on in years. We are not getting any younger each day. By giving your mother a grandson, or even a granddaughter, you would make her very happy. I think you should consider your mother's happiness, and mine too. . . ."

Ben Loy, without saying anything, got up and began edging toward the door. He saw nothing but the bleak dirty cement steps leading to the street.

"If you don't want children when you're young, when do you want them?" the father called after him. "When you're old?"

"What's the difference?" retorted Ben Loy. "You can have them any time you want!" He stormed out of the basement.

As he walked back home, anger made his face flush. If he had known the old man was going to bring up such a topic, he certainly would have stayed away from the club house. Forgotten was his task of finding out from his father if he would permit Mei Oi to go to work. He was in no mood to consult a doctor right now either. He did not feel like going home to Mei Oi, but there was no other place for him to go. When he opened the apartment door, Mei Oi was sitting by the desk in the living room.

"What are you doing, writing letters?" he asked perfunctorily. There was no trace of irritation in his voice.

"Just a few lines to mother," she said, looking up. "Haven't written her for a long time." She was about to get up from her chair when Ben Loy approached and kissed her squarely on the lips, then on her cheeks, on her forehead. She disengaged herself and pulled away. "Did you talk to *Lao Yair?*"

"What's the difference whether I talk to my father or not?" he said. "You know he would say no."

"What did he say?"

"Oh, nothing. I just gave him the letter and left."

Mei Oi disappeared into another room. She reappeared a few moments later. "I almost forgot. Did you see the doctor?"

"No." Ben Loy scrutinized her from top to bottom. She had changed into a blue Chinese gown with a large silver dragon design on the front. He had always admired these sheath dresses on other women, but he never thought that some day he would see his own wife wearing one of them.

"You promised you would see the doctor."

"Okay, okay. I said I would and I will."

"Help me with this button." Mei Oi walked over to the full length mirror on the closet door. She lifted her chin high. She let her fingers drop. "Here, you snap this on for me."

Ben Loy took hold of the collar and struggled with the hook and eye. "There, I've got it!"

Mei Oi turned to face the mirror again. She inspected the collar. She spun around and glanced at the curves reflected in the mirror. She tugged at the lower half of the dress and wiggled a little bit. Her schoolmates back home had told her that when she came to America she would be wearing nothing but western clothes. Now she was glad she had brought several of these Chinese gowns with her. From what she had learned of American dresses they were either too tight, too small, too long, or too short. And she was not familiar with the sizes. As a school girl in Sunwei she had worn nothing but two-piece Chinese suits. She remembered how she and her classmates used to chuckle when they saw a girl wearing a tight-fitting gown. To them, at the time, a girl in a clinging gown was just plain naked. But Mei Oi had come to love these tight-fitting dresses.

She sprayed some perfume on herself. She smelled good and looked good. Ben Loy reached to pull his wife to him, to hold and kiss her, but she pushed him away firmly.

They went to a movie uptown. Mei Oi had discovered that the movies had a relaxing influence on her; so that, after a night out, her inner frustrations became less compelling.

Irritated by the constant reminders from Mei Oi that he consult a doctor, Ben Loy reluctantly stopped by the East Broadway office of Dr. Long the following week. The doctor was sympathetic.

"You said when you first got married in the village," the doctor wanted to make sure, "you were quite adequate?"

"Yes, sir," replied Ben Loy.

"When you came out to Hongkong with your wife and stayed at the All Seas Hotel, you found yourself incapable of an erection?" Ben Loy nodded embarrassedly. "Yet before your marriage, you had been quite adequate with a prostitute at the same hotel?"

"That's right, doctor."

"H'mn." The doctor assumed a pensive pose. "Maybe what you need is a change of scenery. Go away. Go away for a vacation and see what happens. Very often the cause is psychological."

When Ben Loy got home that afternoon, Mei Oi was very anxious to talk to him.

"What did the doctor say?" she asked as soon as her husband stepped inside the door.

"That doctor talked nonsense," said Ben Loy. "He told me to take a vacation. Go away to some other place for a while, he said."

"The doctor said to go away? Where?" Mei Oi was puzzled by Ben Loy's report.

"Anywhere. Just go away," said Ben Loy.

"Are *we* going away?" asked Mei Oi innocently.

"Going away?" Ben Loy wore a startled expression on his face. "What for?"

"But you said the doctor . . ."

"Oh, never mind him. He's crazy. He thinks you can just pack up and go away." He wrinkled his nose.

Weeks passed before Mei Oi brought up the subject of going away again.

"Loy *Gaw*," she said disarmingly. "I have never been to Washington, the capital of the country. It would be fun to see the sights."

Coming from his wife's pretty little mouth, it did not sound like going away to Ben Loy. It was just a visit to Washington. When he realized that he himself had never been to the nation's capital, he agreed to make the trip. He had told himself that someday he would like to see Washington. He decided the time was now. He called his friend Chin Yuen and asked him to work one day for him, the day preceding his day off, so that he would have two days in Washington.

Ben Loy and Mei Oi registered at a hotel not far from Union Station. They went sight-seeing in the daytime. The Lincoln Memorial, the Government Printing Office, the Congress, the Washington Monument, the White House . . .

During their brief stay in the nation's capital, Ben Loy and Mei Oi were happy and carefree. They held hands. They dined in different restaurants. They went window-shopping. Once again they were like a couple of honeymooners.

When night came, they were exhausted from the strenuous activities of sight-seeing. But they were happy and relaxed.

When time came to go to bed, Ben Loy held no feeling of inadequacy. The daytime excitement of the various tours had made him forget his inadequacy. He simply did not have time to think of his past. The bed now merely represented a continuation of the exciting tours on his itinerary. With the cooperation and understanding of Mei Oi, he rediscovered his manliness during his first night in Washington. He was elated. He was also puzzled because the doctor's advice had proven valid. His only regret was that he had to return to New York the following day.

To his dismay and disappointment, he fell back into the old rut of incompetence at his own apartment on Catherine Street in New York.

"Loy *Gaw*," pleaded Mei Oi, "please go back and see Dr. Long again."

Ben Loy waited for his turn at the doctor's office. It was to please his wife that he now found himself thumbing through the pages of a torn magazine, sitting opposite a lady who had followed him in. Momentarily he turned from the magazine to the lady. Young, fairly good looking, of medium build. Shapely legs. Her skirt was slightly above her knees. The well-proportioned legs drew his attention and reminded him of one day in Calcutta.

He had been on a tour of Calcutta's *Chininagar* with two other GI's when they had wandered into a tiny novelty store just off the fringe of Chinatown. At first the conversation was that of a shopkeeper and a potential customer. As Ben Loy and his companions turned to leave, the lady proprietress said in broken English, "My friends, wait. You wait a minute."

She called out something in Hindustani to someone in the back room. Almost instantly a dark-skinned girl came out. She looked no more than sixteen. She had a ready smile and nice shapely legs. She beckoned to Ben Loy. "Come. Come here. I want to show you something."

The twenty-one-year-old Ben Loy had followed her behind the bamboo curtain.

"Aw, com'on. Let's go!" said Ben Loy's fellow soldiers. "We ain't got all day."

But Ben Loy ignored them and followed the girl. As soon as they were shut off from view by the curtain, the girl flipped open her dress, revealing her whole naked front. "See? Nice, huh?"

Ben Loy followed her to another room . . .

*

The door opened and the doctor stepped out. "Who's next?" he called.

Ben Loy's eye jumped from the lady's shapely legs back to the pages of the magazine. A man got up and followed the doctor in. The door closed. Ben Loy's eye went back to the lady's legs.

. . . Two hours later that same afternoon in Calcutta, Ben Loy and his buddies went to another section of the city. There was nothing else to do. Just killing time. On a street corner a youngster came up and accosted them. "Hey, Joe, you likee Chini goil?"

Ben Loy was delighted at the mention of Chinese girls. He had had them all. All different colors and shapes. "Chinese girls? Are you sure?"

"Sure, Chini goil. You come with me. You come." He was a mere boy, about ten or eleven.

Ben Loy and his companions followed the boy to the second floor of a building in a busy section of the city. Coming in from the sun-drenched streets of Calcutta, it felt like entering a cave. The boy called out something and a woman opened the door. They all went in. The woman brought out a girl, but she was not Chinese. She appeared to be Indian.

"You Chini?"

The girl shook her head.

"But the boy said . . . what the hell. A woman is a woman." Ben Loy followed the woman to a wooden bed. . . . Then at the Four Seas Hotel in Hongkong . . . the boy had brought him a different girl every night . . . yet when he came to Hongkong with Mei Oi and stayed at the same hotel . . . he was impotent.

If only he had been less lustful in his youth, he probably would not be in this room waiting to talk to the doctor now. He could have been so happy with Mei Oi, but . . .

He took a last look at the lady's legs before going into the doctor's examination room.

"My name is Wang, doctor," Ben Loy began. "I was here a few weeks ago . . ."

The doctor looked at him blankly; then a flicker of recognition expanded on his face. "Oh, yes," he nodded. "I remember."

Ben Loy began telling the doctor how during his first night in Washington with his wife, he had regained his strength; that when he came back to his apartment in New York, his old condition returned. "It's all my fault," he continued sadly. "Running after women—the many times I've had gonorrhea and syphilis."

"You should have thought of these things a long time ago," the doctor shook his head. "Am I to understand that you are completely impotent now?"

"Almost," replied Ben Loy. "Sometimes I wake up in the middle of the night and my manliness has returned. But at almost the very instant that I . . . possess my wife I have my . . . you know . . . it is all over. My wife does not have a very satisfactory husband," he concluded sadly.

"You have no venereal disease now?" the doctor asked.

"No."

"Are you sure?"

"I think so."

The doctor gave him a thorough examination. He prescribed some tablets for him to take each day and told him to return in two weeks. "Maybe this will help bring back your vitality."

"What about my impotence, doctor, is that a temporary thing or . . . ?"

"Sometimes it is and sometimes it is not," said the doctor. "Come back in two weeks and we'll see. I told you before that sometimes it's psychological."

When he left the doctor's office, Ben Loy was more dejected than he'd been when he entered. He had hoped that Doctor Long would tell him that his impotence would vanish after the medication. The dread possibility of permanent incapacity dawned on him and the thought began to torment him.

Instead of going directly home, he turned into Mott Street. At 91 Mott Street he went up the stairs. A white-haired man in a tan cardigan sweater opened the door in answer to his knocks on apartment two on the second floor.

"Hello," he fidgeted awkwardly. "I want you to look at my sickness."

"Come in." The old man indicated a chair for the caller. "Sit down."

The room was illuminated by the sunlight coming in through the windows of the adjacent room. Ben Loy sat down. The first thing he noticed was the sink, almost directly opposite him, next to the door. Presently the elderly man pulled the light cord and the glow from a 60-watt lamp added to the illumination of the room. He threw a tiny pillow about the size of a brick on the table in front of Ben Loy. He pulled up another chair. The herbalist placed three fingers on Ben Loy's upturned wrist, now resting on the little pillow, feeling the pulse. After several moments, he felt the pulse on the other wrist. He bowed his head and closed his eyes. The moments ticked by slowly. Finally the herbalist lifted his fingers from the wrist. "Kidney weak," he announced thoughtfully. "Kidney weak."

"Yes, I know," said Ben Loy. He wondered if it had been a waste of time to come to the herbalist's. He was now told that his kidney was weak.

"Eat something that would supplement your diet," said the herbalist, who practiced the art of feeling the pulse under the name of Nee Ho. "You need to take some gingsing." Nee Ho took out a pack of cigarettes and offered one to Ben Loy, who declined politely. He lifted his head and blew away the smoke.

"Not right away," he continued. "You have to eat some invigorating tea first. Perhaps after several brewings, you can start taking gingsing. But not before that. Your system is too cool to accept gingsing now."

Ben Loy did not take the prescription to a Chinese herb store. He thought the inter-mixing of medicine might be harmful. If all the modern sciences in America could not bring relief to his marital difficulties, how could he expect a herbalist to work miracles for him? On the other hand, there are undoubtedly tested remedies within the herbalist's realm of knowledge that are good for many ills. He folded the prescription neatly and put it into his coat pocket. He went to the Doyers Street Pharmacy to have Dr. Long's prescription filled. He would give Dr. Long's tablets a trial.

When Ben Loy finally got home that afternoon, Mei Oi had already finished cooking the rice. "What did the doctor say?" she asked, trying to conceal her anxiety.

"He gave me some tablets to take," said Ben Loy. "I don't know if they're any good." He did not mention that he had also gone to the herbalist's.

In the evening, after dinner, he and Mei Oi went to the movies.

CARLOS BULOSAN

Born on the Philippine island of Luzon, Carlos Bulosan (1911?–1956) immigrated to the United States around 1930. The facts of his life in the United States are not altogether clear, particularly because his most celebrated work, *America Is in the Heart*, is ultimately a fictionalized narrative. This book suggests that he worked as a farm laborer on the West Coast but it is not certain whether he actually did so; chronic health problems may have prevented him from doing much hard manual labor. He committed himself passionately to the labor movement, however, through his work as an organizer and writer for the United Cannery and Packing House Workers of America. During his lengthy hospitalization for tuberculosis and kidney disease from 1938 to 1941, Bulosan read voraciously and published short stories and poetry in magazines such as *The Saturday Evening Post* and *The New Yorker*. He published a short-story collection, *The Laughter of My Father*, during the war, followed by *America Is in the Heart* in 1946. That book encapsulated the intensity of his ambivalence toward America as well as his outrage at his adopted country's treatment of Filipinos ("in many ways it was a crime to be a Filipino in California"). His views led to him being placed under surveillance by the FBI. Bulosan's final work, a novel about guerillas in the Philippines entitled *The Cry and the Dedication*, was left unfinished when he died in Seattle in 1956.

from
America Is in the Heart

We arrived in Seattle on a June day. My first sight of the approaching land was an exhilarating experience. Everything seemed native and promising to me. It was like coming home after a long voyage, although as yet I had no home in this city. Everything seemed familiar and kind—the white faces of the buildings melting in the soft afternoon sun, the gray contours of the surrounding valleys that seemed to vanish in the last periphery of light. With a sudden surge of joy, I knew that I must find a home in this new land.

I had only twenty cents left, not even enough to take me to Chinatown where, I had been informed, a Filipino hotel and two restaurants were located. Fortunately two oldtimers put me in a car with four others, and took us to a hotel on King Street, the heart of Filipino life in Seattle. Marcelo, who was also in the car, had a cousin named Elias who came to our room with another oldtimer. Elias and his unknown friend persuaded my companions to play a strange kind of card game. In a little while Elias got up and touched his friend suggestively; then they disappeared and we never saw them again.

It was only when our two countrymen had left that my companions realized what happened. They had taken all their money. Marcelo asked me if I had any money. I gave him my twenty cents. After collecting a few more cents from the others, he went downstairs and when he came back he told us that he had telegraphed for money to his brother in California.

All night we waited for the money to come, hungry and afraid to go out in the street. Outside we could hear shouting and singing; then a woman screamed lustily in one of the rooms down the hall. Across from our hotel a jazz band was playing noisily; it went on until dawn. But in the morning a telegram came to Marcelo which said:

YOUR BROTHER DIED AUTOMOBILE ACCIDENT LAST WEEK

Marcelo looked at us and began to cry. His anguish stirred an aching fear in me. I knelt on the floor looking for my suitcase under the bed. I knew that I had to go out now—alone. I put the suitcase on my shoulder and walked toward the door, stopping for a moment to look back at my friends who were still standing silently around Marcelo. Suddenly a man came into the room and announced that he was the proprietor.

"Well, boys," he said, looking at our suitcases, "where is the rent?"

"We have no money, sir," I said, trying to impress him with my politeness.

"That is too bad," he said quickly, glancing furtively at our suitcases again. "That is just too bad." He walked outside and went down the hall. He came back with a short, fat Filipino, who looked at us stupidly with his dull, small eyes, and spat his cigar out of the window.

"There they are, Jake," said the proprietor.

Jake looked disappointed. "They are too young," he said.

"You can break them in, Jake," said the proprietor.

"They will be sending babies next," Jake said.

"You can break them in, can't you, Jake?" the proprietor pleaded. "This is not the first time you have broken babies in. You have done it in the sugar plantations in Hawaii, Jake!"

"Hell!" Jake said, striding across the room to the proprietor. He pulled a fat roll of bills from his pocket and gave twenty-five dollars to the proprietor. Then he turned to us and said, "All right, Pinoys, you are working for me now. Get your hats and follow me."

We were too frightened to hesitate. When we lifted our suitcases the proprietor ordered us not to touch them.

"I'll take care of them until you come back from Alaska," he said. "Good fishing, boys!"

In this way we were sold for five dollars each to work in the fish canneries in Alaska, by a Visayan from the island of Leyte to an Ilocano from the province of La Union. Both were oldtimers; both were tough. They exploited young immigrants until one of them, the hotel proprietor, was shot dead by an unknown assailant. We were forced to sign a paper which stated that each of us owed the contractor twenty dollars for bedding and another twenty for luxuries. What the luxuries were, I have never found out. The contractor turned out to be a tall, heavy-set, dark Filipino, who came to the small hold of the boat barking at us like a dog. He was drunk and saliva was running down his shirt.

"And get this, you devils!" he shouted at us. "You will never come back alive if you don't do what I say!"

It was the beginning of my life in America, the beginning of a long flight that carried me down the years, fighting desperately to find peace in some corner of life.

When I landed in Seattle for the second time, I expected a fair amount of money from the company. But the contractor, Max Feuga, came into the play room and handed us slips of paper. I looked at mine and was amazed at the neatly itemized expenditures that I was supposed to have incurred during the season. Twenty-five dollars for withdrawals, one hundred for board and room, twenty for bedding, and another twenty for something I do not now remember. At the bottom was the actual amount I was to receive after all the deductions: *thirteen dollars!*

I could do nothing. I did not even go to the hotel where I had left my suit-case. I went to a Japanese dry goods store on Jackson Street and bought a pair of corduroy pants and a blue shirt. It was already twilight and the can-nery workers were in the crowded Chinese gambling houses, losing their season's earnings and drinking bootleg whisky. They became quarrelsome and abusive to their own people when they lost, and subservient to the Chi-nese gambling lords and marijuana peddlers. They pawed at the semi-nude whores with their dirty hands and made suggestive gestures, running out into the night when they were rebuffed for lack of money.

I was already in America, and I felt good and safe. I did not understand why. The gamblers, prostitutes and Chinese opium smokers did not excite me, but they aroused in me a feeling of flight. I knew that I must run away from them, but it was not that I was afraid of contamination. I wanted to see other aspects of American life, for surely these destitute and vicious people were merely a small part of it. Where would I begin this pilgrimage, this search for a door into America?

I went outside and walked around looking into the faces of my country-men, wondering if I would see someone I had known in the Philippines. I came to a building which brightly dressed white women were entering, lifting their diaphanous gowns as they climbed the stairs. I looked up and saw the huge sign:

MANILA DANCE HALL

The orchestra upstairs was playing; Filipinos were entering. I put my hands in my pockets and followed them, beginning to feel lonely for the sound of home.

The dance hall was crowded with Filipino cannery workers and domestic servants. But the girls were very few, and the Filipinos fought over them. When a boy liked a girl he bought a roll of tickets from the hawker on the floor and kept dancing with her. But the other boys who also liked the same girl shouted at him to stop, cursing him in the dialects and sometimes throwing rolled wet papers at him. At the bar the glasses were tinkling, the bottles popping loudly, and the girls in the back room were smoking marijuana. It was almost impossible to breathe.

Then I saw Marcelo's familiar back. He was dancing with a tall blonde in a green dress, a girl so tall that Marcelo looked like a dwarf climbing a tree. But the girl was pretty and her body was nicely curved and graceful, and she had a way of swaying that aroused confused sensations in me. It was evident that many of the boys wanted to dance with her; they were shouting maliciously at Marcelo. The way the blonde waved to them made me think that she knew most of them. They were nearly all oldtimers and strangers to Marcelo. They were probably gamblers and pimps, because they had fat rolls of money and expensive clothing.

But Marcelo was learning very fast. He requested one of his friends to buy another roll of tickets for him. The girl was supposed to tear off one ticket every three minutes, but I noticed that she tore off a ticket for every minute. That was ten cents a minute. Marcelo was unaware of what she was doing; he was spending his whole season's earnings on his first day in America. It was only when one of his friends shouted to him in the dialect that he became angry at the girl. Marcelo was not tough, but his friend was an oldtimer. Marcelo pushed the girl toward the gaping bystanders. His friend opened a knife and gave it to him.

Then something happened that made my heart leap. One of the blonde girl's admirers came from behind and struck Marcelo with a piece of lead pipe. Marcelo's friend whipped out a pistol and fired. Marcelo and the boy with the lead pipe fell on the floor simultaneously, one on top of the other, but the blonde girl ran into the crowd screaming frantically. Several guns banged at once, and the lights went out. I saw Marcelo's friend crumple in the fading light.

At once the crowd seemed to flow out of the windows. I went to a side window and saw three heavy electric wires strung from the top of the building to the ground. I reached for them and slid to the ground. My palms were burning when I came out of the alley. Then I heard the sirens of police cars screaming infernally toward the place. I put my cap in my pocket and ran as fast as I could in the direction of a neon sign two blocks down the street.

It was a small church where Filipino farm workers were packing their suitcases and bundles. I found out later that Filipino immigrants used their churches as rest houses while they were waiting for work. There were two large trucks outside. I went to one of them and sat on the running board, holding my hands over my heart for fear it would beat too fast. The lights in the church went out and the workers came into the street. The driver of the truck in which I was sitting pointed a strong flashlight at me.

"Hey, you, are you looking for a job?" he asked.

"Yes, sir," I said.

"Get in the truck," he said, jumping into the cab. "Let's go, Flo!" he shouted to the other driver.

I was still trembling with excitement. But I was glad to get out of Seattle —to anywhere else in America. I did not care where so long as it was in America. I found a corner and sat down heavily. The drivers shouted to each other. Then we were off to work.

It was already midnight and the lights in the city of Seattle were beginning to fade. I could see the reflections on the bright lake in Bremerton. I was reminded of Baguio. Then some of the men began singing. The driver and two men were arguing over money. A boy in the other truck was playing a violin. We were on the highway to Yakima Valley.

After a day and a night of driving we arrived in a little town called Moxee City. The apple trees were heavy with fruit and the branches drooped to the ground. It was late afternoon when we passed through the town; the hard light of the sun punctuated the ugliness of the buildings. I was struck dumb by its isolation and the dry air that hung oppressively over the place. The heart-shaped valley was walled by high treeless mountains, and the hot breeze that blew in from a distant sea was injurious to the apple trees.

The leader of our crew was called Cornelio Paez; but most of the old-timers suspected that it was not his real name. There was something shifty about him, and his so-called bookkeeper, a pockmarked man we simply called Pinoy (which is a term generally applied to all Filipino immigrant workers), had a strange trick of squinting sideways when he looked at you. There seemed to be an old animosity between Paez and his bookkeeper.

But we were drawn together because the white people of Yakima Valley were suspicious of us. Years before, in the town of Toppenish, two Filipino apple pickers had been found murdered on the road to Sunnyside. At that time, there was ruthless persecution of the Filipinos throughout the Pacific Coast, instigated by orchardists who feared the unity of white and Filipino workers. A small farmer in Wapato who had tried to protect his Filipino workers had had his house burned. So however much we distrusted each other under Paez, we knew that beyond the walls of our bunkhouse were our real enemies, waiting to drive us out of Yakima Valley.

I had become acquainted with an oldtimer who had had considerable experience in the United States. His name was Julio, and it seemed that he was hiding from some trouble in Chicago. At night, when the men gambled in the kitchen, I would stand silently behind him and watch him cheat the other players. He was very deft, and his eyes were sharp and trained. Sometimes when there was no game, Julio would teach me tricks.

Mr. Malraux, our employer, had three daughters who used to work with us after school hours. He was a Frenchman who had gone to Moxee City when it consisted of only a few houses. At that time the valley was still a haven for Indians, but they had been gradually driven out when farming had been started on a large scale. Malraux had married an American woman in Spokane and begun farming; the girls came one by one, helping him on the farm as they grew. When I arrived in Moxee City they were already in their teens.

The oldest girl was called Estelle; she had just finished high school. She had a delightful disposition and her industry was something that men talked about with approval. The other girls, Maria and Diane, were still too young to be going about so freely; but whenever Estelle came to our bunkhouse they were always with her.

It was now the end of summer and there was a bright moon in the sky. Not far from Moxee City was a wide grassland where cottontails and jack rabbits roamed at night. Estelle used to drive her father's old car and would pick up some of us at the bunkhouse; then we would go hunting with their dogs and a few antiquated shotguns.

When we came back from hunting we would go to the Malraux house with some of the men who had musical instruments. We would sit on the lawn for hours singing American songs. But when they started singing Philippine songs their voices were so sad, so full of yesterday and the haunting presence of familiar seas, as if they had reached the end of creation, that life seemed ended and no bright spark was left in the world.

But one afternoon toward the end of the season, Paez went to the bank to get our paychecks and did not come back. The pockmarked bookkeeper was furious.

"I'll get him this time!" he said, running up and down the house. "He did that last year in California and I didn't get a cent. I know where to find the bastard!"

Julio grabbed him by the neck. "You'd better tell me where to find him if you know what is good for you," he said angrily, pushing the frightened bookkeeper toward the stove.

"Let me alone!" he shouted.

Julio hit him between the eyes, and the bookkeeper struggled violently. Julio hit him again. The bookkeeper rolled on the floor like a baby. Julio picked him up and threw him outside the house. I thought he was dead, but his legs began to move. Then he opened his eyes and got up quickly, staggering like a drunken stevedore toward the highway. Julio came out of the house with brass knuckles, but the bookkeeper was already disappearing behind the apple orchard. Julio came back and began hitting the door of the kitchen with all his force, in futile anger.

I had not seen this sort of brutality in the Philippines, but my first contact with it in America made me brave. My bravery was still nameless, and waiting to express itself. I was not shocked when I saw that my countrymen had become ruthless toward one another, and this sudden impact of cruelty made me insensate to pain and kindness, so that it took me a long time to wholly trust other men. As time went by I became as ruthless as the worst of them, and I became afraid that I would never feel like a human being again. Yet no matter what bestiality encompassed my life, I felt sure that somewhere, sometime, I would break free. This faith kept me from completely succumbing to the degradation into which many of my countrymen had fallen. It finally paved my way out of our small, harsh life, painfully but cleanly, into a world of strange intellectual adventures and self-fulfillment.

The apples were nearly picked when Paez disappeared with our money. We lost interest in our work. We sat on the lawn of the Malraux's and sang. They came out of the house and joined us. The moonlight shimmered like a large diamond on the land around the farm. The men in the bunkhouse came with their violins and guitars. Julio grabbed Diane and started dancing with her; then the two younger girls were grabbed by other men.

It was while Estelle was singing that we heard a gun crack from the dirt road not far from the house. Malraux saw them first, saw the clubs and the iron bars in their hands, and yelled at us in warning. But it was too late. They had taken us by surprise.

I saw Malraux run into the house for his gun. I jumped to the nearest apple tree. I wanted a weapon—anything to hit back at these white men who had leaped upon us from the dark. Three or four guns banged all at once, and I turned to see Maria falling to the ground. A streak of red light flashed from the window into the crowd. Estelle was screaming and shouting to her father. Diane was already climbing the stairs, her long black hair shining in the moonlight.

I saw Julio motioning to me to follow him. Run away from our friends and companions? No! *Goddamn you, Julio!* I jumped into the thick of fight, dark with fury. Then I felt Julio's hands pulling me away, screaming into my ears:

"Come on, you crazy punk! Come on before I kill you myself!"

He was hurting me. Blinded with anger and tears, I ran after him toward our bunkhouse. We stopped behind a pear tree when we saw that our house was burning. Julio whispered to me to follow him.

We groped our way through the pear trees and came out, after what seemed like hours of running, on a wide grass plain traversed by a roaring irrigation ditch. Once when we thought we were being followed, we jumped into the water and waited. The night was silent and the stars in the sky were as far away as home. Was there peace somewhere in the world? The silence was broken only by the rushing water and the startled cry of little birds that stirred in the night.

Julio led the way. We came to a dirt road that led to some farmhouses. We decided to stay away from it. We turned off the road and walked silently between the trees. Then we came to a wide desert land. We followed a narrow footpath and, to our surprise, came to the low, uninhabited, wide desert of the Rattlesnake Mountains. The stars were our only guide.

We walked on and on. Toward dawn, when a strong wind came, we jumped into the dunes and covered our heads with dry bushes until it had passed by. We were no longer afraid of pursuit. We were in another land, on another planet. The desert was wide and flat. There were rabbits in the bushes, and once we came upon a herd of small deer. We ran after them with a burning bush, but they just stood nonchalantly and waited for us. When we were near enough for them to recognize our scent, they turned about and galloped down the sand dunes.

When morning came we were still in the desert. We walked until about noon. Then we came to a narrow grassland. We stood on a rise and looked around to see the edge of the desert. Julio started running crazily and jumping into the air. I ran after him. At last we came to the beginning of a wide plain.

The town of Toppenish was behind us now, and the cool wind from the valley swept the plain. We rested under a tree. Julio was different from other oldtimers; he did not talk much. I felt that he had many stories within him, and I longed to know America through him. His patience and nameless kindness had led me away from Moxee City into a new life.

After a while we crossed the plain again, hiding behind the trees whenever we saw anyone approaching us. I was too exhausted to continue when we reached Zillah, where some children stoned us. We hid in an orange grove and rested. At sunset we started again. When we were nearing the town of Granger, I heard the sudden tumult of the Yakima River. Julio started running again, and I followed him. Suddenly we saw the clear, cool water of the river. We sat in the tall grass, cooling our tired bodies beside the bright stream.

I was the first to enter the water. I washed my shirt and spread it to dry on the grass. Sunnyside was not far off. I could hear the loud whistle of trains running seaward.

"This is the beginning of your life in America," Julio said. "We'll take a freight train from Sunnyside and go to nowhere."

"I would like to go to California," I said. "I have two brothers there—but I don't know if I could find them."

"All roads go to California and all travelers wind up in Los Angeles," Julio said. "But not this traveler. I have lived there too long. I know that state too damn well. . . ."

"What do you mean?" I asked.

Suddenly he became sad and said: "It is hard to be a Filipino in California."

Not comprehending what he meant, I began to dream of going to California. Then we started for Sunnyside, listening eagerly to the train whistle piercing the summer sky. It was nearly ten in the evening when we reached Sunnyside. We circled the town, and then we saw the trains—every car bursting with fruit—screaming fiercely and chugging like beetles up and down the tracks. The voices of the trainmen came clearly through the night.

We stopped in the shadow of a water tower. Julio disappeared for a moment and came back.

"Our train leaves in an hour," he said. "I'll go around for something to eat. Wait for me here."

I waited for him to come back for several hours. The train left. Then I began to worry. I went to town and walked in the shadows, looking into the darkened windows of wooden houses. Julio had disappeared like a wind.

I returned to our rendezvous and waited all night. Early the next morning another train was ready to go; I ran behind the boxcars and climbed inside one. When the train began to move, I opened the door and looked sadly toward Sunnyside. Julio was there somewhere, friendless and alone in a strange town.

"Good-bye, Julio," I said. "And thanks for everything, Julio. I hope I will meet you again somewhere in America."

Then the train screamed and the thought of Julio hurt me. I stood peering outside and listening to the monotonous chugging of the engine. I knew that I could never be unkind to any Filipino, because Julio had left me a token of friendship, a seed of trust, that ached to grow to fruition as I rushed toward another city.

ISAAC BASHEVIS SINGER

Born in Leoncin, Poland, Isaac Bashevis Singer (1904–1991) spent
much of his childhood in the village of Bilgoray before moving to Warsaw to embark on a career as a writer. After publishing his novel *Satan
in Goray*, he came to the United States in 1935 and began writing for the
Forward, one of New York City's Yiddish-language newspapers. The stories he wrote drew heavily on the mythology and folklore of the Jewish
shtetl; after the Holocaust it seemed as if he were single-handedly preserving traces of an obliterated world. He also wrote fiction that examined his exile's life in America. With the 1953 publication of Saul Bellow's
translation of his story "Gimpel the Fool," Singer began to be read widely.
His relationship with America was complex and contradictory, and his
views often shifted depending on the forum in which he expressed himself. In interviews and lectures he would adopt a persona of kindly Old
World sage and praise the United States by comparing it with the barba-
rism that had given rise to the Nazi genocide in Europe, but in his fiction,
particularly in works published in Yiddish periodicals but not translated
into English until after his death, he could be far more caustic. In the
novel *Shadows on the Hudson* one character reflects upon how "all kinds
of ethnic groups lived and raised children here: Jews, Italians, Poles and
Irish; black people and yellow people. In these dwellings, cultures
flickered and died out. Here children grew up without any heritage. . . .
Their spiritual fathers were stock Hollywood characters, their literature
trashy novels and the tabloid press. How long could all this last?" "A
Wedding in Brownsville," which follows, is translated by Chana Faerstein and Elizabeth Pollet.

A Wedding in Brownsville

1

T he wedding had been a burden to Dr. Solomon Margolin from the very beginning. True, it was to take place on a Sunday, but Gretl had been right when she said that was the only evening in the week they could spend together. It always turned out that way. His responsibilities to the community made him give away the evenings that belonged to her. The Zionists had appointed him to a committee; he was a board member of a Jewish scholastic society; he had become co-editor of an academic Jewish quarterly. And though he often referred to himself as an agnostic and even an atheist, nevertheless for years he had been dragging Gretl to Seders at Abraham Mekheles', a *Landsman* from Sencimin. Dr. Margolin treated rabbis, refugees, and Jewish writers without charge, supplying them with medicines and, if necessary, a hospital bed. There had been a time when he had gone regularly to the meetings of the Senciminer Society, had accepted positions in their ranks, and had attended all the parties. Now Abraham Mekheles was marrying off his youngest daughter, Sylvia. The minute the invitation arrived, Gretl had announced her decision: she was not going to let herself be carted off to a wedding somewhere out in the wilds of Brownsville. If he, Solomon, wanted to go and gorge himself on all kinds of greasy food, coming home at three o'clock in the morning, that was his prerogative.

Dr. Margolin admitted to himself that his wife was right. When would he get a chance to sleep? He had to be at the hospital early Monday morning. Moreover he was on a strict fat-free diet. A wedding like this one would be a feast of poisons. Everything about such celebrations irritated him now: the Anglicized Yiddish, the Yiddishized English, the ear-splitting music and unruly dances. Jewish laws and customs were completely distorted; men who had no regard for Jewishness wore skullcaps; and the reverend rabbis and cantors aped the Christian ministers. Whenever he took Gretl to a wedding or Bar Mitzvah, he was ashamed. Even she, born a Christian, could see that American Judaism was a mess. At least this time he would be spared the trouble of making apologies to her.

*

Usually after breakfast on Sunday, he and his wife took a walk in Central Park, or, when the weather was mild, went to the Palisades. But today Solomon Margolin lingered in bed. During the years, he had stopped attending the functions of the Senciminer Society; meanwhile the town of Sencimin had been destroyed. His family there had been tortured, burned, gassed. Many Senciminers had survived, and, later, come to America from the camps, but most of them were younger people whom he, Solomon, had not known in the old country. Tonight everyone would be there: the Senciminers belonging to the bride's family and the Tereshpolers belonging to the groom's. He knew how they would pester him, reproach him for growing aloof, drop hints that he was a snob. They would address him familiarly, slap him on the back, drag him off to dance. Well, even so, he had to go to Sylvia's wedding. He had already sent out the present.

The day had dawned, gray and dreary as dusk. Overnight, a heavy snow had fallen. Solomon Margolin had hoped to make up for the sleep he was going to lose, but unfortunately he had waked even earlier than usual. Finally he got up. He shaved himself meticulously at the bathroom mirror and also trimmed the gray hair at his temples. Today of all days he looked his age: there were bags under his eyes, and his face was lined. Exhaustion showed in his features. His nose appeared longer and sharper than usual; there were deep folds at the sides of his mouth. After breakfast he stretched out on the living-room sofa. From there he could see Gretl, who was standing in the kitchen, ironing—blonde, faded, middle-aged. She had on a skimpy petticoat, and her calves were as muscular as a dancer's. Gretl had been a nurse in the Berlin hospital where he had been a member of the staff. Of her family, one brother, a Nazi, had died of typhus in a Russian prison camp. A second, who was a Communist, had been shot by the Nazis. Her aged father vegetated at the home of his other daughter in Hamburg, and Gretl sent him money regularly. She herself had become almost Jewish in New York. She had made friends with Jewish women, joined Hadassah, learned to cook Jewish dishes. Even her sigh was Jewish. And she lamented continually over the Nazi catastrophe. She had her plot waiting for her beside his in that part of the cemetery that the Senciminers had reserved for themselves.

Dr. Margolin yawned, reached for the cigarette that lay in an ashtray on the coffee table beside him, and began to think about himself. His career had gone well. Ostensibly he was a success. He had an office on West End Avenue and wealthy patients. His colleagues respected him, and he was an important figure in Jewish circles in New York. What more could a boy from Sencimin expect? A self-taught man, the son of a poor teacher of Talmud? In person he was tall, quite handsome, and he had always had a way with women. He still pursued them—more than was good for him at his age and with his high blood pressure. But secretly Solomon Margolin had always felt that he was a failure. As a child he had been acclaimed a prodigy, reciting long passages of the Bible and studying the Talmud and Commentaries on his own. When he was a boy of eleven, he had sent for a Responsum to the rabbi of Tarnow who had referred to him in his reply as "great and illustrious." In his teens he had become a master in the *Guide for the Perplexed* and the Kuzari. He had taught himself algebra and geometry. At seventeen he had attempted a translation of Spinoza's *Ethics* from Latin into Hebrew, unaware that it had been done before. Everyone predicted he would turn out to be a genius. But he had squandered his talents, continually changing his field of study; and he had wasted years in learning languages, in wandering from country to country. Nor had he had any luck with his one great love, Raizel, the daughter of Melekh the watchmaker. Raizel had married someone else and later had been shot by the Nazis. All his life Solomon Margolin had been plagued by the eternal questions. He still lay awake at night trying to solve the mysteries of the universe. He suffered from hypochondria and the fear of death haunted even his dreams. Hitler's carnage and the extinction of his family had rooted out his last hope for better days, had destroyed all his faith in humanity. He had begun to despise the matrons who came to him with their petty ills while millions were devising horrible deaths for one another.

Gretl came in from the kitchen.

"What shirt are you going to put on?"

Solomon Margolin regarded her quietly. She had had her own share of troubles. She had suffered in silence for her two brothers, even for Hans, the Nazi. She had gone through a prolonged change of life. She was tortured by guilt feelings toward him, Solomon. She had become sexually frigid. Now her face was flushed and covered with beads of sweat. He earned more than enough to pay for a maid, yet Gretl insisted on doing all the housework herself, even the laundry. It had become a mania with her. Every day she scoured the oven. She was forever polishing the windows of their apartment on the sixteenth floor and without using a safety belt. All the other housewives in the building ordered their groceries delivered, but Gretl lugged the heavy bags from the supermarket herself. At night she sometimes said things that sounded slightly insane to him. She still suspected him of carrying on with every female patient he treated.

Now husband and wife sized each other up wryly, feeling the strangeness that comes of great familiarity. He was always amazed at how she had lost her looks. No one feature had altered, but something in her aspect had given way: her pride, her hopefulness, her curiosity. He blurted out:

"What shirt? It doesn't matter. A white shirt."

"You're not going to wear the tuxedo? Wait, I'll bring you a vitamin."

"I don't want a vitamin."

"But you yourself say they're good for you."

"Leave me alone."

"Well, it's your health, not mine."

And slowly she walked out of the room, hesitating as if she expected him to remember something and call her back.

2

Dr. Solomon Margolin took a last look in the mirror and left the house. He felt refreshed by the half-hour nap he had had after dinner. Despite his age, he still wanted to impress people with his appearance—even the Senciminers. He had his illusions. In Germany he had taken pride in the fact that he looked like a *Junker*, and in New York he was often aware that he could pass for an Anglo-Saxon. He was tall, slim, blond, blue-eyed. His hair was thinning, had turned somewhat gray, but he managed to disguise these signs of age. He stooped a little, but in company was quick to straighten up. Years ago in Germany he had worn a monocle and though in New York that would have been too pretentious, his glance still retained a European severity. He had his principles. He had never broken the Hippocratic Oath. With his patients he was honorable to an extreme, avoiding every kind of cant; and he had refused a number of dubious associations that smacked of careerism. Gretl claimed his sense of honor amounted to a mania. Dr. Margolin's car was in the garage —not a Cadillac like that of most of his colleagues—but he decided to go by taxi. He was unfamiliar with Brooklyn and the heavy snow made driving hazardous. He waved his hand and at once a taxi pulled over to the curb. He was afraid the driver might refuse to go as far as Brownsville, but he flicked the meter on without a word. Dr. Margolin peered through the frosted window into the wintry Sunday night but there was nothing to be seen. The New York streets sprawled out, wet, dirty, impenetrably dark. After a while, Dr. Margolin leaned back, shut his eyes, and retreated into his own warmth. His destination was a wedding. Wasn't the world, like this taxi, plunging away somewhere into the unknown toward a cosmic destination? Maybe a cosmic Brownsville, a cosmic wedding? Yes. But why did God—or whatever anyone wanted to call Him—create a Hitler, a Stalin? Why did He need world wars? Why heart attacks, cancers? Dr. Margolin took out a cigarette and lit it hesitantly. What had they been thinking of, those pious uncles of his, when they were digging their own graves? Was immortality possible? Was there such a thing as the soul? All the arguments for and against weren't worth a pinch of dust.

The taxi turned onto the bridge across the East River and for the first time Dr. Margolin was able to see the sky. It sagged low, heavy, red as glowing metal. Higher up, a violet glare suffused the vault of the heavens. Snow was sifting down gently, bringing a winter peace to the world, just as it had in the past—forty years ago, a thousand years ago, and perhaps a million years ago. Fiery pillars appeared to glow beneath the East River; on its surface, through black waves jagged as rocks, a tugboat was hauling a string of barges loaded with cars. A front window in the cab was open and icy gusts of wind blew in, smelling of gasoline and the sea. Suppose the weather never changed again? Who then would ever be able to imagine a summer day, a moonlit night, spring? But how much imagination—for what it's worth—does a man actually have? On Eastern Parkway the taxi was jolted and screeched suddenly to a stop. Some traffic accident, apparently. The siren on a police car shrieked. A wailing ambulance drew nearer. Dr. Margolin grimaced. Another victim. Someone makes a false turn of the wheel and all a man's plans in this world are reduced to nothing. A wounded man was carried to the ambulance on a stretcher. Above a dark suit and blood-spattered shirt and bow tie the face had a chalky pallor; one eye was closed, the other partly open and glazed. Perhaps he, too, had been going to a wedding, Dr.

Margolin thought. He might even have been going to the same wedding as I. . . .

Some time later the taxi started moving again. Solomon Margolin was now driving through streets he had never seen before. It was New York, but it might just as well have been Chicago or Cleveland. They passed through an industrial district with factory buildings, warehouses of coal, lumber, scrap iron. Negroes, strangely black, stood about on the sidewalks, staring ahead, their great dark eyes full of a gloomy hopelessness. Occasionally the car would pass a tavern. The people at the bar seemed to have something un-earthly about them, as if they were being punished here for sins committed in another incarnation. Just when Solomon Margolin was beginning to sus-pect that the driver, who had remained stubbornly silent the whole time, had gotten lost or else was deliberately taking him out of his way, the taxi entered a thickly populated neighborhood. They passed a synagogue, a funeral par-lor, and there, ahead, was the wedding hall, all lit up, with its neon Jewish sign and Star of David. Dr. Margolin gave the driver a dollar tip and the man took it without uttering a word.

Dr. Margolin entered the outer lobby and immediately the comfortable intimacy of the Senciminers engulfed him. All the faces he saw were familiar, though he didn't recognize individuals. Leaving his hat and coat at the check-room, he put on a skullcap and entered the hall. It was filled with people and music, with tables heaped with food, a bar stacked with bottles. The musi-cians were playing an Israeli march that was a hodgepodge of American jazz with Oriental flourishes. Men were dancing with men, women with women, men with women. He saw black skullcaps, white skullcaps, bare heads. Guests kept arriving, pushing their way through the crowd, some still in their hats and coats, munching hors d'oeuvres, drinking schnapps. The hall re-sounded with stamping, screaming, laughing, clapping. Flash bulbs went off blindingly as the photographers made their rounds. Seeming to come from nowhere, the bride appeared, briskly sweeping up her train, followed by a retinue of bridesmaids. Dr. Margolin knew everybody, and yet knew nobody. People spoke to him, laughed, winked, and waved, and he answered each one with a smile, a nod, a bow. Gradually he threw off all his worries, all his de-pression. He became half-drunk on the amalgam of odors: flowers, sauer-kraut, garlic, perfume, mustard, and that nameless odor that only Senciminers emit. "Hello, Doctor!" "Hello, Schloime-Dovid, you don't recognize me, eh? Look, he forgot!" There were the encounters, the regrets, the reminiscences of long ago. "But after all, weren't we neighbors? You used to come to our house to borrow the Yiddish newspaper!" Someone had already kissed him: a badly shaven snout, a mouth reeking of whiskey and rotten teeth. One woman was so convulsed with laughter that she lost an earring. Margolin tried to pick it up, but it had already been trampled underfoot. "You don't recognize me, eh? Take a good look! It's Zissl, the son of Chaye Beyle!" "Why don't you eat something?" "Why don't you have something to drink? Come over here. Take a glass. What do you want? Whiskey? Brandy? Cognac? Scotch? With soda? With Coca Cola? Take some, it's good. Don't let it stand. So long as you're here, you might as well enjoy yourself." "My father? He was killed. They were all killed. I'm the only one left of the entire family." "Berish the son of Feivish? Starved to death in Russia—they sent him to Kazakhstan. His wife? In Israel. She married a Lithuanian." "Sorele? Shot. Together with her children." "Yentl? Here at the wedding. She was standing here just a moment ago. There she is, dancing with that tall fellow." "Abraham Zilberstein? They burned him in the synagogue with twenty others. A mound of charcoal was all that was left, coal and ash." "Yosele Budnik? He passed away years ago. You must mean Yekele Budnik. He has a delicatessen store right here in Brownsville—married a widow whose husband made a fortune in real estate."

"*Lechayim*, Doctor! *Lechayim*, Schloime-Dovid! It doesn't offend you that I call you Schloime-Dovid? To me you're still the same Schloime-Dovid, the little boy with the blond side-curls who recited a whole tractate of the Talmud by heart. You remember, don't you? It seems like only yesterday. Your father, may he rest in peace, was beaming with pride. . . ." "Your brother Chayim? Your Uncle Oyzer? They killed everyone, everyone. They took a whole people and wiped them out with German efficiency: *gleichgeschaltet!*" "Have you seen the bride yet? Pretty as a picture, but too much make-up. Imagine, a grandchild of Reb Todros of Radzin! And her grandfather used to wear two skullcaps, one in front and one in back." "Do you see that young woman dancing in the yellow dress? It's Riva's sister—their father was Moishe the candlemaker. Riva herself? Where all the others ended up: Auschwitz. How close we came ourselves! All of us are really dead, if you want to call it that. We were exterminated, wiped out. Even the survivors carry

death in their hearts. But it's a wedding, we should be cheerful." "*Lechayim,*
Schloime-Dovid! I would like to congratulate you. Have you a son or daughter
to marry off? No? Well, it's better that way. What's the sense of having children if people are such murderers?"

3

It was already time for the ceremony, but someone still had not come.
Whether it was the rabbi, the cantor, or one of the in-laws who was missing,
nobody seemed able to find out. Abraham Mekheles, the bride's father, rushed
around, scowled, waved his hand, whispered in people's ears. He looked
strange in his rented tuxedo. The Tereshpol mother-in-law was wrangling
with one of the photographers. The musicians never stopped playing for an
instant. The drum banged, the bass fiddle growled, the saxophone blared.
The dances became faster, more abandoned, and more and more people were
drawn in. The young men stamped with such force that it seemed the dance
floor would break under them. Small boys romped around like goats, and
little girls whirled about wildly together. Many of the men were already
drunk. They shouted boasts, howled with laughter, kissed strange women.
There was so much commotion that Solomon Margolin could no longer grasp
what was being said to him and simply nodded yes to everything. Some of
the guests had attached themselves to him, wouldn't move, and kept pulling
him in all directions, introducing him to more and more people from Sencimin
and Tereshpol. A matron with a nose covered with warts pointed a finger at
him, wiped her eyes, called him Schloimele. Solomon Margolin inquired who
she was and somebody told him. Names were swallowed up in the tumult. He
heard the same words over and over again: died, shot, burned. A man from
Tereshpol tried to draw him aside and was shouted down by several Senciminers calling him an intruder who had no business there. A latecomer arrived, a horse and buggy driver from Sencimin who had become a millionaire
in New York. His wife and children had perished, but, already, he had a new
wife. The woman, weighted with diamonds, paraded about in a low-cut gown
that bared a back, covered with blotches, to the waist. Her voice was husky.
"Where did she come from? Who was she?" "Certainly no saint. Her first
husband was a swindler who amassed a fortune and then dropped dead. Of
what? Cancer. Where? In the stomach. First you don't have anything to eat,

then you don't have anything to eat with. A man is always working for the second husband." "What is life anyway? A dance on the grave." "Yes, but as long as you're playing the game, you have to abide by the rules." "Dr. Margolin, why aren't you dancing? You're not among strangers. We're all from the same dust. Over there you weren't a doctor. You were only Schloime-Dovid, the son of the Talmud teacher. Before you know it, we'll all be lying side by side."

Margolin didn't recall drinking anything but he felt intoxicated all the same. The foggy hall was spinning like a carousel; the floor was rocking. Standing in a corner, he contemplated the dance. What different expressions the dancers wore. How many combinations and permutations of being, the Creator had brought together here. Every face told its own story. They were dancing together, these people, but each one had his own philosophy, his own approach. A man grabbed Margolin and for a while he danced in the frantic whirl. Then, tearing himself loose, he stood apart. Who was that woman? He found his eye caught by her familiar form. He knew her! She beckoned to him. He stood baffled. She looked neither young nor old. Where had he known her—that narrow face, those dark eyes, that girlish smile? Her hair was arranged in the old manner, with long braids wound like a wreath around her head. The grace of Sencimin adorned her—something he, Margolin, had long since forgotten. And those eyes, he was in love with those eyes and had been all his life. He half smiled at her and the woman smiled back. There were dimples in her cheeks. She too appeared surprised. Margolin, though he realized he had begun to blush like a boy, went up to her.

"I know you—but you're not from Sencimin?"

"Yes, from Sencimin."

He had heard that voice long ago. He had been in love with that voice.

"From Sencimin—who are you, then?"

Her lips trembled.

"You've forgotten me already?"

"It's a long time since I left Sencimin."

"You used to visit my father."

"Who was your father?"

"Melekh the watchmaker."

Dr. Margolin shivered.

"If I'm not out of my mind then I'm seeing things."

"Why do you say that?"

"Because Raizel is dead."

"I'm Raizel."

"You're Raizel? Here? Oh my God, if that's true—then anything is possible! When did you come to New York?"

"Some time ago."

"From where?"

"From over there."

"But everyone told me that you were all dead."

"My father, my mother, my brother Hershl . . ."

"But you were married!"

"I was."

"If that's true, then anything is possible!" repeated Dr. Margolin, still shaken by the incredible happening. Someone must have purposely deceived him. But why? He was aware there was a mistake somewhere but could not determine where.

"Why didn't you let me know? After all . . ."

He fell silent. She too was silent for a moment.

"I lost everything. But I still had some pride left."

"Come with me somewhere quieter—anywhere. This is the happiest day of my life!"

"But it's night . . ."

"Then the happiest night! Almost—as if the Messiah had come, as if the dead had come to life!"

"Where do you want to go? All right, let's go."

Margolin took her arm and felt at once the thrill, long forgotten, of youthful desire. He steered her away from the other guests, afraid that he might lose her in the crowd, or that someone would break in and spoil his happiness. Everything had returned on the instant: the embarrassment, the agitation, the joy. He wanted to take her away, to hide somewhere alone with her. Leaving the reception hall, they went upstairs to the chapel where the wedding ceremony was to take place. The door was standing open. Inside, on a raised platform stood the permanent wedding canopy. A bottle of wine and a silver goblet were placed in readiness for the ceremony. The chapel with its empty pews and only one glimmering light was full of shadows. The music, so blaring below, sounded soft and distant up here. Both of them hesitated at the threshold. Margolin pointed to the wedding canopy.

"We could have stood there."

"Yes."

"Tell me about yourself. Where are you now? What are you doing?"

"It is not easy to tell."

"Are you alone? Are you attached?"

"Attached? No."

"Would you never have let me hear from you?" he asked. She didn't answer.

Gazing at her, he knew his love had returned with full force. Already, he was trembling at the thought that they might soon have to part. The excitement and the expectancy of youth filled him. He wanted to take her in his arms and kiss her, but at any moment someone might come in. He stood beside her, ashamed that he had married someone else, that he had not personally confirmed the reports of her death. "How could I have suppressed all this love? How could I have accepted the world without her? And what will happen now with Gretl?—I'll give her everything, my last cent." He looked round toward the stairway to see if any of the guests had started to come up. The thought came to him that by Jewish law he was not married, for he and Gretl had had only a civil ceremony. He looked at Raizel.

"According to Jewish law, I'm a single man."

"Is that so?"

"According to Jewish law, I could lead you up there and marry you."

She seemed to be considering the import of his words.

"Yes, I realize . . ."

"According to Jewish law, I don't even need a ring. One can get married with a penny."

"Do you have a penny?"

He put his hand to his breast pocket, but his wallet was gone. He started searching in his other pockets. Have I been robbed? he wondered. But how? I was sitting in the taxi the whole time. Could someone have robbed me here at the wedding? He was not so much disturbed as surprised. He said falteringly:

"Strange, but I don't have any money."

"We'll get along without it."

"But how am I going to get home?"

"Why go home?" she said, countering with a question. She smiled with that homely smile of hers that was so full of mystery. He took her by the wrist and gazed at her. Suddenly it occurred to him that this could not be his Raizel. She was too young. Probably it was her daughter who was playing along with him, mocking him. For God's sake, I'm completely confused! he thought. He stood bewildered, trying to untangle the years. He couldn't tell her age from her features. Her eyes were deep, dark, and melancholy. She also appeared confused, as if she, too, sensed some discrepancy. The whole thing is a mistake, Margolin told himself. But where exactly was the mistake? And what had happened to the wallet? Could he have left it in the taxi after paying the driver? He tried to remember how much cash he had had in it, but was unable to. "I must have had too much to drink. These people have made me drunk—dead drunk!" For a long time he stood silent, lost in some dreamless state, more profound than a narcotic trance. Suddenly he remembered the traffic collision he had witnessed on Eastern Parkway. An eerie suspicion came over him: Perhaps he had been more than a witness? Perhaps he himself had been the victim of that accident! That man on the stretcher looked strangely familiar. Dr. Margolin began to examine himself as though he were one of his own patients. He could find no trace of pulse or breathing. And he felt oddly deflated as if some physical dimension were missing. The sensation of weight, the muscular tension of his limbs, the hidden aches in his bones, all seemed to be gone. It can't be, it can't be, he murmured. Can one die without knowing it? And what will Gretl do? He blurted out:

"You're not the same Raizel."

"No? Then who am I?"

"They shot Raizel."

"Shot her? Who told you that?"

She seemed both frightened and perplexed. Silently she lowered her head like someone receiving the shock of bad news. Dr. Margolin continued to ponder. Apparently Raizel didn't realize her own condition. He had heard of such a state—what was it called? Hovering in the World of Twilight. The Astral Body wandering in semi-consciousness, detached from the flesh, without being able to reach its destination, clinging to the illusions and vanities of the past. But could there be any truth to all this superstition? No, as far as he was concerned, it was nothing but wishful thinking. Besides, this kind of survival would be less than oblivion. "I am most probably in a drunken stupor," Dr. Margolin decided. "All this may be one long hallucination, perhaps a result of food poisoning. . . ."

He looked up, and she was still there. He leaned over and whispered in her ear:

"What's the difference? As long as we're together."

"I've been waiting for that all these years."

"Where have you been?"

She didn't answer, and he didn't ask again. He looked around. The empty hall was full, all the seats taken. A ceremonious hush fell over the audience. The music played softly. The cantor intoned the benedictions. With measured steps, Abraham Mekheles led his daughter down the aisle.

MARJORIE PERLOFF

Marjorie Perloff—then Gabriele Mintz—was six and a half years old when her mother announced to her: "Now we are no longer Austrians. Hitler has taken Austria." Fleeing Vienna in the wake of the 1938 Anschluss, the Mintz family went first to Zurich before sailing to the United States. In her memoir *The Vienna Paradox* (2004), Perloff—who went on to become one of the most influential of American literary critics—traces with wit and nuance her transition from the German high culture into which she was born to the more populist and egalitarian America in which she ultimately grew up. There are, as Perloff remarks elsewhere in the book, no easy answers to the questions she raises: "I remain decidedly ambivalent about my own cultural roots. As a professor of literature, I long for a world where people actually care about the artistic and intellectual life. . . . At the same time, I am aware of the price High Culture exacts and the dangers of nonengagement in the actual public life of one's nation."

from
The Vienna Paradox

The great Saturday adventure of these war years was to go department store shopping with Mother—an outing that involved a long subway ride from 231st to 34th Street, the escalators at Macy's and Gimbel's and—best of all—lunch at Horn & Hardart's, otherwise known as "the Automat." I was usually given $1.25 in quarters which meant that I could choose from the tantalizing windows along the wall the little brown pot of baked beans (25¢), two other vegetables, and a particular white cake with chocolate icing that looked like a squat little tower. To put the quarter into the slot and get *the* thing one wanted instantly: this undoubtedly prepared me for the pleasures of Frank O'Hara's *Lunch Poems*:

> If I rest for a moment near The Equestrian
> Pausing for a liver sausage sandwich in the Mayflower Shoppe,
> That angel seems to be leading the horse into Bergdorf's. . .
> I have in my hands only 35¢, it's so meaningless to eat!

("Music")

Or

> Neon in daylight is a
> great pleasure, as Edwin Denby would
> write, as are light bulbs in daylight.
> I stop for a cheeseburger at JULIET's
> CORNER.

("A Step Away from Them")

Imagine making poetry out of the Mayflower Shoppe, across from Bergdorf Goodman's on Fifth Avenue, out of Juliet's Corner on Times Square! Flexibility and attentiveness, these poems tell us, are the qualities needed to enjoy such city pleasures as "Neon in daylight." It was a matter, as O'Hara put it, of "Grace to be born and live as variously as possible." But in 1941 I could not yet articulate this notion, and although I carefully studied each item in the Horn & Hardart windows, I always chose the same three or four things.

ÉMIGRÉ REINVENTION

One refugee who did display the kind of grace I speak of was Grandfather Schüller. Once he recognized that he had no choice but to accept the demise of the old Austria, the seventy-year-old statesman quickly adapted to the New World. The story of his arrival in New York is itself remarkable. While Grandmama Schüller and her mother had to wait for their visas in Oxford, Grandfather obtained his professor's visa because he had been invited by Alvin Johnson to join the University in Exile at the New School. In July 1940, he sailed on a Dutch ship carrying 900 children, bound for Canada. There he was supposed to remain in custody until his papers were processed, but he got leave to go to the barber, boarded the first train, showed his visa at the border, and, before he knew it, had arrived at Grand Central:

In New York, I left my luggage at Grand Central, asked for a [subway] train to Riverdale, where I got off at about 11.30 at night. Not a soul anywhere, no taxi. Saw a light on in a house, knocked at the door, and asked whether I could call for a taxi, which quickly brought me to Ilse. They were very surprised. Bliss of the reunion after two years. (UV, 185)

Grandfather was soon living with his sister-in-law Ida and her daughter Lotte, a psychiatrist, in the upstairs apartment across the hall from us. He began teaching at the New School—an entirely new experience for him—and supplementing his tiny income by helping the banker Max Warburg write his memoirs as well as acting as consultant for a company called Amertrade. When Grandmother and Great-grandmother arrived a year and a half later, the Schüller-Rosenthal family, now without Lotte, moved around the corner to Cambridge Avenue, where their modest little apartment was reached by a steep flight of outside steps that froze over in the winter. Again, Grandfather made the best of it; he had soon befriended the old German who lived in the basement apartment downstairs—Richard Hoeningswald, a philosophy professor from Munich—and embarked on the serious study, first of classical philosophy, and then the mathematical logic of Frege and the phenomenology of Husserl. On their morning walks, they went over philosophical problems, even as my father did in his letters to Voegelin. Occasionally, they would pass Johnson Avenue, where my friend Eileen Moore and I were roller-skating, and Grandfather would stop to chat for a moment and give me tips derived from his years of figure-skating at the beautiful skating rink near the Ballhausplatz. In making a circle, for instance, the inside shoulder and ankle had to be lowered for balance! And Grandfather would give a little demonstration, much to my embarrassment.

Grandmama was less satisfied with New York. She pronounced the buildings ugly and objected to the dirt, snow, ice, and the cumbersome subway ride downtown. The shabby old apartment and lack of household help were a trial to her. When, at the dinner table, Grandmama, Great-grandmother, and Aunt Ida would engage in their frequent "byunsky" rounds of complaint about New York, Grandfather, who was usually very quiet during meals, would finally lose his temper and say, "*Also jetzt Ruhe!*" Enough! And despite all her caveats, Grandmama soon found the right refugee dressmaker near Central Park, took the subway to museums and concerts, played bridge, and read prodigiously. When I was home with a cold or sore throat (which happened frequently!), she would come over and read to me, as did Great-grandmother. What this meant is that my German literary education was, for many years, way ahead of my English one. By the time I was ten, I knew Schiller's *Wilhelm Tell, Wallenstein, Die Jungfrau von Orleans,* and *Maria Stuart,* as well as Goethe's *Götz von Berlichingen* pretty much by heart. Indeed, I recall that one evening when my father came home from work, I greeted him, much to the amusement of Mother, with the words *"Betrogener törichter Junge!"* ("Betrayed, foolish boy!"). These words come from Act V of *Götz,* when the demonic beauty Adelheid von Walldorf persuades the young steward Franz, who is madly in love with her, to poison her husband, who is also Franz's master. *"Es soll sein!"* ("It will be!"), declares Franz in this most dramatic of scenes.

What I loved in *Götz von Berlichingen,* as in the Schiller historical dramas, was the realistic psychodrama at the core of their Romantic plots. In *Götz,* for example, the noble Weislingen, himself a betrayer, is betrayed in turn by his own man, Franz, who has fallen under the spell of Adelheid. And in *Die Jungfrau von Orleans,* the warrior saint Joan of Arc loses her nerve in battle when she looks into the eyes of the enemy—the young Englishman Lionel—and refuses to kill him. How dramatic this turning point, especially when Joan's peasant father then declares that his daughter is a witch! Or consider the scene in *Maria Stuart,* when Elizabeth learns that "her" Leicester has also been the lover of her hated rival, Maria. There is no English equivalent to these Romantic dramas, with their medieval and rustic trappings, their insoluble conflicts, their dissection of passion, folly, and betrayal, and their sexual undertones. Moreover, the women, unlike the women in, say, Sir Walter Scott's novels, are strong and complex characters, taking charge of their destinies, often despite historical and social odds. In Goethe and Schiller, women are rarely victims: Gretchen in *Faust* is the exception, and even she has the power of insight not found in comparable English innocents.

Turning from these classics to literature in English, I seemed to regress. My library selections ranged from the Lois Lenski books and the famed twin series (e.g., *The Dutch Twins*) to biographies of interesting young girls like

Drina (the young Victoria) and Edna Ferber's big novels like *So Big* and *Giant*. I thus had the oddly skewed notion that Culture was a German commodity. At home, we were always told to speak German, especially when the Grandparents were present, though Mother also employed me, during dishwashing time, to teach her English idioms and correct her mistakes.

In public, having to speak German and be addressed as Gabriele was a regular humiliation. I wanted desperately to "fit in," and hence I hated to accompany Grandmama on the subway, where she immediately spoke German in a loud voice. When I was twelve, Grandmama took me to my first opera at the Met—*Lohengrin*. Wagner was not the ideal choice for a twelve-year-old, and I remember being extremely bored, except during the swan scene. Indeed, although I loved German novels and plays, I never did develop a proper taste for opera, perhaps because every Saturday Walter and I had to tiptoe around the house and be quiet while the opera was on the radio. Forced to listen to *The Marriage of Figaro* and *The Barber of Seville*, we rebelled. At night, I would secretly listen to the *Hit Parade*—at least until Walter, who shared the radio with me, came barging into my room, disconnected the plug, and took the radio into his room so that he could listen to *The Shadow, The Great Gildersleeve,* or *Gangbusters.*

On the whole, however, I accepted the dual culture in which I now functioned without much stress. Speaking German, I was good little Gabriele, who spoke in complete sentences, knew no off-color words, and was interested in "good" books. Speaking English, I was slangier, less polite, more inclined toward popular culture. On occasion, the two modes collided, as when my parents were having a *Jause*—that Austrian cross between a cocktail party and high tea. Mother and Grandmama would work all morning making *Brötchen*—the open-faced sandwiches *de rigueur* on such an occasion —a slice of ham with an asparagus stalk on top, or salmon decorated with hard-boiled egg slices and gherkins. There were also two or three cakes or patisserie. Promptly at four the guests—in those early days, all refugee friends—would arrive and immediately there was very loud German conversation and much laughter. First wine or champagne was served with the *Brötchen* and then immediately tea and cakes. By seven p.m. or so it was all over: the noise stopped as abruptly as it had begun.

Walter and I played a particular role during these "ref parties," as we sarcastically called them. We had to dress up, make a brief appearance, and shake hands with the guests, pausing briefly to eat a *Brötchen* or two. Then we were given the high sign, which meant that we should exit as quickly as we had entered and could now play in our rooms without further disturbance. Although as soon as we were out of the room we joked about some of the guests, it did not seem the least bit strange to us that each and every one of them was a German-speaking refugee.

Indeed, the fact that a large proportion of my parents' Vienna social circle, Geistkreis included, was now living in New York made assimilation into American life that much harder. Refugees who settled in Chicago or San Francisco had to fit in; refugees in New York did not and tried to keep up the old ways, although their names were largely Americanized, so that Redlichs became Redleys, Gärtners Gardeners, and Geiringers Graingers. Later, when I found out that Alfred ("Fredl") Schütz (whose daughter Eva, now Evelyn, I found very boring) was a famous philosopher, whose works some of my colleagues venerated, or that Uncle Max Schur (my father's first cousin) had been Freud's personal physician and was now a leading psychoanalyst, I couldn't quite relate their evident accomplishments to the familiar figures I had seen at Mother's tea parties. And it was also true that, with rare exceptions, only the men did interesting things, whereas the wives, cultured and hence highly opinionated as they were, held entirely subordinate positions. Ilse Schütz, for example, who was a very close friend of Mother's, seemed entirely absorbed in her two children and household. And although there were occasional bachelors like Dr. Winternitz at our parties, I never recall any single women. Indeed, widows like Aunt Gerti, now living at an apartment hotel nearby, or Aunt Ida were invited only by themselves, not to parties. This continued to be the protocol.

In 1942, when I was almost eleven, I was sent, for the first time, to camp. Ironically, Self-Help, the charitable organization that sponsored camp for us Jewish refugee children, sent us to a Y.W.C.A. camp—Camp Owaissa—on Lake Ariel in the Poconos, near Scranton, Pennsylvania. The cost, I remember, was $11.00 per week, and I went for six weeks, three summers in a row. It was one of the happiest times of my young life. I still remember getting on the Greyhound Bus for my very first summer away from home! I sat next to a girl named Ruth Walker (née Wakler), who was to become my best friend.

But on that first day I was so excited I became sick repeatedly: the bus had to stop three times so I could get out and vomit. The first morning at camp, we had to eat Shredded Wheat, which I had never seen before, and I vomited again. After that, everything was perfect.

The morning began with flag-raising followed by Morning Worship—a half-hour of prayer and hymn singing. Here, and again at Evening Worship, we learned such hymns as:

> In Christ there is no East or West.
> In Him no South or North:
> But one great fellowship of love
> Throughout the whole wide earth.

> In Him shall true hearts everywhere
> Their high communion find;
> His service is the golden cord,
> Close binding humankind. . . .

And:

> Be Thou my vision O Lord of my heart;
> Naught be all else to me, save that Thou art
> Thou my best Thought, by day or by night,
> Waking or sleeping, Thy presence my light.

> Be Thou my Wisdom, and Thou my true Word;
> I ever with Thee and Thou with me, Lord;
> Thou my great Father, I Thy true son;
> Thou in me dwelling, and I with thee one.

No one, least of all I, found it at all odd that a group of Jewish refugee girls should be participating in this Christian hymn-singing ritual. The Y.W.C.A., after all, had been kind enough to reach out to us. Besides, what was Goethe's *"Kennst du das Land wo die Zitronen blühn?"* compared to "Be Thou My Vision," sung in the circle of campers by the fire? I was a convert, not to Christianity, but to the sounds and rhythms of these soon-familiar hymns. Many years later, when I read D. H. Lawrence's great essay "Hymns in a Man's Life," with its account of the childhood wonder produced by the "banal Noncomformist hymns that penetrated through and through my childhood," I knew exactly what he meant. Ruthie and another refugee girl named Eve Spitz were somewhat more critical: they reminded me that we were not supposed to sing songs or say prayers to Christ. But I felt the way Lawrence did about "Galilee, Sweet Galilee":

> To me the word Galilee has a wonderful sound. The Lake of Galilee! I don't want to know where it is. I never want to go to Palestine. Galilee is one of those lovely, glamorous worlds, not places, that exist in the golden haze of a child's half-formed imagination. And in my man's imagination it is just the same. It has been left untouched.

Then, too, the daily song ritual included more than hymns. At night, there was the thrilling bugle call of Taps:

> Day is done, gone the sun,
> From the hills, from the lake,
> From the skies.
> All is well, safely rest,
> God is nigh.

I only learned much later that Taps was a military song and that it originated in 1862 during the Civil War. Of our own war, the war raging in Japan and Europe in the summer of '42, we did not speak. While we were making momentous decisions as to whether to choose boating or archery for the nine-to-ten a.m. slot or nature study or arts and crafts from three-to-four p.m., the first Battle of Guadalcanal was underway in the Pacific and the German siege of Stalingrad had begun. I don't remember anyone, whether camper, counselor, or our director, Elsie Borden (known to us as Elsie the Borden Cow), so much as mentioning the war. And indeed at camp, the military bugle call of Taps was followed by a second very unmilitary song, which went like this:

> Now run along home
> And jump into bed,
> Say your prayers
> And cover your head.

The very same thing
I say unto you,
You dream of me,
And I'll dream of you!

No mention of God this time around, only friendship and good feeling. Interestingly, however, I don't remember a single camp friend who was not part of the refugee nexus. I believe I *had* other friends—girls who came from Philadelphia or even Scranton nearby—but I can't now place them. Yet I could give a complete account of the summer's highpoint: learning how to dive. At the beginning of July, I could swim the breast stroke I had learned at Ostia in 1938, but nothing else. Now—so as to become a Green Cap—I learned the crawl, the sidestroke, the elementary backstroke, and back crawl, and then the "spring-dive," performed as gracefully as possible. And having passed the Green Cap test, we swam across the lake with boats beside us for safety. Our happiness was complete.

There was only one major mishap that first summer. In the late afternoon, we were allowed to take out the rowboats for an hour, and one Sunday, Ruthie, Eve, and I went out beyond the island and the boat got caught in the reeds. It took a while to get unstuck, and by the time we approached the Camp Owaissa dock, Evening Worship, which was held down by the lake on Sundays, was in full swing. The whole camp was lined up along the shore, singing "Be Thou My Vision" and other favorites. As we rowed into the dock as quietly as possible, the campers started to giggle and point, and we knew we were in the doghouse. Mrs. Borden was furious, and we were docked for a whole week. To make matters worse, our counselor told us that Mrs. Borden felt the Jewish refugee children had not been sufficiently respectful of the Y.W.C.A. camp's Christian mission. And subconsciously this may well have been true.

It was also true that by seventh grade, P.S. 7 no longer seemed so attractive. These were years when the New York Board of Education was constantly lurching from one pedagogical experiment to another, and when I was in seventh grade, tracking, which had guided all my teaching thus far, was suddenly eliminated. This meant that for the first time we were all in one math or English class and there were students in my class who couldn't multiple nine by five or spell the word *receive*. Some, like Grace Terribile, who was fourteen in seventh grade, had been left back a number of times and were just marking time until they could leave school and get jobs. Many already had boyfriends and paid no attention in class. Our seventh grade teacher, Miss Coyne, who had previously taught in a reform school, always wore dresses with long sleeves because—so rumor had it—she had a huge scar on her right arm where a boy had knifed her. Miss Coyne was a terror, as was the eighth grade teacher, Mrs. Cahill, who had tight white curls and pursed lips and never spoke above a whisper.

My parents had, in the meantime, decided to send me to a private school—the Fieldston School in Riverdale. I received a full scholarship with the proviso that I repeat the eighth grade, because I was a year ahead of myself, having skipped twice at P.S. 7. I didn't like the idea at all: for a thirteen-year-old it is highly humiliating to be put back a grade. I had visited Fieldston for an interview and found it almost too luxurious: it looked more like a country club than a school, and its athletic fields were bigger than all of P.S. 7. But there were two things that happened that changed my mind. The first was the debacle of my graduation dress. In those war years, each girl made her own dress. Mother and I bought five yards of organdy—aqua blue with little white flowers, together with some pink ribbon and a dress pattern. For a while, my sewing efforts (we learned sewing in sixth grade) went quite well, but then I became reckless and made too wide a cut for the square neckline. It was now much too big, and I had to take tucks in it. When I tried it on in sewing class, Mrs. Engel went into a fury. She made me stand up on a chair as an example and announced, much to my humiliation, that Gabriele's dress was the visible emblem of what *not* to do.

The second incident had to do with my eighth-grade penicillin report. Penicillin was a new drug in those days, and I had researched its origins and manufacture as carefully as I could. Then I made the cover for the report with a stencil, the word "penicillin" appearing in yellow at a diagonal against the blue paper background, with the name Gabriele Mintz in the lower right. But, as was my wont, I spilled some glue on the cover, so that there were some faint spots I couldn't quite eliminate. On the last day of school, Mrs. Cahill called me to the front of the room and informed me that I wouldn't graduate unless I made a new cover because of the glue stains on this one. I had the presence of mind to say, "No, Mrs. Cahill. I won't. It doesn't matter, because I am going to a new school." And suddenly I knew I was happy to begin a new life.

All this happened about a week after D-Day, June 6, 1944. I did, in fact, graduate with my class and wear the unfortunate aqua-blue organdy dress. But given the "march of events," my parents paid little attention to this particular nonmilestone. They were glued to the radio every evening, and already their conversation was full of worries that "we" (Britain and the United States) were allowing the Soviets to make too many gains. In December of '44, during the calamitous Nazi-Soviet clash over Budapest, Daddy wrote to Voegelin:

> I fear that Churchill, whom for many reasons, but especially for his prose, I revere, is also responsible for the entirely unnecessary land invasion of Italy. If the Allies had begun the Normandy invasion a year earlier, it would have been an advantage, although it would have helped the Russians too. The Russians, for their part, have succeeded, with their six-month sit-down strike, in dragging out the war, thus helping the Germans hold on to Budapest. . . . Well, the world is ruled with little wisdom, and the prospect that the war may drag on another two or three years and that, in the end, Walter will be sent to Asia, is a source of anxiety.

As it turned out, Daddy was too pessimistic: within five months, the European war was over. I suppose that the calamity of having so grossly misread the Austrian situation a decade earlier made both my parents always expect the worst. On the other hand, Daddy's supposition that the Japanese war might drag on for years and that Walter might have to fight in it was by no means unreasonable in those prenuclear days. Then, too, with victory in May 1945 came the first onsite reports from the concentration camps, guaranteed to strike terror into the hearts of the refugees, who knew that, but for the grace of God, they would have shared the fates of those others, some of whom were their own relatives and friends. One such relative (although I only learned this much later) was Otto Strauss's mother, who could have left with us on the train for Zurich on March 12, 1938, but evidently didn't want to leave her precious jewelry behind. She died at Auschwitz.

For a thirteen-year-old like myself, however, neither the war's end in

Europe nor the cataclysm of Hiroshima three months later seemed very real. At Camp Owaissa that summer, the big event was that an "older girl" named Ruth Oppenheimer finally enlightened the whole cabin about sex. We were incredulous! Was *that* really what men and women did? Surely not our parents! By the time I came home with my newly acquired knowledge, it was time to begin a whole new life at the Fieldston School. Almost the first thing I did was to change my name to Marjorie.

W. H. AUDEN

By the time W. H. Auden (1907–1973) sailed to the United States in
January 1939, he was the most famous living English poet, both for the
extraordinary technical range and assurance of his verse and for his left-
wing viewpoints. He had journeyed to the battlefronts of the Spanish
Civil War and the Sino-Japanese War and espoused a poetry of political
commitment and journalistic observation. His immigration to the United
States—in company with Christopher Isherwood, with whom he had frequently collaborated—marked a shift in his writing away from ideological militancy and toward a reconciliation with the Anglicanism in which
he had been raised. This poem—a lament on the plight of German Jewish refugees written in 1939—typifies the use of song forms that he explored throughout his career. Auden, who came under fire in some quarters for having left England at such a perilous juncture, remained in
America, becoming a naturalized citizen in 1946. For many years he lived
on St. Mark's Place in Manhattan while spending summers on the Italian
island of Ischia and, later, in Vienna, Austria, where he died.

Say this city has ten million souls,
Some are living in mansions, some are living in holes:
Yet there's no place for us, my dear, yet there's no place for us.

Once we had a country and we thought it fair,
Look in the atlas and you'll find it there:
We cannot go there now, my dear, we cannot go there now.

In the village churchyard there grows an old yew,
Every spring it blossoms anew:
Old passports can't do that, my dear, old passports can't do that.

The consul banged the table and said:
"If you've got no passport you're officially dead":
But we are still alive, my dear, but we are still alive.

Went to a committee; they offered me a chair;
Asked me politely to return next year:
But where shall we go to-day, my dear, but where shall we go to-day?

Came to a public meeting; the speaker got up and said:
"If we let them in, they will steal our daily bread";
He was talking of you and me, my dear, he was talking of you and me.

Thought I heard the thunder rumbling in the sky;
It was Hitler over Europe, saying: "They must die";
We were in his mind, my dear, we were in his mind.

Saw a poodle in a jacket fastened with a pin,
Saw a door opened and a cat let in:
But they weren't German Jews, my dear, but they weren't German Jews.

Went down to the harbour and stood upon the quay,
Saw the fish swimming as if they were free:
Only ten feet away, my dear, only ten feet away.

Walked through a wood, saw the birds in the trees;
They had no politicians and sang at their ease:
They weren't the human race, my dear, they weren't the human race.

Dreamed I saw a building with a thousand floors,
A thousand windows and a thousand doors;
Not one of them was ours, my dear, not one of them was ours.

Stood on a great plain in the falling snow;
Ten thousand soldiers marched to and fro:
Looking for you and me, my dear, looking for you and me.

CARL DJERASSI

A research chemist and biomedical entrepreneur best known for his role in the development of the first oral contraceptive pill, Carl Djerassi (born in Austria in 1923) is also a writer of fiction, drama, and poetry as well as an art collector known for his significant collection of the works of Paul Klee. In this chapter from his memoir *The Pill, Pygmy Chimps, and Degas' Horse* (1992), he tells an engaging tale of how, as a resourceful teenager newly arrived in America in 1939 and dropped into a college town in the northwestern corner of Missouri, he managed to transform himself with only the slightest of qualifications into a successful public speaker.

from
The Pill, Pygmy Chimps, and Degas' Horse

"DEAR MRS. ROOSEVELT"

That's how I finally started the letter, after rejecting several more flowery salutations. "Your Excellency" was the one I'd considered most seriously. After all, to me, sixteen years old, a refugee from Hitler, just arrived on these shores, President Roosevelt's wife was clearly queen of America, the woman who could make things happen with the mere wave of her wand. But her shy smile and buckteeth—I'd studied them in countless newspaper photographs —convinced me that such a populist queen would be most comfortable with a simple, everyday sort of address. "Dear Mrs. Roosevelt," I wrote in early 1940, in a letter that, improbably enough, would launch me on the lecture circuit in the Corn Belt.

I

In early September 1939, just after the German army had marched into Poland, my mother had written from London that our American immigration visas had been granted: it was time to leave Europe. I seemed to accept that news with considerable equanimity, the Bulgarian interlude having been a soothing balm to the traumatic disruption of my Viennese childhood. Bulgaria was my father's country—the Djerassis having lived there for hundreds of years since their emigration from Spain during the Inquisition; and I was immediately accepted into my paternal family with true Balkan warmth. But that did not make me a Bulgarian patriot, in spite of my valuable Bulgarian passport. Except for the early, and largely forgotten, years of my infancy in Sofia (I was two months old when I left Vienna the first time), Bulgaria had turned into a synonym for summer vacations. Now it became a remarkably effective preparation for American life, my father having enrolled me in the American College, a private boarding school on the outskirts of Sofia, where I was tutored in a *mélange* of languages that left a permanent imprint on me. (I dream in unaccented English, but when others hear it, they always ask, "Where are you from?") The bulk of the instruction was in English, taught by Yanks, Brits, and Bulgars; but some of the classes were given in Bulgarian (notably mathematics, since American high school texts were not up to local *Gymnasium* standards) and in French—all of them foreign languages to my Viennese ears and tongue. That multilingual sophomore year of my Sofia high school education also introduced me to American literature. For some reason, American history was taught in a later year, but by that time I had already arrived in the country where the fourth of July carried a very different meaning from that embedded in my personal history.

My experience with the Bulgarian language is curious: I must be one of the rare persons who have twice forgotten the same language. While the first five years of my life, shortly after my Viennese birth, were spent in Sofia, we spoke German at home rather than Bulgarian, because my mother never learned that language. My own Bulgarian prattle was carried on largely with our maid and cook, so that I used female endings when referring to myself, and forgot most of it once I·was again settled in Vienna and entering elementary school. (The female aspect of my Viennese youth started on a spectacular scale: The schools were not yet coeducational, and boys and girls went to separate schools in adjacent buildings in the Czerningasse. Since I had arrived from Sofia after the start of the Viennese school year and the boy's school was already full, I, together with three other male latecomers, was put among the girls. Sigmund Freud would doubtless have considered that nugget of information a bonanza.) During my 1938–39 residence in Sofia, I learned teenage Bulgarian from my classmates at the American College, but that second exposure was too feeble to withstand my subsequent, decades-long immersion in American lingo once I had crossed the Atlantic.

When the time came for our departure for America, my father accompanied my mother and me on the train journey to Genoa. I remember him waving his hat from the pier as my mother and I boarded the Italian liner *Rex*, soon to be sunk in the war. There were several reasons my father did not join us. He had a highly successful medical practice in Sofia, and led an intensive and extensive social life (some of which I only discovered shortly before his death) in his native country, where he felt deeply at home. He spoke no English and would have had to start from scratch, living alone in America, since he and my mother would certainly not have lived together. Even if he had wanted to come with us, it would have been impossible, because American immigration quotas were based on place of birth, rather than on citizenship. As my mother and I were born in Vienna, we fell into the Austrian quota, which was enormous compared with the minute Bulgarian one with its ten-year waiting list. Besides, my father did not believe that Bulgaria would be involved in the war, and hence felt neither threatened nor inclined to assume that it would last long. We did not meet again for ten years, by which time I had passed into adulthood and marriage.

My mother and I arrived penniless in New York City in December after a crossing so stormy that our huge ship was delayed more than a day. All that remains in my memory of our steerage accommodations is that I was seasick throughout most of the transatlantic passage. We were not totally penniless when we descended the gangplank—we actually had twenty dollars in precious American currency which had been difficult to secure in Bulgaria; but in less than an hour, we lost that little hoard to the taxi driver, who took us from the pier to the Washington Heights apartment of my mother's Viennese cousins (who had arrived a few months earlier) and knew greenhorns when he saw them.

Within a few days, the Jewish refugee aid organization HIAS (Hebrew Sheltering and Immigrant Aid Society) had found us a studio apartment in a brownstone on West 68th Street in Manhattan and provided us with funds for day-to-day survival until we got something more permanent. My mother, who had no license to practice medicine in the United States, was hired by an Austrian physician, who had arrived the preceding year and already passed the board examinations. He had settled as a country doctor in a small hamlet, Ellenburg Center, near the Canadian border in upstate New York, and my mother served as his assistant and housekeeper. I was luckier.

In terms of grades, I had been only an average student at the *Realgymnasium* in Vienna, sacrificing a good part of scholarship to sports and poker. But I changed dramatically before my fifteenth birthday, when I began my sophomore year at the American College in Sofia. Knowing that it was a steppingstone to my eventual education in America, where grades were bound to count, I became a star student during the two and one-half semesters I spent in Bulgaria, waiting for the magic visa.

Within days of my arrival in Manhattan, clutching my A-studded certificate from Bulgaria, written in plain English—so different from school certificates carried by most other refugees of those days—I visited a faculty member at New York University. He was a friend of one of my former American teachers, who had told me to get advice on where to complete high school. Apparently he paid no attention to my age for, upon learning that I had been at a "college" in Bulgaria, he informed me that though it was too late in the year to apply to New York University, he could probably arrange for the now-defunct Newark Junior College in Newark, New Jersey, to accept me at the start of the January semester. I didn't correct his misapprehension, figuring —correctly—that once I transferred from the junior college to a four-year institution, no one would look again at my high school record and notice that I had missed two years.

While my mother headed for upstate New York, HIAS placed me into the Newark home of an extraordinarily generous family. My relatively painless adjustment to America was helped along by Frank Meier, an inorganic chemist working at Engelhardt Industries; his wife, Clara, a local high school teacher; and their two high school-age sons, August (now a history professor at Kent State University) and Paul (professor of statistics at the University of Chicago). They did not treat me as surrogate parents, but in retrospect their family life was an example of everything good and decent in America: liberal, generous, caring.

In my mind, and most likely also in that of my mother and father (although I recall no concrete conversations on the topic), the tacit assumption was that I would eventually follow in my physician-parents' steps, but no seed of inspiration had yet been sown. Given my fairly logical frame of mind and argumentative nature, I might have turned to law; when I reflect on the ancient-history books I devoured in Europe, and the pleasure I derived in subsequent years from exploring Mayan, Inca, Khmer, and many other sites of early civilizations, I can imagine a career in archeology. As it happened, the person who sowed and sprinkled one of the first chemical seeds was Nathan Washton, the inspiring freshman chemistry teacher at Newark Junior College, where I started with the standard premedical course requirements of chemistry and biology.

It did not take me long to realize that Newark Junior College, aside from providing an effective laundry for my missing years of high school, could serve only as an early launching pad. The following year I would have to find a four-year institution to complete my college education. Rather than waiting until I had exhausted the resources of Newark Junior College, I turned to Eleanor Roosevelt.

II

"I am writing already now because next year I must have a scholarship to continue my schooling." Decades later, my spoken and written English is still sprinkled with "already now" (*schon jetzt*)—a verbal wart from a German-speaking childhood. Never mind the touch of redundancy, the idiomatic flavor. When I make reservations "already now" for next winter's holiday, I do so because my "now" feels naked and incomplete without the security of "already."

Grudgingly I accepted the fact that pressing affairs of state might prevent my letter from rising instantaneously to the top of Mrs. Roosevelt's pile of correspondence. Still, I had to admit to a touch of disappointment when a brief reply finally arrived from the Institute for International Education to which she had forwarded my request. Only in the autumn was my faith in the limitless power of that most democratic of all queens restored in the form of a postcard from an officer of the institute: "I have some good news for you.

You have been awarded a scholarship for the next semester at Tarkio College in Tarkio, Missouri."

Now I had been first exposed to spoken English by a teacher in Vienna who had mispronounced American place names with a certain savoir-faire. His careful enunciation of "Seekaygo, Illinoa" made an indelible impression on me. To this day, I get a jolt whenever I fly to O'Hare Airport and hear the captain announce over the intercom our impending landing in "Sheekahgo." No wonder I managed to give "Meezooree" a Viennese ring when I announced to my mother that in January 1941 I was heading west to a town I couldn't find on any map then at my disposal. Even the Greyhound ticket office in New York had some difficulty discovering that the northwestern corner of Missouri was my ultimate destination. St. Joseph ("Saint Jo, Masura," to many natives) was the city where Greyhound deposited me after changes in Pittsburgh and Kansas City, and where I transferred to a local bus, which eventually passed the sign "Welcome to Tarkio, Queen of the Corn Belt." In that town I launched my career as a public speaker at the age of seventeen.

Within hours of my registration at Tarkio College—a Presbyterian school where a God-fearing student body of one hundred forty was guided by a faculty of twenty (including the business manager, a house mother, and the superintendent of grounds)*—I learned a piece of historical lore that seemed a superb omen to a budding chemistry major like myself: Tarkio's most illustrious alumnus was none other than Wallace Carothers, the inventor of Nylon. (No one mentioned that he'd committed suicide just a few years after making his discovery.)

At the end of my first week, the program chairman of the Tarkio Rotary Club invited me to address its membership on the "Current Situation in Europe." He informed me that I was scheduled to address the local members who had contributed to my scholarship and wanted to inspect the recipient of their largesse. I was too nervous and too innocent of public speaking even to imagine the many pitfalls a teenage, city-bred kid might face in front of an

---

*One would never have guessed that almost exactly fifty years to the day after my arrival, this once conservatively managed college would go bankrupt following major financial shenanigans that propelled it, probably for the first time in its history, onto the front page of the *New York Times*.

audience of middle-aged farmers and businessmen. I was not, however, too innocent to plagiarize ruthlessly John Gunther's *Inside Europe*. His reference to the Balkans—"Must every little language have a country all its own?"— still sticks in my mind.

My peculiar accent gave the speech an air of authenticity that no one— even one who knew the facts—could possibly resist. Its Viennese base from my "Seekaygo, Illinoa" days had been contaminated by my exposure to Bulgarian-speaking classmates at the American College, whose Slavic assaults on the English language had yielded little to the faculty's British and American accents. Already in sophisticated New York City, I'd learned that to the incessant inquiry "Where're you from?" the single word "Bulgaria" was a much more distinctive answer than "Vienna."

At the end of my Rotary debut, the minister of the local Presbyterian church congratulated me on my performance and proposed that I give a similar talk to his congregation after his Sunday sermon. In order not to repeat myself, I rushed back to my source—*Inside Europe* was not only up to date but also full of entertaining tidbits—and shamelessly borrowed new material, which I dressed up in my Viennese-Bulgarian-British accent. This second talk propelled me almost overnight from amateur to professional. In the minister's office that Sunday, with an apologetic reference to the size of the offering, my pleased host shoved toward me the contents of the collection plate—nickels, dimes, and occasional quarters. It was my first lecture honorarium.

The ministerial grapevine apparently crossed denominational boundaries. From that Sunday on, I received almost weekly invitations to address various church groups in northwestern Missouri and southwestern Iowa about the "European Situation." My plagiarism of Gunther became more sophisticated. I mixed his journalistic wisecracks, such as his definitions of *Balkan Peace* ("a period of cheating between two periods of fighting") or *Balkan Revolutions* ("abrupt changes in the form of misgovernment"), with my personal reminiscences of life in prewar Bulgaria. Pre- or post-Anschluss Vienna became *verboten* territory in my speeches. By focusing on Bulgaria, I was unlikely to encounter contradiction from my rural audiences, most of whom probably could not even have named the four countries bordering on Bulgaria. At the same time, I was eliminating potential questions about Viennese experiences I wished to bury rather than resurrect. Just as Tarkio bragged about its basketball team, I boasted about the amazing quality of the Sofia opera, the fact that Bulgaria was the source of most of the world's attar of roses, and that all male students in public schools had to shave their heads. Although long hair was hardly the vogue in the early 1940s in Missouri, my audiences reacted sympathetically when I described the luxurious hair of some of my classmates at the private American College, which did not require such draconian preventive measures against hair lice.

As the weeks passed, the collection plates became the chief source of my pocket money. Instead of waiting on tables or performing other plebeian part-time work, I pontificated to ladies' auxiliaries, church congregations, and even an eighth-grade commencement ceremony with the self-assurance of a so-far-undetected plagiarist. My talks followed the church services, which I always attended because a member of the congregation was usually my host and source of transportation. I found that the small format of the *Reader's Digest* discreetly fit within the covers of all bibles or hymn books. While others lustily sang Christian hymns, I devoured what at that time passed for *au courant* literature and clever humor. The *Reader's Digest* provided a virtuous camouflage which certainly seasoned its otherwise bland contents. But I had an unconscious reason for reading secular literature while others prayed and sang: I was exercising my agnostic Jewishness among the *goyim*.

One Sunday I answered the call of the First Methodist Church of Shenandoah, Iowa. Five decades later, as I review the scene through the double lens of nostalgia and dimming memory, I can still see the collection plate attached to a long handle move slowly in my direction; with a little effort, I can still capture the tinny sound of dimes hitting other dimes or nickels. The fingers in my pocket were already clutching my usual five-cent offering when a daring thought occurred to me: Why not deposit a fifty-cent piece? After all, it would be back in my needy pocket within a couple of hours at the latest. Perhaps it might shame other parishioners into more generous contributions. It's probably my imagination when I now remember that the majestic bong of my half-dollar piece crashing onto the puny pile of small coins startled the neighbor on my right into contributing a quarter. I made a mental note to carry henceforth a half-dollar coin to all my future speaking engagements. To this day, I have the definite impression that on that Sunday in Shenandoah, Iowa, my talk about Bulgaria was particularly polished, my accent unusually mysterious, my anecdotes only faintly schmaltzy. I felt that my prospective honorarium, suitably weighed down by huge half-dollar coins and possibly even blanketed by an unprecedented dollar bill, merited that extra effort.

When the Reverend J. Richard Sneed shook my hand, I felt a particularly firm grasp. His voice seemed almost tremulous as he thanked me. His hope that I should return in the not-too-distant future appeared to emanate straight from his heart. With his hand on my shoulder, he walked me toward the waiting car of the farmer who had offered to drive me back to Tarkio. Only as he removed his hand and gave me an ever so subtle shove toward the vehicle did the infamy of the First Methodist Church of Shenandoah descend on me: I'd paid the outrageous sum of fifty cents—scandalous in those days of nickel Cokes and subway tokens—to listen to myself talk.

"Dear Mrs. Roosevelt," I wanted to write, "warn the President not to trust the Methodists"—but, of course, I did nothing of the sort. By then I was savvy enough to realize that notes from a teenager—even one on the Corn Belt lecture circuit—were unlikely to be read by the President's wife. Besides, it would have been extraordinarily boorish of me to blame the minister of a God-fearing and, on the whole, extraordinarily hospitable congregation for my yearning for a more substantial lecture fee. In any event, this Methodist fiasco was one of my last church appearances before I headed east to spend the summer with my mother in upstate New York. Although I never returned to the northwestern corner of Missouri, I received there an introduction to the heartland of America experienced by relatively few refugee students of my generation, most of whom seldom got beyond the East Coast or were drafted, whereas a knee injury kept me out of the military. Thus, I was able to board a civilian express train that bore me, with one brief, but highly productive stop in industry, straight toward a Ph.D. and a research career in organic chemistry.

LAURA FERMI

Laura Capon Fermi (1907–1977) was born in Rome, the daughter of a nonobservant Jewish naval officer, and studied general science at the university there. In 1928 she married Enrico Fermi (1901–1954), one of the great physicists of the 20th century. A decade later they decided to leave Italy after the Fascists enacted a series of anti-Semitic laws, arriving in New York with their two children in January 1939. The excerpt from Laura Fermi's memoir *Atoms in the Family* (1954) presented here is taken from the chapter entitled "The Process of Americanization" and describes their life in Manhattan and suburban New Jersey. Enrico soon became a crucial figure in the U.S. effort to build an atomic bomb, and on December 2, 1942, his team at the University of Chicago began operating the world's first nuclear reactor. (A colleague reported the achievement to a government official over the telephone with the phrase "the Italian navigator has just landed in the New World.") Laura Fermi also wrote *Atoms for the World*, an account of the 1955 Geneva Conference on the Peaceful Uses of Atomic Energy, and *Illustrious Immigrants: The Intellectual Migration from Europe, 1930–41.*

from
Atoms in the Family

For six months we lived in New York City, within the ten blocks between One Hundred Tenth and One Hundred Twentieth streets, where most Columbia University teachers live, one of the many villages into which the big city is divided. As in many small villages, there also one meets one's acquaintances in the streets and stops to greet them and to exchange some gossip. I seldom needed to go out of the village, for within it I found all the necessities of life; I came to know each street, each corner, each shop of the village: the Chinese laundry and the small tearooms, the bookstore and the post office, the College shop for men and the ladies' ready-to-wear. Only occasionally did I take a trip downtown, and it was an expedition comparable to that of the villager going to town. So I ignored the fact that New York is a huge city, and I did not feel lost in it.

For the first few weeks we stayed at the King's Crown Hotel, an old, well-established hotel in the ten-block village around the university. Then we rented a furnished apartment from a Mrs. Smith. I called her Mrs. Zmeeth and produced the blankest of expressions on the elevator boy's face each time I asked for her. The apartment was on Riverside Drive with the view of the majestic Hudson River and the placid traffic upon it. At night the Palisades glittered with many little lights beyond and across the strip of darkness that the river had become. It was a pleasant apartment. But when I led my children into One Hundred Sixteenth Street, funnel-shaped between two round-cornered buildings at its opening into Riverside Drive, the icy winter winds, which gathered violence and impact in that funnel, made us stagger, and even threw little Giulio onto the ground. Each time he walked that way, he protested and rebelled and had to be dragged by the hand, while huge tears streaked his reddened, babyish face.

That winter Giulio went daily to the playground on the Columbia campus. There he tried to teach Italian to his teachers and proved impervious to the English language. He played quietly by himself, but his big brown eyes did not miss the pleasant sight of a lithe little girl with hair the color of straw and eyes as blue as a piece of sky. She was the first typically Anglo-Saxon little girl he had had leisure to watch and his first sweetheart. He was three years old. And because he refused to learn English, she called him "the little boy who cannot talk"; but both could smile.

On a friend's advice Nella went to Horace Mann School. It was called a progressive school, but I did not know the meaning of the word and did not worry. Nella was placed in third grade, which she had started in Italy, and for a few weeks could not understand what was going on around her. As soon as she caught up with the language, I went to inquire of her teacher about her scholastic achievements. I was told that those did not matter, that the only important thing was that she should be socially adjusted. By the end of the school year I realized that Nella had conscientiously done all of her work except arithmetic. The school did not require any work she did not care to do because of her language difficulties, and she had done all that needed knowledge of the language, omitting only the universally symbolized arithmetic. She was also given an intelligence test at Horace Mann, in which, I was told, she did quite well as a whole, although she failed to answer one of the simplest questions: A little boy has taken a hike in the country where he has played with a small animal. Upon returning home he must wash up thoroughly and change his smelly clothes. What is the animal he has played with? The fact that there are no skunks in Europe or in European children's tales proves the dependence of intelligence tests on environment and vocabulary.

Meanwhile, the nursemaid, now general houseworker, and I had joined forces by tacit agreement to confront and overcome the difficulties of an American ménage. We cooked together. I had never cooked before, but I could hold the American cookbook, translate quantities into sensible metric measures and interpret directions on cans, while she worked deftly with the mixing spoon and the salt shaker. I had no idea how much salt was needed and I spent two hours salting a soup the first time I had to do it alone! Together we made fun of American recipes, in which the main concern is wholesomeness and avoidance of anything rich, rather than taste and giving pleasure to the palate.

For most of the gadgets in the Smiths' apartment I found an explanation, but the refrigerator puzzled me a long time. It was evident that it stayed cold by itself with no need to turn a switch or press a button. But neither the maid nor I could ever foresee the moment when out of deep silence it would suddenly come to life and startle us with its loud buzzing. We stood in questioning watch of the cold white bulk, which was no more willing to yield its secret than the Sphinx of Egypt. Sometimes banging its door seemed to put it in motion, but at other times it resisted the most violent slammings. A more temperamental creature I had never met.

Shopping was a co-operative enterprise shared by the maid and me. She could judge the quality of fruit and vegetables, recognize the cuts of meats. I could better translate dollars into lire to decide whether prices were reasonable; I could explore packages and cans, of which I bought large quantities, for, like any newly arrived European, we went on a canned-food spree which was to last only as long as there were new cans to try. I patronized the small shops where the clerks could take the time to instruct ignorant foreigners in the marvels of pudding powders and of the frozen foods which had just appeared on the market. In almost every grocery store one man at least was Italian born or of Italian descent, and with him my maid and I made friends at once. Not that it helped much: Italians in New York come from the south of Italy, and they bring to their speech so much of their Neapolitan or Sicilian dialects that it is hard to understand them, whether they speak Italian or English.

The maid and I used to slow down our pace while walking by the large market on Broadway, near One Hundred Fifteenth Street. We peeked in with curiosity but dared not enter; how could we have found our way in the midst of that steady agitation of women and shopping bags, of clerks and weighing scales, which filled the little space left in the mysterious pattern of displayed food? Self-service markets were still rare, and there were none in our neighborhood, or I would have become an addict, as I soon became addicted to dime-stores and mail-order houses. There I could obtain what I wanted without talking, even buttons and dress patterns and all the other objects with the unpronounceable double *t* in them. My incapacity for properly pronouncing double *t*'s outlived all other language difficulties. Months later, at a time when I could usually make myself understood and had mustered enough courage to do an occasional bit of shopping over the telephone, I once ordered butter and received bird seed. We never had a canary, and the small unused package followed me across the country, a dusty reminder of difficult times.

After six months in America our maid was due to return to Italy, but she had meanwhile danced with a gentleman in a tuxedo. This dance was a symbol of fallen barriers between the classes, and after it she could no longer accept her lot and go back to a fiancé who would never give her such a social thrill. So she stayed.

Among the several traits that make a strong individualist of Enrico, one is most pronounced: the intolerance of living in a home that he does not own. Accordingly, as soon as we had settled in the furnished apartment that we had rented for six months, we tackled the problem of buying a permanent place in which to live.

It had been simple to buy an apartment in Rome: we had looked at the advertisements in the papers, we had explored a limited number of possible apartments, and we had bought one. In New York it was different. New York was a huge city, but university families were crowded into a remarkably small section of it. In that section there were no small homes, no co-operative apartments, nothing we could buy. Those of our friends who owned their homes lived in the suburbs and practiced that un-European activity, commuting. There were myriads of suburbs, but there was no Greater New York general real estate agent, who could explain the pros and cons of each place and give us an over-all picture of living conditions.

"Several of my colleagues live in a town called Leonia. It is in New Jersey, just across the George Washington Bridge, on the other side of the Palisades," Enrico said one Sunday. "Let's go see what it looks like." It was February, and an icy-cold afternoon. As we got off the bus at the stoplight in Leonia, a gust of wind blew in our faces and blinded us. We did not know where to go.

"Harold Urey, the chemist and Nobel Prize winner for 1934, lives here. We may go visit him and his wife. I know him well enough." This last sentence of Enrico's was an answer to my doubtful expression.

The Ureys were in their large living-room and had a fire going. Our visit was a success. Frieda and Harold Urey were friendly. Bashful, from a distance, their three little girls stared at us with open mouths and rounded eyes. Dr. Urey talked at length to us, in his serious, slightly professorial tone, about Leonia and its excellent public schools, about the advantages of living in a middle-class town where one's children may have all that other children have. He smiled often, but his smile stayed on the surface, as if superimposed over a serious nature. On his round face, which had just begun to become lined, there was purpose and deep concentration, almost constant concern.

Harold Urey was a good orator and sold Leonia to us. Besides, I was anxious to go live where the dirt on my children's knees would not be gray, as in New York, but an honest brown.

By the following summer we were the happy owners of a house on the Palisades, with a large lawn, a small pond, and a lot of dampness in the basement. By the time the house had been redecorated for us and was ready for occupancy, our furniture had arrived from Italy and war had broken out in Europe. We settled, and this time for good, or so we thought.

Neither of us had ever gardened. Enrico is a product of apartment buildings, and I spent most of my childhood and youth in a house whose garden was intrusted to a gardener, except for a peach tree that was under my grandmother's special care.

My grandmother was an intelligent woman, with gray hair neatly parted in the middle and brushed back in tidy bands over her temples. She had had only one daughter, my mother, and so she lived with us. I remember her a few years before she died at seventy, matronly and heavy-set but straight and dignified, clad in the black dress of a widow even when gardening, when with no ease and with sluggish motions she climbed the stepladder against the peach tree to perch on it and carefully remove diseased leaves and buds. She tried to explain to us children the basic rules of gardening, but if I listened to her out of deference for her status in the family, I have since forgotten what I unwillingly learned.

So neither Enrico nor I was qualified to take care of the lawn and the flower beds and the rock garden around the tiny pond. But we wanted to become genuine Americans and were going to do all that others did.

"On Sunday," Harold Urey had told us, "you put on your worst clothes and garden."

I was not concerned about the work in the yard and trusted that Enrico would do it. When we had married, he had told me his plans for the future. He was going to retire at forty. No physicist ever accomplishes anything after forty anyhow. He was of peasant stock and would go back to the soil. The farmer's lot appealed to the individualist in him: a farmer is his own boss and self-sufficient, for he can produce almost all he needs. Enrico had long set his eyes on a piece of land on Monte Mario, a hill on the western outskirts of Rome, with a view of the Eternal City and of the dome of Saint Peter's in the foreground.

When in Enrico's thirty-eighth year of age we settled in Leonia, his peasant blood was not aroused. Whenever the lawn needed mowing Enrico had urgent work to do at the laboratory, even though it was Sunday. By the time he could be persuaded to do the job, the lawn had grown so wild it was impossible to mow it. When it was time to water grass and flowers, Enrico preferred to go for a walk, or to play a game of tennis, claiming that the sprinkling could wait.

So I did my best, gathered all possible advice, filled our flower beds at random as our friends thinned theirs, dug the ground with a cultivator in my right hand and a garden-book in my left. The lawn did not thrive.

"The trouble with lawns around here," Harold Urey said, with serious concern, "is crab grass. You must fight crab grass. Always. Never relent. Walk on your lawn with your eyes on the grass, and when you seen one single strand of crab grass pull it out. Don't give up." He spoke with authority, and each sentence cut the air with the impetus of an ax against a tree.

By the next spring our family was all set to undertake crab-grass extermination. But which was crab grass? We pulled out the most likely plant and dispatched Nella to the Ureys' with it.

"It's not crab grass. Mr. Urey says it can't be. It's too early in the season," Nella reported.

Summer came, and still we did not know which was the crab grass. Harold Urey came by one day. He looked at our lawn, and I saw an intensification of his steady concern in his kindly eyes. He turned to me, and in a soft voice meant to lessen the impact of the news, he said:

"D'you know what's wrong with your lawn, Laura? It's *all* crab grass."

It was the summer of 1940. The phony war had long ended, and France had fallen. With an intensification of concern even stronger than that with which he had viewed our lawn, Harold Urey used to talk of the dangers of war for the United States.

"Would you be surprised," he asked his friends, "if the Germans should land at Nantucket Island by Christmas?"

During the war questions of this kind were asked everywhere and at all times. In the spring of 1941 Enrico and a few other professors at Columbia University organized a "Society of Prophets." On the first day of each month, during the lunch hour at the Men's Faculty Club, society members wrote down ten "Yes or No" questions about events likely to occur during that month. Would Hitler attempt to land in England? Would an American convoy be attacked by German ships in violation of United States neutrality? Would the British be able to hold Tobruk? The "Prophets" wrote down their answers. These were checked on the last day of the month. Records were kept of each Prophet's score.

By the time the society dissolved, Enrico had the highest score, and was *the* Prophet. Ninety-seven per cent of his predictions had come true. In foreseeing events Enrico was helped by his conservatism: he maintains that situations do not change as fast as people expect. Accordingly, Enrico had predicted no changes: Hitler would not attempt a landing in England during the month considered; the British would hold Tobruk; no American convoy would be attacked. His conservatism made him foresee no German attack on Russia during the month of June. Thus he missed a perfect prophet's score.

Meanwhile Harold Urey gardened, and Enrico tried to gain theoretical knowledge about gardening.

"Why are you so concerned about crab grass? It's green, and it covers the lawn. You people are always fighting weeds. What distinguishes weeds from other plants?"

"Weeds grow spontaneously, without being planted," Dr. Urey answered. "They take up space, air, and food from good plants and kill them. At the end of the season they die and nothing is left."

"Therefore, a weed is an unlicensed annual," Enrico concluded, following his need of defining a concept before accepting it.

If Enrico was not helpful in the garden, he was, or at least tried to be, helpful in the house. He realized that with one maid instead of the two we had had in Italy and a house instead of an apartment, there would be more work to do. To help he took up polishing his own shoes. The maid looked at him with disdain, and after several days she reported to me:

"The *professore* polishes only the front of his shoes, not the part over the heels."

Confronted with this accusation, Enrico pleaded guilty. He could not be bothered with the half of his shoes that *he* could not see.

Enrico had manual skill and learned to do the repairs around the house, like a true American husband. When using his hands, Enrico enjoys the novelty of what he is doing but stops a long way this side of refinement, as soon as the functional scope is achieved. Once, when we were still in Italy, our friend Gina Castelnuovo, the mathematician's daughter, sprained an ankle on a mountain hike in the Alps. She had to walk several miles to reach the village and a physiologist, the closest there was to a physician in the small colony of scientists gathered around the Castelnuovos. Her ankle was very swollen. The next day Enrico went to inquire after her condition. He found that the physiologist had put her leg in a cast over the swelling, that the swelling had now subsided, and that Gina's cast felt uncomfortable. It was a challenge for Enrico. Under Professor Castelnuovo's skeptical eyes, he undertook to dampen, tear apart, and reshape the old cast.

"The cast," Gina recalled later, "looked awful, but felt good."

Now in a country where the price of labor advised him to exploit his manual dexterity, Enrico set to work with that same disregard for refinement, with which he had made over Gina's cast. Did our dining-room table need extension leaves because those belonging to it had not arrived from Italy? Very good, Enrico would make them. But they would be rough and unpainted, they would always have to be hidden under a tablecloth and serve a purpose that had nothing to do with aesthetics. Were friends gathering pieces of furniture for their homes? All right! Enrico would build a rocker for them. A rocker is an Anglo-Saxon piece of furniture, not Italian; a new problem. Enrico built it, but never took the time to correct the seat inclination, which kept the sitter at an acute angle, as if bent in pain. The rocker rocked, Enrico contended, and what more can one ask of a rocker?

As soon as the challenge of a new problem was met, Enrico gave up. After all, he is a theoretical physicist and not interested in his projects, once they outlive their theoretical appeal. One set of objects never lost its appeal for Enrico: the gadgets. To him they represent the never ending quest for saving labor, the material proof of human progress, the product of a technology which he considers the symbol, the salvation, and the promise of America. He has never lost interest in gadgets, and, although parsimonious by nature and education, he is always ready to buy one more: from the step-on garbage can, his never-forgiven present of my first Christmas in the United States, through electric razor and electric saw, to the lately acquired television set, we have gone through purchase and use of all available and most automatic household equipment.

In learning the American language and habits, Enrico had a considerable advantage over me: he spent his days at Columbia University among Americans, and inside the very physics building he found an obliging mentor in Herbert Anderson, a graduate student who planned to work for his Ph.D. under Enrico's guidance.

No day went by without Enrico's telling me something that Herbert Anderson had taught him.

"Anderson says we should hire our neighbors' children and pay them a penny for each of our English mistakes they correct. He says it is the only way of learning the language efficiently."

"Anderson says"—and this it was very difficult to believe—"that English words should be pronounced with two accents: vocab´ula´ry." It sounded very unnatural indeed.

"Anderson says that students work their way through college by waiting on tables and selling newspapers. I am afraid they have little time left for study."

"Anderson says that there are no oral examinations in American universities. The multiple-choice tests, Anderson says. . . ."

Altogether, Anderson appeared to be a bottomless well of information, and, duly impressed, I pictured him in my mind as a ponderous person, more mature and professorial than his years. But when I met him I was forced to change my ideas. He was of medium height, as slender as a boy on the threshold of manhood, dressed with the elegance of the young bachelor fond of clothes. Under well-trimmed chestnut hair, his features were small and quiet and his manners unobtrusive. But he was not a self-effacing man, and will power gave strength to his light frame.

Enrico and Anderson were fond of each other. Some young people are occasionally shy of Enrico. Some students complain that he does not know how to give them a "pat on the back." Anderson had no place for shyness and felt no need of special encouragement. Had I been able to understand Americans at that time, I would have recognized in him at least one attribute of the Jeffersonian heritage; the inborn conviction that men are created equal. The older men's position, the public recognition they might receive, the honors shed on them, were to him only indications of the goods available to mankind, and of these Anderson wanted to get his share. So Anderson was not only Enrico's student but his friend and his teacher. He learned physics from Fermi and taught him Americana.

I stayed home most of the time, got Anderson's teachings only at second hand, and learning English was a very slow process.

One day Nella came to me and said in a stern voice:

"Mother, Giulio uses bad language. I heard him call his friend *stinky*."

I could not reply to her, not knowing the meaning of the word. I asked Enrico when he came home.

"As far as I know, it means 'having a bad odor,' " Enrico said. "But I'll ask Anderson in the morning."

From Herbert we had our first authoritative lesson in bad language: *Lousy* is not so bad as *stinky*, Herbert Anderson said. While *gosh* is almost charming in a child's mouth, *golly* is objectionable, and anything stronger is to be frowned upon. *Jerk* and *squirt* are terms which at that time children in the intermediate grades used to designate the teachers they disliked.

Nella and Giulio made me ponder not only on language but also on social philosophy. I started to understand the meaning of democracy and its institutions when nine-year-old Nella asked for "more freedom" and implied I was infringing upon her rights because I requested that she come home after school before going to play and that she let me know at all times where I could find her.

When four-year-old Giulio, whom I had asked to go wash his hands, answered "You can't make me, this is a free country," then we learned some more. To these days Enrico has retained the childish expression "this is a free country" that he acquired from Giulio, who in his turn has entirely outgrown it.

Long would be the list of what we learned from our children, besides bad and good language, the spirit of independence, and the firm belief in human rights. Looking through their young eyes, not dimmed by visions of Old World traditions, we acquired a fresh, if vicarious, perspective of American habits and viewpoints.

In the process of Americanization, however, there is more than learning language and customs and setting one's self to do whatever Americans can do. There is more than understanding the living institutions, the pattern of schools, the social and political trends. There is the absorbing of the background. The ability to evoke visions of covered wagons, to see the clouds of dust behind them in the golden deserts of the West, to hear the sound of thumping hoofs and jolting wheels over a mountain pass. The power to relive a miner's excitement in his boom town in Colorado and to understand his thoughts when, fifty years later, old and spare, but straight, no longer a miner, but a philosopher, he lets his gaze float along with the smoke from his pipe over the ghostlike remnants of his town. The acceptance of New England pride, and the participation in the long suffering of the South.

And there is the switch of heroes.

Suppose that *you* go to live in a foreign country and that this country is Italy. And suppose you are talking to a cultivated Italian, who may say to you:

"Shakespeare? Pretty good, isn't he? There are Italian translations of Shakespeare, and some people read them. As for myself, I can read English and have read some of Lamb's *Tales from Shakespeare*; the dream in midsummer; Hamlet, the neurotic who could not make up his mind; and *Romeo* and *Giulietta*. Kind of queer ideas you Anglo-Saxons have about Italians! Anyhow, as I was saying, Shakespeare is pretty good. But all those historical figures he brings in . . . not the most important ones . . . We have to look up history books to follow him.

"Now you take Dante. *Here* is a great poet for you! A universal poet! Such a superhuman conception of the universe! Such visions of the upper and nether worlds! The church is still walking in Dante's steps after more than six centuries. And his history! He has made history alive. Read Dante and you know history. . . ."

In your hero worship there is no place for both Shakespeare and Dante, and you must take your choice. If you are to live in Italy and be like other people, forget Shakespeare. Make a bonfire and sacrifice him, together with all American heroes, with Washington and Lincoln, Longfellow and Emerson, Bell and the Wright brothers. In the shadow of that cherry tree that Washington chopped down let an Italian warrior rest, and let him be a warrior with a blond beard and a red shirt. A warrior who on a white stallion, followed by a flamboyant handful of red-shirted youths, galloped and fought the length of the Italian peninsula to win it for a king, a warrior whose name is Garibaldi. Let Mazzini and Cavour replace Jefferson and Adams, Carducci and Manzoni take the place of Longfellow and Emerson. Learn that a population can be aroused not only by Paul Revere's night ride but also by the stone

thrown by a little boy named Balilla. Forget that a telephone is a Bell telephone and accept Meucci as its inventor, and remember that the first idea of
an airplane was Leonardo's. Once you have made these adjustments in your
mind, you have become Italianized, perhaps. Perhaps you have not and never
will.

When I travel across the immense plains of the Middle West, plowed and
harvested at night by gremlins, for in the daytime no soul is ever to be seen,
I still feel the impact of emptiness. I miss the crowded terraced fields reclaimed from the stony side of a hill. I miss the many eyes a tourist feels on
his back—as an American friend once told me—each time he stops to eat his
lunch in the most secluded spot in Italy. I miss the people who materialize
from nowhere; the bashful peasant children with their hands behind their
backs; the dark-haired girls who munch apples and throw inquisitive glances
with their spicy eyes; the women who interrupt their chores, who wipe their
hands on faded aprons and emerge from homes hidden out of sight by clumps
of old trees; the men who were slumbering away the hot noon hours sprawled
on the warm earth and now get up to view the tourist with the others.

If I still miss them, I ask myself, and still marvel at the vastness of America, at newly discovered sights, at the mention of some great name still unheard of by me, if I fail to understand the humor in Charles Addams' car-
toons, can I truly say that I am Americanized?

CHRISTOPHER ISHERWOOD

Like W. H. Auden, with whom he crossed the Atlantic in 1939, Christopher Isherwood (1904–1986) came under critical attack for his decision to immigrate to the United States at a time when England faced such imminent peril. As he explains in the opening pages of the diary he was to keep for the rest of his life, the threat of war was not the only thing on his mind. He was already celebrated as the author of the novel *Mr. Norris Changes Trains* (1935) and about to publish its even more successful follow-up, *Goodbye to Berlin* (1939), the source of the 1968 musical *Cabaret*; he had also collaborated with Auden on a series of politically conscious plays and on *Journey to a War*, an account of their trip to battle-torn China. Settling in Los Angeles, Isherwood had a successful career as a screenwriter. His interests also turned decisively from politics to Eastern religion; he became a disciple of the Indian teacher Swami Prabhavananda and with him translated the *Bhagavad Gita*. Isherwood's later books include *Prater Violet* (1946), *The World in the Evening* (1954), *Down There on a Visit* (1962), and *A Single Man* (1964). His diaries are a frank and detailed record of his life at the center of the worlds of writing and filmmaking.

from
Diaries

On January 19, 1939, Auden and I sailed from Southampton in the French liner *Champlain*, bound for New York. It was the first anniversary of our trip to China. I am always on the lookout for coincidences in dates, and I remember that this one flattered my vaguely optimistic belief that my life was somehow running to schedule.

Certainly, at that time, I had every reason to believe in the favorable aspect of my star. This post-Munich winter was the height of my little London success. I lectured, I broadcast, I was welcome at parties. I had plenty of pocket money. The Chinese travel book was finished. I was running an agreeable love affair in which the other partner was more deeply involved than myself, and I kept a second, third and fourth choice waiting on the sidelines in case I got bored. In public, I was carefully modest about all this. In private, to my intimate friends, I boasted, with a vulgarity that still makes me squirm as I write these lines. Auden, particularly, disliked my attitude; it hurt him because he was really fond of me. But I suppose it somehow intrigued him, too—because he once told me, almost admiringly, that I was the cruellest and most unscrupulous person he had ever met. Edward Upward, now only an occasional visitor, didn't say much. Something was broken between us. I couldn't meet his faintly ironical eye. When we were together, I covered my embarrassment with an awkward heartiness.

I think we all sensed that this was a long goodbye. M. cried when I left, I cried, Jacky [Hewit] cried in the taxi to the station and gave me a keepsake, his first champagne cork. Forster, who had come to see us off, asked me: "Shall I join the communist party?" I forget what I answered. I think it was "No." At any rate, the question was oracular. The departing and the dying are credited with a kind of psychic wisdom.

As the train pulled out, there was a nasty sharp wrench, and then, as always when I am the traveler, a quick upsurge of guilty relief. Auden and I exchanged grins—grins which took us back, in an instant, to the earliest days of our friendship. Suddenly, we were twelve and nine years old. "Well," I said, "we're off again." "Goody," said Auden.

Why were we going to America? I suppose, for myself, the chief reason was that I couldn't stop travelling. The mechanism had been set going during those years of wandering around Europe with Heinz [Neddermeyer]. I was also running away from myself: that was why I never stayed anywhere long. I could remain in Portugal, for example, as long as I could believe in an objective Portugal. But, sooner or later, Portugal would dissolve and reveal itself as the all-too-familiar, subjective "Isherwood Portugal." Then I fled in disgust.

America was obviously the next place on the list. I'd had a brief, false, hysterical glimpse of New York the previous summer, under the guidance of George Davis, who has a genius for melodramatic showmanship. We shot up and down skyscrapers, in and out of parties and brothels, saw a fight in a

Bowery dive, heard Maxine Sullivan sing in Harlem, went to Coney Island on July the Fourth, met Maxwell Anderson, Muriel Draper and Orson Welles, drank all day long and took Seconal every night to make us sleep. I came back to England raving about Manhattan, and convinced, like every tourist, that New York is the United States.

Looking forward to our life there, I imagined a milieu in which my London "personality" would function more freely, more cynically, more successfully than ever. I saw myself as a natural citizen of the go-getters' homeland. Oh, I'd talk faster and louder than any of them, I'd learn the slang and the accent, I'd adapt like an Arctic fox. Before long, I'd be writing the great American novel. I was very sure of myself.

The possibility of war, that familiar, six-year-old shadow in the background, had less to do with my emigration than any of my critics will ever believe. At the beginning of 1939, I had honestly begun to think that the crisis had passed over, or had, at any rate, been indefinitely postponed. Even Dr. Katz, that Cassandra of the thirties, had predicted, for the first time, that there would be no war this year. It wasn't until March that the situation began to look really hopeless.

If I were writing a novel—trying, that is to say, to persuade a reader that I was telling him something psychologically plausible—I should have great difficulty at this point. Because now I have to describe a state of mind which introduces a new period in my life.

To put it as simply as possible, for the sake of making a start: while I was on board the *Champlain*, I realized that I was a pacifist.

Maybe it would be more exact to say: I realized that I had always been a pacifist. At any rate, in the negative sense. How could I have ever imagined I was anything else? My earliest remembered feelings of rebellion were against the British army, of which my mother and myself were camp followers, and against the staff of St. Edmund's School, who tried to make me believe in a falsified and sentimentalized view of the 1914 war. My father taught me, by his life and death, to hate the profession of soldiering. I remember his telling me, before he left for France, that an officer's sword is useless except for toasting bread, and that he never fired his revolver because he couldn't hit anything with it, and hated the bang. I came to adore my father's memory, dwelling always upon his civilian virtues, his gentleness, his humor, his musical and artistic talent. Growing up in the postwar world, I learnt—from my history master, from Noël Coward, from Wilfred Owen and Siegfried Sassoon—to loathe the old men who had made the war. Flags, memorials and uniforms made me tremble with rage, because they filled me with terror. I was horribly scared by "war," and therefore secretly attracted to it. I've been into all this at great length in *Lions and Shadows*. No need to repeat it here.

However, these neurotic fears were greatly reduced by our trip to China. True, it wasn't really very dangerous; I think there were only three or four occasions on which we were likely to have been killed by bombs or bullets. But a very little danger will go a long way psychologically. Several times I had been afraid, but healthily afraid. I no longer dreaded the unknown, or feared that I should behave worse than other people. When we were back in England and the Munich crisis began, I was frightened, of course, but I didn't get frantic. I even stayed on in London out of curiosity; I didn't want to miss the first air raid.

Before China, my pacifism was so entangled with cowardice that I could never examine it at all. After China, it was only a matter of time before I should stop repeating slogans and borrowed opinions and start to think for myself. Thinking was impossible as long as I was playing the returned hero, and exploiting it sexually. Thinking was impossible as long as I was lecturing on the Sino-Japanese war and appealing for aid to Chiang Kai-shek. Thinking was impossible during Munich. But the post-Munich hangover brought on the cold, meditative fit, and this boat trip provided the opportunity. A voyage, in this respect, resembles an illness. Time ceases to itch and distract us. We can pause and take stock of our position.

One morning on deck, it seems to me, I turned to Auden and said: "You know, I just don't believe in any of it any more—the united front, the party line, the antifascist struggle. I suppose they're okay, but something's wrong with me. I simply can't swallow another mouthful." And Auden answered: "No, neither can I."

Those were not our words, but psychologically it was as simple as that. It sounds incredible, but Auden's agreement took me completely by surprise. It appears that, since China, we had been living in such a rush that we had never been able to get in five minutes' quiet, sincere conversation—even when alone together. We had merely shouted to each other from two parallel, racing express trains. Auden is always cagey, anyway. Sometimes, when I'm talking, that furrow appears between his eyes, his mouth begins to twitch, and I know he's bothered about something; but he'll only disagree with me in public when the subject we're discussing isn't important to him at all.

Now, in a few sentences, with exquisite relief, we confessed our mutual disgust at the parts we had been playing and resolved to abandon them, then and there. We had forgotten our real vocation. We would be artists again, with our own values, our own integrity, and not amateur socialist agitators, parlor reds.

That was about as far as we went, for the present. Auden, however, had his Anglo-Catholicism to fall back on. Unwillingly, he had denied it, all these years. Now he could admit to it again. I had nothing of this kind, and I didn't yet clearly realize how much I was going to need it. For myself, the positive part of the change consisted in putting my emotions back from a political onto a personal basis. Edward had always said, quite rightly, that my mind was unfitted for abstract ideas; it could only grasp concrete examples, special instances. Anti-Nazism had been possible for me as long as Nazism meant Hitler, Goering and Goebbels, the Gestapo, and the consuls and spies who potentially menaced Heinz on his travels. But now Heinz was caught. He had become, however unwillingly, a part of the Nazi machine, at work in a Berlin factory. Now Werner was helping to build the Siegfried line, and dozens of boys I had known were in the German army.

Suppose I have in my power an army of six million men. I can destroy it by pressing an electric button. The six millionth man is Heinz. Will I press the button? Of course not—even if the 5,999,999 others are hundred per cent Jew-baiting blood-mad fiends (which is absurd). This attitude, which might be called the extreme Sodom and Gomorrha position, where only one Lot is required to save the Cities of the Plain, may be contrasted with the equally violent radicalism of some good democrats of the period, who declared that Hitler was responsible for every crime and that the German people were innocent lambs, and were nevertheless ready to burn down the Just City for the horrible sake of one little sodomite.

Both Auden and I felt it was our duty to tell our friends what had happened. We wrote to most of them, soon after our arrival in New York. M. accepted the change, and I think it pleased her—though she could never quite agree. John Lehmann wrote that he was "puzzled," but this didn't make him hostile, and he has been a faithful friend ever since. Edward, a good while later, sent me two letters, the first disgusted, the second a model of charity towards an attitude one can't understand. Olive [Mangeot], after much bewilderment, remembered only that we cared for each other—like the marvellous woman she is. Forster was greatly interested, and perhaps somewhat influenced. Stephen [Spender] made a typically subtle comment: "I rather envy you."

The voyage was stormy. The *Champlain* seemed very small, slithering down the long grey Atlantic slopes, under a heavy sky. One night I was sick —breaking my round-the-world record. Wrapped in rugs, like invalids, we sipped bouillon, or watched movies in the saloon, where French tapestries flapped out from the creaking, straining walls. We were bored, and amused ourselves by helping with the puppet show in the children's playroom, improvising Franco-English dialogue full of private jokes and double entendres. Off the coast of Newfoundland, we ran into a blizzard. The ship entered New York harbor looking like a wedding cake.

Erika and Klaus Mann were the first to welcome us. They had come out to the ship on the quarantine launch, posing as journalists who wanted our interview. Erika was nervous and ill. She kept coughing. Klaus was full of gaiety and gossip. As we came ashore, I looked around for Vernon [Old], whom I'd radioed from the *Champlain* to meet me. At first, I didn't recognize him among the crowd, his face was so pinched and scarlet with the cold. He had been waiting there for hours.

Somebody had recommended the George Washington Hotel as a place where we should feel "at home." And, indeed, our reception by Donald Neville-Willing was like arriving at the house of a maiden aunt. A short, stout, grey-haired figure, with a beaky nose, jingling keys and a roving eye, Donald ran the hotel, which specialized in Elks and women's clubs conventions, as though he were the Victorian housekeeper of an English ancestral mansion. He was proud of his double-barrelled name, and fervently patriotic. Although he had lived ten years in the United States, he still refused to take out his first papers. In his bedroom, he had signed pictures of the King and Queen, and a framed telegram from an equerry, thanking him for his loyal good wishes on some royal anniversary.

The discovery of some mutual "county" friends in Cheshire meant more to Donald than our dubious literary notoriety. We were respectable, and he couldn't do enough for us. Glasses of hot punch were sent up, free, to our rooms at night. Special prices were quoted on our weekly bills. The telephone frequently rang to summon us down to teas and evening parties in Donald's private sitting room. Donald had many theatrical connections. He introduced us to the English members of the cast of the Stokes Brothers' play *Oscar Wilde*, then running with great success at one of the Manhattan theaters. These actors were all staying at the hotel. One of them, a strikingly handsome boy who played Charlie Parker, tried, unsuccessfully, the effect of water waves in my hair. He was thirty, but looked eighteen, because Marie Tempest had taught him the secret of perpetual youth—to go to bed every afternoon, except matinees, from two to four. I think his name was John Carroll, and I believe he was killed in the war.

Donald not only accepted us, he accepted Vernon, also. It was at his suggestion that Vernon moved over to the hotel from a nearby rooming house. Donald tried to get Vernon a walking-on part in *The American Way*, and, later, a job in Billy Rose's Aquacade. Vernon bought a pair of swimming trunks and practiced diving with a boy at the YMCA, but he wasn't good enough to pass the final test.

Vernon, at this time, was growing up very fast. His various interests, which I indulged as schoolboy crazes, were symptoms of a drive towards self-education. In the next five years, they produced extraordinary results. Auden and I laughed at his barbell exercises, but we offered nothing in their place. As for his drawing, it was a year before I took it seriously, and, by that time, he bitterly resented my lack of interest. It was like my mother's attitude to my writing, all over again. Even now, when we talk about his work, he often seems slightly on the defensive.

At that time, in any case—as the following extract from my diary will show—I was a most unsuitable companion for an eighteen-year-old boy. My conquering, confident mood had abruptly dissolved. I found I couldn't write a line. The European news, and the high costs of our living scared me. Day after day, I moped, a jelly of cowardice, indecision, defeat. We got plenty of invitations, of course; but it seemed to me that all these lunches, suppers and cocktail parties were being offered under false pretences, as far as I was concerned. They wanted to meet Christopher Isherwood. And who was I? A sham, a mirror image, nobody. To M. I wrote: "I believe I have come to the end of my talent." All this was very natural, of course, if I could only have realized it. I was merely going through a "change of life," and change is always uncomfortable.

March 18. Two months since we left England. Here we are—still at the George Washington. What has happened?

This time in New York has been a bad, sterile period for me. I've done practically nothing. Every day, I think: now I must get busy, now I must start work. But at what? My money—including the advance I got from [Bennett] Cerf—is rapidly running out. Wystan still has several hundred dollars, and the prospect of a teaching job, later on. I have no prospects. I don't even know what kind of job I want. My whole instinct is against teaching, or lecturing, or exploiting my reputation in any way. I would like some sort of regular, humble occupation. I got to know Berlin because I was doing something functional—the natural occupation for a poor foreigner—teaching his own language. If I can't do something of the same kind here, I shall never get to know America. I shall never become a part of this city.

Meanwhile, as so often before, I am hypnotized by my own fears. Reading of Hitler's Czechoslovakian coup and his plans against Romania, I feel: After all, what's the use? In a week, or a month, I shall be for it. Wystan is determined to go back to England if war breaks out—and I shall go with him, I suppose. If I were alone, I mightn't. Quite aside from being scared, I am entirely disillusioned about the kind of war this is going to be. Just another struggle for world trade. But they are all over there—all my friends—and the impulse to join them is very strong.

Wystan himself is going through a curious phase. He's as energetic as I'm idle. He takes Benzedrine regularly, in small doses, followed by Seconal at night. He says that "the chemical life" solves all his problems. He writes a great deal—poems and articles and reviews—makes speeches, goes to tea parties and dinners, is quite brilliantly talkative. It's a little as if he and I had changed places. Wystan says, however, that he hates all this. But he's unwilling to return to England, because, there, he's the center of an even more intensive publicity.

There is much that is majestic but nothing that is gracious in this city—this huge, raw, functional skeleton, this fortress of capital, this jungle of absolutely free competition. Every street is partly a slum. Where the banks and the brownstone houses end, the slum tenements begin, with their rusty fire escapes and crowds of baseball-playing Dead End Kids. Beyond, on the mainland, is a wilderness of scrapyards and shacks. This country is insanely untidy.

The Bronx is built almost entirely of billboards and monster advertisements, imploring you to relax. (As if anybody *could*—when every doorknob gives you an electric shock!) Take the advertisements away, and there would be nothing left; no town at all. At the lower end of the island, and uptown in Harlem, huge tribes of Italians, Negroes and Jews have pitched their foul, lively camps—at the feet of the skyscrapers which dominate their heaven like totem poles. Wystan and I call the skyscrapers "the fallen angels." You imagine them crashing down out of the sky, white-hot as meteors, to bury themselves deep in the Manhattan bedrock and slowly cool, through the ages. But the fallen angels are still angels. They are blasphemously insolvent, and utterly without pity. The young, ambitious man tries to climb them—having been told of a heaven at the top, called The Rainbow Room—and when he falls a little crowd collects, and stares. Nobody tries to help—or he might get into trouble with the insurance company. Then, down the street, come the screams of the police car and the clanging of the ambulance bell.

Vernon has been typing a poem of Wystan's with obstinate care, letter by letter. In the middle, he paused to ask me, very seriously, why people like Dickens.

Bennett Cerf, our publisher, and his uncle, who was an intimate friend of Hart Crane, took us to see *Hellzapoppin*. They were rather shocked because we praised it so extravagantly—which shows how little they understand what made us write our plays.

A PEN Club dinner at the Algonquin Hotel. Dorothy Thompson presided, in crimson velvet. I made a facetious speech, with jokes out of the *Reader's Digest*. When I sat down, Thompson said icily: "Delightful." Realized, too late, that we were being deadly serious. Wystan recited his poem on the death of Yeats. A Polish poet recited a Polish poem on Abraham Lincoln. Nobody understood a word—until the last line:

"LINKOLL-NY! Linkoll-ny! *Leen-kool-ny!*" (Wild applause.)

First meeting with Lincoln Kirstein. I had taken one of Wystan's Benzedrine tablets, and the afternoon passed with an effect of terrific, smooth, effortless speed. Neither Lincoln nor I stopped talking for a single moment. We were intimates at once. Almost as soon as we had shaken hands, he began telling us about the American Civil War. He was breathless with it—as though Gettysburg had been fought yesterday.

George Platt Lynes, prematurely grey haired, with the arrogant profile of a late Roman coin, has photographed me peering out from behind a wooden property-pillar. Lincoln calls this picture "The rat with the nervous breakdown."

⁂

[*March 31, 1940.*]

A terrible, shameful, almost insane attack of self-pity and despair. "I hate this place," I told Vernon, "I hate all Americans. I don't belong here. I shall have to go back to Europe." Poor Vernon was much distressed. And of course, I didn't mean what I said about the Americans or the ranch. I meant: I hate myself.

Actually, in my sane moments, I love this country. I love it just because I *don't* belong. Because I'm not involved in its traditions, not born under the curse of its history. I feel free here. I'm on my own. My life will be what I make of it.

I love the ocean, and the orange groves, and the desert, and the big mountains around Arrowhead, where the snow comes down to the shores of the lake and you see the eagles circling above. Nature is unfriendly, dangerous, utterly aloof. However hard I may try, I can't turn her into a stage set for my private drama. Thank God I can't. She refuses to become a part of my neurosis.

THOMAS MANN

The triumphant success of his first novel, *Buddenbrooks*, in 1901 put Thomas Mann (1875–1955) in the forefront of German writers when he was still in his twenties, and his reputation grew ever greater with the publication of *Death in Venice* (1912) and *The Magic Mountain* (1924). In 1929 he won the Nobel Prize in Literature. Mann's political journey took him from enthusiastic support for Germany's goals in World War I to growing dismay at the forces that brought Hitler to power in 1933. After living in Switzerland during the regime's early years, Mann accepted an invitation to teach at Princeton University in 1939 and later settled in Pacific Palisades, California. He became a naturalized citizen in 1944. His later works included *Joseph and His Brothers* (1933–42), *Lotte in Weimar* (1939), *Doctor Faustus* (1949), and *The Confessions of Felix Krull* (1954). In 1945, when this letter to the Austrian writer Walter von Molo was written, it was Mann's intention to remain in the United States, but the political scapegoating of the McCarthy period persuaded him to return to Switzerland in 1952.

from
Letter to Walter von Molo

Pacific Palisades
September 7, 1945

*D**ear Herr von Molo:*
I owe you thanks for a very friendly birthday greeting, as well as for the open letter to me which you gave to the German press and which has also been published in extracts in American newspapers. In it you express even more vehemently than in your private letter the request, in fact the demand, that I return to Germany and live there again, helping "by word and deed."

You are not the only one to direct this summons to me; the Russian-controlled Berlin Radio and the organ of the united democratic parties of Germany have also issued it, so I am told, with the high-sounding argument that I have "a historic task to perform in Germany."

I cannot help rejoicing that Germany wants to have me back again—not only my books, but myself as a person. Yet these appeals also have a somewhat disturbing and depressing effect upon me, and I hear something illogical, even unjust and ill-considered in them. You know only too well, my dear Herr von Molo, how difficult it is to help "by word and deed" in Germany today, given the almost hopeless situation which our unfortunate nation has got itself into. And it seems to me highly dubious whether an already old man whose heart muscle has felt the strains of these grim times can directly, personally, in the flesh, make much of a contribution toward raising up out of their deep abasement the people whom you so movingly describe. This is only by the way. It also seems to me that the Germans making these requests have given little thought to the technical, civil, and psychological difficulties standing in the way of my "reimmigration."

Are these twelve years and their results simply to be wiped from the slate, and is it possible to act as if they had never been? In 1933 the shock of losing the wonted basis of my life, of parting with house and land, books, mementos and all my property, as well as the shock of the deplorable attacks in Germany, the expulsions and repudiations—all that was hard enough, suffocating enough. I shall never forget how Munich's radio and newspapers launched an illiterate and murderous campaign against my Wagner essay, for this was the point at which I fully realized that return was cut off for me. I shall never forget the groping for words, the efforts to write, to reply, to explain myself—those "letters into the night," as René Schickele, one of the many departed friends, called these smothered monologues. What followed was hard enough too: the itinerant life from country to country, the passport anxieties, the hotel existence, while our ears rang with the shameful stories that made their way out of the lost country that was running amok, going from bad to worse, growing more and more alien. All of you who swore loyalty to the "charismatic Leader" (horrible, horrible, besotted education!) and carried on with culture under Goebbels did not go through any of that. I do not forget that later you went through much worse, which I was spared; but you never knew the angina of exile, the uprooting, the nervous shock of homelessness.

At times I was furious at your equanimity. I saw it as a breach of solidarity. If at that time the German intelligentsia, everyone who had a name and meant something in the world—doctors, musicians, teachers, writers, artists —had risen as one man against the disgrace, had declared a general strike, many things might have turned out differently. Instead, the individual, if he happened not to be a Jew, always found himself faced with the question: "Why should I? The others are going along. It can't really be so bad."

I say that at times I felt some fury. But I have never envied you who were sitting there inside, not even in your greatest days. For I knew only too well that those days were nothing but bloody foam which would soon dissipate. I envied Hermann Hesse, in whose companionship I found comfort and strength during the first weeks and months, because he had long been free, had broken away early, with the all too accurate explanation: "A great, important people, the Germans—who can deny it? The salt of the earth, perhaps. But as a political nation, impossible! As such, I want to have nothing to do with them." And he lived in beautiful security in his house in Montagnola, in whose garden he played *boccia* with his troubled, distracted guest.

Slowly, slowly, things subsided and arranged themselves. Some sort of domestic life was resumed, first in France, then in Switzerland; a relative calm, a settling down and sense of belonging emerged from forlornness; I picked up the work that had fallen from my hands, that had begun to seem irremediably shattered. Switzerland, hospitable by tradition but under the pressure of menacing, powerful neighbors and committed to neutrality as a moral principle, naturally showed a mild embarrassment at the presence of a guest without papers who was on such bad terms with his government, and called for "tact." Then came the invitation to the American university; and suddenly in this vast free country there was no longer any talk of "tact"; there was nothing but open, uncowed, outspoken friendliness, joyous, without reservations, in fact with the constant refrain: "*Thank you, Mr. Hitler.*" I have some reason, my dear Herr von Molo, to be grateful to this country, and reason to show my gratitude.

Today I am an American citizen, and long before Germany's frightful defeat I publicly and privately declared that I had no intention of ever again turning my back on America. My children, two of whom are still serving in the American army, are rooted in this country; English-speaking grandchildren are growing up around me. I myself am anchored to this country in many ways, here and there bound by ties of honor (in Washington and at the major universities which have conferred their *honorary degrees* upon me) and have built my house on this glorious, future-oriented coast. In its shelter I should like to pursue my life's work to its end—participating in an atmosphere of power, rationality, abundance, and peace. To put it bluntly, I do not see why I should not enjoy the advantages of my strange lot, after having tasted its disadvantages to the dregs. I especially do not see it because I cannot understand what service I can render the German people—which I could not also render from the State of California. . . .

VLADIMIR NABOKOV

The story of the life of Vladimir Nabokov (1899–1977) up to the moment he sailed, with his wife, Véra, and his son, Dmitri, to New York in 1940 can be found in his incomparable memoir (or, as he described it, "a systematically correlated assemblage of personal recollections") *Speak, Memory* (1951, revised 1966): the uprooting of his family in the Russian revolution, his father's assassination in Berlin in 1922, his early career as a Russian-language writer, his avocation as a lepidopterist. When he came to the United States in 1940 to teach at Stanford and Wellesley, he had already begun writing in English, with *The Real Life of Sebastian Knight* published 1941. In 1955 his masterpiece *Lolita* was published in Paris (American publication was delayed for three years as publisher after publisher recoiled from its provocative subject matter). His 1957 novel *Pnin*, whose first chapter is included here, draws on his American teaching experience to depict a life he might have lived but did not: that of an emigré professor never quite able to master the language or the mores of his adopted country. Nabokov, who settled in Switzerland in 1962, may not have made his peace with American mores, but the American language he may be said to have reinvented after his own fashion.

from
Pnin

The elderly passenger sitting on the north-window side of that inexorably moving railway coach, next to an empty seat and facing two empty ones, was none other than Professor Timofey Pnin. Ideally bald, sun-tanned, and clean-shaven, he began rather impressively with that great brown dome of his, tortoise-shell glasses (masking an infantile absence of eyebrows), apish upper lip, thick neck, and strongman torso in a tightish tweed coat, but ended, somewhat disappointingly, in a pair of spindly legs (now flanneled and crossed) and frail-looking, almost feminine feet.

His sloppy socks were of scarlet wool with lilac lozenges; his conservative black oxfords had cost him about as much as all the rest of his clothing (flamboyant goon tie included). Prior to the nineteen-forties, during the staid European era of his life, he had always worn long underwear, its terminals tucked into the tops of neat silk socks, which were clocked, soberly colored, and held up on his cotton-clad calves by garters. In those days, to reveal a glimpse of that white underwear by pulling up a trouser leg too high would have seemed to Pnin as indecent as showing himself to ladies minus collar and tie; for even when decayed Mme. Roux, the concierge of the squalid apartment house in the Sixteenth Arrondissement of Paris—where Pnin, after escaping from Leninized Russia and completing his college education in Prague, had spent fifteen years—happened to come up for the rent while he was without his *faux col*, prim Pnin would cover his front stud with a chaste hand. All this underwent a change in the heady atmosphere of the New World. Nowadays, at fifty-two, he was crazy about sun-bathing, wore sport shirts and slacks, and when crossing his legs would carefully, deliberately, brazenly display a tremendous stretch of bare shin. Thus he might have appeared to a fellow passenger; but except for a soldier asleep at one end and two women absorbed in a baby at the other, Pnin had the coach to himself.

Now a secret must be imparted. Professor Pnin was on the wrong train. He was unaware of it, and so was the conductor, already threading his way through the train to Pnin's coach. As a matter of fact, Pnin at the moment felt very well satisfied with himself. When inviting him to deliver a Friday-evening lecture at Cremona—some two hundred versts west of Waindell, Pnin's academic perch since 1945—the vice-president of the Cremona Women's Club, a Miss Judith Clyde, had advised our friend that the most convenient train left Waindell at 1:52 P.M., reaching Cremona at 4:17; but Pnin—who, like so many Russians, was inordinately fond of everything in the line of time-tables, maps, catalogues, collected them, helped himself freely to them with the bracing pleasure of getting something for nothing, and took especial pride in puzzling out schedules for himself—had discovered, after some study, an inconspicuous reference mark against a still more convenient train

(Lv. Waindell 2:19 P.M., Ar. Cremona 4:32 P.M.); the mark indicated that Fridays, and Fridays only, the two-nineteen stopped at Cremona on its way to a distant and much larger city, graced likewise with a mellow Italian name. Unfortunately for Pnin, his timetable was five years old and in part obsolete.

He taught Russian at Waindell College, a somewhat provincial institution characterized by an artificial lake in the middle of a landscaped campus, by ivied galleries connecting the various halls, by murals displaying recognizable members of the faculty in the act of passing on the torch of knowledge from Aristotle, Shakespeare, and Pasteur to a lot of monstrously built farm boys and farm girls, and by a huge, active, buoyantly thriving German Department which its Head, Dr. Hagen, smugly called (pronouncing every syllable very distinctly) "a university within a university."

In the Fall Semester of that particular year (1950), the enrollment in the Russian Language courses consisted of one student, plump and earnest Betty Bliss, in the Transitional Group, one, a mere name (Ivan Dub, who never materialized) in the Advanced, and three in the flourishing Elementary: Josephine Malkin, whose grandparents had been born in Minsk; Charles McBeth, whose prodigious memory had already disposed of ten languages and was prepared to entomb ten more; and languid Eileen Lane, whom somebody had told that by the time one had mastered the Russian alphabet one could practically read "Anna Karamazov" in the original. As a teacher, Pnin was far from being able to compete with those stupendous Russian ladies, scattered all over academic America, who, without having had any formal training at all, manage somehow, by dint of intuition, loquacity, and a kind of maternal bounce, to infuse a magic knowledge of their difficult and beautiful tongue into a group of innocent-eyed students in an atmosphere of Mother Volga songs, red caviar, and tea; nor did Pnin, as a teacher, ever presume to approach the lofty halls of modern scientific linguistics, that ascetic fraternity of phonemes, that temple wherein earnest young people are taught not the language itself, but the method of teaching others to teach that method; which method, like a waterfall splashing from rock to rock, ceases to be a medium of rational navigation but perhaps in some fabulous future may become instrumental in evolving esoteric dialects—Basic Basque and so forth—spoken only by certain elaborate machines. No doubt Pnin's approach to his work was amateurish and lighthearted, depending as it did on exercises in a grammar brought out by the Head of a Slavic Department in a far greater college than Waindell—a venerable fraud whose Russian was a joke but who would generously lend his dignified name to the products of anonymous drudgery. Pnin, despite his many shortcomings, had about him a disarming, old-fashioned charm which Dr. Hagen, his staunch protector, insisted before morose trustees was a delicate imported article worth paying for in domestic cash. Whereas the degree in sociology and political economy that Pnin had obtained with some pomp at the University of Prague around 1925 had become by mid-century a doctorate in desuetude, he was not altogether miscast as a teacher of Russian. He was beloved not for any essential ability but for those unforgettable digressions of his, when he would remove his glasses to beam at the past while massaging the lenses of the present. Nostalgic excursions in broken English. Autobiographical tidbits. How Pnin came to the *Soedinyonnïe Shtatï* (the United States). "Examination on ship before landing. Very well! 'Nothing to declare?' 'Nothing.' Very well! Then political questions. He asks: 'Are you anarchist?' I answer"—time out on the part of the narrator for a spell of cozy mute mirth—"'First what do we understand under "Anarchism"? Anarchism practical, metaphysical, theoretical, mystical, abstractical, individual, social? When I was young,' I say, 'all this had for me signification.' So we had a very interesting discussion, in consequence of which I passed two whole weeks on Ellis Island"—abdomen beginning to heave; heaving; narrator convulsed.

But there were still better sessions in the way of humor. With an air of coy secrecy, benevolent Pnin, preparing the children for the marvelous treat he had once had himself, and already revealing, in an uncontrollable smile, and incomplete but formidable set of tawny teeth, would open a dilapidated Russian book at the elegant leatherette marker he had carefully placed there; he would open the book, whereupon as often as not a look of the utmost dismay would alter his plastic features; agape, feverishly, he would flip right and left through the volume, and minutes might pass before he found the right page—or satisfied himself that he had marked it correctly after all. Usually the passage of his choice would come from some old and naïve comedy of merchant-class habitus rigged up by Ostrovski almost a century ago, or from an equally ancient but even more dated piece of trivial Leskovian jollity dependent on verbal contortions. He delivered these stale goods with the rotund gusto of the classical Alexandrinka (a theater in Petersburg), rather than with the crisp simplicity of the Moscow Artists; but since to appreciate whatever fun those passages still retained one had to have not only a sound knowledge of the vernacular but also a good deal of literary insight, and since his poor little class had neither, the performer would be alone in enjoying the associative subtleties of his text. The heaving we have already noted in another connection would become here a veritable earthquake. Directing his memory, with all the lights on and all the masks of the mind a-miming, toward the days of his fervid and receptive youth (in a brilliant cosmos that seemed all the fresher for having been abolished by one blow of history), Pnin would get drunk on his private wines as he produced sample after sample of what his listeners politely surmised was Russian humor. Presently the fun would become too much for him; pear-shaped tears would trickle down his tanned cheeks. Not only his shocking teeth but also an astonishing amount of pink upper-gum tissue would suddenly pop out, as if a jack-in-the-box had been sprung, and his hand would fly to his mouth, while his big shoulders shook and rolled. And although the speech he smothered behind his dancing hand was now doubly unintelligible to the class, his complete surrender to his own merriment would prove irresistible. By the time he was helpless with it he would have his students in stitches, with abrupt barks of clockwork hilarity coming from Charles and a dazzling flow of unsuspected lovely laughter transfiguring Josephine, who was not pretty, while Eileen, who was, dissolved in a jelly of unbecoming giggles.

All of which does not alter the fact that Pnin was on the wrong train.

How should we diagnose his sad case? Pnin, it should be particularly stressed, was anything but the type of that good-natured German platitude of last century, *der zerstreute Professor*. On the contrary, he was perhaps too wary, too persistently on the lookout for diabolical pitfalls, too painfully on the alert lest his erratic surroundings (unpredictable America) inveigle him into some bit of preposterous oversight. It was the world that was absent-minded and it was Pnin whose business it was to set it straight. His life was a constant war with insensate objects that fell apart, or attacked him, or refused to function, or viciously got themselves lost as soon as they entered the sphere of his existence. He was inept with his hands to a rare degree; but because he could manufacture in a twinkle a one-note mouth organ out of a pea pod, make a flat pebble skip ten times on the surface of a pond, shadow-graph with his knuckles a rabbit (complete with blinking eye), and perform a number of other tame tricks that Russians have up their sleeves, he believed himself endowed with considerable manual and mechanical skill. On gadgets he doted with a kind of dazed, superstitious delight. Electric devices enchanted him. Plastics swept him off his feet. He had a deep admiration for the zipper. But the devoutly plugged-in clock would make nonsense of his mornings after a storm in the middle of the night had paralyzed the local power station. The frame of his spectacles would snap in mid-bridge, leaving him with two identical pieces, which he would vaguely attempt to unite, in the hope, perhaps, of some organic marvel of restoration coming to the rescue. The zipper a gentleman depends on most would come loose in his puzzled hand at some nightmare moment of haste and despair.

And he still did not know that he was on the wrong train.

A special danger area in Pnin's case was the English language. Except for such not very helpful odds and ends as "the rest is silence," "nevermore," "weekend," "who's who," and a few ordinary words like "eat," "street," "fountain pen," "gangster," "Charleston," "marginal utility," he had had no English at all at the time he left France for the States. Stubbornly he sat down to the task of learning the language of Fenimore Cooper, Edgar Poe, Edison, and thirty-one Presidents. In 1941, at the end of one year of study, he was proficient enough to use glibly terms like "wishful thinking" and "okey-dokey." By 1942 he was able to interrupt his narration with the phrase, "To make a long story short." By the time Truman entered his second term, Pnin could handle practically any topic; but otherwise progress seemed to have stopped despite all his efforts, and by 1950 his English was still full of flaws. That autumn he supplemented his Russian courses by delivering a weekly lecture in a so-called symposium ("Wingless Europe: A Survey of Contemporary Continental Culture") directed by Dr. Hagen. All our friend's lectures, including sundry ones he gave out of town, were edited by one of the younger members of the German Department. The procedure was somewhat complicated. Professor Pnin laboriously translated his own Russian verbal flow, teeming with idiomatic proverbs, into patchy English. This was revised by young Miller. Then Dr. Hagen's secretary, a Miss Eisenbohr, typed it out. Then Pnin deleted the passages he could not understand. Then he read it to his weekly audience. He was utterly helpless without the prepared text, nor could he use the ancient system of dissimulating his infirmity by moving his eyes up and down— snapping up an eyeful of words, reeling them off to his audience, and drawing out the end of the sentence while diving for the next. Pnin's worried eye would be bound to lose its bearings. Therefore he preferred reading his lectures, his gaze glued to his text, in a slow, monotonous baritone that seemed to climb one of those interminable flights of stairs used by people who dread elevators.

The conductor, a gray-headed fatherly person with steel spectacles placed rather low on his simple, functional nose and a bit of soiled adhesive tape on his thumb, had now only three coaches to deal with before reaching the last one, where Pnin rode.

Pnin in the meantime had yielded to the satisfaction of a special Pninian craving. He was in a Pninian quandary. Among other articles indispensable for a Pninian overnight stay in a strange town, such as shoe trees, apples, dictionaries, and so on, his Gladstone bag contained a relatively new black suit he planned to wear that night for the lecture ("Are the Russian People Communist?") before the Cremona ladies. It also contained next Monday's symposium lecture ("Don Quixote and Faust"), which he intended to study the next day, on his way back to Waindell, and a paper by the graduate student, Betty Bliss ("Dostoevski and Gestalt Psychology"), that he had to read for Dr. Hagen, who was her main director of cerebration. The quandary was as follows: If he kept the Cremona manuscript—a sheaf of typewriter-size pages, carefully folded down the center—on his person, in the security of his body warmth, the chances were, theoretically, that he would forget to transfer it from the coat he was wearing to the one he would wear. On the other hand, if he placed the lecture in the pocket of the suit in the bag *now*, he would, he knew, be tortured by the possibility of his luggage being stolen. On the third hand (these mental states sprout additional forelimbs all the time), he carried in the inside pocket of his present coat a precious wallet with two ten-dollar bills, the newspaper clipping of a letter he had written, with my help, to the New York Times in 1945 anent the Yalta conference, and his certificate of naturalization; and it was physically possible to pull out the wallet, if needed, in such a way as fatally to dislodge the folded lecture. During the twenty minutes he had been on the train, our friend had already opened his bag twice to play with his various papers. When the conductor reached the car, diligent Pnin was perusing with difficulty Betty's last effort, which began, "When we consider the mental climate wherein we all live, we cannot but notice——"

The conductor entered; did not awake the soldier; promised the women he would let them know when they would be about to arrive; and presently was shaking his head over Pnin's ticket. The Cremona stop had been abolished two years before.

"Important lecture!" cried Pnin. "What to do? It is a cata-stroph!"

Gravely, comfortably, the gray-headed conductor sank into the opposite seat and consulted in silence a tattered book full of dog-eared insertions. In a few minutes, namely at 3:08, Pnin would have to get off at Whitchurch; this would enable him to catch the four-o'clock bus that would deposit him, around six, at Cremona.

"I was thinking I gained twelve minutes, and now I have lost nearly two whole hours," said Pnin bitterly. Upon which, clearing his throat and ignoring the consolation offered by the kind gray-head ("You'll make it."), he took off his reading glasses, collected his stone-heavy bag, and repaired to the vestibule of the car so as to wait there for the confused greenery skimming by to be cancelled and replaced by the definite station he had in mind.

JULIA DE BURGOS

Julia de Burgos (1914–1953) was born in a poor rural barrio near Carolina, Puerto Rico, the first of 13 children. She earned a teaching degree at the University of Puerto Rico and soon joined the island's independence movement. *Poema en 20 surcos*, her first book, was published in 1938. She was in Cuba in the early 1940s and there she met Pablo Neruda, who offered to write an introduction for her next collection of verse. She came to the mainland United States around 1942 and lived for a time in Florida. Because of their political activism the Washington, D.C., office that she and her second husband, Armando Marín, shared was raided by the FBI. Burgos then settled in New York City where she continued to write poems promoting her revolutionary and feminist views. "Farewell in Welfare Island," included here, was originally written in English during a 1953 hospital stay. It is an impassioned hymn to the dislocation that Puerto Rican migrants experience in the United States. Burgos died on an East Harlem street without identification; her body was buried in a pauper's grave on the city's Hart Island.

Farewell in Welfare Island

It has to be from here,
right this instance,
my cry into the world.

Life was somewhere forgotten
and sought refuge in depths of tears
and sorrows
over this vast empire of solitude
and darkness.

Where is the voice of freedom,
freedom to laugh,
to move
without the heavy phantom of despair?

Where is the form of beauty
unshaken in its veil simple and pure?
Where is the warmth of heaven
pouring its dreams of love in broken spirits?

It has to be from here,
right this instance,
my cry into the world.
My cry that is no more mine,
but hers and his forever,
the comrades of my silence,
the phantoms of my grave.

It has to be from here,
forgotten but unshaken,
among comrades of silence
deep into Welfare Island
my farewell to the world.

> Goldwater Memorial Hospital
> Welfare Island, NYC
> Feb. 1953

ARIEL DORFMAN

Born in Buenos Aires, Argentina, to a secular Jewish family from Santiago, Chile, Ariel Dorfman (b. 1940) came to the United States at the age of three and grew up for a time in New York City. Because of his father's unpopular leftist political views the family returned to Chile in the mid-1950s. Dorfman became a Chilean citizen and from 1970 to 1973 was the cultural adviser to President Salvador Allende. Forced into exile following the military coup that overthrew Allende, Dorfman returned to the United States and, since 1985, has taught at Duke University. He is a human rights activist and the writer of novels, plays, essays, and studies of popular culture, notably *How to Read Donald Duck* (with Armand Mattelart, published in English in 1975). His 1998 autobiography, *Heading South, Looking North*, recounts his bilingual journey—as does the 2007 essay included here, "Breaking Down the Glass Walls of Language." Immigration, according to Dorfman, is not only physical relocation but linguistic reinvention.

Breaking Down the Glass Walls of Language

T hat's what I'd love to be able to remember: the moment when it happened. Or at least remember the days, the weeks, the way in which English crept into my brain, flooded into my life, hit me like lightning.

It's a memory denied to me, accessible only through others, *através de otros*, through the stories my parents told me later, when I was puzzling about my conversion from Spanish to English, when I searched out *los orígenes* of my love affair with the language of Shakespeare and Ogden Nash, Superman, and, well, Richard Nixon as well.

This I do know: it was February 1945 and snow was falling in New York when I arrived there, a toddler of two and a half, whose skin must still have recollected the sweltering Buenos Aires where he had been born, the Buenos Aires of Borges and Perón that he had only just left behind. Maybe that child was lodging a protest against the first of his many exiles or maybe the reasons were less metaphorical and a tad more medical. Whatever the explanation, the cold and undeniable fact is that I came down with pneumonia.

Recently, as part of a film based on my life, I managed to track down the hospital where I spent those three decisive weeks when I learned English. It was Mount Sinai, way up on Fifth Avenue in front of Central Park, and the woman who had been the head nurse for pediatrics in the 1940s was still volunteering there, though now well into her 90s. She showed me photos of the children's ward, where young patients with my sort of contagious disease were secluded inside large glass-partitioned cubicles, isolated from any outside visitors, only in contact with doctors and nurses and other sick boys and girls. Today they would not segregate that infant. And today he would undoubtedly be surrounded by an array of Hispanics, Latinos, Nuyoricans, whatever you want to call them, today *mi idioma materno*, my mother tongue, Spanish, would be floating around everywhere. Indeed, today Anglo-speaking kids might emerge from that experience with a smattering of *castellano*, knowing how to say *hola* and *gracias* and *quiero más*. But back then it was English and only English wherever I turned, an immersion course *a la fuerza*. *Mi papá y mamá* were allowed to visit only once a week and then, always, they have told me, from the distance, from behind that glass wall watching their son cry and reach out for them. And then what did I do, what else could I do after they had mouthed an adios I was unable to hear, what alternative did I have but to survive, adapt and survive—motivated by the same needs that pressed humans to chance on language as they roamed the plains of Africa so many hundreds of thousands of years ago.

And that's how I learned this language in which I now write these words. Out of sheer necessity. I learned the vocabulary of sustenance and sleep and love from those who healed my lungs and fed me. From those who coddled me at night and played with me in the morning. Almost as if I had to give birth to myself in that hospital ward, midwife myself into a second language.

I must have felt betrayed by my Spanish syllables, by Cervantes and Darío and Sor Juana, even if I had no idea at that point that such future mentors of my literary tongue were awaiting me. And I must have felt abandoned by my parents, *pobrecitos*, my parents who loved me *más que el sol*. Oh, I must have planned my petty revenge.

Because I am told that when I left that hospital after that three-week stay, not only was my pneumonia gone. So was my Spanish. I refused to answer when spoken to in the language into whose waters I had gently been cast, been swimming through, since my inaugural breaths on this Earth. "I don't understand," my mother says that I said, perhaps the first words she ever heard me pronounce in the language in which she would have to speak to me during the next ten years. Except that she never lost her accent, and I never had one, still can "pass" for American.

My forced conversion—like so many captives throughout history—is, of course, only part of the story. English did not come exclusively as a conqueror, merely as a threat. It was awaiting me in the years ahead and in the streets outside. It was the funnies on Sunday in the *New York Herald Tribune*. It was the legend of Babe Ruth's magical sixty home runs. It was the "Teddy Bears' Picnic." It was kindergarten's tales of wonder and two-plus-two-equals-four. And someday it would be William Faulkner and John Wayne, William Blake and Joan Baez, *The Sands of Iwo Jima* and "The Times They Are a-Changin'," and, of course, Ella Fitzgerald.

Later I would return to Latin America, fall in love once more with *el idioma de mi nacimiento*, even come, in a moment of extreme folly, to repudiate English because of its connections to the U.S. Empire that was subjugating *la América de Martí*—only to find myself buffeted by yet another exile, *décadas más tarde*, find myself once again back in the States, back in the land which first gave me the gift of its language.

Except that now, in this land which I have made my own, I am not alone in the quest to make that tongue my own. That initial experience of mine is being repeated and resurrected by millions of other Latino voices, all of us part of a gigantic migratory wave which will transform the language that rushed to my rescue during those dark days of 1945, all of us simply trying to survive. Here I am, more than half a century later, still seduced by those words I first heard, even if I can't remember them, the day I stumbled into that hospital ward and realized that my mouth and tongue and teeth would save me, could save me, from starvation and loneliness.

JOHN LUKACS

The reputation of John Lukacs (b. 1924) as a writer, thinker, and historian of the first rank is so firmly established that "immigrant" might be the last word one would think of applying to him. As he points out in this excerpt from his autobiography *Confessions of an Original Sinner* (1990): "I thought the word *exile* fitted me better than Displaced Person or Refugee or Immigrant." For Lukacs an individual's relationship to history is always "personal and participatory." This is the central point in the historical philosophy of someone whose own past is particularly entwined with the great movements of the 20th century. He was born in Budapest to a well-off Hungarian family and raised with all the educational and material advantages a bourgeois upbringing could furnish. Despite this, having a Jewish mother meant that during World War II he was conscripted into a forced-labor battalion. He saw the Germans advance and retreat and the Russians advance and remain, and decided at the end of the war that it would be best to come to the United States until things settled down. He never returned to Hungary other than as a visitor. A year following his American arrival in 1946, he became a professor of history at Chestnut Hill College outside Philadelphia where he taught until retiring in 1994. His psychological portraits of Churchill and Hitler in *The Duel* and *Five Days in London* have become classics in their field.

from
Confessions of an Original Sinner

Three months from the day that I passed out of my native country, wending my way through a forest on the Austrian border, I came ashore in the United States at Portland, Maine. Owing to my recommendation letters from the American Minister and the American Military Mission in Hungary, the American Consulate in Paris gave me a visa immediately, but it took some time until I could get passage on a ship bound for the United States. A dockers' strike had restricted shipping in more East Coast ports, which was why the Liberty freighter on which I finally sailed from Bordeaux was directed to Portland. It was a warm October day. Remaining in my memory are the gray Maine rocks between which the ship was passing on its way to the port, the flatness of the horizon, the low skyline of the town and the thick woolen anklets of the young girls (bobby socks then) trooping through the streets. This may have been the first time I sensed that I was coming to live in a very old country inhabited by young people—the opposite of my mother continent, which is, by and large, geologically young but whose people are old.

Seven years later I was sworn in as an American citizen. When I walked into the Federal building at Ninth and Market streets in Philadelphia I found myself in a dark cavern of humid gloom. The corridors were formicant with municipal refuse. The court clerk had the expression of a malicious owl. A turtle-like judge pronounced a few dusty clichés. I was sworn in standing next to a South African couple I had met in a Germantown bar some weeks before, when they had been unimpressively drunk. That ceremony was disconcerting. Yet it did not matter much, surely not at the time, the worst years of the Communist oppression in Hungary. I did not for a moment regret the loss (if that was what it was) of my erstwhile Hungarian citizenship. What mattered was the generosity of some of my American relatives and friends, who greeted my American citizenship cheerfully, welcoming me with small presents and an effusive spirit that was very American.

Thirty-six years after that event I still have ambiguous sentiments about being an American. When I talk about Americans or American things, whether here or abroad, I am self-conscious enough to find it difficult, or even impossible, to use the pronoun *we*. (Yet when some years ago a review in *The New Yorker* described me as "a noted American historian," this gave me a mix of amusement and pleasure.) I have often wished for the time before 1840, when one's American passport (then a beautiful quarto folded sheet of parchment paper) was issued by a state or city court and not by Washington, when one traveled and was identified as a Pennsylvanian as well as an American. But that is neither here nor there, being probably part and parcel of my liking for provincial affinities. What belongs here is that modicum of honesty which, I am sorry to say, I find missing in the recollections of many famous immigrants. "I am an American, born in Paris in 1929," I once read in an author's credit line, giving the impression that he was the smart offspring of cosmopolitan Americans of that time, whereas his parents' provenance was not American but Bessarabian, having come to Paris not from the eastern shores of the New World but from the eastern recesses of the Old. I also recall a successful immigrant savant of International Relations who worked his way up to become an American ambassador. He had been born in a provincial town of the Austro-Hungarian Empire, but he must have liked Vienna so much that it eventually became his birthplace. Some years ago Eugene Ormandy, the celebrated director of the Philadelphia Orchestra, received the Medal of Freedom from the President of the United States. To the reporters he said: "People always ask me where I was born. I was born at the age of twenty-one, when I arrived in the United States." Presumably facts such as that his name in Hungary was not Ormandy (being a near-aristocratic monicker), and that he had played a minor role during the sordid and short-lived Communist regime in Hungary in 1919 were now relegated to his preconscious memory.

The memory of immigrants is a complex story that still awaits its exposition by a knowledgeable and sensitive writer. It is complex because for so many immigrants, and even more for their descendants, the Atlantic was a vast psychic chasm, not a bridge between the Old World and the New. If they did not themselves invent the motives of their departure from their native countries, their descendants did it for them. Talking to my students and reading their family history papers year after year, I have been stunned by their sometimes willful ignorance of the provenance of their ancestors, even in instances when they possessed factual data about their grandparents' or great-grandparents' birthplaces in Italy or Ireland or Poland. A split-mindedness is at work there which I may illustrate by two examples. One of my students, Italian-American by name and looks, a third-generation American, wrote emphatically that she knew and wished to know nothing about her Italian ancestors. "We have always regarded ourselves as Americans, nothing more or less." A few sentences later she described one of her American aunts: "She is a full-blooded Italian." Another student, after having written in some detail about the dreadfully humiliating difficulties with which her grandfather, an Irish laborer, had to cope during his first ten years in the United States, went on to write a few lines later that her grandfather was blessed from the day he had set foot in America, where he was newly born.

I was *not* Newly Born. I was *not* An Immigrant. I was *not* one of Emma Lazarus's Huddled Masses. I was a special case: I came to the United States as the United States had allowed my homeland to become a part of the Russian sphere of Europe, having already then demonstrated my dedication to liberty and to the English-speaking nations. I kept telling this to Americans for years. They were not impressed. They listened to me sympathetically, but what I said made no particular impression on them: an immigrant was an immigrant. They were right.

My naturalization (odd word, that) was expedited by the decision of the Immigration and Naturalization Service to classify me as a Displaced Person, a category that the American government established soon after the war, in order to cope with the millions of refugees, of the most various kind (Jews who had escaped Hitler's death camps were often put together with people who had helped the Germans in transporting them there), who were huddled in Western Germany, Austria and Italy after the war. I thought and felt and, on occasion, said that I had little in common with these untutored masses whom I, for one, had preceded by a few years. The very bureaucratic tone of the term Displaced Person grated on my ears. I was wrong. It took me years to realize that every displaced person, including myself, was a *bona et mala fide* immigrant; and that every American immigrant, beginning with 1607 and all that, was a displaced person.

Bona et mala fide: because the vast majority of immigrants had come with the idea of eventually returning to their native countries, an idea that later faded from their minds. This was true, too, of my generation of exiles, but for a different reason: we hoped that sooner or later the United States would force the Russians out of some of their Eastern European satrapies. I had doubts about that from the beginning; still, I thought that the word *exile* fitted me better than Displaced Person or Refugee or Immigrant. The psychology of exiles is interesting enough to fill an entire book. It involves not only aspirations and maladjustments but even dreams. Being an exile has its particular pains and pleasures. The first involve maladjustment in space as well as in time: the inability and, in some cases, the unwillingness to adjust one's mind to the conditions of the host country and to the national mind of its people. This is compounded by the inability to comprehend how one's native country has changed through the years, whereby even the most intelligent exiles can seldom free their minds from the categories and associations of the condition of their native country at the time of their departure.

There are, however, compensatory pleasures in the life of an exile. One of these involves the inflation of one's social status in the old country—a normal human weakness. A vignette of this may be found in the writing of the brilliant French reactionary Rivarol who, in the company of noblemen and noblewomen emigrés in a Hamburg boarding-house in 1793, listened to an aspiring newcomer referring to himself as "*nous aristocrates*," whereupon Rivarol shot back: "*C'est un usage du pluriel que je trouve bien singulier*"— "This is a usage of the plural that I find very singular." In any event, an exile may find it possible to associate with such compatriots whose company in his native country he would have sought largely in vain. The pleasures of this kind of snobbery are easier to come by than in one's native country. Consequently, such social vanities may satisfy even such men and women who were not particularly addicted to social climbing in their earlier lives— as in the instance of a dear old friend of mine who declined my suggestion for a convivial evening in New York with the words, unexpected and strange from his lips: "You don't understand. I may be dining with the Prime Minister at the C.'s tonight." The Prime Minister, a thoroughly honorable man, had been the last constitutional prime minister of Hungary, but that was twenty years before; now he lived in reduced circumstances in New York, where my friend could meet him every day, had he wished to. On the other hand, the C. family *did* live on Park Avenue, a kind of salon of the *gratin* of Hungarian exiledom in New York. Another example of the magnetism of companionship was that of the man-about-town in Budapest now (temporarily) reduced to the status of a factory worker on Long Island, who would appear twice a week in the cocktail lounge of the Sherry-Netherland Hotel in New York, where a Hungarian pianist from Old Budapest was playing and where occasionally Hungarians would amble in. He spent a considerable portion of his paycheck on the glass of cognac and the cover charge; when I asked him why he did this, he said, "One can wave to people there."

Let me repeat: the psychology of exiles still awaits the genius of a master writer who will have to proceed from a position that is rare and difficult, since it must be equidistant from the small world of the exiles and from the larger world of Americans. He must be equidistant and at the same time thoroughly familiar with both, very much including their two languages with all of their nuances. In most cases, the mental life of an exile in the United States goes through three phases. During the first years he lives among other exiles. Then the slow period of his Americanization begins: gradually the number of his American friends and acquaintances and associations (including linguistic associations) increases, while those of his former compatriots decreases. Yet there comes a phase, many years later, when he rediscovers his native roots; among other things, he begins to reread the literature of his native country, and he is no longer unwilling to revisit his native country when that becomes possible. This evolution within the life of a single man is a condensed example of what often happens to immigrant families within three generations. The first generation is still steeped in old habits and ways of thinking. The second generation tears itself away, wishing to be as American as possible. It is the third generation that, fairly secure in its Americanism, sometimes develops a new (and, alas, often abstract or even false) interest in the country of its ancestors. This is different from the acculturation of an immigrant in, say, Britain or France, where he becomes more and more British or French as time goes on; but Americanization is both easier and more complicated than that. It is easier to become an American than to become American, and of course I mean something more than mere citizenship.

I know now that my claim of having been a special kind of immigrant was a distinction without a difference; but there was one difference between me and most of my fellow exiles. As I suggested before, I did not share their hopes for an eventual American liberation of Hungary, not because I was more of a political realist than they but because I knew Americans better than many of them did. Allied with my political pessimism was my conviction that Hungary was lost for a long time. This was one of the reasons I chose to make my academic career and writing into something more than becoming an interpreter of Central European history in English. It was one of the reasons, too, that soon after my arrival in the United States I chose to live among Americans. And this was the time, too, when my engagement to the English language matured into a pursuit of marriage—like all love affairs, full of satisfactions and frustrations, of surprising sudden understandings and depressing misunderstandings: a cohabitation and a concubinage that grew to an extent where I began thinking and counting and dreaming in English, though feeling in Magyar, nonetheless. As Horace said, *"patriae quis exsul se quoque fugit"*—"for a long time the exile flees not only his native country but himself."

JOSEPH PELL

"Purely by chance," as he recalls, did Yosel Epelbaum (born in 1924) survive to become Joseph Pell. The third son of a kosher butcher in rural Poland, Yosel was 18 when, on the night of September 3, 1942, he narrowly and quite by accident avoided Nazi SS and local guard forces as they destroyed the Ukrainian ghetto where he and his family had been transported. The sole survivor from his family, young Epelbaum escaped to nearby woods where he joined a band of partisans, engaging in numerous successful attacks against enemy forces. After the war he became a proficient black-market trader, gradually moving westward from country to country with the resolve to immigrate to the United States, which he did in 1947. He would ultimately settle in San Francisco, with a new name for a new world. Knowing no English and with little formal education, Pell opened an ice cream store soon after arrival. He later founded Pell Development, which became a major real estate company with commercial and residential properties throughout Northern California. His autobiography, *Taking Risks*, from which the following excerpt is taken, was published in 2004.

from
Taking Risks

S tepping off the ferry from Ellis Island and setting foot in Manhattan, I saw other immigrants meet with the excited shouts and warm embraces of relatives. Laughter, cries of joy, and prayers of thanksgiving filled the air.

There were forced moments, too, when people at a loss for words felt they had to say *something*: "Oh, Moishe, I got your pictures in the mail and now I can't believe I'm seeing you in person!" Or, "Mendel, they must have fed you well on the boat; you don't look bad at all." Even that sort of greeting would have meant a lot to me, but there was no one waiting for Yosel Epelbaum. Of the hundred and fifty million people in America, I knew only one, Paul Sade, and he was not about to leave his job in Baltimore and come up to New York just to hug me when I came ashore.

Most of those welcomed by friends or family went off with them. The rest of us stood around, a bit sheepishly, until HIAS (the Hebrew Immigrant Aid Society, which took over for the Joint Distribution Committee once we were in the States) arranged for a bus to take us uptown. Our destination was a hotel on Forty-third Street where I was assigned a small room of my own. There, close to Times Square, I would spend about two weeks. It was a thrilling place for a young man who had grown up in a Polish town without electricity and had lived in the woods for a year and a half. Sure, Katowitz and more so Munich were major cities, but they had been wrecked by war. I was now in the middle of something else—a metropolis throbbing with vitality, the center of the universe.

Everyone was moving fast and with great purpose. Shoppers dashed into the crowded stores, theatergoers hurried to get to the shows on time, and commuters rushed in and out of the packed subways. It was all very stimulating.

But with no place to go, I led an aimless existence. I had not come as a tourist with a list of sights to see, and anyway I had no one to show me around. Even more limiting was my lack of English, causing problems as soon as I left the hotel. That's why I ate most of my meals at the Horn & Hardart Automat where what you saw was what you got. You could look through the glass door of a little compartment, put a few coins in a slot, turn the handle, and, wonder of wonders, pull out your food. But at a regular restaurant some advance planning was required to ensure there would be no surprises. Trying hard not to be rude, I would walk through the place and glance around at the other diners until I saw someone eating a dish I thought I'd like. Then I would sit at a table nearby so when the waiter came over I could order just by pointing at the other person's plate.

I wasn't completely alone in the big city because my girlfriend Eva Rosenzweig had given me the number of some relatives she had in Brooklyn, a family headed by a widow with two grown daughters, one of them single and the other married. The son-in-law, a lawyer, picked me up in his car and drove me over the bridge to meet everyone for a Shabbes dinner. After the meal, the mother got right to the point: Would I be willing to walk around the block a few times with her unmarried daughter? I agreed, felt awkward in such a contrived situation, and nothing came of it. Later I wondered if Eva had made this connection more for the sake of that family than for me. But it didn't matter. I was a lonely guy, and it was good just to have some home cooking and be with people I could talk to.

There was nothing at all positive about my visit to the Biala Podlaska Society, the *landsmanshaft* of former Bialers living in the New York area. I had obtained their phone number from a distant cousin whom I'd met by chance in Munich, and with so much time on my hands figured that I had nothing to lose by going to see them.

I entered a nondescript office and found about half a dozen older men whose dress and manner indicated to me they had immigrated decades before. They listened while I briefly told them about my family and my service in the partisans. Then they invited me to share some food. But when we finished eating, they all got up and huddled together, talking quietly and leaving me at the table with no idea of what was going on. They returned, said goodbye, and handed me a check from the society for twenty-five dollars.

Deeply hurt, I gave it right back to them. I had not gone there asking for money and in any case they hadn't inquired about my financial needs. They just sized me up, and, before sending me on my way, figured that a handout was the right thing. It felt like they were saying: "This nebbish, let's give him twenty-five dollars."

In a city full of strangers, the society was a link to my hometown. Through its members I might have made contact with other Bialers who had known the Epelbaums. At the very least, I could have discovered a sympathetic *landsman* willing to befriend me and relieve the loneliness I felt. But they treated me with all the compassion of government bureaucrats, and I had no desire to return. They were so high-handed in dispensing what I *didn't* need, that I could not bear to ask them for what I truly lacked.

Their behavior was typical of the arrogance and insensitivity I encoun- -

tered from many American Jews in these postwar years. Especially those who had been immigrants themselves tended to look down their noses at newcomers. Someone who had grown up in a Lower East Side tenement early in the century and now lived in a modern apartment building in the Bronx or a row house in Brooklyn enjoyed a wicked delight in referring to us recent arrivals exactly the way they themselves had once been branded— "greenhorns." How I hated that ugly word. And how unfair it was when applied to Holocaust survivors. I understood that green meant a kind of raw immaturity, but even though I was only twenty-three I felt I had been through a lot more than these smug city dwellers. And why "horn"? Did we stick out that much that it appeared we had sprouted an animal-like body part? Thankfully, you rarely hear the term greenhorn today in connection with the wave of Jewish immigrants that has arrived in recent decades from the former Soviet Union.

I know that newcomers from every part of the world and in every era have been met with haughty, stuck-up attitudes by their own countrymen who preceded them. I suppose that's human nature. If you can point to someone else as a bumbling foreigner it must mean that you yourself fit in perfectly.

But we survivors were met with a coldness that went even deeper. Reflecting on the initial conversations I had in the States, I realize now how superficial those exchanges were. "Oh, you survived as a fighter in the forest, but your parents, brothers, and sister didn't make it. I see." And then it was on to a new subject. Maybe they behaved that way out of guilt for not having pressured the Roosevelt administration to rescue us. Or perhaps it was like the uneasiness of a person paying his condolences at a funeral who doesn't know what to say to the immediate family members of the deceased. It may even have been that they wanted to spare themselves the pain of finding out the whole grisly truth of what had so recently happened across the ocean. Whatever the reason, we were snubbed as immigrants and shunned as survivors. This would all change, but in 1947, when I needed it most, I cannot say that American Jewry extended a heartfelt welcome.

Yet I was anything but depressed as I moved through the bustling midtown streets near my hotel. It was a time of being in limbo and yet one of intense anticipation because I had the feeling that after a short period of waiting I would get a fast start in the Golden Land. Through the windows of delicatessens I saw cooks, and I knew I could be one. I saw grocers and butchers and I thought I could do that kind of work, too. And then I'd move up the ladder from there. I'm a quick study, I told myself. I'll learn on the job and perform as well as the Americans themselves.

My hope was that Paul and I would seek our fortune together. His uncles had given him work in their big dry cleaning establishment in Baltimore, and that's where I went to visit him after coming down on the train from New York. The place was so steamy it took a while to spot him. Paul was in the back of the hot, noisy factory, pressing pants with an industrial-strength iron. He told me to wait for him until his shift ended, in the comfortable home of one of his uncles where he occupied the guestroom. When he returned that evening we began a serious discussion about the future.

First, I asked him how much he was getting paid. "Seventy-five cents," he answered. "This is why you came to America," I said, "to press pants for seventy-five cents an hour?" It didn't take him long to realize that he could do a lot better. After talking it over for a couple of days we decided to hit the road, head west, and see what opportunities were out there. I was more than ready to end my stay in New York. And, besides, HIAS, preparing for an even larger wave of immigrants, was encouraging us to relocate elsewhere. So we went back to Manhattan long enough to pick up some belongings I'd left behind and then boarded a train for Chicago.

I don't remember putting a lot of thought into our destination. It was a city known for commerce and seemed to be the most logical next step. "New York, Chicago" had the right ring to it. But about two or three days after we arrived there and rented a cheap room near the Loop, the weather turned raw. It was still October, but the wind blowing off the lake was so strong it almost carried us down the street. You didn't have to walk in that town, you were tossed around by the elements. As an icy blast virtually blew us past the Greyhound bus station I noticed a large, inviting poster in the window beckoning people to San Francisco. It featured, of course, a magnificent bird's-eye photo of the Golden Gate Bridge, an engineering marvel I had read about in the newspapers back in Biala Podlaska in the late thirties. It's the longest suspension bridge in the world, I informed Paul, as we steadied ourselves on the sidewalk. I would sure like to see it, I said.

They also enjoy a mild and sunny climate out there, we told each other. In fact, I had heard a lot about California in just the short time I'd been in the States. Everyone, it seemed, from established American Jews to recently arrived refugees, wanted to move there. But people usually had something holding them in the East—a job, friends, or family. Neither Paul nor I, though, had anything to lose. So, without any hesitation, we went in, walked up to the counter, and bought two one-way tickets on a bus leaving the next day. It wasn't that different than my decision to cross the Atlantic: In Europe, America was everybody's first choice and in America the best place appeared to be California.

It took four days and three nights to get to San Francisco, the longest trip across land that I had taken in my life. I could hardly believe that after going so far in one direction, I remained in the same country. I covered more ground than if I had traveled from Russia to Spain.

Everything impressed me, not least of all the large and powerful motor coach itself. We traveled over broad new highways and on back roads, too. And all along the route people kept getting on and off so I got to see a cross section of the populace as well as the astonishingly vast landscape. There were farmers, factory workers, and soldiers sitting near us; there were blacks, Hispanics, and American Indians. I know of some European immigrants who remained for many years in New York City before venturing west of the Hudson. I was in the country less than a month and, because I was young and unattached, already taking a coast-to-coast trip.

Paul, always a lively conversationalist, made many new friends on the bus and flirted with a few of the single women who came aboard. At night, trading on his good looks and charm, he would steer one of them to the empty seats in the back and try to fool around a little in the darkness.

Meanwhile, I was trying to pick up some English. In addition to my two mother tongues, Yiddish and Polish, I had acquired Ukrainian, Russian, and German just by hearing them spoken or perusing a newspaper in the language. I had never taken a course or studied a grammar book. That's the way I wanted to learn English. Paul gave me his own suggestion for immersion in the foreign words and phrases: Look out the window and read the signs.

I took his advice and was soon baffled. It appeared that most of the property in the American West was owned by one man named Motel. I saw this sign everywhere and thought it was pronounced "*Muh*tel," the same as a cousin of mine back in Poland. I asked Paul how this guy (evidently an East European Jew) accumulated so many buildings. He looked at me as if I were a child and, after setting me straight, repeated his recommendation: "Just keep reading the signs."

DENISE LEVERTOV

Born in Ilford, Essex, in England, Denise Levertov (1923–1997) was the product of a complex heritage: her mother was descended from a Welsh mystic and her father, descended from a Russian rabbi, had converted to Christianity and devoted himself to a dream of uniting the Jewish and Christian faiths. Of her childhood Levertov wrote: "I did lessons at home, and never attended any school or college. . . . Jewish booksellers, German theologians, Russian priests from Paris, and Viennese opera singers visited the house; and perhaps my earliest memory is of being dandled by the ill-fated son of Theodor Herzl, the great Zionist." In Switzerland after the war she met and married the American writer Mitchell Goodman, and in 1948 they settled in the United States, where she became part of a circle of poets that included Robert Creeley, Cid Corman, and Robert Duncan. Levertov became a U.S. citizen in 1955. Of her approach to poetry she wrote: "For me, back of the idea of organic form is the concept that there is a form in all things (and in our experience) which the poet can discover and reveal." This poem is from her 1961 collection *The Jacob's Ladder*.

A Map of the Western Part of the County of Essex in England

Something forgotten for twenty years: though my fathers
and mothers came from Cordova and Vitepsk and Caernarvon,
and though I am a citizen of the United States and less a
stranger here than anywhere else, perhaps,
I am Essex-born:
Cranbrook Wash called me into its dark tunnel,
the little streams of Valentines heard my resolves,

Roding held my head above water when I thought it was
drowning me; in Hainault only a haze of thin trees
stood between the red doubledecker buses and the boar-hunt,
the spirit of merciful Phillipa glimmered there.
Pergo Park knew me, and Clavering, and Havering-atte-Bower,
Stanford Rivers lost me in osier beds, Stapleford Abbots
sent me safe home on the dark road after Simeon-quiet evensong,
Wanstead drew me over and over into its basic poetry,
in its serpentine lake I saw bass-viols among the golden dead leaves,
through its trees the ghost of a great house. In
Ilford High Road I saw the multitudes passing pale under the
light of flaring sundown, seven kings
in somber starry robes gathered at Seven Kings
the place of law
where my birth and marriage are recorded
and the death of my father. Woodford Wells
where an old house was called The Naked Beauty (a white
statue forlorn in its garden)
saw the meeting and parting of two sisters,
(forgotten? and further away
the hill before Thaxted? where peace befell us? not once
but many times?).
All the Ivans dreaming of their villages
all the Marias dreaming of their walled cities,
picking up fragments of New World slowly,
not knowing how to put them together nor how to join
image with image, now I know how it was with you, an old map
made long before I was born shows ancient
rights of way where I walked when I was ten burning with desire
for the world's great splendors, a child who traced voyages
indelibly all over the atlas, who now in a far country
remembers the first river, the first
field, bricks and lumber dumped in it ready for building,
that new smell, and remembers
the walls of the garden, the first light.

FRANK McCOURT

Perhaps no one else in this anthology can claim to have met with a more sudden and explosive success than Frank McCourt (born in 1930), whose memoir *Angela's Ashes* (1996), besides winning the Pulitzer Prize and the National Book Critics Circle Award, has now sold over four million copies, been adapted into a movie, and been translated into 17 languages. Born in Brooklyn to a desperately poor Irish family, McCourt's parents, unable to find steady employment, moved the family to Limerick, Ireland, when he was three. There, living among flooded, decaying houses, continued the miseries that had begun a year earlier with the death of his sister. All of this is movingly recounted in the pages of *Angela's Ashes*: the deaths of his younger brothers, his bout with typhoid when he was ten, his father's drinking. But throughout there is a steady counterpoint of resiliency and hidden joys. The following excerpt is taken from the next installment of his autobiography, *'Tis* (1999), which finds a 19-year-old McCourt coming back to New York City as an immigrant.

*

from
'Tis

T he priest asks if I have anyone meeting me and when I tell him there's no one he says I can travel with him on the train to New York City. He'll keep an eye on me. When the ship docks we take a taxi to the big Union Station in Albany and while we wait for the train we have coffee in great thick cups and pie on thick plates. It's the first time I ever had lemon meringue pie and I'm thinking if this is the way they eat all the time in America I won't be a bit hungry and I'll be fine and fat, as they say in Limerick. I'll have Dostoyevsky for the loneliness and pie for the hunger.

The train isn't like the one in Ireland where you share a carriage with five other people. This train has long cars where there are dozens of people and is so crowded some have to stand. The minute we get on people give up their seats to the priest. He says, Thank you, and points to the seat beside him and I feel the people who offered up their seats are not happy when I take one because it's easy to see I'm nobody.

Farther up the car people are singing and laughing and calling for the church key. The priest says they're college kids going home for the weekend and the church key is the can opener for the beer. He says they're probably nice kids but they shouldn't drink so much and he hopes I won't turn out like that when I live in New York. He says I should put myself under the protection of the Virgin Mary and ask her to intercede with her Son to keep me pure and sober and out of harm's way. He'll pray for me all the way out there in Los Angeles and he'll say a special Mass for me on the eighth of December, the feast of the Immaculate Conception. I want to ask him why he'd choose that feast day but I keep silent because he might start bothering me again about the rich Protestants from Kentucky.

He's telling me this but I'm dreaming of what it would be like to be a student somewhere in America, in a college like the ones in the films where there's always a white church spire with no cross to show it's Protestant and there are boys and girls strolling the campus carrying great books and smiling at each other with teeth like snow drops.

When we arrive at Grand Central Station I don't know where to go. My mother said I could try to see an old friend, Dan MacAdorey. The priest shows me how to use the telephone but there's no answer from Dan. Well, says the priest, I can't leave you on your own in Grand Central Station. He tells the taxi driver we're going to the Hotel New Yorker.

We take our bags to a room where there's one bed. The priest says, Leave the bags. We'll get something to eat in the coffee shop downstairs. Do you like hamburgers?

I don't know. I never had one in my life.

He rolls his eyes and tells the waitress bring me a hamburger with french fries and make sure the burger is well done because I'm Irish and we over-cook everything. What the Irish do to vegetables is a crying shame. He says if you can guess what the vegetable is in an Irish restaurant you get the door prize. The waitress laughs and says she understands. She's half-Irish on her mother's side and her mother is the worst cook in the world. Her husband was Italian and he really knew how to cook but she lost him in the war.

Waw. That's what she says. She really means war but she's like all Americans who don't like to say "r" at the end of a word. They say caw instead of car and you wonder why they can't pronounce words the way God made them.

I like the lemon meringue pie but I don't like the way Americans leave out the "r" at the end of a word.

While we're eating our hamburgers the priest says I'll have to stay the night with him and tomorrow we'll see. It's strange taking off my clothes in front of a priest and I wonder if I should get down on my two knees and pretend to say my prayers. He tells me I can take a shower if I like and it's the first time in my life I ever had a shower with plenty of hot water and no shortage of soap, a bar for your body and a bottle for your head.

When I'm finished I dry myself with the thick towel draped on the bathtub and I put on my underwear before going back into the room. The priest is sitting in the bed with a towel wrapped around his fat belly, talking to someone on the phone. He puts down the phone and stares at me. My God, where did you get those drawers?

In Roche's Stores in Limerick.

If you hung those drawers out the window of this hotel people would surrender. Piece of advice, don't ever let Americans see you in those drawers. They'll think you just got off Ellis Island. Get briefs. You know what briefs are?

I don't.

Get 'em anyway. Kid like you should be wearing briefs. You're in the U.S.A. now. Okay, hop in the bed, and that puzzles me because there's no sign of a prayer and that's the first thing you'd expect of a priest. He goes off to the bathroom but he's no sooner in there than he sticks his head out and asks me if I dried myself.

I did.

Well, your towel isn't touched so what did you dry yourself with?

The towel that's on the side of the bathtub.

What? That's not a towel. That's the bath mat. That's what you stand on when you get out of the shower.

I can see myself in a mirror over the desk and I'm turning red and wondering if I should tell the priest I'm sorry for what I did or if I should stay quiet. It's hard to know what to do when you make a mistake your first night in America but I'm sure in no time I'll be a regular Yank doing everything right. I'll order my own hamburger, learn to call chips french fries, joke with waitresses, and never again dry myself with the bath mat. Some day I'll say war and car with no "r" at the end but not if I ever go back to Limerick. If I ever went back to Limerick with an American accent they'd say I was putting on airs and tell me I had a fat arse like all the Yanks.

The priest comes out of the bathroom, wrapped in a towel, patting his face with his hands and there's a lovely smell of perfume in the air. He says there's nothing as refreshing as aftershave lotion and I can put on some if I like. It's right there in the bathroom. I don't know what to say or do. Should I say, No, thanks, or should I get out of the bed and go all the way to the bathroom and slather myself with aftershave lotion? I never heard of anyone in Limerick putting stuff on their faces after they shaved but I suppose it's different in America. I'm sorry I didn't look for a book that tells you what to do on your first night in New York in a hotel with a priest where you're liable to make a fool of yourself right and left. He says, Well? and I tell him, Ah, no, thanks. He says, Suit yourself, and I can tell he's a bit impatient the way he was when I didn't talk to the rich Protestants from Kentucky. He could easily tell me leave and there I'd be out on the street with my brown suitcase and nowhere to go in New York. I don't want to chance that so I tell him I'd like to put on the aftershave lotion after all. He shakes his head and tells me go ahead.

I can see myself in the bathroom mirror putting on the aftershave lotion and I'm shaking my head at myself feeling if this is the way it's going to be in America I'm sorry I ever left Ireland. It's hard enough coming here in the first place without priests criticizing you over your failure to hit it off with rich Kentucky Protestants, your ignorance of bath mats, the state of your underwear and your doubts about aftershave lotion.

The priest is in the bed and when I come out of the bathroom he tells me, Okay, into the bed. We've got a long day tomorrow.

He lifts the bedclothes to let me in and it's a shock to see he's wearing nothing. He says, Good night, turns off the light and starts snoring without even saying a Hail Mary or a prayer before sleep. I always thought priests spent hours on their knees before sleeping but this man must be in a great state of grace and not a bit afraid of dying. I wonder if all priests are like that, naked in the bed. It's hard to fall asleep in a bed with a naked priest snoring beside you. Then I wonder if the Pope himself goes to bed in that condition or if he has a nun bring in pajamas with the Papal colors and the Papal coat of arms. I wonder how he gets out of that long white robe he wears, if he pulls it over his head or lets it drop to the floor and steps out of it. An old Pope would never be able to pull it over his head and he'd probably have to call a passing cardinal to give him a hand unless the cardinal himself was too old and he might have to call a nun unless the Pope was wearing nothing under the white robe which the cardinal would know about anyway because there isn't a cardinal in the world that doesn't know what the Pope wears since they all want to be Pope themselves and can't wait for this one to die. If a nun is called in she has to take the white robe to be washed down in the steaming depths of the Vatican laundry room by other nuns and novices who sing hymns and praise the Lord for the privilege of washing all the clothes of the Pope and the College of Cardinals except for the underwear which is washed in another room by old nuns who are blind and not liable to think sinful thoughts because of what they have in their hands and what I have in my own hand is what I shouldn't have in the presence of a priest in the bed and for once in my life I resist the sin and turn on my side and go to sleep.

Next day the priest finds a furnished room in the paper for six dollars a week and he wants to know if I can afford it till I get a job. We go to East Sixty-eighth Street and the landlady, Mrs. Austin, takes me upstairs to see the room. It's the end of a hallway blocked off with a partition and a door with a window looking out on the street. There's barely space for the bed and a small chest of drawers with a mirror and a table and if I stretch my arms I can touch the walls on both sides. Mrs. Austin says this is a very nice room and I'm lucky it wasn't snapped up. She's Swedish and she can tell I'm Irish. She hopes I don't drink and if I do I'm not to bring girls into this room under any circumstances, drunk or sober. No girls, no food, no drink. Cockroaches smell food a mile away and once they're in you have them forever. She says, Of course you never saw a cockroach in Ireland. There's no food there. All you people do is drink. Cockroaches would starve to death or turn into drunks. Don't tell me, I know. My sister is married to an Irishman, worst thing she ever did. Irishmen great to go out with but don't marry them.

She takes the six dollars and tells me she needs another six for security, gives me a receipt and tells me I can move in anytime that day and she trusts me because I came with that nice priest even if she's not Catholic herself, that it's enough her sister married one, an Irishman, God help her, and she's suffering for it.

The priest calls another taxi to take us to the Biltmore Hotel across the street from where we came out at Grand Central Station. He says it's a famous hotel and we're going to the headquarters of the Democratic Party and if they can't find a job for an Irish kid no one can.

A man passes us in the hallway and the priest whispers, Do you know who that is?

I don't.

Of course you don't. If you don't know the difference between a towel and a bath mat how could you know that's the great Boss Flynn from the Bronx, the most powerful man in America next to President Truman.

The great Boss presses the button for the elevator and while he's waiting he shoves a finger up his nose, looks at what he has on his fingertip and flicks it away on the carpet. My mother would call that digging for gold. This is the way it is in America. I'd like to tell the priest I'm sure De Valera would never pick his nose like that and you'd never find the Bishop of Limerick going to bed in a naked state. I'd like to tell the priest what I think of the world in general where God torments you with bad eyes and bad teeth but I can't for fear he might go on about the rich Protestants from Kentucky and how I missed the opportunity of a lifetime.

The priest talks to a woman at a desk in the Democratic Party and she picks up the telephone. She says to the telephone, Got a kid here . . . just off the boat . . . you got a high school diploma? . . . na, no diploma . . . well, whaddya expect . . . Old Country still a poor country . . . yeah, I'll send him up.

I'm to report on Monday morning to Mr. Carey on the twenty-second floor and he'll put me to work right here in the Biltmore Hotel and aren't I a lucky kid walking into a job right off the boat. That's what she says and the priest tells her, This is a great country and the Irish owe everything to the Democratic Party, Maureen, and you just clinched another vote for the party if the kid here ever votes, ha ha ha.

The priest tells me go back to the hotel and he'll come for me later to go to dinner. He says I can walk, that the streets run east and west, the avenues north and south, and I'll have no trouble. Just walk across Forty-second to Eighth Avenue and south till I come to the New Yorker Hotel. I can read a paper or a book or take a shower if I promise to stay away from the bath mat, ha ha. He says, If we're lucky we might meet the great Jack Dempsey himself. I tell him I'd rather meet Joe Louis if that's possible and he snaps at me, You better learn to stick with your own kind.

At night the waiter at Dempsey's smiles at the priest. Jack's not here, Fawdah. He's over to the Gawden checkin' out a middleweight from New Joisey.

Gawden. Joisey. My first day in New York and already people are talking like gangsters from the films I saw in Limerick.

The priest says, My young friend here is from the Old Country and he'd prefer to meet Joe Louis. He laughs and the waiter laughs and says, Well, that's a greenhorn talkin', Fawdah. He'll loin. Give him six months in this country and he'll run like hell when he sees a darky. An' what would you like to order, Fawdah? Little something before dinner?

I'll have a double martini dry and I mean dry straight up with a twist.

And the greenhorn?

He'll have a . . . well, what'll you have?

A beer, please.

You eighteen, kid?

Nineteen.

You don't look it though it don't matter nohow long as you with the faw-dah. Right, Fawdah?

Right. I'll keep an eye on him. He doesn't know a soul in New York and I'm going to settle him in before I leave.

The priest drinks his double martini and orders another with his steak. He tells me I should think of becoming a priest. He could get me a job in Los Angeles and I'd live the life of Riley with widows dying and leaving me everything including their daughters, ha ha, this is one hell of a martini excuse the language. He eats most of his steak and tells the waiter bring two apple pies with ice cream and he'll have a double Hennessy to wash it down. He eats only the ice cream, drinks half the Hennessy and falls asleep with his chin on his chest moving up and down.

The waiter loses his smile. Goddam, he's gotta pay his check. Where's his goddam wallet? Back pocket, kid. Hand it to me.

I can't rob a priest.

You're not robbing. He's paying his goddam check and you're gonna need a taxi to take him home.

Two waiters help him to a taxi and two bellhops at the Hotel New Yorker haul him through the lobby, up the elevator and dump him on the bed. The bellhops tell me, A buck tip would be nice, a buck each, kid.

They leave and I wonder what I'm supposed to do with a drunken priest. I remove his shoes the way they do when someone passes out in the films but he sits up and runs to the bathroom where he's sick a long time and when he comes out he's pulling at his clothes, throwing them on the floor, collar, shirt, trousers, underwear. He collapses on the bed on his back and I can see he's in a state of excitement with his hand on himself. Come here to me, he says, and I back away. Ah, no, Father, and he rolls out of the bed, slobbering and stinking of drink and puke and tries to grab my hand to put it on him but I back away even faster till I'm out the door to the hallway with him standing in the door, a little fat priest crying to me, Ah, come back, son, come back, it was the drink. Mother o' God, I'm sorry.

But the elevator is open and I can't tell the respectable people already in it and looking at me that I changed my mind, that I'm running back to this priest who, in the first place, wanted me to be polite to rich Kentucky Protestants so that I could get a job cleaning stables and now waggles his thing at me in a way that's surely a mortal sin. Not that I'm in a state of grace myself, no I'm not, but you'd expect a priest to set a good example and not make a holy show of himself my second night in America. I have to step into the elevator and pretend I don't hear the priest slobbering and crying, naked at the door of his room.

There's a man at the front door of the hotel dressed up like an admiral and he says, Taxi, sir. I tell him, No, thanks, and he says, Where you from? Oh, Limerick. I'm from Roscommon myself, over here four years.

I have to ask the man from Roscommon how to get to East Sixty-eighth Street and he tells me walk east on Thirty-fourth Street which is anyway lively I can walk straight up till I come to my street. He tells me, Good luck, stick with your own kind and watch out for the Puerto Ricans, they all carry knives and that's a known fact, they got that hot blood. Walk in the light along the edge of the sidewalk or they'll be leppin' at you from dark doorways.

Next morning the priest calls Mrs. Austin and tells her I should come get my suitcase. He tells me, Come in, the door is open. He's in his black suit sitting on the far side of the bed with his back to me and my suitcase is just inside the door. Take it, he says. I'm going to a retreat house in Virginia for a few months. I don't want to look at you and I don't want to see you ever again because what happened was terrible and it wouldn't have happened if you'd used your head and gone off with the rich Protestants from Kentucky. Good-bye.

It's hard to know what to say to a priest in a bad mood with his back to you who's blaming you for everything so all I can do is go down in the elevator with my suitcase wondering how a man like that who forgives sins can sin himself and then blame me. I know if I did something like that, getting drunk and bothering people to put their hands on me, I'd say I did it. That's all, I did it. And how can he blame me just because I refused to talk to rich Protestants from Kentucky? Maybe that's the way priests are trained. Maybe it's hard listening to people's sins day in day out when there's a few you'd like to commit yourself and then when you have a drink all the sins you've heard explode inside you and you're like everyone else. I know I could never be a priest listening to those sins all the time. I'd be in a constant state of excitement and the bishop would be worn out shipping me off to the retreat house in Virginia.

EDWARD SAID

Born into an affluent Palestinian family, Edward Said (1935–2003)—
who would come to refer to himself as a "Christian wrapped in a Muslim
culture"—spent his formative years attending secular schools in both
Jerusalem and Cairo that were, according to him, "elite colonial schools,
English public schools, designed by the British to bring up a generation
of Arabs with natural ties to Britain." Kicked out of the last of these,
Victoria College in Cairo (the "VC" of the excerpt below), for trouble-
making, his parents sent him to Mount Hermon, a prep school in Massachusetts. Although homesick and lonely, he managed to graduate at the
top of his class, going on to earn his B.A. at Princeton and his master's
degree and doctorate at Columbia. As a professor of English at Columbia
—besides publishing works of literary criticism that have become
classics—Said wrote extensively on the question of Palestinian state-
hood, U.S. foreign policy in relation to the Arab world, and music. His
autobiography, *Out of Place* (1999), is the source of the selection that
follows. An outsider from the beginning, with a lingering desire to retrieve his Arab past, Said was especially equipped to examine the Palestinian question through a literary prism and to remain, in his words,
"fundamentally critical of a gloating and uncritical nationalism."

from
Out of Place

T hinking back to that last period in Cairo, I recall only the sense of comfort and pleasure I derived from my mother's ministrations; she was obviously thinking of my impending departure, trying to make of those last
days something very special for both of us, while I, not really imagining the
terrible rupture that was to come, enjoyed the time as a liberation from the
hectic schedule I had once followed. No more Tewfiq Effendi, no more Fouad

Etayim, riding was dropped, piano lessons given up, exercises at Mourad's gymnasium terminated. Coming back from school in the late afternoon I'd often find her sitting on the terrace overlooking the Fish Garden, and, inviting me to sit beside her with a glass of rosewater-flavored lemonade, she would encircle me with her arm and reminisce about the old days, how "Edwardo Bianco" had been such a remarkably precocious boy, and how I was what she lived for. We listened to the Beethoven symphonies, particularly the Ninth, which became the piece that meant the most to us. I remember being confused about the nature of her relationship to my father, but also being pacified that she always referred to him as "Daddy," the two of us using the same name for husband and father. All this may have been her way of trying to win me back from America before I went, her way of reclaiming me from my father's plans, which when he sent me to the United States she always disagreed with and rued. But these afternoons had the effect of creating an image of an inviolate union between us, which would have, on the whole, shattering results for my later life as a man trying to establish a relationship of developing, growing, maturing love with other women. It was not so much that my mother had usurped a place in my life to which she was not entitled, but that she managed to have access to it for the rest of her life and, I often feel, after it.

I am only now aware that those talks before we were to leave for the United States constituted a sort of leave-taking ceremony. "Let's go to Groppi's for tea for the last time," or "Wouldn't you like us to go to the Kursaal for dinner once more before you go?" she would ask. But much of it took place in some complicated labyrinth of her own making, which also involved the arrangements she was making for herself and my four sisters, whom she would be alone with after I left. There was something so terribly giving about her attitude in the last week before we packed the house for the first stage of our trip via Lebanon. As I later realized, she thought of that giving as motivated entirely by unselfish love, whereas of course her sovereign ego played a major part in what she was up to, namely, struggling in a limiting domestic household to find a means of self-expression, self-articulation, self-elaboration. These I think were my mother's deepest needs, though she never managed to say it explicitly. I was her only son, and shared her facility of communication, her passion for music and words, so I became her instrument for self-expression and self-elaboration as she struggled against my father's unbending, mostly silent iron will. Her sudden withdrawal of affection, which I dreaded, were her way of responding to my absences. From 1951 until her death in 1990 my mother and I lived on different continents, yet she never stopped lamenting the fact that, alone of all her friends, she suffered the pangs of separation from her children, most particularly me. I felt guilt at having abandoned her, even though she had finally acquiesced in the first and most decisive of my many departures.

The sheer gravity of my coming to the United States in 1951 amazes me even today. I have only the most shadowy notion of what my life might have been had I not come to America. I do know that I was beginning again in the United States, unlearning to some extent what I had learned before, relearning things from scratch, improvising, self-inventing, trying and failing, experimenting, canceling, and restarting in surprising and frequently painful ways. To this day I still feel that I am away from home, ludicrous as that may sound, and though I believe I have no illusions about the "better" life I might have had, had I remained in the Arab world, or lived and studied in Europe, there is still some measure of regret. This memoir is on some level a reenactment of the experience of departure and separation as I feel the pressure of time hastening and running out. The fact that I live in New York with a sense of provisionality despite thirty-seven years of residence here accentuates the disorientation that has accrued to me, rather than the advantages.

We made our annual removal to Lebanon in late June 1951 and spent two weeks in Dhour. Then, on the fifteenth of July, my parents and I departed from Beirut Airport (Khaldé, as it was called then) by Pan-American Stratocruiser for Paris. From almost the moment we stepped off the plane in Paris until we left for London by night sleeper I was afflicted with a plague of styes in both my eyes, which, apart from two small apertures, effectively closed them. This aggravated the sense of drifting and indeterminacy that followed my withdrawal from all aspects of my familiar world, the sense of not *really* knowing what I was doing or where I was going.

Within hours of arriving in London, where we stayed grandly in an imposingly grandiose suite at the Savoy, my cousin Albert was summoned from Birmingham, where he was doing a degree in chemical engineering, and was installed luxuriously with us at the hotel. He appeared to be unaware of the tensions between my father and his brothers, so jolly and admirably rakish did he seem while with us. I spent many hours eating my first fish and chips with Albert, visiting the new Battersea Fun Fair, and going to an unending number of pubs in search of girls and excitement, all the while trying to learn from him the arts of enjoying oneself without feeling either guilty or lonely. He was the one close relative whom for the first twenty years of my life I found myself hoping to emulate because he was everything I was not. He had an erect posture, was an excellent footballer and runner, seemed to be a successful ladies' man, and was a natural leader as well as a brilliant student. London was certainly the most pleasurable interlude of our trip. The moment he left, his tonic effect dissipated, and I settled back into the anxious gloom of the trip.

From Southampton we boarded the *Nieuw Amsterdam*, a larger, more luxurious version of the *Saturnia*. The six-day crossing to New York was uneventfully crammed with sumptuous dinners and lunches, nightly movies, and my parents' ubiquitous presence. "I hate America and Americans," my mother would say. "What are we doing here, Wadie? Please explain this whole crazy business to me. Must we take the boy there? You know he'll never come back. We're robbing ourselves." My mother was querulous and sad, while my father reveled in his pancakes and coffee, apple pie à la mode, excited about America and his determination, now that I was going to be there, to buy a house. I found myself avoiding, except at dinner, the conflicting moods of my parents with no stable idea of where I was going or for how long.

No sooner did we arrive in a steamy, unpleasantly overcast and dark New York than my mother persuaded my father to let us visit her cousin Eva Malik in Washington. We checked in to the Mayflower for only about an hour: Eva came by in her husband's black ambassadorial limousine almost immediately and, brooking no dissent, pried us and our lordly array of luggage out of the hotel and into the nicely comfortable chancellory. In his capacity as Lebanese minister plenipotentiary in the United States, Charles Malik was away at a U.N. meeting in San Francisco, so we had Aunt Eva to ourselves for a few days of tourism and general relaxation. It was she who also insisted that they would be my guardians while I was at boarding school, an arrangement my mother welcomed, as did I, since I might spend my vacations in the splendors of the Lebanese ambassador's residence, in a style that resembled what I thought I had left behind in Cairo. My father was noncommittal, for reasons that I would only later discover. I could sense, however, that both my parents were soon chafing at our stay, which, they kept reminding Eva—who, being alone and otherwise not engaged or obligated by domestic duties, was obviously enjoying our presence—was already too protracted. They both had this notion that one shouldn't in the Arab sense be "heavy"—in effect, not stay anywhere more than three, at most four, days, all the while taking out our hosts for dinner every night, buying lots of flowers and chocolates, making themselves "lighter" by so doing.

Suddenly we embarked for Madison, Wisconsin, which in a recent *National Geographic* had been described to my father's satisfaction as the "nicest" town in the United States. We spent two days in the pretty town, going around with real estate agents who showed us one imposing house after another, each of which the three of us collectively imagined ourselves living in: "That's your mother's desk," said my father, pointing to an unprepossessing corner filled carelessly with a decrepit bridge table. "Here's where we can put the piano," said my mother with noticeably less enthusiasm as the hours wore on. We gathered great quantities of pamphlets and business cards, all of which my father cavalierly tossed into the hotel wastebasket that evening. There was something disconnected and eerie about our house hunting in Madison, but my mother and I played along with my father, although I never grasped what Madison was a fictional projection of for him, except the opportunity to come to the United States like me and settle here, despite his by now elaborate domestic establishment, prospering business, and very full life in Egypt and Lebanon. He always used to say, and my mother repeated often, that had he been twenty years younger after World War II, he would have come to the United States. When we went to Madison he was already fifty-six, but I know that to some extent his interest in the United States was partly theoretical patriotism, partly the invigoration he felt at being out of his family's grasp, partly the desire to make me feel that I was getting the greatest opportunity ever, and that my clinging moroseness and expectant dread about staying on alone would be dissolved in due course. He had an ideological hatred of sentimentality, represented by the regretted effect of his own mother's importunings to return and my mother's behavior toward me just prior to our trip.

We returned to New York via the Milwaukee Road Railroad and a TWA flight from Midway Airport, and the day after Labor Day finally found ourselves on a train leaving Grand Central Station bound for Mount Hermon. The only part of the long journey on the White River Junction train that I remember was our arrival at the tiny, excessively rural Massachusetts station, where a lone taxicab was waiting to take us the final couple of miles to the school. We barely had an hour together, since my parents were to take the return train to New York. When we had found my room, and my parents had had a brief meeting alone with the headmaster, my mother spent fifteen minutes helping me to unpack and make the bed (my unknown roommate was already neatly installed). Then they rapidly departed, leaving me standing with a lump in my throat at the entrance to my imposing dormitory building, Crossley Hall, as they disappeared from view. The void that suddenly surrounded me and that I knew I had to endure for the one academic year I was to be at Mount Hermon seemed unbearable, but I also knew that I had to return to my room to recover some sense of my mother's recent presence—her smell, a trace of her hands, even perhaps a message.

A blond and blue-eyed youth of my own age was there to greet me. "Hi. I'm your roommate, Bob Salisbury," he said pleasantly, leaving me no opportunity to recuperate some of my mother's disappearing aura as I realized that I had now definitively arrived.

Mount Hermon School, originally founded by the evangelist Dwight L. Moody in the late nineteenth century, was larger than Victoria College. It was the male counterpart of the Northfield Seminary for Young Ladies, and the two establishments occupied several thousand acres on opposite sides of the Connecticut River. A six-mile road and a bridge connected the two quite separate but affiliated schools. Mount Hermon, unlike Northfield, was not in a town or village but was entirely self-enclosed and self-sufficient. Unmarried teachers lived among students in the dorm; married faculty with children had little houses scattered over the campus. Although it was in the traditional picture-book sense a beautiful, leafy, hilly, and perfectly maintained New England site, I found it altogether alienating and desolate. The beauties of nature spoke little to me, and at Mount Hermon I found them particularly unseen and repressed.

Crossley Hall was the largest building on campus, a long, glowering redbrick Victorian building that could have been a factory. Salisbury and I were on the second floor; the toilets and showers, which stood in an open row, each exposed to its neighbor, were in the basement. Each student was required to do manual work for ten to twelve hours a week, according to Moody, whose quotations were an early analogue of Chairman Mao's little red book, inculcating in us "the dignity of manual labor." My task with four other boys was to pick the eyes out of potatoes. For the amount that was required each night the job took us a solid one hour and forty-five minutes, during which time we worked nonstop, singing, cracking jokes, but otherwise totally focused on our work, which began right after breakfast, at seven-fifteen, and ended at nine, just before our first class. Our supervisor was a short, stocky middle-aged man—Eddie Benny—a former army sergeant who treated us as recalcitrant, not to say unfit, recruits who had to be ridden constantly.

The daily routine was not only rigorous, it was also long, repetitive, and unrelieved by any of the urban amusements I had grown accustomed to in Cairo. Mount Hermon had a post office and a store, which was open only a few hours a day, where you could buy toothpaste, postcards and stamps, candy bars, and a tiny selection of books. Classes ran until noon. All meals included grace, and lunch was followed by announcements about sports and club meetings. At one we broke for two hours of sports.

Afternoon classes resumed from four till six. Dinner was immediately followed by a short break period for activities. Then we were confined ("locked in" would be a better phrase) in our rooms between eight and ten-fifteen for a two-and-a-quarter-hour study period, policed by floor officers. These were students elevated to this position not because of seniority or academic accomplishment but for mysterious reasons having to do with "leadership," a word I heard for the first time at Mount Hermon. Talking during study hall was forbidden. At ten-fifteen we were allowed a fifteen-minute bathroom and tooth-brushing seance, then lights out and silence.

Each student was allowed two Saturday afternoons per semester to go to Greenfield, a miserable little place about ten miles away. Other than that, except for sport team trips, we were imprisoned in Mount Hermon's stifling, claustrophobic regimen for three months. Phones were both scarce and rare. My parents called me once from New York before they returned to Cairo to break the news that "Dr. Rubendall and we thought that you should repeat your junior year, even though technically you passed Upper Five." My father came on the line. "If you graduate next spring you'll only be sixteen. That's too young to go to university. So you'll be at that school"—he often forgot the school's name—"for two years. You're a lucky fellow!" he said cheerily, and without irony. "I wish I had had your chances." I knew he meant this, although I realized that as someone who had struggled hard earlier in his life he also slightly resented the privileged life he was giving me. I remembered the shock I had felt a few weeks earlier in London, when, having put us and Albert in rooms and suites at the Savoy with no expense spared, and having taken us to fancy restaurants, theaters, or concerts every night (including the most memorable musical comedy I ever saw, *Kiss Me Kate* with Alfred Drake and Patricia Morison, and a super *H.M.S. Pinafore* with Martyn Green at the Savoy Theatre), he rounded on me angrily for spending sixpence to buy a theater program. "Do you think you're the son of a rich man, throwing money away like that?" he said harshly. When I turned to my mother for help and comfort, she explained, "He had to work so hard," leaving me speechless and shamed, unable to point out the disparity between the rage over sixpence and the vast expenses being disbursed in luxury hotels and restaurants.

"Goodbye, sweetheart. When you feel blue," my mother ended the call impetuously, "try not to be alone. Find someone and sit with them." Her voice started to quiver disturbingly. "And think of me and how much I miss you." The void around me increased. "Daddy says we must go. I love you, darling." Then, nothing. Why, I remember asking myself in the silence, had I been sent so far away to this dreadful, godforsaken place? But these thoughts were blown away by the dry New England voice of Mr. Fred McVeigh, the French teacher, in whose tiny Crossley apartment I had just received my parents' call. "Okay?" he asked me laconically as if to say, if you're done, please return to your room. Which I did, with the dawning realization that here were no lingering, suggestive communications but only cut-and-dry, mean-what-you-say exchanges, which in their own way, I discovered, were just as coded and complex as the ones I had supposedly left behind.

A day later I wandered over to see Mr. Edmund Alexander, the tennis coach and English teacher. Aside from Dr. Rubendall, "Ned" Alexander was the only other Cairo connection at Hermon. I had been told about him by Freddie Maalouf, a close family friend who had been a classmate of Ned's.

Small, dark, and wiry, wearing a white wool tennis sweater, Alexander was not at all welcoming. We stood facing each other across a tan station wagon parked in the driveway of his large white clapboard house. "Yes?" he asked curtly. "I'm from Cairo," I said enthusiastically. "Freddie Maalouf urged me to look you up and say hello." Not a line softened in his hard, leathery expression. "Oh, yes, Freddie Maalouf," was all he said, without a single additional comment. Undaunted I switched into Arabic, thinking that his and my native language might open up a more generous avenue of interaction. It had exactly the opposite effect. Stopping me in midsentence, Alexander held up his right hand, "No brother"—a very Arab locution, I thought, even though uttered in English—"no Arabic here. I left all that behind. Here we are Americans"—another Arabic turn of phrase, instead of "We're in America now"—"and we should talk and act like Americans."

It was worse than I thought. All I wanted was some friendly contact emanating from home, something to make an opening in the immense fabric of loneliness and separation that I felt surrounding me. Alexander revealed himself as not only unfriendly but something of an antagonist. He immediately placed me on the varsity–junior varsity tennis ladder, which meant weeks of challenge matches that protected the varsity from newcomers, and when those ended with the first onset of snow in early November I was established (unfairly I thought) on the JV list. Then for a year I had nothing more to do with Alexander, whom I would see with his wife, the senior Mount Hermon farmer's daughter, tooling around on campus in their station wagon, being as American as could be. I became a charge of the British JV coach and American history teacher, Hugh Silk, to whose "coaching" I brought all my residual anti-British sentiment. Even though I had won the top spot, he kept me at number 2 because, he once told me admonishingly, I wasn't fit to be number 1. Too many gestures, too many complaints, too many temperamental outbursts proved that I wasn't, he said, "equable enough."

Alexander's behavior proved the sagacity of my father's minatory observation that in the United States one should stay away from the Arabs. "They'll never do anything for you and will always pull you down." He illustrated this by putting out his hands flat and bringing them down to two feet from the floor. "They'll always be a hindrance. They neither keep what's good about Arab culture, nor show any solidarity with each other." He never gave examples, but the graphic figure he made with his hands and the definitive way he said it suggested no exception or qualification to the *aperçu*. Both Alexander's reaction to my banal overture and Silk's disciplinary iron fist–velvet glove approach turned out to be a more subtle form of moral pressure than what I had encountered in years of often brutal confrontations with British authority in my Egyptian or Palestinian schools. There, at least you knew that *they* were your enemies. At Hermon, the going currency was "common or shared values," care and concern for the student, interest in such intangibles as leadership and good citizenship, words of encouragement, admonishment, praise administered with a kind of fastidiousness I never dreamed of in VC, where war was a constant feature of daily life, with no palliatives either offered by the authorities or accepted by us, the students. Judgment in the United States was constant but concealed under a teasing fabric of softly rolling words and phrases, all of them in the end borne up by the unassailable moral authority of the teachers.

I also soon learned that you could never really find out why or on what basis you were judged, as I was, inadequate for a role or status that relatively objective indicators like grades, scores, or match victories entitled you to. While I was at Mount Hermon I was never appointed a floor officer, a table head, a member of the student council, or valedictorian (officially designated as number 1 in the class) and salutatorian (officially number 2) although I had the qualifications. And I never knew why. But I soon discovered that I would have to be on my guard against authority and that I needed to develop some mechanism or drive not to be discouraged by what I took to be efforts to silence or deflect me from being who I was rather than becoming who they wanted me to be. In the process I began a lifelong struggle and attempt to demystify the capriciousness and hypocrisy of a power whose authority depended absolutely on its ideological self-image as a moral agent, acting in good faith and with unimpeachable intentions. Its unfairness, in my opinion, depended principally on its prerogative for changing its bases of judgment. You could be perfect one day, but morally delinquent the next, even though your behavior was the same. For example, Silk and Alexander taught us not to say things like "Good shot!" to our tennis opponents. Never give them anything or concede anything; make your opponent work extra hard. But I recall that once during a close match against Williston Academy I was taken aside and reprimanded for having made my opponent pick up a ball that *may* have been closer to me. "Take the extra step," I was told, and was made silently furious at the shifting grounds for judgment. But what developed in my encounters with the largely hypocritical authority at Mount Hermon was a newfound will that had nothing to do with the "Edward" of the past but relied on the slowly forming identity of another self beneath the surface.

It soon became clear to me in my homesick disorientation that except for the words of advice in my weekly letter from my mother I had to deal with the daily routine at Hermon entirely on my own. Academically, the going was relatively easy and sometimes actually enjoyable. Whereas in VC we had only the dry material itself to deal with, none of it prettified or packaged, at Mount Hermon much that was required of us was prepared for by elaborate, simplifying instructions. Thus, our forceful and articulate English teacher (also the golf coach), Mr. Jack Baldwin, took us through one month of reading and analyzing *Macbeth* by minute studies of character, motivation, diction, figural language, plot pattern, all of the topics broken down into subgroups, steps, progressions that led cumulatively to a notebookful of short essays capped by a summary paragraph or two on the meaning of the play. Altogether more rational and thoughtful than in previous schools, this system invigorated and challenged me, particularly by comparison with the Anglo-Egyptian style of studying literary texts where all we were required to do was to articulate the very narrowly defined "correct" answers.

During the first weeks Baldwin assigned us an essay topic of a very unpromising sort: "On Lighting a Match." I dutifully went to the library and proceeded through encyclopedias, histories of industry, chemical manuals in search of what matches were; I then more or less systematically summarized and transcribed what I found and, rather proud of what I had compiled, turned it in. Baldwin almost immediately asked me to come and see him during his office hours, which was an entirely novel concept, since VC's teachers never had offices, let alone office hours. Baldwin's office was a cheery little place with postcard-covered walls, and as we sat next to each other on two easy chairs he complimented me on my research. "But is that the most interesting way to examine what happens when someone lights a match? What if he's trying to set fire to a forest, or light a candle in a cave, or, metaphorically, illuminate the obscurity of a mystery like gravity, the way

Newton did?" For literally the first time in my life a subject was opened up for me by a teacher in a way that I immediately and excitedly responded to. What had previously been repressed and stifled in academic study—repressed in order that thorough and correct answers be given to satisfy a standardized syllabus and a routinized exam designed essentially to show off powers of retention, not critical or imaginative faculties—was awakened, and the complicated process of intellectual discovery (and self-discovery) has never stopped since. The fact that I was never at home or at least at Mount Hermon, out of place in nearly every way, gave me the incentive to find my territory, not socially but intellectually.

The Browsing Room in the library basement provided me an escape from the often insufferable daily routine. It housed a record player (33 rpm records had just been introduced) and several bookshelves of novels, essays, and translations. I listened to a heavy three-record album of *The Marriage of Figaro* conducted by von Karajan, with Erich Kunz, Elisabeth Schwartzkopf, George London, and Irmgaard Seefried, over and over again; I read some of the many sets of American literary classics (Cooper's *The Leatherstocking Tales*, Twain's travels and novels, Hawthorne and Poe stories) with considerable excitement, since they revealed a complete, parallel world to the Anglo-Egyptian one in which I had been immersed in Cairo.

But the major breakthrough for me was in music, which, along with religion, played a substantial role in the school's programs. I tried out for and made the chapel choir, as well as the entirely secular glee club. We were all required to go to chapel services four times a week (including Sunday), where the organist, one Carleton L'Hommedieu, played a robust prelude and postlude, generally by Bach, but occasionally by second-rate American composers such as John Knowles Paine and George Chadwick. During one of these early services I found myself impulsively driven to go to speak to L'Hommy, as everyone called him behind his back, about piano lessons. My wasteful years at VC had taken the life out of my piano career, but listening to records and L'Hommy's playing inspired me to begin again.

L'Hommy was about five feet eight inches and cadaverously thin, given to plaid bow ties and striped shirts, always very well put together (no one ever saw him tieless or in shorts). He had a disconcertingly mincing walk, with his two exceptionally fine and slender hands often held out (like a rabbit's) as he tripped along, but at the keyboard he cut a very confident, even authoritative figure. I owe him the fact that he took me seriously and was never impatient with me as a pianist. Still, L'Hommy typified the cautious, often pedantic kind of teacher who would constantly try to hold the student back. His teaching style notwithstanding, his superb playing and music history teaching filled me with enthusiasm. Soon music was an all-consuming knowledge as well as experience: I listened, played, read, and read about it systematically (in the library's *Grove's Dictionary of Music and Musicians*) for the first time in my life, and I have never stopped. But there had to be, I now realize, a L'Hommedieu figure for me to react against, someone whose competence gave him the right to an on-the-whole "measured" (not wildly enthusiastic) judgment. We rarely saw eye to eye, but at least I had a hard taskmaster's ear to prod me on my way, *against* his, always held in check, as, for example, by his excessively polite "Oh yes, Ed! That was very nice. But don't you think that the insecurities of the opening could be fixed up," etc., after my playing the gavotte of the Bach G-minor English Suite for him, and toned down a bit. I remember one steamy Sunday afternoon practicing the gavotte with the windows open, and after working meticulously on the little things that my teacher had caught me with, I decided to let out all stops, playing the piece through passionately, the way I felt it. At that moment L'Hommy and Mr. Mirtz, an elderly English teacher, walked by the very window and obviously heard and saw me. "Hey, that's great, Ed," was Mirtz's unbuttoned expostulation. "Uh-uh," was L'Hommy's own rather disapproving response. I played on, giving myself even more steam. I remember that on the next meeting we switched abruptly from the Bach to (in my view) a dinky, tinkly C-major Haydn Sonata: "Solomon, the very fine British pianist, played it in his last recital." So there it was, his Solomon versus my Rubinstein.

The abrasive rough and tumble of my daily life in the six-hundred-student boarding school was nonetheless unpleasant and sometimes intolerable. There was no cultural background for friendship of the kind I had experienced at VC. I roomed with Bob Salisbury (who was one class below me) for two years, but we were never close in any but superficial ways. I felt that there was no depth, no ease, to the Americans, only the surface jokiness and anecdotal high spirits of teammates, which never satisfied me. There was always the feeling that what I missed with my American contemporaries was other languages, Arabic mainly, in which I lived and thought and felt along with English. They seemed less emotional, with little interest in articulating their attitudes and reactions. This was the extraordinary homogenizing power of American life, in which the same TV, clothes, ideological uniformity, in films, newspapers, comics, etc., seemed to limit the complex intercourse of daily life to an unreflective minimum in which memory has no role. I felt myself to be encumberingly full of memories, and the best friends I made at Mount Hermon were recent immigrants like Gottfried Brieger, an extremely ironic German student, and the socially awkward but intellectually curious Neil Sheehan.

The mythology of D. L. Moody dominated the school and made it the not-quite-first-rate place it was. There was the "dignity of manual labor" part, which seemed to me totally silly. There seemed to be unquestioned assent to the man's incredible importance: it was my first encounter with enthusiastic mass hypnosis by a charlatan, because except for two of us, not one teacher or student expressed the slightest doubt that Moody was worthy of the highest admiration. The only other dissenter was Jeff Brieger, who cornered me in the Browsing Room and said, "*Mais c'est dégoûtant,*" pointing at one of the many hagiographical studies we were meant to read.

And so it was with religion—the Sunday service, the Wednesday evening chapel, the Thursday noon sermon—dreadful, pietistic, nondenominational (I disliked that form of vacillation in particular), full of homilies, advice, how-to-live. Ordinary observations were encoded into Moodyesque sturdy Christianity in which words like "service" and "labor" acquired magical (but finally unspecifiable) meaning, to be repeated and intoned as what gave our lives "moral purpose." There had been nothing of that at VC; now it was a full load of the stuff. And no beatings, or bullying prefects. We were all Hermon boys, six hundred of us marching on after Moody and Ira Sankey, his faithful sidekick.

Clothes were a problem for me. Everyone wore corduroys, jeans, lumber jackets, boots. While in London my father had taken me to a Dickensian establishment next door to the Savoy called Thirty Shilling Tailors and bought me a very dark gray suit. I also had the VC assortment of gray slacks, a blazer, and a few dress shirts, all of them packed into two gigantic beige leather suitcases, along with a stamp collection, two albums of family photos, and a mounting pile of my mother's letters, each of which I preserved carefully. I had to write my parents to get permission to buy a more appropriate wardrobe and by October I was almost but not quite like everyone else. It took me another month to master the academic system completely, and by late November I was (to my surprise) astonishing my classmates with my intellectual performances. Why or how I did well I do not really know to this day, since following my mother's injunction not to be blue or alone I was both, and alienated from the extended stag sessions in the Blue Cloud (the smoking and pool room), or the little cliques that formed in Crossley, or around the various athletic teams. I longed to be back in Cairo; I kept calculating the time difference of seven hours (leaving my bedside alarm set on Cairo time), missing our family's Cairo food during school meals, an unappetizing regime that began with chicken à la king on Monday and ended with cold cuts and potato salad on Sunday night—and above all missing my mother, each of whose letters deepened the wound of abandonment and separation I felt. Sometimes I would pull out one of my massive suitcases from under the bed, leaf through the albums or letters and begin gently to cry, quickly reminding myself of my father's "Buck up boy; don't be a sissy. Pull your back up. Back, back."

I experienced the changing of seasons from fall to winter with dread, as something unfamiliar, having come from a basically warm and dry climate. I have never gotten over my feelings of revulsion for snow, which I first saw on my sixteenth birthday, November 1, 1951. Since that time, try as I might, I have found little to enjoy or admire about snow. For me snow signified a kind of death. But what I suffered from was the social vacancy of Mount Hermon's setting. I had spent all my life in two rich, teeming, historically dense metropolises, Jerusalem and Cairo, and now I was totally bereft of anything except the pristine woods, apple orchards, and the Connecticut River valley and hills stripped of their history. The nearest town of Greenfield has long symbolized for me the enforced desolation of middle America.

On the other hand, a small number of teachers and students, as well as subjects like literature and music, gave me moments of great pleasure, normally somewhat tinged with guilt. "Don't forget how much I miss and love you; your absence has made everything seem so empty," my mother would repeat down the years, making me feel that I couldn't, mustn't feel all right unless she was with me, and that it was a serious betrayal for me to do something that I liked doing if she wasn't present. This gave my American days a sense of impermanence, and even though I spent three quarters of the year in the United States, it was always Cairo to which I accorded stability.

GREGORY DJANIKIAN

Armenian-American poet Gregory Djanikian was born in Alexandria, Egypt, in 1949, and raised in Williamsport, Pennsylvania, where he moved with his family at age six. In "Immigrant Picnic," first published in *Poetry* magazine in July 1999 and later collected in *So I Will Till the Ground* (2007), he takes a lighthearted look at the jumbled tongues and traditions in evidence at a family Fourth of July barbecue. Djanikian's earlier collections of poetry include *Man in the Middle* (1984), *Falling Deeply into America* (1989), *About Distance* (1995), and *Years Later* (2000). He teaches English and creative writing at the University of Pennsylvania.

Immigrant Picnic

It's the Fourth of July, the flags
are painting the town,
the plastic forks and knives
are laid out like a parade.

And I'm grilling, I've got my apron,
I've got potato salad, macaroni, relish,
I've got a hat shaped
like the state of Pennsylvania.

I ask my father what's his pleasure
and he says, "Hot dog, medium rare,"
and then, "Hamburger, sure,
what's the big difference,"
as if he's really asking.

I put on hamburgers *and* hot dogs,
slice up the sour pickles and Bermudas,
uncap the condiments. The paper napkins
are fluttering away like lost messages.

"You're running around," my mother says,
"like a chicken with its head loose."

"Ma," I say, "you mean *cut off*,
loose and *cut off* being as far apart
as, say, *son* and *daughter*."

She gives me a quizzical look as though
I've been caught in some impropriety.
"I love you and your sister just the same," she says.
"Sure," my grandmother pipes in,
"you're both our children, so why worry?"

That's not the point I begin telling them,
and I'm comparing words to fish now,
like the ones in the sea at Port Said,
or like birds among the date palms by the Nile,
unrepentantly elusive, wild.

"Sonia," my father says to my mother,
"what the hell is he talking about?"
"He's on a ball," my mother says.

"That's *roll*!" I say, throwing up my hands,
"as in hot dog, hamburger, dinner roll. . . ."

"And what about *roll out the barrels*?" my mother asks,
and my father claps his hands, "Why sure," he says,
"let's have some fun," and launches

into a polka, twirling my mother
around and around like the happiest top,

and my uncle is shaking his head, saying
"You could grow nuts listening to us,"

and I'm thinking of pistachios in the Sinai
burgeoning without end,
pecans in the South, the jumbled
flavor of them suddenly in my mouth,
wordless, confusing,
crowding out everything else.

THOM GUNN

In this excerpt from his autobiographical essay "My Life Up to Now" (included in the 1982 collection *The Occasions of Poetry*), Thom Gunn (1929–2004) captures a moment of transition. Acclaimed early on as a poet associated with the so-called Movement, the group of English poets who espoused a formalist and anti-romantic approach, Gunn after settling in the United States in 1954 would evolve well beyond the manner and subject matter of his early work in such volumes as *Touch* (1967), *Moly* (1971), and *The Passages of Joy* (1982). Perhaps best known for his poems confronting the devastation of the AIDS epidemic in *The Man with Night Sweats* (1992), Gunn forged a singular poetic identity fusing English verse traditions and American realities. He was, in the words of his friend August Kleinzahler, "an Elizabethan poet in modern guise, though there's nothing archaic, quaint, or sepia-toned about his poetry."

from
My Life Up to Now

A lso at Cambridge I met Mike Kitay, an American, who became the leading influence on my life, and thus on my poetry. It is not easy to speak of a relationship so long-lasting, so deep, and so complex, nor of the changes it has gone through, let alone of the effect it has had on my writing. But his was, from the start, the example of the searching worrying improvising intelligence playing upon the emotions which in turn reflect back on the intelligence. It was an example at times as rawly passionate as only Henry James can dare to be.

In my last year at Cambridge, I edited an anthology of undergraduate (and some graduate) poetry of the previous two years. It says something about the literary climate in Cambridge at the time: I was not alone in being influenced by the metaphysical poets of the seventeenth century, for example. The prevailing tone is clever, bookish, and spirited.

After I left Cambridge I spent some months in Rome on a studentship (though I came back to Cambridge for the following spring and summer to stay in the Central Hotel). In front of a new notebook I wrote:

> A style is built with sedentary toil
> And constant imitation of great masters.

The master I chose to imitate that winter was the author of these lines, Yeats. Little got finished, as a result: Yeats was too hypnotic an influence, and my poetry became awash with his mannerisms. Of the great English poets he is probably the second most disastrous influence after Milton. The skills to be learned are too closely tied in with the mannerisms.

I found that the only way to get to the United States, where I intended to eventually join Mike (who had to go into the air force) was to get a fellowship at some university. An American friend, Donald Hall, wrote suggesting that I should apply for a creative-writing fellowship at Stanford University, where I would work under Yvor Winters, with whose very name I was unfamiliar. I applied, and was fortunate enough to get it, so in 1954 I set out for America, spending my twenty-fifth birthday in mid-Atlantic and landing in New York during a hurricane. What followed was a beautiful year, during which I wrote most of what was to become my second book. I had a room, for fifteen dollars a month, at the top of an old shingled house on Lincoln Avenue in Palo Alto. The eaves stretched down beside the window where I sat at my desk; I could watch the squirrels leaping about on it as I wrote.

I went several times into San Francisco. It was still something of an open city, with whore-houses flourishing for anybody to see. A straight couple took me to my first gay bar, the Black Cat. It excited me so much that the next night I returned there on my own. And I remember walking along Columbus Avenue on another day, thinking that the ultimate happiness would be for Mike and me to settle in this city. It was foggy and I remember exactly where I thought this, right by a cobbler's that still stands there.

But for most of that year I was some thirty miles away down the Peninsula, and the person I had most to do with was Yvor Winters. It was wonderful luck for me that I should have worked with him at this particular stage of my life, rather than earlier when I would have been more impressionable or later when I would have been less ready to learn. As it was, he acted as a fertilizing agent, and opened the way to many poets I had known little of— most immediately Williams and Stevens, whom he insisted I read without delay. He was a man of great personal warmth with a deeper love for poetry than I have ever met in anybody else. The love was behind his increasingly strict conception of what a poem should and should not be. It would have seemed to him an insult to the poem that it could be used as a gymnasium for the ego. Poetry was an instrument for exploring the truth of things, as far as human beings can explore it, and it can do so with a greater verbal exactitude than prose can manage. Large generalized feelings (as in Whitman) were out, and rhetoric was the beginning of falsification. However, taken as I was with the charm and authority of the man and with the power of his persuasiveness, it already seemed to me that his conception of a poem was too rigid, excluding in practice much of what I could not but consider good poetry, let us say 'Tom o' Bedlam' and 'The force that through the green fuse drives the flower'. The rigidity seemed to be the result of what I can only call an increasing distaste for the particulars of existence.

The Sense of Movement, then, was a much more sophisticated book than my first collection had been, but a much less independent one. There is a lot of Winters in it, a fair amount of Yeats, and a great deal of raw Sartre (strange bedfellows!). It was really a second work of apprenticeship. The poems make much use of the word 'will'. It was a favourite word of Sartre's, and one that Winters appreciated, but they each meant something very different by it, and would have understood but not admitted the other's use of it. What *I* meant by it was, ultimately, a mere Yeatsian wilfulness. I was at my usual game of stealing what could be of use to me.

It is still a very European book in its subject-matter. I was much taken by the American myth of the motorcyclist, then in its infancy, of the wild man part free spirit and part hoodlum, but even that I started to anglicize: when I thought of doing a series of motorcyclist poems I had Marvell's mower poems in my mind as model.

At the end of the year I went, for the second time, to Texas by rail, but this time stopped off for a few days in Los Angeles. It was mid-1955, and Los Angeles was a place of wonder to me: it was already the city of *Rebel*

Without a Cause, a movie that had not yet been made. The place was as foreign and exotic to me as ever Venice or Rome had been—the huge lines of palms beside the wide fast streets, the confident shoddiness of Hollywood Boulevard, and the dirty glamour of a leather bar called the Cinema, which was on Santa Monica Boulevard, almost a part of a closed gas station and right across from a vast cemetery.

I had been given an introduction to Christopher Isherwood. He asked me over to the set of a movie for which he had written the script, *Diane*, starring Lana Turner as Diane de Poitiers. He was all warmth and kindness to the rather pushy English boy who had turned up out of the blue, and ended up by asking me to a dinner he had already been invited to, at Gerald Heard's. I had my own ideas about Heard, and argued brashly with him for much of the evening.

I can hardly say that meeting Isherwood was the start of the influence he has had on me, but it strengthened it and made it personal. In his talk, as in his books, he is able to present complexity through the elegance of simplicity, but without ever reducing it *to* mere simplicity. And such a manner was just what I needed to learn from.

I joined Mike in San Antonio, Texas, where I taught for a year. English friends thought it sounded an amusing place to be: we found it distinctly boring, starting with the hot and humid climate. However, the sand storms were of interest to one who had never seen them. Also, I got a motorcycle which I rode for about one month, and it was in San Antonio that I heard Elvis Presley's songs first and that I saw James Dean's films. I wrote only three poems during the whole year.

Then, full of nostalgia for the smell of eucalyptus in the dry sunshine of the San Francisco Peninsula, I dragged Mike back with me to do graduate work at Stanford, where I had got a teaching assistantship. On the way, while he stayed with his parents, I spent a few weeks in New York, beginning a lifelong romance with it. If England is my parent and San Francisco is my lover, then New York is my own dear old whore, all flash and vitality and history.

Back at Stanford, Winters encouraged me to attend his workshops regularly, but I went to them less and less, from something of an instinct for self-preservation. The man was too strong; and for all my gratitude to him I knew

I had, if necessary, to write my own bad poetry and explore its implications for myself. And I never did get a PhD. Most of the graduate work began to seem pointless after a while, and I had already decided not to go on with it when I was lucky enough to get an offer to teach English at the University of California at Berkeley, in 1958.

I lived for a couple of years in Oakland, a drab town next to Berkeley, then in 1960 spent several months on leave in Berlin, where I wrote the last poems to be included in my next book. When I returned, it was to San Francisco, across the Bay, and I still live there. San Francisco is a provincial town that goes in and out of fashion, but it is never boring and has much of the feel of the big city without trying to master you as the big city does. It leaves you alone: sitting in my yard, now, I could be a hundred miles away from San Francisco.

CHARLES SIMIC

Born in Belgrade in 1938 on the eve of World War II, Charles Simic experienced a childhood of chaos, displacement, and pervasive violence. "My family, like so many others," he writes in his autobiography, *A Fly in the Soup* (2000), "got to see the world for free, thanks to Hitler's wars and Stalin's takeover of East Europe." His family was finally reunited in America in the early 1950s, as he recounts here in a passage that makes clear the special perspective that Simic brought to his experience of post-war American culture. He would emerge as a poet with an utterly distinctive voice in such collections as *Dismantling the Silence* (1971), *Unending Blues* (1986), *Hotel Insomnia* (1992), and *Jackstraws* (1999).

from
A Fly in the Soup

The most important thing we did in Paris was study English. My mother found out that there were free night classes, twice a week, given by the World Church Service. All three of us went. Previously, I don't believe I knew ten words of English. My mother knew some, but not much. In any case, here we were in a class with a bunch of refugees from all over Eastern Europe and a very friendly American minister as a teacher. I worked hard for once. I liked the language immediately.

We began buying the *Saturday Evening Post* and *Look* magazine to practice reading. I understood little of what I read, but the pictures and advertisements were very interesting. The American colors were so bright. One didn't see such yellows, reds, and oranges in Europe. The pictures of children terrified me; they looked so clean, so happy. The girls often had freckles. They smiled a lot. Everybody smiled. The old people with perfect teeth, the movie stars, the politicians, too, all had their mouths stretched from ear to ear. In

France nobody smiled like that. Certainly not the barbers. I remember a Norman Rockwell–like cover of a little redhead kid in a barber's chair with a smiling barber bending over him with scissors. The barbers in Paris gave me dirty looks when I walked in to have one of my rare haircuts.

When we went to the American Embassy for the obligatory physical examination given to every prospective immigrant, I expected the doctor to be grinning. He looked glum while he listened to my chest. I must be very sick, I told myself. None of the nurses smiled either. It was clear; I'd be rejected. My brother and mother will go to America, and I'll stay here in France wasting away from some incurable disease in a crowded and filthy state hospital.

Weeks passed before we got the results of the examination. In the meantime, we worried and turned the pages of American magazines, studying the cars, the baked hams out of a can, the rich, many-layered desserts. The summer was approaching. We walked all the time. One evening, just after dusk, on the fashionable Avenue Victor Hugo, we saw Prince Paul, the brother of the assassinated Yugoslav King who himself was deposed in 1941 in an act that got Yugoslavia into the war. My mother went up to him to say we were Yugoslavs. I remember an impeccably dressed, elderly man bowing stiffly to my mother and asking me my name. I could tell he didn't care one way or another what it was.

In those days, both in Paris and United States, we ran into famous politicians, people who were responsible, if anyone was solely responsible, for Yugoslavia's troubles. Here, sitting in somebody's kitchen slicing salami, would be a face you remembered from an old newspaper, signing some treaty with Hitler or Mussolini. It was hard to believe they were the same people. They looked pretty ordinary and talked nonsense just like everybody else. They expected to return next week and no later than the week after. Their villas and bank accounts would be restored. Great crowds would welcome them, shouting, "You were right! You were always right!" They didn't like one bit what my mother and I had to say about Yugoslavia. They insisted that nothing had changed since they left. They felt sorry for us falling so obviously for Commie propaganda.

In early June of 1954 we received our American visas. It took several more weeks to book our passage. The World Church Service paid our way and in style. We were to sail on the *Queen Mary* on August 5. What excitement! "You'll be starting a whole new life," everybody said. Even our grocer was sure it was going to be wonderful.

Our remaining days in Paris dragged on. My mother took us to museums daily so we'd remember the great art treasures of France. We also started eating modest meals in modest neighborhood restaurants. At night we went to the movies, watching the American films from the first rows, looking for clues to our future.

In school I had flunked everything except drawing and music, so I avoided my friends. I was ashamed of myself. After the terror of waiting for the results of my physical, I felt somewhat more optimistic but not entirely. Who could be sure I was not going to be a complete failure in America?

The *Queen Mary* was all lit up the night we boarded it. It was huge and a veritable labyrinth on the inside. We were traveling in the cheapest class, but the accommodations seemed luxurious to us. It took a couple of days to discover that we were not supposed to leave our class. There was a door with a sign that spelled it out. I snuck through it once, walked through the magnificent Cabin Class, and made my way to the First Class. There were shops and restaurants there as elegant as anything they have in Paris. I saw ladies in evening gowns cut so low their breasts were about to fall out, men in dark suits smoking cigars, little children who wore neckties and looked snotty. I remember a bejeweled old woman in a wheelchair pushed by a very beautiful nurse in white. It didn't take long before a steward spotted me ogling and directed me politely back to the Tourist Class.

We had no complaints about our class. Far from it. Our cabins were small and windowless but otherwise comfortable. The food was excellent, and there was a new film shown every day. Everybody was friendly and in a good mood, especially at the beginning of the trip.

A day or two after we left Le Havre there was a storm. It started during the night. The ship heaved and creaked as if starting to come apart. It was impossible to sleep, and many got seasick. In the morning only a few showed up for breakfast. By the afternoon, with the storm still raging, the movie theater was empty. They showed the movie anyway. The boat rocked, the waves pounded its sides, but the people on the screen went on talking with perfect composure.

My mother was back in the cabin throwing up, but my brother and I refused to stay in bed. We liked the food so much, we didn't allow ourselves to get sick. We roamed our section of the ship. It was difficult to walk, of course. We had to hold onto the walls and railings. It never occurred to us to be scared. We sat in the empty lounge for hours watching the waves crest and slide under the ship. There was a lot of water out there. It was absolutely amazing. We couldn't get over it.

The next day the storm subsided. The sky was cloudless. The chart outside the purser's office indicated the progress of our voyage. We were more than halfway across. The next day we were even closer. We kept asking the crew when we would be able to see the land.

The sighting occurred at night. By the time we rose in the morning the land was clearly visible. We were speeding into the New York harbor. After breakfast everyone was on deck. We began to make out details on the land. There was a road on which a car was traveling. Everybody kept pointing to it! Next, there were some neat white houses. One even had laundry hung out to dry in its backyard. Then a fishing boat came by. There were a couple of black men on deck, waving. Pretty soon there were small boats everywhere. We could see the Statue of Liberty. I think a cheer went up.

What stunned me, left me speechless with excitement, was the first sight of Manhattan with its skyscrapers. It was just like in the movies, except this was the real thing. The enormous city before us with its docks, its big ships, its traffic on the outer highways, its billboards and crowds. My father was out there somewhere waiting for us. We tried to spot him. We didn't realize we would have to go back down and spend hours clearing immigration. With our past experiences of border crossing, we were a bit nervous. You never knew. What if they pulled a surprise on us and sent us back to Yugoslavia?

My father waited past the customs. A tall man. We recognized him from the pictures. We waved. He waved back. He was wearing a white suit under which we could see a blue shirt and suspenders. Very American, we thought. He smoked a long thin cigar and smiled in a friendly way.

Then the confusion of embraces and kisses, the emotion of his seeing my brother for the first time, the search for a porter, the wait for a taxi, and everybody talking at the same time. It was all incredible and wonderful! The trash on the streets, the way people were dressed, the tall buildings, the dirt, the heat, the yellow cabs, the billboards and signs. It was nothing like Europe. It was terrifically ugly and beautiful at the same time! I liked America immediately.

In the hotel room another surprise awaited us. There was a television set. While my mother and father talked, my brother and I sat on the floor and watched a Dodgers-Giants game. I remember who was playing because my brother fell in love with baseball that afternoon, and with the Dodgers in particular, and insisted on being outfitted immediately with a baseball cap and glove.

That evening, after a stroll around Times Square and Broadway, we went to a restaurant where we dined on hamburgers, french fries, and milk shakes, followed by banana splits. I don't know what my mother thought of the meal, but we loved it. American food is kid's food, and no kid in the world can resist it. "Remember this day," my father kept saying. Indeed, it was August 10, 1954. Tomorrow he was going to buy us American clothes and shoes and all sorts of other things.

Who could possibly sleep? My mother and brother did. My father and I watched TV and talked. It was still early. "Let's go for a walk," he said. The hotel was only a couple of blocks away from Times Square. We found ourselves there again, watching the crowd. I felt comfortable with my father right away. He never treated anyone younger differently. He talked to everybody the same way. He would address a five-year-old selling lemonade on the street as if he were the head of a major corporation.

We ended up in a jazz club that night. It was called the Metropole, on Broadway and Forty-eighth Street. A long narrow room with a bar on one side and small booths on the other. The bandstand was just above the bar. There were six black musicians blasting away.

We took a booth, and my father ordered some whiskey for himself and ginger ale for me. This must have been some day for him too. I was all absorbed in the music. This was definitely better than any radio. It was heaven.

We stayed a long time. My father even gave me a few sips of his whiskey.

Between sets we talked. I told him about my life, and he told me about his. This was just the beginning. We spent many nights together like that. My father loved the nightlife. He was happiest in bars and restaurants. In the company of friends and with something good to eat and drink, he'd glow. It was pure joy to be around him then. He was full of life and interesting talk. I didn't want to go to bed, but we finally had to.

"This is wonderful," he said. He always wanted to come to America and had a chance to do so when, in 1926, he won some kind of scholarship to Columbia University, but then he didn't, to his everlasting regret and for reasons that were entirely trivial. "Even in prison in Italy," he told me, "I sat in solitary confinement dreaming of New York."

One morning the Germans took him out into the courtyard at daybreak, and he figured they were going to shoot him. There was a squad of armed soldiers and an officer with them, but then a photographer with a tripod came and took several pictures of my father standing against the wall. He had no idea what for.

"I want to see New York before I die," he told the Germans as they were leading him back to his cell.

My father was still employed by the same telephone company he used to work for back in Yugoslavia. Their headquarters were in Chicago, but he spent all his time on the road. Whenever one of their client companies needed more telephone lines, my father was sent to examine the facilities, draw up the blueprints, and stay there until the job was completed. As it was, he spent the years 1950–54 moving from one small town to another, spending in each place anywhere from a couple of months to a year. He had no home. At the time we arrived, he was working in Middletown, New York. After his vacation was over, and having found an apartment for us in Queens, he went back to Middletown. I went with him.

The idea was, I would study English on my own and not enroll in school till the second semester. We would spend the week in Middletown and come to New York on weekends. That's what we did. I stayed in the rooming house, while my father worked. In the evenings we ate out then either went to the movies or came back to our room to talk and drink wine.

My father, as was his custom, had a lot of books, two trunks full. At that time his ambition was to write a critical history of Marxism, so most of the books were on that subject. He read late into the night and took voluminous notes. He made occasional comments about the project as he told me about his life. There was his life, and there was Marxism and fascism and everything else. He was trying to make sense of it all.

His stories were tremendously entertaining. He was also interested in my own. We had a lot of catching up to do. What made it exciting for me was that for the first time in my life I could be absolutely frank. I told him everything, and he did the same to me. We were both, in our own way, very lonely people. The ten years that we didn't see each other made it difficult to reestablish our relationship on a father-son basis. It was much easier to be friends, to talk like friends. When people overheard us they were shocked. "The way that boy speaks to his father!"

During this time he was teaching me English. The first book I read in English was Whittaker Chambers's *Witness*. I don't remember a thing about it today, but at that time it gave me the confidence necessary to attempt to read others. When in New York, my father would spend Saturday mornings going from bookstore to bookstore. He bought books, and it was understood I could pick some for myself. I did that often, picking out something much too difficult for me. I read Hemingway and Twain and God-knows-what-else! It was a slow process, since I had to look up a lot of words in the dictionary, and there were long passages that I simply didn't understand. Still, I had so much time to myself while he was at work.

My return to school terrified me. It had been a long time since I was properly a student. I had no confidence in my ability. I also had no idea what grade I'd be in. I would see young people my age going to school, and I would shudder. The way I spoke English anybody could tell immediately I was a foreigner.

The closer Christmas came and the beginning of the second semester, the more miserable I became. My father was still a lot of fun, but the mood at home was tense. It was clear my parents were not getting along. The ten years of separation, plus their completely different personalities, made them strangers. Whatever one liked, the other did not. My mother, for example, had no interest in things American. She had already found some Yugoslavs, was seeing them, and, aside from wanting to improve her English so that she could get a job, she had no curiosity about this country. Since my brother and I sided with my father, there were constant conflicts. She grew jealous. "You don't love me anymore," she'd blurt out. "We have more fun with him," we'd make the mistake of saying.

Still, for a while appearances were preserved. We sat around the dinner table making plans for the future. My brother and I would go to college and that sort of thing. I had my doubts, but I said nothing.

The high school I was supposed to attend was in Elmhurst, Queens. My parents had gone there to make inquiries. I was invited to come shortly after the New Year, before the classes resumed, and take some tests so I could be placed in the proper grade.

I didn't sleep the night before the appointment. My father was back in Middletown. It was a windy and bitterly cold morning, and the walk from our place to the school was very long. I was numb with cold and terror when I arrived.

As usually happens in life, things turned out quite differently from what I had anticipated. Luckily, there was no question of writing to Belgrade or Paris for a transcript. The European education system is very different, and it would be very difficult to interpret such a document whenever it eventually arrived. So they made it simple. They gave me an IQ test, and, as for the rest, they just asked me to write down the subjects I had studied in Europe.

That was easy enough. I wrote down things like algebra, physics, French, Russian, world history, biology. They asked me a couple of questions in each area and in the process found out that in Paris we had read Homer and Virgil. That did it. I was made a second-semester junior on the spot. The whole process did not take more than a couple of hours.

I was greatly relieved. I still had some apprehension about actually doing the schoolwork, but this was a miraculous beginning. My love for America was infinite. No more Monsieur Bertrand and his crummy jokes at my expense. Even the Yugoslav teachers had given me hard times after I stayed back. School was not for dummies like me, they reminded me daily. Years later, I heard they were incredulous when told that I had gone to college. "That little bum! Don't Americans have any sense?"

The school itself was amazing. Newton High School may have been the model for the movie *Blackboard Jungle*. I had met all kinds of juvenile delinquents in my life, but never so many. This was like reform school. The teachers had their hands full maintaining discipline. If you kept your mouth shut, as I did, you passed all your subjects.

I remember a large class in something called "Hygiene." I sat in the last row playing chess with a black kid. Up front the teacher was arguing about something with a couple of punks in leather jackets. That's the way it was every day, half of the class harassing the teacher while the other half daydreamed. I never did any work. Nobody called on me. I don't think I even had a clue what I was supposed to do, but I kept my mouth shut. I received a B for my silence at the end of the semester.

The other classes were more or less the same. In English the old lady who was our teacher kept trying to read aloud one of Edgar Allan Poe's tales. The class, against her objections, provided the sound effects. There were the sinister creaking doors and coffin lids, clocks ticking at midnight, and the wind blowing through the ruined tower. She pleaded with us to stop. When we were reading *Julius Caesar*, it was the same. More sound effects and muffled laughter. I came to see her once after class to ask for an extension on my term paper, blaming my delay on the ignorance of the English language. "Don't worry," the poor woman told me. "I know you're a good boy." I certainly was. I behaved in class and did my homework. The girls interested me, but I was too shy to speak to them in my heavily accented English. As for the boys, many of them were trouble bound, and I'd had enough of that for a while. Also, I had no time to hang around. I was working after school and all day Saturdays.

It was a terrific job as far as I was concerned. I worked for a small company that supplied special screws for airplanes. I helped the stock clerk. I counted screws. The screws were very expensive, so you had to be super-careful counting them. I was. It wasn't difficult, and I got paid. I bought a cheap phonograph and my first jazz records. On Sundays I went to Manhattan and the movies. I was beginning to feel very comfortable in America.

The big event that spring was buying a television set. It was a huge twenty-one-inch model that my father and I had a hell of a time lugging from the store. Once we turned it on, it stayed on. We watched television all the time. It was good for our English, everybody said. It certainly was. I stopped reading books and just watched TV. Everything interesting from breakfast shows to late, late movies. I think that it was while watching television that my brother and I started speaking English to each other. We heard certain expressions on TV and wanted to use them immediately.

I am surprised how quickly we felt at home in the United States. My father's attitude had a lot to do with it. He thought America was the most exciting place on earth and wanted us to share his excitement. He had no desire to go back to Yugoslavia. He wanted us to be real Americans. My mother, on the other hand, had always retained the conviction that Europeans were superior. She missed Europe. I did not. I was a flop there. Here I had managed to finish a grade. I had a job, and summer was coming.

Then we had another surprise. My father's request for a transfer to the company's headquarters, which he didn't expect to be approved, suddenly came through. We were moving to Chicago. From now on we would live together, see him all the time, and have a normal life.

I wasn't entirely happy about being uprooted again, nor was my mother. She worried about leaving New York, where there were more opportunities to find work in the music business. She was trying to resume her career as a voice teacher but had no luck. Still, she also desired some kind of regular family life. There really was not much choice. It was decided that my father and I would go first, find an apartment, and then my mother and brother would follow.

JUDITH ORTIZ COFER

Born in Hormigueros, Puerto Rico, in 1952, Judith Ortiz Cofer came to mainland America at four. She moved with her family into a house in Paterson, New Jersey, her father having just joined the navy and been assigned a post at the Brooklyn Navy Yard. Though forced to learn English quickly in order to help her mother, Cofer would return to Puerto Rico periodically when her father went to sea. The sense of a dual identity common to many immigrants must have been especially marked in someone who was able to travel back and forth with relative ease between her old and adopted lands. As she writes, "I am a composite of two worlds. . . . I lived with . . . conflictive expectations: the pressures from my father to become very well versed in the English language and the Anglo customs, and from my mother not to forget where we came from. That is something that I deal with in my work all the time." This poem, from her 1995 collection *Reaching for the Mainland*, is a fine example of Cofer's ability to convey lucidly the most jarring aspects of the immigrant experience.

Arrival

When we arrived, we were expelled
like fetuses
from the warm belly of an airplane.
Shocked by the cold,
we held hands as we skidded
like new colts on the unfamiliar ice.
We waited winter in a room sealed
by our strangeness.
Watching the shifting tale of the streets,

our urge to fly toward the sun
etched in nailprints like tiny wings
in the gray plaster of the windowsill,
we hoped all the while
that lost in the city's monochrome
there were colors we couldn't yet see.

MARIE ARANA

Marie Arana (born in 1949) spent the first ten years of her life in Peru—a childhood she describes as "rooted in the Andean dust." Her mother, a classical violinist, and her father, an engineer for a multinational corporation, each embracing the cultures of old and adopted lands respectively, aggravated the already considerable sense of displacement Arana felt: she was the "fifty-fifty" to their "wholes." In the long run it worked to her advantage; forcing herself to adapt to the strong cultural presence of each parent meant she was able to accommodate herself to *other* cultures. After studying Russian at Northwestern, she earned a certificate in Mandarin through Yale's program in China in 1976, and was awarded the following year an M.A. in linguistics from the University of Hong Kong. On coming back to the United States she began a career in publishing, eventually becoming editor-in-chief of the book supplement of the *Washington Post*. During this time she wrote her memoir *American Chica* (2001), from which this excerpt is drawn. Arana originally arrived in Rawlins, Wyoming, where her maternal grandparents lived. Determined to become a native and speak like one, her first American ambition was to "learn how to spit."

from
American Chica

There were no swans at the Dutch Maid Motel on Route 22 in Springfield, New Jersey. The discount emporia rose up beside it like floats in a carnival day parade. MOTHER GOOSE SHOES, said one billboard, and behind it—as though to deliver on an uncle's warning—a giant's shoe, big as a building, with smiling gringos streaming through its doors. BIG BOY LUMBER, said another sign, and looming above it, a musclebound Gog in a red plaid shirt with his head shaved clean as a tub.

The Dutch Maid Motel was shell pink with white lace in its windows, a picket fence leading the way. Two yellow-haired dolls in frilled aprons framed the front lawn marquee, cocking their wooden toes and bending over so that their underpants showed. In the back garden, freshly planted shrubs stood at attention, and white lawn chairs waited for swimmers to clamber out of the pool. It was the antithesis of anything we had ever known in Wyoming. We'd never seen a highway so busy, with so many people and such enormous stores. We had never seen such shiny long cars, such a webwork of roads. We looked around for the familiar: open prairie, cattle, horses, and boots. But none of these was in evidence. This America was different.

We had come to New Jersey for the public schools. Not because it would be the most convenient commute for my father. It was not. It took nearly an hour for the hulking Erie-Lackawanna to cart a clamoring army of worsted wool to the Hudson River every weekday morning. Nor were we there, as far as we could tell, because of my mother. She didn't have a relative within a five-state radius.

"Because of the public schools?" said Papi, scratching his head with wonder. To him, the notion of building a life around children was alien, bizarre, inexplicable. In Peru, it had been the other way around: children built lives around their parents. The elders defined the world.

While Papi traveled to Hoboken on the lurching, squealing Erie-Lackawanna, then ferried across the Hudson to Fulton Street, snapping a newspaper as smartly as any itinerant company man, Mother sallied forth with school ratings and a real-estate map in hand.

George and I headed for the Dutch Maid's lobby, where we'd discovered how well we were going to fare in these United States. "See that?" I said to George, pointing a finger at Lucy and Desi in the lobby's box. "She's the wife, and her husband speaks Spanish. Their family's just like us!" "See that?" said my brother, as Hoss Cartwright swung a leg over a horse. "He's a guy with a ranch, just like Grandpa. This place is gonna be great!" Only Vicki reserved opinion, peering at us from a far corner, seeing that those lambent shadows bore no resemblance to the trawl of highway outside.

"Ey! *Mangia, mangia!*" crowed an Italian waitress with high hair in the Howard Johnson across the road from the lumber giant. Her lips were beige patent, her eyes winged like Nefertiti's, her black hairdo leaning like a tower about to crash. "You people *paesan*? You just get hee or what?"

"No, no," said Papi, flashing a smile and flirting. "That's Spanish you're hearing."

"Zat right?" She stared at us for a while, cracking her gum, thinking it over. "Don't hee mucha that around hee. I don't speak Italian myself, but for a minute, you sounded like *paesan'*." She walked away, keeling against the cant of her hair, wiping her hands on her hips.

I was living on strawberry milk shakes. Was there a nectar so silky, so sweet on the tongue, so satisfying to the eye in its prettily tapered glass? Afternoons would come and Mother would bring hot dogs and french fries wrapped in wax paper, with mustard and relish on the side. George tore in happily. He was pudgy now, constantly eating. The yellow pills he'd been taking ever since Boston had made him jolly and fat. He polished off his frankfurters, praising their tidy ingenuity, but I could hardly take more than a bite. It would take time before I could eat from cardboard, sitting on the edge of a bed, with paper spread out on my knees. I longed for fragrant *sopa de albahaca* from my abuelita's table, with her well-ironed napkins and over-size spoons. As it was, I consumed very little in that wholesale paradise. I sat in the pink motel, awaited my fluted shakes, checked on Desi's progress in his wife's country, listened to the thrum of the road, and read neon messages that squiggled from the giant's chest like fortunes down a *bruja*'s braid. *Shop here, America. We build you.*

Not Paramonga, not Cartavio, not Rawlins could have prepared me for Summit, New Jersey. Mother chose it for the excellence of its schools, but she might as well have chosen it for its polarity to everything we'd known. Moving from Lima to Summit was like wandering into Belgrade from Bombay, the differences were so marked.

It was a small-town suburb of New York City, bedroom community for company presidents and businessmen. Split between Anglos and Italians, the residents were largely prosperous, but there was a hierarchy to that prosperity I was slow to see. The rich were the commuters, WASPs who had graduated from the Ivy League, played golf at the Beacon Hill Country Club, shopped at Brooks Brothers, and sent their children to prep schools nearby: Pingry, Lawrenceville, Kent Place. The less rich were the Italians—merchants, landscapers, restaurateurs, mechanics—who serviced the town. There was another notable category: scientists who worked in nearby Bell Labs or Ciba-Geigy, and their brainy, musical children. But there were no indigents: no beggars in the streets, no *señoras* hawking fruit.

Ours was the only Hispanic family. There were few Jews. The relative sizes of the town's churches told the story. Summit Presbyterian was the largest, most prestigious. That imposing stone structure sat squarely in the middle of town, and the rich could be seen strutting in and out of it in their finery. The Catholic Church of St. Theresa, with steps sweeping up to its portals as if they led to salvation itself, was situated several blocks away, next to its own school. The Episcopal, Methodist, and Baptist churches were scattered about town, signaling lesser lights.

By June we were in Troy Court, a cluster of brick apartment buildings on New England Avenue. It was a modest district, on the other side of town from the mansions, and it would have been clear to anyone but us children that it was home to people on the fringes of society. There were strings of apartments up and down the avenue, where transients came and went, and old ramshackle houses, where nurses and waitresses lived.

Mother had her eye on a house in the middle range of the Summit spectrum, but it would be months before the owners vacated it. She had decided we would be wise to wait. When we moved into the apartment, it was empty save for an upright piano, the one thing we had bought on Route 22. We took our meals on it, plinking while we chewed, sleeping on the floor, waiting for our crate to arrive.

Within a week, we had recreated Lima on New England Avenue—*huacos* on the shelves, llama skins draped through the rooms. The display looked odd, even to us. The Lima we had come from had been a jumble, a place where Spanish and indigenous objects mixed freely—where modern and ancient accompanied each other, where a rich man's house might be flanked by a tenement—but here, in this quiet, suburban setting, our possessions looked out of place. When the truck finally pulled away, two neighbors came over to see.

They were ten and eight, as sunny and frisky as Dutch maids on a road-side billboard. "You new?" said the older one. "*We're* new. We just moved in a few days ago."

They were from Westfield, a few towns over. George and I told them we were from Peru, but they puckered their mouths, rolled their eyes, and allowed as how they didn't know where that was.

"Your parents are Westfieldian people?" I asked, trying to make conversation, figuring Westfield to be a country, like Peru.

"Were," the tall one said. "Our mother got married last week."

I was taking that information in, but she sailed ahead breezily. "My name is Suzi Hess. This is my sister, Sara. My mother used to be called Hess, too. Like us. But she's Mrs. Loeb now."

There it was. The gringo roulette.

"Oh, I know all about that," I said, flaunting my urbanity. "My mother has a different name, too."

"Different from you?"

"No." I rushed to explain. "But different from her parents."

"Well, of course, silly. Every married woman has a different name from her parents."

My head felt fat as a blowfish. I needed to say that in Peru women strung their married and maiden names together, and that when my mother did that, her maiden name had turned out to be married, too, but it was going to take so much explanation. It was more complicated than I was willing to say: I was ashamed of my mother; ashamed that she was ashamed. In Peru, divorce was unthinkable. These girls, on the other hand, spoke of it so freely. I wanted them to be my friends. I burbled, dithered, stared down my nose, pulled on my ear. It didn't take long for Suzi to take pity. "Okay, let's see now. Your mother is divorced like ours, right?" she said, trying to help me along.

"Unh, yeah," I said, and my head filled with the miracle that we might have this great flaw in common.

"So she has children by another marriage?" she said.

"Unh, yeah. I dunno."

"You don't know? You don't know whether or not you have sisters or brothers somewhere else?"

"I dunno," I repeated.

"You mean they could be walking around and you wouldn't have any idea they're there?"

I hadn't thought of that. Now I genuinely tried to squeeze that possibility into my brain. "No idea," I responded.

"Jee-zee-kew-zee. They do things crazy in Pay-roo," Suzi said. She laughed merrily, a tinkly, high titter as sweet as a canary's. Freckly Sara flashed her big, buck teeth and put out a hand. "Friends?"

"Yip. Sure."

While George and I were running up and down the driveway behind those apartments, working to seal a friendship with these girls, Mother was humming through our rooms, settling into the life she had dreamed of for so long. She'd whisk outside from time to time, smoothing her hair, trotting to a cab, pointing to our big sister's face in the window. "You mind Vicki, you hear?" When we asked where she was going, she'd reply, "To Summit Food Market!" Or "Off to your school!" Or "Off to see about the house!" Off!

She seemed enraptured with her new life, was a bundle of energy. I watched her cook meals, wash dishes, scrub floors—do tasks I had never seen her do before—but she dug in with relish, singing as she went, looking up joyfully when I walked in, pushing the hair from her eyes.

If it had never been clear before, it was crystal clear now: My mother had been a sad woman in Peru. There was nothing sad about her now. It didn't seem to matter that she wasn't with the Clapps. She did not visit them, nor did she call or write them, as far as I knew. She didn't seem to need them at all. It began to dawn on me that it wasn't *them* she had missed in Peru; she'd missed these American streets and her freedom to roam around in them.

Papi was another story: He dragged out to the train station earlier and earlier in the morning, shuffled home beat at the end of the day. He grew more and more disengaged. He missed his Peruvian family and his *compadres*. You could see it in the way he slumped through the door, headed for his chair, heaved himself down with a sigh. "Write to your abuelita," he'd tell me day after day, pointing to the stack of letters from her. "She wants to know how you are."

In town, he had trouble understanding the fast-talking, slang-slinging suburbanites; he'd cast a weary look my way to signal me to translate. At first, I was as puzzled by accents as he was. But his reliance on me made an impression. In Peru I had always thought he and I were similar, that Mother was the different one. But here in Summit, I felt more kinship with my mother, my father the odd one out. "You kids are turning into gringos," he'd say, staring at us in amazement. But I knew our mother was the only gringo among us; she was it a full hundred percent. My father was the only Peruvian; he, too, was one hundred percent. They were wholes. They were complete. They were who they were. They would never *become* anything like the other. We children, on the other hand, were becoming others all the time, shuttling back and forth. We were the fifty-fifties. We were the cobbled ones.

Summit was nothing like Mother, really, nor was it anything like the American school in Lima, nor like Rawlins, Wyoming, whose lingo we heard in our dreams. At first, we swaggered around, George and I, like cowboys, a-yawin' and a-struttin', thinking we knew what America was. But when Easterners looked at us, they drew their chins into their necks, pocketed their hands, and sidled away. We trotted down Springfield Avenue, hiking our jeans, jiggling our heels, only to find that the places that drew these gringos were Roots haberdashery and Summit Athletic. Not bars with decapitated fauna. Not general stores with buckshot and beans. There were men in hats, plenty of them, but they were scurrying out of the Summit train station with their faces pulled down and their collars pulled up, repairing to Brookdale Liquors, then tearing home with their wives behind the wheel. On weekends, a different breed swept down Main Street: in pastel cardigans, with bags of charcoal briquets, golf clubs, and Roots merchandise dangling from their hands, pennies winking out of their shoes.

It was the way they spoke that was most puzzling. Why didn't it sound like English we'd heard before? It certainly didn't sound like Nub, or Grandpa Doc, or Old Joe Krozier. "Ah'll take a pack uh this here Juicy Fruit, mister," I drawled to Summit's version of a corner-store Wong, a scrubbed little man in a white jacket and spectacles behind the counter at Liss Pharmacy.

"Beg your pardon, miss?"

I cleared my throat and tried again, raising my voice this time. "This here Jee-you-see Fah-root, mister. How much yew want?"

"Oh, ho! No need to shout, my dear. That'll cost you . . . a nickel."

"Nekel? *Qué quiere decir* nekel?" I whispered to George.

"That big *moneda* there," he hissed, pointing into my palm. "The five-cent one."

"Oh." I surrendered it to the man. He pursed his lips.

"Y'ever chaw weed?" I asked Suzi, sitting on the stair step of our apartment, looking out at the pristine grass where children were not to go.

"Chaw weed?"

"Yip. My cousin Nub, he's a cowboy, and he larned me how."

"Taught me how."

"O-keh, o-keh. Taught me how. Have you ever done it?"

"No, I haven't. Gee, Marie, you gotta stop talking weird. You say things all wrong. And I don't know why. I hear your mother talking just like everybody else. If you don't talk right you'll never fit in school. Kids are gonna make fun of you, for sure."

Suzi and Sara became our tutors, whiling away summer days until fireflies bumped our faces, teaching us what to say. You said *okay*, not *o-keh*. You went to a *movie*, not a *cinema*. You caught *colds*, not *constipations*. You wrote on a clean, spanking new *sheet* of paper. Not a fresh *shit*. It was clear we had entered a new phase, far from our dirt-lot hankerings on Avenida Angamos. We weren't hoping to be thought of as better. We just hoped we wouldn't be made "fun of." We hoped not to be noticed at all.

MARILYN CHIN

Born in 1955, Marilyn Chin came to Portland, Oregon, from Hong Kong with her family when she was seven. Her father, a cook and restaurant owner, was not able to hold down a job, and by the end of the decade he had estranged himself from the family. Such turmoil notwithstanding, Chin managed to earn a B.A. in ancient Chinese literature from the University of Massachusetts and an M.F.A. in poetry from the University of Iowa. She has published three books of poetry: *Dwarf Bamboo* (1987), *The Phoenix Gone, The Terrace Empty* (1994), and *Rhapsody in Plain Yellow* (2002). The following poem from her 1994 collection is representative of the general tenor of her poetry: a reluctance to embrace her adopted homeland wholeheartedly while at the same time a refusal to sentimentalize her Chinese heritage. "How can we remake ourselves?" she asks in her poem "Chinaman's Chance." "The railroad killed your great-grandfather. / His arms here, his legs there."

How I Got That Name
an essay on assimilation

I am Marilyn Mei Ling Chin.
Oh, how I love the resoluteness
of that first person singular
followed by that stalwart indicative
of "be," without the uncertain i-n-g
of "becoming." Of course,
the name had been changed
somewhere between Angel Island and the sea,
when my father the paperson
in the late 1950s
obsessed with a bombshell blonde

transliterated "Mei Ling" to "Marilyn."
And nobody dared question
his initial impulse—for we all know
lust drove men to greatness,
not goodness, not decency.
And there I was, a wayward pink baby,
named after some tragic white woman
swollen with gin and Nembutal.
My mother couldn't pronounce the "r."
She dubbed me "Numba one female offshoot"
for brevity: henceforth, she will live and die
in sublime ignorance, flanked
by loving children and the "kitchen deity."
While my father dithers,
a tomcat in Hong Kong trash—
a gambler, a petty thug,
who bought a chain of chopsuey joints
in Piss River, Oregon,
with bootlegged Gucci cash.
Nobody dared question his integrity given
his nice, devout daughters
and his bright, industrious sons
as if filial piety were the standard
by which all earthly men were measured.

Oh, how trustworthy our daughters,
how thrifty our sons!
How we've managed to fool the experts
in education, statistics and demography—
We're not very creative but not adverse to rote-learning.
Indeed, they can *use* us.
But the "Model Minority" is a tease.
We know you are watching now,
so we refuse to give you any!
Oh, bamboo shoots, bamboo shoots!

The further west we go, we'll hit east;
the deeper down we dig, we'll find China.
History has turned its stomach
on a black polluted beach—
where life doesn't hinge
on that red, red wheelbarrow,
but whether or not our new lover
in the final episode of "Santa Barbara"
will lean over a scented candle
and call us a "bitch."
Oh God, where have we gone wrong?
We have no inner resources!

Then, one redolent spring morning
the Great Patriarch Chin
peered down from his kiosk in heaven
and saw that his descendants were ugly.
One had a squarish head and a nose without a bridge.
Another's profile—long and knobbed as a gourd.
A third, the sad, brutish one
may never, never marry.
And I, his least favorite—
"not quite boiled, not quite cooked,"
a plump pomfret simmering in my juices—
too listless to fight for my people's destiny.
"To kill without resistance is not slaughter"
says the proverb. So, I wait for imminent death.
The fact that this death is also metaphorical
is testament to my lethargy.

So here lies Marilyn Mei Ling Chin,
married once, twice to so-and-so, a Lee and a Wong,
granddaughter of Jack "the patriarch"
and the brooding Suilin Fong,
daughter of the virtuous Yuet Kuen Wong

and G. G. Chin the infamous,
sister of a dozen, cousin of a million,
survived by everybody and forgotten by all.
She was neither black nor white,
neither cherished nor vanquished,
just another squatter in her own bamboo grove
minding her poetry—
when one day heaven was unmerciful,
and a chasm opened where she stood.
Like the jowls of a mighty white whale,
or the jaws of a metaphysical Godzilla,
it swallowed her whole.
She did not flinch nor writhe,
nor fret about the afterlife,
but stayed! Solid as wood, happily
a little gnawed, tattered, mesmerized
by all that was lavished upon her
and all that was taken away!

JULIA ALVAREZ

Although born in New York City in 1950, Julia Alvarez spent the first ten years of her life in the Dominican Republic. She was forced to flee with her family in 1960 after her father participated in an unsuccessful plot to overthrow the dictator Rafael Trujillo. Since then she has returned to the Dominican Republic periodically. A born storyteller, Alvarez was encouraged to write at a young age. After attending boarding school, she graduated from Middlebury College in 1971 and went on to earn an M.F.A. from Syracuse University four years later. Her first (and best-known) novel, *How the Garcia Girls Lost Their Accents* (1991), comprises 15 interrelated stories based on her own experiences. The bulk of these stories deal with the painful realities of cultural assimilation, a dominant theme in much of her writing. The plaintive note struck at the end of the following essay, from *Something to Declare* (1998), is echoed in her poem "Exile," where she describes the flight from her native land as a "loss much larger than I understood."

Our Papers

We never went on trips abroad when I was a child. In the Dominican Republic no one could travel without papers, and the dictatorship rarely granted anyone this special permission.

There were exceptions—my grandparents went to New York regularly because my grandfather had a post in the United Nations. My godmother, who was described as one of the most beautiful widows in the country, got permission to go on a trip because she was clever. At a state function, she told El Jefe that she knew he was a gentleman, and a gentleman would not refuse a lady a favor. She wanted so much to travel. The next morning a black limousine from the National Palace rolled up to her door to deliver her papers, along with some flowers.

"Where did you want to go?" I asked her, years later.

"*Want* to go?" she looked at me blankly. "I didn't want to go anywhere. I just wanted to get away from the hell we were living in."

Those trips were not vacations—though they did share an aspect of vacations: they were escapes, not from the tedium of daily routines, but from the terror of a police state.

When I was a child, then, vacations meant a vacation from school. That was vacation enough for me! Summer vacations also meant a move. During the long, hot months of July and August, the whole extended family—uncles, aunts, sisters, cousins, grandparents—left the capital to get away from the heat and diseases that supposedly festered in the heat. My grandfather had bought an old house a short walk from the beach in the small fishing village of Boca Chica, close to where the new airport was being built. The house itself was nothing elegant: two stories, wood frame, a wraparound porch on the first floor, a large screened-in porch on the second, a big almond tree that dropped its fruit on the zinc roof. Ping! in the middle of the night. *What was that?*

We slept on cots, all the cousins, in that screened-in porch. Meals were eaten in two shifts on a big picnic table—first, the whole gang of children, our seating arrangement planned to avoid trouble, the rowdy ones next to the well-behaved ones, the babies with bibs in high chairs, looking like the little dignitaries of the gathering. The grown-ups ate after we were sent up to our cots to nap so we could "make our digestions" and be able to go swimming in the late afternoon. Our lives, which were communal during the rest of the year, since we all lived in neighboring houses, grew even more communal when we were all under the same roof. The men stayed on in the capital during the week, working hard, and appeared on Friday afternoons to a near stampede of children running up from the beach to see what our papis had brought us from the city. During the rest of the week, it was just the cousins and our mothers and grandmother and aunts and nursemaids, and the great big sea that splashed in our dreams all night long.

It seemed then that we were not living in a dictatorship but in a fairyland of sand and sun and girlish mothers who shared in our fun. The perpetual worried look disappeared from my mother's face. She went barefoot on the beach, a sea breeze blew her skirt up in the air, she tried to hold it down. We chose the fish for our dinner right off the fishermen's boats. The women gossiped and told stories and painted their fingernails and toenails and then proceeded down the line to do the same for the girl children. They always had some little intrigue going. They especially loved to tease the husbands alone in the capital, making funny phone calls, pretending they were other women ("Don't you remember me, Edy querido?!") or pretending they were salesladies calling to say that their wives' order of a hundred dollars' worth of Revlon cosmetics had just arrived. Could payment be sent immediately?

Ha, ha, ha! The women held their sides and laughed wildly at the men's embarrassment. It was fun to see them having such a good time for a change.

And then, suddenly, in 1960, summers at the beach stopped altogether. We stayed home in the capital. The women were too worried to leave the men by themselves. Nightly, a black Volkswagen came up our driveway and sat there, blocking our way out. We were under virtual house arrest by the SIM. The men talked in low, worried voices behind closed doors. The shadows under my mother's eyes grew darker. When we begged and pleaded to go to Boca Chica for the summer, she blurted out, "¡Absolutamente no!" before she was hushed by a more circumspect aunt.

That's when talk of a vacation began in my family—vacation as in the American understanding of vacation, a trip far away, for fun.

"Wouldn't you love to go to the United States and see the snow?" one aunt asked my sisters and me one day out of the blue.

"That would be so much fun!" another aunt chimed in.

We sisters looked from one to the other aunt, unsure. Something about the conversation seemed rehearsed. Some adult intrigue was afoot. This one would not involve giggles on the phone and howls of laughter over how gullible the men were. This one would be serious, but just how serious I did not understand until years later.

My father's activities in the underground were suspected, and it would be only a matter of time before he would be hauled away if we stayed. And who knew where else the ax might fall—on his wife and children? Friends in the States rigged up a fellowship for my father. The pretext was that he would study heart surgery there since there wasn't a heart surgeon in the Dominican Republic. What if our dictator should develop heart trouble? Papi was petitioning for a two-year visa for himself and his family. No, he told the authorities, he would not go without us. That would be a hardship.

"You bet," my mother tells me now. "We would have been held hostage!"

"Why didn't you tell us any of this back then?" I ask her. All we ever heard about was that we were taking a vacation to the United States. "Why didn't you just say, we're leaving forever?"

"Ay sí, and get ourselves killed! You had the biggest mouth back then—" She shakes her head, and I know what is coming, "and you still do, writing, writing, writing."

She is right, too—about the big mouth. I remember my three sisters and I were coached not to mention that we were going to the United States of America—at least not till our papers came, if they ever came.

Before the day was over, I had told our secret to the cousins, the maids, the dog, and the corner candy man, who was always willing to exchange candy for my schoolbooks and school supplies. I hadn't meant to disobey, but it was so tempting to brag and get a little extra respect and a free box of cinnamon Chiclets.

"I'm going to see the snow!" I singsang to my boy cousin Ique.

"So?" he shrugged and threw me a shadow punch. Needless to say, we were two of the rowdy ones.

Toys made a better argument. I was going to the land where our toys came from.

He raised his chin, struggling with the envy he did not want to admit to feeling. "Bring me back something?" he finally pleaded.

"Okay," I said, disarmed. No one had mentioned our return until this very moment. Surely, vacations were something you came back from?

When our papers finally arrived one morning in early August, Papi booked us on the next flight off the Island. The vacation was on. We could tell anybody we wanted. Now, I was the one who grew silent.

"Hello, very pleased to make your acquaintance?" one uncle joked in English, holding out his hand to me. He had come by to say good-bye, for we were leaving that very night. Meanwhile, we girls better practice our English! We would get so tall and pale and pretty in the United States, and smart!

Maybe we would marry Americans and have little blue-eyed babies that didn't know how to speak Spanish!

That gripped my braggart's heart. We were going to be gone *that* long?

As the hours ticked by and more and more visitors and relatives snuck in the back way to say good-bye, my sisters and I grew pale with fear. We didn't really want to go to a place where buildings scraped the sky and everyone spoke English all the time, not just at school in English class. We didn't want to go someplace if all the cousins and aunts couldn't come along.

The uncles mocked us, lifting their eyebrows in shock. "How crazy! Do you know how many children would give their right arms to go to the United States of America?" Their argument, a variation on the starving Chinese children who would give their right arms to eat our vegetables, did not convince us. Our protests increased as the hour drew near.

I don't know which aunt it was, or perhaps it was our own distraught mother, who decided to trick us to calm us down. Never mind the United States, we were really going to Boca Chica! The story wasn't a total untruth. The new airport was on the way to the fishing village.

We were suspicious. Why were we dressed in party dresses if we were going to the beach? Why did we have suitcases like foreign people, instead of the big hampers of clothes and provisions we took with us when we left for the summer for the beach house?

"That's enough, girls!" Mami snapped. "One more word from you and you can all stay here by yourselves!"

Now there was a threat worth its weight in silence. Abandonment was far worse than a long, maybe permanent vacation somewhere strange. By the time we boarded the plane, long past midnight, none of us had raised any further objections. Besides by now, it had been drummed into us—how lucky we were to have our papers, to be free to go on this long vacation.

Soon after the roar of takeoff, we fell asleep, so we did not see the little lights flickering in some of the houses as we flew over Boca Chica. Hours before dawn, the fishermen would already be casting their nets out in the ocean. By midmorning, when we would be gaping at the buildings in New York City, the fish would be laid out on a big board across the rowboats' length, their pink and silver scales iridescent with the water scooped over them to make them look fresher.

For weeks that soon became months and years, I would think in this way. What was going on right this moment back home? As the leaves fell and the air turned gray and the cold set in, I would remember the big house in Boca Chica, the waves telling me their secrets, the cousins sleeping side by side in their cots, and I would wonder if those papers had set us free from everything we loved.

CZESLAW MILOSZ

A member of the Polish resistance against the Nazis and an exile from the former Soviet bloc, Vilnius-born Czeslaw Milosz (1911–2004) first came to prominence in the West with *The Captive Mind* (1953), a devastating study of communism in Eastern Europe that was translated into French, German, and English soon after its initial publication in Polish in France. At that time he was living in Paris, during the first phase of a long exile that began in 1951 when he was granted political asylum. In 1960 he came to the United States to teach at the University of California; Berkeley remained his home base for most of his later life. He translated Walt Whitman and Robinson Jeffers into Polish and fashioned English translations of the Polish poems in his groundbreaking anthology *Post-War Polish Poetry* (1965). He also wrote poems inspired by the California landscape and published the essay collection *Visions from San Francisco Bay* (1969). Banned in Poland, most of his poetry was not available in English until the 1970s, a decade of increasing acclaim that culminated in his winning the Nobel Prize in Literature in 1980. His poems written in America often consider his Lithuanian and Polish past or address concerns rooted in European history and its calamitous 20th century. Despite strong ties to several American poets, Milosz was influenced by American poetry in a relatively limited way. Some of his more incisive reflections on his experience in the United States are the diary *A Year of the Hunter* (1994) and *Milosz's ABCs* (2001). The translation below is by Madeline Levine.

from
Milosz's ABC's

A merica. What splendor! What poverty! What humanity! What in humanity! What mutual goodwill! What individual isolation! What loyalty to the ideal! What hypocrisy! What a triumph of conscience! What perversity! The America of contradictions can, not must, reveal itself to immigrants who have made it here. Those who have not made it will see only its brutality. I made it, but I have always tried to remember that I owe it to my lucky star, not to myself, and that right next door are entire neighborhoods of unfortunates. I will say even more: the thought of their grueling labor and unfulfilled hope, of the gigantic prison system in which the unneeded are kept, taught me to look skeptically at its decorations—those well-kept houses amidst the suburbs' greenery.

During my school years America rose to meet me as a loaf of white bread and a mug of cocoa from Hoover's postwar relief effort, as blue-striped shirts, and then as films with Mary Pickford and Charlie Chaplin. When a few years later I adored the actress Sylvia Sidney, how astonished I would have been had someone told me that some day my photograph and hers would be neighbors in the pages of *American Biography*. The movies meant that America was already beginning its expansion, but a number of streets signaled this, too—German Street in Wilno, or the one in Drohobycz that Bruno Schulz depicted as the Street of Crocodiles. As I was able to confirm later on in my life, the poorer streets on Manhattan's East Side were just like them.

During the course of this century "the beast emerging from the sea" overwhelmed, one after the other, its enemies and rivals. The most important of these rivals was Soviet Russia, because this clash was not only about military might, but about a model for man as well. The attempt to create a "new man" according to utopian principles was an enormous undertaking, and those who dismiss it after the fact apparently do not understand what were the stakes in this game. The "old man" won, and with the help of mass media is imposing its model on the entire planet. Looking at it from a distance, one should seek the causes of the Soviet defeat in the cultural sphere. Russia, expending astronomical sums of money on propaganda, was unable to persuade anyone to adopt its model, even in the conquered countries of Europe which accepted its efforts with derision, seeing in them the unattractive self-adornment of barbarians.

The Cold War, that conflict between democratic America and gloomy Eastern totalism, deprived many people of their freedom of judgment and even of clear-sightedness, since a lack of enthusiasm for America could be perceived as an inclination toward the Communist side.

The twentieth century brought America into a new dimension which she had previously not known. At the beginning of the century, artists and writers fled to the old cultural centers of Paris and London from a country known to be dull, materialistic, concerned only with making money. At the end of the century, artists and writers from all kinds of countries journey to America as to a land of opportunities. By now, New York, not Paris, is the world capital of painting. Poetry, reduced to something akin to coin collecting in Western Europe, has found an audience in America on university campuses, and also entire departments, institutes, and prizes. I realize that had I remained in France I would not have received the Neustadt Prize in 1978 (which is referred to as the Little Nobel and is usually a first step toward the Nobel), or the Nobel Prize after that.

Today it is difficult to imagine how distant America was from Europe at the beginning of the century. An ocean separated the two continents, and voyages were accompanied by images of shipwrecks, which appear in illustrated magazines throughout the nineteenth century. My first voyage to America from England in the winter of 1945–46 took some twelve days. The little vessel climbed earnestly up the watery mountain only to find itself in a trough and to clamber up again. Then transatlantic flights became commonplace, and once I even flew on the French *Concorde*: dinner accompanied by wine had barely progressed to the cheese plate, and we were already in Paris.

People traveled to America, but they rarely came back. It did happen on occasion, though. In the wealthy and beautifully laid-out village of Peiksva, not far from the manor where I was born, "the American's house" stood out. Then something took place that provides, in brief, a glimpse of what happened to Lithuania under Soviet rule: collectivization. The village, bordering on great forests, had given aid to the "forest brotherhood." The family from "the American's house" were murdered, the house was burned down, the villagers were deported to the Siberian taiga, and the village itself was leveled.

Janka's father also was one who returned from America. Before World War I Ludwik Dłuski worked for several years in various metallurgical plants on the East Coast. I thought of him when I looked at the rusted skeletons of abandoned factories in the Hudson River Valley north of New York City. In those old-fashioned factories Mr. Dłuski shared the fate of the disinherited of the earth who labor from dawn to dusk, without the rights and privileges won later on by labor unions. In the Warsaw he returned to, life may have been difficult, but without that exhausting labor (he became a court bailiff), and, at least, not as lonely.

LUC SANTE

A cultural archeologist of omnivorous curiosity and idiosyncratic
tastes, Luc Sante (born in 1954) recreated a lost New York in his classic
Low Life (1991) and has gone on to explore many other byways—from
the origin of the blues to the photography of Walker Evans—in the essays that he publishes regularly in *New York Review of Books*, some of
which were collected in *Kill All Your Darlings* (2008). In his 1996 memoir
The Factory of Facts (from which the piece below is taken) Sante, who
was born in Belgium and came to the United States with his family in the
early 1960s, in effect dismantles his identity to take a look at the cultural
materials that have shaped it, in the process casting an unsettling light
on the very notions of culture and personal identity.

from
Cargo

Like many children, I had more than once entertained the idea that my
parents were stand-ins, that I had been adopted or somehow switched at
birth, that I was descended from more worthy, more interesting beings. It had
not, however, crossed my mind that these spectral progenitors might be rich.
I had imagined them as vagabonds, mountebanks, carnies, thieves. They
were everything my parents were not—adventurous, daring, roguish, *bad*—
but only up to a point, since the romance did not involve money, not even fugitive sums deposited under false names in the vaults of scattered South American banks.

Maybe my father had once had a corresponding fantasy, though. Not
knowing where our name came from or what it meant, he had suggested that
it might represent a corrupted form of *Saint* or *Sainte*. He had gone so far as
to sketch a scenario for me in which our ancestors were French aristocrats
whose name was some sort of compound on the order of *Saint-Médard* or

Sainte-Euphrosine. They had fled the guillotine during the Terror, running as far as darkest southern Belgium, where they had insinuated themselves among the populace and taken up suitably humble identities. A few generations later, their descendants did not suspect the glory that lay dormant in their bloodline. My father, who had left school at fourteen, as young people of the working class did then, nevertheless was a prodigious autodidactic reader, fascinated by the French Revolution, so I could see where the idea had in part germinated.

The rest might have been inspired by the tale of his cousin Alphonse Faniel, the son of his father's sister Bertha. This Faniel, nearly a generation older than my father, like virtually all his first cousins, had been a layabout, the despair of his parents. At length, though, he had found work in a factory, assembling bicycle frames. He was sufficiently adept at it that he proposed starting his own enterprise, and his parents had set him up in a small business in the Belgian Congo, where he imported disassembled bicycles, put them together and sold them. He hired Congolese help and kept them on by giving them bicycles as bonuses. He initially parlayed his profits into a truck, to ferry his wares from the port of Matadi to Léopoldville, the capital, and then bought another truck, and eventually a whole fleet. Then he started buying houses, which he rented out at inflated rates to American military and diplomatic personnel during the war. When he made his long-delayed visit to his native Verviers after V-E Day, he came in a late-model Buick—in that time and place, he could not have caused more of a sensation had he arrived on the back of an elephant. A few years later he retired to Spain, buying a substantial tract of land that came with a castle and a title, and lived out his days as the Marquis de Mirmas. That was the closest anyone had come to establishing a Sante fortune.

I never met Alphonse Faniel, and it is more than probable that he never knew of my existence, nor would he have cared. He existed throughout my childhood as a distant mythic figure, and I came to believe he was fictitious; indeed I conflated his title with that of the Marquis de Carabas, which Puss in Boots bestowed on his master. If his story seemed improbable even to a child, it was because money had never otherwise smiled upon the Santes, or for that matter on my mother's family, the Nandrins, nor upon the host of accessory lineages: the Hermants, the Remacles, the Éloys, the Cornets, the

Sauvages, the Werners. My father's side seemed to consist entirely of factory workers—day laborers, not artisans—while my mother's family was apparently an undifferentiated mass of subsistence farmers, not even smallholders but (as it happened) tenant farmers, who might have considered themselves prosperous had they possessed a single cow. I accepted from an early age that we were just that way—*p'tites gens*—folks meant to scratch out a living by the sweat of their brows, whose every meager advance would be met with a consequent reversal.

I had concrete evidence of this within my own three-person nuclear family. My father, after leaving school, worked for the railroad for a while, as a track inspector, and briefly for a textile job-lot dealer and in a wool-carding plant. After the war, which he spent mostly hiding from the Germans, he found work in a fulling mill, then in an iron foundry that manufactured carding machines. There, around the time of my birth, he ascended from the shop floor to a position in junior management. Then the place shut down. My parents spent a year of misery, running a Bata Shoe franchise in a grimy industrial suburb. Then the foundry reopened, my father got his job back, my parents bought themselves a new house on a corner lot in a brand-new development. They hardly had time to enjoy it, however, before my father's employer shut down again, this time apparently for good, and in a severe economic climate that all but precluded other employment possibilities. Which is how we wound up emigrating to America. Where my father was back once again on the factory floor. His advances had come through hard work and application, his reversals from sheer bad luck. One step forward and one step back—this was our lot, like a curse, a mark of Cain.

Thus the dream's identification of my parents with a militant dynasty would seem particularly tendentious, on the face of it. On the other hand, my role as the repressed masses had some internal validity. I could reasonably claim to have been kept in an ahistorical bubble during part of my childhood, not that my parents themselves were particularly to blame. For every year that stretches between my current age and my early years, some sort of psychological logarithmic expansion seems to occur, so that by the time I hit my fortieth birthday my childhood felt a century removed. I didn't become aware of this curious relativistic phenomenon until my late twenties. Around that time, I developed a consuming interest in the turn of the last century, prompted in part by the place where I was living, the Lower East Side of New York City, where every hundred-year-old tenement shell, with its scalloped cornice and ornately detailed window frames ornamenting vacancy and rot, appeared on my retina accompanied by a grimly ironic caption: THE NINE-TEENTH CENTURY. I was haunted by those ruins, as if every one of them said, I am Ozymandias King of Kings. I wanted desperately to see them when they were newly built, convinced that such a time must have been sunnier, more humane (I was wrong).

As I immersed myself in the nineteenth century, I was struck again and again by a personal identification that verged on cryptomnesia. I *knew* that time, as if I had lived in it myself. In impressionable adolescence I had toyed with the idea of reincarnation, but I was no longer vulnerable to that sort of nonsense, I told myself. At length I realized that the haze gathering around my peripheral vision as I pawed through documents and photographs and attempted to bore my way ocularly, Superman-like, through ten decades of grit on the inner and outer surfaces of neighboring hovels was my own child-hood. The distance between the atmosphere of my infancy and that of my fledgling adulthood was something measurable in epochs.

I spent my early years in factory towns and their adjacent suburbs, amid bricks and soot and smokestacks and cobbled roads. We took streetcars for short trips and trains for long ones. We bought food fresh for every meal, not because we were gourmets but because we lacked a refrigerator (less perish-able substances were kept in the root cellar). My mother got up every morning in the chill and made a fire in the parlor stove. Running water came in only one temperature: frigid. We communicated by mail and got our news chiefly from newspapers (we were sufficiently modern, though, in that we owned a radio roughly the size of a filing cabinet). My early classrooms featured pot-bellied stoves and double desks with inkwells, into which we dipped our nibs. We boys wore short pants until the ceremony of *communion solennelle*, at age twelve. And so on. But this wasn't any undiscovered pocket of the Car-pathians, it was postwar western Europe, where "postwar" was a season that stretched for nearly twenty years.

Seen from that angle, the dream's decadent aristocracy might be my par-ents, but it could as well stand for Belgian culture in general, although such a distinction might easily be perceived as academic by the Metaphor Central whose offices lie in my back brain. The Belgium of my youth certainly had a vacuum-sealed quality about it. Material deprivation aside, its relation to the modern world was ambiguous at best. On the one hand, it could hardly be said to lie outside history; it had, after all, recently undergone five years of rampaging, furious, deadly history. On the other, Belgium—especially, it seemed to me, the southeastern portion of the country, the provinces of Liège and Luxembourg that contained nearly all my family—was determinedly monochrome. Although this rump brushed the borders of four other countries, it only held one tribe. However much the surnames might apparently vary, French or Flemish or Walloon or German or Dutch or Luxembourgeois, the people themselves were visibly of a single stock. They followed one religion—in my mother's pious family it was said that there were two sects: Catholics and people who had had a fight with a priest. They were monolingual, or almost. The old Walloon tongue was dying out, and only a few people knew the language of their neighbors just over the border.

People generally stayed put. Rare were the ambitious youths who made it as far as Brussels; going to Paris for more than a once-in-a-lifetime holiday was unheard of, except maybe among the rich, but we didn't know any of those. In the country, people remained in their native villages unless they were driven out by misfortune. Neighboring lands were inhabited by the Other, variously indolent, mendacious, thieving, irreligious, cruel, dirty—and for that matter the next province or the nearest town might be just as foreign and unwholesome. The rest of the world was composed of heathens, who lived in huts and presumably ate each other. Of course, Belgium possessed that extraordinary appendage in Africa, but that was perceived as a job more than as a place—you'd go for a year, working for high wages under what were understood to be supremely trying circumstances, then get three to six months off at home, and a few decades of this would finance your retirement. America, of course, was a myth. It existed in the movies, but was there more to it than that? Everyone had heard of somebody's cousin's mother's uncle who had gone there and prospered, living in sultanesque luxury on a ranch on the Great Plains, driving a Cadillac among buffalo herds when not dodging bullets in Chicago—but all such stories were legendary, unverifiable, and believed only wishfully.

The fact that Belgium is a monarchy, however constitutional, unquestionably lent it a Ruritanian quality. The rich were phantoms, who wore titles and inhabited châteaux. Maybe you'd met one—my parents had some fancy friends at whose home they once dined with a baron—but they chiefly existed on another plane, touching on common soil only briefly and magnanimously. The royal family held a place in the popular imagination akin to that of Hollywood stars. People spoke of them, speculating on their relationships and personalities, as if they knew them, but the materialization of one or more in the town square, to dedicate a monument or commemorate a feast, was clearly a sacred occasion. One would bathe in the projected radiance even as one felt it somewhat untoward to stare directly at those elevated beings. A pilgrimage to the gardens and greenhouses of the royal palace at Laeken, on the week in May when they were opened to the public, represented nearly as much of a hajj as the trip to the miracle sites of Lourdes or Fatima for which poor people might save their centimes for decades. And the king—the shy, modest, bespectacled Baudouin, who assumed the throne in 1951 upon the abdication of his rather questionable father, Leopold III—was perceived as nearly Christlike in his humility, his wisdom, his love for his subjects. His common touch, his lack of affect, was the very quality that marked him most evidently as a divinely appointed monarch. Belgians, whatever their individual opinions or attitudes, were cast in the role of subjects; the delineations of class were indelibly inscribed.

I had inherited Belgian culture as a package of fragments. I had my impressionistic memories—a heap of short strips of film, blurred stills, muffled or corroded sound recordings, waxily unreliable scratch-'n'-sniff cards, as well as a box of startlingly efficient emotional triggers. I had my mother's definition of the national character, which was rural, pious, familial, severe, sentimental, and unquestioning, and came with culinary, botanical, and zoological annexes. I had my father's, likewise sentimental but otherwise urban, far less reverent, class-conscious in a somewhat feistier vein, humorous but scarred by war and striving. And I had scattered glimpses of my contemporaries and their experience, a little bit through my infrequent contact with friends over there, much more from the books and magazines that I got in the mail by subscription or courtesy of my godfather and his wife my aunt, newsagents in Lambermont. This collection of elements, of wildly uneven size and impact, accounted for perhaps three-quarters of my personality, or at least my self-definition, even in late childhood. My rebellion was a complex matter, since I wanted to break free of the influence of my parents without jettisoning what I valued, and they stood as both guardians and embodiments of everything connected with my early life.

But dump I did. Willfully, accidentally, organically, negligently, crudely, systematically, inevitably I got rid of a section of myself, a part that was once majority and shrank to accessory. I went from being the little Belgian boy, polite and diffident and possessed of a charming accent, to a loutish American adolescent. This was nothing special: I drank, I smoked, I stole, I swore, I stopped going to church. I went in for the usual extremes of hair length and took drugs and listened to abrasive music and hung (timidly enough) around various countercultural scenes, that sort of thing. I grew increasingly bored with school, cutting classes and skipping days at every possible opportunity—eventually getting myself expelled—and used the time to, among other things, read books that would have made my parents blanch, beginning with *Naked Lunch* when I was thirteen. I pursued girls, although haltingly, because I was still an awkward little Belgian boy. Otherwise, of course, none of these activities distinguished me from my contemporaries, and I would likely have engaged in them no matter where I lived, but my mother was convinced that Belgian children did not do such things, her view of Belgium becoming more idealized with every year she spent away from it. My view of Belgium became correspondingly more hostile, because it represented authority and also because I was certain its taint was what made me timid and awkward and unpopular and unattractive and solitary. I began a project to reinvent myself, acknowledge no bonds or ties or background, pass myself off as entirely self-made.

At least this is one way of looking at things; it could also be said that I subtracted nothing, but merely added. It never occurred to me to change my name or adapt its pronunciation or stop using French; I would never become one of *them*. I would never pledge allegiance to the flag—or any flag, for that matter—and I would never eat soft white bread or drink Budweiser or watch the Super Bowl or refer to my parents as Mom and Dad or refer to or even think of Americans as "we." This defiance was impelled in part by rage at the country that made me feel like a pariah—jumbled up indiscriminately with issues of taste and belief or the lack thereof—but also by a vestigial pride. And yet along the way a fundamental loss took place, something that the dream transformed into a treasure. Certainly the theme of loss is constant for exiles, even two-bit job-seekers and their offspring. My parents lost friends, lost family ties and patterns of mutual assistance, lost rituals and habits and favorite foods, lost any link to an ongoing social milieu, lost a good part of the sense they had of themselves. We lost a house, several towns, various landscapes. We lost documents and pictures and heirlooms, as well as most of our breakable belongings, smashed in the nine packing cases that we took with us to America. We lost connection to a thing larger than ourselves, and as a family failed to make any significant new connection in exchange, so that we were left aground on a sandbar barely big enough for our feet. I lost friends and relatives and stories and familiar comforts and a sense of continuity between home and outside and any sense that I was normal. I lost half a language through want of use and eventually, in my late teens, even lost French as the language of my internal monologue. And I lost a whole network of routes through life that I had just barely glimpsed.

Hastening on toward some idea of a future, I only half-realized these losses, and when I did realize I didn't disapprove, and sometimes I actively colluded. At some point, though, I was bound to notice that there was a gulf inside me, with a blanketed form on the other side that hadn't been uncovered in decades. My project of self-invention had been successful, so much so that I had become a sort of hydroponic vegetable, growing soil-free. But I had been formed in another world; everything in me that was essential was owed to immersion in that place, and that time, that I had so effectively renounced. Continuing to believe that I had just made myself up out of whole cloth was self-flattering but hollow. I once wrote a rock and roll song whose chorus went, "If I only have one life, let me live it as a lie," and I really believed it, then, at twenty-five. But later on I could no longer ignore the contradictions. Shame and pride, self-loathing and rage, arrogance and solipsism all blurred together insupportably, so that I could truly be myself only when under attack. I was in danger of being devoured by my own negativity. I took cover in nostalgia, perversely enough a nostalgia for times and places that were not my own. There was nothing wrong with that, of course, except that I was in part using it as a blind, and the details I uncovered became substitutes for my own constituent ingredients. It is fascinating and often fruitful to try on another skin, but it is ultimately meaningless if one hasn't acknowledged one's own. I already had a history, intriguingly buried. It might even be an interesting one. Eventually I came to the conclusion that if I did nothing else, I at least needed to uncover it. Maybe some of what I thought I had lost was merely hidden.

Like it or not, each of us is *made*, less by blood or genes than by a process that is largely accidental, the impact of things seen and heard and smelled and tasted and endured in those few years before our clay hardens. Offhand remarks, things glimpsed in passing, jokes and commonplaces, shop displays and climate and flickering light and textures of walls are all consumed by us and become part of our fiber, just as much as the more obvious effects of upbringing and socialization and intimacy and learning. Every human being is an archeological site. What passes for roots is actually a matter of sediment, of accretion, of chance and juxtaposition. Recent research on genetic inheritance has been deformed into legend by chatter, and made to serve old and often destructive notions of destiny, ethnic or racial or social or economic. Behavior, though, gets passed down less by encoding than by example; tendencies and inclinations and limits and the ability to surpass them are formed not in the womb but out in the air. Parents exert an overwhelming effect on their children by their words, their deeds, their omissions and concealments, but children simultaneously conduct their own education, absorbing everything that crosses their field of reception, and that is a matter over which parents have little or no control. So the damnedest bits of fugitive trivia may show up years later, recombined and inexplicable, prominent in the baggage of the adult self. The archeological detective who can trace their passage in detail does not exist and never will. I don't claim any special ability in my own case, but I do possess a circumstantial advantage. Emigration, like a natural upheaval, sheared my foundation when the ground was soft, laying open expanses of strata. Pieces of matter and machinery protruded that would otherwise have dissolved or been driven underground. Time has blunted their contours, so that identification is rarely certain, but enough remains visible to allow for guesses, at least to suggest the whereabouts of the template that cast them. I can't in any way be conclusive about what made me. All I can do is to reconstruct the site, and imagine the factory at work.

LUCETTE LAGNADO

Long an investigative reporter and later an editor for newspapers such as the *New York Post, Village Voice, Forward,* and *Wall Street Journal,* Lucette Lagnado (born in 1957) published her first book, *Children of the Flame: Dr. Josef Mengele and the Untold Story of the Twins of Auschwitz* (written with Sheila Cohn Dekel) in 1991. Her next book, *The Man in the White Sharkskin Suit* (2007), recounts her family's journey from Nasser's Egypt in 1962 when she was a small child. Her sensitive memoir is at once an elegy for a vanished Cairo, a meditation on family, and a story of uneasy adjustment in America—even if the family's new home in Bensonhurst, Brooklyn, "was a sort of faux Cairo when we got there. . . . All those refugees from the Levant were there. We tried to have what we had before." The title refers to Lagnado's father, once a dashing businessman in Egypt, whose life in exile is one of bewilderment, disappointment, and longing for home.

from
The Man in the White Sharkskin Suit

We were officially welcomed to America by an HIAS bureaucrat, who apologized profusely for being late. She handed my father $50 to help tide us over those first few days, and arranged for a taxi to transport us and our suitcases to our hotel.

The Broadway Central was a lumbering old hotel, long past its prime, perched between Greenwich Village and the Bowery. It had once housed any number of illustrious guests and visitors, from Diamond Jim Brady to James Fisk, the railroad tycoon who was shot there, to Leon Trotsky, who waited tables before hastening back to Russia to lead the Red Army.

But now, in the early 1960s, it was so down-at-the-heels it catered mostly to needy low-income families and stray out-of-towners and refugees like us who couldn't afford any better—a forerunner of the welfare hotels that would become commonplace.

Though we were given a suite, our accommodations were, if possible, even more squalid than at the Violet Hotel. We had a small kitchenette and two large drafty rooms, where beds were lined up one next to the other as in a hospital ward. There were only five beds for the six of us, so I doubled up with my mom in a small bed, close to a wall with a large gaping hole.

We were used to balmy winters, and even Paris had been mild the year we were there, but here it was freezing cold. I went to bed every night in my street clothes—a pair of gray wool slacks from Cairo and a turtleneck sweater.

My mother thought I was being silly, as did the rest of the family. No one could understand why I insisted on sleeping in scratchy woolen street clothes instead of the soft and toasty flannel pajamas they had managed to retrieve from one of the suitcases, and I am not sure I understood myself.

We fell back into the nerve-racking rituals of people with nothing to do. I took walks with various members of my family—slow walks with my father, who was in constant pain, aggravated by the frigid temperatures; brisk walks with César, who was curious about America but not in love with it the way he had been in love with Paris; anxious walks with my mom, who seemed bewildered by the Village and New York in general; quiet walks with my sister, who took me again and again to Washington Square Park.

On the benches were people clad entirely in black, who looked like no one I had ever seen before. I couldn't help staring at these strange creatures seated amid the snowy white splendor of Washington Square Park. "Ce sont des bohémiens, des 'beatniks,'" my sister explained. We'd sit in one of the benches and stare at them, hoping they would approach us. They had eyes only for each other, and neither I nor my sister, all bundled up in our layers of Mediterranean garb, could possibly be part of any group. We were still outsiders, even to the beatniks, the quintessential outsiders.

When she walked alone, Suzette would occasionally find herself accosted by a beatnik, asking her for a handout. She'd shake her head no and continue walking. But she felt strangely guilty about turning them down, though she had even less than they did.

More inviting even than Washington Square Park was our local supermarket. I'd never been inside a supermarket before, and I found it dazzling, especially the fruits and vegetables, which I was used to buying loose by the pound, in outdoor stalls or from the vendors who roamed around Malaka Nazli. Here, they came packaged in green paper cartons, tightly wrapped in a layer of cellophane, so that even ordinary grapes or pears seemed remote and shiny and untouchable. I wondered why anyone would take the trouble to cover bananas or green beans in plastic, when anywhere else in the world, it was possible to simply reach for some. That must be America, I decided: a country where even commonplace items like apples sparkled and looked expensive and desirable beneath their plastic sheathing.

Bread was another mystery. I was used to tall thin golden baguettes purchased fresh from bakeries all over Paris, and in Cairo, we enjoyed hot round pita bread that came from the oven. But here, the package of white bread looked nothing like the bread I knew. It was all dough with practically no crust, while I was used to crust and very little dough.

I was anxious to sample some, but my father seemed horrified: "Loulou, ce n'est pas du pain, ça," he said; This is not bread. We never bought white bread from the supermarket near the Broadway Central and rarely, if ever, later on.

A few days after we'd arrived, the resettlement agency called, asking to see us. HIAS had discharged us from its files; our only remaining contact involved the debt we had incurred for the tickets to sail aboard the *Queen Mary*, and which my father had agreed to repay over time. Now we were in the care of NYANA, the New York Association for New Americans. Mom, who loved to Frenchify every English name, promptly dubbed it *la Nyana*.

My father and César made their way to the agency's lower Manhattan office to meet with the social worker in charge of our Americanization. Sylvia Kirschner, a tough-talking veteran, seemed from the start to take an active, almost visceral dislike to my father. She offered so much advice it was dizzying. Our stay at the Broadway Central had to be as brief as possible. The family needed to find a place to live. My dad, my older siblings, and even my mom all had to go out and find work. We had to master English and meet people and make friends and lead normal lives again.

The initial meeting had the feel of a police interrogation. Why hadn't we begun to look for an apartment? Where were my mother and the other children? Why hadn't they come, too? Had we made any contact with relatives who could help us find work or a place to live? We had been in America all of five days; Mrs. Kirschner seemed in an awful hurry.

My father sat there, listening politely, talking only when she lobbed questions his way. He was so quiet and deferential that the social worker misunderstood—the way that she would consistently misunderstand him. She mistook his silence for contempt, and decided he was being obsequious when he was simply trying to be gentlemanly, more so than usual because he knew that this woman held our fate in her hands.

Unwittingly, Dad had incurred the wrath of Sylvia Kirschner.

It wasn't that Mrs. Kirschner was blind to my father's frailties—his advancing age, his deepening infirmities, his growing dependency. On the contrary, in page after page of notes that read almost like a diary, she chronicled my dad's failing strength, observing that he "looks considerably older than his age, walks with a pronounced limp and also very slowly due to his leg fracture," and "was obviously in pain." Even in the relative comfort of her office, she noticed that he could barely sit still without shifting his leg or grimacing, and he was so "very tired."

Yet, faced with a man clearly in decline, Mrs. Kirschner seemed unmoved. She found him troubling. Though skilled and vastly experienced, a professional who'd helped thousands of immigrants make the transition from the old world, making that transition had been based on the act of *letting go*— abandoning belief systems that were quaint and out of date in favor of the modern, the new, the progressive ideas that were so uniquely American.

That is what assimilation was all about, yet the overly polite gentleman with the vaguely British accent and the severe limp rejected the notion out of hand.

My father was by no means convinced the values of New York trumped those of Cairo. He couldn't see abandoning a culture he loved and trusted in favor of one he barely knew, and which he instinctively disliked. He preferred being an old Egyptian to a new American. He had, in short, no desire whatsoever to assimilate. "We are Arab, madame," he told Mrs. Kirschner.

It was a tragic clash of cultures and personalities. Both strong-willed people, my father and Sylvia Kirschner were set in their ways, and adhered to belief systems that were worlds apart and could never, ever be reconciled.

Like boxers in a ring, they stood in their respective corners, determined to fight to the final bell for the principles they cherished.

And in a way, the test of wills between Sylvia Kirschner and Leon Lagnado in a small refugee agency in early 1964 presaged the conflicts my family would face for years to come in America, where our values and feelings about the importance of God and family and the role of women would constantly collide with those of our American friends. It also hinted at the larger, more terrifying and far deadlier conflict that would break out between the United States and the Muslim world decades later, when the United States would seek to spread its belief in freedom and equality only to find itself spurned at every turn by cultures that viewed America as a godless and profoundly immoral society.

Leon could have been a criminal, a jewel thief, a philanderer, a swindler: nothing could have offended our social worker more than his refusal to conform and change and cast aside those values she clearly viewed as virtually un-American and utterly repugnant.

In her eyes, my father was a patriarch in a land where there were no patriarchs. He wanted to rule over his wife and children—perhaps even his social worker—even though men weren't supposed to do that anymore. "He is an extremely rigid person, with limited horizons, has an Oriental psychology, covered up by a veneer of manners," she wrote. My dad and his views were hopelessly at odds with the enlightened society he had been fortunate to enter.

Or maybe not so fortunate. In one of her more insightful moments, Mrs. Kirschner remarked that my father "regards the immigration as a calamity rather than as an opportunity."

Barely a week later, the six of us trooped down to the tip of Lower Manhattan to meet with the redoubtable Mrs. Kirschner.

She looked us up and down, taking notes, then came to me, peered closely my way, and took more notes. The only one she approved of unreservedly was Suzette. From the start, the two laughed and chatted as if they were old friends. My sister turned on the charm. "A very attractive, articulate young lady," Mrs. Kirschner raved in her case files.

Not all of us fared as well.

César seemed to annoy her almost as much as my father. She didn't accuse my teenage brother of being old-world; she simply resented a sense of ambition she felt went beyond his natural abilities. Mrs. Kirschner seemed troubled by my older brother's outsize dreams, the fact he resisted taking an entry-level job as a messenger or a clerk. She stressed the need for him to be practical and start working.

Over the years, my brother would blame Sylvia Kirschner and *la Nyana* for the path he had taken, for the fact he had gone to work at eighteen, stuck in a series of menial and low-paying jobs, when he should have been attending school and building his career.

Instead, because of the fateful decree that he land a job, any job, the college degree that César could have earned in four years took him a decade to complete. He had no choice but to attend night school, where most students were immigrants like himself, which only underscored his feelings of apartness and alienation. His master's degree, which should have taken two years, took five instead. By the time he was done, César was thirty-five.

Mrs. Kirschner was deeply sympathetic to my mother and anxious to help her, to change her, to help her take advantage of the opportunities that had been denied to her as a woman in Egypt.

Mrs. Kirschner became obsessed with my mother's appearance, the fact that she was toothless and looked older than she was. The idea that a forty-two-year-old woman would walk around without any teeth struck her as almost barbaric. In the social worker's eyes, Edith was timid, quiet, anxious, and clearly under my father's spell. Mom "gave the impression of a frightened person," the social worker wrote, "emphasized by her enormous black eyes which stare almost childlike for protection." Leon was to blame. All the conflicts and problems and pathology she saw in my family were largely the result of his impossibly domineering personality.

🍂　🍂

Mrs. Kirschner wanted us out of the Broadway Central immediately. She had threatened to stop paying our bills, which would have effectively left us homeless.

We would be like normal people again, with a real address. It was, as far as I was concerned, our most exciting day in America: we were going shopping for furniture. We would have our own beds, chairs, couches, tables—all that we'd missed for so long.

As we trooped to Macy's in single file, I noticed the cold didn't bother me a bit. I spotted the sign from blocks away: "Macy's: The World's Largest Store."

I was in awe. But once upstairs, as we wandered through the vast showrooms, we realized there was nothing we could actually afford.

The salesman showed us magnificent king-size beds that looked as if they were out of a movie set but weren't even remotely within our budget. Noting our dismay, he escorted us to a corner where Macy's kept its least expensive merchandise. He pointed out several spartan metal cots. The low-lying folding beds were small and forbidding, with thin striped foam mattresses barely a couple of inches thick.

"*C'est comme dans l'armée*," my mom remarked acidly; It's like the army.

We walked out of Macy's having spent our entire furniture budget on six folding steel cots.

Mrs. Kirschner blanched at the bill—$254—and accused my father of being a spendthrift. Why Macy's? she demanded to know. Why not a neighborhood shop?

She continued to see him as the cause of all our mishaps. A feminist before the flowering of the feminist movement, she viewed my father with such suspicion and hostility that even his attributes in her eyes turned into flaws. Why did a refugee from Egypt shop only in first-rate department stores? Why did he speak with an upper-crust British accent? she wondered. Surely it was an affectation.

My father had lived his entire life by a code of honor. In Egypt, he had been respected and admired precisely for his principles. Yet the chasm was so immense between him and our social worker she found almost nothing to admire—not even his lovely English. His insistence on tradition made him obdurate in her eyes. His devotion to faith and ritual was hopelessly quaint. She cast a wary eye on the religious passion that had always defined my father; because she was so secular, the product of a secular society, she didn't share that passion and dismissed it as superficial and devoid of sincerity.

There was also the notion that he was unemployable—or at least, that was the verdict rendered by *la Nyana* within weeks of our arrival. The agency simply couldn't envision a place for my father in the vast and abundant land of opportunity known as America.

"I have always worked, madame," he told Mrs. Kirschner. Though he had always been secretive with us about his business dealings, he spoke at length with her about his experience as a grocer, an investor, and a pharmaceutical and chemical salesman.

He was desperate to work. When Mrs. Kirschner pointed out his physical limitations, he exclaimed, "Le bon Dieu est grand." But this only led her to complain in her case notes about Dad's tendency to always invoke God. My father, she wrote, "resorts to denials, distortions, and evasion, and his philosophy is that 'God is Great,' which he constantly expresses in French."

She cast a cold eye on his impassioned plea that he *needed* to work to support all six of us, as he had always done. The social worker suggested he apply for welfare, instead. It was, again, a quintessentially American idea, certainly for the early 1960s. But nothing she said could have offended him more. He didn't want charity, he told her coldly. Besides, he had a better idea.

In his walks around Manhattan, he'd noticed the hundreds of little stalls and stands that were everywhere, in the subway stations, on street corners, by bus stops, near any crowded venue, manned by one or two people selling cigarettes, newspapers, chocolate bars, candy, chips, cookies, magazines. Now *there* was a business that seemed manageable. It reminded him of the old days when he and Oncle Raphael had peddled groceries together.

He was prepared to start small, and besides, in his mind, these micro-businesses had enormous potential: New Yorkers wanted their morning paper and their Almond Joy and their pack of Camels in the same way that in Cairo, the typical Egyptian could be counted on to purchase a bottle of olive oil and a can of sardines.

My father decided he was going to open a candy store.

He started combing the classifieds for newsstands and tobacco stalls that were for sale. If no one in America would hire him, it seemed the ideal solution. He decided to appeal to Mrs. Kirschner and *la Nyana* to help him. A loan of $2,000 would do the trick, and then he would be able to support my mom and the rest of us entirely on his own as he always had.

Mrs. Kirschner wouldn't hear of it.

She didn't think she was being arbitrary or unkind. On the contrary, she felt she was being solicitous of my father, whose limp had gotten worse in the months since we had arrived. Prominent doctors the agency consulted said he should stay off his feet and give himself time to heal, yet there he was, proposing a venture that would require him to stand all day. Besides, he didn't even have a coherent business plan—only supreme self-confidence that he could support us.

My dad's impossibly modest wish was turned down. The man who had done business with Coca-Cola couldn't be trusted to sell cigarettes and bubble gum.

In the middle of January, a major blizzard hit New York and left more than a foot of snow. It was more snow than we thought possible. A few days later, we left the Broadway Central for the second floor of the Cohens' brick two-family on Sixty-sixth Street in Brooklyn. Mr. and Mrs. Cohen were waiting to greet us. "Etfadalou," they cried, Arabic for welcome, and with typical Syrian hospitality, they offered us a platter of *khak*, salty ring-shaped biscuits covered with sesame. We hadn't eaten them since Cairo, and biting into the delicious treats made us realize both that we were far from home and that we'd finally arrived. The cots from Macy's were waiting for us. We still didn't have a table, and there was one chair for all six of us.

Yet even here we couldn't quite escape Sylvia Kirschner's wrath.

Six months after our move, she decided to make a home visit. That morning, my father asked me if I wanted to go into Manhattan with him. I nodded yes, eager to accompany him on what seemed like an adventure. I didn't realize that my dad was whisking me out of the house so I wouldn't run into our social worker.

The two were now openly at war, any semblance of civility gone. He had watched as she befriended Suzette, encouraging her to flout his authority by telling her that in America, it was fine for a young woman to be independent. My sister was now threatening to leave the family and live on her own. My distraught father called Mrs. Kirschner and complained she had sent Suzette hurtling down a path that could only lead to disaster. "We will be ruined, madame," he told the social worker. She shrugged and scribbled in her notes that he was being "extremely melodramatic."

My father had other plans for my sister.

At the end of our block, my father had found a new home for himself—the Congregation of Love and Friendship. There it was, the old Cairo synagogue he thought was lost forever, resurrected from the dead, even down to its original Hebrew name, Ahabah ve Ahavah. The Congregation was warm and inviting, and he was reunited with several of his old friends from Egypt, who had undertaken the same sad journey. They prayed with the familiar melodies of Cairo Jewry, in the cherished cadence and rhythm of the temples around Malaka Nazli.

Many of the men had sons Suzette's age who were eager to get married and rebuild their lives. He told the social worker he had suitors lined up for my sister. He couldn't help boasting how skilled he was at arranging marriages—he had helped each one of his five sisters find a husband. Surely he could make a fine match for his own daughter.

Mrs. Kirschner wasn't impressed. In America, girls didn't have to be married off while they were young. They could leave the hearth, pursue an education, have a career. She didn't think my sister had any obligation to get married—or to obey my father.

Dad found all of this unconscionable. On that hot summer day, he determined that he wasn't going to let Sylvia Kirschner get anywhere near me.

I helped him carry the large brown box he carted everywhere these days. My father hadn't found a job, but he was working. He had become a necktie salesman. Inside the box were dozens of ties, soft and silky and patterned in the most wonderful shapes and colors I had ever seen—a treasure trove that any adult male would be certain to want.

An hour or so later, Mrs. Kirschner arrived to find my mother alone. Where was my father? she asked. And where was I? She seemed dismayed we weren't all there, as she'd specified. She was also annoyed. What on earth was Leon doing taking a little girl out on such a scorching day?

My mom tried to soothe her. She brought out a platter piled high with cakes and cookies, and some lemonade, and said I had gone with him to work.

Sylvia Kirschner was beside herself. She decided that he must be using me to boost his chances of making more sales. With my dark hair and dark eyes, I "could easily attract attention," she scribbled furiously. She couldn't imagine why he would take me with him "unless of course, it was for the purpose of using" me to "get a sympathetic reaction" from customers.

I was very lucky: decades would pass before the country embraced a "Take Your Daughter to Work" day and little girls began joining their dads in cubicles and at computer screens and in corporate boardrooms, and having the time of their lives.

It was clear he was struggling in his new business venture, and there were days he didn't make any sales. But on that hot summer morning, as we walked hand in hand, he was hopeful and tender and solicitous. He smiled as he asked me, "Loulou, tu vas m'aider à vendre les cravates?"; Will you help me sell some ties?

He thought that I would bring him luck.

JESSICA HAGEDORN

Born in Manila in 1949, the Filipina-American novelist, poet, musician, and performance artist Jessica Hagedorn has called America "the loneliest of countries." She has written with anger and savage wit about the immigrant's feelings of estrangement: "in new york / they ask me if i'm puerto rican / and do i live in queens? // i listen to pop stations / chant to iemaja / convinced i'm really brazilian." Coming to the United States as a teenager in 1963, she lived in San Francisco before moving to New York City in the late 1970s. In addition to her poems, plays, and performance pieces, Hagedorn is the author of the novels *Dogeaters* (1990), *The Gangster of Love* (1996), and *Dream Jungle* (2003), and is also the editor of the collection *Charlie Chan Is Dead: An Anthology of Contemporary Asian American Fiction* (1993).

from

The Gangster of Love

J imi Hendrix died the year the ship that brought us from Manila docked in San Francisco. My brother, Voltaire, and I wept when we read about it in the papers, but it was Voltaire who was truly devastated. Hendrix had been his idol. In homage to Jimi, Voltaire had learned how to play electric guitar, although he'd be the first to admit he wasn't musically gifted. "It's okay for me to dream, isn't it?" He'd laugh. Voltaire grew his bushy hair out and teased it into what he called a "Filipino Afro." Voltaire caused a sensation whenever he appeared in his royal purple bell-bottoms and gauzy shirts from India. My parents were appalled, especially when Voltaire took the next logical step and adopted an "indigenous Filipino" hippie look. The crushed velvet was replaced by batik fabric; the corny peace medallions replaced by carabao horn, scapulars, and amulets he purchased from bemused market vendors in front of Baclaran Church.

My father once threatened to have Voltaire arrested by the Marcos secret police for looking like an effeminate *bakla*. Then there was the incident of Voltaire's guitar, which he set fire to in a very public ritual in Luneta Park. According to my father, Voltaire was on the military's growing shitlist of subversives and hippie dissidents. Nothing much came of my father's threats, except after one of their more physical confrontations when Voltaire disappeared for weeks. My mother was sure he was dead. "He's probably holed up in some Ermita drug den," my father scoffed, though he was plainly worried. Voltaire eventually showed up without explaining himself, but by then no one cared: my mother's announcement that she was finally leaving my father overshadowed everything.

Voltaire and I convinced ourselves that our parents' breakup was temporary, that the journey we were taking with our mother was some sort of weird vacation. Our lives as the children of Milagros Rivera had often consisted of startling events and irreversible showdowns. We were relieved to be away from the Philippines after the bang-bang, shoot-'em-up elections. Who gave a damn about voting anyway? Even my father was forced to admit that the elections were a joke. Everyone knew Crocodile had fixed it to win. That's what Voltaire called Marcos now—Crocodile. Imelda was Mrs. Croc, or Croc of Shit, as Voltaire sometimes said when he was in a truly bitchy mood. Voltaire blamed Marcos, the CIA, and the Catholic Church for everything that was wrong with our country. He once said the CIA had contaminated the Pasig River with LSD as part of their ongoing chemical warfare experiments against the Vietcong. He also claimed that we were the original gooks. He and our sister, Luz, the eldest, used to argue about politics all the time. "Didn't you know the term *gook* originated in the Philippine-American war?" he once yelled at her. "Enough!" Luz yelled back at Voltaire.

Excited and distracted by our sudden trip to America, we didn't dare ask too many questions—even when Luz stubbornly refused to leave Manila and my father.

Voltaire croons softly to himself as he leans over the deck railing and studies the faces of the motley crowd waiting on the pier. " 'Purple Haze was in my brain, lately things don't seem the same . . .' There she is!" He waves to a tiny woman bundled up like an Eskimo in a hooded down parka and pants.

Voltaire must've recognized Auntie Fely from those Kodak cards she sends every Christmas with photos of her with her stepchildren and husband stiffly posed under a lavishly decorated artificial tree and "Merry Xmas & a Happy New Year to You & Yours from the Cruz Family" embossed in gold.

According to my brother, I was three when Auntie Fely left to find work in America. A few years older than my mother, Auntie Fely was unmarried then, and she doted on all of us. She stopped by our house on her way to the airport for one last teary goodbye, though family and friends had already bid their farewells at numerous ceremonial breakfasts, lunches, *meriendas*, and dinners held a month before my aunt's scheduled departure. Luz was the first to receive kisses and hugs, then Voltaire. My aunt gave each of them envelopes stuffed with peso bills. "Don't spend it all on sweets." Because I'm the baby of the family, Auntie Fely saved me for last. She scooped me up with her strong arms and peered into my face as if to memorize it. The intensity of her gaze, magnified through Coke-bottle eyeglasses, frightened me.

Auntie Fely was a nurse, and since I'd been diagnosed as borderline anemic by our family physician, Dr. Katigbak, she had the dubious honor of administering my dreaded vitamin B shot every Tuesday. I would run and hide whenever I saw my aunt approaching in her starched cap and uniform— Auntie Fely took her profession very seriously—carrying that ominous black medical kit packed with glass vials and a sinister array of gleaming silver needles. She'd huff and puff up the winding, graveled pathway, drenched in sweat by the time she reached the front door. "Where's my little patient?" I'd hear her call out in a sweet, singsong voice, as she and my *yaya* Emy hunted for me in every shadowy nook of our rambling ruin of a house.

"Your Auntie Fely's going to miss her little patient so much." She kissed me noisily several times on both cheeks and wept. "Don't ever forget your Auntie Fely."

My right arm still throbbing from yesterday's injection, I howled in terror for my mother, my *yaya* Emy—anyone who could rescue me from my aunt's smothering embrace.

Shortly after she found a job in a public hospital in San Francisco, Auntie Fely was set up by her supervisor, another Filipino nurse named Mrs. Garcia, with a flashy widower from Stockton named Basilio Cruz. Basilio's wife,

Dolly, had recently died in the ICU after a mysterious ailment. There were rumors of foul play—worrisome *tsismis* my mother heard all the way back in Manila—but only rumors. Dolly Cruz had worked as a managing house-keeper at the Hilton Hotel, leaving behind a bubblegum pink, two-bedroom tract home in Daly City, quite a bit of insurance money, and no debts. There were three grown children. The eldest was a postal worker named Boni—short for Bonifacio—who moved back to Stockton after his father remarried and never spoke to him again. The twins, Peachy and Nene, seemed more adaptable and took to calling our aunt Mama Fely. They were unbelievable academic achievers, graduating from high school with honors, then majoring in medicine at the University of San Francisco on scholarships. "USF is the best," Auntie Fely had written my mother proudly in her last Christmas card. "A strict Catholic school."

"Look! We're approaching the Golden Gate." My mother points at the shad-owy outline of the bridge through the thick morning fog.

"But it's not gold," I say, disappointed.

On the windy pier, a burnished man in a dapper felt hat and fur-trimmed overcoat makes face talk, eyebrows going up and down in furious Filipino sign language: *Welcome! Hurry up! What are you waiting for? Everything okay,* ba?

My mother can't help scowling. "That must be the famous Bas." Then she forgets herself, blowing kisses and making twisted crazy faces of her own. Another passenger hands her confetti and streamers, which she flings at the people huddled and waiting below. "Fely! Fely!" Her eyes are moist and I could swear she is sniffling. Is it possible? I nudge Voltaire with my elbow. My mother has always been too tough to let anyone see her cry. "Fely!" She is jumping up and down in her four-inch heels. Voltaire and I exchange amused glances as the other passengers on deck turn to gawk at her.

Our passports are stamped, our suitcases inspected. "My sister is a citi-zen," my mother informs the warehouse crowded with immigration officials and customs agents. Voltaire's long hair, beads, and fringed buckskin jacket (bought off an enterprising Australian hippie in Manila) inspire hostile stares as we exit the customs area into the biting wind. "Thinks he's Tonto," I hear one of the officials saying. Someone laughs.

Auntie Fely is weeping and smiling. Her exclamations and questions overlap, uttered with that same lilting, singsong cadence. "Raquel! *Dios ko!* Remember me? My little patient! *Naku!* How old are you now! Not even a teenager yet! Ay! *Talaga!* So big!" She means mature when she says big. Even after all her years in America, Auntie Fely still says "Open the light . . . close the light" when she orders someone to turn a light switch on or off and "for a while" when she has to put a phone call on hold.

My mother is holding back tears. "Fely, we finally made it."

In my childhood, my mother was a volatile presence, vampy, haughty, impulsive. "Who the fuck do you think you are?" my father used to yell at her. He was a mystery to me, aloof and distracted, anxious about money. I was never sure what he did for a living, except that he employed eleven people. The sign at the entrance to his cramped office read RIVERA TRADING CO.

Whenever she fought with my father, my mother would hop on the next plane bound for Hong Kong or Tokyo. Glamorous cities, distant and exotic enough to provide a distraction, yet only a few hours away from Manila. We were her reluctant, loyal, sullen companions, tagging along on our mother's spur-of-the-moment adventures. That time in Hong Kong, for example. Luz, Voltaire, and I were the only children present in Patsy Lozano's presidential suite at the Peninsula Hotel, brought along by my mother for who knows what reason. Patsy and my mother were both pretty drunk, having a grand time with a rather decadent crew. The men all vaguely resembled my father, with feline Chinese Portuguese nymphets clinging to their sharkskin suits.

The radio was on loud, blaring Perez Prado's heated music. My mother danced with a fat, graceful man, and they showed off some breathtaking mambo moves. Suddenly she pulled away from her sweaty partner and climbed up on the coffee table. Lost in her own world, lithe and exuberant in her green mermaid dress, she shook her bare perfumed shoulders and tossed her head back with abandon. I was enthralled and ashamed of my mother's torrid performance. The music ended, and the fat man helped my mother down as Patsy Lozano applauded. More drinks were consumed, and everyone forgot about us. The fat man whispered in my mother's ear.

*

Luz locked herself in the bathroom to sulk. Voltaire snuck out and was later found by hotel security, aimlessly going up and down the elevators. No one even noticed he was missing. I stayed, sure I was going to die from having to sit there and watch my mother make a spectacle of herself. An eternity later, back in the safety of our much humbler hotel, Luz, Voltaire, and I got in my mother's king-size bed and watched unfunny British comedies on the king-size television. Our mother went nightclubbing with Patsy and the fat man. To spite them all, we ran up a huge bill ordering junk food from room service—making ourselves sick on soda pop, banana splits with chocolate syrup, hot dogs and club sandwiches doused in ketchup and mayonnaise. I threw up all night long, alternating between chills, diarrhea, and a burning fever.

"There, there," Voltaire murmured, helping me wash up for the hundredth time. We ran out of clean towels.

"Are you playacting?" Luz asked me snidely, suspicious as always.

Then there was Tokyo. Voltaire wasn't with us, so there was no one to mediate between my mother and Luz. Now a tall, sour adolescent, Luz shadowed my mother relentlessly like a stern, disapproving chaperone. "Why don't you go sightseeing and let me breathe?" my mother wailed in desperation.

The day we arrived, we ran into a smooth businessman from Manila named Alfonso Something-or-Other. Alfonso's last name was too baroque, too Spanish, and too long to take seriously. We were in the midst of checking in, exhausted and surrounded by luggage, most of it my mother's. "You remember Mr. Something-or-Other, don't you?" My mother gave us one of her warning glances. "He plays golf with your father."

"Ah," Luz said.

"I don't," I chimed in.

We were in no mood for being nice to yet another one of my mother's insincere and fawning admirers. Plus, I never forgot what Sister Immaculada at Our Lady of Perpetual Sorrow had drummed into us in daily catechism class: sex in any form was a mortal sin, and the sin of adultery the absolute worst. Sister Immaculada was the oldest living nun at my school, with bushy gray eyebrows that curled over her eyes. "Not only will you end up in hell forever," Sister Immaculada droned in a raspy voice, "but Lucifer himself will make a special point of torturing you personally. He'll carve out your private parts, barbecue while you watch, then make you eat yourself slowly, morsel by morsel."

"Call me Tito Alfonso," the man said in Spanish to Luz and me. He smelled of leather and expensive soap.

I spoke to him in English. "You're not my uncle."

Luz pinched me, but said nothing.

Alfonso invited us to eat with him in the hotel dining room that evening, and we were annoyed with our mother for accepting his invitation. Luz and I were determined not to leave her alone with him, however, so we tagged along. We made Alfonso suffer by pretending not to hear every time he spoke to us, or else by responding with a terse yes or no. Luz made things worse by speaking to me only in Tagalog.

I drank iced Coca-Cola in a very tall glass, aware of the flirtation going on between my mother and Alfonso. She kept laughing at every other thing he said and leaning closer and closer to him. They had both simply decided to ignore Luz and me. I felt impotent and wished Voltaire was with us, sure that Alfonso wouldn't take as many liberties in his presence. Suddenly I bit down hard on the rim of my glass. The sliver felt cold and dangerous on my tongue. Luz squealed like a pig. "She's going to die! Mama, Raquel ate glass and she's going to die!"

Alfonso and my mother stared at the cracked glass I held in my hand. It took a moment for what I'd done to register in their minds. "Open your mouth," my mother commanded, a strange look on her face. I froze, afraid of what she might do. "Open your mouth," she repeated, glaring at me. The diners from nearby tables looked in our direction.

"Are you all right, *hija*?" Alfonso asked solicitously. He put a hand on my mother's braceleted arm, as if to restrain her from attacking me. The sliver of sharp glass prevented me from speaking.

"She's *insane*," Luz said, to no one in particular. I had gone too far and upset them all, including my sister. The waiter hurried over just as the band onstage began playing "Begin the Beguine." "Filipino," I managed to croak to Luz, pointing at the band. I attempted a smile.

"You're *insane*," Luz repeated.

"*Eb-ri-ting* okay?" our Japanese waiter asked.

"Spit," my mother growled, holding out her napkin. I did as I was told. She wrapped the shard of glass in the napkin, handed it to the startled waiter, then casually ordered another Coke for me.

Our deluded, beautiful mother thought that by running away and spending money my father didn't really have, she could force him to mend his ways. She was a romantic, defiant, and proud woman who sometimes got what she wanted. My father would actually show up and surprise her with presents and flowers, making promises he couldn't or wouldn't keep. He'd take us children on fatherly outings, making a supreme effort not to look bored. We all fell for his charm. When my father didn't feel up to the chase, he would simply wait for my mother to run out of money and return to Manila. He punished her by flaunting his mistress in public. We all knew about his *querida*, a long-legged beauty queen named Evelyn "Baby" Guzman. Another Baby in a long line of Babys. To this day, my mother can't bring herself to speak Baby's name. "That woman" is about all she can manage.

I have made it a point to try and remember everything. I remember that Baby wasn't much older than my sister, Luz—and therefore more threatening to my youth-obsessed mother than any of my father's other women. I always thought it quite fitting and funny that my mother refused to grant my father, Francisco Rivera, a proper divorce. Two years after we moved to America, he chose to bribe Judge Ramos and marry Baby Guzman in an illegal civil ceremony on September 21, 1972, the day Ferdinand Marcos declared martial law in the Philippines.

EVA HOFFMAN

Eva Hoffman was born in 1945 in Krakow, Poland, and immigrated to Canada with her parents as a teenager in 1963. Her first book, the memoir *Lost in Translation: Life in a New Language* (1989), recounts her sense of displacement—at once geographical, cultural, and linguistic (because she knew no English)—as she adjusted to her new home. After attending Rice University, Yale (where she studied music), and Harvard, she taught at several American colleges and worked for the *New York Times* in the 1980s, including a stint as an editor of the *Book Review*. "I think every immigrant becomes a kind of amateur anthropologist," Hoffman once observed. "You do notice things about the culture or the world that you come into that people who grow up in it, who are very embedded in it, simply don't notice. . . . Very gradually you start understanding the inner life of the culture, the life of those both large and very intimate values." She has published a novel, *The Secret* (2001), as well as *Exit into History: A Journey Through the New Eastern Europe* (1993), *Shtetl: The Life and Death of a Small Town and the World of Polish Jews* (1997), and *After Such Knowledge: Memory, History and the Legacy of the Holocaust* (2004).

from
Lost in Translation

The way to jump over my Great Divide is to crawl backward over it in English. It's only when I retell my whole story, back to the beginning, and from the beginning onward, in one language, that I can reconcile the voices within me with each other; it is only then that the person who judges the voices and tells the stories begins to emerge.

The tiny gap that opened when my sister and I were given new names can never be fully closed up; I can't have one name again. My sister has returned to her Polish name—Alina. It takes a while for me to switch back to it; Alina, in English, is a different word than it is in Polish: it has the stamp of the unusual, its syllables don't fall as easily on an English speaker's tongue. In order to transport a single word without distortion, one would have to transport the entire language around it. My sister no longer has one, authentic name, the name that is inseparable from her single essence.

When I talk to myself now, I talk in English. English is the language in which I've become an adult, in which I've seen my favorite movies and read my favorite novels, and sung along with Janis Joplin records. In Polish, whole provinces of adult experience are missing. I don't know Polish words for "microchips," or "pathetic fallacy," or *The Importance of Being Earnest*. If I tried talking to myself in my native tongue, it would be a stumbling conversation indeed, interlaced with English expressions.

So at those moments when I am alone, walking, or letting my thoughts meander before falling asleep, the internal dialogue proceeds in English. I no longer triangulate to Polish as to an authentic criterion, no longer refer back to it as to a point of origin. Still, underneath the relatively distinct monologue, there's an even more interior buzz, as of countless words compressed into an electric blur moving along a telephone wire. Occasionally, Polish words emerge unbidden from the buzz. They are usually words from the primary palette of feeling: "I'm so happy," a voice says with bell-like clarity, or "Why does he want to harm her?" The Polish phrases have roundness and a surprising certainty, as if they were announcing the simple truth.

Occasionally, the hum makes minute oscillations. "I'm learning a lot about intimacy in this relationship," I tell myself sternly, and a barely discernible presence whispers, pianissimo, I love him, that's all. . . . "The reason he's so territorial is because he's insecure," I think of a difficult colleague, and an imp of the perverse says, "Well, simply, he's a bastard. . . ." But I'm less likely to say the latter to my American friends, and therefore the phrase has a weaker life. In order to translate a language, or a text, without changing its meaning, one would have to transport its audience as well.

No, there's no returning to the point of origin, no regaining of childhood unity. Experience creates style, and style, in turn, creates a new woman. Polish is no longer the one, true language against which others live their secondary life. Polish insights cannot be regained in their purity; there's something

I know in English too. The wholeness of childhood truths is intermingled with the divisiveness of adult doubt. When I speak Polish now, it is infiltrated, permeated, and inflected by the English in my head. Each language modifies the other, crossbreeds with it, fertilizes it. Each language makes the other relative. Like everybody, I am the sum of my languages—the language of my family and childhood, and education and friendship, and love, and the larger, changing world—though perhaps I tend to be more aware than most of the fractures between them, and of the building blocks. The fissures sometimes cause me pain, but in a way, they're how I know that I'm alive. Suffering and conflict are the best proof that there's something like a psyche, a soul; or else, what is it that suffers? Why would we need to suffer when fed and warm and out of the rain, were it not for that other entity within us making its odd, unreasonable, never fulfillable demands?

But in my translation therapy, I keep going back and forth over the rifts, not to heal them but to see that I—one person, first-person singular—have been on both sides. Patiently, I use English as a conduit to go back and down; all the way down to childhood, almost to the beginning. When I learn to say those smallest, first things in the language that has served for detachment and irony and abstraction, I begin to see where the languages I've spoken have their correspondences—how I can move between them without being split by the difference.

The gap cannot be fully closed, but I begin to trust English to speak my childhood self as well, to say what has so long been hidden, to touch the tenderest spots. Perhaps any language, if pursued far enough, leads to exactly the same place. And so, while therapy offers me instruments and the vocabulary of self-control, it also becomes, in the long run, a route back to that loss which for me is the model of all loss, and to that proper sadness of which children are never really afraid; in English, I wind my way back to my old, Polish melancholy. When I meet it, I reenter myself, fold myself again in my own skin. I'm cured of the space sickness of transcendence. It is possible that when we travel deep enough, we always encounter an element of sadness, for full awareness of ourselves always includes the knowledge of our own ephemerality and the passage of time. But it is only in that knowledge—not its denial—that things gain their true dimensions, and we begin to feel the simplicity of being alive. It is only that knowledge that is large enough to cradle a tenderness for everything that is always to be lost—a tenderness for each of our moments, for others and for the world.

The gap has also become a chink, a window through which I can observe the diversity of the world. The apertures of perception have widened because they were once pried apart. Just as the number "2" implies all other numbers, so a bivalent consciousness is necessarily a multivalent consciousness.

Multivalence is no more than the condition of a contemporary awareness, and no more than the contemporary world demands. The weight of the world used to be vertical: it used to come from the past, or from the hierarchy of heaven and earth and hell; now it's horizontal, made up of the endless multiplicity of events going on at once and pressing at each moment on our minds and our living rooms. Dislocation is the norm rather than the aberration in our time, but even in the unlikely event that we spend an entire lifetime in one place, the fabulous diverseness with which we live reminds us constantly that we are no longer the norm or the center, that there is no one geographic center pulling the world together and glowing with the allure of the real thing; there are, instead, scattered nodules competing for our attention. New York, Warsaw, Tehran, Tokyo, Kabul—they all make claims on our imaginations, all remind us that in a decentered world we are always simultaneously in the center and on the periphery, that every competing center makes us marginal.

It may be only in my daily consciousness of this that the residue of my sudden expulsion remains. All immigrants and exiles know the peculiar restlessness of an imagination that can never again have faith in its own absoluteness. "Only exiles are truly irreligious," a contemporary philosopher has said. Because I have learned the relativity of cultural meanings on my skin, I can never take any one set of meanings as final. I doubt that I'll ever become an ideologue of any stripe; I doubt that I'll become an avid acolyte of any school of thought. I know that I've been written in a variety of languages; I know to what extent I'm a script. In my public, group life, I'll probably always find myself in the chinks between cultures and subcultures, between the scenarios of political beliefs and aesthetic credos. It's not the worst place to live; it gives you an Archimedean leverage from which to see the world.

*

I'm writing a story in my journal, and I'm searching for a true voice. I make my way through layers of acquired voices, silly voices, sententious voices, voices that are too cool and too overheated. Then they all quiet down, and I reach what I'm searching for: silence. I hold still to steady myself in it. This is the white blank center, the level ground that was there before Babel was built, that is always there before the Babel of our multiple selves is constructed. From this white plenitude, a voice begins to emerge: it's an even voice, and it's capable of saying things straight, without exaggeration or triviality. As the story progresses, the voice grows and diverges into different tonalities and timbres; sometimes, spontaneously, the force of feeling or of thought compresses language into metaphor, or an image, in which words and consciousness are magically fused. But the voice always returns to its point of departure, to ground zero.

This is the point to which I have tried to triangulate, this private place, this unassimilable part of myself. We all need to find this place in order to know that we exist not only within culture but also outside it. We need to triangulate to something—the past, the future, our own untamed perceptions, another place—if we're not to be subsumed by the temporal and temporary ideas of our time, if we're not to become creatures of ephemeral fashion. Perhaps finding such a point of calibration is particularly difficult now, when our collective air is oversaturated with trivial and important and contradictory and mutually canceling messages. And yet, I could not have found this true axis, could not have made my way through the maze, if I had not assimilated and mastered the voices of my time and place—the only language through which we can learn to think and speak. The silence that comes out of inarticulateness is the inchoate and desperate silence of chaos. The silence that comes after words is the fullness from which the truth of our perceptions can crystallize. It's only after I've taken in disparate bits of cultural matter, after I've accepted its seductions and its snares, that I can make my way through the medium of language to distill my own meanings; and it's only coming from the ground up that I can hit the tenor of my own sensibility, hit home.

LI-YOUNG LEE

Born to Chinese parents in Jakarta, Indonesia, in 1957, Lee's family moved to escape persecution, first going to Hong Kong, Macao, and Japan, then settling in the United States in 1964. His books of poetry include *Rose* (1986), *The City in Which I Love You* (1990), *Book of My Nights* (2001), and *Behind My Eyes* (2008), from which the following poem is taken. He is the recipient of a Guggenheim Fellowship, three Pushcart Prizes, the Lannan Literary Award, the American Book Award, the William Carlos Williams Award, and the Delmore Schwartz Memorial Poetry Award. Lee is also the author of a memoir entitled *The Winged Seed* where he probes dislocation, exile, accents, and the adoption by an immigrant of a new persona, all the time asking, "What makes a person want to disavow his own life?" He lives in Chicago.

Self-Help for Fellow Refugees

If your name suggests a country where bells
might have been used for entertainment

or to announce the entrances and exits of the seasons
or the birthdays of gods and demons,

it's probably best to dress in plain clothes
when you arrive in the United States,
and try not to talk too loud.

If you happen to have watched armed men
beat and drag your father
out the front door of your house
and into the back of an idling truck

before your mother jerked you from the threshold
and buried your face in her skirt folds,
try not to judge your mother too harshly.

Don't ask her what she thought she was doing
turning a child's eyes
away from history
and toward that place all human aching starts.

And if you meet someone
in your adopted country,
and think you see in the other's face
an open sky, some promise of a new beginning,
it probably means you're standing too far.

Or if you think you read in the other, as in a book
whose first and last pages are missing,
the story of your own birthplace,
a country twice erased,
once by fire, once by forgetfulness,
it probably means you're standing too close.

In any case, try not to let another carry
the burden of your own nostalgia or hope.

And if you're one of those
whose left side of the face doesn't match
the right, it might be a clue

looking the other way was a habit
your predecessors found useful for survival.
Don't lament not being beautiful.

Get used to seeing while not seeing.
Get busy remembering while forgetting.
Dying to live while not wanting to go on.

Very likely, your ancestors decorated
their bells of every shape and size
with elaborate calendars
and diagrams of distant star systems,
but with no maps for scattered descendants.

And I bet you can't say what language
your father spoke when he shouted to your mother
from the back of the truck, "Let the boy see!"

Maybe it wasn't the language you used at home.
Maybe it was a forbidden language.
Or maybe there was too much screaming
and weeping and the noise of guns in the streets.

It doesn't matter. What matters is this:
The kingdom of heaven is good.
But heaven on earth is better.

Thinking is good.
But living is better.

Alone in your favorite chair
with a book you enjoy
is fine. But spooning
is even better.

JAMAICA KINCAID

"I was always being told I should be something, and then my whole upbringing was something I was not: it was English." Born in 1949 as Elaine Potter Richardson on Antigua, a British colony in the Caribbean, she came to the United States in 1965 initially as an au pair in a New York City suburb. After that she worked at *Art Direction* magazine, took courses in photography at The New School, and began writing for *The New Yorker*. In 1973 she started signing her name as Jamaica Kincaid because of her family's disapproval of her writing. In the essays in *A Small Place* (1988) she challenges the restrictions of colonialism as well as the exploitations of postcolonialism, especially on her native island (of which she is still a citizen), a theme that continues in her novel *The Autobiography of My Mother* (1996). *Lucy* (1990), the novel from which the excerpt below is taken, is a reworking of her first months in a foreign country, a slow rite of passage that continues her fictionalized personal history begun in the novel *Annie John* (1985).

from
Lucy

It was my first day. I had come the night before, a gray-black and cold night before—as it was expected to be in the middle of January, though I didn't know that at the time—and I could not see anything clearly on the way in from the airport, even though there were lights everywhere. As we drove along, someone would single out to me a famous building, an important street, a park, a bridge that when built was thought to be a spectacle. In a daydream I used to have, all these places were points of happiness to me; all these places were lifeboats to my small drowning soul, for I would imagine myself entering and leaving them, and just that—entering and leaving over and over again—would see me through a bad feeling I did not have a name for. I only knew it felt a little like sadness but heavier than that. Now that I saw these places, they looked ordinary, dirty, worn down by so many people entering and leaving them in real life, and it occurred to me that I could not be the only person in the world for whom they were a fixture of fantasy. It was not my first bout with the disappointment of reality and it would not be my last. The undergarments that I wore were all new, bought for my journey, and as I sat in the car, twisting this way and that to get a good view of the sights before me, I was reminded of how uncomfortable the new can make you feel.

I got into an elevator, something I had never done before, and then I was in an apartment and seated at a table, eating food just taken from a refrigerator. In the place I had just come from, I always lived in a house, and my house did not have a refrigerator in it. Everything I was experiencing—the ride in the elevator, being in an apartment, eating day-old food that had been stored in a refrigerator—was such a good idea that I could imagine I would grow used to it and like it very much, but at first it was all so new that I had to smile with my mouth turned down at the corners. I slept soundly that night, but it wasn't because I was happy and comfortable—quite the opposite; it was because I didn't want to take in anything else.

That morning, the morning of my first day, the morning that followed my first night, was a sunny morning. It was not the sort of bright sun-yellow making everything curl at the edges, almost in fright, that I was used to, but a pale-yellow sun, as if the sun had grown weak from trying too hard to shine; but still it was sunny, and that was nice and made me miss my home less. And so, seeing the sun, I got up and put on a dress, a gay dress made out of madras cloth—the same sort of dress that I would wear if I were at home and setting out for a day in the country. It was all wrong. The sun was shining but the air was cold. It was the middle of January, after all. But I did not know that the sun could shine and the air remain cold; no one had ever told me. What a feeling that was! How can I explain? Something I had always known—the way I knew my skin was the color brown of a nut rubbed repeatedly with a soft cloth, or the way I knew my own name—something I took completely for granted, "the sun is shining, the air is warm," was not so. I was no longer in a tropical zone, and this realization now entered my life like a flow of water dividing formerly dry and solid ground, creating two banks, one of which was my past—so familiar and predictable that even my unhappiness then made me happy now just to think of it—the other my future, a gray blank, an overcast seascape on which rain was falling and no boats were in sight. I was no longer in a tropical zone and I felt cold inside and out, the first time such a sensation had come over me.

In books I had read—from time to time, when the plot called for it—someone would suffer from homesickness. A person would leave a not very nice situation and go somewhere else, somewhere a lot better, and then long to go back where it was not very nice. How impatient I would become with such a person, for I would feel that I was in a not very nice situation myself, and how I wanted to go somewhere else. But now I, too, felt that I wanted to be back where I came from. I understood it, I knew where I stood there. If I had had to draw a picture of my future then, it would have been a large gray patch surrounded by black, blacker, blackest.

What a surprise this was to me, that I longed to be back in the place that I came from, that I longed to sleep in a bed I had outgrown, that I longed to be with people whose smallest, most natural gesture would call up in me such a rage that I longed to see them all dead at my feet. Oh, I had imagined that with my one swift act—leaving home and coming to this new place—I could leave behind me, as if it were an old garment never to be worn again, my sad thoughts, my sad feelings, and my discontent with life in general as it presented itself to me. In the past, the thought of being in my present situation had been a comfort, but now I did not even have this to look forward to, and so I lay down on my bed and dreamt I was eating a bowl of pink mullet and green figs cooked in coconut milk, and it had been cooked by my grandmother, which was why the taste of it pleased me so, for she was the person I liked best in all the world and those were the things I liked best to eat also.

The room in which I lay was a small room just off the kitchen—the maid's room. I was used to a small room, but this was a different sort of small room. The ceiling was very high and the walls went all the way up to the ceiling, enclosing the room like a box—a box in which cargo traveling a long way should be shipped. But I was not cargo. I was only an unhappy young woman living in a maid's room, and I was not even the maid. I was the young girl who watches over the children and goes to school at night. How nice everyone was to me, though, saying that I should regard them as my family and make myself at home. I believed them to be sincere, for I knew that such a thing would not be said to a member of their real family. After all, aren't family the people who become the millstone around your life's neck? On the last day I spent at home, my cousin—a girl I had known all my life, an unpleasant person even before her parents forced her to become a Seventh-Day Adventist—made a farewell present to me of her own Bible, and with it she made a little speech about God and goodness and blessings. Now it sat before me on a dresser, and I remembered how when we were children we would sit under my house and terrify and torment each other by reading out loud passages from the Book of Revelation, and I wondered if ever in my whole life a day would go by when these people I had left behind, my own family, would not appear before me in one way or another.

There was also a small radio on this dresser, and I had turned it on. At that moment, almost as if to sum up how I was feeling, a song came on, some of the words of which were "Put yourself in my place, if only for a day; see if you can stand the awful emptiness inside." I sang these words to myself over and over, as if they were a lullaby, and I fell asleep again. I dreamt then that I was holding in my hands one of my old cotton-flannel nightgowns, and it was printed with beautiful scenes of children playing with Christmas-tree decorations. The scenes printed on my nightgown were so real that I could actually hear the children laughing. I felt compelled to know where this night-gown came from, and I started to examine it furiously, looking for the label. I found it just where a label usually is, in the back, and it read "Made in Australia." I was awakened from this dream by the actual maid, a woman who had let me know right away, on meeting me, that she did not like me, and gave as her reason the way I talked. I thought it was because of something else, but I did not know what. As I opened my eyes, the word "Australia" stood between our faces, and I remembered then that Australia was settled as a prison for bad people, people so bad that they couldn't be put in a prison in their own country.

My waking hours soon took on a routine. I walked four small girls to their school, and when they returned at midday I gave them a lunch of soup from a tin, and sandwiches. In the afternoon, I read to them and played with them. When they were away, I studied my books, and at night I went to school. I was unhappy. I looked at a map. An ocean stood between me and the place I came from, but would it have made a difference if it had been a teacup of water? I could not go back.

Outside, always it was cold, and everyone said that it was the coldest winter they had ever experienced; but the way they said it made me think they said this every time winter came around. And I couldn't blame them for not really remembering each year how unpleasant, how unfriendly winter weather could be. The trees with their bare, still limbs looked dead, and as if someone had just placed them there and planned to come back and get them later; all the windows of the houses were shut tight, the way windows are shut up when a house will be empty for a long time; when people walked on the streets they did it quickly, as if they were doing something behind someone's back, as if they didn't want to draw attention to themselves, as if being out in the cold too long would cause them to dissolve. How I longed to see someone lingering on a corner, trying to draw my attention to him, trying to engage me in conversation, someone complaining to himself in a voice I could overhear about a God whose love and mercy fell on the just and the unjust.

I wrote home to say how lovely everything was, and I used flourishing words and phrases, as if I were living life in a greeting card—the kind that has a satin ribbon on it, and quilted hearts and roses, and is expected to be so precious to the person receiving it that the manufacturer has placed a leaf of plastic on the front to protect it. Everyone I wrote to said how nice it was to hear from me, how nice it was to know that I was doing well, that I was very much missed, and that they couldn't wait until the day came when I returned.

One day the maid who said she did not like me because of the way I talked told me that she was sure I could not dance. She said that I spoke like a nun, I walked like one also, and that everything about me was so pious it made her feel at once sick to her stomach and sick with pity just to look at me. And so, perhaps giving way to the latter feeling, she said that we should dance, even though she was quite sure I didn't know how. There was a little portable record-player in my room, the kind that when closed up looked like a ladies' vanity case, and she put on a record she had bought earlier that day. It was a song that was very popular at the time—three girls, not older than I was, singing in harmony and in a very insincere and artificial way about love and so on. It was very beautiful all the same, and it was beautiful because it was so insincere and artificial. She enjoyed this song, singing at the top of her voice, and she was a wonderful dancer—it amazed me to see the way in which she moved. I could not join her and I told her why: the melodies of her song were so shallow, and the words, to me, were meaningless. From her face, I could see she had only one feeling about me: how sick to her stomach I made her. And so I said that I knew songs, too, and I burst into a calypso about a girl who ran away to Port-of-Spain, Trinidad, and had a good time, with no regrets.

The household in which I lived was made up of a husband, a wife, and the four girl children. The husband and wife looked alike and their four children looked just like them. In photographs of themselves, which they placed all over the house, their six yellow-haired heads of various sizes were bunched as if they were a bouquet of flowers tied together by an unseen string. In the pictures, they smiled out at the world, giving the impression that they found everything in it unbearably wonderful. And it was not a farce, their smiles. From wherever they had gone, and they seemed to have been all over the world, they brought back some tiny memento, and they could each recite its history from its very beginnings. Even when a little rain fell, they would admire the way it streaked through the blank air.

At dinner, when we sat down at the table—and did not have to say grace (such a relief; as if they believed in a God that did not have to be thanked every time you turned around)—they said such nice things to each other, and the children were so happy. They would spill their food, or not eat any of it at all, or make up rhymes about it that would end with the words "smelt bad." How they made me laugh, and I wondered what sort of parents I must have had, for even to think of such words in their presence I would have been scolded severely, and I vowed that if I ever had children I would make sure that the first words out of their mouths were bad ones.

It was at dinner one night not long after I began to live with them that they began to call me the Visitor. They said I seemed not to be a part of things, as if I didn't live in their house with them, as if they weren't like a family to me, as if I were just passing through, just saying one long Hallo!, and soon would be saying a quick Goodbye! So long! It was very nice! For look at the way I stared at them as they ate, Lewis said. Had I never seen anyone put a forkful of French-cut green beans in his mouth before? This made Mariah laugh, but almost everything Lewis said made Mariah happy and so she would laugh. I didn't laugh, though, and Lewis looked at me, concern on his face. He said, "Poor Visitor, poor Visitor," over and over, a sympathetic tone to his voice, and then he told me a story about an uncle he had who had gone to Canada and raised monkeys, and of how after a while the uncle loved monkeys so much and was so used to being around them that he found actual human beings hard to take. He had told me this story about his uncle before, and while he was telling it to me this time I was remembering a dream I had had about them: Lewis was chasing me around the house. I wasn't wearing any clothes. The ground on which I was running was yellow, as if it had been paved with cornmeal. Lewis was chasing me around and around the house, and though he came close he could never catch up with me. Mariah stood at the open windows saying, Catch her, Lewis, catch her. Eventually I fell down a hole, at the bottom of which were some silver and blue snakes.

When Lewis finished telling his story, I told them my dream. When I finished, they both fell silent. Then they looked at me and Mariah cleared her throat, but it was obvious from the way she did it that her throat did not need clearing at all. Their two yellow heads swam toward each other and, in unison, bobbed up and down. Lewis made a clucking noise, then said, Poor, poor Visitor. And Mariah said, Dr. Freud for Visitor, and I wondered why she said that, for I did not know who Dr. Freud was. Then they laughed in a soft, kind way. I had meant by telling them my dream that I had taken them in, because only people who were very important to me had ever shown up in my dreams. I did not know if they understood that.

CHANG-RAE LEE

Chang-rae Lee's first novel, *Native Speaker* (1995), is set in Queens, the quintessential "outer borough" of New York City that now holds the distinction of being the "most diverse" county in the United States, with a foreign-born population approaching 50 percent. In the excerpt that follows, Lee's protagonist Henry Park witnesses a tense minor standoff between a Korean-American store owner and an African-American customer, and hints at some of the complex rivalries and alliances that emerge in an intensely competitive, multicultural place like Queens. Late at night, exploiting *themselves* as cheap labor, the proprietors of the Korean store, the Vietnamese deli, and the West Indian takeout vie for a marginal extra dollar or two.

Lee, born in Seoul in 1965, moved to the United States at the age of three and was raised mainly in Flushing—a Queens neighborhood in which new arrivals from Asia have been replacing a former generation of immigrants from Southern Europe for several decades. He has gone on to write the novels A *Gesture Life* (1999), *Aloft* (2004), and *The Surrendered* (2009) in addition to directing the Program in Creative Writing at Princeton University.

from
Native Speaker

A s we passed the rows of Korean stores on the boulevard, John could tell me the names of the owners and previous owners. Mr. Kim, before him Park, Hong, then Cho, Im, Noh, Mrs. Yi. He himself once ran a wholesale shop on this very row, long before all of it became Korean in the 1980s. He sold and leased dry-cleaning machines and commercial washers and dryers, only high-end equipment. He expanded quickly from the little neighborhood business, the street-front store, for he had mastered enough language to deal with non-Korean suppliers and distributors in other cities and Europe. Other Koreans depended on him to find good deals and transact them. Suddenly, he existed outside the intimate community of his family and church and the street where he conducted his commerce. He wasn't bound to 600 square feet of ghetto retail space like my father, who more or less duplicated the same basic store in various parts of the city. Those five stores defined the outer limit of his ambition, the necessary end of what he could conceive for himself. I am not saying that my father was not a remarkable and clever man, though I know of others like him who have reached farther into the land and grabbed hold of every last advantage and opportunity. My father simply did his job. Better than most, perhaps.

Kwang, though, kept pushing, adding to his wholesale stores by eventually leasing plants in North Carolina to assemble in part the machines he sold for the Italian and German manufacturers. He bought into car and electronics dealerships, too, though it was known that some of the businesses had been troubled in recent years, going without his full attention. The rumor was that he'd lost a few million at least. But he seemed to have plenty left. At the age of forty-one he started attending Fordham full-time for his law and business degrees. I have seen pictures of the graduation day hung about his house, Kwang and his wife, May, smiling in the bright afternoon light, bear-hugging each other. He passed the bar immediately, though I know he never intended to practice the law or big corporate business. He wanted the credentials. But that sounds too cynical of him, which would be all wrong. He wasn't vulnerable to that kind of pettiness. He was old-fashioned enough that he believed he needed proper intellectual training and expertise before he could serve the public.

"Henry," he said, "over there, on the far corner." There were two men talking and pointing at each other in the open street display of a wristwatch and handbag store. The lighted sign read H&J ENTERPRISES with smaller Korean characters on the ends. He pulled us over and I followed him out.

The owner recognized Kwang immediately, and stopped arguing with the other man and quickly bowed. The man was shaking a gold-toned watch: it had stopped working and he wanted his money back. The Korean explained to us that he only gave exchanges, no refunds, he seemed to say again for all, pointing continually at the sign that said so by the door. Besides, he told Kwang in Korean, this man bought the watch many months ago, during the winter, and he was being generous enough in offering him another one. He added, *You know how these blacks are, always expecting special treatment.*

Kwang let the statement pass. He introduced himself to the man, telling him he was a councilman. He asked the man if he had bought other things at the store.

"I stop here every couple weeks," the man answerer. "Maybe pick out something for my wife."

"One time a muhnt!" the Korean insisted.

The man shook his head and mouthed, "Bullshit." He explained he'd originally come to get an exchange, but the owner was so rude and hard to understand (intentionally, he thought) that he decided to demand a full refund instead. He wasn't going to leave until he got one. He showed us the receipt. Kwang nodded and then gestured for the storekeeper to speak with him inside the store. I waited outside with the customer. I remember him particularly well because his name, Henry, was embossed on a tag clipped to his shirt pocket. When I told him my name he smiled weakly and looked in the store for Kwang. I didn't say anything else and he coughed and adjusted his glasses and said he was tired and frustrated and just wanted his money or an exchange so he could get on home. He was a salesman at the big discount office furniture store off 108th Street.

"I don't know why I keep shopping here," he said to me, searching the wares in the bins. "It's mostly junk anyway. My wife kind of enjoys the jewelry, though, and it's pretty inexpensive, I suppose. Buying a watch here was my mistake. I should know better. Thirteen ninety-nine. And *I know* I wasn't born yesterday."

We laughed a little. Henry explained that it was easy to stop here on Fridays to buy something for his wife, a pair of earrings or a bracelet. "She works real hard all week and I like to give her a little present, to let her know I know what's going on." She was a registered nurse. He showed me a five-dollar set of silver earrings. "I was gonna buy these, but I don't know, you don't expect anybody to be *nice* anymore, but that man in there, he can be cold."

I didn't try to explain the store owner to Henry, or otherwise defend him. I don't know what stopped me. Maybe there was too much to say. Where to begin?

Certainly my father ran his stores with an iron attitude. It was amazing how successful he still was. He generally saw his customers as adversaries. He disliked the petty complaints about the prices, especially from the customers in Manhattan. "Those millionaires is biggest trouble," he often said when he got home. "They don't like anybody else making good money." He hated explaining to them why his prices were higher than at other stores, even the other Korean ones, though he always did. He would say without flinching that his produce was simply the best. The freshest. They should shop at other stores and see for themselves. He tried to put on a good face, but it irked him all the same.

With blacks he just turned to stone. He never bothered to explain his prices to them. He didn't follow them around the aisles like some storekeepers do, but he always let them know there wasn't going to be any *funny business* here. When a young black man or woman came in—old people or those with children in tow didn't seem to alarm him—he took his broom and started sweeping at the store entrance very slowly, deliberately, not looking at the floor. He wouldn't make any attempt to hide what he was doing. At certain stores there were at least two or three incidents a day. Shoplifting, accusations of shoplifting, complaints and arguments. Always arguments.

To hear those cries now: the scene a stand of oranges, a wall of canned ham. I see my father in his white apron, sleeves rolled up. A woman in a dirty coat. They lean in and let each other have it, though the giving is almost in turns. It's like the most awful and sad opera, the strong music of his English, then her black English; her colorful, almost elevated, mocking of him, and his grim explosions. They fight like lovers, scarred, knowing. Their song circular and vicious. For she always comes back the next day, and so does he. It's like they are here to torture each other. He can't afford a store anywhere else but where she lives, and she has no other place to buy a good apple or a fresh loaf of bread.

In the end, after all those years, he felt nothing for them. Not even pity. To him a black face meant inconvenience, or trouble, or the threat of death. He never met any blacks who measured up to his idea of decency; of course he'd never give a man like Henry half a chance. It was too risky. He personally knew several merchants who had been killed in their stores, all by blacks, and he knew of others who had shot or killed someone trying to rob them. He had that one close call himself, of which he never spoke.

For a time, he tried not to hate them. I will say this. In one of his first stores, a half-wide fruit and vegetable shop on 173rd Street off Jerome in the Bronx, he hired a few black men to haul and clean the produce. I remember my mother looking worried when he told her. But none of them worked out. He said they either came to work late or never and when they did often passed off fruit and candy and six-packs of beer to their friends. Of course, he never let them work the register.

Eventually, he replaced them with Puerto Ricans and Peruvians. The "Spanish" ones were harder working, he said, because they didn't speak English too well, just like us. This became a kind of rule of thumb for him, to hire somebody if they couldn't speak English, even blacks from Haiti or Ethiopia, because he figured they were new to the land and understood that no one would help them for nothing. The most important thing was that they hadn't been in America too long.

I asked Henry instead if he had known of Kwang before. He didn't, not caring much for politics or politicians. "But you know," he said, "he's not like all the other Koreans around here, all tense and everything."

When they returned, the shop owner approached Henry and nodded very slightly, in the barest bow, and offered him another watch, this one boxed in clear plastic. "I give you betteh one!" he said, indicating the higher price on the sticker. "Puh-rease accept earring too. Pfor your wifuh. No chargeh!"

Henry looked confused and was about to decline when John Kwang reached over and vigorously shook his hand, pinning the jewelry there. "This is a gift," he said firmly. "Mr. Baeh would like you to accept it."

Henry shook our hands and left for home. As we waited for the traffic to pass so we could pull away from the curb, I saw Baeh inside his tiny store shaking his head as he quickly hung handbags. Every third or fourth one he banged hard against the plastic display grid. He wouldn't look back out at us. Kwang saw him, too. We drove a few blocks before he said anything.

"He knows what's good for us is good for him," Kwang said grimly. "He doesn't have to like it. Right now, he doesn't have any choice."

At the time I didn't know what Kwang meant by that last notion, what kind of dominion or direct influence he had over people like Baeh. I only considered the fact of his position and stature in the community as what had persuaded the storekeeper to deal fairly with Henry. I assumed Baeh was honoring the traditional Confucian structure of community, where in each village a prominent elder man heard the townspeople's grievances and arbitrated and ruled. Though in that world Baeh would have shown displeasure only in private. He would have acted as the dutiful younger until the wise man was far down the road.

But respect is often altered or lost in translation. Here on 39th Avenue of old Queens, in the mixed lot of peoples, respect (and honor and kindness) is a matter of margins, what you can clear on a $13.99 quartz watch, or how much selling it takes to recover when you give one away. I knew that Mr. Baeh would stay open late tonight, maybe for no more of a chance than to catch the dance club overflow a full five hours later, drunk and high kids who might blow a few bucks on one of his gun-metal rings or satin scarves or T-shirts. The other merchants on the block would do the same. The Vietnamese deli, the West Indian takeout. Stay open. Keep the eyes open. You are your cheapest labor. Here is the great secret, the great mystery to an immigrant's success, the dwindle of irredeemable hours beneath the cheap tube lights. Pass them like a machine. Believe only in chronology. This will be your coin-small salvation.

SHIRLEY GEOK-LIN LIM

Although she did not immigrate to the United States until she was 24, Shirley Geok-lin Lim (born in 1944) was unusual in that she arrived with a full and easy command of the English language, along with a university degree. From an early age, growing up destitute in British Malaya, Lim had sought refuge from the painful realities of her life in literature, and had her first poem published in the *Malacca Times* when she was ten years old. She calls her relationship with this "imperial language" the "only constant in my life": a language "which, to my mind, now plainly belongs to the entire human species, like rice, cotton, or paper." A Fulbright scholarship took her to Brandeis University where she earned an M.A. in 1971. To date Lim has written five books of poetry, a novel, three short-story collections, and a memoir (from which the following excerpt is drawn): the award-winning *Among the White Moon Faces* (1996).

from
Immigrant Mother

I became an American politically with the birth of my child. I may have been a blackbird, flying into Boston as a disheveled traveler uncertain whether I was choosing expatriation, exile, or immigration. But I had no such doubts about my unborn child. He would be an American child of Jewish and Asian descent.

Native-born children carry the cultural imprint of Americanism in a way that their immigrant parents cannot. If they become encumbered by nostalgia and regret, like their parents, this consciousness of another country cannot undermine the infant primacy of an American homeland. I wanted my child to possess the privileges of a territorial self, even as I had as a young Malaysian. "Out of the cradle endlessly rocking," the folding into and unfolding out of a social space and a people. While all citizens are guaranteed juridically their claim to a place in the United States, not every claim is unquestioned, nor is that place certain. Poverty, skin color, sex, disease, disability, any difference can arouse suspicion and exclusion. I did not expect my child to be safe from these discriminations, but I wished, at least for his infancy, the primal experience of bonding with an American homeland. In this desire, I marked myself as a U.S. citizen, and I finally began the process for citizenship.

Without relatives and with only my college colleagues for a community, pregnancy was a lonely, isolating experience. One morning I had to be in New York City for an interview with the Immigration and Naturalization Office. The train rattled through the underground tunnels into Grand Central Station, shaking its entire length. On any other morning I would have been absorbing its energy, bouncing with it, waiting eagerly to emerge into the day outside and to merge into the anonymity of coats and boots and shining shop windows.

Now, overcome with nausea, I munched furiously on Saltine crackers. My seatmate pretended not to see the crumbs that fell like dandruff over my black winter coat. My stomach heaved and rumbled. It was aching to throw up, but there was nothing inside, only dry lumps of baked flour like wet cement chuting down to settle my hunger pangs.

The doors opened and everyone pushed out. I was a black fish gathered up in the net of bodies. The bodies carried me out of the train and up the stairs through other tunnels. I could not slow my stride; my legs trundled like part of a centipede's hundred pairs. I had no will in this morning rush hour's masses. Slowly my head was turning dark, and I felt myself lose consciousness. The centipede was rushing down a flight of steps toward the downtown Lexington. Just ahead the subway cars were spilling with other bodies, and a mechanical voice was announcing, "Keep clear of the closing doors. Keep clear of the closing doors." The feet rushed faster, faster down the steps.

But I could not keep up. I sat down on the steps, despite the press of bodies behind me. The river backed up, split open, then swirled around the boulder that was myself. I put my head down between my knees. The concrete steps were black and brown with grime. The dirt had piled up along the backs of the steps, bits of fresh candy wrappers still colored blue and gold, brown filter tips and butts with shredded tobacco falling out. I could see only a little piece of concrete. The rest was filled with moving legs, tan and khaki pants, blue dungarees, suede heels, frayed hems and silk-bound hems, unwashed sneakers split at the sides, white leather sneakers squeaking new, dirt-crusted workboots with soles like floors. No one stopped to ask why I was sitting on the steps of Grand Central Station. I was grateful for the city's impersonality: I could have been sitting by the abyss of the Grand Canyon listening to the rush of the wind among the bent piñon and ponderosa pines. The huge ingrained ugliness of New York's subways appeared as much a force of nature as the Grand Canyon's wind-scrubbed beauty; I was as invisible in the midst of thousands of hurrying feet as a hiker lost on the canyon's red-scarp edge.

On Saint Valentine's Day, 1980, four months pregnant, I stood in a hall in White Plains and swore allegiance to the flag and to the republic for which it stands. There must have been about two hundred others there that morning, more white than brown, and there was a festive mood in the hall as the black-robed justice congratulated us. This is the crucible of America, the moment when the machinery of the state opens its gate and admits irrevocably those aliens who have passed the scrutiny of its bureaucrats—language tests, history tests, economic tests, social tests. Tests that impress with the enormous and amazingly indifferent power of representative Americans to deny you identity, tests that force you to compliance, tests for inclusion that threaten exclusion. So my patriotism on my first day as an American citizen was not unbounded. Scooping a piece of buttermilk pancake from its puddle of maple syrup at the International House of Pancakes where I had gone to celebrate my passage into American identity, I felt alien in a different way, as if my ambivalence toward the United States must now extend inward to an ambivalence toward myself. No longer a traveler, I was included in my accusations of America.

My morning sickness disappeared after three months. I swelled and swelled, fifty pounds above my normal weight, half as much as I was, a red plum tomato in my cotton summer frock. We had moved to Westchester County, fifty miles out of Manhattan, two years earlier, and while Charles commuted to teach in Manhattan, I fell in love with the Westchester suburbs for the first time. The May days were busy with Queen Anne's lace, day lilies, Dutchmen's-breeches, and flourishing sumac. I fretted over a strand of bright orange butterfly weed that had sprung up by Route 100, waving above the still gray water of the Croton Reservoir, just below our white-and-green colonial home. It was too exotic, an endangered wildflower, in plain view, with the red-winged blackbirds flashing among the sumac bushes. Sure enough in a few days the butterfly weed blossoms, winged like palpitating floaters that its milky sap invites, were gone. Some passing human had picked them, robbing the seeds that would have borne more orange wings for the years after.

We practiced huffing and puffing. The gynecologist's receptionist had me down as a *mater primigravida*. The term conjured the images of the Virgin Mary from those faraway convent days: the gravely tragic countenance, the graceful folds of cloak and robes concealing a thickened waistline. A pregnant woman oppressed by secrets, social isolation, poverty, married to a man not the father of her baby, that central story never told directly, the story of woman's delight in childbearing. The narrowing of the story to simply mother and infant, the man far away in the clouds or discreetly in the background, together with the oxen and donkeys. A celibate woman's fantasy, a revenge story for women harrowed by men's demands and commands.

I was lucky. Charles was tender and attentive, but all that deep breathing and panting came to nothing. At almost nine pounds, the baby had to be sprung out of my bony pelvic cage by a scalpel. As the nurses rushed me into the operating room, my temperature rising precipitously each minute and the fetal temperature mounting to life-threatening degrees, I focused on the life in my body. It, he, she was ready to emerge from the container which was myself. The event of childbirth is violent and bloody. As if experiencing her death, the mother cannot change course. She endures and, if she is able and wise, assists in the moment of expulsion. When the anesthesiologist crammed the plastic apparatus into my throat like a giant obscene penis, I willed my body to relax, to float like the lotus yielding its seeds to the light.

At that moment I felt the cold swab of the anesthetic-soaked cotton like the curve of a scimitar across my abdomen and lost consciousness.

The nine months of pregnancy had been a slowly swelling swoon into domesticity, marked by giddy strolls through aisles of baby perambulators, crib mobiles, bath toys, terry-cloth books, hooded towels, fuzzy blue, brown, and white rabbits, dogs, lions, unicorns, Smurfs, bears and more bears, an instant cornucopia of infant goods for infant-obsessed Americans. But once my son was born, strenuously hungry and alert, it became clear I could not simply buy him a life.

I had entered U.S. society through the workplace, taking my seat in department meetings and at conference sessions as a colleague. My husband's parents were dead, he was estranged from his only brother, and all my brothers were in Malaysia. It mattered that we spent Easter, Passover, Memorial Day, Labor Day, Hanukkah, Christmas, and New Year's Eve alone, but it didn't matter that much. Occasionally a colleague invited us to a department picnic or a department brunch. But babies do not socialize through English departments. I was tormented by the fear that my son would grow up isolated, as I was, in the United States. I did not wish my son to be lonely the way we were. He was an American, whatever that was, and I wanted him to have the full plenitude of his world, not the shadowy existence of a green-card holder.

The myth of assimilation became a pressing reality as soon as I brought my son home from Northern Westchester Hospital. A child's society is his parents': cut off from the umbilical cord, he is nonetheless tied to the company his mother keeps. Or does not keep, in my case. It may have been important for my imagination to maintain the distance of the resident alien, but I wanted something different for my son. Despite the absence of an extended community, I wanted for him to have a pride of belonging, the sense of identity with a homeland, that which I had possessed as a Chinese Malaysian for a brief time in my youth. I wanted Gershom to be able to run for the presidency of the United States if that was what he wished.

The passage of assimilation began at the earliest age. Anxiously I accepted every birthday invitation that came his way from the Montessori mothers. Together, Gershom and I shopped for Mattel educational toys, boxes with differently shaped mouths and blocks, cobblers' benches, multicolored xylophones, huge plastic contraptions that invited baby fists to punch and ring and pull and pat. I chose the opulent set, the more expensive version of a brand-name product, while Gershom sat in his thrift-store stroller, pointing at each large package within reach. We drove down numerous Yorktown and Somers circular dead-ends, clutching party invitations and directions in one hand. His bottom still padded with diapers, he waddled among pink-cheeked, blond, and blue-eyed toddlers. I sat with the mommies, an alien among a dozen or so white women, an awkward mismatch among the grandmothers furiously snapping Nikons at the cake and chubby faces and the fathers with rolling video cameras. A college teacher years older than the young home-makers with junior-executive husbands, I held my breath and sat very gingerly on the new sofas in these strangers' split-level ranches, where lavish bathrooms were cleaner than the shelters of billions of other humans. I could not afford contemptuous segregation or condescending kinship if I wished Gershom to have a full human connection with America.

Malls and department-store aisles do not discriminate. Everything is for sale to everyone. But women do. Mothers, keeping a wary eye on their scrambling pebble-picking children in playgrounds, do. Fathers, arriving to pick up their toddlers after work, loosening their ties by the Montessori entrance, do. If I could hope to have Gershom pass into Middle America in wall-to-wall carpeted living rooms, we never succeeded in the public playgrounds among anonymous whites.

Weekends and summers Gershom and I set forth to Reis Park, Leonard Park, Muscoot Farm, and assorted town fairs and parades. Cautiously I let him loose in the sandbox, retreated to one side where other mothers stood under the shade of birches and oaks and cast their eyes sidewise on the little spaders and grubbers. There were no homesteaders here, only transient visitors who might or might not return another afternoon. Was it the chip on my shoulder that sounded the alarm? I watched enviously as strangers veered toward each other and began exchanging intimacies of toilet training and bed-wetting. I imagined their eyes were already measuring their toddlers' compatibility, one pink hand patting another pink hand's castle.

My olive-skinned child had dark handsome eyes and thick dark hair. He was oblivious to social slight as he scrambled up the teeter-totter. There was no one to teeter with him. The other children had wandered away with their parents who strolled off deep in conversation. I called out to him, placed my weight on two legs so that my body did not pull the balance down, and planted the illusion that between us we could move the teeter-totter up and down, up and down.

I had approached being alone in the United States as inevitable. It was a lonely society, even lonelier for an Asian immigrant whose train seat next to her usually remained untaken till the car was full. But what I accepted as my position in the United States I felt keenly as unacceptable for my son. A grievance gnawed in me, perhaps the displaced desires for assimilation, a growing anger that, despite his birth here in the United States, his childhood was still marked by the perception of my foreignness.

I began to ask my colleagues, "When did your family come to the United States?"

"Oh, I don't know. My grandfather was a Prussian officer, so I must be third generation."

"My mother came after World War I; got out just before Hitler. What does that make me? A second generation?"

"I came over from Manchester to do my master's at New York University. Never went home."

"Well, I'm not an American citizen. I still have my Canadian passport."

"Of course, my husband's parents are from Sicily. They are horribly traditional."

All these recent origins. All these immigrants. But the stiffness and tentativeness, the distinct charge of distance that marked one as alien and outsider, was directed chiefly to those who did not look white European.

There are many ways in which America tells you you don't belong. The eyes that slide around to find another face behind you. The smiles that appear only after you have almost passed them, intended for someone else. The stiffness in the body as you stand beside them watching your child and theirs slide down the pole, and the relaxed smile when another white mother comes up to talk. The polite distance as you say something about the children at the swings and the chattiness when a white parent makes a comment. A polite people, it is the facial muscles, the shoulder tension, and the silence that give away white Americans' uneasiness with people not like them. The United States, a nation of immigrants, makes strangers only of those who are visibly different, including the indigenous people of the continent. Some lessons begin in infancy, with silent performances, yet with eloquent instructions.

OLGA BROUMAS

Born in Hermoupolis, Greece, in 1949, Olga Broumas came to the United States in the late 1960s on a Fulbright scholarship to the study at the University of Pennsylvania. Her first published poems were in Greek, but her 1977 book *Beginning with O*—from which the poem "Sometimes, as a child" is taken—was selected by Stanley Kunitz for the Yale Series of Younger Poets. Her books of poetry since then include *Soie Sauvage* (1980), *Pastoral Jazz* (1983), *Perpetua* (1989), and *Rave: Poems, 1975–1999* (1999); she has also translated work by the Greek poet Odysseas Elytis. Her poetry frequently explores themes of lesbian sexuality and the oppression of women, in language often charged with echoes of Greek literature, mythology, and landscape. Currently she is poet-in-residence at Brandeis University.

Sometimes, as a child

when the Greek sea
was exceptionally calm
the sun not so much a pinnacle
as a perspiration of light, your brow and the sky
meeting on the horizon, sometimes

you'd dive
from the float, the pier, the stone
promontory, through water so startled
it held the shape of your plunge, and there

in the arrested heat of the afternoon
without thought, effortless
as a mantra turning

you'd turn
in the paused wake of your dive, enter
the suck of the parted waters, you'd emerge

clean caesarean, flinging
live rivulets from your hair, your own
breath arrested. Something immaculate, a chance

crucial junction: time, light, water
had occurred, you could feel your bones
glisten
translucent as spinal fins.

                    In rain-
green Oregon now, approaching thirty, sometimes
the same
rare concert of light and spine
resonates in my bones, as glistening
starfish, lover, your fingers
beach up.

TAHIRA NAQVI

A native of Lahore, Pakistan, Tahira Naqvi (born in 1952) moved to the United States in 1971. She has taught Urdu at New York University and Columbia University, among other institutions, and is the author of two story collections, *Attar of Roses and Other Stories of Pakistan* (1997) and *Dying in a Strange Country* (2001). The latter volume (from which the following selection is taken) presents a portrait of the Pakistani diaspora in America through a series of interconnected tales told in multiple voices. "The connection between the home country and the acquired immigrant culture has always fascinated me," she has observed, "and I'm always being compelled to think or write about it." Naqvi has also published English translations of a number of Urdu writers, including Ismat Chughtai, Khadija Mastur, and Saadat Hasan Manto.

Dying in a Strange Country

S akina Bano was afraid. Afraid not of the fact that she was on an airplane larger than her house for the first time in her life, nor of travelling alone, companionless, on a twenty-two hour journey with four stops in cities she had not heard of before with names she could not pronounce correctly, although this was something that would surely crowd fear into the heart and mind of any sixty-nine year old widow. No, it was not the journey that troubled her. Why, when the plane lifted itself from the ground and the noise and vibration rattled her skull, it was not fear that laid its hand upon her heart, but an exhilaration, as if she were being lifted like a cloud toward the sky. No, her fear had little to do with such concerns.

"Son, I can't come," she had written to Asad. "I'm old, I want to take my last breath in my own country, and be buried among my own people. Tell me this, if I die there, what will happen to me?"

First Asad tried to scold her in his letters, telling her she was stubborn, childish. "What example are you setting for the others?" he wrote irately. Sakina Bano was amused when her son scolded her. How ridiculous to be drowned in a storm of anxiety over something like this, he reproached. Ridiculous? What did he, a young man whose whole life lay ahead of him like a stretch of fertile fields, know of such things? Letter after letter fell into the tinny silence of her letterbox on 73 Sabir Street, Gujranwala. Then Asad gave her an ultimatum: he said pointblank he would not come home until she first visited him in Amreeka. "I had not imagined that you would deny me this little comfort, but you have and so I too will be stubborn," he added. She smiled to think that is what she often did, complain and give him ultimatums, but now it was his turn.

She relented. Dragging her fear along with her like a tenacious shadow, she boarded the plane and thought, "He'll never come back and live on 73 Sabir Street so I must now see where his new home will be. Everyone is talking about Amreeka, I should see what's the fuss about."

A clinking, clattering noise interrupted her reverie. Within minutes the air in the cabin was redolent with the smell of richly spiced food, seasoned heavily with garam masala, like wedding fare. "We're going to eat," Sakina Bano told herself nervously. She wasn't hungry, having eaten dinner at Kubra's house an hour before her departure from Lahore. "Here Amma, just a little more, who knows what you'll get on the plane," her daughter had said, depositing another helping of pulao with green peas on her mother's plate.

The food carts began to crowd the aisles. Sakina Bano had been warned about the possibility of pork in airline food and elsewhere, and "I hear the meat isn't always halal," her daughter had said in a cautionary tone. There was also alcohol. She could smell it, like urine left overnight in the open drain along a street wall. Well, then she must ask, she could lose nothing by asking. But how difficult that was! Food trays were being passed with such rapidity that she found it impossible to hold the stewardess's attention long enough for a question. Also, she felt awkward, overcome by a diffidence she could not account for. Was she one who had difficulty speaking her mind?

Her tray remained untouched. She did not even try to slip her finger under the silvery wrapping and lift a corner to see what she was about to eat, and then, when coffee and tea were being passed out, she swiftly laid a restraining hand on the stewardess's arm. Her reserve disguised with a self-conscious smile, she asked in a small voice, "This is all halal meat, isn't it?"

"We serve only halal meat, Ammaji," the woman replied with a condescending inflection, her eyes, heavy-lidded from the weight of mascara and layers of green and blue makeup, flickering only momentarily with interest.

Rid of her dilemma, Sakina Bano turned to the food. She removed the silver foil on the tray and looked down, with surprise, on biryani and korma. Some of the buttery brown rice slipped onto her kurta front as she neatly rounded off small portions with her fingers, and after the first morsel was chewed and swallowed, she realized she was hungry after all. The food was well cooked, spicy, and although she would have preferred a fluffy, steaming chappati and some daal of maash, this was something to talk about when she returned to Sabir Street. Wedding food on the plane. Well, why not, after the thousands of rupees for one ticket.

As she wiped her hands later with a white paper napkin, she thought, What a waste. Could she not have walked to the bathroom and washed her hands? But where was the bathroom, could she easily walk to it? she asked herself in sudden consternation. "There will be many new things, Amma," Asad had written. "Just watch what the others are doing." No one was running to the bathrooms to wash hands, she saw.

On her left sat a dour-looking man, in his late sixties perhaps, or maybe older, with a stomach flabby like risen dough and a peppery, bristly beard, and she wasn't about to learn anything from watching him. He was probably as much a novice as she; he had dropped cutlery at least twice and his paper napkin was lying forlornly on the floor while he used his handkerchief to wipe his hands. But now the young girl on her right, in the window seat, who had told Sakina Bano earlier that her name was Abida and she was returning to college, now she seemed like a person who had made this trip more than once. She had handled the paper napkin deftly, making no fumbling moves with the cutlery that came wrapped in a narrow plastic bag. Sakina Bano briefly fidgeted with the bag in the hopes of getting a spoon out, but she soon discovered she would have to wrestle with it before she gained access to what was buried inside. Why, who needed the spoon, and anyway, was she going to flounder clumsily with a fork and knife and make herself look foolish? She had enough sense not to reveal her shortcomings. So she ate as she had always done, with her fingers. The lissome young girl with bright, almond-shaped eyes and long, black hair that fell on her shoulders like strands of silk, was Pakistani, and therefore no stranger to old customs.

But what was all this compared to the cacophonous noise that clamored in her head? That threatened to drown out all other sounds?

What if . . . yes, what if she suffered a heart attack just this instant and died? Why, don't people often die quietly and without a fuss? And if she were a corpse, would the airline transport her back to Pakistan? What if the plane was forced to make a landing in the country they were flying over when she took her last breath, and her body was abandoned there, in a strange country? She knew Cairo was their first stop, but were they near Cairo? She couldn't be certain. However, the thought that Egypt might be the place where she was left for burial provided some comfort, for at least then she would be among fellow Muslims.

Sakina Bano swallowed the spit in her mouth which felt like a cotton ball, leaned back in her seat, her hand firmly wrapped around the hot cup of tea in front of her. She took a deep breath. For the moment, just for the moment, the fear was put to rest.

Cairo was a hurried stop. The passengers were not allowed to get off, something about terrorism, she heard one of the passengers remark. She imagined men rushing about with guns, spraying strangers with bullets and felt unnerved by sudden dread. But to die was to die. She smiled the smile of a fatalist. What was important was where one died. What could a terrorist do to her in Cairo?

After Cairo she lost track of time. Day and night seemed to cross over so rapidly she didn't know whether to sleep or remain awake. When the plane came down at Frankfurt it was nearly morning she saw. Below her, when the plane descended in sudden swoops as if it were about to fall, were dark smoky whorls streaked with orange and red and fringed with gold.

Inside, the airport looked isolated, the only passengers in sight wandering about like mindless creatures, faces ashen from exhaustion and lack of sleep, their bodies slouched with fatigue, their steps leaden. Some were stretched out on shiny, slippery benches in the transit lounge to snatch whatever fitful sleep they could. Airport officials, usually crisp and alert no doubt, also wore crestfallen looks and moved about unhurriedly. The clock on a white wall above a red sign she couldn't read said three.

No sooner did she deposit her weary, aching body into one of the chairs that lined a large glass wall than a tiny spurt of anxiety crawled out of her thoughts like a worm, edged its way into her blood, spreading like an arrhythmic flurry. What if? The possibility was too frightful for her to weigh. Sakina Bano stiffened in her chair. She must not fall asleep. Her eyes strayed to the clock, she looked for the seconds hand. But the hand was stationary, it seemed, stilled. A German clock keeping German time; what could it mean to her? Turning away, she looked about her anxiously and observed Abida, her young companion from the plane, slumped in a seat not too far from her. Her thin arms crossed over a large canvas bag in her lap, the girl slept soundly. How Sakina Bano envied the untroubled and tranquil expression on her face. How happy her dreams must be, unencumbered and free.

Later, back on the plane, before the food carts came clattering down the aisles again, Sakina Bano decided she would talk to Abida. The two women reminisced about places they both knew in Lahore, Abida's hometown; Anarkali Bazaar where every day men, women, and children roamed about as if a carnival was in progress, Bano Bazaar where a woman may find all she ever wanted, McLeod Road where all the cinema houses were and where mammoth film posters rose like walls guarding a city, and the shrine of Data Sahib where you made vows and prayers were answered.

"Is this your first visit, Ammaji?" the girl asked, placing the book she had been reading face down in her lap.

"Yes," Sakina Bano said, sighing wistfully. "My son has been asking me for a long time, but it's not easy you know. Kubra, my daughter, was having her first baby, and then the house had to be whitewashed before the rains. Asad, my son, lives in Dan-bury, Con-necti-cut." Her lips stretched back, her tongue rolling, she emphasized each syllable as Kubra had instructed her. Such difficult names. "And where are you going?"

"I live in New York City," Abida replied, searching the older woman's face for a glimmer of recognition, "a place called Manhattan. It's not too far from Danbury, your son will know where it is. Your son's married?"

"No, but Kubra and I have found a girl for him. If he likes her we will have the wedding next year." She rubbed her forehead with her fingers in a nervous gesture and lowered her head. "If I'm still alive then," she muttered sadly, her face turned away.

The girl's eyes widened in alarm. "You're not sick, Ammaji, are you?"

Sakina Bano shook her head and smiling sheepishly, lifted a hand and gesticulated. "No, no, I'm not sick, except for the pain in the legs, in my back, the cataracts that keep growing too fast. No, but old age is a kind of sickness too, isn't it, child? I only pray my maker allows me to die in my own country." Sakina Bano felt immense relief after this confession.

"You shouldn't talk like this, Ammaji. In America men and women in their seventies get married and start new lives." Abida smiled mischievously.

"Ai hai, child, what nonsense is this? And when do they prepare for death? Or is it that they think they will live forever? New attachments, new pain, who wants it all over again?"

Abida broke into a laugh. Sakina Bano wondered if the young woman could help. "Child," she whispered with her hand resting on Abida's arm, "tell me this, what happens if someone dies? I mean how do they bring the body back?" She was intent on knowing the truth, all of it, however ugly and menacing.

"What?" Abida turned to her in surprise. Then, realizing her companion was serious, she said, "Ammaji, I don't know too much about these things, but I'm sure arrangements can be made to transport the body. Actually I think four airline tickets have to be bought. It's expensive, I've heard. But you know, Ammaji," she looked at Sakina Bano solicitously, "nowadays there are burials right there in special cemeteries that have been allotted by Muslim communities."

This piece of information proved distressing. There was little solace in what the girl said. Asad could never afford four tickets, and then she'd have to be buried in . . . Dan-bury! Sakina Bano collapsed in her seat, her spirits fallen, her desire to continue the conversation waned.

Perhaps he can get a loan, she brooded over her next cup of tea. Surely it would be a burden, but he could have all of her savings, nearly fifty thousand rupees, and all the other property would be his anyway. She will not mind, although her husband's soul would be agitated, it's been in the family for nearly sixty years, but Asad could sell the house on 73 Sabir Street and invest the money, and there was also some agricultural land that had belonged to

Asad's grandfather. The picture began to appear a little less bleak. She arranged a pillow behind her head and settling into a comfortable position, shut her eyes.

"At the airport, keep your wits about you," Asad had shouted into the phone. Although he had described the airport to her in detail, at Kennedy Airport she was still like a child lost among strangers in a crowded bazaar. Her son's instructions were explicit: "Have your passport in your hand when you're in line at Immigration, stay close to people from your flight, if you're in doubt ask someone, ask Amma, don't be afraid to ask. At customs, open your suitcases quickly if told to, but don't volunteer, tell the officer what you're carrying if he inquires, and please, Amma, don't bring mangoes. Carrying fruit is not permitted." Instructions or no instructions, she was on her own, she realized with sudden panic.

At customs a tall, thin man with a deeply lined, ashen-white face, thin red nose and probing eyes pointed to her suitcase and asked her if she had any mangoes. She knew the English word. She shook her head, secretly wondering if he would question her further. Deep inside her suitcase, carefully wrapped in a plastic bag were two bottles of pickled mangoes that she had prepared with her own hands. The small, dark green, tart mangoes she had taken down from her own tree growing in the front garden. No, he didn't want to know more. Anyway, snug in those bottles was not fruit, just tiny pickled raw mangoes that Asad favored.

Afterward, a dark, stocky man, distinguishable from the others by a uniform he wore, silently piled her two cases along with Abida's on a large trolley, and signaling them, strode toward gray double doors that seemed to dominate a seemingly endless white wall.

Beyond the doors, around the corner, was Amreeka. Never before had Sakina Bano seen so many people gathered in one place. Not even on Eid shopping days in the bazaars when the city's inhabitants spilled into the streets as if a catastrophe had forced them to suddenly vacate their homes. So different from each other, the people here milled about restlessly, speaking languages that seemed like babbling noises to her. Some of the people looked familiar, men, women and children from either India or Pakistan, but there were also others who must be from countries she was aware existed on a map, a geography of strangeness.

The two women followed the dark man in the uniform. As she lifted a trembling hand to adjust the slipping dupatta from her head, Sakina Bano felt overcome by a wave of dizziness, and if she hadn't caught on to the railing on her left she might have stumbled and fallen. Where is Asad? she wondered, gnawed by anxiety, and suddenly, feeling his attentive gaze upon her, she spotted him. He rushed toward her, his face drawn and his brow creased with concern, as if she were a child who had gone away and was returning.

Once they were outside, Abida said goodbye to her and got into a car with a young man who couldn't be much older than she. Her brother? Her husband? Maybe just a friend. Sakina Bano waved, saddened by the thought that she would probably never see her again.

It was cool. The sky was a dark blue. She saw stars. In the midst of all the strangeness the sky seemed to afford a sense of comfort, for was it not the same sky she saw every night in Gujranwala, now thousands of miles away? Her fear receded as she trudged alongside her son, her hands nervously clutching a corner of her dupatta.

Asad's apartment was small. Just one bedroom. Barely enough space for a low, three-drawer bureau and a bed that had no headboard and shook and rattled as if it had a loose bottom when you sat on it. The kitchen, tiny and doorless, was the size of a bathroom in her house, and the area between the bedroom and the kitchen her son had set up as the drawing room with one upholstered sofa not very clean, a low table scratched and marked with circular cup stains, and two chairs on which the paint was peeling untidily. Is this what he had come to Amreeka for? He had left the long, circular veranda of 73 Sabir Street, the spacious rooms with elevated, beamed ceilings and windows everywhere, the wide, open red-brick courtyard with the large mulberry tree where the winter sun warmed you and where you slept under dark blue starry skies on hot summer nights. For this? There must be something she could not see as yet, something that eluded her because she was old and because her mind was clogged with uneasy thoughts.

On a Friday, nearly a week after her arrival in Danbury, Sakina Bano accompanied her son to what he informed her was the local Islamic Center.

Having envisioned, if not a mosque, at least a place which had some trappings of the Islamic, she was stupefied by what she saw.

"This is the Salvation Army Church," Asad whispered in her ear as the two of them entered a long passage where she was greeted by dark-haired children shrieking playfully, many of them running, chasing the others. As she drew her dupatta about her, a girl no older than seven or eight, her plaits ribboned, her eyes wide with excitement, ran into her and almost fell. Sakina Bano bent over quickly to hold her, buffing the girl's fall with her arm. The girl looked up at her, stiffened and moved away awkwardly.

A church, she wondered in amazement. Muhammad and Issa in the same place! What would her husband say if he were alive? She saw a few women. Some wore shalwar and kameez, three others were in long robes with scarves covering their hair. Who are these women? Sakina Bano wondered. Egyptian, Saudi, maybe Iranian? A group of men stood in the narrow passage; removed from the women, many young like her son, a few older and gray-haired with somber and wearied faces, they talked in low voices.

Not used to being in the company of strange men, unless she was in the bazaar or on a train or the bus stop, Sakina Bano felt uncomfortable when Asad introduced her to the people in the passage. Of course he wants them to know his mother has come to visit him in his new home, she thought, trying to placate herself.

"Walekumsalaam, walekumsalaam," she mumbled with her head lowered as she sidled away from their intrusive attention. Asad led her to a room where more women sat, most of them tending infants.

Asad introduced her. A woman, who reminded her of Abida because of her boyish figure, long hair open to her shoulders and was younger than all the rest, came forward quickly to greet her. Soon all of them engulfed her excitedly as if she were a special guest.

"Do you like Amreeka?" a plump, attractive woman with a chubby baby on her arm, asked genially. She was rocking a baby who, his head lolling on her shoulder, drooled on the sparkling gold bangles on her wrist.

"Yes, yes, I like it, what is there not to like?" Sakina Bano wondered if any of them knew anything about transporting bodies by air.

"You must come and visit us soon," the plump woman said, smiling again, and before Sakina Bano could respond to her invitation, the child began to whimper and the young woman walked away, patting the infant and cooing softly.

Her name, Sakina Bano soon discovered, was Husna, while the one who resembled Abida was Sabiha. They were all so eager, these women. Eager to be friendly, to be hospitable, and as they talked their solemn enthusiasm lighted up their faces, imbuing their voices with energy so that the most trivial topics of conversation seemed to assume undue importance. One day Asad's wife will be here, among them, first alone and then with a child on her arm, while on Sabir Street, Sakina Bano will wait out her days by herself, expecting the postman's rattle at the letterbox, running out for letters, for photographs charting the progress of her daughter-in-law, her new grandchild.

The children were assembling for class. One of the men, fair skinned, with a beard that was black like the overused surface of a tawa, a short, chubby man no more than thirty-five or thirty-six, came in and started talking to the children. Why, Arabic is his mother tongue, Sakina Bano realized with surprise. When he began reciting from the Koran, how buoyantly the words of the ayaats fell from him, like unhurried rain from the heavens.

"He's from Egypt," Asad told her later. Class was being held in a section of the large hall in which everyone was congregated, and separated from the place where the women sat by a tall, movable partition. The women in the long dresses and scarves had come in too, and Sabiha chatted energetically with them in English. Asad and the other men had moved in somewhere behind the partition as well; perhaps on the other side was another movable wall.

Her attention was suddenly snagged by the drop of a word that wiggled its way into her consciousness and was suspended there. Like a kite trapped precariously in the branches of a tree. Because she had been deeply engrossed in the melodic recitation, she missed the first part of the conversation, but the word "buried" didn't elude her. She turned to a slightly older woman, closer to her in age perhaps, her hair thickly patched with gray, large glasses with thick, opaque lenses hiding nearly all of her diminutive nose, who was now talking.

". . . she had cancer so her family knew she didn't have too long to live, and her son didn't take her back to Pakistan when she passed away. It was a Sunday, and all the stores were closed. Do you know, they couldn't even buy white cotton for her shroud? Isn't it just terrible?" She shook her head gravely and chafed her hands together.

"What did they do?" It was Husna, the baby now asleep with its head resting peacefully on her shoulder, the small pink mouth open.

Sakina Bano's heart convulsed. The ground seemed to slip from under her feet. She held her breath. Her gaze was riveted on the older woman's face.

"What can I say, it was just dreadful. May Allah save us from such a fate. All the friends of the family donated whatever new white bed sheets they had, and the women made a kaffan. She was buried in the town cemetery. Thank God there was a Turkish maulvi who could say the burial prayers."

Sakina Bano's mouth went dry. She felt sweat rise like tiny thorns on her skin. A thousand little invisible insects seemed to have set down their furry legs upon her person, and were moving, slowly. Bedsheets! What an unfortunate woman. And what guarantee they were all cotton? Wash and wear is what they are making these days. And to be buried among strangers—such a dismal fate. Poor woman, to be so far from home and die. To be wrapped in bed sheets which said, on small tags somewhere, "Made in Amreeka." Will the angels condescend to enter a grave where a body lay draped in a shroud made by Christians? Sakina Bano shuddered at the possibility of being abandoned by God's messengers at the hour of reckoning.

Conversation veered off to other subjects, but Sakina Bano remained entangled in a web of irreversible anxiety. Later that night, agitated and unsolaced, she tossed and turned on her bed as if she was on live coals. Sleep evaded her. Finally she decided to pray and sat on the janamaz with her prayer beads for a long time.

"Ya Allah," she entreated with outstretched hands, "I ask you only this. Let me return to my home, and then my life is yours to do what you want with it. I have no fear of death. I ask not to live forever. But there is great fear in my heart of dying here. In your infinite mercy grant me this one wish and I will never want anything for myself again."

She didn't know when she dozed off, the words gathering thickly on her tongue like molasses, but clear in her head. When she fell forward on the prayer mat she woke up with a start. Extending both arms out, she slowly brought the edge of the mat toward her, folding the rest of it as she rose to her feet slowly. It was time to sleep.

Sunny and humid, the day was warm, but nothing like a warm day in Gujran-wala. The temperature there must have already climbed to a torrid, pasty hundred-and-two degrees. Here, it was pleasant. With the car windows down, a small breeze quietly fanned her face, making her drowsy.

She could not pronounce the name of the place Asad was taking her to. They were on their way to visit her niece Zenab, her cousin's daughter, a dear girl who always visited her in Gujranwala even though it was an out of the way town, always bringing gifts. Today Sakina Bano was taking her a hand-blocked brick-red tablecloth and a set of matching napkins. She knew what Zenab liked. And for Zenab's husband she had brought a vest that all the young men were wearing these days, and for the year-old baby it was an embroidered cotton kurta and pajama.

Sakina Bano would soon be asleep, except that the leafage astounded and mesmerized her and she had to constantly move her head to see it all. Never had she seen such density of foliage. Of such variety. No two trees seemed alike. Like walls, they rose on either side of the road until the sky, when she gazed up, was only a narrow strip of sharp, unclouded blue. Like a clear well-lighted path.

Something seemed to grasp at her attention when Asad stopped the car at one of the traffic lights. She glanced to her right and stared in wide-eyed wonder at the image before her. A hill, sloping lazily upward from the edge of the road, carpeted with grass so finely clipped it was like a velvet mantle, greener than any green she had ever known. Fresh, washed color interlaced with a trellis of sunlight filtered through tall trees lining the hill's highest borders. And little clusters of the brightest, sharpest red flowers, each cluster attended by a small, squat slab of gray stone. Sakina Bano gasped at the beauty of what she saw.

The question was squelched as soon as it raised its head in her thoughts.

She knew the place. The perfect little slabs of stone had a voice that fell plainly into her ears. The car was moving again, and Sakina Bano fell against her seat as if she had travelled a great distance on foot and must rest now to catch her breath.

Her eyes shut, she found herself in another dwelling, a portion of land where her husband and so many of her relatives were resting. Dismal, overgrown with weeds and wildly tangled shrubbery, the only color was brought into the place by those who came to visit the graves. A red tinge from a dupatta here, a green kurta, a dab of purple chador, a brightly white cotton shirt, spotless like a new shroud. The earth here was dry, cakey and cracking, gashed where the pressure from the countless heavy stone mounds had dragged it open. The ocher of the earth presented no other hue. The trees that bent over the crumbling graves in postures of despair, were thin and untended, their spindly branches forever bare and shriveled. Spring seemed not to touch them, even lightly. It was like a place forgotten, by time, by nature, by life. The tall brick wall that enclaved the cemetery and which half stood and half fell, as everything else did there, seemed to shut out nature's benevolence just as it shut out the living world.

Sakina Bano moved restlessly in her seat. She emitted a long sigh.

"Amma, are you all right?" Asad cast a worried glance at her.

"Yes, yes I'm all right," she lied. How could she bring herself to tell him she wished she would be as fortunate as her husband. That she longed to be buried like him in the cemetery where earth had lost color. Her father was also there and her mother, her uncles and also her grandparents. There, she would not be alone.

She was assailed by fear again. Words in your head are like dreams; no one knows of them except you, the dreamer. She must let her son hear the words that milled through her thoughts like a winter dust storm, thick, suffocating, cleaving through what stood in its path. She had made up her mind.

"Asad?" she said casually, as if she were going to ask him about Zenab's husband, whether he had decided to go back to Pakistan after he finished his training, or whether the baby had begun teething.

"Yes Amma?"

"Listen, now don't get upset . . ." Her voice cracked.

"What is it? Are you feeling all right?" Asad slowed down and she thought he might stop. So much traffic around them, he might get into an accident. What a burden she was, and she wasn't even dead as yet.

"I said I'm fine, I just want to discuss something, now don't get worried." She patted his arm and cleared her throat. "If something were to happen . . ." she increased the pressure on his arm as he opened his mouth to protest. "If, if something should happen, I want you to send me back to Pakistan." There. The words had escaped, ponderous, no longer erasable.

Shaken for a moment, he shook his head. "Amma, what kind of silly talk is this?" he said irritably. "Are you still carrying that absurd notion in your head? By God's grace you're healthy and there's no reason to suppose anything will happen." He was angry at her obstinacy.

"Don't get upset, son, you must understand, you can't get upset. I'm serious." She pleaded tearfully.

A smile appeared on his face. "Amma, Amma," he chuckled, "what's the matter with you?" Aware that she had not taken kindly to his humor he assumed a straight face. "All right, I promise, I promise. Are you satisfied?" His eyes pinned on the road, he struggled again with a smile.

"I think you will have to buy two tickets."

"What?" He turned again, to look at her in amazement this time.

She continued. "Keep your eyes on the road. You might have to get a loan because you need forty thousand rupees to send a body back to Pakistan, but don't worry, I've got fifty saved in my account in Pakistan, and it's all yours."

Asad started to laugh, catching himself when she sniffled and tugged at his sleeve.

"I said I am serious. Why are you laughing? Promise you won't bury me in—what's the place called—Dan-bury." With a corner of her dupatta she wiped the tears on her cheeks.

"I promise, Amma," Asad said in an apologetic tone.

"Promise you will take me home to Sabir Street." She clutched her son's arm.

"Yes, I will," her son said earnestly, "I promise."

Sakina Bano blew her nose with her handkerchief and leaned back in her seat. The strip of blue sky seemed to have vanished. The branches of trees formed a crested canopy, hiding the sky from her. Feeling weightless, as if a cumbersome burden she had been carrying all this time had suddenly dislodged itself, she shut her eyes. Her thoughts, which only moments ago held her down like a chain of steel, became amorphous and flew inside her head, like a kite cut off from its restraining cord, free.

JHUMPA LAHIRI

"When I first started writing I was not conscious that my subject was the Indian-American experience. What drew me to my craft was the desire to force the two worlds I occupied to mingle on the page as I was not brave enough, or mature enough, to allow in life." Jhumpa Lahiri was born in London in 1967 of Bengali descent and raised in small-town Rhode Island after her family came to the United States in 1970. Her first collection of stories, *An Interpreter of Maladies* (1999), from which the work that follows is drawn, deftly maps this terrain of overlapping worlds, where small misunderstandings and simple gestures reveal the complexity of the immigrant experience. *An Interpreter of Maladies* has been translated into 29 languages and was a bestseller in the United States and abroad. Lahiri's second collection of stories, *Unaccustomed Earth* (2008), debuted at number one on the *New York Times* bestseller list.

The Third and Final Continent

I left India in 1964 with a certificate in commerce and the equivalent, in those days, of ten dollars to my name. For three weeks I sailed on the SS *Roma*, an Italian cargo vessel, in a cabin next to the ship's engine, across the Arabian Sea, the Red Sea, the Mediterranean, and finally to England. I lived in north London, in Finsbury Park, in a house occupied entirely by penniless Bengali bachelors like myself, at least a dozen and sometimes more, all struggling to educate and establish ourselves abroad.

I attended lectures at LSE and worked at the university library to get by. We lived three or four to a room, shared a single, icy toilet, and took turns cooking pots of egg curry, which we ate with our hands on a table covered with newspapers. Apart from our jobs we had few responsibilities. On weekends we lounged barefoot in drawstring pajamas, drinking tea and smoking

Rothmans, or set out to watch cricket at Lord's. Some weekends the house was crammed with still more Bengalis, to whom we had introduced ourselves at the greengrocer, or on the Tube, and we made yet more egg curry, and played Mukesh on a Grundig reel-to-reel, and soaked our dirty dishes in the bathtub. Every now and then someone in the house moved out, to live with a woman whom his family back in Calcutta had determined he was to wed. In 1969, when I was thirty-six years old, my own marriage was arranged. Around the same time I was offered a full-time job in America, in the processing department of a library at MIT. The salary was generous enough to support a wife, and I was honored to be hired by a world-famous university, and so I obtained a sixth-preference green card, and prepared to travel farther still.

By now I had enough money to go by plane. I flew first to Calcutta, to attend my wedding, and a week later I flew to Boston, to begin my new job. During the flight I read *The Student Guide to North America*, a paperback volume that I'd bought before leaving London, for seven shillings six pence on Tottenham Court Road, for although I was no longer a student I was on a budget all the same. I learned that Americans drove on the right side of the road, not the left, and that they called a lift an elevator and an engaged phone busy. "The pace of life in North America is different from Britain as you will soon discover," the guidebook informed me. "Everybody feels he must get to the top. Don't expect an English cup of tea." As the plane began its descent over Boston Harbor, the pilot announced the weather and time, and that President Nixon had declared a national holiday: two American men had landed on the moon. Several passengers cheered. "God bless America!" one of them hollered. Across the aisle, I saw a woman praying.

I spent my first night at the YMCA in Central Square, Cambridge, an inexpensive accommodation recommended by my guidebook. It was walking distance from MIT, and steps from the post office and a supermarket called Purity Supreme. The room contained a cot, a desk, and a small wooden cross on one wall. A sign on the door said cooking was strictly forbidden. A bare window overlooked Massachusetts Avenue, a major thoroughfare with traffic in both directions. Car horns, shrill and prolonged, blared one after another. Flashing sirens heralded endless emergencies, and a fleet of buses rumbled past, their doors opening and closing with a powerful hiss, throughout the night. The noise was constantly distracting, at times suffocating. I felt it deep in my ribs, just as I had felt the furious drone of the engine on the SS *Roma*. But there was no ship's deck to escape to, no glittering ocean to thrill my soul, no breeze to cool my face, no one to talk to. I was too tired to pace the gloomy corridors of the YMCA in my drawstring pajamas. Instead I sat at the desk and stared out the window, at the city hall of Cambridge and a row of small shops. In the morning I reported to my job at the Dewey Library, a beige fort-like building by Memorial Drive. I also opened a bank account, rented a post office box, and bought a plastic bowl and a spoon at Woolworth's, a store whose name I recognized from London. I went to Purity Supreme, wandering up and down the aisles, converting ounces to grams and comparing prices to things in England. In the end I bought a small carton of milk and a box of cornflakes. This was my first meal in America. I ate it at my desk. I preferred it to hamburgers or hot dogs, the only alternative I could afford in the coffee shops on Massachusetts Avenue, and, besides, at the time I had yet to consume any beef. Even the simple chore of buying milk was new to me; in London we'd had bottles delivered each morning to our door.

In a week I had adjusted, more or less. I ate cornflakes and milk, morning and night, and bought some bananas for variety, slicing them into the bowl with the edge of my spoon. In addition I bought tea bags and a flask, which the salesman in Woolworth's referred to as a thermos (a flask, he informed me, was used to store whiskey, another thing I had never consumed). For the price of one cup of tea at a coffee shop, I filled the flask with boiling water on my way to work each morning, and brewed the four cups I drank in the course of a day. I bought a larger carton of milk, and learned to leave it on the shaded part of the windowsill, as I had seen another resident at the YMCA do. To pass the time in the evenings I read the *Boston Globe* downstairs, in a spacious room with stained-glass windows. I read every article and advertisement, so that I would grow familiar with things, and when my eyes grew tired I slept. Only I did not sleep well. Each night I had to keep the window wide open; it was the only source of air in the stifling room, and the noise was intolerable. I would lie on the cot with my fingers pressed into my ears, but when I drifted off to sleep my hands fell away, and the noise of the traffic would wake me up again. Pigeon feathers drifted onto the windowsill, and one evening, when I poured milk over my cornflakes, I saw that it had soured. Nevertheless I resolved to stay at the YMCA for six weeks, until my wife's passport and green card were ready. Once she arrived I would have to rent a proper apartment, and from time to time I studied the classified section of the newspaper, or stopped in at the housing office at MIT during my lunch break, to see what was available in my price range. It was in this manner that I discovered a room for immediate occupancy, in a house on a quiet street, the listing said, for eight dollars per week. I copied the number into my guidebook and dialed from a pay telephone, sorting through the coins with which I was still unfamiliar, smaller and lighter than shillings, heavier and brighter than *paisas*.

"Who is speaking?" a woman demanded. Her voice was bold and clamorous.

"Yes, good afternoon, madame. I am calling about the room for rent."

"Harvard or Tech?"

"I beg your pardon?"

"Are you from Harvard or Tech?"

Gathering that Tech referred to the Massachusetts Institute of Technology, I replied, "I work at Dewey Library," adding tentatively, "at Tech."

"I only rent rooms to boys from Harvard or Tech!"

"Yes, madame."

I was given an address and an appointment for seven o'clock that evening. Thirty minutes before the hour I set out, my guidebook in my pocket, my breath fresh with Listerine. I turned down a street shaded with trees, perpendicular to Massachusetts Avenue. Stray blades of grass poked between the cracks of the footpath. In spite of the heat I wore a coat and a tie, regarding the event as I would any other interview; I had never lived in the home of a person who was not Indian. The house, surrounded by a chain-link fence, was off-white with dark brown trim. Unlike the stucco row house I'd lived in in London, this house, fully detached, was covered with wooden shingles, with a tangle of forsythia bushes plastered against the front and sides. When I pressed the calling bell, the woman with whom I had spoken on the phone hollered from what seemed to be just the other side of the door, "One minute, please!"

Several minutes later the door was opened by a tiny, extremely old woman. A mass of snowy hair was arranged like a small sack on top of her head. As I stepped into the house she sat down on a wooden bench positioned at the bottom of a narrow carpeted staircase. Once she was settled on the bench, in a small pool of light, she peered up at me with undivided attention. She wore a long black skirt that spread like a stiff tent to the floor, and a starched white shirt edged with ruffles at the throat and cuffs. Her hands, folded together in her lap, had long pallid fingers, with swollen knuckles and tough yellow nails. Age had battered her features so that she almost resembled a man, with sharp, shrunken eyes and prominent creases on either side of her nose. Her lips, chapped and faded, had nearly disappeared, and her eyebrows were missing altogether. Nevertheless she looked fierce.

"Lock up!" she commanded. She shouted even though I stood only a few feet away. "Fasten the chain and firmly press that button on the knob! This is the first thing you shall do when you enter, is that clear?"

I locked the door as directed and examined the house. Next to the bench on which the woman sat was a small round table, its legs fully concealed, much like the woman's, by a skirt of lace. The table held a lamp, a transistor radio, a leather change purse with a silver clasp, and a telephone. A thick wooden cane coated with a layer of dust was propped against one side. There was a parlor to my right, lined with bookcases and filled with shabby claw-footed furniture. In the corner of the parlor I saw a grand piano with its top down, piled with papers. The piano's bench was missing; it seemed to be the one on which the woman was sitting. Somewhere in the house a clock chimed seven times.

"You're punctual!" the woman proclaimed. "I expect you shall be so with the rent!"

"I have a letter, madame." In my jacket pocket was a letter confirming my employment from MIT, which I had brought along to prove that I was indeed from Tech.

She stared at the letter, then handed it back to me carefully, gripping it with her fingers as if it were a dinner plate heaped with food instead of a sheet of paper. She did not wear glasses, and I wondered if she'd read a word of it. "The last boy was always late! Still owes me eight dollars! Harvard boys aren't what they used to be! Only Harvard and Tech in this house! How's Tech, boy?"

"It is very well."

"You checked the lock?"

"Yes, madame."

She slapped the space beside her on the bench with one hand, and told me to sit down. For a moment she was silent. Then she intoned, as if she alone possessed this knowledge:

"There is an American flag on the moon!"

"Yes, madame." Until then I had not thought very much about the moon shot. It was in the newspaper, of course, article upon article. The astronauts had landed on the shores of the Sea of Tranquillity, I had read, traveling farther than anyone in the history of civilization. For a few hours they explored the moon's surface. They gathered rocks in their pockets, described their surroundings (a magnificent desolation, according to one astronaut), spoke by phone to the president, and planted a flag in lunar soil. The voyage was hailed as man's most awesome achievement. I had seen full-page photographs in the *Globe*, of the astronauts in their inflated costumes, and read about what certain people in Boston had been doing at the exact moment the astronauts landed, on a Sunday afternoon. A man said that he was operating a swan boat with a radio pressed to his ear; a woman had been baking rolls for her grandchildren.

The woman bellowed, "A flag on the moon, boy! I heard it on the radio! Isn't that splendid?"

"Yes, madame."

But she was not satisfied with my reply. Instead she commanded, "Say 'splendid'!"

I was both baffled and somewhat insulted by the request. It reminded me of the way I was taught multiplication tables as a child, repeating after the master, sitting cross-legged, without shoes or pencils, on the floor of my one-room Tollygunge school. It also reminded me of my wedding, when I had repeated endless Sanskrit verses after the priest, verses I barely understood, which joined me to my wife. I said nothing.

"Say 'splendid'!" the woman bellowed once again.

"Splendid," I murmured. I had to repeat the word a second time at the top of my lungs, so she could hear. I am soft-spoken by nature and was especially reluctant to raise my voice to an elderly woman whom I had met only moments ago, but she did not appear to be offended. If anything the reply pleased her because her next command was:

"Go see the room!"

I rose from the bench and mounted the narrow carpeted staircase. There were five doors, two on either side of an equally narrow hallway, and one at the opposite end. Only one door was partly open. The room contained a twin bed under a sloping ceiling, a brown oval rug, a basin with an exposed pipe, and a chest of drawers. One door, painted white, led to a closet, another to a toilet and a tub. The walls were covered with gray and ivory striped paper. The window was open; net curtains stirred in the breeze. I lifted them away and inspected the view: a small back yard, with a few fruit trees and an empty clothesline. I was satisfied. From the bottom of the stairs I heard the woman demand, "What is your decision?"

When I returned to the foyer and told her, she picked up the leather change purse on the table, opened the clasp, fished about with her fingers, and produced a key on a thin wire hoop. She informed me that there was a kitchen at the back of the house, accessible through the parlor. I was welcome to use the stove as long as I left it as I found it. Sheets and towels were provided, but keeping them clean was my own responsibility. The rent was due Friday mornings on the ledge above the piano keys. "And no lady visitors!"

"I am a married man, madame." It was the first time I had announced this fact to anyone.

But she had not heard. "No lady visitors!" she insisted. She introduced herself as Mrs. Croft.

My wife's name was Mala. The marriage had been arranged by my older brother and his wife. I regarded the proposition with neither objection nor enthusiasm. It was a duty expected of me, as it was expected of every man. She was the daughter of a schoolteacher in Beleghata. I was told that she could cook, knit, embroider, sketch landscapes, and recite poems by Tagore, but these talents could not make up for the fact that she did not possess a fair complexion, and so a string of men had rejected her to her face. She was twenty-seven, an age when her parents had begun to fear that she would never marry, and so they were willing to ship their only child halfway across the world in order to save her from spinsterhood.

For five nights we shared a bed. Each of those nights, after applying cold cream and braiding her hair, which she tied up at the end with a black cotton string, she turned from me and wept; she missed her parents. Although I would be leaving the country in a few days, custom dictated that she was now a part of my household, and for the next six weeks she was to live with my brother and his wife, cooking, cleaning, serving tea and sweets to guests. I did nothing to console her. I lay on my own side of the bed, reading my guidebook by flashlight and anticipating my journey. At times I thought of the tiny room on the other side of the wall which had belonged to my mother. Now the room was practically empty; the wooden pallet on which she'd once slept was piled with trunks and old bedding. Nearly six years ago, before leaving for London, I had watched her die on that bed, had found her playing with her excrement in her final days. Before we cremated her I had cleaned each of her fingernails with a hairpin, and then, because my brother could not bear it, I had assumed the role of eldest son, and had touched the flame to her temple, to release her tormented soul to heaven.

The next morning I moved into the room in Mrs. Croft's house. When I unlocked the door I saw that she was sitting on the piano bench, on the same side as the previous evening. She wore the same black skirt, the same starched white blouse, and had her hands folded together the same way in her lap. She looked so much the same that I wondered if she'd spent the whole night on the bench. I put my suitcase upstairs, filled my flask with boiling water in the kitchen, and headed off to work. That evening when I came home from the university, she was still there.

"Sit down, boy!" She slapped the space beside her.

I perched beside her on the bench. I had a bag of groceries with me— more milk, more cornflakes, and more bananas, for my inspection of the kitchen earlier in the day had revealed no spare pots, pans, or cooking utensils. There were only two saucepans in the refrigerator, both containing some orange broth, and a copper kettle on the stove.

"Good evening, madame."

She asked me if I had checked the lock. I told her I had.

For a moment she was silent. Then suddenly she declared, with the equal measures of disbelief and delight as the night before, "There's an American flag on the moon, boy!"

"Yes, madame."

"A flag on the moon! Isn't that splendid?"

I nodded, dreading what I knew was coming. "Yes, madame."

"Say 'splendid'!"

This time I paused, looking to either side in case anyone were there to overhear me, though I knew perfectly well that the house was empty. I felt like an idiot. But it was a small enough thing to ask. "Splendid!" I cried out.

Within days it became our routine. In the mornings when I left for the library Mrs. Croft was either hidden away in her bedroom, on the other side of the staircase, or she was sitting on the bench, oblivious to my presence, listening to the news or classical music on the radio. But each evening when I returned the same thing happened: she slapped the bench, ordered me to sit down, declared that there was a flag on the moon, and declared that it was splendid. I said it was splendid, too, and then we sat in silence. As awkward as it was, and as endless as it felt to me then, the nightly encounter lasted only about ten minutes; inevitably she would drift off to sleep, her head falling abruptly toward her chest, leaving me free to retire to my room. By then, of course, there was no flag standing on the moon. The astronauts, I had read in the paper, had seen it fall before they flew back to Earth. But I did not have the heart to tell her.

Friday morning, when my first week's rent was due, I went to the piano in the parlor to place my money on the ledge. The piano keys were dull and discolored. When I pressed one, it made no sound at all. I had put eight one-dollar bills in an envelope and written Mrs. Croft's name on the front of it. I was not in the habit of leaving money unmarked and unattended. From where I stood I could see the profile of her tent-shaped skirt. She was sitting on the bench, listening to the radio. It seemed unnecessary to make her get up and walk all the way to the piano. I never saw her walking about, and assumed, from the cane always propped against the round table at her side, that she did so with difficulty. When I approached the bench she peered up at me and demanded:

"What is your business?"

"The rent, madame."

"On the ledge above the piano keys!"

"I have it here." I extended the envelope toward her, but her fingers, folded together in her lap, did not budge. I bowed slightly and lowered the envelope, so that it hovered just above her hands. After a moment she accepted, and nodded her head.

That night when I came home, she did not slap the bench, but out of habit I sat beside her as usual. She asked me if I had checked the lock, but she mentioned nothing about the flag on the moon. Instead she said:

"It was very kind of you!"

"I beg your pardon, madame?"

"Very kind of you!"

She was still holding the envelope in her hands.

At the end of August, Mala's passport and green card were ready. I received a telegram with her flight information; my brother's house in Calcutta had no telephone. Around that time I also received a letter from her, written only a few days after we had parted. There was no salutation; addressing me by name would have assumed an intimacy we had not yet discovered. It contained only a few lines. "I write in English in preparation for the journey. Here I am very much lonely. Is it very cold there. Is there snow. Yours, Mala."

I was not touched by her words. We had spent only a handful of days in each other's company. And yet we were bound together; for six weeks she had worn an iron bangle on her wrist, and applied vermilion powder to the part in her hair, to signify to the world that she was a bride. In those six weeks I regarded her arrival as I would the arrival of a coming month, or season—something inevitable, but meaningless at the time. So little did I know her that, while details of her face sometimes rose to my memory, I could not conjure up the whole of it.

A few days after receiving the letter, as I was walking to work in the morning, I saw an Indian woman on the other side of Massachusetts Avenue, wearing a sari with its free end nearly dragging on the footpath, and pushing a child in a stroller. An American woman with a small black dog on a leash was walking to one side of her. Suddenly the dog began barking. From the other side of the street I watched as the Indian woman, startled, stopped in her path, at which point the dog leapt up and seized the end of the sari between its teeth. The American woman scolded the dog, appeared to apologize, and walked quickly away, leaving the Indian woman to fix her sari in the middle of the footpath, and quiet her crying child. She did not see me standing there, and eventually she continued on her way. Such a mishap, I realized that morning, would soon be my concern. It was my duty to take care of Mala, to welcome her and protect her. I would have to buy her her first pair of snow boots, her first winter coat. I would have to tell her which streets to avoid, which way the traffic came, tell her to wear her sari so that the free end did not drag on the footpath. A five-mile separation from her parents, I recalled with some irritation, had caused her to weep.

Unlike Mala, I was used to it all by then: used to cornflakes and milk, used to Helen's visits, used to sitting on the bench with Mrs. Croft. The only thing I was not used to was Mala. Nevertheless I did what I had to do. I went to the housing office at MIT and found a furnished apartment a few blocks away, with a double bed and a private kitchen and bath, for forty dollars a week. One last Friday I handed Mrs. Croft eight one-dollar bills in an envelope, brought my suitcase downstairs, and informed her that I was moving. She put my key into her change purse. The last thing she asked me to do was hand her the cane propped against the table, so that she could walk to the door and lock it behind me. "Good-bye, then," she said, and retreated back into the house. I did not expect any display of emotion, but I was disappointed all the same. I was only a boarder, a man who paid her a bit of money and passed in and out of her home for six weeks. Compared to a century, it was no time at all.

At the airport I recognized Mala immediately. The free end of her sari did not drag on the floor, but was draped in a sign of bridal modesty over her head, just as it had draped my mother until the day my father died. Her thin brown arms were stacked with gold bracelets, a small red circle was painted on her forehead, and the edges of her feet were tinted with a decorative red dye. I did not embrace her, or kiss her, or take her hand. Instead I asked her, speaking Bengali for the first time in America, if she was hungry.

She hesitated, then nodded yes.

I told her I had prepared some egg curry at home. "What did they give you to eat on the plane?"

"I didn't eat."

"All the way from Calcutta?"

"The menu said oxtail soup."

"But surely there were other items."

"The thought of eating an ox's tail made me lose my appetite."

When we arrived home, Mala opened up one of her suitcases, and presented me with two pullover sweaters, both made with bright blue wool, which she had knitted in the course of our separation, one with a V neck, the other covered with cables. I tried them on; both were tight under the arms. She had also brought me two new pairs of drawstring pajamas, a letter from my brother, and a packet of loose Darjeeling tea. I had no present for her apart from the egg curry. We sat at a bare table, each of us staring at our plates. We ate with our hands, another thing I had not yet done in America.

"The house is nice," she said. "Also the egg curry." With her left hand she held the end of her sari to her chest, so it would not slip off her head.

"I don't know many recipes."

She nodded, peeling the skin off each of her potatoes before eating them. At one point the sari slipped to her shoulders. She readjusted it at once.

"There is no need to cover your head," I said. "I don't mind. It doesn't matter here."

She kept it covered anyway.

I waited to get used to her, to her presence at my side, at my table and in my bed, but a week later we were still strangers. I still was not used to coming home to an apartment that smelled of steamed rice, and finding that the basin in the bathroom was always wiped clean, our two toothbrushes lying side by side, a cake of Pears soap from India resting in the soap dish. I was not used to the fragrance of the coconut oil she rubbed every other night into her scalp, or the delicate sound her bracelets made as she moved about the apartment. In the mornings she was always awake before I was. The first morning when I came into the kitchen she had heated up the leftovers and set a plate with a spoonful of salt on its edge on the table, assuming I would eat rice for breakfast, as most Bengali husbands did. I told her cereal would do, and the next morning when I came into the kitchen she had already poured the cornflakes into my bowl. One morning she walked with me down Massachusetts Avenue to MIT, where I gave her a short tour of the campus. On the way we stopped at a hardware store and I made a copy of the key, so that she could let herself into the apartment. The next morning before I left for work she asked me for a few dollars. I parted with them reluctantly, but I knew that this, too, was now normal. When I came home from work there was a potato peeler in the kitchen drawer, and a tablecloth on the table, and chicken curry made with fresh garlic and ginger on the stove. We did not have a television in those days. After dinner I read the newspaper, while Mala sat at the kitchen table, working on a cardigan for herself with more of the bright blue wool, or writing letters home.

At the end of our first week, on Friday, I suggested going out. Mala set down her knitting and disappeared into the bathroom. When she emerged I regretted the suggestion; she had put on a clean silk sari and extra bracelets, and coiled her hair with a flattering side part on top of her head. She was prepared as if for a party, or at the very least for the cinema, but I had no such destination in mind. The evening air was balmy. We walked several blocks down Massachusetts Avenue, looking into the windows of restaurants and shops. Then, without thinking, I led her down the quiet street where for so many nights I had walked alone.

Together we explored the city and met other Bengalis, some of whom are still friends today. We discovered that a man named Bill sold fresh fish on Prospect Street, and that a shop in Harvard Square called Cardullo's sold bay leaves and cloves. In the evenings we walked to the Charles River to watch sailboats drift across the water, or had ice cream cones in Harvard Yard. We bought an Instamatic camera with which to document our life together, and I took pictures of her posing in front of the Prudential building, so that she could send them to her parents. At night we kissed, shy at first but quickly bold, and discovered pleasure and solace in each other's arms. I told her about my voyage on the SS *Roma*, and about Finsbury Park and the YMCA, and my evenings on the bench with Mrs. Croft. When I told her stories about my mother, she wept. It was Mala who consoled me when, reading the *Globe* one evening, I came across Mrs. Croft's obituary. I had not thought of her in several months—by then those six weeks of the summer were already a remote interlude in my past—but when I learned of her death I was stricken, so much so that when Mala looked up from her knitting she found me staring at the wall, the newspaper neglected in my lap, unable to speak. Mrs. Croft's was the first death I mourned in America, for hers was the first life I had admired; she had left this world at last, ancient and alone, never to return.

As for me, I have not strayed much farther. Mala and I live in a town about twenty miles from Boston, on a tree-lined street much like Mrs. Croft's, in a house we own, with a garden that saves us from buying tomatoes in summer, and room for guests. We are American citizens now, so that we can collect social security when it is time. Though we visit Calcutta every few years, and bring back more drawstring pajamas and Darjeeling tea, we have decided to grow old here. I work in a small college library. We have a son who attends Harvard University. Mala no longer drapes the end of her sari over her head, or weeps at night for her parents, but occasionally she weeps for our son. So we drive to Cambridge to visit him, or bring him home for a weekend, so that he can eat rice with us with his hands, and speak in Bengali, things we sometimes worry he will no longer do after we die.

Whenever we make that drive, I always make it a point to take Massachusetts Avenue, in spite of the traffic. I barely recognize the buildings now, but each time I am there I return instantly to those six weeks as if they were only the other day, and I slow down and point to Mrs. Croft's street, saying to my son, here was my first home in America, where I lived with a woman who was 103. "Remember?" Mala says, and smiles, amazed, as I am, that there was ever a time that we were strangers. My son always expresses his astonishment, not at Mrs. Croft's age, but at how little I paid in rent, a fact nearly as inconceivable to him as a flag on the moon was to a woman born in 1866. In my son's eyes I see the ambition that had first hurled me across the world. In a few years he will graduate and pave his way, alone and unprotected. But

I remind myself that he has a father who is still living, a mother who is happy and strong. Whenever he is discouraged, I tell him that if I can survive on three continents, then there is no obstacle he cannot conquer. While the astronauts, heroes forever, spent mere hours on the moon, I have remained in this new world for nearly thirty years. I know that my achievement is quite ordinary. I am not the only man to seek his fortune far from home, and certainly I am not the first. Still, there are times I am bewildered by each mile I have traveled, each meal I have eaten, each person I have known, each room in which I have slept. As ordinary as it all appears, there are times when it is beyond my imagination.

LUIS H. FRANCIA

In poetry and nonfiction that foregrounds his origins, Manila-born journalist, film critic, editor, and poet Luis H. Francia (born in 1945) has explored the myriad effects of colonialism on Filipinos, including immigrants. Francia came to the United States in 1970. He has remarked that many Filipino writers who write in English "are engaged in the literary equivalent of guerilla warfare, using the very same weapon that had been employed to foist another set of foreign values upon a ravished nation"—an insight that informs the strand of defiance one encounters in his poem "In Gurgle Veritas": "Raise the banners / Of your reason, Jack, and feast on / Your white gods, I'll / Raise my dark lyrics, and toast and / Roast you with my sweet kiss, and the / Lucifer lunacy of gurgle." His books include *Eye of the Fish: A Personal Archipelago* (2001), *Memories of Overdevelopment* (1998), and the poetry collections *The Arctic Archipelago* (1991) and *Museum of Absences* (2004). He has also edited or co-edited the anthologies *Brown River, White Ocean: An Anthology of Twentieth-Century Philippine Literature in English* (1993), *Flippin': Filipinos on America* (1997), and *Vestiges of War: The Philippine-American War and the Aftermath of an Imperial Dream* (2002).

Tío

I first laid eyes on him more than a decade ago on a trip to Los Angeles. He was at the airport, slim, erect, still spry at 70 years of age, and pleased to meet me, just as I was to have finally met him. Of what we initially said to one another, I retain little. But I distinctly remember a strong spirit, the same imperiousness his older brother, my late father, had, now tempered by time. Retired, he now worked for another retired gentleman, as some sort of majordomo, cooking and running errands for him.

He and his wife, Barbara—a hearty, sociable Colombian woman 20 years his junior—lived in a pleasant bungalow near the foothills of the San Gabriel mountains, across from Pasadena. They had a garden that bore manifold and glorious evidence of Barbara's green thumb: flowering bushes, shade and fruit trees. Barbara had had two sons, Jairo and Alvaro, by a previous marriage, whom he took as his own; in the process, they became my cousins.

How was I to address him, Uncle Andy or Tío Andres? Though this was America, I instinctively decided on "Tío." That at any rate would have been how we would address an uncle back home. Tío Andres had never returned home and never would, but I wanted him to feel that some part of home had come seeking him out. Partly it was for my own benefit: to imagine him still in the context of a Philippine landscape, a landscape in which I, too, could be detected. The reality of it was that California had been woven into his life far longer than the emerald-green paddies, coconut trees, and the tropical heat of his youth.

The second eldest in his family after my father, Tío had left Manila when he was barely 20, disappointed in love as only the young can be. His father, my Lolo Pepe, did not approve of the girl Tío Andres was mad about and wanted to marry. Lolo was a strict, land-owning Spanish mestizo from Laguna who died before I was born. He and Tío Andres were stubborn, headstrong men, a trait many of the younger generation of Francias share. So it was that Tío Andres left for California, having been given passage money by his mother. Disagreement, a falling-out, corrosive bitterness would have been inevitable as a typhoon during monsoon season. As for my kind, gentle Lola Morang who hated confrontation (I don't recall her ever raising her voice even when chiding her grandchildren), she wished for nothing more than that the two would cool off. Exile, displacement, was to be temporary—a naive expectation, to be sure. And so it was that Tío Andres lived and died in a land that breeds both dreams and nightmares.

My siblings and cousins, a whole generation, never knew Tío Andres as we were growing up. We knew him only as a young man who left because of a broken heart. He kept in touch intermittently with his mother and siblings (there were nine of them), but gradually his image became ghostly, vaporous, an abstraction.

That image reacquired some solidity when Tía Margarita, Tío Andres' youngest sister, moved to New York, and reestablished contact with her brother.

On that first visit of several days Tío Andres and I would sit on lawn chairs in the mornings, amidst the leafy profusion of Barbara's garden, basking in the sun, and talking casually about his life in America. He had crossed the Pacific Ocean and arrived at what the Chinese termed the Golden Mountain, just before the Depression, at a time when Filipinos were neither citizens nor immigrants—they had the limbo-like status of "nationals." When to be a Filipino in California was, in Carlos Bulosan's words, "a crime." Attempting to build a brown life in a white world, with amor propio and dignity intact, became an endeavor fraught with peril.

Not that he expected life to be a bowl of roses. But as one of the heirs to a considerable estate, he was used to a comfortable life. By the time of my childhood, those lands had long been gone, the result of Lolo Pepe's uncritical generosity: he would pay for close friends' gambling debts by pawning parcels of land to a family notorious for its usurious habits and one of whose descendants I courted briefly. (But that's another story.) Had he been born during the last century, in the age of Rizal and Luna, he would have gone instead to Madrid as an *ilustrado*. Indeed, he, like my father, spoke Spanish. So his class and education set him apart from the other Filipinos who arrived in California at the same time, the *manong*, those from the working class and the peasantry, from the hardscrabble lands of the Ilocos region, or the Visayas, leaving home not because of family and female trouble but to try and become the economic mainstay of their families. Socially he was from the same class as the *pensionados*—young men and women on educational scholarships provided by the U.S. colonial government, so they could come back and administer the colony—though the world he inhabited intersected both that of the *pensionados* and the *manong*. In a way he was like that character Ambo in some of Bienvenido Santos's short stories, a man who had witnessed the lonely, desperate lives of the *manong*, hemmed in by a society that looked at Filipinos and white women together as an affront, and who recounted these stories to Ben Santos's eponymous narrator.

Tío Andres didn't have to pick crops the way a lot of other *manong* had to, didn't have to endure backbreaking work in the heat-clogged fields or in the bleak canneries of Alaska. He was a pianist/composer, a good tennis player, and a whiz at billiards: talents that served him well. He had used all his skills to survive in an America that could be and often was dangerously hostile. For a while he was the pianist of an all-Filipino dance band and he got to see quite a bit of the West, mainly from dance halls and pool rooms. Something of the youthful rake came through when he, smiling, said there were always women around. He no longer played the piano, though there was an upright near his bedroom. I asked him to play but he would only shake his head.

We were driving somewhere once at a fast clip—he was an assured demon behind the wheel, and would have fit perfectly into Manila's traffic — when he asked me to open the glove compartment. I did. It was full of watches. He asked me to pick one out. I looked through the odd assortment, and selected a slim gold wristwatch. He nodded, "That's a fine watch, older than you. Keep it." I thanked him and asked him why he had so many. He said they were winnings from pool games, when his opponents couldn't pay up. He had his own pool cue that he kept in the trunk of his car. He no longer played, however, but had gotten used to bringing his cue wherever he went, in case there was an occasion for a pickup game and some easy money.

He still had the gambler's penchant for superstitions, for auguries. On my first visit, he brought me to downtown San Gabriel to purchase a lottery ticket. He felt I would bring him luck. We joked about becoming millionaires. Alas, my value as a talisman proved illusory.

The second time I saw him was one Christmas Eve about six years ago. I found myself unexpectedly with Tío—for the last time, as it turned out—a serendipitous result of having missed my Manila-bound flight from Los Angeles. He was close to 80 that Christmas, now a little stooped, weaker, forbidden by his family from driving.

He seemed pretty content with where he had arrived, the kind of contentment survivors of a storm at sea, now on terra firma and gazing at a green, calm horizon, possessed, thankful for small mercies obtained along the way. I don't doubt that he had experienced racism, even violence. As an Asian in a xenophobic society, how could it have been otherwise? Tío Andres chose not to dwell on the racism, the social inequities of his time. He exhibited no bitterness, much to my surprise. I was a little disappointed, for I had unconsciously expected someone along the lines of a militant *manong*, someone like Allos in *America Is in the Heart*, someone who would have articulated my own anger and rage in a way I could never do. I wanted him to be my voice as well as a bridge to that past, to link me up to all those Filipinos we had read about and seen in photographs; young bucks nattily dressed, with slicked-back hair, the worm of nostalgia eating away at their hearts but making their eyes light up even more with the desire of living life to the fullest. I wondered then, as I wonder now, if I stayed in this country that long, would I have a similar grace and forgive?

My uncle hated to complain, to dwell on the past. Why, I asked him, did he never go back? He shrugged, didn't say anything for a while. Then he said something about how it was too late now. Everything would be different anyway, wouldn't it? It wasn't an answer, to be sure. But then it was a question one couldn't really answer or explain to anyone else. You had to arrive at that point and then see for yourself.

The Christmas Eve celebration is still clearly etched in my memory: food, gifts, and the comforting noises of family—Tia Barbara, my cousins Alvaro and Jairo, Jairo's wife and children, and Tío Andres. He marks time, a warrior unafraid of that good night. The next morning, Christmas, we sit in the sun, but this time in the car parked on the driveway, with Tío in the driver's seat, the only time he's allowed to be in there. He moves the car intermittently up the driveway, following the sun's progress, the heat reminding him of the Philippines to which he would never return, except perhaps in those moments when he would wonder if anyone back home, in his hometown of Magdalena, Laguna, or even Manila, still remembered him. Life, now pared to essential rituals of memory and contemplation, would end two years later in this other home.

Airborne the night after, towards a familiar and beloved archipelago, though it wouldn't have mattered to him, I knew that one day I would write about him, so he needn't have worried about disappearing from the radar of our memory. I thought of what he had given me: his strength of spirit, his generosity, and calm resignation. They may have been intangible, unlike the gold wristwatch I now wore, but they were far more valuable gifts.

JOSEPH BRODSKY

"To be an exiled writer is like being a dog or a man, hurtled into outer space in a capsule," wrote Leningrad-born poet Joseph Brodsky (1940–1996). "And your capsule is your language." Brodsky's exile was foisted upon him by the Soviet authorities; even after his arrest, imprisonment, and 18 months of hard labor in the Arctic because of his supposedly "pornographic and anti-Soviet" poetry (circulated in *samizdat* publications), he refused two invitations to migrate to Israel in 1971. He was nonetheless forced out of the Soviet Union and arrived in the United States the following year, accepting the position of poet-in-residence at the University of Michigan. Translated into English and complemented by a substantial body of essays collected in volumes such as *Less Than One* (1986) and *On Grief and Reason* (1995), Brodsky's poetry met with wide acclaim over the next two decades, resulting in a Nobel Prize in Literature in 1987 and a term as Poet Laureate of the United States. As Czeslaw Milosz observed, his writings represent "no less than an attempt to fortify the place of man in a threatening world."

from

The Condition We Call Exile

L ife in exile, abroad, in a foreign element, is essentially a premonition of your own book-form fate, of being lost on the shelf among those with whom all you have in common is the first letter of your surname. Here you are, in some gigantic library's reading room, still open . . . Your reader won't give a damn about how you got here. To keep yourself from getting closed and shelved you've got to tell your reader, who thinks he knows it all, about something qualitatively novel—about his world and himself. If this sounds a bit too suggestive, so be it, because suggestion is the name of the whole game anyhow, and because the distance exile puts between an author and his protagonists indeed sometimes begs for the use of astronomical or ecclesiastical figures.

This is what makes one think that "exile" is, perhaps, not the most apt term to describe the condition of a writer forced (by the state, by fear, by poverty, by boredom) to abandon his country. "Exile" covers, at best, the very moment of departure, of expulsion; what follows is both too comfortable and too autonomous to be called by this name, which so strongly suggests a comprehensible grief. The very fact of our gathering here indicates that, if we indeed have a common denominator, it lacks a name. Are we suffering the same degree of despair, ladies and gentlemen? Are we equally sundered from our public? Do we all reside in Paris? No, but what binds us is our book-like fate, the same literal and symbolic lying open on the table or the floor of the gigantic library, at various ends, to be trampled on or picked up by a mildly curious reader or—worse—by a dutiful librarian. The qualitatively novel stuff we may tell that reader about is the autonomous, spacecraft-like mentality that visits, I am sure, every one of us, but whose visitations most of our pages choose not to acknowledge.

We do this for practical reasons, as it were, or genre considerations. Because this way lies either madness or the degree of coldness associated more with the pale-faced locals than with a hot-blooded exile. The other way, however, lies—and close, too—banality. All of this may sound to you like a typically Russian job of issuing guidelines for literature, while, in fact, it's simply one man's reactions to finding many an exiled author—Russian ones in the first place—on the banal side of virtue. That's a great waste, because one more truth about the condition we call exile is that it accelerates tremendously one's otherwise professional flight—or drift—into isolation, into an absolute perspective: into the condition at which all one is left with is oneself and one's language, with nobody or nothing in between. Exile brings you overnight where it would normally take a lifetime to go. If this sounds to you like a commercial, so be it, because it is about time to sell this idea. Because I indeed wish it got more takers. Perhaps a metaphor will help: to be an exiled writer is like being a dog or a man hurtled into outer space in a capsule (more like a dog, of course, than a man, because they will never retrieve you). And your capsule is your language. To finish the metaphor off, it must be added that before long the capsule's passenger discovers that it gravitates not earthward but outward.

For one in our profession the condition we call exile is, first of all, a linguistic event: he is thrust from, he retreats into his mother tongue. From being his, so to speak, sword, it turns into his shield, into his capsule. What started as a private, intimate affair with the language in exile becomes fate—even before it becomes an obsession or a duty. A living language, by definition, has a centrifugal propensity—and propulsion; it tries to cover as much ground as possible—and as much emptiness as possible. Hence the population explosion, and hence your autonomous passage outward, into the domain of a telescope or a prayer.

In a manner of speaking, we all work for a dictionary. Because literature *is* a dictionary, a compendium of meanings for this or that human lot, for this or that experience. It is a dictionary of the language in which life speaks to man. Its function is to save the next man, a new arrival, from falling into an old trap, or to help him realize, should he fall into that trap anyway, that he has been hit by a tautology. This way he will be less impressed—and, in a way, more free. For to know the meaning of life's terms, of what is happening to you, is liberating. It would seem to me that the condition we call exile is up for a fuller explication; that, famous for its pain, it should also be known for its pain-dulling infinity, for its forgetfulness, detachment, indifference, for its terrifying human and inhuman vistas for which we've got no yardstick except ourselves.

We must make it easier for the next man, if we can't make it safer. And the only way to make it easier for him, to make him less frightened of it, is to give him the whole measure of it—that is, as much as we ourselves can manage to cover. We may argue about our responsibilities and loyalties (toward our respective contemporaries, motherlands, otherlands, cultures, traditions, etc.) ad infinitum, but this responsibility or, rather, opportunity to set the next man—however theoretical he and his needs may be—a bit more free shouldn't become a subject for hesitation. If all this sounds a bit too lofty and humanistic, then I apologize. These distinctions are actually not so much humanistic as deterministic, although one shouldn't bother with such subtleties. All I am trying to say is that, given an opportunity, in the great causal chain of things, we may as well stop being just its rattling effects and try to play causes. The condition we call exile is exactly that kind of opportunity.

Yet if we don't use it, if we decide to remain effects and play exile in an old-fashioned way, that shouldn't be explained away as nostalgia. Of course, it has to do with the necessity of telling about oppression, and of course, our condition should serve as a warning to any thinking man toying with the idea of an ideal society. That's our value for the free world: that's our function.

But perhaps our greater value and greater function are to be unwitting embodiments of the disheartening idea that a freed man is not a free man, that liberation is just the means of attaining freedom and is not synonymous with it. This highlights the extent of the damage that can be done to the species, and we can feel proud of playing this role. However, if we want to play a bigger role, the role of a free man, then we should be capable of accepting —or at least imitating—the manner in which a free man fails. A free man, when he fails, blames nobody.

LAN CAO

The U.S. Census Bureau estimated over 1.6 million Vietnamese Americans in 2006. Granted special status by the Indochina Migration and Refugee Assistance Act of 1975 and the Refugee Act of 1980, Vietnamese refugees fled first on naval vessels and later in small makeshift boats, and by land through camps in Thailand and other Southeast Asian countries. Their exodus is one of the lasting legacies of the Vietnam War and has changed the face of communities across America. In 2008 Louisiana's 2nd district elected the first Vietnamese American to Congress. Lan Cao (born in 1961), a native of Saigon, left Vietnam with her parents when she was 13. She is now professor of law at the College of William and Mary. In her semiautobiographical novel *Monkey Bridge* (1997)—described as the first novel by a Vietnamese-American writer about the immigrant experience—she ponders the ongoing presence, in memory, of a missing family member, Baba Quan, and the persistence of old wounds.

from
Monkey Bridge

The smell of blood, warm and wet, rose from the floor and settled into the solemn stillness of the hospital air. I could feel it like an unhurried chill in my joints, a slow-moving red that smoldered in a floating ether of dull, gray smoke. All around me, the bare walls expanded and converged into a relentless stretch of white. The bedsheet white of the hallway was an anxious white I knew by heart. White, the color of mourning, the standard color for ghosts, bones, and funerals, swallowed in the surface calm of the hospital halls.

A scattering of gunshots tore through the plaster walls. Everything was unfurling, everything, and I knew I was back there again, as if the tears were always pooled in readiness beneath my eyes. It was all coming back, a fury of whiteness rushing against my head with violent percussive rage. The automatic glass doors closed behind me with a sharp sucking sound.

Arlington Hospital was not a Saigon military hospital. Through the hydraulic doors, I could see the lush green lawn that stretched languidly across an immense parking lot. A few feet beyond, a spray of water blossomed upward, then rotated in a soundless circle wide enough to reach the far outcropping of grass. The American flag, flown sky-high from a sturdy iron pole, still swelled and snapped in the wind. I knew I was not in Saigon. I was not a hospital volunteer. It was not 1968 but 1978. Yet I also knew, as I passed a wall of smoked-glass windows, that I would see the quick movement of green camouflage fatigues, and I knew. I knew the medic insignia on his uniform and I knew, I knew, what I would see next. His face, not the face before the explosion, but the face after, motionless in a liquefied red that poured from a tangle of delicate veins. "Oh God, oh God, oh my God!" people cried. The doctor, the medic, and the operating-room crew killed in a cramped, battered room reinforced by rows of military-green sandbags. The calm of Saigon had always been unreliable, narcotically unreal. Who could have known before the man was cut up that an unexploded grenade, fired from a launcher—not a dead bullet—had lodged in the hollowness of his stomach?

"Look," Bobbie said. "See how it pops in your hand?" Bobbie was my best friend from high school. She was squeezing a rubber toy shaped like a bowling pin with a round mouth and two round eyes that bugged out with each squeeze like a pair of snake eyes. A toy that doubled as a physical therapist's rehabilitation tool, it could make my mother laugh, and at the same time would exercise her left hand. "Good for a weak hand," she proclaimed.

Bobbie had no subverted interior and would never see the things I saw. I could feel the sharp, unsubdued scent of chemicalized smoke settle in my nostrils as I watched her meander among a collection of toys. The very idea of a gift shop in a hospital, with stuffed rabbits and teddy bears and fresh roses and carnations, was new to me. Despite the immediacy of illness, an American hospital, after all, was still a place where one could succumb to the perplexing temptations of hope.

This is Arlington Hospital, I reminded myself. There, beyond the door, was the evenly paved lot, its perimeters unenclosed by barbed wire or sandbags. Visitors mingled in the lobby; I had been taught to avoid the front portion of buildings. In Saigon, it would have been a danger zone, as was any zone that a hand grenade could conceivably reach if thrown from a passing vehicle.

My mother was still in her bed, a cranked-up baby bed reinforced with piles of pillows pushed against the fully extended metal railings. She lay with one arm diagonally shielding her face, breathing hard. I avoided looking too closely at it, her red blotchy face that had been burned by a kitchen fire years ago. As she told it, she had been preparing caramelized pork when flames from one of the burners had caught on a silk scarf loosely wrapped around her neck. This web of tender skin that she referred to as The Accident had been diagnosed as permanent, and, worse still, she seemed to accept it as such without question. French night cream I bought was simply put away on the bathroom shelf, behind my moisturizers and cleansing lotions. Cucumber and tomato treatments I prepared remained in the refrigerator for days, until they soured and thickened and had to be discarded. I knew the wound could flare into a lurid red, because it was at those moments that strangers adopted an attitude of polite abandon and courteously dropped their eyes, as I too dropped mine.

She had once been beautiful, in an old wedding picture years ago, her skin the smooth, slightly flushed alabaster of a mere fifteen-year-old bowing happily before the family altar. Even now, the delicate feline features showed, in spite of the singed and puckered flesh.

The nurses moved in and out, coaxing a needle into my mother's thick, unyielding veins, whispering. Their white canvas shoes made soft shuffling noises against the linoleum tiles, maintaining a constant and instinctive distance of several feet from my mother's bed.

"She's talking in her sleep again, calling out to Baba Quan," Bobbie said. The expanse of white blinded my eyes. In spite of the darkness in her curtain-drawn room, the walls and the tiles and the stark white of my mother's twisted sheets and pillows emitted a flurry of bright, funeral-white lights.

Since she was first admitted to the hospital almost one month before, after Mrs. Bay, our neighbor, found her slumped on the bathroom floor, she had been calling out for my grandfather.

"Baba Quan. Baba Quan," she repeated, his name coming out of her throat as a long infernal moan, like none I had heard come out of her before. Although partially paralyzed and restrained by a band tightened across her chest like one giant tourniquet, my mother could still move, even if only with the random force and strength of a trapped and frustrated eel.

I knew my mother to be the sort of daughter who had always been devoted to her father. She had never truly recovered from the mishap that left him without the means to leave Saigon. For some unknown reason, they had missed each other at their place of rendezvous on the 30th of April, 1975, and the preapproved car that was supposed to take both of them, along with a few other Vietnamese, to an American plane, had had to leave without him. Because I was already living in America with Uncle Michael, as I called him —the American colonel we befriended in Saigon—my mother left her father, her only remaining family member, behind. From that day on, my grandfather's absence glistened just beyond the touch of our fingertips. During those moments when my mother sat alone by the window, I could almost see her hand trying to make contact with the moment when her father had failed to appear. The memory of that day continued to thrash its way through her flesh, and there were times when I thought she would never be consoled.

"Do you remember your grandfather?" Bobbie asked. Bobbie seemed to think I was a baby and not a teenager when I left Vietnam, so young that memory could not possibly have taken hold.

"Yes," I said, "although I could count on my fingers the number of times I actually spent with him at family gatherings and holidays." My grandfather was born in Ba Xuyen, a rice-growing province in the Mekong Delta. He was a traditional man, a devout Confucian who did not like to travel away from his village home. According to my mother, he was always preoccupied with tending the spirits of his ancestors, their burial grounds. "The spirits stay with the ancestral land," my mother had explained.

I leaned over the railing and rubbed moisturizing cream into my mother's skin. My house in Saigon had been stocked with mementos from her village in Ba Xuyen. Coconut halves, smoothed and hollowed into bowls and filled with brown earth and a handful of well-worn pebbles; a rusty iron scythe that hung like a half-moon on the walls of my mother's bedroom; and a fountain my grandfather kept filled and replenished with water from a fast-moving brook by the outer edge of the village. A patch of earth and a sprinkle of water from the province of Ba Xuyen in the Mekong Delta. That is what "country" means in Vietnamese—"earth" and "water" combined.

"We must all maintain a loyalty to our beginnings," Baba Quan had told my mother once. "We tend to our souls, not our bodies." And to me he whispered, "Burn a candle for your grandmother, little granddaughter, and ask for her blessings from the world beyond."

My grandfather was a farmer. He brought the fertile blackness of the earth with him. When I looked at his face, I could almost see the rice fields I had never seen. I could say the words "plows" and "water buffaloes" as if they were as unsurprising as "notebook" and "Citroën." Even then, when I was a mere seven-year-old, but certainly more often now, I wondered about his history, and the fables and myths of our ancestral land. "Take me with you to Ba Xuyen," I had begged. I had adored him with a fierceness that distance made completely possible.

"I want to meet him. The way Mrs. Bay talks, he sounds like the flashiest guy in town," Bobbie said.

Mrs. Bay was my mother's best friend, her sole friend in Virginia. They were both widows whose husbands had died around the same year in Vietnam. We lived in the same building in Little Saigon, on the same floor, our apartments facing prosperously in the same lucky direction. She and my mother had lived in the same village. Mrs. Bay's parents and my mother's parents had both been tenant farmers to Mr. Khan, the most powerful landowner in Ba Xuyen, with holdings so vast that, as the saying goes, a stork would have to stretch the full majestic length of its wings to fly the expanse of his land.

Baba Quan, according to Mrs. Bay, had been considered odd by the villagers, a man more concerned about staking out his one-hectare leasehold with lions he carved from mahogany and infused with fierce protective spells, than about tending and harvesting the land. He was simply more flamboyant than most of the farmers of Ba Xuyen, Mrs. Bay would explain. "He wore the strangest clothes for a farmer," she said, "colorful pants and shirts with various patterns and designs, while everyone else would be wearing black or brown." And after a moment's pause, she would say, with a wink and a definitive nod, "He was certainly an eccentric." I interpreted this to mean that my grandfather had many talents. I could see him in his work shed, his hammer and saw hung neatly on nails tacked to the walls, his screws and bolts, and a few cans of paint, scattered by the foot of a sawhorse.

"Someday maybe we'll have airplanes that go from Saigon to Washington," I said. "And maybe my grandfather will be able to fly over here, just like that."

"That's what we're hoping for, right?" Bobbie replied. One way or another, Bobbie and I would find a way to bring my grandfather to the United States. Or at least that was our plan.

I turned toward my mother. Her firefly eyes clicked open and closed, and along her forehead the horizontal grooves had deepened into sharp narrow ruts. Slowly, she extended the full length of her arm, a straight profile of skin and bone, and sliced the air with long diagonal slashes. Her body had become a battlefield, she a war wound fastened to a bed in a suburban hospital more equipped to deal with cesarean sections and other routine operations.

I took her hand and pinned it under mine. A salty smell of pickled plums Mrs. Bay brought from the Mekong Grocery rose from her mouth. She had gone from eating by tubes to sipping liquid and recently to pureed baby food and finally, last week, to pickled plums and pho, a Hanoi beef-noodle soup. I could smell the fierce immediacy of cinnamon, anise, and fish sauce on the tips of her nails. My mother was getting better.

The sleeping pill must have worn off, because she plucked her hand from my grasp and started poking around, jabbing, punching the remote-control buttons with faltering fingers. She was getting excited, waving her hand, her good right hand, in rapid movements, her parched purple lips chewing air, mumbling, sputtering—a furnace flinging hot grease.

"You've been calling out to Baba Quan again," I said.

She shrugged. Her body went rigid, her arms slapping and flailing the bed. She pointed to the mustard-colored plastic pitcher on the stainless-steel table by the bedside. On cue, I poured water into the paper cup and left it within easy reach near the edge of the night table. "You pick it up yourself," I said. A month ago, I would have handed it over to her with perfect Confucian etiquette—clasped in both hands. The right hand would have been too flippant, the left hand an insult, but both hands were perfectly, exquisitely polite.

"That's what the nurses said. Let Mrs. Nguyen do everything herself," Bobbie piped up. They had issued their warnings: my mother was capable of doing many more things than she let on. "Force her to use her hands, especially her left hand," they had commanded. "They're full of threats," Mrs. Bay had complained in turn. If she doesn't do this, if she doesn't do that, her muscles will dissolve, she won't be able to move, she'll forget she has a left side. How could they have known it was not muscular but karmic movements and the collapse of Heaven that frightened my mother?

I took her hands, thick with calluses gone soft, and positioned them toward the Dixie cup. She stared at me with importunate eyes, and I could see frustration, nostalgia in the looks she gave me, beneath the fault line of rage that threatened always to crack open and explode. In the eerie silence of the room, I could practically hear the sound of old memories ripping their way through her face. I stood back and watched. Even the unruly thatch of black hair could not completely cover the splotches of very old burn on her cheeks that still occasionally ignited into a fresh, rampaging red. It wasn't summer, and yet the threat of heat from the radiator had been enough to seduce old wounds.

The television screen flipped from sitcom to sitcom. A few months in the hospital and already my mother was switching channels like a native-born American child. She laughed along with the artificial laughter on screen.

"What are you looking for, Ma?" I asked.

"Jaime . . . Jaime Sommers." She looked around the room. The Bionic Woman delighted my mother. Jaime could very well materialize out of drawers, ceilings, and walls. They both shared bionic ears. Hers, my mother believed, empowered her to hear things no one else could. Like the Chinese, the Vietnamese believed a set of long ears was a sign of longevity and luck. The Buddha, for example, had ears that spanned half the length of his face, and every painting or statue, my mother used to say with pride, depicted him with gracefully long and perfectly enlightened ears.

The Bionic Woman was a little bit of Shaolin kung fu mixed with American hardware, American know-how.

"I'll get it for you, Mrs. Nguyen," Bobbie whispered.

The television screen became a rectangle of icy aquamarine. Against the bleached electronic glow, the Bionic Woman crouched, then stretched her body, propelling it off the ground onto a tall building while supersonic vibrations accompanied each sequence of movements in the background.

A look of satisfaction registered on my mother's face. These were her sustaining sounds, the Dopplerized sound effects and metallic vibrations that signified Jaime's superhuman abilities. She pushed a button, cranking the bed to a more upright position. This appeared to be a particularly good episode. Jaime was especially alert tonight and was not making any move that would lead her down the wrong path.

A rattling cough raked through my mother's chest. "Baba Quan, Baba Quan," she suddenly gasped, drumming her right fingers against her left wrist, tying a ferocious knot with the sheet corners, carrying on in her usual convoluted language about karma I could not make out. "Karma," that word alone, whose sacred formula I could not possibly know, had become her very own singular mantra. This was alien territory, very alien, even for me. I checked Bobbie's eyes. To her, it was simply another foreign language, the thick, guttural sounds, the rises and drops in the voice, all simply a bit more exotic than her high-school French.

"I'm trying to reach him for you, Ma," I promised. "I've written." I flashed a coconspirator's glance at Bobbie. "We'll figure something out."

For the past three and a half years, my mother and I had lived quietly with the tragedy of my grandfather's disappearance, and I, in moments alone, had tried to piece together the missing minutes that led to his absence. The muffled stillness of that day continued to cast a long, heavy pall over our lives. What had happened to my grandfather? This question continued to linger in our midst and shroud our lives in a ravenous expanse with no discernible seams or edges.

Now my mother looked at me with urgent, inquisitive eyes, dull one minute, glowing the next, drifting in and out of consciousness, my grandfather's name reverberating through her chest. I eased her head onto the pillow. By the hospital's standards, my mother was behaving abnormally. But what was abnormal was not the behavior, only that it had been so public.

We each had our own way. My mother had hers, I had mine. My philosophy was simply this: if I didn't see it at night, in nightmares or otherwise, it never happened. I had my routines: constant vigilance, my antidote to the sin of sleeping and the undomesticated world of dreams. I reached for the pills, my kind of comfort—verifiable peace in every hundred-milligram pellet of reliable, synthetic caffeine. What harm could there be in that?

*

It was almost midnight. Alone in our apartment, I looked out the window. There was nothing but darkness outside, a fierce silence fractured by the occasional sound of black ghosts making their marks. Even the bare winter branches, tidy and muted like dry bones, had become a disturbance of tangled nerves. I closed my eyes. Simplify. Simplify. Everything will be all right.

There, in front of my eyes, were the sutures stitched zigzag across my mother's head. A stroke that struck as she stood on a stool and reached toward the ceiling to change the bathroom light, and she was now in a hospital with a blood clot in her brain, hallucinations and nightmares about a missing father, and "complications," as the hospital personnel referred to it.

"She's getting better, slowly, every day. We have great hopes that, with rigorous rehabilitation, she'll have full control of her right side very soon. The left side will need more work. But over all, she'll more or less be able to do most of what she used to do—as long as she sticks to her physical-therapy routine, of course," one of the nurses had told me.

Of course. My mother had had a hemorrhage, after all. I willed my mind blank and tried to keep a calm, steady gaze. "One wrong move," as my father used to say, and the force of too many things abruptly rammed inside my brain. I was already back there, in the military hospital in Saigon. This had been how the war entered the capital city. Pulsing flesh, exposed cartilage and bone fastened to mattresses shoved against hospital walls. With a notepad and a pen in hand, I had walked the halls, acted as a scribe, writing down battlefield memories and dying declarations from those war-wounded who were too weak to write letters. A fierce explosion: shards of metal flying from a large gaping wound. Too late to shove anything back now. One wrong move and something had tipped one notch too far and everything was pouring inside out, a live current of nervous wires connecting me to disorder, to insanity. A sliver of metal. Pinched arteries. Singed eyelids and exploded pupils, dislodged and burned black like two charred yolks.

I slipped under the blanket and waited for the NoDoz to do its job. Against a pillow wedged sandbag-tight behind me, my head felt full and heavy and exposed like an open root canal, throbbing inside my palms.

JUNOT DÍAZ

The writing of Junot Díaz (born in 1968) is a hybrid prose style that interweaves Spanish colloquialisms with a rapid-fire New York City street patois. In his critically acclaimed and Pulitzer Prize–winning novel *The Brief Wondrous Life of Oscar Wao* (2007), this style is especially pronounced, in order, as he has noted, to make the reader "feel like an immigrant . . . that there'd be one language chain that you might not get." Díaz, the middle of five children, came to New Jersey (where most of his stories are set) from the Dominican Republic with his family when he was six years old. In the collection the following story is taken from, *Drown* (1996), Díaz explores, through his protagonist Yunior (also the narrator of *Oscar Wao*), conflicting ideas about masculinity in both the old and the adopted lands.

from
Drown

Mami's youngest sister—my tía Yrma—finally made it to the United States that year. She and tío Miguel got themselves an apartment in the Bronx, off the Grand Concourse and everybody decided that we should have a party. Actually, my pops decided, but everybody—meaning Mami, tía Yrma, tío Miguel and their neighbors—thought it a dope idea. On the afternoon of the party Papi came back from work around six. Right on time. We were all dressed by then, which was a smart move on our part. If Papi had walked in and caught us lounging around in our underwear, he would have kicked our asses something serious.

He didn't say nothing to nobody, not even my moms. He just pushed past her, held up his hand when she tried to talk to him and headed right into the shower. Rafa gave me the look and I gave it back to him; we both knew Papi had been with that Puerto Rican woman he was seeing and wanted to wash off the evidence quick.

Mami looked really nice that day. The United States had finally put some meat on her; she was no longer the same flaca who had arrived here three years before. She had cut her hair short and was wearing tons of cheap-ass jewelry which on her didn't look too lousy. She smelled like herself, like the wind through a tree. She always waited until the last possible minute to put on her perfume because she said it was a waste to spray it on early and then have to spray it on again once you got to the party.

We—meaning me, my brother, my little sister and Mami—waited for Papi to finish his shower. Mami seemed anxious, in her usual dispassionate way. Her hands adjusted the buckle of her belt over and over again. That morning, when she had gotten us up for school, Mami told us that she wanted to have a good time at the party. I want to dance, she said, but now, with the sun sliding out of the sky like spit off a wall, she seemed ready just to get this over with.

Rafa didn't much want to go to no party either, and me, I never wanted to go anywhere with my family. There was a baseball game in the parking lot outside and we could hear our friends, yelling, Hey, and, Cabrón, to one another. We heard the pop of a ball as it sailed over the cars, the clatter of an aluminum bat dropping to the concrete. Not that me or Rafa loved baseball; we just liked playing with the local kids, thrashing them at anything they were doing. By the sounds of the shouting, we both knew the game was close, either of us could have made a difference. Rafa frowned and when I frowned back, he put up his fist. Don't you mirror me, he said.

Don't you mirror me, I said.

He punched me—I would have hit him back but Papi marched into the living room with his towel around his waist, looking a lot smaller than he did when he was dressed. He had a few strands of hair around his nipples and a surly closed-mouth expression, like maybe he'd scalded his tongue or something.

Have they eaten? he asked Mami.

She nodded. I made you something.

You didn't let him eat, did you?

Ay, Dios mío, she said, letting her arms fall to her side.

Ay, Dios mío is right, Papi said.

I was never supposed to eat before our car trips, but earlier, when she had put out our dinner of rice, beans and sweet platanos, guess who had been the first one to clean his plate? You couldn't blame Mami really, she had been busy—cooking, getting ready, dressing my sister Madai. I should have reminded her not to feed me but I wasn't that sort of son.

Papi turned to me. Coño, muchacho, why did you eat?

Rafa had already started inching away from me. I'd once told him I considered him a low-down chickenshit for moving out of the way every time Papi was going to smack me.

Collateral damage, Rafa had said. Ever heard of it?

No.

Look it up.

Chickenshit or not, I didn't dare glance at him. Papi was old-fashioned; he expected your undivided attention when you were getting your ass whupped. You couldn't look him in the eye either—that wasn't allowed. Better to stare at his belly button, which was perfectly round and immaculate. Papi pulled me to my feet by my ear.

If you throw up—

I won't, I cried, tears in my eyes, more out of reflex than pain.

Ya, Ramón, ya. It's not his fault, Mami said.

They've known about this party forever. How did they think we were going to get there? Fly?

He finally let go of my ear and I sat back down. Madai was too scared to open her eyes. Being around Papi all her life had turned her into a major-league wuss. Anytime Papi raised his voice her lip would start trembling, like some specialized tuning fork. Rafa pretended that he had knuckles to crack and when I shoved him, he gave me a *Don't start* look. But even that little bit of recognition made me feel better.

I was the one who was always in trouble with my dad. It was like my God-given duty to piss him off, to do everything the way he hated. Our fights didn't bother me too much. I still wanted him to love me, something that never seemed strange or contradictory until years later, when he was out of our lives.

By the time my ear stopped stinging Papi was dressed and Mami was crossing each one of us, solemnly, like we were heading off to war. We said, in turn, Bendición, Mami, and she poked us in our five cardinal spots while saying, Que Dios te bendiga.

This was how all our trips began, the words that followed me every time I left the house.

None of us spoke until we were inside Papi's Volkswagen van. Brand-new, lime-green and bought to impress. Oh, we were impressed, but me, every time I was in that VW and Papi went above twenty miles an hour, I vomited. I'd never had trouble with cars before—that van was like my curse. Mami suspected it was the upholstery. In her mind, American things—appliances, mouthwash, funny-looking upholstery—all seemed to have an intrinsic bad-ness about them. Papi was careful about taking me anywhere in the VW, but when he had to, I rode up front in Mami's usual seat so I could throw up out a window.

¿Cómo te sientes? Mami asked over my shoulder when Papi pulled onto the turnpike. She had her hand on the base of my neck. One thing about Mami, her palms never sweated.

I'm OK, I said, keeping my eyes straight ahead. I definitely didn't want to trade glances with Papi. He had this one look, furious and sharp, that always left me feeling bruised.

Toma. Mami handed me four mentas. She had thrown three out her window at the beginning of our trip, an offering to Eshú; the rest were for me.

I took one and sucked it slowly, my tongue knocking it up against my teeth. We passed Newark Airport without any incident. If Madai had been awake she would have cried because the planes flew so close to the cars.

How's he feeling? Papi asked.

Fine, I said. I glanced back at Rafa and he pretended like he didn't see me. That was the way he was, at school and at home. When I was in trouble, he didn't know me. Madai was solidly asleep, but even with her face all wrinkled up and drooling she looked cute, her hair all separated into twists.

I turned around and concentrated on the candy. Papi even started to joke that we might not have to scrub the van out tonight. He was beginning to loosen up, not checking his watch too much. Maybe he was thinking about that Puerto Rican woman or maybe he was just happy that we were all together. I could never tell. At the toll, he was feeling positive enough to actually get out of the van and search around under the basket for dropped coins. It was something he had once done to amuse Madai, but now it was habit. Cars behind us honked their horns and I slid down in my seat. Rafa didn't care; he grinned back at the other cars and waved. His actual job was to make sure no cops were coming. Mami shook Madai awake and as soon as she saw Papi stooping for a couple of quarters she let out this screech of delight that almost took off the top of my head.

That was the end of the good times. Just outside the Washington Bridge, I started feeling woozy. The smell of the upholstery got all up inside my head and I found myself with a mouthful of saliva. Mami's hand tensed on my shoulder and when I caught Papi's eye, he was like, No way. Don't do it.

The first time I got sick in the van Papi was taking me to the library. Rafa was with us and he couldn't believe I threw up. I was famous for my steel-lined stomach. A third-world childhood could give you that. Papi was worried enough that just as quick as Rafa could drop off the books we were on our way home. Mami fixed me one of her honey-and-onion concoctions and that made my stomach feel better. A week later we tried the library again and on this go-around I couldn't get the window open in time. When Papi got me home, he went and cleaned out the van himself, an expression of askho on his face. This was a big deal, since Papi almost never cleaned anything himself. He came back inside and found me sitting on the couch feeling like hell.

It's the car, he said to Mami. It's making him sick.

This time the damage was pretty minimal, nothing Papi couldn't wash off the door with a blast of the hose. He was pissed, though; he jammed his finger into my cheek, a nice solid thrust. That was the way he was with his punishments: imaginative. Earlier that year I'd written an essay in school called "My Father the Torturer," but the teacher made me write a new one. She thought I was kidding.

We drove the rest of the way to the Bronx in silence. We only stopped once, so I could brush my teeth. Mami had brought along my toothbrush and a tube of toothpaste and while every car known to man sped by us she stood outside with me so I wouldn't feel alone.

*

Tío Miguel was about seven feet tall and had his hair combed up and out, into a demi-fro. He gave me and Rafa big spleen-crushing hugs and then kissed Mami and finally ended up with Madai on his shoulder. The last time I'd seen Tío was at the airport, his first day in the United States. I remembered how he hadn't seemed all that troubled to be in another country.

He looked down at me. Carajo, Yunior, you look horrible!

He threw up, my brother explained.

I pushed Rafa. Thanks a lot, ass-face.

Hey, he said. Tío asked.

Tío clapped a bricklayer's hand on my shoulder. Everybody gets sick sometimes, he said. You should have seen me on the plane over here. Dios mio! He rolled his Asian-looking eyes for emphasis. I thought we were all going to die.

Everybody could tell he was lying. I smiled like he was making me feel better.

Do you want me to get you a drink? Tío asked. We got beer and rum.

Miguel, Mami said. He's young.

Young? Back in Santo Domingo, he'd be getting laid by now.

Mami thinned her lips, which took some doing.

Well, it's true, Tío said.

So, Mami, I said. When do I get to go visit the D.R.?

That's enough, Yunior.

It's the only pussy you'll ever get, Rafa said to me in English.

Not counting your girlfriend, of course.

Rafa smiled. He had to give me that one.

Papi came in from parking the van. He and Miguel gave each other the sort of handshakes that would have turned my fingers into Wonder bread.

Coño, compa'i, ¿cómo va todo? they said to each other.

Tía came out then, with an apron on and maybe the longest Lee Press-On Nails I've ever seen in my life. There was this one guru motherfucker in the *Guinness Book of World Records* who had longer nails, but I tell you, it was close. She gave everybody kisses, told me and Rafa how guapo we were— Rafa, of course, believed her—told Madai how bella she was, but when she got to Papi, she froze a little, like maybe she'd seen a wasp on the tip of his nose, but then kissed him all the same.

Mami told us to join the other kids in the living room. Tío said, Wait a minute, I want to show you the apartment. I was glad Tía said, Hold on, because from what I'd seen so far, the place had been furnished in Contemporary Dominican Tacky. The less I saw, the better. I mean, I liked plastic sofa covers but damn, Tío and Tía had taken it to another level. They had a disco ball hanging in the living room and the type of stucco ceilings that looked like stalactite heaven. The sofas all had golden tassels dangling from their edges. Tía came out of the kitchen with some people I didn't know and by the time she got done introducing everybody, only Papi and Mami were given the guided tour of the four-room third-floor apartment. Me and Rafa joined the kids in the living room. They'd already started eating. We were hungry, one of the girls explained, a pastelito in hand. The boy was about three years younger than me but the girl who'd spoken, Leti, was my age. She and another girl were on the sofa together and they were cute as hell.

Leti introduced them: the boy was her brother Wilquins and the other girl was her neighbor Mari. Leti had some serious tetas and I could tell that my brother was going to gun for her. His taste in girls was predictable. He sat down right between Leti and Mari and by the way they were smiling at him I knew he'd do fine. Neither of the girls gave me more than a cursory one-two, which didn't bother me. Sure, I liked girls but I was always too terrified to speak to them unless we were arguing or I was calling them stupidos, which was one of my favorite words that year. I turned to Wilquins and asked him what there was to do around here. Mari, who had the lowest voice I'd ever heard, said, He can't speak.

What does that mean?

He's mute.

I looked at Wilquins incredulously. He smiled and nodded, as if he'd won a prize or something.

Does he understand? I asked.

Of course he understands, Rafa said. He's not dumb.

I could tell Rafa had said that just to score points with the girls. Both of them nodded. Low-voice Mari said, He's the best student in his grade.

I thought, Not bad for a mute. I sat next to Wilquins. After about two seconds of TV Wilquins whipped out a bag of dominos and motioned to me. Did I want to play? Sure. Me and him played Rafa and Leti and we whupped their collective asses twice, which put Rafa in a real bad mood. He looked at me like maybe he wanted to take a swing, just one to make him feel better. Leti kept whispering into Rafa's ear, telling him it was OK.

In the kitchen I could hear my parents slipping into their usual modes. Papi's voice was loud and argumentative; you didn't have to be anywhere near him to catch his drift. And Mami, you had to put cups to your ears to hear hers. I went into the kitchen a few times—once so the tíos could show off how much bullshit I'd been able to cram in my head the last few years; another time for a bucket-sized cup of soda. Mami and Tía were frying tostones and the last of the pastelitos. She appeared happier now and the way her hands worked on our dinner you would think she had a life somewhere else making rare and precious things. She nudged Tía every now and then, shit they must have been doing all their lives. As soon as Mami saw me though, she gave me the eye. Don't stay long, that eye said. Don't piss your old man off.

Papi was too busy arguing about Elvis to notice me. Then somebody mentioned María Montez and Papi barked, María Montez? Let me tell *you* about María Montez, compa'i.

Maybe I was used to him. His voice—louder than most adults'—didn't bother me none, though the other kids shifted uneasily in their seats. Wilquins was about to raise the volume on the TV, but Rafa said, I wouldn't do that. Muteboy had balls, though. He did it anyway and then sat down. Wilquins's pop came into the living room a second later, a bottle of Presidente in hand. That dude must have had Spider-senses or something. Did you raise that? he asked Wilquins and Wilquins nodded.

Is this your house? his pops asked. He looked ready to beat Wilquins silly but he lowered the volume instead.

See, Rafa said. You nearly got your ass *kicked*.

I met the Puerto Rican woman right after Papi had gotten the van. He was taking me on short trips, trying to cure me of my vomiting. It wasn't really working but I looked forward to our trips, even though at the end of each one I'd be sick. These were the only times me and Papi did anything together.

When we were alone he treated me much better, like maybe I was his son or something.

Before each drive Mami would cross me.

Bendición, Mami, I'd say.

She'd kiss my forehead. Que Dios te bendiga. And then she would give me a handful of mentas because she wanted me to be OK. Mami didn't think these excursions would cure anything, but the one time she had brought it up to Papi he had told her to shut up, what did she know about anything anyway?

Me and Papi didn't talk much. We just drove around our neighborhood. Occasionally he'd ask, How is it?

And I'd nod, no matter how I felt.

One day I was sick outside of Perth Amboy. Instead of taking me home he went the other way on Industrial Avenue, stopping a few minutes later in front of a light blue house I didn't recognize. It reminded me of the Easter eggs we colored at school, the ones we threw out the bus windows at other cars.

The Puerto Rican woman was there and she helped me clean up. She had dry papery hands and when she rubbed the towel on my chest, she did it hard, like I was a bumper she was waxing. She was very thin and had a cloud of brown hair rising above her narrow face and the sharpest blackest eyes you've ever seen.

He's cute, she said to Papi.

Not when he's throwing up, Papi said.

What's your name? she asked me. Are you Rafa?

I shook my head.

Then it's Yunior, right?

I nodded.

You're the smart one, she said, suddenly happy with herself. Maybe you want to see my books?

They weren't hers. I recognized them as ones my father must have left in her house. Papi was a voracious reader, couldn't even go cheating without a paperback in his pocket.

Why don't you go watch TV? Papi suggested. He was looking at her like she was the last piece of chicken on earth.

We got plenty of channels, she said. Use the remote if you want.

The two of them went upstairs and I was too scared of what was happening to poke around. I just sat there, ashamed, expecting something big and fiery to crash down on our heads. I watched a whole hour of the news before Papi came downstairs and said, Let's go.

About two hours later the women laid out the food and like always nobody but the kids thanked them. It must be some Dominican tradition or something. There was everything I liked—chicharrones, fried chicken, tostones, sancocho, rice, fried cheese, yuca, avocado, potato salad, a meteor-sized hunk of pernil, even a tossed salad which I could do without—but when I joined the other kids around the serving table, Papi said, Oh no you don't, and took the paper plate out of my hand. His fingers weren't gentle.

What's wrong now? Tía asked, handing me another plate.

He ain't eating, Papi said. Mami pretended to help Rafa with the pernil.

Why can't he eat?

Because I said so.

The adults who didn't know us made like they hadn't heard a thing and Tío just smiled sheepishly and told everybody to go ahead and eat. All the kids—about ten of them now—trooped back into the living room with their plates a-heaping and all the adults ducked into the kitchen and the dining room, where the radio was playing loud-ass bachatas. I was the only one without a plate. Papi stopped me before I could get away from him. He kept his voice nice and low so nobody else could hear him.

If you eat anything, I'm going to beat you. ¿Entiendes?

I nodded.

And if your brother gives you any food, I'll beat him too. Right here in front of everybody. ¿Entiendes?

I nodded again. I wanted to kill him and he must have sensed it because he gave my head a little shove.

All the kids watched me come in and sit down in front of the TV.

What's wrong with your dad? Leti asked.

He's a dick, I said.

Rafa shook his head. Don't say that shit in front of people.

Easy for you to be nice when you're eating, I said.

Hey, if I was a pukey little baby, I wouldn't get no food either.

I almost said something back but I concentrated on the TV. I wasn't going to start it. No fucking way. So I watched Bruce Lee beat Chuck Norris into the floor of the Colosseum and tried to pretend that there was no food anywhere in the house. It was Tía who finally saved me. She came into the living room and said, Since you ain't eating, Yunior, you can at least help me get some ice.

I didn't want to, but she mistook my reluctance for something else.

I already asked your father.

She held my hand while we walked; Tía didn't have any kids but I could tell she wanted them. She was the sort of relative who always remembered your birthday but who you only went to visit because you had to. We didn't get past the first-floor landing before she opened her pocketbook and handed me the first of three pastelitos she had smuggled out of the apartment.

Go ahead, she said. And as soon as you get inside make sure you brush your teeth.

Thanks a lot, Tía, I said.

Those pastelitos didn't stand a chance.

She sat next to me on the stairs and smoked her cigarette. All the way down on the first floor and we could still hear the music and the adults and the television. Tía looked a ton like Mami; the two of them were both short and light-skinned. Tía smiled a lot and that was what set them apart the most.

How is it at home, Yunior?

What do you mean?

How's it going in the apartment? Are you kids OK?

I knew an interrogation when I heard one, no matter how sugar-coated it was. I didn't say anything. Don't get me wrong, I loved my tía, but something told me to keep my mouth shut. Maybe it was family loyalty, maybe I just wanted to protect Mami or I was afraid that Papi would find out—it could have been anything really.

Is your mom all right?

I shrugged.

Have there been lots of fights?

None, I said. Too many shrugs would have been just as bad as an answer. Papi's at work too much.

Work, Tía said, like it was somebody's name she didn't like.

Me and Rafa, we didn't talk much about the Puerto Rican woman. When we ate dinner at her house, the few times Papi had taken us over there, we still acted like nothing was out of the ordinary. Pass the ketchup, man. No sweat, bro. The affair was like a hole in our living room floor, one we'd gotten so used to circumnavigating that we sometimes forgot it was there.

By midnight all the adults were crazy dancing. I was sitting outside Tía's bedroom—where Madai was sleeping—trying not to attract attention. Rafa had me guarding the door; he and Leti were in there too, with some of the other kids, getting busy no doubt. Wilquins had gone across the hall to bed so I had me and the roaches to mess around with.

Whenever I peered into the main room I saw about twenty moms and dads dancing and drinking beers. Every now and then somebody yelled, ¡Quisqueya! And then everybody else would yell and stomp their feet. From what I could see my parents seemed to be enjoying themselves.

Mami and Tía spent a lot of time side by side, whispering, and I kept expecting something to come of this, a brawl maybe. I'd never once been out with my family when it hadn't turned to shit. We weren't even theatrical or straight crazy like other families. We fought like sixth-graders, without any real dignity. I guess the whole night I'd been waiting for a blowup, something between Papi and Mami. This was how I always figured Papi would be exposed, out in public, where everybody would know.

You're a cheater!

But everything was calmer than usual. And Mami didn't look like she was about to say anything to Papi. The two of them danced every now and then but they never lasted more than a song before Mami joined Tía again in whatever conversation they were having.

I tried to imagine Mami before Papi. Maybe I was tired, or just sad, thinking about the way my family was. Maybe I already knew how it would all end up in a few years, Mami without Papi, and that was why I did it. Picturing her alone wasn't easy. It seemed like Papi had always been with her, even when we were waiting in Santo Domingo for him to send for us.

The only photograph our family had of Mami as a young woman, before she married Papi, was the one that somebody took of her at an election party that I found one day while rummaging for money to go to the arcade. Mami had it tucked into her immigration papers. In the photo, she's surrounded by laughing cousins I will never meet, who are all shiny from dancing, whose clothes are rumpled and loose. You can tell it's night and hot and that the mosquitos have been biting. She sits straight and even in a crowd she stands out, smiling quietly like maybe she's the one everybody's celebrating. You can't see her hands but I imagined they're knotting a straw or a bit of thread. This was the woman my father met a year later on the Malecón, the woman Mami thought she'd always be.

Mami must have caught me studying her because she stopped what she was doing and gave me a smile, maybe her first one of the night. Suddenly I wanted to go over and hug her, for no other reason than I loved her, but there were about eleven fat jiggling bodies between us. So I sat down on the tiled floor and waited.

I must have fallen asleep because the next thing I knew Rafa was kicking me and saying, Let's go. He looked like he'd been hitting those girls off; he was all smiles. I got to my feet in time to kiss Tía and Tío good-bye. Mami was holding the serving dish she had brought with her.

Where's Papi? I asked.

He's downstairs, bringing the van around. Mami leaned down to kiss me.

You were good today, she said.

And then Papi burst in and told us to get the hell downstairs before some pendejo cop gave him a ticket. More kisses, more handshakes and then we were gone.

I don't remember being out of sorts after I met the Puerto Rican woman, but I must have been because Mami only asked me questions when she thought something was wrong in my life. It took her about ten passes but finally she cornered me one afternoon when we were alone in the apartment. Our upstairs neighbors were beating the crap out of their kids, and me and her had been listening to it all afternoon. She put her hand on mine and said, Is everything OK, Yunior? Have you been fighting with your brother?

Me and Rafa had already talked. We'd been in the basement, where our parents couldn't hear us. He told me that yeah, he knew about her.

Papi's taken me there twice now, he said.

Why didn't you tell me? I asked.

What the hell was I going to say? *Hey, Yunior, guess what happened yesterday? I met Papi's sucia!*

I didn't say anything to Mami either. She watched me, very very closely. Later I would think, maybe if I had told her, she would have confronted him, would have done something, but who can know these things? I said I'd been having trouble in school and like that everything was back to normal between us. She put her hand on my shoulder and squeezed and that was that.

We were on the turnpike, just past Exit 11, when I started feeling it again. I sat up from leaning against Rafa. His fingers smelled and he'd gone to sleep almost as soon as he got into the van. Madai was out too but at least she wasn't snoring.

In the darkness, I saw that Papi had a hand on Mami's knee and that the two of them were quiet and still. They weren't slumped back or anything; they were both wide awake, bolted into their seats. I couldn't see either of their faces and no matter how hard I tried I could not imagine their expressions. Neither of them moved. Every now and then the van was filled with the bright rush of somebody else's headlights. Finally I said, Mami, and they both looked back, already knowing what was happening.

JOSIP NOVAKOVICH

In the 33 years since coming to the United States from Croatia (then part of Yugoslavia), Josip Novakovich (born in 1956) has written trenchantly about immigration and his Balkan roots in the story collections *Yolk* (1995), *Salvation and Other Disasters* (1998), and *Infidelities* (2005), as well as in the essays gathered in *Apricots from Chernobyl* (1995) and *Plum Brandy* (2002), from which "Grandmother's Tongue" is taken. Also the author of the novel *April Fool's Day* (2004) and co-editor of the immigrant-writing anthology *Stories in the Stepmother Tongue* (2000), Novakovich has described himself as "an expatriate who occasionally is tempted to become an ex-expatriate, to return home. The problem is, home has changed. I am perfectly happy to be an American in search of a lost place and time through multiple views and perspectives and visits."

Grandmother's Tongue

As a kid in Croatia I learned that I had an American grandmother through eavesdropping on my parents during tax time, when my father, a clogmaker—that is, a "private entrepreneur," a residue of capitalism to be gotten rid of in socialism—feared that he would be thrown into jail for lack of money.

"Why don't you write to your mother?" Father said. "She could get us out of this crap."

"No, she couldn't. She's old and can barely take care of herself."

"Nonsense, she's an American."

"So?"

"Write to her. She could send us papers, and we could move there."

"Yeah, right, like they need wooden shoes over there."

"I've had it with your pessimism. When I married you, I thought you were some kind of American; that means optimism. We'd manage there; let's just get the hell out of here."

"Is that why you married me?"

"Come on!"

They talked in Croatian, but I remember it in English. I've forgotten the sound of my father's voice in Croatian; he died when I was eleven. He had often dreamed of America. I remember how he and I stared at a postcard of Lincoln Center's golden Atlases holding up the gilded, hollow globe. A Baptist minister had mailed it to him.

If it weren't for my grandfather Pavle's poverty at the turn of the century, Mary would not have become my grandmother, and I would not exist, so no matter how absurd the meeting between Pavle and Mary appears to be, I must respect it as the source of my life. Pavle emigrated from Austria-Hungary; in that pre-photograph passport era, he managed to use an Austrian cow's export certificate to get into the States. He spoke no English, so when looking for the address of an acquaintance who would help him settle, the bus driver stopped in front of the address and found it easier to pull Pavle to the house than to speak to him. Pavle advanced in his job at a screw factory, and on the day when he was promoted to a managerial position, at the age of twenty-eight, he felt self-confident. He walked by a yard where he saw a pretty girl of fifteen. He went to the house, rang the bell, introduced himself to the girl's father, told him where he worked and how much he made, and asked whether he could marry the girl. The father said yes. They married the following weekend; it's not clear whether Mary had any say over this. This was before World War I. Mary gave birth to my mother, and they lived in Cleveland until she was three, when Pavle, a Greek-Catholic Croat, heard that a wonderful new country was formed: Kingdom of Serbs, Croats, and Slovenes, small nations which were hitherto victims of empires. Together the South Slavs would be strong. He sold everything he had and moved his family to what would soon be renamed Yugoslavia. He did not want to live in a city, so he bought a piece of land in the hills near the Sava River in Medjuric, not far from Kutina, and tilled the stingy soil for the rest of his days as, to my mind, one of the first American hippies.

He was a poor peasant, barely subsisting in an old wooden house next to that of his older brother, who often stole Pavle's wheat and chickens. Pavle's high taxes mostly went to the Serb king in Belgrade. Pavle believed in Yugoslavia nevertheless, unlike his wife, who hated the village mud and listened to the shortwave radio, pining for America.

Pavle got offers to work in Zagreb as a clerk and interpreter but declined them, though Mary wanted to live there. Their suffering together lasted twenty years before a greater one arrived—World War II. She joined the Partisans as a nurse. He preached against all the armies that passed through the village—Croatian, German, Serb, Partisan—declaring them all rapists and plunderers, which many of them were. At the end of the war he talked against the Partisans, who had executed several local Croat peasants as collaborators, and for that he went to jail, probably to be shot. My mother went there asking for him several times, not knowing whether he was dead or alive, and finally when she argued that since he had lived in America his head was filled with strange notions and he could not think straight, the police freed him.

Mary did not come back to Pavle. She could not forgive him that instead of fighting fascism, he had used his courage to offend everybody. That was the high interpretation of their divorce, which I heard repeatedly as a kid.

The communist government gave Mary an apartment near the Square of the Victims of Fascism in Zagreb as a reward for her being a Partisan. Though she could now live well, she got her American passport in the United States consulate and went back to Cleveland. I did not know what she did in Cleveland; people never bothered to tell me, nor did I ask. Just being an American was a lucrative profession.

Years later she visited her relatives in Zagreb, so my family went to Zagreb to see her. She gave me orange pencils, thinner and longer than the Yugoslav ones, which came blue or brown, and never with an eraser. Now I had an eraser, too, a whole apparatus in one elongated finesse. I stared at the transatlantic grandmother; she wore a blue skirt of a thin fabric and a string of nearly-white beads around her neck. Her hair was gray and blue and so were her small eyes, which blinked from the camera's flash that my older brother, a medical student at the time, was blasting at her. He had good reason to be so fascinated with her: when our father nearly disowned him for marrying a woman from the coast, she would send my brother a monthly stipend. Mary spoke in a funny way, slurring her r's, softening her consonants, and lengthening her vowels; she was a foreigner.

My father was vexed because she gave our family, except my older brother, no financial assistance, and helped her two sons build houses. One used the money to buy an apartment too small for his family and spent the rest on good living. I liked that uncle because whenever I visited him, he let me eat as much paté as I wished, thickly spread over warm, white bread, while at home I could eat meat only once a week and paté now and then, which Mother spread so thin that the brown bread stayed dry and barely swallowable. Uncle Ivo smoked cigarettes—the only member of our family to do so—and told me hundreds of jokes he had collected as a truck driver on his noble mission of distributing wine and brandy throughout the Federation. The other uncle (a member of the party and many bars) was Grandmother's favorite because he had joined the Partisans right at the beginning of the war, when there were few. He built a house in the suburbs of Zagreb, Dubrava, with the agreement that one apartment would belong to Grandmother so that she could retire there.

And one year she did live there. Mother, my brother, and I visited several times. My cousin showed me Mary's room, with her wigs. "She's almost bald, you know?" he said. As she had a large aquiline nose, he called her the bald eagle. He showed me her dentures in a glass, and her bracelets and earrings. Most of the grandmother seemed to be detachable; she was a composite of American products, a true industrial person. Yet to my eyes she was also folklorically natural: in her hooked nose and the wig, I saw a reflection of the American Indian culture—her wig was the scalp of an enemy, a powerful one: capitalism. We all wanted the spoils, impudently begging. She had bought my cousin a dovecote, with letter carriers. Seeing that he got so much, I asked her to buy me a tape recorder. She did. Other cousins got record players, flutes, and none of us were grateful because she was an American. The greed of her relatives who hung around her expecting money and bricks, the failure of socialism to create a feeling of community, her not getting along with her daughter-in-law (a Czech peasant woman with rabbit teeth and a jovial temperament, which apparently could become its opposite), all drove her away. "I have better socialism in America than this," she said, and left. Supposedly, she was a communist in Cleveland.

Everything American enchanted me. I would read the words on the pencil sides and memorize *Made in America*; I scrutinized American stamps and dollar bills with a magnifying glass. The dollar bill was as clean as a starched bedsheet, self-confident, almost uncreasable, washable, unlike the Yugoslav bills: the hundred and the thousand dinar notes creased; creases became cottony and oily, and slowly disintegrated, or would, if we did not tape over the folds and over variegated pictures of bosomy women harvesters bending over wheat stalks and factory workers baring their body-builder quality chests, clenching their fists, and bulging their jaw muscles, emotionally out of control, probably in hatred of the West. In contrast to this hypermasculine and hyperfeminine socialist expressionism on dusty paper, the sturdy, nearly imperishable American dollar bill exhibited a tranquil, monochromatic green gentleman (or a gentlewoman, I was not sure) resembling my grandmother, the neck wrapped up in cloth, in no need of baring anything, yet baring much to me. I could count in English, Hungarian, and German from one to ten before going to school—no achievement since this was one of the childhood games on our block. But from the dollar bill, once I understood what dictionaries were for, I learned *God, We, Trust, Great, Seal,* and the full name, *The United States of America,* and this gave me a feeling of out-distancing my neighborhood. And distance I wanted because of daily fistfights and quarrels on the block, and violent teachers at school—a physical education teacher once punched me in the jaw, knocking me, and my upper molar, out. I admired how Grandmother Mary could stay away from Yugoslavia, and I wished to do the same. Perhaps though born in Yugoslavia I was not doomed to be a Yugoslav?

As though sensing my love for geography, Grandmother Mary mailed me a world map. From the political Rand McNally map with America in the middle and Asia split in half, I learned most countries' English names. I smoked stolen Winstons and stared for hours at pink China, yellow Soviet Union, green France—all without mountains but with black rivers of ink. For politics rivers seemed more important than mountains, or they were easier to do, which itself must have been some kind of political statement of

American leisure. And leisure I wanted because I'd hated work since the age of nine when I had to spend several nights fastening leather on wooden soles, hammering thousands of nails, missing, and pounding my thumb into blue pain, helping my father meet a Belgrade glass factory's deadline for wooden shoe delivery. This large glass factory saved him from bankruptcy-jail time; that a Serbian factory saved us Croats from the local communist sharks and a local factory did not reminds me that in the sixties Serbs and Croats got along.

Even more than trade work I detested the communist work rhetoric and communal work projects. As students, a couple of days a month we'd go to state farms and pick corn in muddy fields, or rake leaves in the park, or wheelbarrow gravel on the roads. Out of spite, I rooted for capitalist America in the cold war. Most of my friends rooted for the Soviet Union. I rooted for Israel in the Six-Day War, they for the Arab League, as did the whole non-aligned world; I rooted for Bobby Fischer, my friends for Boris Spassky. To this siding with the West, I made an exception in literature. I read the complete works of Gogol, Dostoyevski, and Tolstoy, and no American writers excited me as much as these. I was such an avid Gogolite that I punched a friend of mine in the mouth and cut his lip because he said that *Dead Souls* bored him. I often went through bouts of Russofilia despite my spite.

I was the only student at our high school who publicly refused membership in the League of the Yugoslav Socialist Youth—not a smart move because it cost me participation in the exchange program with a high school in Michigan. As our high school's best student in English I had been nominated to go, but now I was blacklisted as politically inappropriate, which intensified my determination to go West. Not that I disliked the communist theories. On the contrary, I enjoyed them a great deal. But I disliked the Yugoslav Communist Party's totalitarian dictatorship, with soldiers and policemen on every corner and spies in every tavern.

(That's a high interpretation. The low one: I abhorred the quasi-folk music bands with accordions, electric guitars, and gold teeth who shrieked suicidal songs through the failing audio systems of many bars. A song entitled "Jugoslavija" caused the most wailing, tears, and drunken, violent sentimentality. No wonder Yugoslavia fell apart. So I'm probably more a music exile than a political and linguistic exile, but I'll admit this only in the parentheses.)

I believed that if communism was needed, only America could make it, and I found out that Karl Marx had believed similarly. I thought the American hippie movement and communes—that's where it's at!—would create an enjoyable kind of communism, that America would manufacture communism as it did TV (which gave everybody the same images) and nuclear weapons (which could obliterate everybody).

For the time being I could not physically go to America, but mentally I could, through English—my grandmother's tongue. (It should have been my mother's tongue, but when she moved to Yugoslavia at the age of three, she quickly forgot her English and learned Croato-Slovene; there's no such language, but in my grandparents' home, there was.) I learned English everywhere, walking with a dictionary, sometimes memorizing fifty words an hour during boring sermons and lectures, but mostly I learned through rock: Jimi Hendrix ("I don't live today. Will I live tomorrow"), Janis Joplin, and Jim Morrison ("Love me two times baby . . . one for tomorrow, one just for today . . . , I'm goin' away")—without noticing that this rock music was just as suicidal as Yugo folk music. I subscribed to the *Melody Maker*, glued its pages to the walls and the ceiling, so that wherever I turned English words burst at me like popcorn on the stove. At night I listened to shortwave radio—BBC and Christian programs with apocalyptic messages of fear and trembling. The waves themselves trembled up and down and slipped out of range and hisses and buzzes startled me from nightmares as though reptiles had crawled from under my pillow. Then a John Wayne-like voice would depict the joys of the millennium. To me the millennium meant America.

In 1974 when I was eighteen, I wrote to Mary asking for a visa. She sent me the papers and enough money for the fare. I flew from Belgrade to New York, sitting next to a young woman from Sarajevo. We had such a good conversation about our vague dreams and hopes that we declared we would be friends for life, but at the end of the flight, in eagerness to get out of the JFK customs corridors into the glamour of America (cocktails of coffee stains and urine in the subway), we lost track of each other. Since this was a charter flight, we would later fly back together to Belgrade and there I would be so terrified of the Yugoslav customs police that my friend for life and I would again forget about each other, without exchanging addresses and names. Later, I would have a similar experience with many Americans: quick friendship, and quicker forgetting.

After JFK I went to Port Authority from where, I thought by the sound of it, I would take a boat to Cleveland. I was glad to find out that I could take a bus instead; on the bus a man kept shouting that he was seeing flying cows, and he felt sorry for me that I was not. Once I got off the bus in Cleveland, I saw no people in the street, only cars, and in each car only one person, and this frightened me as though I had landed in a bad science-fiction scenario where the landscape conformed transparently to one idea: individualism and isolation, as though each person were a turtle with a steel shell. A panzer.

My grandmother greeted me excitedly. "Oh my, all the way from the old country, all by yourself, my little grandson!" We kissed on the cheeks. We rushed up the drumming stairs to her apartment. She did not have a house of her own but lived on the second floor of a family house on East 65th, south of St. Clair Avenue, in an old Slovene-Croat neighborhood. She had no car, not even a TV set, but she had hundreds of paperbacks, mostly war novels. She shared her apartment with an excommunicated Croat priest, who filled his room with altars, crucifixes, books in Latin, and incense. He was an anti-vernacularist. It turned out he spoke Croatian badly anyhow, and in that respect reminded me of Tito, who spoke a strange mélange of Slovene, Croatian, or Serbian, with German and Russian vocabulary. The priest held services in Latin to a small congregation of Latin purists in Cleveland. He constantly muttered prayers in Latin, *per omnia saecula saeculorum.*

Mary took me downtown to the May Company and proudly introduced me, her blood, to the cashiers. She walked with me around the neighborhood to meet a hundred old Slovenes. One old man wanted to give me his forest in Slovenia because he had no progeny; he thought that despite communism his old papers should be valid. I yawned. I did not come to the States to meet decrepit semi-Slovenes. I wanted to meet real Americans. And I wasn't interested in my grandmother's war memories, though she would often slip into them. I had heard enough about the damned war. There were hundreds of ugly war memorials wherever you turned in Croatia, so one more old person sentimentalizing about the heroic times made me close my ears. She talked about gangrene, worms in wounds, Ustashi, and about staying back in a hotel room with several doctors so that if there was an assassination attempt on Tito, they could help him right away. I am sure her stories were good, but they are gone. I did not listen because Yugoslavia did not interest me.

But I did try to find out about Mary Volcensek's background. It irked her when I asked what her grandparents' ethnicities were. "You should know better than to ask such nonsense!" she said. "Let the dead bury the dead. Don't you see what nationality has done to Yugoslavia? Forget it!" Considering the past and the future Balkan wars, she had an excellent point.

I visited Mary for only a month, greedily trying to soak up America, sure that I would never be able to afford another visit. I did not know this: You can leave another country to go to the States, but once you get into the States, the States get into you, and there's hardly any way of leaving. Even if you do, you carry America with you; you shower once a day, use mouthwash and dental floss, and feel guilty when you butter your bagel. I came back to the States two years later as a student and stayed, occasionally visiting Mary.

Grandmother later moved to East 55th Street and Carry Avenue, which continued westward as a cobbled street with rusting rails, flanked by old gutted foundries. Nobody walked there; the western extension of the street had died. On St. Clair, one block south, a store sold Croatian newspapers, books, and memorabilia, and down the street was a Croatian hall. Grandmother now lived with her brother, who stayed quiet and drunk on Scotch. He said nothing, so when he had a stroke nobody noticed it for days. His wife, a retired police clerk, talked all the time, smoked cigarettes, and wore miniskirts, proud of her legs. "Not too bad for sixty, are they?" she asked me as she gave us all a ride to an outdoor concert/picnic with Frank Jankovic playing polkas. She talked about all kinds of crime cases she'd dealt with in her career, and I did not listen. I excelled at not listening. When Grandmother was away, she asked me, "Have you thought of your grandmother's death?"

"No," I said.

"Well, you should. Do you know how much a casket costs? The funeral? Guess who's gonna be stuck with the bill?"

What a practical and cruel way of talking, I thought.

Mary again took me for walks around her neighborhood. She went for coffee every afternoon to the fire station at the corner. All the firemen knew her and jested with her. "She's something, you'd be surprised, things she comes up with!" I was surprised. She would not stand for loneliness. She was sociable. I guess to her firemen were like soldiers, like Partisans. This must have recaptured something for her.

For lunch she took me to a Lutheran church. She was no Lutheran, but the church had a program for the elderly. Slovenes, Croats, Czechs, Germans, chatted in their mélange of languages. As long as she could walk and take church buses this was good, better than a nursing home.

But the visit was not altogether pleasant. Once when she felt quite relaxed, she confided to me, with a voice of emotion and compassion, in English, "Your mother should have never married that brute, your father!"

"How can you say something like that?" I said. I thought this again was something political. My father had spent the war as a deserter. First he was in the Croat Regulars, then he deserted to the Partisans, then when he was sent to the front lines, he deserted the Partisans, hid in woods, and perhaps did more jumping back and forth to avoid fighting. He was, from a military standpoint, a coward, though as a pacifist he had his areas of courage. He had enough trouble with communists in Yugoslavia; now even here he got insulted. He was dead a long while, and his memory for me was a painful one. To top it off, Mary said my older sister, Nada, should never have married "that factory worker," who had six brothers. "She should have become a lady, and that factory worker made her wear galoshes and long, thick fabrics all the way down to her ankles! She was so bright, brighter than all of you, and she had to end up with that mule, permanently pregnant with his children!"

Instead of being understanding and realizing that there was probably some justifiable subtext to these statements, I put on airs. Of course, when I was leaving, I dropped them, and shook hands with her. I wanted to obey the tradition and kiss her on the cheek, but she said: "Don't bother. I am an old woman. My mouth doesn't feel good, it stinks, I am sure. And forget what I said."

In 1981 I visited her on my trip from Wyoming, where I had worked on coal mine silo construction. I hitchhiked to Cleveland. I walked in cautiously and lied that I had taken a bus from Wyoming because I did not want to disappoint Grandmother by appearing to be a bum. To her mind, I was the first of her line to attend an Ivy League school, so the education should amount to something more than hitchhiking and a back injury that would yield no workmen's compensation. Her sister-in-law asked me what I would become— Mary never did; she probably considered it a personal question—and I said I'd studied philosophy, so a college teacher. The police clerk viewed me suspiciously, and as soon as Grandmother was away, said, "She's not gonna last. Neither is your grand-uncle. All these funerals are coming up for me! You think there's any money to inherit here? Forget it. She's spent all of it on her thankless relatives in the old country. Do you think any of them will care if she dies? Sure they will: they'll wonder whether they've inherited anything. But the little she had, it's all gone. Medical bills. She's had two heart attacks! You didn't know, did you?"

Later Mary had her third one. I talked to her on the phone. All she wanted to do was die. She quit eating and drank only ginger ale. "I close my eyes and hope I don't ever have to open them again. The last time I nearly made it, but when I was unconscious they took me to the hospital! And I had told them to leave me alone. I came to with IVs, oxygen, the works. I've lived long enough. There's nothing I need to see or know anymore. Good-bye!"

I learned of her death in my mother's letter from Croatia. It wasn't even a cable since Mother probably could not afford one. The letter took two weeks to reach me. I don't know what I was doing when the letter arrived. I know what I was doing when John Lennon was shot: I was eating a dry French baguette in a basement in New Haven. I know what I was doing when I heard JFK was shot. I was seven, yet I remember I was walking uphill past the library on a startlingly sunny morning with stone cobbles glistening between the Serb Orthodox church and the Catholic church when I saw black flags and heard JFK was dead. But when Mary died time did not stop, nor did the place freeze or burn itself, or whatever, into my memory. I was almost glad she had died. She wanted this. I did not call Cleveland. I suspected that her brother had died too. I did not wonder how much I should contribute for the funeral costs; I had nothing.

When I visited Croatia the summer after that, all kinds of distant and close relatives asked me about her money and inheritance, and I said, "What inheritance? Don't you know she had nothing. Be glad you don't have to pay for the burial." I think some of them thought I must have got everything, and

in a way they were right but not the way they thought. Nobody was sentimental for her except my mother. She understood that her mother must have
been poor. She never thought that everybody in America was rich. She never
wanted me to give anybody any dollars. Of course, I felt the pressure to give
dollars wherever I went, whenever I saw my poor nephews and nieces, but
my mother said, "Don't be like your grandmother, or you'll end up like her, a
forgotten pauper."

And there the story would end, I thought, but last year, when I visited my
brother, a theology student in Switzerland, he made an addendum: the low
interpretation of why Grandmother had left Yugoslavia. Right after World
War II, while Grandfather worked in the fields, our uncle, father's younger
brother, and Grandmother carried on in the house. Pavle, or perhaps our
father, caught them. This was such a disgrace that Mary ran away from the
village to Zagreb, quickly had her papers made, and went back to Cleveland.
The uncle was excommunicated from the Baptist church and never rejoined.
Our strict Baptist father may have chased her away, and for the rest of his
days, he despised his brother Drago and shunned him. Nobody talked about
Drago gladly. When he died half the relatives refused to go to his funeral. It
was not incest but still, our father's brother sleeping with our mother's mother
was adultery close enough to incest to cause the first divorce in our family
history. But then, what history? Who's kept it? Traces of our ancestors vanish. So, who knows. Mary's hatred for our father could stem from this disgrace at least as much as from politics. But this low interpretation may not be
true, may be just a rumor.

But after whatever brought them apart, Grandfather Pavle sent her messages to please come back. Years later he remarried but often still wept for
his first wife, my mother said. He'd loved Mary till his death. His second wife
had to put up with this, but she understood it. She raised him a marble tombstone in the small Protestant cemetery (he had become a Baptist in the States)
near the rail tracks. My mother respected her more than her mother, for her
humility and unrequited love for Pavle. Whenever the train passed that spot,
I leaned my head against the windowpane and saw Pavle's stone. I remember
walking in his long funeral, the oration at his grave, the feast after the burial.
How sociably he had died. And how desolately Mary did.

I don't know where my maternal grandmother's grave is. I think it is in Cleveland, but what cemetery? What kind of memoirist could I be with so little knowledge, and perhaps respect, for my ancestry? One day I will drive north and look for Volcenseks (originally Volzehntscheck, Wohlzehnsheck?); maybe I will find her grave. I don't know whether there's an epitaph on her tombstone, whether there's any stone. But there's an epitaph in this for me—she gave me English and courage (or cowardice) to leave Croatia. I probably gave her nothing in return, but she wanted nothing. "Let the dead bury the dead."

My language of choice—if this was a choice—is matrilineal. Croatian as patrilineal I have rejected: I don't write in it, and now I don't even know what Croatian is since it's been changing under political pressures. It was always politicized; first it had to conform to Germanization and Magyarization, then to Yugoslavization (with Serb syntax and vocabulary), and now under the new nationalist government it's been "ethnically cleansed" to some archaic form. By now to educated Croats my Croatian appears to be a mélange of all kinds of things. Several years ago, I myself shrank back when I heard a man who could speak neither Croatian nor English. In each sentence he'd mix the two, and to understand him, you'd have to be bilingual. I've let my father's tongue atrophy. This may appear callous and unpatriotic of me, but if I were feelingly patriotic, I would be open to criticism just as well since this charge easily befalls Croats and other weak nations. (Ivo Andric, the Croatian writer who won the Nobel Prize for Literature in 1961, considered himself strictly Yugoslav, not Croat, and he wrote almost exclusively about Serbs and Muslims; he was so little "patriotic.") The politics of language—almost as much as bad music—probably drove me away from Yugoslavia, and Grandmother's tongue attracted me overseas, and this all made me become an American, if that's what I've become.

Most language is matrilineal anyhow. *Lingua* is a feminine noun. My wife breast-feeds and teaches our son English. At the age of fifteen months he knows two dozen words. I taught him only two, *tree* (he says it as "tzi") and *bath* (as "bah"). Jeanette has encouraged him to say his first sentence: "Go-go zoo." As soon as he wakes up, he brings his little sneakers to our bed, balances them on our heads and shouts, "Go-go!" I don't bother him with Croatian even if one day he might decide to look for his roots in Croatia. I think they are in Cleveland.

GARY SHTEYNGART

Born in 1972, Shteyngart arrived in the United States with his family when he was seven years old. Thrust into an environment at once hostile and welcoming, he sought refuge in the one thing that seemed stable to him: the Russian language. This love permeates his work as does his nostalgia for his childhood in Leningrad in the Soviet Union, which as Shteyngart said in an interview "only became horrible once you were an adult." The two novels that Shteyngart has written to date, *The Russian Debutante's Handbook* (2003) and *Absurdistan* (2006), develop the themes touched on in the following short memoir written in 2004: nostalgia, displacement, the reconciling of two very different cultures—all in a lively but caustic style filled with pop culture and literary references.

The Mother Tongue
Between Two Slices of Rye

When I return to Russia, my birthplace, I cannot sleep for days. The Russian language swaddles me. The trilling r's tickle the underside of my feet. Every old woman cooing to her grandson is my dead grandmother. Every glum and purposeful man picking up his wife from work in a dusty Volga sedan is my father. Every young man cursing the West with his friends over a late morning beer in the Summer Garden is me. I have fallen off the edges of the known universe, with its Palm Pilots, obnoxious vintage shops, and sleek French-Caribbean Brooklyn bistros, and have returned into a kind of elemental Shteyngart-land, a nightmare where every consonant resonates like a punch against the liver, every rare vowel makes my flanks quiver as if I'm in love.

Lying in bed in my hotel room I am hurt to the quick by the words from an idiotic pop song: "Please don't bother me," a cheerful young girl is singing on a Russian music channel, "I'm going back to my mama's house."

If I'm in some cheap Soviet hell-hole of a hotel, I can hear the house-keepers screaming at each other. "Lera, bitch, give me back my twenty."

"You, Vera, are the bitch," says her colleague. These words Ti, Vera, suka replay themselves as an endless mantra as I sink my face into a skimpy, dandruff-smelling pillow from Brezhnev times. For the time being, Lera and Vera are my relatives, my loved ones, my everything. I want to walk out of my room and say, in my native tongue, "Lera, Vera, here is twenty rubles for each of you. Ladies, dear ones, let's have some tea and cognac in the bar downstairs."

If I'm in a Western hotel, one of Moscow's Marriotts, say, I try to tune into the airplane-like hum of the central AC and banish Russian from my mind. I am surrounded by burnished mahogany, heated towel racks, and all sorts of business class accoutrements ("Dear Guest," little cards address me in English, "your overall satisfaction is our ultimate goal"), but when I open the window I face a stark Soviet-era building, where the Veras and Leras carry on at full pitch, grandmas coo to children, young men while away the morning hours in the courtyard with beer and invective.

In order to fall asleep, I try speaking to myself in English. "Hi there! Was' up? What are you doing Thursday? I have to see my analyst from 4:00 to 4:45. I can be downtown by 5:30. When do you get off work?" I repeat the last words to my phantom New York friend over and over, trying to regain my American balance, the sense that rationalism, psychiatry, and a few sour-apple martinis can take care of the past, because, as the Marriott people say, overall satisfaction is our ultimate goal. "When do you get off work? When do you get off work? When do you get off work? Hi there!" But it's no use.

Please don't bother me, I'm going back to my mama's house.
Lera, you bitch, give me my twenty rubles.

And in a final insult, an old Soviet anthem from my youth, hummed through the back channels of memory, the little chutes and trap doors that connect the right brain and the left ventricle through which pieces of primor-dial identity keep falling out.

The seagull is flapping its wings
Calling us to our duty
Pioneers and friends and all our comrades
Let us set out for the journey ahead

Sliced down the middle, splayed like a red snapper in a Chinatown restaurant, stuffed with kh and sh sounds instead of garlic and ginger, I lie in a Moscow or St. Petersburg hotel bed, tearful and jet-lagged, whispering to the ceiling in a brisk, staccato tone, maniacally naming all the things for which the Russian language is useful—ordering mushroom and barley soup, directing the cab driver to some forgotten grave, planning the putsch that will for once install an enlightened government. *Khh . . . Shh . . . Rrrr*

Home at last.

Veliky moguchi russki yazik. The Great and Mighty Russian Tongue is how my first language bills itself. Throughout its seventy-year tenure, bureaucratic Soviet-speak had inadvertently stripped it of much of its greatness and might (try casually saying the acronym OSOAVIAKHIM, which denotes the Association for Assistance of Defense, Aircraft and Chemical Development). But in 1977 the beleaguered Russian tongue can still put on quite a show for a five-year-old boy in a Leningrad metro station. The trick is to use giant copper block letters nailed to a granite wall, signifying both pomp and posterity, an upper-case paean to an increasingly lower-case Soviet state. The words gracing the walls of the Technological Institute station read as follows:

1959—SOVIET SPACE ROCKET
REACHES THE SURFACE OF THE MOON

Take that, Neil Armstrong.

1934—SOVIET SCIENTISTS CREATE
THE FIRST CHAIN REACTION THEORY

So that's where it all began.

1974—THE BUILDING OF THE BAIKAL-AMUR
MAIN RAILROAD TRUNK HAS BEEN INITIATED

Now what the hell does that mean? Ah, but Baikal-Amur sounds so beautiful—Baikal the famous (and now famously polluted) Siberian lake, a centerpiece of Russian myth; Amur (amour?) could almost be another word Russian has gleefully appropriated from the French (it is, in fact, the name of a region in the Russian Far East).

I'm five years old, felt boots tight around my feet and ankles, what might be half of a bear or several Soviet beavers draped around my shoulders, my mouth open so wide that, as my father keeps warning me, "a crow will fly in there." I am in awe. The metro, with its wall-length murals of the broad-chested revolutionary working class that never was, with its hectares of granite and marble vestibules, is a mouth-opener to be sure. And the words! Those words whose power seems not only persuasive, but, to this five-year-old kid already obsessed with science fiction, extra-terrestrial. The wise aliens have landed and WE ARE THEM. And this is the language we use. The great and mighty Russian tongue.

Meanwhile, a metro train full of sweaty comrades pulls into the station, ready to take us north to the Hermitage or the Dostoyevsky museum. But what use is there for the glum truth of Rembrandt's returning prodigal son or a display of the great novelist's piss pots, when the future of the human race, denuded of its mystery, is right here for all to see? SOVIET SCIEN-TISTS CREATE THE FIRST CHAIN REACTION THEORY. Forget the shabby polyester-clad human element around you, the unique Soviet metro smell of a million barely washed proletarians being sucked through an enormous marble tube. There it is, kid, in copper capital letters. What more do you want?

Some two years later, in Queens, New York, I am being inducted into a different kind of truth. I am standing amidst a gaggle of boys in white shirts and skullcaps and girls in long dresses wailing a prayer in an ancient language. Adults are on hand to make sure we are all singing in unison; that is to say, refusing to wail is not an option. "*Sh'ima Yisrael*," I wail, obediently, "*Adonai Eloheinu, Adonai echad.*"

Hear, O Israel, the Lord is our God, the Lord is One.

I'm not sure what the Hebrew words mean (there is an English translation in the prayer book, only I don't know any English either), but I know the tone. There is something plaintive in the way we boys and girls are beseeching the Almighty. What we're doing, I think, is supplicating. And the members of my family are no strangers to supplication. We are Soviet Jewish refugees in America ("refu-Jews," the joke would go). We are poor. We are at the mercy of others: Food Stamps from the American government, financial aid from refugee organizations, second-hand Batman and Green Lantern T-shirts and scuffed furniture gathered by kind American Jews. I am sitting in the cafeteria of the Hebrew school, surrounded first by the walls of this frightening institution—a gray piece of modern architecture liberally inlaid with panes of tinted glass—with its large, sweaty rabbi, its young, underpaid teachers, and its noisy, undisciplined American Jewish kids, and, in a larger sense, surrounded by America: a complex, media-driven, gadget-happy society, whose images and language are the lingua franca of the world and whose flowery odors and easy smiles are completely beyond me. I'm sitting there, alone at a lunch table, a small boy in over-sized glasses and a tight checkered Russian shirt, perhaps the product of some Checkered Shirt Factory #12 in Sverdlovsk, and what I'm doing is, I'm talking to myself.

I'm talking to myself in Russian.

Am I saying "1959—SOVIET SPACE ROCKET REACHES THE SURFACE OF THE MOON"? It's very possible. Am I recounting the contents of the Vorontsovski Palace in Yalta, where, just a year ago, I proved myself smarter than the rest of the tour group (and won my mother's undying love) by pointing out that the palace resembled the contours of a neighboring mountain? It could be. Am I nervously whispering an old Russian childhood ditty (one that would later find its way into one of my stories written as an adult): "Let it always be sunny, let there always be Mommy, let there always be blue skies, let there always be me"? Very possible. Because what I need now, in this unhappy, alien place, is Mommy, the woman who sews my mittens to my overcoat, for otherwise I will lose them, as I have already lost the bottle of glue, lined notebook, and crayons that accompany me to first grade.

One thing is certain—along with Mommy, and Papa, and one sweet kid, the son of liberal American parents who have induced him to play with me, the Russian language is my friend. It's comfortable around me. It knows things the noisy brats around me, who laugh and point as I intone my Slavic sibilants, will never understand. The way the Vorontsovski Palace resembles the mountain next to it. The way you get frisked at the Leningrad Airport, the customs guard taking off your hat and feeling it up for contraband diamonds. The way SOVIET SCIENTISTS CREATE[D] THE FIRST CHAIN REACTION THEORY in 1934. All this the great and mighty Russian language knows. All this it whispers to me at night, as I lie haunted by childhood insomnia.

Teachers try to intervene. They tell me to get rid of some of my Russian furs. Trim my bushy hair a little. Stop talking to myself in Russian. Be more, you know, normal. I am invited to play with the liberals' son, a gentle, well-fed fellow who seems lost in the wilderness of Eastern Queens. We go to a pizza parlor and, as I inhale a slice, a large string of gooey Parmesan cheese gets stuck in my throat. Using most of my fingers, I try to pull the cheese out. I choke. I gesture about. I panic. I moo at our chaperone, a graceful American mama. *Pomogite!* I mouth. Help! I am caught in a world of cheap endless cheese. I can see a new placard for the Leningrad metro. 1979—FIRST SOVIET CHILD CHOKES ON CAPITALIST PIZZA. When it's all over, I sit there shuddering, my hands covered with spittle and spent Parmesan. This is no way to live.

And then one day I fall in love with cereal. We are too poor to afford toys at this point, but we do have to eat. Cereal is food. It tastes grainy, easy and light, with a hint of false fruitiness. It tastes the way America feels. I'm obsessed with the fact that many cereal boxes come with prizes inside, which seems to me an unprecedented miracle. Something for nothing. My favorite comes in a box of a cereal called Honey Combs, a box featuring a healthy white kid—as a sufferer of asthma, I begin to accept him as an important role-model—on a bike flying through the sky (many years later I learn he's probably "popping a wheelie"). What you get inside each box of Honey Combs are small license plates to be tied to the rear of your bicycle. The license plates are much smaller than the real thing but they have a nice metallic heft to them. I keep getting MICHIGAN, a very simple plate, white letters on a black base. I trace the word with my finger. I speak it aloud, getting most of the sounds wrong. MEESHUGAN.

When I have a thick stack of plates, I hold them in my hand and spread them out like playing cards. I casually throw them on my dingy mattress, then scoop them up and press them to my chest for no reason. I hide them under my pillow, then ferret them out like a demented post-Soviet dog. Each plate is terribly unique. Some states present themselves as a "America's Dairyland," others wish to "Live Free or Die." What I need now, in a very serious way, is to get an actual bike.

In America the distance between wanting something and having it delivered to your living room is not terribly great. I want a bike, so some rich American (they're all rich) gives me a bike. A rusted red monstrosity with the spokes coming dangerously undone, but what do you want? I tie the license plate to the bicycle, and I spend most of my day wondering which plate to use, citrus-sunny FLORIDA or snowy VERMONT. This is what America is about: choice.

I don't have much choice in pals, but there's a one-eyed girl in our building complex whom I have sort of befriended. She's tiny and scrappy, and poor just like us. We're suspicious of each other at first, but I'm an immigrant and she has one eye, so we're even. The girl rides around on a half-broken bike just like mine, and she keeps falling and scraping herself (rumor is that's how she lost her eye) and bawling whenever her palms get bloodied, her head raised up to the sky. One day she sees me riding my banged-up bicycle with the Honey Combs license plate clanging behind me and she screams "MICHIGAN! MICHIGAN!" And I ride ahead, smiling and tooting my bike horn, proud of the English letters that are attached somewhere below my ass. Michigan! Michigan! with its bluish-black license plate the color of my friend's remaining eye. Michigan, with its delicious American name. How lucky one must be to live there.

Vladimir Girshkin, the struggling young immigrant hero of my first novel, *The Russian Debutante's Handbook*, shares a few characteristics with me, notably his penchant for counting money in Russian, which, according to the book, is "the language of longing, of homeland and Mother, his money-counting language." And also, I might add, the language of fear. When the ATM coughs out a bushel of cash or I am trying to perform a magic trick with my checkbook, trying to glean something from nothing, I leave English behind. American dollars, the lack of which constitutes an immigrant's most elemental fright, are denominated entirely in the Russian language. And so with shaking hands, the fictional Vladimir Girshkin and the all-too-real Gary Shteyngart count a short stack of greenbacks, a record of our worth and accomplishment in our adopted land: *"Vosemdesyat dollarov . . . Sto dollarov . . . Sto-dvadtsat' dollarov . . ."*

Many of my dreams are also dreamt in Russian, especially those infused with terror. There's one, for instance, where I emerge into a sepia-toned Manhattan, its skyscrapers covered by the chitinous shells of massive insects with water-bug antennae waving menacingly from their roofs. "What has happened?" I ask an unmistakably American passer-by, a pretty young woman in a middle-class pullover.

"Nichevo," she answers in Russian ("it's nothing"), with a bored Slavic shrug of the shoulders, just as I notice a pair of insect-like mandibles protruding from the base of her jaw. And I wake up whispering *bozhe moi, bozhe moi.* My God, my God.

And when terror informs my waking world, when an airplane's engines for some reason quit their humming mid-flight, when a big man with murder in his nostrils turns the corner and walks right into me, I think *Za shto?* What for? Why me? Why now? Why am I to die like this? Is it fair? It's a question addressed not to the Heavens, which I'm guessing are fairly empty of God, but to the Russian language itself, the repository of my sense of unfairness, a language in which awful things happen inexplicably and irrevocably.

After we come to the States, many of my more adaptable fellow immigrants quickly part ways with their birth languages and begin singing Michael Jackson's "Billy Jean" with remarkable accuracy and hip-swinging panache. The reason I still speak, think, dream, quake in fear, and count money in Russian has to do with a series of decisions my parents make when we're still greenhorns. They insist that only Russian be spoken in the home. It's a trade-off. While I will retain my Russian, my parents will struggle with the new language, nothing being more instructive than having a child prattle on in English at the dinner table.

Our house is Russian down to the last buckwheat kernel of kasha. When English does make its appearance, it is scribbled on a series of used IBM punch cards from my father's computer classes. I handle the punch cards with the same awe as I do the Honey Comb license plates, intrigued as much by their crisp, beige, American feel as by the words and phrases my father has written upon them, English on one side, Russian on the other. I remember, for some reason, the following words—"industry" (*promishlenost*), "teapot" (*chainik*), "heart attack" (*infarkt*), "symbolism" (*symvolizm*), "mortgage" (*zaklad*), and "ranch" (*rancho*).

The second decision is mostly economic. We cannot afford a television, so instead of *The Dukes of Hazzard*, I turn to the collected works of Anton Chekhov, eight battered volumes of which still sit on my bookshelves. And when we find a little black-and-white Zenith in the trash can outside our building, I am only allowed to watch it for half an hour a week, not enough time to understand why Buck Rogers is trapped in the twenty-fifth century or why the Incredible Hulk is sometimes green and sometimes not. Without television there is absolutely nothing to talk about with any of the children at school. It turns out these loud little porkers have very little interest in "Gooseberries" or "Lady with Lapdog," and it is impossible in the early 1980s to hear a sentence spoken by a child without an allusion to something shown on TV.

So I find myself doubly handicapped, living in a world where I speak neither the actual language, English, nor the second and almost just as important language—television. For most of my American childhood I have the wretched sensation that fin-de-siècle Yalta with its idle, beautiful women and conflicted, lecherous men lies somewhere between the Toys R Us superstore and the multiplex.

Around this time, I start writing in English with gusto. I write for the same reasons other curious children write: loneliness, boredom, the transgressive excitement of building your own world out of letters, a world not sanctioned by family and school. The latter becomes my target. While I patiently wail my *"Sh'ma Yisrael,"* praying that God will indeed take mercy on me, that he will make the young Hebrew School Judeans stop teasing me for my cardboard sweater and my anxious, sweaty brow, for being a bankrupt Russian in a silver-tinseled American world, I also decide to act.

I write my own Torah. It's called the Gnorah, an allusion to my nickname Gary Gnu, the name of an obscure television antelope which I have never seen. The Gnorah is a very libertine version of the Old Testament, with lots of musical numbers, singing prophets, and horny eleven-year-old takes on biblical themes. Exodus becomes Sexodus, for instance. Henry Miller would have been proud.

The Gnorah is written on an actual scroll, which I somehow manage to type up sideways so that it looks like an actual Torah. I hit the IBM Selectric keyboard with a giddy, nerdish excitement. Thousands of sacrilegious English words pour out in a matter of days, words that aren't inflected with my still-heavy Russian accent. Impatiently, I blow on passages deleted with white-out, knowing somehow that my life is about to change. And it does. The Gnorah receives wide critical acclaim from the students of the Solomon Schechter Hebrew Day School of Queens—a relief from the rote memorization of the Talmud, from the aggressive shouting of blessings and counterblessings before and after lunch, from the ornery rabbi who claims the Jews brought on the Holocaust by their over-consumption of delicious pork products. The Gnorah gets passed around and quoted. It doesn't quite make me acceptable or beloved. Only owning a twenty-seven-inch Sony Trinitron and a wardrobe from Stern's department store can do that. But it helps me cross the line from unclubbable fruitcake to tolerated eccentric. Tell me, is there anything writing can't do?

The Gnorah marks the end of Russian as my primary tongue and the beginning of my true assimilation into American English. I want to be loved so badly, it verges on mild insanity. I devote most of my school hours, time that should be spent analyzing Talmudic interpretations of how a cow becomes a steak, writing stories for my classmates, stories that poke fun at our measly lives, stories filled with references to television shows I barely know, stories shorn of any allusion to the Russia I've left behind or to the pages of Chekhov patiently yellowing on my bookshelves. A progressive young teacher sets aside time at the end of the English class for me to read these stories, and, as I read, my classmates yelp and giggle appreciatively, a great victory for the written word in this part of Queens.

But soon my pre-adolescent writing career is cut short. My family is not so poor anymore and can afford to shell out one thousand dollars for a salmon-colored twenty-seven-inch Sony Trinitron. The delivery of this Sony

Trinitron is possibly the happiest moment of my life. Finally, in a real sense, I become a naturalized citizen of this country. I turn it on, and I never turn it off. For the next ten years, I will write almost nothing.

I have begun this essay with a sleepless trip to contemporary Russia, a trip bathed in the anxious sounds of the mother tongue, and I have come to the end with a child's farewell to the language that once choreographed his entire world. But memory, which in the Russian sense is often just a flimsy cover for nostalgia, begs for a different ending.

So I will conclude elsewhere, at a place called the Ann Mason Bungalow Colony in the Catskill Mountains. Even the poorest Russian cannot live without a summer *dacha*, and so every June we, along with other Russian families, rent one of a dozen of little barrack-style bungalows (white plaster exterior with a hint of cheap wood around the windows) not far from the old Jewish Borscht Belt hotels. My mother and I sneak into the nearby Tamarack Lodge, where Eddie Fisher and Buddy Hackett once shared a stage, to witness giant, tanned American Jews lying belly-up next to an Olympic-size outdoor pool or sleep-walking to the auditorium in bedroom slippers to watch Neil Diamond in *The Jazz Singer*. This is probably the grandest sight I have come across in the ten or eleven years of my existence. I immediately vow to work hard so that one day I can afford this kind of lifestyle and pass it on to my children (the Tamarack Lodge has since closed; I have no children).

Back at the Ann Mason Bungalow Colony, we survive without daily screenings of *The Jazz Singer* and the pool can fit maybe a half-dozen small Russian children at a time. Ann Mason, the proprietor, is an old Yiddish-spouting behemoth with three muumuus to her wardrobe. Her summer population during weekdays consists almost entirely of Soviet children and the grandmothers entrusted with them—the parents are back in New York working to keep us all in buckwheat. The children (there are about ten of us from Leningrad, Kiev, Kishinev, and Vilnius) adore Ann Mason's husband, a ridiculous, pot-bellied, red-bearded runt named Marvin, an avid reader of the Sunday funny papers whose fly is always open and whose favorite phrase is "Everybody in the pool!" When Ann Mason cuts enough coupons, she and Marvin take some of us to the Ponderosa Steakhouse for T-bones and mashed potatoes. The all-you-can-eat salad bar is the nexus of capitalism and glut-tony we've all been waiting for.

Ann Mason's Bungalow Colony sits on the slope of a hill, beneath which lies a small but very prodigious brook, from which my father and I extract enormous catfish and an even larger fish whose English name I have never learned (in Russian it's called a *sig*; the Oxford-Russian dictionary tells me, rather obliquely, that it is a "freshwater fish of the salmon family"). On the other side of the brook there is a circular hay field which belongs to a rabidly anti-Semitic Polish man who will hunt us down with his German shepherd if we go near, or so our grandmothers tell us.

Our summers are spent being chased by these grandmothers, each intent on feeding us fruits and farmer's cheese, which, along with kasha in the morning, form the cornerstones of our mad diets. Shouts of *"frukti!"* (fruits) and *"tvorog!"* (farmer's cheese) echo above the anti-Semite's mysterious hay-field. By sundown a new word is added to the grandmother's vocabulary, *"sviter!"*—a desperate appeal for us to put on sweaters against the mountain cold.

These children are as close as I have come to compatriots. I look forward to being with them all year. There is no doubt that several of the girls are maturing into incomparable beauties, their tiny faces acquiring a round Eur-asian cast, slim-hipped tomboyish bodies growing soft here and there. But what I love most are the sounds of our hoarse, excited voices. The Russian nouns lacing the barrage of English verbs, or vice versa (*"babushka, oni poshli* shopping *vmeste v ellenvilli "*—"grandma, they went shopping together in Ellenville").

Fresh from my success with the Gnorah, I decide to write the lyrics for a music album, popular American songs with a Russian inflection. Madonna's "Like a Virgin" becomes "Like a Sturgeon." There are paeans to babushkas, to farmer's cheese, to budding sexuality rendered with a trilled "r" that sounds sexier than we think. We record these songs on a tape recorder I buy at a drugstore. For the album cover photograph I pose as Bruce Springsteen on his *Born in the USA* album, dressed in jeans and a T-shirt, a red baseball cap sticking out of my back pocket. Several of the girls pose around my "Bruce." They are dressed in their finest skirts and blouses, along with hopeful application of mascara and lipstick. "Born in the USSR" is what we call the album. (*"I was bo-ho-rn down in-uh Le-nin-grad . . . wore a big fur shapka on my head, yeah . . ."*)

We await the weekends when our parents will come, exhausted from their American jobs, the men eager to take off their shirts and point their hairy chests at the sky, the women to talk in low tones about their husbands. We cram into a tiny station wagon and head for one of the nearest towns, where, along with a growing Hasidic population, there is a theater that shows last summer's movies for two dollars (giant bag of popcorn with fake butter —fifty cents). On the return trip to the Ann Mason Bungalow Colony, sitting on each other's laps, we discuss the finer points of *E.T.: The Extra-Terrestrial.* I wonder aloud why the film never ventured into outer space, never revealed to us the wrinkled fellow's planet, his birthplace and true home.

We continue our Russo-American discussion into the night, the stars lighting up the bull's-eye of the anti-Semitic hayfield, our grandmothers mumbling the next day's rations of kasha and sweaters in their sleep. Tomorrow, a long stretch of non-competitive badminton. The day after that, Marvin will bring out the funny papers and we will laugh at Beetle Bailey and Garfield, not always knowing why we're laughing. It's something like happiness, the not knowing why.

GREG DELANTY

One of the most acclaimed Irish poets of his generation, Greg Delanty (born in 1958) has taught for many years at St. Michael's College in Vermont. He first came to the United States in the late 1970s and became an American citizen in 1994; he now divides his time between Ireland and the United States. As the Irish critic Terence Brown has noted, Delanty speaks for a generation of Irish immigrants to America whose experience has been vastly different from that of their 19th-century forebears: "Since the 1980s ease of trans-Atlantic travel, communication . . . and a common popular culture has made emigration an ambiguous experience with the Irish and American worlds superimposed upon one another. . . . Greg Delanty's poetry has been markedly alert to this new Irish-American condition of life." Delanty's collections include *American Wake* (1995), *The Hellbox* (1998), *The Blind Stitch* (2002), and *Collected Poems 1986–2006* (2006).

We Will Not Play the Harp Backward Now, No

> *If in Ireland*
> *they play the harp backward at need*
> Marianne Moore, 'Spenser's Ireland'

We, a bunch of greencard Irish,
   vamp it under the cathedral arches
   of Brooklyn Bridge that's strung like a harp.
But we'll not play
the harp backward now, harping on
   about those Micks who fashioned
this American wind lyre

and about the scores
    who landed on Ellis Island
or, like us, at Kennedy and dispersed
through this open sesame land

in different directions like the rays
    of Liberty's crown, each ray
    forming a wedge or caret.
We'll refrain from inserting
how any of us craved for the old country
    and in our longing composed a harp,
pipe, porter and colleen Tir na nOg.
And if we play
    the harp right way round now
we'll reveal another side of the story
told like the secret of Labraid the Exile: how

some, at least, found a native genius for union
    here, and where, like the Earl Gerald,
    who turned himself into a stag
and a green-eyed cat
of the mountain, many of us
    learned the trick
of turning ourselves into ourselves,
free in the *fe fiada** anonymity
    of America. Here
we could flap the horse's ears
of our singularity and not have to fear,

nor hide from the all-seeing Irish
    small town, blinking evil eyes.
    Nor does this landscape play that unheard,
but distinctly audible

---

*Fe fiada (fay fee-da): a mist or veil in Irish mythology which renders those under it invisible.

mizzling slow air
    that strickens us with the plaintive notes
of the drawn-out tragedy
of the old country's sorry history.
    No, we'll not play the harp backward
any more, keeping in mind the little people's harp
and how those who hear it never live long afterward.

REINALDO ARENAS

In April 1980—in one of the most surprising and dramatic episodes in the recent history of immigration to the United States—a vast, makeshift, sometimes barely seaworthy armada began arriving off the Florida coast, crammed with refugees departing from the Cuban port of Mariel. These *Marielitos* quickly numbered about 125,000 by official estimates, severely straining the resources of the INS, the Coast Guard, and Miami's expatriate Cuban community. This strain only intensified when it was discovered that the Castro regime had used the boatlift to purge the nation of counterrevolutionary elements including not only political agitators and prisoners of conscience, but felons, prostitutes, the mentally ill, and homosexuals. Within a few years the myth of the violent *Marielito* was cemented in the popular imagination by the film *Scarface*. In his memoir *Before Night Falls* (1993)—first published in Spain as *Antes que anocheza* (1992)—Reinaldo Arenas (1943–1990) offers a very different account of the event. A Castro sympathizer in his youth, Arenas had become a pariah in Cuba for his open homosexuality and his dissident writings, and when he saw his chance, he concealed his identity from authorities and joined the exodus. Arenas' new life in America was filled with new hardships and cut short by suicide after a lengthy struggle with AIDS. But in America he also found a "sense of freedom and the thrill of adventure without feeling persecuted." These years were marked by intense literary creativity including his "Pentagonía" novels about post-revolutionary Cuba: *Singing from the Well* (1987), *Farewell to the Sea* (1987), *The Palace of White Skunks* (1990), *The Color of Summer* (1990), and *The Assault* (1992). In 2000 director Julian Schnabel adapted *Before Night Falls* into an acclaimed film.

from

Before Night Falls

MARIEL Around the beginning of April 1980, a driver on the number 32 bus route drove a bus full of passengers through the doors of the Peruvian embassy asking for political asylum. Strangely enough, all the passengers on the bus also decided to ask for political asylum. Not one of them wanted to leave the embassy.

Fidel Castro demanded that all the people be returned, but the ambassador from Perú stated that they were on Peruvian territory, and according to international law, they had the right to political asylum. Days later, during one of his fits of anger, Fidel Castro decided to withdraw the Cuban guards from the embassy, perhaps trying in this way to pressure the ambassador to give in and force the people out of the embassy.

This time he miscalculated. When it became known that the Peruvian embassy was no longer guarded, thousands upon thousands of people, young and old, entered the grounds asking for political asylum. One of the first to do so was my friend Lázaro. I did not believe in the possibility of asylum because the news was even published in *Granma*; I thought it was a trap, and that once all the people were inside the embassy, Castro would arrest them. As soon as he knew who his enemies were—that is, all those who wanted to leave—he could then easily put them in jail.

Lázaro said good-bye to me before going to the embassy. The following day the embassy doors were closed again, but there were 10,800 people inside and 100,000 more outside, trying to get in. From all over the country, trucks were arriving full of young people who wanted to get in, but at that point Fidel Castro knew he had made a big mistake by withdrawing the guard from the Peruvian embassy. Not only was the embassy closed but only people living in Miramar were allowed near the site.

Electricity and water to the embassy were cut off, and for 10,800 people, 800 food rations were delivered. In addition, State Security smuggled in numerous undercover agents who went as far as to murder former high government officials requesting asylum. The area surrounding the embassy was scattered with Communist Youth Organization and Communist Party IDs, discarded by the people inside.

All the world press agencies were wiring the news, but the Cuban government tried to play down the incident. Even Julio Cortázar and Pablo Armando Fernández, stalwart champions of Castro who were in New York at the time, declared that there were only six or seven hundred people inside the embassy.

One taxi driver drove his car at full speed trying to break into the embassy, and was machine-gunned down by State Security; wounded, he still tried to get out of his car and into the embassy, but he was carried away in a patrol car.

The events at the Peruvian embassy were the first mass rebellion by the Cuban people against the Castro dictatorship. After that, people tried to enter the U.S. Interest Section office in Havana. Everybody was seeking an embassy to get into, and police persecution reached alarming proportions. In the end, the Soviet Union sent a high official of the KGB to Cuba, to hold a number of meetings with Fidel Castro.

Fidel and Raúl Castro had personally taken a look at the Peruvian embassy. There, for the first time, Castro heard the people insulting him, calling him a coward, a criminal, and demanding freedom.

It was then that Fidel ordered that they be gunned down, and those people—who had gone for fifteen days with almost no food, sleeping on their feet because there was no space to lie down, trying to survive amid the filth of their own excrement—faced up to the bullets by singing the old national anthem. Many were wounded.

To avoid the danger of a popular uprising, Fidel and the Soviet Union decided that a breach must be opened to allow a number of those nonconformists to leave; it was like curing sickness by bleeding.

During a desperate and angry speech, accompanied and applauded by Gabriel García Márquez and Juan Bosch, Castro accused those poor people in the embassy of being antisocial and sexually depraved. I'll never forget that speech—Castro looked like a cornered, furious rat—nor will I forget the hypocritical applause of García Márquez and Juan Bosch, giving their support to such a crime against the unfortunate captives.

The port of Mariel was then opened, and Castro, after stressing that all those people were antisocial, said that precisely what he wanted was to have that riffraff out of Cuba. Posters immediately started to appear with the slogans LET THEM GO, LET THE RIFFRAFF GO. The Party and State Security organized a "voluntary" march against the refugees at the embassy. People had no choice but to take part in the march; many went with the hope of perhaps being able to jump the fence and get inside. But the marchers could not get close, not with three rows of cops between them and the fence.

Thousands of boats full of people started to leave for the United States from the port of Mariel. Of course, not all those at the embassy who wanted to leave were able to do so, but only those whom Fidel Castro wanted to get rid of: common prisoners and criminals from Cuban jails; undercover agents whom he wanted to infiltrate in Miami; the mentally ill. And all this was paid for by the Cuban exiles who sent boats to get their relatives out. The majority of those families in Miami spent all their resources renting boats to rescue their loved ones, and when they arrived at Mariel, Castro would often fill their boats with criminals and insane people, and they could not get their relatives out. But thousands of honest people also managed to escape.

Of course, to be able to depart from the Port of Mariel, people had to leave the Peruvian embassy with a safe-conduct issued by State Security, and had to return to their homes and wait until the Castro government gave them the order to leave. From that moment on, State Security, not the Peruvian embassy, was making the decisions as to who could leave the country and who could not. Many resisted, not wanting to abandon the embassy, especially those most involved with the Castro regime.

The mobs organized by State Security waited outside the embassy for those leaving with safe-conducts and in many instances tore up their permits. Besides losing their right to exile, they were beaten up by the rabble.

Lots of people were physically attacked, not only for being at the Peruvian embassy but merely for sending telegrams asking their relatives in Miami to come for them at the Port of Mariel. I saw a young man beaten unconscious and left on the street just as he was coming out of the post office after sending one of those telegrams. This happened daily, everywhere, during the months of April and May 1980.

Twenty days later, Lázaro returned from the embassy and was hardly recognizable; he weighed less than ninety pounds. He had gone to a lot of trouble to avoid being beaten, but he was starving. Now all he could do was wait for his exit permit. The day it came, I accompanied him in a taxi to where the documents were being issued, and he said to me: "Don't worry, Reinaldo, I am going to get you out of here." When he left the taxi, I saw the mob attack him and hit him on the back with steel bars as he ran under a shower of rocks and rotten fruit; in the midst of all that, I saw him disappear toward freedom, while I remained behind, alone. But in my building almost everyone wanted to leave the country, so it felt like a sort of refuge.

During that civil strife, terrible things were happening. To escape being beaten by the mob, one man got in his car and drove it into some of the people who were attacking him. An agent of State Security immediately shot him in the head, killing him. The incidents were even published in *Granma*; to have killed such an antisocial person was considered a heroic act.

The homes of those waiting for exit permits were surrounded by mobs and stoned; in the Vedado, several people were stoned to death. All the terrors suffered for twenty years were now reaching their peak. Anyone who was not Castro's agent was in danger.

Opposite my room someone had put up various posters reading: HOMO-SEXUALS, GET OUT; SCUM OF THE EARTH, GET OUT. To get out was exactly what I wanted, but how? Ironically, the Cuban government hurled insults at us and demanded that we leave, but at the same time prevented us from leaving. At no point did Fidel Castro open the Port of Mariel to all who wanted to leave; his trick was simply to let go the ones who posed no danger to the image of his government. Professionals with university degrees could not leave, nor could writers who had published abroad, such as myself.

However, since the order of the day was to allow all undesirables to go, and in that category homosexuals were in first place, a large number of gays were able to leave the Island in 1980. People who were not even homosexual pretended to be gay in order to obtain permission to leave from the Port of Mariel.

The best way to obtain an exit permit was to provide any documentary proof of being a homosexual. I did not have such a document, but I had my ID, which stated that I had been in jail because of a public disturbance; that was good enough proof, and I went to the police.

At the police station they asked me if I was a homosexual and I said yes; then they asked me if I was active or passive and I took the precaution of saying that I was passive. A friend of mine who said he played the active role was not allowed to leave; he had told the truth, but the Cuban government did not look upon those who took the active male role as real homosexuals. There were also some women psychologists there. They made me walk in front of them to see if I was queer.

I passed the test, and a lieutenant yelled to another officer, "Send this one directly." This meant that I did not have to go through any further police investigation. They made me sign a document stating that I was leaving Cuba for purely personal reasons, because I was unworthy to live within the marvelous Cuban Revolution. They gave me a number and told me not to leave my home. The cop filling out my papers said: "Listen carefully, if you are going to have a 'clothes-hanger party' you must have it at home, because if you are not there when the exit permit arrives, you'll miss your chance." I think that cop would have been delighted to go to the imaginary nude party that he said I would have at home.

My exit permit had been negotiated at the neighborhood level, the police station. The mechanisms of persecution in Cuba were not yet technically sophisticated; for that reason, I could leave without State Security finding out about it; I was leaving as just another queer, not as a writer; in the middle of that pandemonium, none of the cops who authorized my exit knew anything about literature or had any reason to know my books, almost none of which, in any case, had ever been published in Cuba.

When I had finally dozed off one night, after a sleepless week locked up in my unbearably hot room, there was a knock at my door. It was Marta Carriles and Lázaro's father calling out: "Get up, your exit permit is here! We knew Saint Lazarus would help you!" I ran downstairs in my pajamas and right there at the building's entrance, holding a sheet of paper, was a cop who asked me if I was Reinaldo Arenas. I answered affirmatively, in as low a voice as I could, and he told me I had thirty minutes to get ready and show up at a place called Cuatro Ruedas to leave the country.

Rushing up the stairs I ran into Pepe Malas, who was always on the watch, and he said: "There is a cop down there looking for you. What does he want?" With panic in my face I told him that they had come to take me in again, that there was going to be another trial. I was so terrified at the thought that he could discover my real reasons, that he believed me.

In those days it was very difficult to get to Cuatro Ruedas in thirty minutes. When the bus came, I told the driver I had an exit permit, and that I would give him a gold chain if he got there in less than half an hour. The driver stepped on the gas and drove at full speed, without making any stops, and I made it on time. I quickly said good-bye to Fernando, Lázaro's father, and ran to the place where a soldier was waiting. I surrendered my ration booklet and the document I had received from the police officer at home, and was immediately given a passport and a safe-conduct stating that I was one of the exiles from the Peruvian embassy. I left for Mariel on the first bus of the day. To cap it all, the bus broke down on the way and we had to wait about two hours for another bus to pick us up and take us to our destination.

We arrived at El Mosquito, the concentration camp near Mariel; it was aptly named because of the swarms of mosquitoes there. We had to wait two or three days for our turn to leave Mariel. During this time I met some friends, and also many who I knew were undercover agents; I tried to stay out of their way so they would not notice me. We were searched, since we were not allowed to take any letters, not even the telephone number of someone in the United States. I had memorized the number of my aunt in Miami.

Before entering the area for people already authorized to leave the country, we had to wait in a long line and submit our passports to an agent of State Security who checked our names against those listed in a huge book; they were the names of people not authorized to leave the country. I was terrified. I quickly asked someone for a pen and since my passport was handwritten and the *e* of *Arenas* was closed, I changed it to *i* and became Reinaldo Arinas. The officer looked up my new name, and of course never found it.

Before we boarded the buses for the Port of Mariel, another officer told us that we were all leaving "clean," that is, that no passport contained any criminal records, and that, therefore, when we arrived in the United States all we had to say was that we were exiles from the Peruvian embassy. There was, no doubt, a dirty and sinister game behind these procedures; the Revolutionary government purposefully intended to create an enormous confusion so that authorities in the United States would not know who were the actual exiles and who were not.

Before boarding the boats, we were sorted into categories and sent to empty warehouses: one for the insane, one for murderers and hard-core criminals, another for prostitutes and homosexuals, and one for the young men who were undercover agents of State Security to be infiltrated in the United States. The boats were filled with people taken from each of these different groups.

It should be remembered that there were 135,500 people in that exodus; the majority were people like myself; all they wanted was to live in a free world, to work and regain their lost humanity.

Finally, at one in the morning of May 4, my turn came. The name of my boat was *San Lázaro* and I remembered Marta Carriles's words. A soldier took several pictures of us and minutes later we were under way. We were escorted by two Cuban police launches; it was a precaution to prevent people who had not received exit permits from illegally boarding those boats.

Something horrendous happened just then. As we were leaving, a member of the coast guard threw his rifle into the water and quickly started to swim toward us. The other coast guard launches approached the swimmer, and the men killed him, while he was still in the water, with their bayonets.

The *San Lázaro* continued sailing away from the coast. The Island turned into a jumble of blinking lights, and then everything became a deep shadow. We were now on the open sea.

For me, who for so many years had wanted nothing more than to abandon that land of horrors, it was easy not to cry. But there was a youth, perhaps seventeen years old, forced on board in Mariel having to leave all his family behind, who was crying disconsolately. There were some women with children who, like me, had not eaten in five days. There were also several mental patients.

The captain of the boat was an exile who had left Cuba for the United States twenty years ago, and had now returned just to get his family out. Instead, he was carrying a ship full of strangers, with the promise that, on his next trip, he would be allowed to take his family with him. He was the navigator because he had no other choice. He told me he knew nothing about navigation, and had chartered that boat in order to rescue his family. There was, to make the situation even worse, nothing to eat on board.

The trip from Havana to Key West is only seven hours. However, we had been sailing for more than a day without seeing that blessed Key West. Finally the captain confessed that he was completely off course and did not know where we were. He did have a radio and was trying to contact other vessels, but to no avail.

On the second day, the boat ran out of gas, and we began drifting in the powerful current of the Gulf Stream. We had not eaten for so many days that we couldn't even throw up; we only vomited bile. One of the mental patients tried to jump overboard several times and had to be held down while some of the ex-convicts yelled at him to control himself, telling him that he was going to "Yuma." The poor man shouted back, "To hell with Yuma, I want to go home." He had no idea that we were going to the United States of America. Sharks were circling around us, waiting to devour anyone unlucky enough to fall overboard.

At last the captain was able to raise another boat, which then called the U.S. Coast Guard, who in turn ordered a helicopter search. Three days later the U.S. helicopter appeared; it dropped almost to water level, shot some photos, and left. It radioed rescue orders to the coast guard and that very night a coast guard vessel came by. They threw us lines and brought us aboard, tied our boat to their stern, and we were soon on our way. They fed us, and little by little, we recovered our strength and began to feel a great joy. At last we reached Key West.

KEY WEST   As I was leaving my building on Monserrate Street, the president of my CDR approached me and said, "Don't worry, I won't inform on you; what I want from you is that if you see my son, you tell him that I am all right." Strangely enough, when I arrived at Key West, her son was one of the first persons I met, so I was able to deliver his mother's message. He then took me to a warehouse where Cuban exiles in Miami had stored all donations for the arrivals from Mariel, and he gave me a new pair of shoes, jeans, and a resplendent new shirt. He also gave me a cake of soap, and a huge amount of food. I took a bath, shaved, and started once again to feel like a human being.

Later I met a dancer from Alicia Alonso's ballet company, who told me that shortly after I left Mariel, my name was being paged over all the loudspeakers; the police were after me. Still later I found out that they were checking all passports at boarding time, and were even stopping all the buses and asking for me. The Cuban State Security and UNEAC had been alerted and, believing I was still at El Mosquito camp, had organized an intensive search to prevent my leaving the country.

We were lodged in Key West, waiting for immigration to decide where to place us. In the midst of that crowd I ran across Juan Abreu; we could finally embrace outside Cuba, at last free.

Upon reaching Miami I tried to contact Lázaro, as well as Margarita and Jorge Camacho, who were then in Spain. I was lucky to meet Lázaro when I arrived at my uncle's house; he was waiting for me, and we found it still hard to believe that the two of us, with only a week's difference, were now in the United States. I wrote Margarita and Jorge Camacho; they knew about my escape from a news cable in the Spanish press. I was now trying to recover my manuscripts, and I knew Jorge and Margarita, who were in their country home, did not have them there. They had delivered them to Severo Sarduy in Paris. I called him, and on that first call Severo told me that he did not have them either. I wrote a desperate letter to my friends the Camachos. They told me not to worry; they had the originals and Severo only had copies. It was fortunate they had taken such precautions, because apparently it seemed that Severo Sarduy had no intention whatsoever of returning those manuscripts to me.

MIAMI   The International University of Florida invited me to speak at a conference in June of 1980. I entitled my talk "The Sea Is Our Jungle and Our Hope." This was my first lecture before a free audience. Heberto Padilla was next to me; he spoke first. He was in a really pitiful state; completely drunk and stumbling, he faced the audience and improvised incoherently. The public reacted violently against him. I felt pity for the man, destroyed by the system, unable to come to terms with his own ghost and the fact that he had made a public confession in Cuba. In all truth, Heberto has never recovered from that confession. The system managed to destroy him in the most perfect way, and even now seemed to make use of him for its own benefit.

As soon as I started denouncing the tyranny I had been suffering for twenty years, even my own publishers, who had made enough money from my books, covertly turned against me. Emmanuel Carballo, who had published more than five editions of *El mundo alucinante* [in Mexico] and never paid me a penny, now wrote me an indignant letter saying I should have never left Cuba, while, at the same time, refusing to make any payment to me. There were countless promises, but the money never came: it was a very profitable way of exercising his communist militancy.

The same thing happened with Angel Rama, who had published a collection of my short stories in Uruguay. Instead of at least writing me a letter to congratulate me for having left Cuba (he knew of my situation, having met me there in 1969), he wrote a lengthy newspaper article for *El Universal* of Caracas, which he entitled "Reinaldo Arenas on His Way to Ostracism." In that article Rama stated that my leaving Cuba was a mistake, that all my problems had been only bureaucratic, and that now I would be condemned to ostracism. All this was extremely cynical and, moreover, preposterous, considering that Rama was referring to someone who since 1967 had not been able to publish anything in his own country, and who had suffered repression and imprisonment there and had indeed already been condemned to ostracism. I realized that the war had started all over again, now in a much more underhanded manner; it was less terrible than Fidel's war against the intellectuals in Cuba, albeit no less sinister.

To top it all, after numerous phone calls to Paris, Sarduy not only paid me a mere one thousand dollars for the French editions, but one day called my aunt in Miami and told her I had lots of money. And my aunt, of course, never doubted that I am a millionaire.

None of this surprised me: I already knew that the capitalist system was also sordid and money-hungry. In one of my first statements after leaving Cuba I had declared that "the difference between the communist and capitalist systems is that, although both give you a kick in the ass, in the communist system you have to applaud, while in the capitalist system you can scream. And I came here to scream."

DINAW MENGESTU

Dinaw Mengestu (born in 1978) was only two years old when he left Ethiopia to rejoin his father, who had already fled the Red Terror of the Mengistu Haile Mariam regime. He grew up in Chicago, studied at Georgetown and Columbia (where he received an M.F.A. in fiction), and went on to write for periodicals including *Rolling Stone* (for whom he reported on the situation in Darfur), *Harper's*, and the *Wall Street Journal*. His first novel, *The Beautiful Things That Heaven Bears*, from which the following excerpt is taken, was published in 2007 and won wide acclaim and many awards. A study of the intersecting lives of three immigrants from different parts of Africa (Congo, Kenya, and Ethiopia) who find themselves in a rapidly gentrifying neighborhood in Washington, D.C., the book has been described by Chris Abani as "a retelling of the immigrant experience . . . in which immigrants must come to terms with the past and find a way to be loyal to two ideas of home: the one they left and the one they've made in America."

from
The Beautiful Things That Heaven Bears

A t eight o'clock Joseph and Kenneth come into the store. They come almost every Tuesday. It's become a routine among the three of us without our ever having acknowledged it as such. Sometimes only one of them comes. Sometimes neither of them. No questions are asked because nothing is expected. Seventeen years ago we were all new immigrants working as valets at the Capitol Hotel. According to the plaque outside the main entrance, the hotel was built to resemble the Medicis' family house in Italy. On weekends tourists lined the rooftop to stare at the snipers perched on the White House roof. It was there that Kenneth became Ken the Kenyan and Joseph, Joe from the Congo. I was skinnier then than I am now, and as our manager said, I didn't need a nickname to remind him I was Ethiopian.

"You close the store early today?" Kenneth asks, as he walks in and glances at the empty aisles. He comes straight from his job, his suit coat still on despite the early May heat. His shirt is neatly pressed, and his tie is firmly fastened around his neck. Kenneth is an engineer who tries not to look like one. He believes in the power of a well-tailored suit to command the attention and respect of those who might not otherwise give him a second thought. Every week he says the same thing when he walks in. He knows there's no humor in it, but he's come to believe that American men are so successful because they say the same thing over and over again.

"Don't take it from me," he said in his defense once. "Listen to them. Every day. The same thing. Every day my boss comes in, and he says to me, 'You still fighting the good fight, Kenneth?' And I put my fist in the air and say, 'Still fighting.' And he says, 'That's what I like to hear.' He makes ninety thousand a year. Ninety thousand. So, I say, 'You close the store early today?' And you say, 'Fuck you.'"

"Fuck you, Ken," I say as the door closes behind him. He smiles gratefully at me whenever I say that. As much as Kenneth has ever needed anything in his life, he has needed order and predictability, small daily reassurances that the world is what it is, regardless of how flawed that may be. He has a small mouth, with full lips that would be considered beautiful on a woman, but that on him come off as overly puckered. He's self-conscious about his teeth, which are slightly brown and bent in the same direction. Joseph pressed him once into saying why, even now with all that he earns, he has never had them fixed. Kenneth smiled a full, wide smile for us before he responded. When he speaks in front of strangers he buries his mouth behind his hand. He rubs his lower lip between his thumb and forefinger, making everything he is embarrassed about disappear.

"You can never forget where you came from if you have teeth as ugly as these," he said. He grinned once more. He tapped a slightly brown front tooth for effect.

Kenneth looks Kenyan. His skin is dark, his nose is long and thin, and yet his features are soft, almost delicate, like a child's. He's six feet tall, but it's only in the past two years, since he got his job, that he's ever weighed more than a hundred and fifty pounds. When he's drunk he lifts up his shirt, blows out his stomach, and pats his protruding belly proudly. "God bless America," he says with each pat. "Only here can someone become the Buddha."

I go to the back of the store and pull out the fold-up table and chairs the three of us always sit at. I have a small deli counter in the front, now empty, behind which used to lie wasted slabs of roast beef, ham, and turkey cut to look like the upper half of a cow's thigh, just before it becomes the ass. I spent two thousand dollars of borrowed money on it with the idea that perhaps my store could become a deli, and in becoming a deli, a restaurant, and in becoming a restaurant, a place that I could sit back and look proudly upon. I place the chairs right in front of the empty deli counter. I sit with my back against the glass. It's May 2. Since January, I've had exactly three deli orders (turkey, no mayo, wheat bread; turkey, mustard, wheat bread; turkey, just one slice), not a single one after lunchtime. Despite my recent efforts, there is nothing special to my store. It's narrow, shabby, and brightly lit, with a ceiling of fluorescent bulbs that hum for over an hour every morning after being turned on. I sell twenty-five-cent bags of potato chips, two-liter bottles of Pepsi, boxes of macaroni and cheese, diapers, soap, detergent, condensed milk in narrow aisles haphazardly arranged.

"Jo-Jo here yet?" Kenneth asks. Some days it's Joe from the Congo, or Joe-Joe Congo, or Congo Joe.

"Not yet."

"Africans. Congolese. You can never trust us to be on time."

"You are."

"I'm an engineer. I have to be precise. Precision is the name of my game. You say to be somewhere at eight-thirty, I'm there at eight-thirty. Not a minute later."

He pulls out a bottle of Johnnie Walker Black from his bag and places it on the table.

"How was today?" he asks me.

"Three hundred seventy-three dollars and eighty-four cents."

Kenneth shakes his head mournfully at the number. Almost nobody comes into the store anymore. It's been this way for months now, with each month a little worse than the one before. Business is slow, money is tight, and ever since Judith moved out of the neighborhood, I've been opening and closing my store at odd hours, driving away what few regular customers I still have left. Recently Kenneth tried to bring the subject up while we were alone in the store. He was looking at my accounts for April and shaking his head in dismay while tsking loudly to himself. There were ten days last month that were marked with a red zero, days that I hadn't even bothered to open the store, or that I had closed before any customers had a chance to come in.

"Why are you doing this?" he finally asked me. He held open the book so I could see exactly what he was talking about. "Do you even care?"

I shook my head, not knowing how to explain to him that there were no one-word responses or common phrases that I could turn to for an answer.

On a good day I have forty or maybe fifty customers. Most of them are stay-at-home moms or dads who've moved into one of the newly refurbished houses surrounding Logan Circle. They stop in during an afternoon stroll with their children dangling around their necks like amulets to ward off age, sickness, unemployment, rain, death. They buy bottled water, toothpaste, cleaning supplies, and, if their kids are old enough, one of the small five-cent pieces of candy I've learned to keep next to the register for just this purpose. On those good days, which come once or twice a week, I make just over four hundred dollars. I walk home at the end of the night feeling better, not only about my store, but about this country. I think to myself, America is beautiful after all. There is more here. Gas is cheap. This is not a bad place. Things could be worse. And what else could I have done?

"So then, you hate America today?" Kenneth says. He smiles a half-smile. He pours a little scotch into a Styrofoam cup he stole from his office and hands it to me. I know that if I let him, he would pull from his pocket the missing $26.16 and slide it into the cash register. Anything to make me feel better.

"With all my heart," I say to him.

Joseph's already drunk when he comes into the store. He strolls through the open door with his arms open. You get the sense when watching him that even the grandest gestures he may make aren't grand enough for him. He's constantly trying to outdo himself, to reach new levels of Josephness that will ensure that anyone who has ever met him will carry some lingering trace of Joseph Kahangi long after he has left. He's now a waiter at an expensive downtown restaurant, and after he cleans each table he downs whatever alcohol is still left in the glasses before bringing them back to the kitchen. I can tell by his slight swagger that the early dinnertime crowd was better than usual today.

Joseph is short and stout like a tree stump. He has a large round face that looks like a moon pie. Kenneth used to tell him he looked Ghanaian.

"You have a typical Ghanaian face, Joe. Round eyes. Round face. Round nose. You're Ghanaian through and through. Admit it, and let us move on."

Joseph would stand up then and theatrically slam his fist onto the table, or into his palm, or against the wall. "I am from Zaire," he would yell out. "And you are a ass." Or, more recently, and in a much more subdued tone: "I am from the Democratic Republic of the Congo. Next week, it may be something different. I admit that. Perhaps tomorrow I'll be from the Liberated Land of Laurent Kabila. But today, as far as I know, I am from the Democratic Republic of the Congo."

Joseph kisses me once on each cheek after he takes his coat off.

"That's my favorite thing about you Ethiopians," he says. "You kiss each other on the cheeks all the time. It takes you hours to say hello and good-bye because you're constantly kissing each other. Kiss. Kiss. Kiss."

Kenneth pours Joseph a scotch and the three of us raise our cups for a toast.

"How is America today, Stephanos?" Joseph asks me.

"He hates it," Kenneth says.

"That's because he doesn't understand it." Joseph leans closer toward me, his large moon-pie face eclipsing my view of everything except his eyes, which are small and bloodshot, and look as if they were added onto his face as an afterthought.

"I've told you," he says. "This country is like a little bastard child. You can't be angry when it doesn't give you what you want."

He leans back deliberately in his chair and crosses his legs, holding the pose for two seconds before leaning over and resting both arms on his thighs.

"But you have to praise it when it comes close, otherwise it'll turn around and bite you in the ass."

The two of them laugh and then quickly pour back their drinks and refill their glasses. There is a brief silence as each struggles to catch his breath. Before either of them can tell me something else about America ("This country cares only about one thing . . ." "There are three things you need to know about Americans . . ."), I call out, "Bukassa." The name catches them off guard. They both turn and stare at me. They swirl their cups around and around to make sure it looks like they're thinking. Kenneth walks over to the map of Africa I keep taped on the wall right next to the door. It's at least twenty years old, maybe older. The borders and names have changed since it was made, but maps, like pictures and journals, have a built-in nostalgic quality that can never render them completely obsolete. The countries are all color-coded, and Africa's hanging dour head looks like a woman's head wrapped in a shawl. Kenneth rubs his hand silently over the continent, working his way west to east and then south until his index finger tickles the tip of South Africa. When he's finished tracing his hand over the map, he turns around and points at me.

"Gabon." He says it as if it were a crime I was guilty of.

"What about it?" I tell him, "I hear it's a fine country. Good people. Never been there myself, though."

He turns back to the map and whispers, "Fuck you."

"Come on. I thought you were an engineer," Joseph taunts him. "Whatever happened to precision?" He stands up and puts his large fat arm over Kenneth's narrow shoulders. With his other hand he draws a circle around the center of Africa. He finds his spot and taps it twice.

"Central African Republic," he says. "When was it?"

He scratches his chin thoughtfully like the intellectual he always thought he was going to become, and has never stopped wanting to be.

"Nineteen sixty-four? No. Nineteen sixty-five."

"Nineteen sixty-six," I tell him.

"Close."

"But not close enough."

So far we've named more than thirty different coups in Africa. It's become a game with us. Name a dictator and then guess the year and country. We've been playing the game for over a year now. We've expanded our playing field to include failed coups, rebellions, minor insurrections, guerrilla leaders, and the acronyms of as many rebel groups as we can find—the SPLA, TPLF, LRA, UNITA—anyone who has picked up a gun in the name of revolution. No matter how many we name, there are always more, the names, dates, and years multiplying as fast as we can memorize them so that at times we wonder, half-jokingly, if perhaps we ourselves aren't somewhat responsible.

"When we stop having coups, we can stop playing," Joseph said once. It was the third or fourth time we had played, and we were guessing how long we could keep it up.

"I should have known that," Kenneth says. "Bukassa has always been one of my favorites."

We all have favorites. Bukassa. Amin. Mobutu. We love the ones known for their absurd declarations and comical performances, the dictators who marry forty women and have twice as many children, who sit on golden thrones shaped like eagles, declare themselves minor gods, and are surrounded by rumors of incest, cannibalism, sorcery, and magic.

"He was an emperor," Joseph says. "Just like your Haile Selassie, Stephanos."

"He didn't last as long, though," I remind him.

"That's because no one gave him a chance. Poor Bukassa. Emperor Bukassa. Minister of Defense, Education, Sports, Health, War, Housing, Land, Wildlife, Foreign Affairs, His Royal Majesty, King of the Sovereign World, and Not Quite But Almost the Lion of Judah Bukassa."

"He was a cannibal, wasn't he?" Kenneth asks Joseph.

"According to the French, yes. But who can believe the French? Just look at Sierra Leone, Senegal. Liars, all of them."

"The French or the Africans?"

"What difference does it make?"

We spend the next two hours alternating between shots and slowly sipped glasses of Kenneth's scotch. Inevitably, predictably, our conversations find their way home.

"Our memories," Joseph says, "are like a river cut off from the ocean. With time they will slowly dry out in the sun, and so we drink and drink and drink and we can never have our fill."

"Why do you always talk like that?" Kenneth demands.

"Because it is true. And that is the only way to describe it. If you have something different to say, then say it."

Kenneth leans his chair back against the wall. He's drunk and on the verge of falling.

"I will say it," he says.

He pours the last few drops of scotch into his cup and sticks his tongue out to catch them.

"I can't remember where the scar on my father's face is. Sometimes I think it is here, on the left side of his face, just underneath his eye. But then I say to myself, that's only because you were facing him, and so really, it was on the right side. But then I say no, that can't be. Because when I was a boy I sat on his shoulders and he would let me rub my hand over it. And so I sit on top of a table and place my legs around a chair and lean over and I try to find where it would have been. Here. Or there. Here. Or there."

As he speaks his hand skips from one side of his face to the other.

"He used to say, when I die you'll know how to tell it's me by this scar. That made no sense but when I was a boy I didn't know that. I thought I needed that scar to know it was him. And now, if I saw him, I couldn't tell him apart from any other old man."

"Your father is already dead," I tell him.

"And so is yours, Stephanos. Don't you worry you'll forget him someday?"

"No. I don't. I still see him everywhere I go."

"All of our fathers are dead," Joseph adds.

"Exactly," Kenneth says.

It's the closest we've ever come to a resolution.

It's a few minutes past midnight when Joseph and Kenneth stand to go home. They both live in the suburbs, right outside of the city, in nearly identical, fully carpeted apartments with hardly any furniture besides the oversize televisions that they leave on even when they're not home. They both hate the city now.

Joseph kisses me once on each cheek before leaving. Kenneth slaps me on the back and says one more time, for good measure, "Keep fighting the good fight, Stephanos."

They pull away in Kenneth's badly worn used red Saab. Buying that car was Kenneth's first entry into a long-awaited form of American commerce that I think he imagined would lift him above the fray. Three years ago I went with him to a used-car dealership on the outskirts of a distant Virginia suburb to buy that car. He picked me up early on a Saturday morning when business was already slow and a few lost hours in the store didn't amount to much. He had rented a car for the occasion, a midsize sedan that placed him squarely in the middle class, of which he had just recently become a member. He wore a suit for the occasion, one cheaper than the ones he wears these days, but a suit nonetheless. He pulled the car up to my house and waited for me downstairs while leaning coolly against the passenger-side window, legs crossed. I wish for his sake there had been more people out there to see him because he looked wonderful. It wasn't just the clothes and the rented car, but an unadorned confidence that I had never seen him with before.

"How do I look, Stephanos?" he asked me as I walked out the front door. "Good, no?"

He had a habit back then, only recently abandoned, of ending his sentences with a question. He lifted his arms just high enough to reveal that the cuffs on his jacket were almost half an inch too short.

"Top class," I told him.

"You mean that, no? I really look good?"

"Of course you do."

Our drive to the dealership was a slow one. He eased his way prematurely into fading green lights, and took a slow, extended route around the neighborhood to reach the expressway. I didn't mind any of it. We had all suffered enough mockery and humiliation to last us well beyond our lifetimes, and if my role now was to serve as a blind, unflaggingly devoted cheerleader through whatever challenges and victories lay ahead, then I was all the happier for it.

We pulled into the dealership cautiously, as if every minor gesture of ours were being judged. We got out of the car, and rather than walk around the lot or enter the main office, Kenneth grabbed me by the wrist and said, "Wait, Stephanos. Let them come to us."

He resumed the pose he had taken in front of my house, except now, with the sun a little higher, he put on a pair of sunglasses to complete the portrait.

As we stood outside and waited against the hood of the car, middle-aged American men in white short-sleeve shirts came in and out of the main office, walked leisurely through the aisles of cars, dabbed their brows with handkerchiefs that they then refolded back into their pockets, and never once passed anything more than a brief, one-eyed glance in our direction. We waited ten and then twenty minutes before we finally realized that no one was coming to us, regardless of what we wore or how long we stood there.

"Come on, Stephanos. Let's go," Kenneth finally said. "They don't have what I want."

Kenneth showed up at the store three days later in the red Saab. He came near the end of the day and dropped the keys on the register as if he had just plucked them from one of the aisles.

"Look at the label," he said.

There was a red-and-blue Saab key chain, and the heads of the two keys were each wrapped in rubber and stamped with the company logo.

"A Saab?" I asked him.

"Not bad, no?"

"Where is it?"

"Right out front. Go see for yourself."

Kenneth stayed in the store while I went to inspect his car. There were webs of rust along the rear tires, a dented front fender, and patches of faded paint along the passenger-side door. When I went back into the store I gave him a high-five. I lied and told him that the car was beautiful.

"Really? Beautiful?" he asked me.

"Beautiful," I told him.

I watch the car through the windows as Kenneth and Joseph miss their turn off the circle and have to drive around it again. The second time, they honk just for me as they pass by.

EDWIDGE DANTICAT

The most prominent and widely read of Haitian-American writers, Edwidge Danticat (born in 1969) is the author of the story collection *Krik? Krak!* (1995) and the novels *Breath, Eyes, Memory* (1994), *The Farming of Bones* (1998), and *The Dew Breaker* (2004). In her memoir *Brother, I'm Dying* (2007) she writes about the last days of her father suffering from pulmonary fibrosis as well as her 81-year-old uncle who sought asylum in the United States after a battle between gang members and U.N. peacekeepers led to the burning of his church and threats on his life. Uncle Joseph, the family patriarch, had been a crucial presence in Danticat's childhood, having helped raise her for the ten years she remained in Haiti after her father immigrated to the United States in 1971. When Joseph fled Port-au-Prince he was struggling with throat cancer and could speak only with the aid of a voice box; yet when detained by immigration authorities in Miami his medications were taken from him and he was denied the medical care he needed. He died a few days later. Danticat's unembellished account of her uncle's death, which closely follows the official report on the case, is a restrained yet fiercely eloquent indictment of the way incarcerated immigrants are treated at detention centers, particularly the Krome facility.

from
Brother, I'm Dying

Alien 27041999

My uncle was now alien 27041999. He and Maxo had left Port-au-Prince's Toussaint Louverture Airport on American Airlines flight 822. The flight was scheduled to leave at 12:32 p.m., but was a bit delayed and left later than that.

On the plane, my uncle attempted to write a narrative of what had happened to him on a piece of white paper. He titled his note "Epidemie du 24 octobre 2004."

"Un groupe de chimères ont détruit L'Eglise Chrétienne de la Rédemption," it began. "A group of chimères destroyed Eglise Chrétienne de la Redemption." He then gave up writing sentences to simply list what had been removed or burned from the church, including the pews, two padded ballroom chairs used at wedding ceremonies, a drum set, some speakers and microphones.

Once they got off the plane at around two thirty p.m., my uncle and Maxo waited their turn with a large group of visitors in one of the long Customs and Border Protection lines. When they reached the CBP checkpoint, they presented their passports and valid tourist visas to a CPB officer. When asked how long they would be staying in the United States, my uncle, not understanding the full implication of that choice, said he wanted to apply for temporary asylum. He and Maxo were then taken aside and placed in a customs waiting area.

I don't know why my uncle had not simply used the valid visa he had to enter the United States, just as he had at least thirty times before, and later apply for asylum. I'm sure now that he had no intention of staying in either New York or Miami for the rest of his life. This is why, according to Maxo, he had specified "temporary." Had he acted based on someone's advice? On something he'd heard on the radio, read in the newspapers? Did he think that given all that had happened to him, the authorities—again those with the power both to lend a hand and to cut one off—would have to believe him? He planned to stay at most a few weeks, a few months, but he was determined to go back. This was why he'd gotten his police report from the anti-gang unit. This was why he had wanted the officer, a justice of the peace or an investigative judge, to go to Bel Air to witness and inspect, so he could return when things were calmer and reclaim his house, school and church. He had said as much to Tante Zi the day before.

I can only assume that when he was asked how long he would be staying in the United States, he knew that he would be staying past the thirty days his visa allowed him and he wanted to tell the truth.

*

Maxo and my uncle were approached by another Customs and Border Protection officer again at 5:38 p.m., at which point it was determined that my uncle would need a translator for his interview. Maxo, a fluent English speaker, could not as his son act as his translator.

Documents from the Bureau of Customs and Border Protection indicate that my uncle was interviewed by an Officer Reyes with help from a translator. A standard CBP interview form would have had Officer Reyes begin by saying, "I am an officer of the United States Immigration and Naturalization Service. I am authorized to administer the immigration laws and take sworn statements. I want to take your sworn statement regarding your application for admission to the United States."

A digitized picture attached to my uncle's interview form shows him looking tired and perplexed. His head is cropped from the tip of his widow's peak down to his chin. The picture shows a bit of his shoulder, which is slumped back, away from the frame. He is wearing a jacket, the same one that, according to Maxo, he'd been wearing since he left his house in Bel Air. Though he is facing the camera, his eyes are turned sideways, possibly toward the photographer.

The interview began with Officer Reyes asking my uncle, "Do you understand what I have said to you?"

"Yes," answered my uncle.

"Are you willing to answer my questions at this time?"

After making my uncle swear and affirm that all the statements he was about to make would be true and complete, Officer Reyes asked him to state his full name.

"Dantica Joseph Nosius," answered my uncle.

"Of what country are you a citizen?"

"Haiti."

"Do you have any reason to believe you are a citizen of the United States?"

"NO."

"Do you have any family, mother, father, brother, sister, spouse, or child who are citizens or permanent residents of the United States?"

My uncle replied that he had two brothers in the United States, one—my father—a naturalized U.S. citizen, and the second—my uncle Franck—a permanent resident.

"What is your purpose in entering the United States today?" asked Officer Reyes.

"Because a group that is causing trouble in Haiti wants to kill me," my uncle answered.

According to the transcript, Officer Reyes did not ask for further explanation or details.

"How much money do you have?" he asked, proceeding with the interview.

My uncle answered that he had one thousand and nine U.S. dollars with him.

"What is your occupation?" asked Officer Reyes.

The transcriber/translator has my uncle saying, "I am a priest," but he most likely said he was an evèk, a bishop, or elder pastor.

"What documents did you present today to the first Customs and Border Protection officer that you encountered?" asked Officer Reyes.

"My Haitian passport and immigration forms," my uncle answered.

"What name is on those documents?"

"Dantica Joseph Nosius."

"Is the name on the documents your true and correct name?"

"Yes."

"Have you ever used any other names?"

"No."

"Are you currently taking any prescription medication for any health condition?" asked Officer Reyes.

The transcriber/translator has my uncle saying, "Yes, for back pain and chest." And in parentheses, writes, "ibuprofen."

The transcript has neither my uncle nor the interviewer mentioning two rum bottles filled with herbal medicine, one for himself and one for my father, as well as the smaller bottles of prescription pills he was taking for his blood pressure and inflamed prostate.

"How would you describe your current health status?" Officer Reyes continued.

According to the transcript, my uncle answered, "Not bad." He had probably said, "Pa pi mal," just as my father continued to, even as he lay dying.

"Have you ever been arrested before at any time or any place?"

"No."

"Why exactly are you requesting for [sic] political asylum in the United States today?"

"Because they burned down my church in Haiti and I fear for my life."

Again no further explanation or details were requested and my uncle did not offer more.

"Have you had [sic] applied for political asylum before in the United States or any other country?"

"No."

"Have anyone [sic] ever petition for you to become a United States Legal Permanent Resident?"

"No."

"Were you in the United States in the year 1984?"

"Yes, but I do not remember."

(I couldn't remember either whether or not he'd been in the United States in 1984. I knew he had been the year before, during the summer of 1983, when he got the voice box, but could not recall if he'd returned the following year.)

"Have you have any encounter [sic] the United States Immigration Services before?"

"No."

"Why did you leave your home country of last residence?"

"Because I fear for my life in Haiti. And they burned down my church."

"Do you have any fear or concern about being returned to your home country or being removed from the United States?"

"Yes."

"Would you be harmed if you are returned to your home country of last residence?"

"YES."

"Did you understand my questions?"

"Yes."

"Do you have any questions or is there anything you'd like to add?"

"No."

My uncle was then asked to sign the statement. He was supposed to have initialed each page of the translated transcript, but instead he signed his name on all five pages. A CBP log shows he was then returned to the waiting area, where at 7:40 p.m. he was given some soda and chips.

*

At 10:03 p.m., my uncle Franck received a call at his home in Brooklyn. The male CBP officer who called him asked Uncle Franck whether Uncle Joseph had filed an application to become a U.S. resident in 1984. Uncle Franck said no.

Later, Department of Homeland Security files would show that a September 22, 1983, request had been made by Kings County Hospital, where my uncle had had his surgery and subsequent follow-up visits, to the United States Department of Justice, about my uncle's immigration status. As a result of this, on February 14, 1984, an immigration "alien" file, number 27041999, a file he was never aware of, was opened for my uncle. The file was subsequently closed.

"He's been coming to the United States for more than thirty years," Uncle Franck remembers telling the CPB officer who called him. "If he wanted to stay, he would have stayed a long time ago."

Uncle Franck then asked if he could speak to Uncle Joseph.

"They say they're going to put me in prison," Uncle Franck remembers Uncle Joseph saying. It was difficult to register emotion on the voice box, but Uncle Franck thought he sounded like he was caught up in something he had no way of understanding.

"It's not true. They can't put you in prison," Uncle Franck recalls telling him. "You have a visa. You have papers. Did you tell them how long you've been coming here?"

Uncle Franck then asked Uncle Joseph to put the CBP officer on the phone again.

"He's going to Krome," the officer said.

"He can't," Uncle Franck said. "He's eighty-one years old, an old man."

Uncle Franck then asked if he could speak to my uncle one more time.

The CBP officer told him, "We already have a translator for him," and hung up.

At 11:00 p.m., my uncle was given some chips and soda again. At 11:45 p.m., he signed a form saying his personal property was returned to him. The form lists as personal property only his one thousand and nine dollars and a silver-colored wristwatch. At 1:30 a.m., I received my phone call. At 4:20 a.m., my uncle and Maxo were transported to the airport's satellite detention area, which was in another concourse. By then my uncle was so cold that he wrapped the woolen airplane blanket he was given tightly around him as he curled up in a fetal position on a cement bed until 7:15 a.m. At around 7:30 a.m., they left the detention area to board a white van to Krome. Maxo was handcuffed, but asked if my uncle could not be handcuffed because of his age. The officer agreed not to handcuff my uncle, but told Maxo to tell my uncle that if he tried to escape he would be shot.

There is a form called a Discretionary Authority Checklist for Alien Applicants, which is meant to assist examining Customs and Border Protection officers in deciding whether to detain or release a person like my uncle. On the checklist are questions such as: Does the alien pose a threat to the United States, have a criminal history or terrorist affiliations or ties? Is s/he likely to contribute to the illegal population or pose some other credible threat?

Noting the "nature" of my uncle's inadmissibility, Officer Reyes cited a positive Central Index System search involving the 1984 immigration file.

In the remarks section beneath his check mark, he wrote, "Subject has an A#" or an alien registration number. In a more detailed memo, he would later write, "The Central Index System revealed that subject had an existing A (27041999) number which revealed negative results to him being a resident. The Central Index System did not contain any information on the subject except his name and date of birth and activity date of 02/14/1984."

Still, I suspect that my uncle was treated according to a biased immigration policy dating back from the early 1980s when Haitians began arriving in Florida in large numbers by boat. In Florida, where Cuban refugees are, as long as they're able to step foot on dry land, immediately processed and released to their families, Haitian asylum seekers are disproportionately detained, then deported. While Hondurans and Nicaraguans have continued to receive protected status for nearly ten years since Hurricane Mitch struck their homelands, Haitians were deported to the flood zones weeks after Tropical Storm Jeanne blanketed an entire city in water the way Hurricane Katrina did parts of New Orleans. Was my uncle going to jail because he was Haitian? This is a question he probably asked himself. This is a question I still ask myself. Was he going to jail because he was black? If he were white, Cuban, anything other than Haitian, would he have been going to Krome?

"Are age and health factors in this situation?" demands the Discretionary Authority Checklist for Alien Applicants.

In spite of my uncle's eighty-one years and his being a survivor of throat cancer, which was obvious from his voice box and tracheotomy, when answering whether there were age and health factors to be taken into consideration, Officer Reyes checked No.

Is the applicant a well-known public figure?

No.

Congressional or media interest?

No.

Does the applicant have a legitimate reason for entering the U.S.?

No.

Is the applicant's reason for entry based on an emergency?

No.

Credible claim of official misinformation?

No.

Is there a relationship to a U.S. employer or resident?

Yes.

Intent to circumvent admissibility requirements?

No.

Misrepresentations made by applicant during inspection process?

No.

Would the applicant be admissible if s/he had a valid passport and/or visa? (My uncle had both.)

Yes.

Is there relief for the applicant through the parole or visa waiver process?

No.

Tomorrow

My father's rough patch had continued. He was becoming agitated, panicked at times over his decreasing ability to speak for extended periods. His anxiety sent us on a renewed search. During his monthly visit with Dr. Padman, Bob asked if he could be considered for any experimental treatment programs and procured a referral to a pulmonologist at Columbia Presbyterian in upper Manhattan.

Suddenly my father had a place and time on which to pin his hopes. He was so looking forward to his appointment that he would end each of our brief conversations by saying, "We'll see what they tell me at Columbia."

On Saturday morning, as my father struggled for breath and dreamed of Columbia, I had to tell him that his brother was at Krome, a place that he, like all Haitians, knew meant nothing less than humiliation and suffering and more often than not a long period of detention before deportation.

"So it's true," he said. Uncle Franck had called the night before to tell him that Uncle Joseph might be going there.

"I hate to put this on you," my father said. "You're pregnant, but you're the only family he has down there. It's in your hands."

I told him that Fedo and I had already called a few immigration lawyers and they'd all advised us that there was nothing we could do before Monday morning.

"You mean," my father said, "Uncle has to spend the whole weekend in jail?"

When he arrived at Krome, my uncle was lined up with a dozen or so other detainees and his briefcase inventoried and taken away from him. A Krome property inventory form lists one softcover religious book, his Bible, one thousand U.S. dollars—he was allowed to keep the nine dollars to buy phone cards—one airline ticket, one tube of Fixodent for his dentures, and two nine-volt batteries for his two voice boxes. Again there's no mention of the herbal medicine or the pills he was taking for his blood pressure and inflamed prostate.

My uncle's initial medical screening involved a daylong examination of his vital signs, chest X-rays, and a physical and mental history interview. In the notes jotted down by the examining nurse, he is described as composed, friendly and "purposeful." To the question "Does the detainee understand and recognize the significance and symptoms of the situation in which he finds himself?" the nurse answers, "Yes," adding elsewhere, "Patient uses a traditional Haitian medicine for prostate & says if he doesn't take it he pees blood & has pain." Russ Knocke, a spokesman for U.S. Immigration and Customs Enforcement, would later derogatorily refer to my uncle's traditional medicine as "a voodoolike potion."

At the end of his first day at Krome, my uncle's blood pressure was so high that he was assigned to the Short Stay Unit, a medical facility inside the prison. He and Maxo were separated.

I am acquainted with Ira Kurzban, author of *Kurzban's Immigration Law Sourcebook*, one of the most widely used immigration manuals in the United States. Ira had represented Haitian immigrant clients for more than thirty years and had worked as general counsel to the governments of Panama, Nicaragua, Cuba and Haiti and as former president Aristide's attorney. On the recommendation of a mutual friend, I called his office early Monday morning and asked for his help.

"I'm sending one of my best guys on this," he said, after I explained the entire situation to him. "Because of his age and health condition, we'll first try to get your uncle out as soon as possible."

Soon after Ira hung up, John Pratt, a stern-sounding man with a slight southern drawl, called.

"I'm heading to Krome now," he said. "I'll need as much information as you have about the situation."

I told him all I knew. I hadn't been able to speak to my uncle since his arrival, so I couldn't offer much insight into his state of mind or how he might come across at a credible fear hearing, an inquiry into his claims of persecution that would be held before an asylum officer at Krome.

"Are you willing to take him in if they release him?" Pratt asked.

"Of course," I said.

"Hang on tight then and stay by the phone," he said.

Once there was only waiting to do, my husband left for work. I called some Brooklyn ambulette companies about transporting my father to Columbia Presbyterian the next day. My father had so little fat and muscle left on his body that it was agonizing for him to sit for any stretch of time, so I basically wanted to rent him a bed on wheels.

"The only way you get a bed is if you call 911," a Russian dispatcher told me, so I booked a van with a recliner.

All morning, I hoped that John Pratt would call and tell me he was going to walk out of Krome with my uncle, news I would have loved to share with my father. However, when Pratt did call that afternoon the only good news was that my uncle's credible fear hearing had been scheduled for nine o'clock the next morning.

"So he's not coming home?" I said. Even as I said it, the word "home" felt inappropriate, unsuitable. My uncle no longer had a home.

"Can I visit him?" I asked.

"Only weekend visits are allowed at Krome," he said, "and he'd have to put you on a list a couple of days before the fact, but there's a good chance they'll release him tomorrow."

That night at around six o'clock, my uncle called me from Krome.

"Bon dye," I shouted, so overjoyed to hear that motorized voice. "My God. It's so good to hear you."

"Oh, I can't tell you how good it is to hear you," he said.

Then I slipped into a repartee I had fallen into with my father in the last weeks or so as he'd grown sicker. I called him cher, amour, mon coeur, darling, my love, my heart.

"How are you, my heart?"

"M nan prizon," he said. I'm in jail.

"Oh I know," I said, now missing his real voice, the one that didn't always sound the same, the one I could no longer fully remember. "I know and I am so sad. I'm so sad and sorry for everything that's happened both in Haiti and here. But you met with the lawyer?"

"Yes," he said. "Maxo and I both did."

"He's going to get you out," I said. "He's a very good lawyer. He's going to get you out."

"Okay," he said. He'd had so many horrible surprises in the last few days, why should he believe that things would start going well now?

"Nèg nan prizon," he said. "Fò w mache pou wè." If you live long enough you'll see everything.

"Don't worry," I said. "We'll get you out."

"They took my medicine." The machine produced some static as if his finger had slipped off the button that he pressed to keep the voice going. "I also had something for your father, some liquid vitamins. They took that too. And my papers, my notepads, they're gone. Burned."

"Don't worry about all that," I said. "Just concentrate on getting out tomorrow."

"Does he know?" he asked. "Does Mira know I'm in here? I didn't want him to know. He's so sick. I don't want him to have this on his mind."

"Don't worry," I said. "He knows you're getting out tomorrow."

"Do people in Haiti know?" he asked. He was most concerned about his sisters, Tante Zi and Tante Tina.

"I think they know," I said.

Now even the motorized voice betrayed a hint of shame, the kind of shame whose only reprieve is silence.

"I have to go," he said. "Others are waiting."

"How do you feel?" I asked. "If you don't feel well, tell them."

"I will," he said. "I have to go."

I heard a muffled voice in the background, someone demanding a turn at the pay phone.

"You're strong," I said. "Very strong. You have so much more strength than even you know."

And reluctantly he agreed and said, "Oh yes. It's true."

"Just get through tonight," I said. "Tomorrow, God willing, you'll be free."

Afflictions

My father every now and then would quote from the book of Genesis, paraphrasing his favorite lines from the story of Joseph, the youth who was ousted and sold into unfriendly territory by his brothers. My uncle Joseph was named after the rainbow-coated man, but I'd never heard Papa look for parallels between my uncle's life and the biblical story before.

"Uncle is in his own Egypt this morning, in his land of afflictions," my father said, when we talked just before nine a.m. the next day.

"He's going to be all right," I said. "You just concentrate on Columbia Presbyterian."

As I was talking to my father, my uncle was waiting with John Pratt outside an asylum unit trailer office at Krome. Leaning over to one of three other detainees also waiting for hearings, my uncle asked the English-speaking Haitian man to tell Pratt that his medication had been taken away. Before Pratt could respond, he and my uncle were called in by asylum officer

Castro, a woman who appeared to be in her mid-forties. The asylum interview was about to begin.

My uncle and Pratt were seated at a desk close to the back wall, facing Officer Castro. A certified translator was needed for the proceedings, and since there wasn't one on the premises, a telephone translation service was called and the interpreter put on speakerphone. The phone was on the desk in front of my uncle, next to Pratt's lawbooks, notepads and other materials.

The interpreter had trouble understanding my uncle's voice box, so Officer Castro asked my uncle to move his mouth closer to the phone. As my uncle leaned forward, his hand slipped away from his neck and he dropped his voice box.

The records indicate that my uncle appeared to be having a seizure. His body stiffened. His legs jerked forward. His chair slipped back, pounding the back of his head into the wall. He began to vomit.

Vomit shot out of his mouth, his nose, as well as the tracheotomy hole in his neck. The vomit was spread all over his face, from his forehead to his chin, down the front of his dark blue Krome-issued overalls. There was also vomit on his thighs, where a large wet stain showed he had also urinated on himself.

"Somebody call for help!" Pratt jumped from his chair and pulled his papers away from the spreading vomit.

Officer Castro rushed over to the desk and grabbed the sleeves of my uncle's uniform. She pulled his body forward, straightening his head. Grabbing a nearby wastebasket, she placed it in front of my uncle. My uncle continued to vomit into the wastebasket as he opened and closed his eyes, which wandered aimlessly in their sockets.

When he stopped vomiting, my uncle's body grew rigid and cold, his arms falling limply at his side. Officer Castro called out to the guards keeping watch over the other detainees outside her office and asked them to call the medical unit. A guard radioed for help but said that Krome was in lockdown and that it might take some time for help to arrive.

Officer Castro grabbed the phone in front of my uncle to see if the interpreter was still there. The phone was dead. She asked if there was anyone around who could speak to my uncle in Creole. The guard brought the English-speaking Haitian detainee to whom my uncle had spoken about his medication into the asylum office. The man said a few words to my uncle, but there was no reaction. Pratt asked Officer Castro to send for Maxo. The guard said he needed special permission from his supervisor to have Maxo come. The guard radioed for special permission.

Fifteen minutes had passed since my uncle first started vomiting. A registered nurse and medic finally arrived. By then my uncle looked "almost comatose," Pratt recalled. "He seemed somewhat unconscious and couldn't move."

Pratt told the medic and nurse that right before he became sick, my uncle had told him his medication had been taken away. Pratt then turned to Officer Castro and asked if my uncle could be granted humanitarian parole given his age and condition.

"I think he's faking," the medic said, cutting Pratt off.

To prove his point, the medic grabbed my uncle's head and moved it up and down. It was rigid rather than limp, he said. Besides, my uncle would open his eyes now and then and seemed to be looking at him.

"You can't fake vomit," Pratt shot back. "This man is very sick and his medication shouldn't have been taken away from him."

The medications were indeed taken away, replied the medic, in accordance with the facility's regulations, and others were substituted for them.

The medic and the nurse then moved my uncle from the asylum office to a wheelchair in the hallway.

When Maxo arrived, he ran over to his father and seeing him slumped over in the wheelchair and leaning over the side, began to cry. Except for the occasional flutter of his eyelids, it seemed to Maxo that his father was unconscious. The first thing Maxo wanted to do was clean the vomit from his face. Though his father was in distress, he knew that underneath the sticky heave and chunks of still undigested food, this very proud man would feel humiliated by his appearance.

"He wouldn't be like this if you hadn't taken away his medication," Maxo said, sobbing.

"He's faking," repeated the medic. "He keeps looking at me."

The medic then turned to Pratt and told him that based on his many years of experience at Krome, he could easily make such determinations.

"Please just let me clean him," Maxo sobbed.

The medic told him that he'd been called only to help his father communicate with them. "If you can't help, then we'll send you back."

"He can't speak without his voice box," Maxo said. Covered in vomit, the voice box was no longer operable.

During that discussion, it seemed to Maxo that his father's eyes were fluttering a bit more. Maybe he could hear them. Maybe he was getting better, coming out of whatever had overcome him.

"Papa," Maxo pleaded, "please try to move. Maybe they'll let you go."

My uncle opened his eyes and looked up at Maxo. He raised his hands from his lap, but they fell limply back to his knees. It seemed to Maxo that he was trying to mouth, "M pa kapab." I can't.

My uncle's eyes remained open, but they seemed cloudy and dazed, set on something way beyond Maxo, the guards, the medic, John Pratt and all the others around him.

"He's not cooperating," the medic said. For a moment Maxo wasn't sure whether the medic was talking about him or his father.

"His eyes are open and he's not unconscious," added the medic. "I still think he's faking, but we'll take him to the clinic."

A stretcher was brought and my uncle placed on it.

Pratt asked Officer Castro if they could continue the credible fear interview at the clinic.

No, he was told. That was against the rules.

I was on the phone with the medical transport service that was taking my father to Columbia Presbyterian when John Pratt called to tell me that my uncle had become ill. I was expecting good news, great news even. Before Pratt could even speak, I wanted to say, "Where do I go? How do I get him?"

"Your uncle became ill during the credible fear interview." Pratt's solid voice was shaken. There was even a hint of horror in it.

"They've taken him to the clinic at Krome," he said. "I'm in the lobby, waiting to see if we can continue the interview in a while. Mr. Kurzban is making calls to the Miami district office to see if your uncle can receive a humanitarian parole."

Later that morning, in the Krome medical unit, my uncle's condition worsened and according to Krome records, he was transported to Miami's

Jackson Memorial Hospital with shackles on his feet. That same morning was the first time in nine weeks that my father had been out of his house. It was a crisp autumn day in New York and most of the leaves had already fallen off the trees. Speeding down the Prospect Expressway toward Manhattan, my father felt every stop and turn, every painful jolt and bounce of the ride in his bones. Still, between coughing spells, he told my mother and Bob, "At least I'm outside."

Being outside was all my father got out of the visit. The lung specialist who saw him made him take off his shirt, listened to his labored breathing, and asked him if he had a DNR.

"What's a DNR?" my father asked Bob in Creole.

"It's a piece of paper that says if you die, you don't want to be brought back to life and kept alive by machines," Bob explained.

"No," my father told the doctor. "I don't want to be kept alive by machines. There's already been enough suffering."

Let the Stars Fall

My uncle's medical records indicate that he arrived in the emergency room at Jackson Memorial Hospital around 1:00 p.m. with an intravenous drip in progress from Krome. He was evaluated by a nurse practitioner at 1:10 p.m., his pulse (80), temperature (97.0), blood pressure (169/78) checked and noted. At 2:00 p.m., he signed, in an apparently firm hand, a patient consent form stating, "I [he did not fill in his name in the blank spot] consent to undergo all necessary tests, medication, treatments and other procedures in the course of the study, diagnosis and treatment of my illness(es) by the medical staff and other agents and/or employees of the Public Health Trust/Jackson Memorial Hospital (PHT/JMH) and the University of Miami School of Medicine, including medical students."

At 3:24 p.m., blood and urine samples were taken. His urine analysis showed some blood and a high level of glucose. His CBC, or complete blood count test, displayed a higher than normal number of white blood cells, which hinted at a possible infection. The test also showed elevated bilirubin or abnormal gallbladder and liver functions.

At 4:00 p.m., during a more thorough evaluation by the nurse practitioner, he complained of acute abdominal pain, nausea and loss of appetite.

A new IV was administered. Chest X-rays and abdominal films were taken. Pneumonia and intestinal obstruction were ruled out.

At 5 p.m., he was transferred to the hospital's prison area, Ward D. His Ward D admission note, which was also prepared by a registered nurse, remarks, "No acute distress, ambulatory. To IV hydrate and reevaluate. Patient closely observed."

Once in Ward D, where no lawyers or family members are allowed to visit, and where prisoners are restrained to prevent escapes, to protect the staff, the guards and the prisoners from one another, his feet were probably shackled once more, just as, according to Krome records, they'd been during the ambulance ride. He was given another IV at 10:00 p.m., at which time it was noted by the nurse on duty that he was "resting quietly." He was to be further observed and followed up, she added.

His vital signs were checked again at midnight, then at 1:00 a.m. and 7:00 a.m. the next day, when his temperature was 96 degrees, his heart rate a dangerous 114 beats per minute and his blood pressure 159/80. At 9:00 a.m. he was given another IV and 5 mg of Vasotec to help lower his blood pressure. By 11:00 a.m., his heart rate had decreased to 102 beats per minute, still distressingly high for an eighty-one-year-old man with his symptoms.

The records indicate that he was seen for the first time by a physician at 1:00 p.m., exactly twenty-four hours after he'd been brought to the emergency room. The physician, Dr. Hernandez, noted his test results, namely his high white cell count, his elevated liver enzymes and his persistent abdominal pain. He then ordered an abdominal ultrasound, which was performed at 4:56 p.m. The ultrasound showed intra-abdominal fluid around my uncle's liver and sludge, or thickened bile, in his gallbladder. Before the test was administered, my uncle was given another patient consent form to sign. He signed it less comprehensibly than the first, next to a stamped hospital declaration of "PATIENT UNABLE TO SIGN."

At 7:00 p.m., after more than twenty hours of no food and sugarless IV fluids, my uncle was sweating profusely and complained of weakness. He was found to be hypoglycemic, with a lower than normal blood sugar level of 42 mg/dl. The doctor on duty prescribed a 5 percent dextrose drip and twenty minutes later, my uncle's blood glucose stabilized at 121 mg/dl. It was then noted that he was awake and alert and his mental response "appropriate."

At 7:55 p.m., his heart rate rose again, this time to 110 beats per minute. An electrocardiogram (EKG) was performed at 8:16 p.m. The next note on the chart shows that he was found pulseless and unresponsive by an immigration guard at 8:30 p.m. There is no detailed account of "the code" or the sixteen minutes between the time he was found unresponsive and the time he was pronounced dead, at 8:46 p.m. Only a quick scribble that cardiopulmonary resuscitation (CPR) and advanced cardiac life support (ACLS) "continued for 11 mins."

Aside from the time he had throat cancer, my uncle nearly died on one other occasion. It was the summer of 1975, and I was six years old. He was stricken with malaria. Fever, chills, nausea and diarrhea had sent him to his doctor, who'd hospitalized him.

I hadn't seen him in several days when Tante Denise brought Nick, Bob and me to the hospital to visit him. When we walked into his small private room, he was curled in a fetal position, and though he was wrapped in several blankets, was shivering. His face was ashen and gray and his eyes the color of corn.

"The children are here," Tante Denise had told him.

He seemed not to see us. Grunting, he closed his eyes as if to protect them from the ache coursing through the rest of his body. When he opened his eyes again, he glared at us as if wondering what we were doing there.

"I brought the children," Tante Denise said again. "You asked for them." He looked at each one of us carefully, then said, "Ti moun, children." "Wi," we answered, a weak chorus of five- and six-year-olds.

Looking at Nick, my uncle said, "Maxo, I'll be sad to die without seeing you again." Then turning to Bob, he said, "Isn't that right, Mira?"

He called me Ino, the name of his dead sister.

"Ino knows I'm right," he said. Then closing his eyes once more, he added, "Kite zetwal yo tonbe." Let the stars fall.

His words evoked a loud wail from Tante Denise, who grabbed us by the hands and pulled us away from the bed.

"He's gone," she wailed. "My husband's dying. He's only speaking to people who aren't here."

The fact that my uncle had asked the stars to fall was also not lost on Tante Denise, who believed, and had groomed us to accept, that each time a star fell out of the sky, it meant someone had died.

I wasn't looking at the sky when my uncle died at Jackson Memorial Hospital, but maybe somewhere a star did fall down for him.

Thinking, as Pratt had been told, that my uncle was only being tested and observed, I spent the day waiting for his discharge and release. But late in the afternoon, I had a terrible feeling and began to frantically call the hospital until I reached a nurse in Ward D, the hospital's prison ward.

My uncle was resting, she said, but she couldn't allow me to speak to him since any contact with the prisoners, either by phone or in person, had to be arranged through their jailers, in my uncle's case, through Krome. While Pratt pleaded with the higher-ups at Krome to let us visit, I pleaded with the nurse to let me speak to my uncle. But neither one of us got anywhere, not even after my uncle died.

When a close friend of Maxo's, whom Maxo had used his one allowable phone call from Krome to tell, telephoned to break the news to me, I called Ward D again to ask if indeed it was true that a Haitian man named Joseph Dantica had just died there. The man who answered curtly told me, "Call Krome." And when I did telephone Krome—thinking I should have an official answer before calling my relatives—I was told by another stranger that I should try back in the morning.

By then it was nearly midnight.

"Don't tell your family now," my husband said, rocking me as I sobbed in his arms. "At least let them get *this* good night sleep."

We spent most of the night awake, cradling along with my large belly this horrendous news that those who most loved my uncle were not yet aware of. Some, like my father, were probably still praying for his release and recovery. Others, like his sisters in Haiti, were surely worrying, dreading perhaps, yet never expecting this particularly heartbreaking ending.

Waiting for daybreak, we reorganized the room in which my uncle was to have stayed, removing the paintings from the walls and stripping the bed of the sheets he was supposed to have slept on. As we slid the bed from one side of the room to the other, I worried for my father. Would he survive the shock?

Placing a new set of curtains on the windows, after my husband had collapsed into bed, I worried for my daughter too. How would this stress, my sleeping so little, my lifting and lowering things and stooping in and out of closets in the middle of such a painful night affect her?

The next morning, my first call was to Karl, who conferenced the rest of the calls with me. We called Uncle Franck, who moaned loudly over the phone, then my mother, who, as always, was the most composed.

It was best that she, Bob and Karl tell my father in person, she said.

My father was in bed, weakened but tranquil after yet another sleepless night, when they told him. For a moment he was absolutely still, then he pushed his head back and looked up at the ceiling and then again at my mother and brothers. He didn't say anything at all. Perhaps he was numb, in shock. He didn't appear surprised either, my mother said. It was, she said, as if he already knew.

❧ ❧

My uncle was buried in a cemetery in Queens, New York. His grave sits by an open road, overlooking the streets of Cyprus Hills and the subway tracks above them. During his life, my uncle had clung to his home, determined not to be driven out. He had remained in Bel Air, in part because it was what he knew. But he had also hoped to do some good there. Now he would be exiled finally in death. He would become part of the soil of a country that had not wanted him. This haunted my father more than anything else.

"He shouldn't be here," my father said, tearful and breathlessly agitated, shortly before drifting off to sleep that night. "If our country were ever given a chance and allowed to be a country like any other, none of us would live or die here."

MAJID NAFICY

Born in Isfahan, Iran, in 1952, Majid Naficy began writing poetry at an early age, and went on to publish work in a wide range of genres. After briefly attending UCLA he returned to Iran to study at Tehran University, where he became a political activist opposing the regime of the shah. After the Islamic revolution in 1979 his wife and brother were executed by the new government and he fled the country, settling in Los Angeles in 1983. He has published poetry in both English and Farsi and is an editor of the journal of the Iranian Writers' Association in Exile. His collections include *Muddy Shoes* (1999) and *Father and Son* (2003). "Night" was translated by Niloufar Talebi.

Night

Midnight approaches in Texas
And in New York midnight has passed
A new day dawns in Sweden.
It is only in the City of Angels
That night will not forsake me.

I clasp my arms around myself
Close my eyelids
And cast myself into the night
Like a lone rock.
Maybe in Texas
It will knock on a bedroom window
Or land on a rooftop in New York.
But the world is round
And the heavy loneliness of this night
Sits only on my soul.

Time has turned its back on me
And the earth
Like a black well
Has spread its mouth open
Under my feet.

I let myself cross all borders
And spin like a meteor
Around myself.
But suddenly
The soft ring of a call
Brings me back to earth.

The day has not yet
Approached noon in Esfahan
And my mother
Who is clipping my father's nails
On the balcony
Has heard the sound
Of a rock
Plunging into the courtyard pool.

ILAN STAVANS

Born in Mexico City in 1961 to a Jewish family who had left Poland and Ukraine, Stavans himself immigrated to the United States in 1985 to work as a newspaper reporter. He has written about this double move in his memoir *On Borrowed Words* (2001). Stavans' interest in language as a prism for understanding identity is the subject of *Dictionary Days* (2005) and *Love and Language* (2007). In *Resurrecting Hebrew* (2008) he explored the odyssey of that language from pre-biblical times to present-day Israel. He has edited the poetry of Pablo Neruda and the short stories of Isaac Bashevis Singer. Stavans is known for his explorations of Spanglish, the tongue resulting from the crossbreeding of Spanish and English. In 2002 he translated into Spanglish the first chapter of Cervantes' *Don Quixote* and has subsequently produced a lexicon of the hybrid language. Stavans teaches at Amherst College.

from

Autobiographical Essay

KALEIDOSCOPE

Bizarre combination—Mexican Jews: some 60,000 frontier dwellers and hyphen people like Dr. Jekyll and Mr. Hyde, a sum of sums of parts, a multiplicity of multiplicities. Although settlers from Germany began to arrive in "Aztec Country" around 1830, the very first synagogue was not built in the nation's capital until some fifty-five years later. From then on, waves of Jewish immigrants came from Russia and Central and Eastern Europe— Ashkenazim whose goal was to make it big in New York (the Golden Land), but since an immigration quota was imposed in the United States in 1924, a little detour places them in Cuba, Puerto Rico, or the Gulf of Mexico (the Rotten Land). Most were Yiddish-speaking Bundists: hardworking peasants, businessmen, and teachers, nonreligious and entrepreneurial, escaping

Church-sponsored pogroms and government persecution whose primary dream was never Palestine. Hardly anything physical or ideological differentiated them from the relatives that did make it north, to Chicago, Detroit, Pittsburgh, and the Lower East Side—except, of course, the fact that they, disoriented immigrants, couldn't settle where they pleased. And this sense of displacement colored our future.

Migration and its discontents: I have often imagined the Culture Shock, surely not too drastic, my forefathers experienced at their arrival: from *mujik* to *campesino*, similar types in a different milieu. Mexico was packed with colonial monasteries where fanatical nuns prayed day and night. Around 1910 Emiliano Zapata and Pancho Villa were making their Socialist Revolution, and an anti-Church feeling (known in Mexico as La Cristiada and masterfully examined in Graham Greene's *The Power and the Glory*) was rampant. Aztecs, the legend claims, once sacrificed daughters to their idols in sky-high pyramids, and perhaps were cannibals. Undoubtedly this was to be a transitory stop, it had to. It was humid, and at least in the nation's capital, nature remained an eternal autumn. I must confess never to have learned to love Mexico. I was taught to retain a sense of foreignness—as a tourist without a home. The best literature I know about Mexico is by Europeans and U.S. writers: Italo Calvino, André Breton, Jack Kerouac, Greene, Joseph Brodsky, Antonin Artaud, Katherine Anne Porter, Malcolm Lowry, Harriet Doerr . . . I only love my country when I am far away. Elsewhere—that's where I belong: the vast diaspora. Nowhere and everywhere. (Am I a name dropper? Me, whose name no one can pronounce?)

OUT OF THE BASEMENT

When the Mexican edition of *Talia in Heaven* (1989) came out, my publisher, Fernando Valdés, at a reception, talked about the merits of this, my first (and so far only) novel. He applauded this and that ingredient, spoke highly of the innovative style, and congratulated the author for his precocious artistic maturity. Memory has deleted most of his comments. I no longer remember what he liked and why. The only sentence that still sticks in my mind, the one capable of overcoming the passing of time, came at the end of his speech, when he said: "For many centuries, Latin America has had Jews living in the basement, great writers creating out of the shadow. And Ilan Stavans is the one I kept hidden until now." A frightening metaphor.

In the past five hundred years, Jews in the Hispanic world have been forced to convert to Christianity or somehow to mask or feel ashamed of their ancestral faith. Their intellectual contribution, notwithstanding, has been enormous. Spanish letters cannot be understood without Fray Luis de León, Arcipreste de Hita, and Ludovicus Vives, without Fernando de Roja's *La Celestina* and the anti-Semitic poetry of Francisco de Quevedo, author of the infamous sonnet "A man stuck to a nose" (*Erase un hombre a una nariz pegado, érase una nariz superlativa, érase una alquitara medio viva, érase un peje espada mal barbado . . .*). In the Americas, a safe haven for refugees from the Inquisition and later on for Eastern Europeans running away from the Nazis, Jewish writers have been active since 1910, when Alberto Gerchunoff, a Russian immigrant, published in Spanish his collection of interrelated vignettes, *The Jewish Gauchos of the Pampas*, to commemorate Argentina's independence. He switched from one language to another to seek individual freedom, to validate his democratic spirit, to embrace a dream of plurality and progress: Yiddish, the tongue of Mendel Mokher Sforim and Sholem Aleichem, was left behind; Spanish, Cervantes's vehicle of communication— Gerchunoff was an admirer of *Don Quixote*—became the new tool, the channel to entertain, educate, and redeem the masses. Like Spinoza, Kafka, Nabokov, and Joseph Brodsky, he was the ultimate translator: a bridge between idiosyncrasies. The abyss and the bridge. Many decades later, some fifty astonishing writers from Buenos Aires and Mexico to Lima and Guatemala, including Moacyr Scliar, Clarice Lispector, and Mario Szichman, continue to carry on Gerchunoff's torch, but the world knows little about them. The narrative boom that catapulted Gabriel García Márquez, Carlos Fuentes, and others from south of the Rio Grande to international stardom in the sixties managed to sell a monolithic, suffocatingly uniform image of the entire continent as a Banana Republic crowded with clairvoyant prostitutes and forgotten generals, never a multicultural society. To such a degree were ethnic voices left in the margin that readers today know much more about Brazilians and Argentines thanks to Borges's short stories "Emma Zunz" and "El milagro secreto" ("The Secret Miracle") and Vargas Llosa's novel *The*

Storyteller, than to anything written by Gerchunoff and his followers. Sadly and in spite of his anti-Semitic tone, my Mexican publisher was right: In the baroque architecture of Latin American letters, Jews inhabit the basement. And yet, *la pureza de sangre* in the Hispanic world is but an abstraction: native Indians, Jews, Arabs, Africans, Christians . . . the collective identity is always in need of a hyphen. In spite of the "official" image stubbornly promoted by governments from time immemorial, Octavio Paz and Julio Cortázar have convincingly used the salamander, the *axólotl*, as a symbol to describe Latin America's popular soul, always ambiguous and in mutation.

AMERICA, AMERICA

I honestly never imagined I could one day pick up my suitcases to leave home once and for all. And yet, at twenty-five I moved to New York; I was awarded a scholarship to study for a master's at the Jewish Theological Seminary and, afterwards, perhaps a doctorate at Columbia University or elsewhere. I fled Mexico (and Spanish) mainly because as a secular Jew—what Freud would have called "a psychological Jew"—I felt marginalized, a stereotype. (Little did I know!) A true chameleon, a bit parochial and nearsighted, a nonconformist with big dreams and few possibilities. Like my globe-trotting Hebraic ancestors, I had been raised to build an ivory tower, an individual ghetto. By choosing to leave, I turned my past into remembrance: I left the basement and ceased to be a pariah. *Talia in Heaven* exemplifies that existential dilemma: Its message simultaneously encourages Jews to integrate and openly invites them to escape; it alternates between life and memory. Paraphrasing Lionel Trilling, its cast of characters, victims of an obsessive God (much like the Bible's) who enjoys ridiculing them, are at the bloody crossroad where politics, theology, and literature meet. To be or not to be. The moment I crossed the border, I became somebody else: a new person. In *Chromos: A Parody of Truth*, Felipe Alfau says: "The moment one learns English, complications set in. Try as one may, one cannot elude this conclusion, one must inevitably come back to it." While hoping to master the English language during sleepless nights, I understood James Baldwin, who, already exiled in Paris and quoting Henry James, claimed it is a complex fate to be an American. "America's history," the black author of *Nobody Knows My Name* wrote, "her aspirations, her peculiar triumphs, her even more peculiar defeats, and her position in the world—yesterday and today—are all so profoundly and stubbornly unique that the very word 'America' remains a new, almost completely undefined, and extremely controversial proper noun. No one in the world seems to know exactly what it describes." To be honest, the rise of multiculturalism, which perceives the melting pots, a soup of diverse and at times incompatible backgrounds, has made the word "America" even more troublesome, more evasive and abstract. Is America a compact whole, a unit? Is it a sum of ethnic groups unified by a single language and a handful of patriotic symbols? Is it a Quixotic dream where total assimilation is impossible, where multiculturalism is to lead to disintegration? And Baldwin's statement acquires a totally different connotation when one goes one step beyond, realizing that "America" is not only a nation (a state of mind) but also a vast continent. From Alaska to the Argentine pampa, from Rio de Janeiro to East Los Angeles, the geography Christopher Columbus mistakenly encountered in 1492 and Amerigo Vespucci baptized a few years later is also a linguistic and cultural addition: America the nation and America the continent. America, America: I wanted to find a room of my own in the two; or two rooms, perhaps?

ON BEING A WHITE HISPANIC AND MORE

Once settled, I suddenly began to be perceived as Hispanic (i.e., Latino)—an identity totally alien to me before. (My knowledge of spoken Latin is minimal.) To make matters worse, my name (once again?), accent, and skin color were exceptions to what gringos had as the "Hispanic prototype." In other words, in Mexico I was perceived as Jewish; and now across the border, I was Mexican. Funny, isn't it? (In fact, according to official papers I qualify as a white Hispanic, an unpleasant term if there was ever one.) Once again, an impostor, an echo. (An impostor, says Ambrose Bierce in *The Devil's Dictionary*, is a rival aspirant to public honors.)

Themselves, myself: Hispanics in the United States—white, black, yellow, green, blue, red . . . twice Americans, once in spite of themselves. They have been in the territories north of the Rio Grande even before the Pilgrims of the *Mayflower*; and with the Guadalupe Hidalgo Treaty signed in 1848, in which Generalísimo Antonio López de Santa Ana gave away and subsequently sold half of Mexico to the White House (why only half?), many of them unexpectedly, even unwillingly, became a part of an Anglo-Saxon, English-speaking reality. Today after decades of neglect and silence, decades of anonymity and ignorance, Latinos are finally receiving the attention they deserve. The second fastest-growing ethnic group after the Asians, their diversity of roots—Caribbean, Mexican, Central and South American, Iberian, and so on—makes them a difficult collectivity to describe. Are the Cuban migrations from Holguín, Matanzas, and Havana similar in their idiosyncratic attitude to those of Managua, San Salvador, and Santo Domingo? Is the Spanish they speak their true lingua franca, the only unifying factor? Is their immigrant experience in any way different from that of previous minorities—Irish, Italian, Jewish, what have you? How do they understand and assimilate the complexities of what it means to be American? And where do I, a white Hispanic, fit in?

Nowhere and everywhere. In 1985 I was assigned by a Spanish magazine to interview Isaac Goldemberg, a famous Jewish-Peruvian novelist who wrote *The Fragmented Life of Don Jacobo Lerner*. When we met at the Hungarian Pastry Shop at Amsterdam Avenue and 110th Street, he told me, among many things, he had been living in New York for over two decades without mastering the English language because he didn't want his Spanish to suffer and ultimately evaporate. Borges says in his short story "The Life of Tadeo Isidoro Cruz (1829–1874)": "Any life, no matter how long or complex it may be, is made up essentially of a single moment—the moment in which a man finds out, once and for all, who he is." That summer day I understood my linguistic future lay in the opposite direction from Goldemberg's: I would perfect my English and thus become a New York Jew, an intellectual animal in the proud tradition celebrated by Alfred Kazin. And I did. In just a single moment I understood who I could be.

NORMAN MANEA

Now a professor and writer-in-residence at Bard College, Norman
Manea (born in 1936) fled his native Romania in 1986, after two decades
of life under Nicolae Ceauşescu and a childhood spent partly in a concentration camp. Given this history, it is perhaps no wonder that an ordinary
day on New York City's Upper West Side—as described in his 2003 memoir *The Hooligan's Return*—seems in some ways like a day in Paradise.
And yet in spite of the abundance that spills out onto the city's sidewalks, the exiled writer is by turns amused and haunted by recognitions
of contradiction, deracination, and loss—as if the past were inevitably
and uncannily present, or as if the present were entirely spectral.
Manea—whose works translated into English also include *On Clowns:
The Dictator and the Artist* (essays, 1992), *October, Eight O'Clock* (stories,
1992), *Compulsory Happiness* (novellas, 1994), and *The Black Envelope*
(novel, 1995)—writes less about Romania or his adopted United States
than about states of in-betweenness and the struggle to find a home in a
broken world. "Barney Greengrass" is from *The Hooligan's Return*. The
translation is by Angela Jianu.

Barney Greengrass

T he bright spring light, like an emanation from Paradise, streams through
the large picture window wide as the room itself. There is a man in the
room, looking down from his tenth-floor apartment at the hubbub below, at
the buildings, the shop signs, the pedestrians. In Paradise, he must remind
himself again this morning, one is better off than anywhere else.

Across the street is a massive red-brick building. His eye catches groups
of children going through their paces in dance and gym classes. Yellow lines
of taxicabs, stuck in traffic at the juncture of Broadway and Amsterdam
Avenue, are screaming, driven mad by the morning's hysterical metronome.

The observer, however, is now oblivious to the tumult below, as he scrutinizes the sky, a broad expanse of desert across which drift, like desert beasts, slow-moving clouds.

Half an hour later, he stands on the street corner in front of the forty-two-story building where he lives, a stark structure, no ornamentation, a simple shelter, nothing less, or more, than an assemblage of boxes for human habitation. A Stalin-era apartment block, he thinks. But no Stalinist building ever reached such heights. Stalinist nonetheless, he repeats to himself, defying the stage set of his afterlife. Will he become, this morning, the man he was nine years ago, when he first arrived here, bewildered now, as he was then, by the novelty of life after death? Nine years, like nine months brimming with novel life in the womb of the adventure giving birth to this brand-new morning, like the beginning before all beginnings.

On the left, the drugstore where he regularly buys his medicines. He is idly looking at the store's sign—RITE AID PHARMACY, spelled out in white letters on a blue background—where suddenly five fire engines, like metallic fortresses, advance on the street in a screech of sirens and horns. Hell's fires can rage in Paradise, too.

But it is nothing serious, and in an instant everything is back in place—the photo shop where he is having the photo for his new ID processed; the neighborhood diner; the local Starbucks; and, of course, a McDonald's, its entrance graced by a pair of panhandlers. Next come the Pakistani newsstand, the Indian tobacconist, the Mexican restaurant, the ladies' dress shop, and the Korean grocery, with its large bunches of flowers and displays of yellow and green watermelons, black and red and green plums, mangoes from Mexico and Haiti, white and pink grapefruit, grapes, carrots, cherries, bananas, Fuji and Granny Smith apples, roses, tulips, carnations, lilies, chrysanthemums. He walks past small buildings and tall buildings, a mixture of styles and proportions and destinies, the Babylon of the New World, and of the Old World, too. There is a population to match—the tiny Japanese man in a red shirt and cap, swaying between two heavy loads of packages; the fair-haired, bearded, pipe-smoking man in shorts, walking between two big blond female companions in pink shorts and dark sunglasses; the tall, slim barefoot girl, with cropped red hair, skimpy T-shirt, and shorts the size of a fig leaf; the heavy, bald man with two children in his arms; the short fat man with a black mustache and a gold chain dangling down his chest; beggars and policemen and tourists as well, and none seem irreplaceable.

He crosses to Amsterdam Avenue at Seventy-second Street and is now in front of a small park, Verdi Square, a triangle of grass bordered on three sides by metal railings and presided over by a statue of Giuseppe Verdi, dressed in a tailcoat, necktie, and hat, surrounded by a bevy of characters from his operas on which the placid pigeons of Paradise have come to rest. A scattering of neighborhood denizens sit on the nearby benches, the pensioners, the disabled, the bums swapping stories and picking at their bags of potato chips and slices of pizza.

There is nothing lacking in Paradise—food and clothing and newspapers, mattresses, umbrellas, computers, footwear, furniture, wine, jewelry, flowers, sunglasses, CDs, lamps, candles, padlocks, dogs, cars, prostheses, exotic birds, and tropical fish. And wave after wave of salesmen, policemen, hairdressers, shoeshine boys, accountants, whores, beggars. All the varieties of human faces and languages and ages and heights and weights people that unlikely morning, on which the survivor is celebrating the nine years of his new life. In this new Afterlife world, all the distances and interdictions have been abolished, the fruit of the tree of knowledge is available on computer screens, the Tree of Eternal Life offers its pickings in all the pharmacies, while life rushes at breakneck speed and what really matters is the present moment.

Suddenly hell's alarm bells break out again. No fire this time, but a white, roaring juggernaut leaving behind the blur of a blood-red circle with a red cross and red letters reading AMBULANCE.

No, nothing is missing in this life-after-death, nothing at all. He raises his eyes toward the heavens that allowed this miracle to happen. An amputated firmament it is, for the concrete rectangles of the buildings narrow the prospect to a chink of blue sky. The façade on the right, blocking the view, is formed by a brownish wall flanked by a waste pipe; on the left, a yellow wall. Against this golden background, spelled out in iridescent blue, is the message DEPRESSION IS A FLAW IN CHEMISTRY NOT IN CHARACTER. Warning, or mere information—hard to tell. DEPRESSION IS A FLAW IN CHEMISTRY NOT IN CHARACTER, displayed on five separate lines, one after the other.

He stares at the lines of sacred text, his head tilted backward. Jolted out of his reverie, he steps back and finds himself walking along Amsterdam Avenue again. There is an advantage to his new life—immunity. You are no longer chained to all the trivia, as in the previous life, you can walk on in indifference. He heads toward the restaurant/delicatessen Barney Greengrass, famous for its smoked fish. "The place will remind you of your previous life," his friend has promised.

The buildings along Amsterdam Avenue have been reclaimed from the past, old houses, reddish, brown, smoke-gray, four-five-six stories, iron balconies, fire escapes blackened by time. These streets of the Upper West Side, when he first encountered them, reminded him of the Old World. However, over the nine—or is it ninety?—years since he moved into the neighborhood, the tall buildings have multiplied, dwarfing even the forty-two stories of his apartment building to the proportions of a paltry Stalinist construction—there is that insidious adjective again.

On the ground floor of the building, the old shops, as before—Full Service Jewelers, Utopia Restaurant, Amaryllis Florist, Shoe Store, Adult Video, Chinese Dry Cleaning, Nail Salon, Roma Frame Art, and, at the corner of Seventy-sixth Street, Riverside Memorial Chapel. A young girl with thick legs and long dark hair, wearing a black short-sleeved dress, black stockings, and thick, dark sunglasses, comes out of the building. Three long black cars with darkened windows, like huge coffins, are parked at the curb. Out of them step smartly dressed gentlemen in black suits and black hats, elegant ladies in black dresses and black hats, teenagers in sober dress. Once more the metronome has struck the hour of eternity for some poor soul. Life is movement, he has not forgotten, and he hurries away. One step, two, and he is out of danger.

On the sidewalk in front of the venerable Ottomanelli Bros. meat market (SINCE 1900, a sign proclaims) are two wooden benches. An old woman sits on the one on the right. He collapses onto the other, keeping an eye on her. She stares vacantly into space, but he feels she is observing him. They seem to recognize each other. Her presence is familiar, as if he has felt it before on certain evenings, in certain rooms suddenly charged with a protective silence that would envelop him. Never has he felt this way in broad daylight amid the hubbub of the workaday world.

The old lady gets up from the bench. He waits for her to take a few steps, then follows her. He walks behind her in the slow rhythm of the past. He observes her thin legs, fine ankles, sensible shoes, cropped white hair, bony shoulders bent forward, her sleeveless, waistless dress, made of a light material in red and orange checks on a blue background. In her left hand, as in time before, she carries a shopping bag. In her right hand, as in time before, she holds a folded gray sweater. He overtakes her and makes a sudden turn. She gives a start. She probably recognizes the unknown man who had collapsed, exhausted, on the other bench at Ottomanelli's. They look at each other, startled. A ghost, out of the blue, on a bench, on a city sidewalk.

All is familiar—the gait, the dress, the sweater, the cropped white hair, the face half-seen in a fraction of a second. The forehead and the eyebrows and the eyes and the ears and the chin are all as before, only the mouth has lost its full contour and is now just a line, the lips too long, lacking shape; and the nose has widened. The neck sags, with wrinkled skin.

Enough, enough . . . He turns around and follows her from a distance. Her silhouette, the way she walks, her whole demeanor. You do not need any distinguishing marks, you always carry everything with you, well-known, immutable; you have no reason to follow a shadow down the street. He slows down, lost in thought, and the vision, as he had wished, vanishes.

Finally, at Eighty-sixth Street, he reaches his destination: Barney Greengrass. Next to the window, the owner sits sprawled in a chair, his hunched back and big belly enveloped in a loose white shirt with long sleeves and gold buttons. The neck is missing; the head, topped by a rich mane of white hair, is ample, the nose, mouth, forehead, and ears firmly drawn. On the left, behind the salami-halvah counter, stands a worker in a white coat. Another counterman tends the bread-bagels-buns-cakes section.

He greets the owner and the young man standing next to him, who has a telephone glued to each ear. Then he walks into the room on the left, the restaurant area. At the table next to the wall a tall, thin man with gold-rimmed spectacles raises his eyes from his newspaper and calls out the customary greeting: "How're you doing, kid?" A familiar face, a familiar voice. Exiles are always grateful for such moments. "What's up?"

"Not much. 'The social system is stable and the rulers are wise,'" as our colleague Zbigniew Herbert says. "'In Paradise one is better off than any-where else.'" The novelist, to whom these quotations are directed, is not keen on poetry, but luckily, it sounds more like prose.

"How are you? Tell me the latest. News from here, not from Warsaw."

"Well, I'm celebrating nine years of life in Paradise. On March 9, 1988, I was shipwrecked on the shore of the New World."

"Children love anniversaries, and Barney Greengrass's is the ideal place for such things. It has all the memories of the ghetto, pure cholesterol, *Oy mein Yiddishe mame.* The old world and the old life."

He hands me the plastic-covered menu. Yes, the temptations of the ghetto are all here: pickled herring in cream sauce, fillet of schmaltz herring (very salty), corned beef and eggs, tongue and eggs, pastrami and eggs, salami and eggs, homemade chopped chicken liver, gefilte fish with horseradish. The chicken liver is no pâté de foie gras, nor are incubator-bred American chickens East European chickens. The fish isn't like the fish of the Old World, the eggs aren't like the eggs we used to know. But people keep trying, and so here are the substitutes for the past. Russian dressing with everything, with roast beef, turkey . . . Yes, the myth of identity, the surrogates of memories translated into the language of survival.

A handsome young waiter approaches. He recognizes the famous novelist and says to him, "I've read your latest book, sir." Philip seems neither flattered nor upset by this greeting. "Indeed? And did you enjoy it?" He had, the waiter avowed, but not as much as the previous book, much sexier.

"Good, good," the novelist says, without raising his eyes from the menu. "I'll have the scrambled eggs with smoked salmon and orange juice. Only the whites, no yolks." The waiter turns to the customer's unknown companion. "What about you, sir?"

"I'll have the same," I hear myself mumbling.

Barney Greengrass offers acceptable surrogates of East European Jewish cuisine, but it is not enough to add fried onions or to affix bagels and knishes to the menu to produce a taste of the past.

"So, how did you like Barney's cuisine?"

No reply.

"Okay, you don't have to answer that. Are you going to go back to Romania or not, what have you decided?"

"I haven't decided anything yet."

"Are you afraid? Are you thinking of that murder in Chicago? That professor . . . what was his name? The professor from Chicago."

"Culianu, Ioan Petru Culianu. No, I'm not in the least like Culianu. I am not a student of the occult like Culianu, nor, like him, have I betrayed the master, nor, like him, am I a Christian in love with a Jewish woman and about to convert to Judaism. I'm just a humble nomad, not a renegade. The renegade has to be punished, while I . . . I am just an old nuisance. I cannot surprise anybody."

"I don't know about surprises, but you've been quite a nuisance occasionally. A suspect, becoming more suspicious. This is not to your advantage."

Professor Ioan Petru Culianu had been assassinated on the twenty-first of May 1991, in broad daylight, in one of the buildings of the University of Chicago. A perfect murder, apparently—a single bullet, shot from an adjacent stall, straight into the professor's head, as he sat on the plastic seat in the staff toilets of the Divinity School. The unsolved mystery of the assassination had, naturally, encouraged speculation—the relations between the young Culianu and his mentor, the noted Romanian scholar of religion Mircea Eliade, with whose help he had been brought to America; his relations with the Romanian community of Chicago, with Romania's exiled King, his interest in parapsychology. There was, in addition, the Iron Guard connection, that movement of extreme-right-wing nationalists whose members were known as *legionari*, the Legionnaires. The Iron Guard, which Mircea Eliade had supported in the 1930s, still had adherents among the Romanian expatriates of Chicago. It was said that Culianu was on the verge of a major reassessment of his mentor's political past.

The Chicago murder, it was true, coincided with the publication of my own article about Eliade's Legionnaire past, in *The New Republic*, in 1991. I had been warned by the FBI to be cautious in my dealings with my compatriots, and not only with them. It was not the first time I had talked about this with my American friend. Culianu, Eliade, Mihail Sebastian—Eliade's Jewish friend—these names had come up frequently in our conversations over the previous months.

As the date of my departure for Bucharest approached, Philip insisted that I articulate the nature of my anxieties. I kept failing. My anxieties were ambiguous. I did not know if I feared meeting my old self there, or if I feared bringing back my new image, complete with the expatriate's laurels and the homeland's curses.

"I can understand some of your reasons," Philip says. "There must be others, probably. But this trip could cure you, finally, of the East European syndrome."

"Perhaps. But I'm not ready yet for the return. I am not yet indifferent enough to my past."

"Exactly! After this trip, you will be. Those who come back, come back healed."

We have reached the same old dead end. But this time, he persists.

"What about seeing a few old friends? A few old places? You did say you would be willing to see some of them, despite not being quite ready for it. Last week, you said something about going to the cemetery to visit your mother's grave."

A long pause follows. "I saw her again," I finally say. "This morning, half an hour ago. I was on my way here, and suddenly there she was, seated on this bench, on Amsterdam Avenue, in front of Ottomanelli's."

We fall silent again. When we leave Barney Greengrass's, our conversation returns to familiar topics and resumes its jovial tone. We say goodbye, as we always do, at the corner of Seventy-ninth Street. Philip turns left, toward Columbus Avenue. I continue down Amsterdam to Seventieth Street and my non-Stalinist Stalinist apartment building.

ANITA DESAI

Born Anita Mazumdar in Mussoorie, India, in 1937, Anita Desai, the daughter of a Bengali father and a German mother, grew up speaking a number of languages: German, Bengali, Urdu, Hindi, and English. In 1957 she earned a bachelor's degree in English literature from the University of Delhi and published her first story. She wrote numerous works for adults and children in India before becoming a visiting fellow at Cambridge University in 1986 and immigrating to the United States the following year. She taught first at Smith and Mount Holyoke before joining the faculty at Massachusetts Institute of Technology where she is now John E. Burchard Professor of Humanities Emeritus. Desai's works include *Clear Light of Day* (1980), *In Custody* (1984), and *Fasting, Feasting* (1999)—all three short-listed for the Booker Prize for Fiction. In 1993 Merchant Ivory Productions released a film adaptation of *In Custody*, directed by Ismail Merchant.

Various Lives

For the sake of simplicity, I would like to say that I was born in India at a time when it was a meeting place for two cultures, Indian and British, but the truth is that these are merely umbrella terms, for both cultures were split into an infinitely larger number of spokes and panels that came together to form not an elegant object but a conveniently usable one. In my home in Old Delhi, a rambling old bungalow weighed down with bougainvilleas of the kind the British left behind all across their empire in Asia, we listened to my mother sing us German lullabies and play Schubert on her piano (always out of tune because warped by Delhi's ferocious temperatures) while my siblings and I spoke Hindi to each other and our neighbours, a Hindi that actually was mixed with Urdu to form—conveniently, usably—the hybrid Hindustani spoken in north India. We bicycled to school past the Nicholson Gardens and the

British cemetery where many of the stalwarts of the British Empire—and their more frail offspring—were buried. At Queen Mary's High School for Girls we sang hymns (curious, when one thinks of it, that the mild English missionaries who taught us so enjoyed hearing assemblies of a hundred or more girls, Hindu and Muslim every one of them, lustily and unthinkingly bellow "Onward Christian Soldiers"), and we played rounders and badminton in the playgrounds. In the evening we went for a walk to the Qudsia Gardens, where we played hide-and-seek amongst the tombs of emperors and empresses of the Moghul Empire mouldering under the palm trees, or to the Jumuna River, where at twilight the bells of the temples along the riverbank clanged and banged while we played in the sands till dark. We came home and read for the hundredth time our treasured copies of the works of Dickens, the Brontë sisters, Wordsworth and Milton, or old copies of comic books like Superman and Beano that we had bought with our pocket money in the arcades of Connaught Circus. Or we listened to my mother tell us one of Grimm's fairy tales or of Christmastime or Easter in Germany, or heard my father talk of his childhood among the rivers and rice fields of Bengal, so far to the east and in the past as to be quite mythical.

So for me the European section of the umbrella had panels made up of both colonial Britain and the more distant, less physical world of my mother's prewar Germany while the Indian section had stripes that were Hindu—festivals, dress, food—and also Muslim—other festivals, foods, and dress. Was this ridiculous, this object that we held over our heads, fashioned by our motley ancestors? Was it schizophrenic?

We gave it little thought and got on with our lives. Its pied, patchwork structure seemed to us quite commonplace, normal. Turned upside down, we could use it to sail into wider seas, experience different worlds. And England, when I first visited it, seemed vaguely familiar, one knew what to expect—daffodils blowing on a hill, little dark pubs and red letterboxes; and in America the high rises, the neon lighting, the spaghetti of highways sprawling across the continent. And yet, and yet how confusing the actual experience proved. This world had been a part of my reading and my imagination, comfortably so, which made settling into the life of a visiting fellow at Cambridge University a dreamlike experience of recognition rather than the unsettling one of discovery. The latter was the experience that America provided when I arrived on this third continent to teach, initially at a small liberal arts college in western Massachusetts that was close to where two of my children were studying. This experience proved far more unsettling: India had prepared me for England but not, I found, for America.

I found it hard to understand what was said to me, and people found it equally hard to understand me. I could not make the switch from tom-ah-toe to tom-a-to or frag-ile to frag-il; my jaw was too stubborn, my tongue too stiff. Also I found that I laughed at things others considered serious and that they spoke at length of matters I would not think of divulging in public. I was a foreigner. Mystified, I observed other foreigners—of a younger generation— brought up not on literature but on the common currency of movies and pop music, who on arrival jumped in feet first, laughing with confidence, and bobbed up fully baptised first-generation Americans. I was too old for this, my joints too stiff: When I tried to pump gas or pour myself coffee in a busy cafeteria, all my fingers turned to thumbs, distressingly. It was a chastening experience to find myself, at my age, a callow beginner. I studied once again Mark Twain's *Huckleberry Finn*, Nabokov's *Lolita*, Frost's austere poems, Eugene O'Neill's great tragedies. I prowled the streets, looking through the big picture windows I passed at lighted interiors. The sounds of lawnmowers, of boom boxes in passing cars, the smoke and smells of summer barbecues were items I studied anxiously for clues. But a glass pane separated us; I found myself trying to lip-read, puzzled.

Every few months I returned to India. It was comforting to put my feet into slippers again, dress in old soft cotton clothes, know what everyone was saying, or leaving unsaid, or thinking. But I could also see that my American experience had interposed itself between us, created an unease. Here too I was on the outside now, looking in. So much had happened while I was away, so much that I had not experienced or participated in, and I no longer had the right to comment. And while some things remained unchanged, stood still— the family, the circle of friends, the way of life—so much else had changed or was in flux—the economy, the media and, above all, the politics of the time. Fluid, volatile, powerful, they were carrying everyone in their tide, except myself. I was not part of it and did not understand it.

How can one write of scenes and worlds one does not understand? One may write of one's bewilderment, but that has its limitations. And these scenes, these times have their own writers to interpret them, writers whose materials it rightfully is. I had neither the experience nor the understanding nor even the language to tackle this new territory. Both the old and the new territory could equally well do without my contribution. Having plunged off one coast, I had not really arrived on another. Instead I found myself floundering midway; like the person in Stevie Smith's poem, "I was much further out than you thought / And not waving but drowning."

Yet other writers had traveled, had found their new worlds rich, challenging, and rewarding—even more so than the ones they had left, sometimes. E. M. Forster's greatest book was the one he wrote about India, Henry James's greatest books his European ones, Nabokov's masterpiece American. Joseph Brodsky and Czeslaw Milosz had even taken to writing their poetry in their adopted language. How, I wanted to know, how?

It was evidently true that the experience of travel, the novelty of the scenes you visited, could lend your writing a certain vividness, like scenes lit up by flashes of lightning in the dark. But you also needed a language for these unfamiliar places and experiences; the old language did not always do. What I knew was the literary language—and it had sufficed in England, where it had originated; what was proving difficult to master was the living one into which it had evolved and that I now heard around me—and to a novelist it is this that is essential since it is the key that unlocks the world you struggle to describe.

In India I had picked up words, languages, customs, costumes, and cuisines from the litter left behind by the tides of history as a magpie might pick up bright objects to line its nest. I wrote in English, that first language I had been taught to read and write by the missionary ladies of Queen Mary's School, but could not restrict myself to it; if I did, I was pursued by a sense of leaving other parts of my tongue locked, unused. What about the Indian languages I used every day? What about German, my "family secret"? It created a lingual unease, this need to bring them into my writing. And yet my work needed to be comprehensible to readers who did not share my precise inheritance. For that, my prose had to be as clear as a pane of glass, transparent.

Perhaps that was the key: to use transparency so that it would allow the buried languages, the hidden languages, to appear beneath the glass of my prose.

I first consciously attempted to do that in *In Custody*, a novel about an Urdu poet, Nur. Now, Urdu is a gorgeously rich language in its sounds—Zindagi for Life! Zamana for Time!—but its literary tradition is also strict, formal. In writing about a poet, and concocting poetry I attributed to him, I had to write verses in English that echoed their Persian origin. I employed traditional images and metaphors and tried to follow the Persian verse forms in lines such as:

> Night ends, dawn breaks, and sorrow reappears,
> Addressing us, in morning light, with a cock's shrill crow.

and:

> The breeze enters, the blossom on the bough wafts its scent.
> The opened window lets in the sweet season, Spring.

I was immensely gratified by a scolding I received: "You really should have acknowledged the poet you quoted; why is there no acknowledgment?" But it was accompanied by a rumble of unease: I knew, even if the person who scolded me did not, that it was only pastiche, not poetry. The greatest gratification actually came about when these verses were translated into Urdu by the Urdu translator who adapted the screenplay I wrote for the Urdu version filmed by Ismail Merchant. Hearing the translated lines spoken, I felt myself translated into an Urdu poet—a surreal experience.

Then there was the German strand in my linguistic being: I searched for years and years for a subject that would allow me to use German in an Indian setting, the German buried, hidden, locked up within me. I could not use a German subject—I had never lived in that country even if I grew up singing "Hoppe, hoppe Reiter" and quoting Goethe's line "Kennst du das Land . . . ?"

Finally I found him: Baumgartner. His name dropped out of a tree and struck me on the head as I walked in Lodi gardens in Delhi on a dusty summer evening, and I went home and started writing a book about a German emigré who escapes from the Holocaust to India. This is how I have him react to the languages he hears in a foreign land:

He had had trouble recognising her language as English; it had seemed to him more like the seeds of a red hot chilli exploding out of its pod into his face. He mopped his face . . .

And:

He found he had to build a new language to suit these conditions— German no longer sufficed, and English was elusive. Languages sprouted around him like tropical foliage and he picked out words from it without knowing if they were English or Hindi or Bengali— they were simply words he needed: chai, khana, baraf, lao, jaldi, joota, chota peg, pani, kamra, soda, garee . . . what was this language he was wrestling out of the air, wrenching it around to his own purpose? He suspected it was not Indian, but India's, the India he was marking out for himself.

This Baumgartner, this golem, then became my guide. Like him I too wandered, quite haphazardly, into a world about which I knew nothing, that was totally foreign to me—or so I thought. Driven by a bitter, grey northern winter in search of light and colour to Mexico, I experienced a shock of recognition: This was India! Or, at any rate, an Indian world. True, its language was Spanish, its religion Christianity, but there was that same sense of history, of every stone being old and containing centuries of time. And so it was I went further still, south to Guatemala. This is the new continent I explore now and where I find myself at one time a stranger and a native. To live in that state one needs to make oneself porous and let languages and impressions flow in and flow through, to become the element in which one floats.

Once one has torn up one's roots, one becomes a piece of driftwood, after all, or flotsam. It is the tides and currents that become one's fluid, uncertain home.

I found it interesting that Brodsky chose as his final resting place Venice, that island in a lagoon where continents wash into each other, creating a confluence that belongs to poetry, to art and spirit rather than to humdrum reality. I understand that wish—to have the wash and flow of water as one's final home. It is a very Indian urge, after all.

ANYA ULINICH

Born in Moscow in 1973, Anya Ulinich immigrated to the United States with her family when she was 17. Living poor and isolated in Phoenix with "about 20 English words between the four of us," she began to feel she was also "living split in two." She soon learned to read, write, and speak English fluently and managed to graduate from the Art Institute of Chicago (she was a painter before she wrote), eventually earning an M.F.A. from the University of California at Davis. In 2000 she moved to Brooklyn where she began working on her first novel, *Petropolis* (2007), while raising two children. "The Nurse and the Novelist," the 2008 short story that follows, is an attack on what she calls "atrocity kitsch"—on the idea of characters who "fashion heaps of bones into tiny missing pieces of themselves."

The Nurse and the Novelist

1. The Butterfly

The entire book is set in two columns. The narrower one is in *italics. It tells a story of a village woman who falls in love with a boy hiding in her cellar.* The wider column is about a depressed young man. In his Manhattan apartment, the depressed young man keeps a jar of toenail clippings that he has been collecting since he was a boy. He doesn't know why he collects the clippings, and he hides the jar from his advertising executive girlfriend. One day, the young man is summoned to his grandfather's deathbed. The grandfather hands him a gold charm shaped like a wing of a butterfly. The charm bears the initials E. S. "Find Evgeniya," the grandfather whispers. "Who is Evgeniya?" the young man demands of his parents. Your grandfather is confused, his parents insist, the necklace most likely belonged to your granny Elaine, she adored asymmetric jewelry. But the S? The depressed young man loses sleep over the S. He takes the charm to a jeweler, who discovers miniature, unintelligible foreign writing along the wing's edge. The young man pesters his parents for grandfather's birthplace. Ah, but the village no longer exists. It is now a suburb of Minsk. The young man decides to travel there. He has never seen such devastation: crumbling apartment blocks, leaning adobe shacks, rusted debris among ten-foot-tall weeds. The young man rents an apartment in one of the buildings, and enlists a bright local boy as an interpreter. At first, no one remembers the Jews, or their village. Finally, the young man hears rumors of a shut-in, an old woman whom local children call the Witch. The Witch peers at the wing necklace through her keyhole, and opens the door. She is a tiny, emaciated woman. She leans heavily on a crutch, but her eyes shine with luminous resolve. She had rescued fourteen children of the Jews. She could have saved more if only their parents had trusted her, she explains. Why didn't they trust you, the young man asks. Think about it, the old woman says—people didn't know what was going to happen to them. They considered it safer to keep their children by their side rather than give them to a stranger. The young man starts to cry. Magical realism kicks in, a man in the yard unlocks a dovecot, and the allegorical souls of the Jews soar above the Belarusian wasteland. "How is Mischa, my darling?" the old woman asks. The young man can't bear to speak the truth, to tell her that his grandfather is dead. Did his parents let you save him? "He was an orphan, and he was older, sixteen," the old woman answers. "I hope you don't mind me telling you, but we loved each other. He lived in my cellar by day and came out by night. We were lovers." The young man urges her to go on. "Then my husband came from the war. Mischa had to leave. The Germans were gone by then." The Witch gives the young man another charm, the left wing of the butterfly. "Now that you have come to me, I may die in peace," she adds. Back in his own apartment, the young man hears screaming and cries through the wall. Soon, he realizes that a human smuggling operation is happening next door. Three young girls are held captive and beaten. The young man rescues the most beautiful one and takes her to a women's shelter, where he falls in love with a scrappy social worker. Together, they return to the States. A year later, they have a baby girl. They name her Evgeniya. As the young man hangs the butterfly necklace, now complete, on little Evgeniya's chest, it becomes clear to him why he has been collecting nail clippings in a jar all along, and he is able to stop.

2. What Happened to Felix

Officially, my grandmother's apartment building is called Greenway Views, but everyone calls it the Cliff, for the way its massive towers jut out over the Brooklyn-Queens Expressway. These days, my grandmother is mostly confined to her sixth floor apartment in the Cliff, but ages ago she had been a young woman in the Russian city of Leningrad.

Grandma Rita was beautiful, with thin arched eyebrows and soft wavy hair. My grandfather Dima, on the other hand, had always been homely. He had protuberant watery eyes, saucer ears, and an overbite. However, he was brilliant, witty, and successful. Now, their friend Felix was so handsome that I caught my twelve-year-old daughter, Nina, sleeping with his photo under her pillow. I don't blame her: I did the same at her age. Rita, Dima, and Felix met during their third year at Leningrad University, and became inseparable. There is a photograph of the three of them, leaning on the parapet above the Neva. Felix is holding a bicycle.

Dima was in the physics department, Rita studied biology, and Felix was a violinist. The family legend is that my grandfather, who died when I was twenty, had been in love with my grandmother since the moment he first laid eyes on her. Grandma Rita doesn't dispute the legend, though she never talks about her own early feelings for my grandfather. Here is the story she does tell, sipping Snapple in her apartment in the Cliff. They just finished the university when the war started. Dima, with his excellent grades and his science background, was designated a "worker valuable for the Motherland," and shipped off to Siberia to head the production floor in a weapons plant. Felix was drafted to the front. My grandmother remained in Leningrad.

All three survived the war. In the summer of 1945, Felix returned from the front. By then, Dima had come back, too. There was a party at Felix's parents' apartment. It was a small party: just Rita, Dima, Felix, and two other friends. According to my grandmother, Felix's parents had a very nice apartment. They had a beaded chandelier and a seven-string guitar that hung on the wall with a silk bow tied around its neck. No one had touched the guitar in four years, but during the party Felix picked it up, tuned it, and played romansy. ("I used to enjoy music," grandma Rita says. My father disagrees.

He had never heard music in his parents' house. They didn't own a record player. "Before your time," grandmother objects.) Everyone drank spirt. When they were quite drunk, Felix showed them a souvenir he'd brought from the front: a German leaflet he'd found in the battlefield—the kind that the enemy threw down from airplanes. "Comrade Fighters," it said, in Russian. "Following Stalin's orders will lead to your annihilation! Choose while you still have the choice. Cross over to freedom!" They laughed at the leaflet's arrogance—Berlin lay in ruins, and they were drinking and singing in Leningrad.

"Afterwards, Dima left, and Felix and I went for a walk," grandmother says.

Expressway traffic sounds like the surf below the Cliff. A fly lands on the edge of the Snapple bottle. My grandmother picks up a sugar cube and gingerly places it between her four remaining teeth. Lately, all she seems to be eating is Snapple and sugar cubes, trying to consume energy in its purest, most efficient form. Nina says that old age is evolution backwards. She also says that shopping should be illegal, and that she wishes she were never born. As much as I love my daughter, her utterances couldn't contain less meaning if they were randomly generated by a computer.

"We spent the night by the river," grandma Rita tells me. The next morning, Felix disappeared. His hysterical mother told Rita that he was arrested for disseminating enemy propaganda. Three months later, my grandmother married my grandfather.

"Dima was persistent. He treated me like his treasure. All his life. He went to Iran in the '60s. Everyone in his delegation was bringing back rugs, things for the home. Not him—he brought this." Grandma points to a gold ring with an emerald that she always wears. The ring is approximately the size, and, I imagine, the weight, of a human eyeball. "When my mother got sick, Dima took care of her. He came from work, fed and washed her—every night, while I couldn't bear. He was an extraordinary person."

"What about Felix?" I ask.

Grandma shrugs, and her stare turns glassy. A fire truck screeches below the Cliff. "Those were difficult times," she says.

3. Sunset Bleu

Last year, a new condominium building grew in the weeded lot next to the Cliff. On summer nights, residents of the Cliff set up folding tables and play dominos on the sliver of brown grass between the buildings, shouting over the traffic din. Small boys, trusted with buying chips and beer for the grown-ups, dash between the cars at the mouth of the BQE onramp on their way to a bodega. The residents of Sunset Bleu condominiums are outdoorsy people —Bianchis and Specializeds hang like colorful vines over the railings of their undersized balconies. But they never seem to appear on the ground. On hot spring nights, they stew in their loft-like apartments, watching their toddlers bounce around angular mid-century furniture.

The novelist lives there too. He is about my age. He has the body of a man who spends too much time at Daddy-and-Me classes, but his face still looks like his jacket photo. I was out with my grandmother when I spotted him at ShopRite buying a mop, and introduced myself.

He inquired where my grandmother was from. His twins were screaming in the jogger. I said I had a story for him, if he wanted to get coffee. That Satur-day, we met at Hubcap—a coffee house that, when I was a kid, used to be an auto repair place that blasted Spanish music all the way down the block and infused sidewalk puddles with happy rainbows of gasoline. This time, the block's soundtrack was a loop of Edith Plaf and Radiohead. I told the novel-ist about my grandparents and Felix, and asked if he'd like to come to my place to look at old photographs. At home, I poured us both scotch, and then another, and we lay side by side on my bed, not touching, but knowing that it would only be a matter of time before we did, simply because his toddlers were not there, Nina was away, and the fan was blowing in the window. In-stead, we just fell asleep.

We woke up sweaty and middle-aged.

My ex was a serious man, I told the novelist. We got married and had Nina right after college. He went on to get his Ph.D. in English, while I always worked as a nurse. It made me happy to be a family provider. For years, as part of his course work, my husband read novels about dictators, real and imaginary. I read a couple, on his recommendation. In both of them, a chump from the dictator's inner circle contemplated a minute, private act of courage (squeaking against the rape of his daughter in one; loving the wrong girl in another), and was immediately crushed, the daughter raped, the girl kidnapped, the chump left for dead in a public toilet pit before he even knew what hit him. These stories reminded me of jogging on a track, or of life itself—you ended up exactly where you began. Frankly, I had no patience for them. Coming home from the night shift, my swollen ankles spilling over the straps of my Mary-Jane clogs, I needed stories of journeys from point A to point B, so I read your books.

The novelist grinned.

Right before my husband left, he started reading your books too. But he was a snob. I think he felt your novels were beneath him, because he sneaked them. He took them to the bathroom hidden inside *Harper's*. After a while, he became addicted, though he was still ashamed. I caught him wrapping *The Butterfly* in a newspaper before he left for the subway. And then he left me for one of his grad students.

The novelist's smile stiffened. You know, there is one thing I vowed never to write about: divorce. It's so fucking boring.

Let me tell you a few things, I said.

Jewelry gets lost very easily. I mean, these are tiny things.

Where no one remembers the Jews, no one remembers the Jews.

But here is the main reason why my husband was ashamed of carrying your books, I think. In your novels, past calamities are nothing but milestones of self-discovery. The central question is: "Why am I collecting toenails in a jar?" It only takes a village of dead Jews to figure it out. Your characters are monsters who fashion heaps of bones into tiny missing pieces of themselves. My husband was not a selfish man, who was preparing to commit what he saw as a selfish act. He must have found *The Butterfly* a real celebration of narcissism, a tutorial of sorts.

The novelist sat up and coughed into his fist. I've got to go, he sighed. Did you want to show me some photos?

But listen, there is more to the story, I said. During the blockade of Leningrad, my grandmother worked at Vavilov's seedbank. Have you ever heard of it? No doubt a novel or two has been written about the heroes who worked there—several starved to death among the seeds but didn't eat a single one, preserving the genetic wealth of the world's largest collection. Well, my grandma Rita snacked on Vavilov's seeds. She boiled Vavilov's roots for lunch, and made soup with Vavilov's bulbs for dinner. She was hungry and didn't care about biodiversity. Then she married a man who sent his rival to near-certain death. In your books, people like her normally kill themselves, don't they? Because if they didn't, how would your characters discover what's really important in life and solve the riddle of their neuroses?

You need therapy, the novelist said. Seriously, have you ever tried . . .

Just listen to me for a second, I said. I lived in Russia until I was eleven. Then, it was still the Soviet Union. In school, we read stories and watched films about young heroes, our would-be role models. Fourteen-year-old Zina Portnova, for instance, poisoned German officers' food at her cafeteria job. To avoid blowing her cover, she ate the poisoned soup and miraculously survived. Later, she was arrested. At an interrogation, she grabbed a gun from the desk, shot two Gestapo men dead, fled, was captured, savagely tortured, and killed. Or take the friggin Eaglet. At the end of the movie, he's hiding out in a field, saving the last hand grenade to blow himself up. We had to write essays about these children. In conclusion we had to state that, should our country be in peril again, we would act in a similar manner. Anything different would earn a lower grade. These writing lessons terrified me. I felt completely alone. I was convinced that all of my classmates were calmly planning to withstand torture, while I knew that I would become a collaborator the minute some Nazi yelled at me.

No one knows for sure, the novelist said.

I asked him if he can ever stop lying.

In my daughter's room, I found the picture of Felix tucked into Nina's diary. The photo smells of incense, just like all of Nina's possessions lately. The contours of Felix's face come together like the novelist's storylines. It's no wonder he didn't survive. I handed the picture to the novelist.

He could still be alive, he suggested. And what if it wasn't your grandfather who betrayed him?

Uh-huh. You can write that, I told him.

I haven't seen the novelist since. Then I read that he got mugged in the lobby of Sunset Bleu (someone followed him into the building), put the condo on the market, and moved to Woodstock. His latest book was a moving tale of love and forgiveness written from the point of view of a dog lost in the aftermath of Katrina.

4. The Novelist

Things have been so much better for Jen and me since we moved upstate. To be honest, I grew up in the Midwest, and always had a real ambivalent relationship with the city. On one hand, it's beautiful. On the other hand, it can be a kind of hell. There are things I've done that I'm not particularly proud of, and, well, I have never told Jen about. Like the time I almost slept with this creepy, geeky nurse I met at a supermarket.

ALEKSANDAR HEMON

In early 1992, when Serbian nationalist forces began their march into Bosnia, Aleksandar Hemon (born in 1964)—a young journalist from Sarajevo—happened to be visiting Chicago on an exchange program. He applied successfully for political asylum, worked odd jobs (including two years as a canvasser for Greenpeace), got an M.A., and by 2000 had published his first book in English, a story collection, *The Question of Bruno.* In *Nowhere Man* (2002), the novel from which the following excerpt is taken, protagonist Jozef Pronek, another Sarajevan, finds himself reluctantly drawn back into violent Old World antipathies as he tries to get ahead in the Chicago he now calls home. Like Hemon, Pronek refuses to identify himself as "Muslim" or otherwise; he is simply Sarajevan, "complicated." Fears of the kind of "Balkanization" that descended on the post-Yugoslav world in the 1990s haunt discussions of assimilation and ethnic identity in the United States. Hemon continues to write in his native Bosnian (or Serbo-Croatian) as well as in English. He was a 2004 MacArthur Fellowship winner, and has published *The Lazarus Project* (novel, 2008) and *Love and Obstacles* (stories, 2009).

from

Nowhere Man

The slumbering guard, about to slide off his chair, had his fingers on the holstered revolver. Pronek passed him by, pushed the grill door aside, and stepped into the elevator. The elevator was rife with a woman's fragrant absence: peachy, skinny, dense. Pronek imagined the woman who might have exuded that scent, and she was worth a stare. She was tall and rangy and strong-looking; her hair was black and wiry and parted in the middle; she had black eyes and a sulky droop to her lips. She took a cigarette out of her purse, which was heavier than it needed to be, turned to him and said, expecting a friendly lighter: "I've been searching for someone, and now I know who."

Pronek's eyes narrowed as he looked at the space where the woman would have stood, and he saw himself through her eyes: tall, formerly lanky, so his relaxed movements did not match his fat-padded trunk; his head almost shaved, marred by a few pale patches (he cut his own hair); a gray sweatshirt that read ILLINOIS across his chest; worn-out jeans with a few pomegranate-juice splotches; and boots that had an army look, save for the crack in his left sole—September rains had already soaked his left sock. As he stepped out of the elevator, a whiff of the fragrant cloud followed him out. He stood in the empty hall: on the left and on the right, there were rows of doors standing at attention in the walls. Above a door on the right was a lit exit sign. Pronek made an effort to remember the position—in case he was too much in a hurry to wait for an elevator. He was looking for office number 909 and decided to go right. The colorless carpet muffled his careful steps. The elbow-shaped hall reeked of bathroom ammonia and sweet cigars, and the fragrant whiff dissipated in it. Pronek tried to open the bathroom door—green, sturdy, with a silhouette of a man—but it was locked. When he pushed the door with his shoulder, it rattled: he could break it open without too much force. He figured that there would be fire stairs behind a milky bathroom window, and that the alley would lead to Michigan Avenue, where he could safely disappear in the street mass.

All of a sudden, Pronek became aware of a sound that had been in his ears for a while but not quite reaching his brain: it was a smothered, popping sound—first one, then two—with a click at the end. Much like the sound of a gun with a silencer. Pronek's muscles tensed and his heart started thumping like a jungle drum—he was convinced that the hall was echoing his accelerating pulse. He felt his eyebrows dewing, thick loaves of pain forming in his calves. He tiptoed past the doors: 902 (Sternwood Steel Export); 904 (Marlowe Van Buren Software); 906 (Bernard Ohls Legal Services); 908 (empty); 910 (Riordan & Florian Dental Office)—the popping, along with the murky light, came from behind the dim glass of 910. Pronek imagined bodies lined up on the floor facedown, some of them already dead, with their blood and hair on the wall, their brains bubbling on the carpet. They were shivering, waiting for a quiet man with a marble-gray face to pop them in their napes, knowing they would end up in unmarked graves. They reacted to the surprising bullet with a spasm, then death relaxation, then their blood placidly soaking the carpet. There was another pop. There had been at least six of them, and Pronek reckoned that the killer must be running out of bullets. It was risky, it was none of his business, so he twisted the door handle and peeked in.

A large man in a yellow helmet was pressing his orange staple gun against the far wall. He sensed Pronek and turned around slowly. His skin was pale and he needed a shave. He had dirty overalls and a green shirt underneath, with tiny golf balls instead of buttons. He stood firmly facing Pronek, his jaw tense, as if expecting a punch, his staple gun pointing to the floor. "Can I help you with something?" he said, frowning under his helmet. Pronek could see his eyebrows almost encountering each other above his nose. "Sorry," Pronek said. "I look for the office 909."

Office 909 had a sign that read GREAT LAKES EYE and a black-and-white eye with long, upward-curling eyelashes. Pronek hesitated for a moment before knocking at the door—his fingers levitated, angled, in front of the eye. Pronek knocked, using three of his knuckles, the glass shook perilously, then he opened the door and entered an empty waiting room. There was another door, closed, and there were magazines strewn on the few chairs, even on the musty floor, as if someone had searched through them all. The waiting room was lit by a thin-necked lamp in the corner, leaning slightly as if about to snap. There was an underdeveloped cobweb without a spider in the upper left corner. A picture of an elaborate ocean sunset—as if somebody lit a match under the water—hung on the opposite wall. ACAPULCO, it said in the lower right corner, WHERE YOU WANT TO DREAM. Pronek stood in front of the picture, imagining himself playing the guitar on a beach in Acapulco, tears welling up in his eyes.

The door opened and a man and a woman came out. They were laughing convivially with someone who remained invisible. The man—tall and black —put on a fedora with a little bluish feather, which went perfectly with his dapper navy blue suit, snug on his wide shoulders, and his alligator boots with little explosions on his toes. The woman was pale and slim, with blond boyish hair and a pointy chin. She had a tight, muscular body, like a long-distance runner, and a beautiful lean neck. She kept the tip of her finger on her chin as she listened to the man inside, who said: "What you wanna do is get some pictures." Pronek imagined touching gently the back of her neck, below the little tail of hair on her nape, and he imagined the tingle that would make her shudder. "You bet," the woman said, stepping out of the waiting room, barely glancing at Pronek. "You got yourself a client, Owen," the dapper man said, following the woman, and a head sprung out of the door, eyes bulging to detect Pronek. "Gee, a client," the head said, and the couple giggled as they closed the door. "Why don't you come in."

Pronek followed the man inside, closing the croaking door behind him. The room was bright, its windows looking at Grant Park and the dun lake beyond it, waves gliding toward the shore. There was a sofa with a disintegrating lily pattern and a coffee table with a chess board on it. Pronek landed in the sofa and the fissures between the cushions widened and gaped at Pronek's thighs.

"My name is Taylor Owen," the man said.

"I am Pronek," Pronek said. "Jozef Pronek."

"Good to meet you, Joe," Owen said.

Owen had sweat shadows under his armpits and a hump on his back, as if there were a pillow under his beige shirt. His tie was watermelon red, tightly knotted under his Adam's apple, which flexed sprightly like a Ping-Pong ball as he spoke. He was bald, with a little island of useless hair above his forehead and a couple of grayish tufts fluffing over his ears. He sat behind a narrow desk piled with papers, the back of his head touching the wall as he leaned in his chair.

"I called. I talked to somebody," Pronek said, "about the job. I thought you need the detective."

"The detective?" Owen chortled. "Lemme guess: you seen a few detective movies, right? The Bogart kind of stuff?"

"No," Pronek said. "Well, yes. But I know it is not like that."

Owen stared at him for a long instant, as if deciding what to do with him, then asked: "Where you from?"

"Bosnia."

"Never heard of it."

"It was in Yugoslavia."

"Ah!" Owen said, relieved. "It's a good place not to be there right now."

"No," Pronek said.

"You a war veteran?"

"No. I came here just before the war."

"You have a blue card?"

"What?"

"You have any security experience?"

"No."

"See, son, we don't have detectives around here no more. Detectives are long gone. We used to be private investigators, but that's over too. We're operatives now. See what I mean?"

"Yeah," Pronek said. There was a black-and-gray pigeon on the windowsill, huddled in the corner, as if freezing.

"No Bogey around here, son. I been in this business for a good long time. Started in the sixties, worked in the seventies. Still work. Know what I mean?"

"Yeah."

"I worked when Papa Daley was running the Machine . . ."

The phone rang behind the parapet of papers, startling Pronek. Owen snatched the receiver out of its bed and said: "Yup." He turned away from Pronek toward the window, but looked over the shivering pigeon, out to the lake. It was a sunny day, cold and blustery still. The wind gasped abruptly, then pushed the windowpane with a thump, overriding the grumbling hum of Michigan Avenue. Above Owen's hump there was a picture of an army of bulls chasing a throng of men with red scarves down a narrow street. Some of the men were being trampled by bulls who didn't seem to notice them.

"You can kiss that sonovabitch good-bye," Owen said, throwing his feet up on the corner of his desk and rocking in his chair. "You're kidding me. Shampoo? You gotta be kidding me."

On the desk, there was a pile of letters ripped open, apparently with little patience, and a couple of thick black files. Owen scratched the hair island, the size of a quarter, with his pinkie, beginning to rock faster. The pigeon barely had its eyes open, but then it turned its head back and looked straight at Pronek, smirking. Pronek crossed his legs and tightened his butt muscles, repressing a flatulence.

"I know what you up against. It sure is tough. Join the rest of the fucking world." He listened for a moment. "Skip the wisecracks, darling, all right?"

The pigeon was bloated, as if there were a little balloon under the feathers. What if the pigeon was a surveillance device, Pronek thought, a dummy pigeon with a tiny camera in its head, pretending to be sick, watching them.

"All right, I'll see you after the fight tonight. Love ya too," Owen said, and hung up. He swung back on his chair toward Pronek, sighed and said: "My wife is a boxing judge. Can you believe that? A boxing judge. She sits by the rink, watching two guys pummel each other, counting punches. Hell, people think I'm making that up when I tell them."

"It's normal," Pronek said, not knowing what to say.

Owen opened a drawer in his desk, the drawer resisting with a bloodcurdling screech, and produced a bottle of Wild Turkey. He poured a generous gulp in a cup that had CHICAGO BULLS written around it, shaking his head as if already regretting his decision. He slurped from the cup and his face cramped, as if he had swallowed urine, then it settled down, a little redder now. He looked at Pronek, trying to see through him.

"So you wanna be an operative?"

"I would like to be," Pronek said.

"We don't solve big cases here. Rich women don't make passes at us. We don't tell off big bosses, and we don't wake up in a ditch with a cracked head. We just earn our daily bread doing divorces, checking backgrounds, chasing down deadbeat dads, know what I mean? It's all work, no adventure, pays the rent. Got it?"

"Yeah," Pronek said.

"Do you know where the Board of Education is?"

"In the downtown," Pronek said.

"Do you know where Pullman is?"

"No."

"Way south. Do you know where the Six Corners is?"

"No."

"Irving Park and . . . Oh, fuck it! Do you have a car?"

"No. But I want to buy the car." Pronek started fidgeting in his chair. A drop of sweat rolled down from his left armpit.

"Do you have a camera?"

"No."

"Do you know how to tail."

"Tale?" Pronek asked, perplexed. "You mean, tell the tale?"

Owen formed a pyramid with his hands and put its tip under his nose, then pushed his nose up a little, so the bridge of his nose wrinkled. He glared at Pronek, as if affronted by his sheer presence, curling his lips inward, until his mouth was just a straight line. Pronek wanted to tell him that he could learn, that he was really smart, that he used to be a journalist, talked to people—he could make himself over to be an operative. But it was too late: Owen was blinking in slow motion, gathering strength to finish the interview off. He dismantled the pyramid, unfurled his lips and said:

"Listen, son, I like you. I admire people like you, that's what this country is all about: the wretched refuse coming and becoming American. My mother's family was like that, all the way from Poland. But I ain't gonna give you a job just 'cause I like you. Gotta pay my rent too, know what I mean? Tell you what I'll do: give me your phone and I'll call you if something comes up, okay?"

"Okay," Pronek said.

Owen was watching him, probably expecting him to get up, shake hands and leave, but Pronek's body was suddenly heavy and he could not get up from the sofa. Nothing in the room moved or produced a sound. They could hear the ill cooing of the pigeon.

"Okay," Owen repeated, as if to break the spell.

Pronek stood at the corner of Granville and Broadway, watching his breath clouding and dissolving before his eyes, waiting for Owen. The picture-frame shop across the street had nicely framed Halloween paintings in the window —ghosts hovering over disheveled children, ghouls rising out of graves. The shop window was brightening as the sun was moving slowly out of the lake, most of it still underwater. A man with a rotund goiter growing sideways on his neck was entering the diner on Granville. Pronek thought that the man was growing another, smaller head and imagined a relief of a little, wicked face under the taut goiter skin. Across Broadway, they were tearing down a Shoney's: what used to be its parking lot was just a mud field now. The building was windowless; floors ripped out; cables hanging from the ceiling like nerves. Just in front of Pronek, a throbbing car stopped at the street light, inhabited by a teenager who had a shield of gold chains on his chest. He was drumming on the wheel with his index fingers, then looked up, pointed one of his fingers at Pronek, and pretended to shoot him. Pronek smiled, as if getting the joke, but then the teenager turned east and disappeared down Granville. Pronek was cold, Owen was late. A *Chicago Tribune* headline, behind the filthy glass of a newspaper box, read THOUSANDS KILLED IN SREBRENICA. In the distance, Pronek saw a boxy Broadway bus stopping every once in a while on the empty street, sunlight shimmering on its windshield.

Owen pulled up, materializing out of nowhere, brakes screeching, right in front of Pronek. He drove an old Cadillac that looked like a hideous off-spring of a tank and a wheel cart. Before Pronek could move toward the car, Owen honked impatiently, and the sound violated the early morning hum. Pronek opened the door, and an eddy of cigarette smoke and coffee smell escaped into the street. Owen said nothing, put the car in gear and drove off—a bus whizzed by, barely missing them. He drove with both of his hands on top of the wheel, alternately looking at the street and frowning at the tip of his cigarette as it was being transformed into its own ashen ghost. Finally, the ash broke off and fell into his lap. Owen said, as if on cue: "Damn, it's early. But what can we do? We gotta get this guy while he's home sleeping."

Pronek was silent, mulling over a question that would not require too many words. They were waiting at the light on Hollywood. The car in front of them had a bumper sticker reading: IF YOU DON'T LIKE MY DRIVING CALL 1–800–EATSHIT.

"Who is this man?" Pronek asked.

"He's a character, lemme tell you. He's Serbian, I believe. Been here for fifteen years or so, married an American girl, had a child, and then split after years of marriage. He's a runaway daddy, is what he is. Couldn't find the son-ovabitch, wouldn't show up in court, the lady couldn't get child support. I gotta get him to accept the court summons, so if he doesn't show up in court, we can get cops on his ass. Are you all like that over there, sonovabitches?"

He put out his cigarette in the ashtray already teeming with butts, a few of them falling on the floor. Pronek imagined himself snorting up all those ashes and butts: it would be a good way to exhort a confession under torture. He coughed nauseatedly.

"What are you?" Owen asked. "It's Serbs fighting Muslims over there, right? Are you a Serb or a Muslim?"

"I am complicated," Pronek said, and retched. The car was like a gas chamber, and Pronek felt an impulse to rise and breathe from the pocket of air just under the roof. "You can say I am the Bosnian."

"I don't give a damn myself, as long as you speak the same language. You speak the same language, right? Yugoslavian or something?"

"I guess," Pronek said.

"Good," Owen said. "That's what we need here. That's why I called you. You get the job done, you get sixty bucks, you're a happy man."

Owen lit another cigarette, snapped his Zippo shut, and inhaled solemnly, as if inhaling a thought. The hair island had developed into a vine growing out of his forehead, nearly reaching his eyebrows. He drove past Bryn Mawr, where a crew of crazies was already operating: a man who kept lighting matches over a bunch of cigarettes strewn on the pavement before him, muttering to himself, as if performing a recondite ritual; an old toothless woman in tights with a wet stain spreading between her thighs; a man with thick oversized glasses hollering about Jesus. They drove past the funeral home: a man in a black coat was unlocking the front door and adjusting the welcome mat, yawning all along—there must have been an early death. They stopped at Lawrence, then turned right.

As they were moving westward, Pronek felt the warmth of a sunbeam tickling his neck. The windshield had thick eyebrows of dirt and a few splattered insects under them. As if reading his mind, Owen said:

"Lemme ask you something: what's the last thing that goes through a fly's head as it hits the windshield?"

He glanced sideways at Pronek with a mischievous grin, apparently proud of his cleverness. "What is it?" he asked again, and slammed the brakes, honking madly at the car in front.

"I don't know," Pronek said. "I should have gone the other way."

"Went," Owen said.

"What?"

"Went. You say I should've went the other way." He slammed the brakes again. "But no, that's not what it is. Think again."

"I don't know."

"It's the ass. The last thing that goes through a fly's head as it hits the windshield is its ass." He started laughing, nudging Pronek, until his guffawing turned into coughing, and then nearly choking. They stopped at the Clark light and he thumped his chest like a gorilla, his vine of hair quivering, his throat convulsing.

Pronek realized that there was an entire world of people he knew nothing about—the early morning people. Their faces had different colors in the morning sunlight. They seemed to be comfortable so early in the morning, even if they were already tired going to work: he could tell they had had their breakfast, their eyes were wide open, their faces developed into alertness—in contrast to Pronek's daze: the itching eyes, the tense, tired muscles, the crumpled face, the growling stomach, the pus taste in his mouth, and a general thought shortage. The six A.M. people, the people who existed when Owen and his people were sleeping: old twiggy ladies, with a plastic cover over their meticulously puffed-up hair, like wrapped-up gray lettuce heads; old men in nondescript suits, obviously performing their morning-walk ritual; kids in McDonald's uniforms on their way to the morning shift, already burdened with the midday drowsihead; joggers with white socks stretched to their knees, who seemed to be running in slow motion; sales associates in black stockings, freshly made up, dragging screaming children into a bus; workers unloading crates of pomegranates onto a stuck-up dolly—they all seemed to be involved in something purposeful.

Owen completed his coughing, cleared his throat confidently, and asked: "You still have family there?"

"Where?" Pronek responded, confused by a sudden change in the communication pace.

"Phnom Penh, that's where! Wherever you're from, you still have folks there?"

"Yeah, my parents are still there. But they are still alive."

"Now, who's trying to kill them? I can never get this right. Are they Muslim?"

"No," Pronek said. "They are in Sarajevo. Some Serbs try to kill the Muslims in Sarajevo and Bosnia, and also the people who don't want to kill the Muslims."

"You probably gonna hate this sonovabitch then."

"I don't know yet," Pronek said. What if, he thought, what if he were dreaming this. What if he were one of those six A.M. people, just about to wake up, slap the snooze button, and linger a few more minutes in bed. Owen hit the brakes again, and Pronek slapped the dashboard, lest he go through the windshield. They were at Western: a Lincoln statue was making a step forward, worried as ever, his head and shoulders dotted with dried pigeon shit. "That sonovabitch lives around here," Owen announced. He crossed Western, almost running over a chunky businessman who was hugging his briefcase as he scurried across the street.

They parked the car on an empty street with two rows of ochre-brick houses facing each other. Owen adjusted his curl, adhering it to his dome. He was looking in the rearview mirror, his hump breathing on his back, his eyes shrunken because of the fuming cigarette in his mouth. The houses all looked the same, as if they were made in the same lousy factory, but the lawns were different: some were trimmed and orderly like soccer pitch; some had strewn litter, little heaps of dog turd, and wet leaves raked together. Owen pointed at the house that had a FOR SALE sign, like a flag, in front of it.

"What I want you to do," he said, handing him a stern envelope, "is to go to that door, ring the bell, and when he asks who it is, you talk to him in your monkey language and give him this. He takes it, you leave, I give you sixty bucks, we all happy and free. How's that?"

"That is fine," Pronek said, and wiped his sweaty palms against his pants. He considered getting out of the car, passing the house, and running away—it would take him forty minutes to walk back to his place.

"You all right?" Owen asked. "Piece of cake, just do it."

"What is his name?" Pronek asked.

"It's Branko something. Here, you can read it." He pointed at the envelope.

Pronek read: "Brdjanin. It means the mountain man."

"Whatever," Owen said, and excavated a gun from under his armpit—two black, perpendicular, steely rectangles, the nozzle eye glancing at Pronek. He looked at it as if he hadn't seen it for a while and offered it to Pronek: "You want it?"

"No, thanks," Pronek said. He wondered what would be the last thing going through his head.

"Nah, you probably don't need it," Owen said. "I'll be right here, caring about you."

Pronek stepped out of the car and walked toward the house. The number on the brass plate next to the door was 2345, and the orderliness of the digits seemed absurd against the scruffy house: blinds with holes, dusty windows, a mountain of soggy coupon sheets at the bottom of the stairs, blisters of paint on the faded-brown door with a red-letter sign reading NO TRESPASSING in its window. There was a squirrel sitting in an empty bird bath padded with damp leaves, watching him, with its little paws together, as if ready to applaud. Pronek walked up the stairs to the door, clenching the envelope, his heart steadily thumping. He pressed the hard bell-nipple, and heard a muffled, deep ding-dong. He looked toward Owen in the car, who looked back at him over the folded *Sun-Times*, with an eager pen in his hand. "If this is a detective novel," Pronek thought, "I will hear shooting now." He imagined going around the house, jumping over the wire fence, looking in, and seeing a body in the middle of a carmine puddle spreading all over the floor, a mysterious fragrance still in the air. Then running back to Owen, only to find him with a little powder-black hole in his left temple, his hand petrified under his armpit, too slow to save him. There was no doubt that he would have to find the killer and prove his own innocence. Maybe Mirza could come over and be his partner, they could solve the crime together. He rang the bell again. The squirrel moved to a better position and was sitting on a tree branch, watching him intently. "*Dobro jutro*," Pronek muttered, rehearsing the first contact with Brdjanin. "*Dobro jutro. Evo ovo je za Vas.*" He would give him the envelope then, Brdjanin would take it, confused by the familiarity of the language. Piece of cake.

But then he heard keys rattling, the lock snapping, and a bare-chested man, with a beard spreading down his hirsute front and a constellation of brown birthmarks on his pink dome—a man said: "What?" Pronek stared at him paralyzed, his throat clogged with the sounds of *dobro jutro*.

"What you want?" The man had a piece of lint sticking out of his navel and a cicatrice stretching across his stomach.

"This is for you," Pronek garbled, and handed him the envelope. The man snatched it out of Pronek's hand, looked at it, and snorted.

Should've went the other way.

"You no understand nothing," the man said, waving the envelope in front of Pronek's face.

"I don't know," Pronek said. "I must give this to you."

"Where you from?"

"I am," Pronek said reluctantly, "from Ukraine."

"Oh, *pravoslavni* brother!" the man exclaimed. "Come in, we drink coffee, we talk. I explain you."

"No, thank you," Pronek uttered. "I must go."

"Come," the man growled, and grabbed Pronek's arm and pulled him in. "We drink coffee. We talk."

Pronek felt the disturbed determination of the man's fingers on his forearm. The last thing he saw before he was sucked in the house by the man's will was Owen getting out of the car with an unhappy, worried scowl on his face.

As Pronek was walking in Brdjanin's onionesque wake, he saw a gun handle—gray with two symmetrical dots, like teeny beady eyes—peering out of his pants, which were descending down his butt. Brdjanin led him through a dark hall, through a couple of uncertainly closed doors, into a room that had a table in its center and five chairs summoned around it. On the lacy tablecloth, there was a pear-shaped bottle of reddish liquid with a wooden Orthodox cross in it. There were five shot glasses and a platoon of crushed McDonald's bags surrounding it.

"Sit," Brdjanin said. "Here."

"I must go," Pronek uttered, and sat down, facing a window. A fly was buzzing against the windowpane as if trying to cut through it with a minikin circular saw. There was an icon on the wall: a sad saint with a tall forehead and a triangular beard, his head slightly tilted under the halo weight, his hands touching each other gently.

"Sit," Brdjanin said, and pulled the gun out of his ass, only to slam it on the table. The five glasses rattled peevishly. The window looked out at the garden: there was a shovel sticking out of the ground like a javelin, next to a muddy hole and a mound of dirt overlooking it. Brdjanin sat across the table from Pronek, and pushed the gun aside. "No fear. No problem," he said, then turned toward the kitchen and yelled: *"Rajka, kafu!"* He put the envelope right in front of himself, as if about to dissect it. "We talk with coffee," he said.

A woman with a wrinkled, swollen face and a faint bruise on her cheek, like misapplied makeup, peeked in from the kitchen, pulling the flaps of her striped black-and-white bathrobe together, and then retreated. There was a din of drawers and gas hissing, ending with an airy boom.

"You Ukrainian," Brdjanin said, and leaned toward him, as if to detect Ukrainianness in his eyes. "How is your name?"

"Pronek," Pronek said, and leaned back in his chair.

"Pronek," Brdjanin repeated. "Good *pravoslav* name. *Pravoslavni* brothers help Serbs in war against crazy people."

Pronek looked at Brdjanin, whose beard had a smile crevice in the middle, afraid that a twitch on his face, or a diverted glance would blow his feeble cover. Brdjanin was staring at him enthusiastically, then pushed the envelope aside with contempt, leaned further toward Pronek, and asked fervently:

"You know what is this?"

"No," Pronek said.

"Is nothing," Brdjanin said, and thrust his right hand forward (the gun comfortably on his left-hand side), all his fingers tight together and his thumb erect, as if he were making a wolf hand-shadow. His thumb was a grotesque stump, like a truncated hot dog, but Pronek was cautious not to pay too much attention to it.

"You must understand," Brdjanin said. "I was fool, *budala*. Wife to me was whore, was born here, but was Croat. Fifteen years. Fifteen years! I go see her brothers, they want to kill me." He made the motion of cutting his throat with the thumb stump, twice, as if they couldn't kill him on the first try. "They Ustashe, want to cut my head because I Serb. Is war now, no more wife, no more brothers. My woman is Serb now, you brother to me now. I trust only *pravoslav* people now. Other people, other people . . ." He shook his head, signifying suspicion, and pulled his thumb across his throat again.

Pronek nodded automatically, helpless. He wanted to say that Croats are just like everyone else: good people and bad people, or some reasonable platitude like that, but in this room whatever it was he used to think just an hour ago seemed ludicrous now. He wanted the woman to be in the room with him, as if she could protect him from Brdjanin's madness and his cutthroat thumb stump. The room reeked of coffee and smoke, stale sweat and Vegeta, a coat of torturous, sleepless nights over everything. The woman trudged out of the kitchen and put a tray with a coffee pot and demitasse between the two of them, and then dragged her feet back, as if she were ready to collapse. Pronek looked after her longingly, but Brdjanin didn't notice. "This Serbian coffee. They say Turkish coffee. It's Serbian coffee," Brdjanin said, lit a cigarette and let two smoke-snakes out of his nostrils. Pronek imagined saving the woman from this lair, taking her home (wherever it may be) and taking care of her, until she recovered and regained her beauty, slouching somewhere in her heart now—and he would ask for nothing in return. Brdjanin slurped some coffee from his demitasse, then reached behind his chair and produced a newspaper. The headline said: THOUSANDS KILLED IN SREBRENICA.

"Killed?" Brdjanin cried. "No killed. Is war. They kill, they killed."

He threw the paper across the table and it landed right in front of Pronek, so he had to look at it: a woman clutching her teary face wrapped in a colorless scarf, as if trying to unscrew her head.

"Hmm," Pronek said, only because he thought silence might be conspicuous.

"You know what is this?" Brdjanin asked, and spurted out an excited flock of spit drops. "You know?"

"Nothing," Pronek mumbled.

"No, is not nothing. Is Muslim propaganda."

"Oh," Pronek said. Where was Owen? If Owen broke in now, taking out Brdjanin as he was trying to reach his gun, Pronek would run to the kitchen, grab the woman's hand, and escape with her. "Come with me," he would say. *"Podji sa mnom."*

"You know when bomb fall on market in Sarajevo?" Brdjanin asked, frowning and refrowning, sweat collecting in the furrows. "They say hundred people die. They all dolls, *lutke*. Muslims throw bomb on market. Propaganda! Then they put dolls for television, it look bad, like many people killed."

Pronek's mother had barely missed the shell. She had just crossed the street when it landed. She wandered back, dazed, and trudged through bloody pulp, torn limbs hanging off the still-standing counters, shell-shocked people slipping on brains. She almost stepped on someone's heart, she said, but it was a tomato—what a strange thing, she thought, a tomato. She hadn't seen a tomato for a couple of years.

"I have the friend," Pronek said, trying to appear disinterested, his heart throttling in his chest, "from Sarajevo. He says the people really died. His parents are in Sarajevo. They saw it."

"What is he?"

"He is the Bosnian."

"No, what is he? He is Muslim? He is Muslim. He lie."

"No, he's not Muslim. He is from Sarajevo."

"He is from Sarajevo, he is Muslim. They want Islamic Republic, many *mudjahedini.*"

Pronek slurped his coffee. The gun lay on the left-hand side, comfortably stretched like a sleeping dog—he wouldn't have been surprised if the gun scratched its snout with its trigger. Pronek could see the woman's shadow moving around the kitchen. Brdjanin sighed, and put both of his hands on the table, pounding it slowly as he spoke:

"How long you been here? I been here twenty years. I don't come from nowhere. I leave my parents, my sister. I come here. Good country, good people. I work in factory, twenty years. But not my country. I die for my country. American die for his country. You die for Ukraine. We all die. Is war."

Pronek looked out and saw Owen getting around the shovel, the paper and pen still in his hands, almost falling into the hole. Owen looked up at the window, saw Pronek and nodded upward, asking if everything was all right. Pronek quickly looked at Brdjanin, who was looking at his hand, gently hacking the table surface, muttering: "I Serb, no nothing."

"I must go," Pronek said. "I must go to work."

"You go." Brdjanin shrugged and stroked his beard. "No problem."

Pronek stood up. Brdjanin put his hand on the gun. Pronek walked toward the door. Brdjanin held the gun casually, no finger near the trigger. Pronek opened the door, Brdjanin behind him. It was the bathroom: a radiator was wheezing, a cat-litter box underneath was full of sandy lumps. As Pronek was turning around, slowly, Brdjanin grasped Pronek's jacket, his left hand still holding the gun, and looked at him: he was shorter than Pronek, with an exhausted yeasty smell, his eyes were moist green. He had a coffee shadow on the beard around his mouth. Pronek nodded meaninglessly, paralyzed with fear. Brdjanin bowed his head, saying nothing. Pronek could see the woman framed by the kitchen door, watching them. He looked at her, hoping she would come and save him from Brdjanin's grasp. She would come and embrace him and say it was all okay. But she was not moving, as if she were used to seeing men in a clinch. She had her hands in her robe pockets, but then took out a cigarette and a lighter. She lit the cigarette and Pronek saw the lighter flame flickering with uncanny clarity. She inhaled with a deep sough and tilted her head slightly backward, keeping the smoke in for the longest time, as if she had died an instant before exhaling. Brdjanin was sobbing: squeally gasps ending with stertorous, shy snorts, his shoulders heaving in short leaps, his hand tightening its grip on Pronek's jacket. Pronek imagined Brdjanin's gun rising to his temple, the index finger pulling the trigger in slow motion—a loud pop and brains all over Pronek, blood and slime, dripping down. The woman looked down, drained, her bosom rising, patiently not looking up, as if waiting for the two men to disappear.

"It is okay," Pronek said, and put his hand on Brdjanin's shoulder. It was sticky and soft, with a few solitary hairs curling randomly. "It will be okay."

"What the hell were you doing in there?" Owen asked curtly, standing at the bottom of the stairs with his hands on his hips. "I almost went in there shooting to save your ass."

Pronek descended the stairs. The sun was creeping up from behind the building across the street, making the black trees gray. The same squirrel stopped, now upside down, midway down a tree and looked at Pronek. It was skinny and its tail fluff was deflated—it was going to be a long winter.

"Did he take the thing?"

"Yeah," Pronek said. "But I don't think he cares."

"Oh, he'll have to care, believe you me, he'll care."

"There is the woman in there," Pronek said, wistfully.

"There always is," Owen said.

Owen patted Pronek on the back, and softly pushed him toward the car. All the weight of Pronek's body was in his feet now, and his neck hurt, as if it were cracking under his head. They walked slowly, Owen offered him a cigarette and Pronek took it. Owen held the lighter in front of Pronek's face, and Pronek saw the yellow flame with a blue root, flickering under his breath—he recognized with wearisome detachment that he was alive. He inhaled and said, exhaling:

"I don't smoke."

"Now you do," Owen said.

They drove up Western, past the cemetery wall, past the used car shops—cars glittering in the morning silence, like a timorous army. Owen turned on the radio: Dan Ryan was congested, Kennedy moving slowly, the day was to be partly cloudy, gusty winds, high in the fifties. They turned right on Granville. Pronek felt his muscles tense, a cramp in his fingers, as if they were transforming into talons, clutching the dollar bills Owen had given him.

"I used to know a guy like you in Vietnam," Owen said. "Never said a fucking word. Kept to himself. He was a sniper, popped them like bottles on a fence. He would sit in a tree camouflaged, for hours, not moving, not making a sound. Guess you get used to it. He'd watch a village, wait for Charlie to crawl out, and then bam! Once we were—"

"You can leave me here," Pronek said abruptly. "I'm the next block."

"Sure. Thanks again, man," Owen said, and pulled up. "I'll sure call if I have something for you. Okay?"

"Thanks," Pronek said, and got out of the car. The morning was crisp, with just enough snap in the air to make one's life simple and sweet. But he was sleepy, with the feeling that he had just spent time with someone who didn't exist, a feeling that was slowly turning into anger. Way down Broadway, there was a quick shimmer coming off a moving bus windshield. Pronek stood on the corner, letting his eyelids slide down like blinds, gathering strength before walking home. He looked at the Shoney's being razed, and imagined himself destroying it with a huge hammer, slamming the walls, ripping out pipes, until there was just a pile of rubble. And then he would go on, until there was nothing left.

LARA VAPNYAR

Lara Vapnyar (born in 1971) is another representative (along with Gary Shteyngart and Anya Ulinich) of the new generation of Russian emigré writers. Vapnyar immigrated from Moscow to Brooklyn in 1994, and like Ulinich she arrived with only a handful of English words. Thanks to a steady diet of television, Alice Munro, and Jane Austen, she soon acquired an excellent command of the language, and by 2002 had begun publishing her first stories in English. These were collected a year later in *There Are Jews in My House*, from which the following excerpt is drawn. Vapnyar's most recent book is *Broccoli and Other Tales of Food and Love* (2008).

Mistress

A t home, Misha did his homework in their long white kitchen, because in his mother's opinion this was the only place that had proper light for him to work and wasn't too drafty. For about a year, the four of them—he, his mother, his grandfather, and his grandmother—had been living in this one-bedroom apartment with unevenly painted walls, faded brown carpet, and secondhand furniture. Everything in the apartment seemed to belong to some-body else. Misha and his mother slept in the bedroom, Misha on a folding bed. The grandmother and grandfather slept on the sofa bed in the living room. Or rather it was the grandmother who slept, snoring softly. The grandfather seemed to be awake all night. Whenever Misha woke up, he heard the old man tossing and groaning or pacing heavily on the creaky kitchen floor.

In Russia, they'd had separate apartments. They even lived in different cities. His grandparents lived in the south of Russia, in a small town over-grown with apple and peach trees. Misha and his parents lived in Moscow. Then his father left to live with another woman. In Moscow, Misha had his own room, a very small one, not bigger than six square meters, where the wallpaper was patterned with tiny sailboats. Misha had his own bed and his own desk with a lamp shaped like a crocodile. His books were shelved neatly above the desk, and his toys were kept in two plywood boxes beside his bed. When his parents argued, they used to say, "Misha, go to your room!" But during the last months before his father left, they didn't have time to send him to his room. They argued almost constantly: they started suddenly, without any warning, in the middle of a matter-of-fact conversation, during dinner, or while playing chess, or while watching TV, and stopped after Misha had gone to bed, or maybe they didn't stop at all. Misha went to his room himself. He sat on a little woven rug between his bed and his desk, playing with his building blocks and listening to the muffled sounds of his parents yelling. He played very quietly.

Misha liked doing his homework, although he would never have admitted that. He laid out his glossy American textbooks so that they took up nearly the entire surface of the table. He loved coloring maps, drawing diagrams, solving math problems: he even loved spelling exercises—he was pleased with the sight of his handwriting, the sight of the firm, clear, rounded letters. Most of all, he loved that during homework time nobody bothered him. "Shh! Michael's studying," everybody said. Even his grandmother, who usually cooked dinner while Misha was studying, was silent, or almost silent—she quietly hummed a theme from a Mexican soap opera that she watched every day on the Spanish channel. Her Spanish was not much better than her English, but she said that in Mexican shows you didn't need words to understand what was going on. The other thing she loved to watch on TV was the weather reports, where you didn't need words either: a picture of the sun meant a good day, raindrops meant drizzle, rows of raindrops meant heavy rain. Misha's mother was against subscribing to a Russian TV channel, because she thought it would prevent them from adjusting to American life. For the same reason, she insisted that everybody call Misha "Michael." Misha's mother was well adjusted. She watched the news on TV, rented American movies, and read American newspapers. She worked in Manhattan and wore the same clothes to work that Misha had seen in the magazines in the waiting room, but her skirts were longer and the heels of her shoes weren't as high.

The problem with the homework was that it took Misha only about forty minutes. He tried to prolong it as much as he could. He did all the extra math problems from the section called "You Might Try It." He brought his own book and read it, pretending that it was an English assignment. He stopped from time to time as if he had a problem and had to think it over, but in truth he just sat there, watching his grandmother cook.

She took all these funny packages, string bags, plastic bags, paper bags, bowls, and wrapped plates out of the refrigerator and put them on the counter, never forgetting to sniff at each of them first. Then she opened the oven with a loud screech, gasping and saying, "Sorry, Michael," took out saucepans and skillets, put them on the stove, filled some of them with water and greased others with chicken fat (she always kept some chicken fat handy, not trusting oil). While the saucepans and skillets gurgled and hissed on the stove, the grandmother washed and chopped the contents of packages and bowls, using two wooden boards—one for meat, the other for everything else. Misha always marveled at how fast her short and swollen fingers moved. In a matter of seconds, handfuls of colorful cubes disappeared in the saucepans and skillets under chipped enameled lids. "I was wise," the grandmother often said to her waiting-room friends. "I brought all the lids here. In America, it's impossible to find a lid that fits." The women agreed, something was definitely wrong with American lids.

To make ground meat, the grandmother used a hand-operated metal meat-grinder, also transported from Russia. She had to summon the grandfather into the kitchen, because the grinder was too heavy. She couldn't turn the handle herself; she couldn't even lift it. The grandfather put his newspaper down and came in obediently, shuffling his slippered feet as he walked, with the same tired, resigned expression that he had worn when he followed the grandmother home from the Russian food store, carrying bulging bags printed with a stretched red THANK YOU. He took off his dark checkered shirt and put it on the chair. (The grandmother insisted that he do that. "You don't want pieces of raw meat all over your shirt!") He put an enameled bowl of meat cubes in front of him and secured the grinder on the windowsill. He stood leaning over it, dressed in a white undershirt and dark woolen trousers. He had brought to America five good suits that he used to wear to work in Russia. Now he wore the trousers at home and the jackets hung in a closet with mothballs in their pockets. The grandfather took hold of the rusty meat-grinder handle and turned it slowly, with effort at first, then faster and faster. His flabby pale shoulders were shaking and tiny beads of sweat came out on his puffy cheeks, his long rounded nose, and his shiny head. The grandmother sometimes tore herself away from her cooking to offer comments: "What have you got, crooked fingers?" or "Here, you dropped a piece again" or "I hope I will have this meat ground by next year." She had never talked to him like that in Russia. In Russia, when he came home from work, she rushed to serve him dinner and put two spoonfuls of sour cream into his shchi herself. The grandfather slurped the soup loudly and talked a lot during dinner. Now he didn't even answer the grandmother back. He just stood there, clutching the meat-grinder handle with yellowed knuckles, turning it even faster, which made his face redden and the blue twisted veins on his neck bulge. His stare was focused on something far away, out the window. Misha thought that maybe he wanted to jump, like Misha had wanted to in the doctor's office. But their apartment was on the sixth floor.

While the food was cooking, the grandmother went to get her special ingredient, dill. She kept darkened, slightly wilted bunches spread out on an old newspaper on the windowsill. She took one and crushed it into a little bowl with her fingers, to add it to every dish she cooked. At dinner, everything had the taste of dill: soup, potatoes, meat stew, salad. In fact, dinner hardly tasted like anything else but dill—the grandmother didn't trust spices; she put very little salt in their food and no pepper at all. Misha watched how she moved from one saucepan to another, dressed in a square-shaped dark cotton dress, drying her moist red face and her closely cropped gray hair with a piece of cloth, sweeping potato peels off the counter, groaning when one fell to the floor and she had to pick it up. He couldn't understand why she put so much work into the preparation of this food, which was consumed in twenty minutes, in silence, and didn't even taste good.

Misha couldn't pretend to be busy with his homework forever. Eventually, the grandmother knew that he was done. She watched a weather report on TV and if nothing indicated a natural disaster sent Misha to a playground with his grandfather. "Go, go," she would yell at the grandfather, who sat on the sofa in his unbuttoned checkered shirt, buried in a Russian newspaper. "Go, walk with the boy, make yourself useful for a change!" And the grandfather would stand up, groaning, go to the bathroom mirror to check if he should shave, and usually decide against it. Then he would button his shirt, tuck it into his trousers, and say gloomily: "Let's go, Michael." Misha knew that after they left, the grandmother would take over the Russian newspaper. She would put her glasses on (she had two pairs, both made from cheap plastic, one light blue, the other pink), and slump on the sofa, making the springs creak. She would sit there with her feet planted far apart and read the classifieds section, the singles ads. She would circle some with a red marker she had borrowed from Misha, to show them later to Misha's mother, who would laugh at first, then get irritated, then get upset and yell at the grandmother.

All the way to the playground, while they passed red brick apartment buildings and rows of private houses with little boys in yarmulkes and little girls in long flowery dresses playing on the sidewalks, Misha's grandfather walked a few steps ahead, with his hands folded against his back, staring down at his feet, never saying a word.

Back in Russia, it was different, maybe because Misha was younger then. When he spent summers at his grandparents' place, the grandfather took him to a park willingly, without being asked. He talked a lot while they strolled along the paths of a dark, dense forest: about trees, animals, about how fascinating even the most ordinary things that surround us could be. Little Misha didn't try to grasp the meaning of his words. They just reached him along with other noises: the rustle of a tree, a bird's squawk, a nasty scrape of gravel as he ran his sandal-clad toes through it. It was the sound of the grandfather's voice that was important to him. They walked slowly, Misha's little hand lying securely in the grandfather's big sweaty one. From time to time, Misha had to release his hand and wipe it against his pants, but then he hurried to take the grandfather's hand again.

Now, once they reached the playground and stepped on its black spongy floor, the grandfather said, "Okay, go play, Michael." Then he strolled around the place, searching for Russian newspapers left behind on the benches. He usually found two or three. He walked to a big flat tree stump, in the farthest corner from the domino tables where a heated crowd of old Russian men gathered, and where old Russian women sat on benches discussing their own ailments and other people's mistresses. There, for the full hour that they spent in the playground, the grandfather sat unmoving, except to turn the newspaper pages. Misha didn't know how he was supposed to play.

Three-year-olds on their tricycles rode all over the soft black surface of the playground. The slide was occupied by shrieking six-year-olds, and the swings were filled with little babies rocked by their mothers, or with fat teenage girls who had to squeeze their bottoms tightly to fit between the chains. Misha usually walked to the tallest slide, stepping over dabs of chewing gum and pools of melted ice cream. He climbed up to the very top and crawled into a plastic hut. There he sat huddled on a low plastic bench. Sometimes he brought a book with him. He liked thick, serious books about ancient civilizations, archaeological expeditions, and animals who'd become extinct millions of years ago. But most of the time, it was too noisy to read. Then Misha simply stared down at the playground that seemed to move and stir like a big restless animal, and at his immobile grandfather.

The notice about the English class was printed in bold black letters on pink neon paper. The color was so bright that it arrested everyone's gaze no matter where it was lying. Since the beginning of March, it could be seen lying anywhere in the apartment: on the kitchen table, in the bedroom on a crumpled pillow, on the toilet floor between a broom and a Macy's catalog, stuffed under the sofa (the grandmother pulled it out from there, blew the pellets of dust off it, smoothed it with her hands, and scolded the grandfather angrily). Everybody studied it, read it, or at least looked at it. They were discussing whether the grandfather should go. He fit the description perfectly. Any legal immigrant who had lived in the country less than two years and possessed basic knowledge of English was invited to attend a three-month-long class on American conversation. "Rich in Idioms" was printed in letters bigger than the rest. "Free of Charge," in even bigger letters. "It's an excellent program, Father!" Misha's mother raved at dinner, removing the bones from the catfish stew on her plate. "Taught by American teachers, real teachers, native speakers! Not by Russian old ladies, who confuse all the tenses and claim that it's classic British grammar." At first, the grandfather tried to ignore her. But Misha's mother was persistent. "You're rotting alive, Father! Think how wonderful it would be if you had something to do, something to look forward to." Misha's grandmother clattered dishes, moved chairs with a screech, and often interrupted this conversation with questions like "Where are the matches? I just put them right here" or "Do you think this fish is overcooked?" She was offended that nobody suggested that she go to the class, even though she knew that the words "basic knowledge of English" hardly applied to her. The best she could do was spell her first name. The last name required Misha's help. But Misha's mother couldn't be distracted by the grandmother's questions or the clattering of dishes. "You'll begin to speak in no time, Father. You know grammar, you have vocabulary, you just need a push." The grandfather only bent his neck lower and sipped his tea, muttering that it was all nonsense and that in their area of Brooklyn you hardly ever needed English. "What about yours and mother's appointments?! Michael and I are tired of taking you there all the time. Right, Michael?" As she said this, Misha's mother moved their large porcelain teapot, preventing her from seeing Misha's face across the table. Misha nodded. It was decided that the grandfather would go.

On the first day of class, the grandfather took one of his jackets from a hanger and put it on, on top of his usual checkered shirt. He asked Misha if he had a spare notebook. Misha gave him a notebook with a marble cover, a sharp pencil, and a ballpoint pen. The grandfather put it all in a plastic THANK YOU bag. In the hall, he took the box with his Russian leather shoes from the top shelf of the closet and asked Misha if they needed shining. Misha did not know, and the grandfather shoved the box back and put his sneakers on. He shuffled out to the elevator, holding the THANK YOU bag under his arm.

From then on, two nights a week—the class was held on Mondays and Wednesdays—they had dinner without the grandfather. His absence didn't make much difference, except maybe that Misha's mother and the grandmother bickered a little more. It usually started with a clipping from a Russian newspaper, a big colorful ad—COME TO OUR PARTY AND MEET YOUR DESTINY. PRICE: FIFTY DOLLARS (FOOD AND DRINK INCLUDED)—and ended with Misha's mother yelling: "Why do you want to marry me off? So you can drive the next one away?" and the grandmother reaching for a bottle of valerian root drops. "I never said a bad word to your husband," the grandmother said plaintively. "You said plenty of your words to me. Didn't spare money in long-distance calls!" "I only wanted to open your eyes!" Then Misha's mother rushed out of the kitchen, and the grandmother yelled after her, carefully counting the drops into her teacup: "How can you be so ungrateful! I came to America to help you. I left everything and came here for your sake!"

Misha's mother had come to America for Misha's sake. She said it to him once, after she got back from a parent-teacher conference. She returned home and said, "Come with me to the bedroom, Michael." He went, feeling his hands grow sweaty and his ears turn red, although he knew that he hadn't done anything bad at school. His mother sat on the edge of the bed and removed her high-heeled shoes, then pulled off her pantyhose. "The teacher says you don't talk, Michael. You don't talk at all. Not in class, not during the recess." She was rubbing her pale feet with small, crooked toes. "Your English is fine, you have excellent marks on your tests. You have excellent marks in every subject. Yet you're not going to make it to the top of the class!" She left her feet alone and began to cry, her black eye makeup running around her eyes. She said to him, sniffling, that he—his future—was the only reason she came to America. Then she went into the bathroom to wash her face, leaving her rolled-up pantyhose on the floor—two soft, dark circles joined together. From the bathroom, she yelled to him: "Why don't you talk, Michael?"

It wasn't true that he didn't talk at all. When asked a question, he gave an accurate answer, but he tried to make it as brief as possible. He never volunteered to talk. He registered everything that was said in class; he made comments and counterarguments in his head; he even made jokes. But something prevented these already-formed words from coming out of his mouth. He felt the same way when his father called on Saturdays. Misha spent a whole week preparing for his call; he had thousands of things to tell him. In his head, he related everything that had happened to him at school; he described his classmates, his teachers. He wanted to talk about things he had read in books, about lost cities, volcanoes, and weird animals. In his head, Misha even laughed, imagining how he would tell his father all the funny stories he read about dinosaurs, and how his father would laugh with him. But when his father called, Misha went numb. He answered questions but never volunteered to speak and never asked anything himself. He sat with the phone on his bed, facing the wall and picking at old layers of paint with his fingernail. He could hear his father's impatient, disappointed breathing on the other end of the line. Misha thought that his reluctance to talk might explain why his father had not called in several weeks.

Now the grandfather had to do his homework too. Misha came home from school and found him sitting at the kitchen table in Misha's usual place with his notebooks and dictionaries spread across the table. The grandfather would even cut himself little colorful cards out of construction paper and copy down difficult words from the dictionary: an English word on one side, the Russian meaning on the other. He studied seriously and couldn't be bothered during that time. The grandmother had to go to the Russian food store alone, and she brought back smaller, lighter bags because she couldn't carry heavy things. Nobody used the meat-grinder now. It was stored in a cupboard along with other useless things brought from Russia: baking sheets, funny-shaped molds, a small, dented samovar, a gadget for removing sour cherrystones. The grandmother wasn't happy about this. She muttered that she had the whole household on her shoulders and threw looks of reproach at her husband. Misha's mother said: "Please leave him alone—Father has to learn something. It's only for three months anyway." Misha wondered if the grandfather enjoyed his homework as much as he did. He also wondered if the grandfather cheated like he did, pretending that his homework took much more time than it really did.

RICHARD RODRIGUEZ

"I write about race in America in hopes of undermining the notion of race in America," declares Richard Rodriguez in *Brown: The Last Discovery of America* (2002). Raised in Sacramento, California, the son of Mexican parents, Rodriguez (born in 1944) has also written eloquently about immigration, bilingualism, education, religion, and the nuances of identity in contemporary America. After abandoning graduate degree work in English literature because he felt he was the undeserving beneficiary of affirmative action, Rodriguez embarked on a career as a journalist, which has included positions with PBS and the Pacifica News Service. His books as an essayist and memoirist include *Hunger of Memory: The Education of Richard Rodriguez* (1982), *Mexico's Children* (1990), and *Days of Obligation: An Argument with My Mexican Father* (1992).

from
Hunger of Memory

I remember to start with that day in Sacramento—a California now nearly thirty years past—when I first entered a classroom, able to understand some fifty stray English words.

The third of four children, I had been preceded to a neighborhood Roman Catholic school by an older brother and sister. But neither of them had revealed very much about their classroom experiences. Each afternoon they returned, as they left in the morning, always together, speaking in Spanish as they climbed the five steps of the porch. And their mysterious books, wrapped in shopping-bag paper, remained on the table next to the door, closed firmly behind them.

An accident of geography sent me to a school where all my classmates were white, many the children of doctors and lawyers and business executives. All my classmates certainly must have been uneasy on that first day of school—as most children are uneasy—to find themselves apart from their families in the first institution of their lives. But I was astonished.

The nun said, in a friendly but oddly impersonal voice, 'Boys and girls, this is Richard Rodriguez.' (I heard her sound out: *Rich-heard Road-ree-guess.*) It was the first time I had heard anyone name me in English. 'Richard,' the nun repeated more slowly, writing my name down in her black leather book. Quickly I turned to see my mother's face dissolve in a watery blur behind the pebbled glass door.

Many years later there is something called bilingual education—a scheme proposed in the late 1960s by Hispanic-American social activists, later endorsed by a congressional vote. It is a program that seeks to permit non-English-speaking children, many from lower-class homes, to use their family language as the language of school. (Such is the goal its supporters announce.) I hear them and am forced to say no: It is not possible for a child—any child—ever to use his family's language in school. Not to understand this is to misunderstand the public uses of schooling and to trivialize the nature of intimate life—a family's 'language.'

Memory teaches me what I know of these matters; the boy reminds the adult. I was a bilingual child, a certain kind—socially disadvantaged—the son of working-class parents, both Mexican immigrants.

In the early years of my boyhood, my parents coped very well in America. My father had steady work. My mother managed at home. They were nobody's victims. Optimism and ambition led them to a house (our home) many blocks from the Mexican south side of town. We lived among *gringos* and only a block from the biggest, whitest houses. It never occurred to my parents that they couldn't live wherever they chose. Nor was the Sacramento of the fifties bent on teaching them a contrary lesson. My mother and father were more annoyed than intimidated by those two or three neighbors who tried initially to make us unwelcome. ('Keep your brats away from my sidewalk!') But despite all they achieved, perhaps because they had so much to achieve, any deep feeling of ease, the confidence of 'belonging' in public was withheld from them both. They regarded the people at work, the faces in crowds, as very distant from us. They were the others, *los gringos.* That term was interchangeable in their speech with another, even more telling, *los americanos.*

I grew up in a house where the only regular guests were my relations. For one day, enormous families of relatives would visit and there would be so many people that the noise and the bodies would spill out to the backyard and front porch. Then, for weeks, no one came by. (It was usually a salesman who rang the doorbell.) Our house stood apart. A gaudy yellow in a row of white bungalows. We were the people with the noisy dog. The people who raised pigeons and chickens. We were the foreigners on the block. A few neighbors smiled and waved. We waved back. But no one in the family knew the names of the old couple who lived next door; until I was seven years old, I did not know the names of the kids who lived across the street.

In public, my father and mother spoke a hesitant, accented, not always grammatical English. And they would have to strain—their bodies tense—to catch the sense of what was rapidly said by *los gringos.* At home they spoke Spanish. The language of their Mexican past sounded in counterpoint to the English of public society. The words would come quickly, with ease. Conveyed through those sounds was the pleasing, soothing, consoling reminder of being at home.

During those years when I was first conscious of hearing, my mother and father addressed me only in Spanish; in Spanish I learned to reply. By contrast, English (*inglés*), rarely heard in the house, was the language I came to associate with *gringos.* I learned my first words of English overhearing my parents speak to strangers. At five years of age, I knew just enough English for my mother to trust me on errands to stores one block away. No more.

I was a listening child, careful to hear the very different sounds of Spanish and English. Wide-eyed with hearing, I'd listen to sounds more than words. First, there were English (*gringo*) sounds. So many words were still unknown that when the butcher or the lady at the drugstore said something to me, exotic polysyllabic sounds would bloom in the midst of their sentences. Often, the speech of people in public seemed to me very loud, booming with confidence. The man behind the counter would literally ask, 'What can I do for you?' But by being so firm and so clear, the sound of his voice said that he was a *gringo*; he belonged in public society.

I would also hear then the high nasal notes of middle-class American speech. The air stirred with sound. Sometimes, even now, when I have been traveling abroad for several weeks, I will hear what I heard as a boy. In hotel lobbies or airports, in Turkey or Brazil, some Americans will pass, and suddenly I will hear it again—the high sound of American voices. For a few seconds I will hear it with pleasure, for it is now the sound of *my* society—a reminder of home. But inevitably—already on the flight headed for home—the sound fades with repetition. I will be unable to hear it anymore.

When I was a boy, things were different. The accent of *los gringos* was never pleasing nor was it hard to hear. Crowds at Safeway or at bus stops would be noisy with sound. And I would be forced to edge away from the chirping chatter above me.

I was unable to hear my own sounds, but I knew very well that I spoke English poorly. My words could not stretch far enough to form complete thoughts. And the words I did speak I didn't know well enough to make into distinct sounds. (Listeners would usually lower their heads, better to hear what I was trying to say.) But it was one thing for *me* to speak English with difficulty. It was more troubling for me to hear my parents speak in public: their high-whining vowels and guttural consonants; their sentences that got stuck with 'eh' and 'ah' sounds; the confused syntax; the hesitant rhythm of sounds so different from the way *gringos* spoke. I'd notice, moreover, that my parents' voices were softer than those of *gringos* we'd meet.

I am tempted now to say that none of this mattered. In adulthood I am embarrassed by childhood fears. And, in a way, it didn't matter very much that my parents could not speak English with ease. Their linguistic difficulties had no serious consequences. My mother and father made themselves understood at the county hospital clinic and at government offices. And yet, in another way, it mattered very much—it was unsettling to hear my parents struggle with English. Hearing them, I'd grow nervous, my clutching trust in their protection and power weakened.

There were many times like the night at a brightly lit gasoline station (a blaring white memory) when I stood uneasily, hearing my father. He was talking to a teenaged attendant. I do not recall what they were saying, but I cannot forget the sounds my father made as he spoke. At one point his words slid together to form one word—sounds as confused as the threads of blue and green oil in the puddle next to my shoes. His voice rushed through what he had left to say. And, toward the end, reached falsetto notes, appealing to his listener's understanding. I looked away to the lights of passing automobiles. I tried not to hear any more. But I heard only too well the calm, easy tones in the attendant's reply. Shortly afterward, walking toward home with my father, I shivered when he put his hand on my shoulder. The very first chance that I got, I evaded his grasp and ran on ahead into the dark, skipping with feigned boyish exuberance.

But then there was Spanish. *Español:* my family's language. *Español:* the language that seemed to me a private language. I'd hear strangers on the radio and in the Mexican Catholic church across town speaking in Spanish, but I couldn't really believe that Spanish was a public language, like English. Spanish speakers, rather, seemed related to me, for I sensed that we shared— through our language—the experience of feeling apart from *los gringos*. It was thus a ghetto Spanish that I heard and I spoke. Like those whose lives are bound by a barrio, I was reminded by Spanish of my separateness from *los otros, los gringos* in power. But more intensely than for most barrio children—because I did not live in a barrio—Spanish seemed to me the language of home. (Most days it was only at home that I'd hear it.) It became the language of joyful return.

A family member would say something to me and I would feel myself specially recognized. My parents would say something to me and I would feel embraced by the sounds of their words. Those sounds said: *I am speaking with ease in Spanish. I am addressing you in words I never use with* los gringos. *I recognize you as someone special, close, like no one outside. You belong with us. In the family.*

(*Ricardo.*)

At the age of five, six, well past the time when most other children no longer easily notice the difference between sounds uttered at home and words spoken in public, I had a different experience. I lived in a world magically compounded of sounds. I remained a child longer than most; I lingered too long, poised at the edge of language—often frightened by the sounds of *los gringos*, delighted by the sounds of Spanish at home. I shared with my family a language that was startlingly different from that used in the great city around us.

For me there were none of the gradations between public and private society so normal to a maturing child. Outside the house was public society; inside the house was private. Just opening or closing the screen door behind me was an important experience. I'd rarely leave home all alone or without reluctance. Walking down the sidewalk, under the canopy of tall trees, I'd warily notice the—suddenly—silent neighborhood kids who stood warily watching me. Nervously, I'd arrive at the grocery store to hear there the sounds of the *gringo*—foreign to me—reminding me that in this world so big, I was a foreigner. But then I'd return. Walking back toward our house, climbing the steps from the sidewalk, when the front door was open in summer, I'd hear voices beyond the screen door talking in Spanish. For a second or two, I'd stay, linger there, listening. Smiling, I'd hear my mother call out, saying in Spanish (words): 'Is that you, Richard?' All the while her sounds would assure me: *You are home now; come closer; inside. With us.*

'*Sí,*' I'd reply.

Once more inside the house I would resume (assume) my place in the family. The sounds would dim, grow harder to hear. Once more at home, I would grow less aware of that fact. It required, however, no more than the blurt of the doorbell to alert me to listen to sounds all over again. The house would turn instantly still while my mother went to the door. I'd hear her hard English sounds. I'd wait to hear her voice return to soft-sounding Spanish, which assured me, as surely as did the clicking tongue of the lock on the door, that the stranger was gone.

Plainly, it is not healthy to hear such sounds so often. It is not healthy to distinguish public words from private sounds so easily. I remained cloistered by sounds, timid and shy in public, too dependent on voices at home. And yet it needs to be emphasized: I was an extremely happy child at home. I remember many nights when my father would come back from work, and I'd hear him call out to my mother in Spanish, sounding relieved. In Spanish, he'd sound light and free notes he never could manage in English. Some nights I'd jump up just at hearing his voice. With *mis hermanos* I would come running into the room where he was with my mother. Our laughing (so deep was the pleasure!) became screaming. Like others who know the pain of public alienation, we transformed the knowledge of our public separateness and made it consoling—the reminder of intimacy. Excited, we joined our voices in a celebration of sounds. *We are speaking now the way we never speak out in public. We are alone—together,* voices sounded, surrounded to tell me. Some nights, no one seemed willing to loosen the hold sounds had on us. At dinner, we invented new words. (Ours sounded Spanish, but made sense only to us.) We pieced together new words by taking, say, an English verb and giving it Spanish endings. My mother's instructions at bedtime would be lacquered with mock-urgent tones. Or a word like *sí* would become, in several notes, able to convey added measures of feeling. Tongues explored the edges of words, especially the fat vowels. And we happily sounded that military drum roll, the twirling roar of the Spanish *r*. Family language: my family's sounds. The voices of my parents and sisters and brother. Their voices insisting: *You belong here. We are family members. Related. Special to one another. Listen!* Voices singing and sighing, rising, straining, then surging, teeming with plea-sure that burst syllables into fragments of laughter. At times it seemed there was steady quiet only when, from another room, the rustling whispers of my parents faded and I moved closer to sleep.

At last, seven years old, I came to believe what had been technically true since my birth: I was an American citizen.

But the special feeling of closeness at home was diminished by then. Gone was the desperate, urgent, intense feeling of being at home; rare was the experience of feeling myself individualized by family intimates. We remained a loving family, but one greatly changed. No longer so close; no longer bound tight by the pleasing and troubling knowledge of our public separateness. Neither my older brother nor sister rushed home after school anymore. Nor did I. When I arrived home there would often be neighborhood kids in the house. Or the house would be empty of sounds.

Following the dramatic Americanization of their children, even my par-ents grew more publicly confident. Especially my mother. She learned the names of all the people on our block. And she decided we needed to have a telephone installed in the house. My father continued to use the word *gringo*. But it was no longer charged with the old bitterness or distrust. (Stripped of any emotional content, the word simply became a name for those Americans not of Hispanic descent.) Hearing him, sometimes, I wasn't sure if he was pronouncing the Spanish word *gringo* or saying gringo in English.

Matching the silence I started hearing in public was a new quiet at home. The family's quiet was partly due to the fact that, as we children learned more and more English, we shared fewer and fewer words with our parents. Sentences needed to be spoken slowly when a child addressed his mother or father. (Often the parent wouldn't understand.) The child would need to repeat himself. (Still the parent misunderstood.) The young voice, frustrated, would end up saying, 'Never mind'—the subject was closed. Dinners would be noisy with the clinking of knives and forks against dishes. My mother would smile softly between her remarks; my father at the other end of the table would chew and chew at his food, while he stared over the heads of his children.

My *mother*! My *father*! After English became my primary language, I no longer knew what words to use in addressing my parents. The old Spanish words (those tender accents of sound) I had used earlier—*mamá* and *papá*— I couldn't use anymore. They would have been too painful reminders of how much had changed in my life. On the other hand, the words I heard neighborhood kids call *their* parents seemed equally unsatisfactory. *Mother* and *Father*, *Ma*, *Papa*, *Pa*, *Dad*, *Pop* (how I hated the all-American sound of that last word especially)—all these terms I felt were unsuitable, not really terms of address for *my* parents. As a result, I never used them at home. Whenever I'd speak to my parents, I would try to get their attention with eye contact alone. In public conversations, I'd refer to 'my parents' or 'my mother and father.'

My mother and father, for their part, responded differently, as their children spoke to them less. She grew restless, seemed troubled and anxious at the scarcity of words exchanged in the house. It was she who would question me about my day when I came home from school. She smiled at small talk. She pried at the edges of my sentences to get me to say something more. (What?) She'd join conversations she overheard, but her intrusions often stopped her children's talking. By contrast, my father seemed reconciled to the new quiet. Though his English improved somewhat, he retired into silence. At dinner he spoke very little. One night his children and even his wife helplessly giggled at his garbled English pronunciation of the Catholic

Grace before Meals. Thereafter he made his wife recite the prayer at the start of each meal, even on formal occasions, when there were guests in the house. Hers became the public voice of the family. On official business, it was she, not my father, one would usually hear on the phone or in stores, talking to strangers. His children grew so accustomed to his silence that, years later, they would speak routinely of his shyness. (My mother would often try to explain: Both his parents died when he was eight. He was raised by an uncle who treated him like little more than a menial servant. He was never encouraged to speak. He grew up alone. A man of few words.) But my father was not shy, I realized, when I'd watch him speaking Spanish with relatives. Using Spanish, he was quickly effusive. Especially when talking with other men, his voice would spark, flicker, flare alive with sounds. In Spanish, he expressed ideas and feeling he rarely revealed in English. With firm Spanish sounds, he conveyed confidence and authority English would never allow him.

The silence at home, however, was finally more than a literal silence. Fewer words passed between parent and child, but more profound was the silence that resulted from my inattention to sounds. At about the time I no longer bothered to listen with care to the sounds of English in public, I grew careless about listening to the sounds family members made when they spoke. Most of the time I heard someone speaking at home and didn't distinguish his sounds from the words people uttered in public. I didn't even pay much attention to my parents' accented and ungrammatical speech. At least not at home. Only when I was with them in public would I grow alert to their accents. Though, even then, their sounds caused me less and less concern. For I was increasingly confident of my own public identity.

🐚   🐚

I grew up victim to a disabling confusion. As I grew fluent in English, I no longer could speak Spanish with confidence. I continued to understand spoken Spanish. And in high school, I learned how to read and write Spanish. But for many years I could not pronounce it. A powerful guilt blocked my spoken words; an essential glue was missing whenever I'd try to connect words to form sentences. I would be unable to break a barrier of sound, to speak freely. I would speak, or try to speak, Spanish, and I would manage to utter halting, hiccuping sounds that betrayed my unease.

When relatives and Spanish-speaking friends of my parents came to the house, my brother and sisters seemed reticent to use Spanish, but at least they managed to say a few necessary words before being excused. I never managed so gracefully. I was cursed with guilt. Each time I'd hear myself addressed in Spanish, I would be unable to respond with any success. I'd know the words I wanted to say, but I couldn't manage to say them. I would try to speak, but everything I said seemed to me horribly anglicized. My mouth would not form the words right. My jaw would tremble. After a phrase or two, I'd cough up a warm, silvery sound. And stop.

It surprised my listeners to hear me. They'd lower their heads, better to grasp what I was trying to say. They would repeat their questions in gentle affectionate voices. But by then I would answer in English. No, no, they would say, we want you to speak to us in Spanish. ('. . . *en español.*') But I couldn't do it. *Pocho* then they called me. Sometimes playfully, teasingly, using the tender diminutive—*mi pochito.* Sometimes not so playfully, mockingly, *Pocho.* (A Spanish dictionary defines that word as an adjective meaning 'colorless' or 'bland.' But I heard it as a noun, naming the Mexican-American who, in becoming an American, forgets his native society.) '*¡Pocho!*' the lady in the Mexican food store muttered, shaking her head. I looked up to the counter where red and green peppers were strung like Christmas tree lights and saw the frowning face of the stranger. My mother laughed somewhere behind me. (She said that her children didn't want to practice 'our Spanish' after they started going to school.) My mother's smiling voice made me suspect that the lady who faced me was not really angry at me. But, searching her face, I couldn't find the hint of a smile.

Embarrassed, my parents would regularly need to explain their children's inability to speak flowing Spanish during those years. My mother met the wrath of her brother, her only brother, when he came up from Mexico one summer with his family. He saw his nieces and nephews for the very first time. After listening to me, he looked away and said what a disgrace it was that I couldn't speak Spanish, '*su proprio idioma.*' He made that remark to my mother; I noticed, however, that he stared at my father.

Chronology
Sources and Acknowledgments
Index

CHRONOLOGY

1607   The first permanent English colony is established at Jamestown, Virginia.

1619   Dutch traders sell 20 Africans into servitude at Jamestown, beginning the importation of slaves into the English colonies in North America.

1620   English Separatists (the Pilgrims) leave Holland and establish a settlement at Plymouth.

1624   Dutch begin settlement of New Netherland along the Hudson River.

1630   Puritans begin their migration to the Massachusetts Bay Colony.

1638   Colony of New Sweden founded on the Delaware River.

1655   Dutch take control of New Sweden.

1664   English conquer New Netherland.

1672   Royal African Company is chartered by Charles II of England; its success in the slave trade increases the number of Africans imported into the English North American colonies as the number of white indentured servants used in plantation agriculture declines.

1715   Population of British North American colonies is estimated at 434,600, including 375,750 whites and 58,850 blacks.

1754   Colonial population is estimated at about 1,486,000, including 1,193,000 whites and 293,000 blacks.

1776   Declaration of Independence accuses George III of endeavoring "to prevent the population of these States" by obstructing naturalization laws and discouraging immigration.

1787   Article I, Section 8 of the Constitution gives Congress the power to "establish an uniform Rule of Naturalization"; Article I, Section 9 prohibits Congress from ending the importation of slaves before 1808.

1790   Naturalization Act provides that any "free white person" who is of "good character" and has resided in the United States for two years may become a citizen after taking an oath or affirmation to support the Constitution. First U.S. census reports population of 3,929,214, including more than 3,172,000 whites and 756,000 blacks, of whom 697,000 are slaves. The national origins of the white population are approximately 60 percent English, 8 percent German, 8 percent Scottish, 6 percent Scots-Irish, 3 percent Irish, and 3 percent Dutch.

1795   New naturalization act extends the necessary residence period to five years and requires prospective citizens to renounce allegiance to other countries.

1798   Congress extends residence period to 14 years (measure is passed along with the Alien and Sedition Acts).

1802   Congress restores five-year naturalization period.

1803   United States purchases Louisiana from France; the territory has approximately 50,000 non-Indian inhabitants, including 28,000 slaves.

1807   The importation of slaves is banned by Congress, effective January 1, 1808, although illegal slave trading continues until the 1860s. (It is estimated that between 10 and 11 million Africans were brought to the western hemisphere by the slave trade, mostly from ports between Senegambia and Angola; 560,000 slaves were landed in the British North American colonies and in the United States, and more than 1 million Africans died during the Atlantic passage.)

1819   United States purchases Florida from Spain (1830 census counts Florida population of nearly 35,000). Congress requires annual reporting of the number of immigrants entering the country. An estimated 226,000 immigrants arrive in the United States, 1790–1819.

1820   Census reports population of 9,638,453.

1830   151,824 immigrants arrive, 1820–30. Census reports population of 12,866,020.

1840   599,125 immigrants arrive, 1831–40. Census reports population of 17,068,953.

1845–49   Potato famine causes about 1 million people to emigrate from Ireland, mostly to the United States.

1848   Treaty of Guadalupe Hidalgo is signed, ending Mexican-American War; under its terms, U.S. citizenship is offered to 80,000 Mexicans living in California and New Mexico.

1849   California Gold Rush begins significant Chinese immigration to the United States. Approximately 300,000 Chinese immigrants arrive by 1882, although many return to China; the 1880 census reports a Chinese population of 105,000.

1850   1,713,251 immigrants arrive, 1841–50. Census reports population of 23,191,876.

1854   427,833 immigrants arrive during the year, the highest figure ever in relation to the total population. Know Nothings, a nativist political movement opposed to Catholic immigration, sweep Massachusetts state elections.

1856   Know Nothing ticket wins 21 percent of the popular vote and 8 electoral votes in presidential election, but movement soon breaks apart along sectional lines.

1860   2,598,214 immigrants arrive, 1851–60. Census reports population of 31,443,321, including 3,950,528 slaves and 476,748 free people of color. Between 1831 and 1860 more than 1.9 million Irish and 1.5 million German immigrants enter the United States.

1865   Thirteenth Amendment to the Constitution abolishes slavery.

1868   Fourteenth Amendment grants national citizenship to all persons born or naturalized in the United States.

1870   2,314,824 immigrants arrive, 1861–70. Census reports population of 38,558,371. Congress extends naturalization to "aliens of African nativity and persons of African descent," but the new law continues to exclude Asians from becoming naturalized citizens. (The children of Asian immigrants born in the United States become citizens under the Fourteenth Amendment.)

1880   2,812,191 immigrants arrive, 1871–80. Census reports population of 50,189,209. Between 1861 and 1880 approximately 1.5 million German, 870,000 Irish, and 370,000 Scandinavian immigrants enter the country.

1881   Series of pogroms in the Russian empire prompts significant Jewish immigration from Eastern Europe; about 2 million Jewish immigrants arrive, 1881–1924. (Jewish population of the U.S. in 1881 is estimated to be 250,000, mostly of German origin.)

1882 Congress passes Chinese Exclusion Act, forbidding the entry of Chinese laborers into the United States for ten years. (Ban is broadened in 1884 to include almost all Chinese immigrants, extended for another decade in 1892, and made permanent in 1902.) New Immigration Act imposes 50-cent head tax on immigrants (increased to $2 in 1903 and $4 in 1907) and bars entry of the mentally disabled and the insane, paupers, and persons convicted of non-political offenses.

1885 Congress severely restricts importation of contract laborers.

1890 5,246,613 immigrants are admitted, 1881–90. Census reports population of 62,979,766. Polish immigration increases after 1890 (about 950,000 Poles arrive between 1850 and 1900).

1891 Congress bars entry of polygamists and prostitutes and establishes Office of the Superintendent of Immigration within the Treasury Department (renamed the Bureau of Immigration in 1895).

1893 U.S. Supreme Court upholds 1892 extension of the Chinese Exclusion Act.

1894 Immigration Restriction League is founded in response to increased immigration from Eastern and Southern Europe.

1898 United States annexes Hawaii and is ceded Puerto Rico and the Philippines by Spain.

1900 3,687,564 immigrants are admitted, 1891–1900 (decline in number from previous decade is a result of the economic depression in the United States, 1893–97). Census reports population of 76,212,168. Between 1881 and 1900 approximately 2 million German, 1 million Irish, 1 million Scandinavian, and 1 million Italian immigrants enter the country. Puerto Ricans and Chinese and Japanese residents of Hawaii become American nationals; their status allows them to move to the continental United States, although Asians are still barred from becoming naturalized.

1902   Residents of the Philippines become American nationals.

1903   Congress bars anarchists and violent revolutionaries from entering the country. Bureau of Immigration is transferred to the new Department of Commerce and Labor (bureau is reorganized as the Bureau of Immigration and Naturalization in 1906).

1907   Congress passes Expatriation Act requiring women who marry aliens to assume the citizenship of their husbands. (Act is modified in 1922 to cover only women who marry Asians, and is repealed entirely in 1931.) Informal "gentlemen's agreement" with Japan severely limits Japanese immigration to the United States (about 150,000 Japanese arrive, 1891–1910).

1910   8,795,386 immigrants are admitted, 1901–10. Census reports population of 92,228,496.

1913   Bureau of Immigration and Naturalization is transferred into the new Department of Labor (in 1933 it is reorganized as the Immigration and Naturalization Service).

1914   Outbreak of World War I reduces immigration.

1917   Congress passes new immigration act that raises head tax to $8, imposes a literacy test on immigrants, and prohibits immigration from South and Southeast Asia and the Pacific Islands (excluding the Philippines and Guam). Puerto Rico is made a commonwealth and its residents become American citizens.

1920   5,735,811 immigrants are admitted, 1911–1920. Census reports population of 106,021,537. Between 1901 and 1920 about 3.1 million Italian, 1 million Polish, and 700,000 Scandinavian immigrants enter the country.

1921   Congress passes act establishing quota system for European immigration, limiting total immigration to 357,000 and setting national quotas at 3 percent of the immigrants from that country residing in the U.S. in 1910.

1922   Quota system is extended until 1924. Supreme Court upholds exclusion of Asians from naturalization, ruling in *Ozawa v. United States* that the Japanese-born plaintiff is not Caucasian and therefore not a "white person."

1923   Supreme Court rules in *United States v. Thind* that an immigrant from India, although Caucasian, is not a "white person" by custom and is therefore ineligible for naturalization.

1924   Congress passes new immigration quota act, limiting annual European immigration to 164,000 and setting national quotas at 2 percent of the immigrants from that country residing in the U.S. in 1890. Immigration from Canada and from independent nations in the Caribbean and Latin America is exempted from the quota system, while all Asian immigration (except from the Philippines) is prohibited.

1929   Under provisions of 1924 act the immigration quota is reduced to 150,000, with quotas for each country based on the national origins of the U.S. population as reported by the 1920 census.

1930   4,107,209 immigrants are admitted, 1921–30. Census reports population of 123,202,624.

1931   Great Depression causes sharp decline in immigration; from 1932 to 1935, emigrants outnumber immigrants.

1933   Refugees begin fleeing Nazi Germany; about 150,000 German émigrés, mostly Jewish, eventually enter the U.S. (Number admitted is less than the maximum national quota, as many applicants are denied visas by consular officials on technical grounds.)

1934   Congress passes law providing for the self-government and eventual independence (in 1946) of the Philippines; legislation reclassifies Filipinos as alien and sets immigration quota of 50 persons per year.

1939   Outbreak of World War II reduces immigration to the United States.

1940   528,431 immigrants are admitted, 1931–40. Census reports population of 132,164,569. Immigration and Naturalization Service is transferred to the Department of Justice. Congress passes act requiring the registration and fingerprinting of all aliens in the United States.

1942   U.S. government interns more than 120,000 Japanese resident aliens and Japanese-American citizens living on the West Coast.

1943   Congress repeals the 1882 Chinese Exclusion Act, establishes a highly restricted quota for Chinese immigrants, and makes them eligible for naturalization.

1946   Congress establishes highly restricted immigration quotas for Indians and Filipinos and permits their naturalization.

1948   Displaced Persons Act results in the admission by 1952 of 400,000 European refugees over and above national quota limits.

1950   1,035,039 immigrants are admitted, 1941–50. Census reports population of 151,325,798.

1952   Congress passes Immigration and Nationality Act that continues quota system based on national origins, allows for highly restricted immigration from Asia, and bars entry to persons considered politically subversive.

1954   Immigration and Naturalization Service launches "Operation Wetback," aimed at illegal immigrants in the Southwest, and deports 130,000 people to Mexico.

1959   Refugees begin fleeing Cuban Revolution (more than 800,000 Cubans are admitted to the U.S., 1959–2000).

1960   2,515,479 immigrants are admitted, 1951–60. Census reports population of 179,323,175.

1965   Congress passes new Immigration and Nationality Act, abolishing national origin quotas and establishing annual limit of 170,000 immigrants from the eastern hemisphere and 120,000 from the western hemisphere (hemispheric limits are abolished in 1978, and annual worldwide limit is set at 290,000). The spouses, unmarried minor children, and parents of U.S. citizens are exempt from numerical limits, and preference in issuing visas is given to cases involving family reunification and to workers in needed occupations.

1970   3,321,677 immigrants are admitted, 1961–70. Census reports population of 203,302,031.

1975   Refugees from Indochina begin arriving in the United States (more than 1.1 million Vietnamese enter the country by 2000).

1980   4,493,314 immigrants are admitted, 1971–80. Census reports population of 226,542,199. Congress passes Refugee Act that lowers worldwide annual limit for immigrants to 270,000 and provides for an additional 50,000 refugee admissions each year (refugee limits are often exceeded).

1986   Immigration Reform and Control Act results in amnesty being granted to 3 million illegal immigrants.

1990   7,338,062 immigrants are admitted, 1981–90. Census reports population of 248,709,873. Congress raises annual worldwide numerical limit for immigrants to 675,000.

1996   Immigration and Naturalization Service estimates that there are 5 million illegal immigrants living in the United States.

2000   9,095,417 immigrants are admitted, 1991–2000. Census reports population of 281,421,906. Between 1971 and 2000 approximately 4.5 million Mexican, 1.4 million Filipino, 1.2 million Chinese, 777,000 Indian, 764,000 Korean, and 735,000 Dominican immigrants are admitted to the United States. Census Bureau estimates that there are 8.5 million illegal immigrants in the country.

2003   Immigration and Naturalization Service is transferred to new Department of Homeland Security and divided into separate bureaus for Customs and Border Protection, Immigration and Customs Enforcement, and Citizenship and Immigration Services.

2008   Approximately 8.3 million immigrants are admitted, 2001–8. Census estimates population of 304 million.

SOURCES AND ACKNOWLEDGMENTS

Great care has been taken to locate and acknowledge all owners of copyrighted material included in this book. If any owner has inadvertently been omitted, acknowledgment will gladly be made in future printings.

Louis Adamic. *From* Laughing in the Jungle: *Laughing in the Jungle* (New York: Harper & Brothers, 1932), pp. 3–6, 41–45, 99–104. Copyright ©1932 by Louis Adamic. Copyright © renewed 1960 by Stella Adamic. Reprinted by permission of HarperCollins Publishers.

Felipe Alfau. *From* Chromos: *Chromos* (Urbana, Ill.: Dalkey Archive Press, 1990), pp. 7–22. Copyright © 1990 by Felipe Alfau. Reprinted by permission of the Dalkey Archive Press.

Julia Alvarez. Our Papers: *Something to Declare* (Chapel Hill, N.C.: Algonquin Books of Chapel Hill, 1998), pp. 13–19. Copyright © 1995, 1998 by Julia Alvarez. Reprinted by permission of Susan Bergholz Literary Services, New York, N.Y. and Lamy, N.M. All rights reserved.

Mary Antin. *From* The Promised Land: *The Promised Land* (Boston: Houghton Mifflin Company, 1912), pp. 222–40.

Marie Arana. *From* American Chica: *American Chica* (New York: Dial Press, 2001), pp. 258–67. Copyright © 2001 by Marie Arana. Used by permission of The Dial Press/Dell Publishing, a division of Random House, Inc.

Reinaldo Arenas. *From* Before Night Falls: *Before Night Falls* (New York:

Penguin Books, 1993), pp. 276–88. Copyright © by the Estate of Reinaldo Arenas and Dolores M. Koch. Used by permission of Viking Penguin, a division of Penguin Group (USA) Inc.

W. H. Auden. Say this city has ten million souls: *Collected Poems*, ed. Edward Mendelson (New York: Vintage International, 1991), pp. 265–66. Copyright © 1976 by Edward Mendelson, William Meredith, and Monroe K. Spears, Executors of the Estate of W. H. Auden. Used by permission of Random House, Inc. Written in 1939.

John James Audubon. *From* Myself: *Writings and Drawings*, ed. Christoph Irmscher (New York: Library of America, 1999), pp. 772–75. Originally published in 1893.

Ayuba Suleiman Diallo. *From* Some Memoirs of the Life of Job . . . Who Was a Slave about Two Years in Maryland: *Documenting the South* (Chapel Hill, N.C.: University of North Carolina digitized text, 1999), pp. 12–26. Originally published in 1734.

Joseph Brodsky. *From* The Condition We Call Exile: *On Grief and Reason* (New York: Farrar, Straus and Giroux, 1995), pp. 31–34. Copyright © 1995 by Joseph Brodsky. Reprinted by permission of Farrar, Straus and Giroux, L.L.C.

Olga Broumas. Sometimes, as a child: *Beginning with O* (New Haven: Yale University Press, 1977), p. 1. Copyright © 1977 by Olga Broumas. Reprinted by permission of Yale University Press.

Carlos Bulosan. *From* America Is in the Heart: *America Is in the Heart* (Harcourt, Brace and Company, 1946), pp. 99–101, 104–12.

Julia de Burgos. Farewell in Welfare Island: *Song of the Simple Truth*, ed. Jack Agüeros (Willimantic, Conn.: Curbstone Press, 1997), p. 357. Copyright © 1997. Reprinted by permission of Curbstone Press. Distributed by Consortium. Written in 1953.

Abraham Cahan. *From* The Education of Abraham Cahan: *The Education of Abraham Cahan* (Philadelphia: Jewish Publication Society of America, 1969), pp. 217–29. Copyright © 1969 by Abraham Cahan. Translated by Leon Stein, Abraham P. Conan, and Lynn Davidson. Published by The Jewish Publication Society of America, with the permission of the publisher.

Ludovico Caminita. *From* On the Island of Tears: Ellis Island: *Voices of*

Italian America, ed. Martino Marazzi (Madison, N.J.: Fairleigh Dickinson University Press, 2004), pp. 125–31. Translated by Ann Goldstein. Copyright © 2004. Reprinted by permission of Fairleigh Dickinson University Press.

Lan Cao. *From* Monkey Bridge: *Monkey Bridge* (New York: Viking, 1997), pp. 1–12. Copyright © 1997 by Lan Cao. Used by permission of Viking Penguin, a division of Penguin Group (USA) Inc.

Charles Chaplin. *From* Charlie Chaplin's Own Story: *Charlie Chaplin's Own Story*, ed. Harry M. Geduld (Bloomington, Ind.: Indiana University Press, 1985), pp. 110–14.

Marilyn Chin. How I Got That Name: *The Phoenix Gone, The Terrace Empty* (Minneapolis, Minn.: Milkweed Editions, 1994), pp. 16–18. Copyright © 1994 by Marilyn Chin. Reprinted with permission from Milkweed Editions.

Louis Chu. *From* Eat a Bowl of Tea: *Eat a Bowl of Tea* (New York: Kensington Publishing Corporation, 2002), pp. 79–89. Copyright © 1961. All rights reserved. Reprinted by arrangement with Kensington Publishing Corporation, www.kensingtonbooks.com. Originally published in 1961.

Judith Ortiz Cofer. Arrival: *Reaching for the Mainland* (Tempe, Ariz.: Bilingual Press, 1995), p. 26. Copyright © 1995 by Judith Ortiz Cofer. Reprinted by permission of Bilingual Press, Tempe, Arizona.

J. Hector St. John de Crèvecoeur. *From* Letters from an American Farmer: *Letters from an American Farmer* (New York: Albert and Charles Boni, 1925), pp. 48–56. Originally published in 1782.

Lorenzo Da Ponte. *From* Memoirs: *Memoirs*, ed. Arthur Livingston (New York: Dover Publications, 1959), pp. 353–65. Translated by Elisabeth Abbott. Originally published in Italian in 1823–27.

Edwidge Danticat. *From* Brother, I'm Dying: *Brother, I'm Dying* (New York: Alfred A. Knopf, 2007), pp. 214–43, 251. Copyright © 2007 by Edwidge Danticat. Used by permission of Alfred A. Knopf, a division of Random House, Inc.

Greg Delanty. We Will Not Play the Harp Backward Now, No: *Collected Poems, 1986–2006* (Manchester, U.K.: Carcanet Press Ltd., 2007) Copyright © Greg Delanty. Reprinted by permission of the author.

Anita Desai. Various Lives: *Lives in Translation*, ed. Isabelle de Courtivron

(Basingstoke, U.K.: Palgrave Macmillan, 2003), pp. 11–17. Copyright © 2003 by Anita Desai, Reprinted by permission of Melanie Jackson Literary Agency, L.L.C.

Junot Díaz. From Drown: *Drown* (New York: Riverhead Books, 1996), pp. 23–43. Copyright © 1996 by Junot Díaz. Used by permission of Riverhead Books, an imprint of Penguin Group (USA) Inc.

Gregory Djanikian. Immigrant Picnic: *The Best American Poetry 2000*, ed. Rita Dove (New York: Scribner, 2000), pp. 48–49. Copyright © 2007 by Gregory Djanikian. Reprinted by permission of the author.

Carl Djerassi. From The Pill, Pygmy Chimps and Degas' Horse: *The Pill, Pygmy Chimps and Degas' Horse* (New York: Basic Books, 1992), pp. 14–21. Copyright © 1992 by Carl Djerassi. Reprinted by permission of the author.

Ariel Dorfman. Breaking Down the Glass Walls of Language: *How I Learned English*, ed. Tom Miller (Washington: National Geographic, 2007), pp. 217–19. Copyright © 2007 by Ariel Dorfman. Reprinted with permission of the Wylie Agency L.L.C.

Edith Maude Eaton (Sui Sin Far). Mrs. Spring Fragrance: *Mrs. Spring Fragrance* (Chicago: A. C. McClurg and Company, 1912), pp. 1–21.

Laura Fermi. From Atoms in the Family: *Atoms in the Family* (Chicago: University of Chicago Press, 1954), pp. 141–53. Copyright © 1954 by the University of Chicago. Reprinted by permission of the University of Chicago Press.

Luis H. Francia. Tío: *Memories of Overdevelopment* (Pasig City, Philippines: Anvil, 1998), pp. 202–6. Copyright © 1998. Reprinted by permission of Luis H. Francia.

Richard Frethorne. Letter to his mother and father: *The Records of the Virginia Company of London*, ed. Susan Kingsbury (Washington: U.S. Government Printing Office, 1935), pp. 58–62. Written in 1623.

Ernesto Galarza. From Barrio Boy: *Barrio Boy* (Notre Dame, Ind.: University of Notre Dame Press, 1971), pp. 193–212. Copyright © 1971 by the University of Notre Dame Press. Reprinted with permission.

Thom Gunn. From My Life Up to Now: *The Occasions of Poetry* (Ann Arbor, Mich.: University of Michigan Press, 1999), pp. 175–78. Copyright ©

1992, 1999 by Thom Gunn. Reprinted by permission of Farber & Farber, Ltd. Originally published in 1982.

Jessica Hagedorn. *From* The Gangster of Love: *The Gangster of Love* (Boston: Houghton Mifflin Company, 1996), pp. 5–13. Copyright © 1996 by Jessica Hagedorn. Reprinted by permission of Houghton Mifflin Harcourt Publishing Company. All rights reserved.

Moyshe-Leyb Halpern. In the Golden Land: *In New York*, ed. and trans. Kathryn Hellerstein (Philadelphia: Jewish Publication Society of America, 1982), pp. 19, 21. Copyright © 1982 by Kathryn Hellerstein, editor. Published by The Jewish Publication Society of America, with the permission of the publisher. Originally published in 1919.

Aleksandar Hemon. *From* Nowhere Man: *Nowhere Man* (New York: Doubleday, 2002), pp. 137–59. Copyright © 2002 by Aleksandar Hemon. Used by permission of Doubleday, a division of Random House, Inc.

Eva Hoffman. *From* Lost in Translation: *Lost in Translation* (New York: E. P. Dutton, 1989), pp. 272–76. Copyright © 1989 by Eva Hoffman. Used by permission of Dutton, a division of Penguin Group (USA) Inc.

Christopher Isherwood. *From* Diaries: *Diaries: Volume One: 1939–1960*, ed. Katherine Bucknell (HarperFlamingo, 1996), pp. 3–11, 94. Copyright © 1996 by Don Bachardy. Reprinted by permission of HarperCollins Publishers. Written in 1939–40.

Frances (Fanny) Kemble. *From* Journals: *Fanny Kemble's Journals*, ed. Catherine Clinton (Cambridge: Harvard University Press, 2000), pp. 41–49. Copyright © 2000 by the President and Fellows of Harvard College. Reprinted by permission of the publisher.

Jamaica Kincaid. *From* Lucy: *Lucy* (New York: Farrar, Straus and Giroux, 1990), pp. 3–15. Copyright © 1990 by Jamaica Kincaid. Reprinted by permission of Farrar, Straus and Giroux, L.L.C.

Lucette Lagnado. *From* The Man in the White Sharkskin Suit: *The Man in the White Sharkskin Suit* (New York: HarperCollins, 2007), pp. 204–9, 214–18. Copyright © 2007 by Lucette Lagnado. Reprinted by permission of HarperCollins Publishers.

Jhumpa Lahiri. The Third and Final Continent: *Interpreter of Maladies* (Boston: Houghton Mifflin Company, 1999), pp. 173–84, 189–93, 196–98.

by Joseph Pell. Reprinted by permission of RDR Books, Muskegon, Michigan.

Menotti Pellegrino. *From* The Mysteries of New York: *Voices of Italian America*, ed. Martino Marazzi (Madison, N.J.: Fairleigh Dickinson University Press, 2004), pp. 65–66, 68–69. Translated by Ann Goldstein. Copyright © 2004. Reprinted by permission of Fairleigh Dickinson University Press.

Marjorie Perloff. *From* The Vienna Paradox: *The Vienna Paradox* (New York: New Directions, 2004), pp. 147–61. Copyright © 2003 by Marjorie Perloff. Reprinted by permission of New Directions Publishing Corporation.

Poetry by Chinese Immigrants. *Island: Poetry and History of Chinese Immigrants on Angel Island, 1912–1940*, ed. and trans. Him Mark Lai, Genny Lim, and Judy Yung (Seattle: University of Washington Press, 1991), pp. 36, 38, 40, 42. Copyright © 1980 by the History of Chinese Detained on Island Project. Reprinted by arrangement with the authors and the University of Washington Press.

James Revel. The Poor Unhappy Transported Felon's Sorrowful Account: *American Poetry: The 17th and 18th Centuries* (New York: Library of America, 2007), pp. 156–63. Written circa 1680.

Jacob Riis. *From* The Making of an American: *The Making of an American*, ed. Roy Lubove (New York: Harper & Row, 1966), p. 35–46. Originally published in 1901.

Richard Rodriguez. *From* Hunger of Memory: *Hunger of Memory* (New York: David R. Godine, 1982), pp. 9–17, 22–25, 28–29. Copyright © 1982 by Richard Rodriguez. Reprinted by the permission of David R. Godine, Publisher, Inc.

O. E. Rølvaag. *From* The Third Life of Per Smevik: *The Third Life of Per Smevik* (New York: Harper & Row, 1971), pp. 115–29. Translated by Ella Valborg Tweet and Solveig Zempel. Copyright © 1971. Reprinted by permission of Solveig Zempel.

Henry Roth. *From* Call It Sleep: *Call It Sleep* (New York: Farrar, Straus and Giroux, 1992), pp. 9–16. Copyright © 1934, renewed 1962 by Henry Roth. Reprinted by permission of Farrar, Straus and Giroux, L.L.C. Originally published in 1934.

Edward Said. *From* Out of Place: *Out of Place* (New York: Alfred A. Knopf, 1999), pp. 221–35. Copyright © 1999 by Edward W. Said. Used by permission of Alfred A. Knopf, a division of Random House, Inc.

Luc Sante. *From* Cargo: *The Factory of Facts* (New York: Pantheon Books, 1998), pp. 23–34. Copyright © 1998 by Luc Sante. Used by permission of Pantheon Books, a division of Random House, Inc.

Carl Schurz. *From* Reminiscences: *The Reminiscences of Carl Schurz*, volume II (London: John Murray, 1909), pp. 3–12, 17–18. Originally published in 1907.

Gary Shteyngart. The Mother Tongue Between Two Slices of Rye: *Threepenny Review* (Spring 2004). Copyright © 2004 by Gary Shteyngart. First appeared in *Threepenny Review*. Reprinted with permission of Denise Shannon Literary Agency, Inc. All rights reserved.

Charles Simic. *From* A Fly in the Soup: *A Fly in the Soup* (Ann Arbor, Mich.: University of Michigan Press, 2000), pp. 64–73. Copyright © 2000 by Charles Simic. Reprinted with permission of University of Michigan Press.

Isaac Bashevis Singer. A Wedding in Brownsville: *Collected Stories: Gimpel the Fool to The Letter Writer* (New York: Library of America, 2004), pp. 488–501. Originally published in *Short Friday and Other Stories* (New York: Farrar, Straus and Giroux, 1964). Translated by Chana Faerstein and Elizabeth Pollet. Copyright © 1964 by Isaac Bashevis Singer and renewed 1992 by Alma Singer. Reprinted by permission of Farrar, Straus and Giroux, L.L.C.

Ilan Stavans. *From* Autobiographical Essay: *The Essential Ilan Stavans* (New York: Routledge, 2000), pp. 78–82. Copyright © by Ilan Stavans. Reprinted by permission of Routledge.

Thomas Tillam. Upon the First Sight of New England: *Proceedings* of the American Antiquarian Society, new series LIII (1944), p. 331. Written circa 1638.

Anya Ulinich. The Nurse and the Novelist: *Pen: America 9* (2008). Copyright © 2008 by Anya Ulinich. Reprinted by permission of the author.

Lara Vapnyar. Mistress: *There Are Jews in My House* (New York: Pantheon Books, 2003), pp. 96–108. Copyright © 2003 by Lara Vapnyar. Used by permission of Pantheon Books, a division of Random House, Inc.

Bernardo Vega. *From* Memoirs: *Writing New York* (New York: Library of America, 1998), pp. 785–802. Copyright © 1984 by Monthly Review Press. Reprinted by permission of the Monthly Review Foundation.

Phillis Wheatley. On being brought from Africa to America: *American Poetry: The 17th and 18th Centuries* (New York: Library of America, 2007), p. 776.

Anzia Yezierska. *From* Children of Loneliness: *How I Found America* (New York: Persea Books, 1995), pp. 178–90. Originally published in *Children of Loneliness* (New York: Funk & Wagnalls Company, 1923). Copyright © 1985, 1991 by Louise Levitas Henriksen. Reprinted by permission of Persea Books, Inc.

Editor's Acknowledgments

I am grateful for the support and advice of countless people. My thanks are due to Edna Acosta-Belén at SUNY-Albany; André Aciman at CUNY-Graduate Center; Verónica Albin at Rice University; Julia Alvarez at Middlebury College; Harold Augenbraum, executive director of the National Book Foundation; Chris Benfey at Mount Holyoke College; Jules Chametzky at the University of Massachusetts in Amherst and editor emeritus of the *Massachusetts Review*; Isabelle de Courtivron at MIT.; Morris Dickstein at CUNY-Graduate Center; Ariel Dorfman at Duke University; Dalia Feldman in Boston; Luis H. Francia at New York University; Nora Gerard, Aaron Lansky, and Nancy Sherman at the National Yiddish Book Center; Alan Johnson at the University of Chicago Press; Steven G. Kellman at the University of Texas in San Antonio; Eliezer Nowodworski in Tel Aviv; Thomas Phelps at the National Endowment for the Humanities; Rachel Rubinstein at Hampshire College; Jonathan Rosen at Nextbook; Stephen A. Sadow at Northeastern University; Neal Sokol in St. Louis; Werner Sollors at Harvard University; Matthew Warshawsky at the University of Oregon; and the members of Double Edge Theatre, especially Stacy Klein, Carlos Uriona, and Matthew Glassman, with whom I discussed some of the selections.

Also thanks to Rachel S. Edelman, my research assistant at Amherst

College; Bobbie Helinski and Elizabeth Eddy at Amherst College for secretarial support; Daria D'Arienzo, Margaret Adams Groesbeck, Michael Kasper, Susan Kimball, John Lancaster, Tracy Sutherland, and Susan Sheridan at Frost Library, Amherst College, in helping to locate sources.

Finally, *gracias de todo corazón* to my parents, Abraham and Ofelia Stavchansky, for enabling me as an immigrant by projecting their love across the geographical divide.

INDEX